The Evangelical Conversion Narrative

Whitefield Preaching in Moorfields, AD 1742 by Eyre Crowe (1824–1910).
The painting appeared in the summer exhibition of the Royal Academy in
1865 (no. 559) and an engraving was published in the *Illustrated London
News* on 22 July 1865. The subject is drawn from Whitefield's own account
in letters written on 11 and 15 May 1742.

The Evangelical Conversion Narrative

Spiritual Autobiography in Early Modern England

D. BRUCE HINDMARSH

OXFORD

UNIVERSITY PRESS

OXFORD
UNIVERSITY PRESS

Great Clarendon Street, Oxford OX2 6DP

Oxford University Press is a department of the University of Oxford.
It furthers the University's objective of excellence in research, scholarship,
and education by publishing worldwide in

Oxford New York

Auckland Cape Town Dar es Salaam Hong Kong Karachi
Kuala Lumpur Madrid Melbourne Mexico City Nairobi New Delhi
Shanghai Taipei Toronto

With offices in

Argentina Austria Brazil Chile Czech Republic France Greece
Guatemala Hungary Italy Japan South Korea Poland Portugal
Singapore Switzerland Thailand Turkey Ukraine Vietnam

Published in the United States
by Oxford University Press Inc., New York

© D. Bruce Hindmarsh 2005

The moral rights of the author have been asserted
Database right Oxford University Press (maker)

First published 2005

British Library Cataloguing in Publication Data

Data available

Library of Congress Cataloging-in-Publication Data

Hindmarsh, D. Bruce
The evangelical conversion narrative : spiritual autobiography in
early modern England/D. Bruce Hindmarsh.

1. Evangelical Revival—Biography—History and criticism.
2. Christian converts—England—Biography—History and criticism. 3. Autobiography—
Religious aspects—Christianity—History—18th century. I. Title.
BR758.H56 2005
248.2′4′092242—dc22   2004029048

ISBN 0–19–924575–4

EAN 9780199245758

1 3 5 7 9 10 8 6 4 2

Typeset by Kolam Information Pvt, Ltd., India
Printed in Great Britain by
Biddles Ltd., King's Lynn

To Carolyn

Preface

THE idea for this book emerged while I was still writing *John Newton and the English Evangelical Tradition* (Oxford, 1996). In that book I devoted a chapter to studying Newton's famous autobiography, *An Authentic Narrative* (1764), and I became intrigued by the whole genre of conversion narrative and more attentive to how widespread this form of spiritual autobiography was during the eighteenth century. But although I could find dozens of studies of the Puritan conversion narrative in the seventeenth century, I could not point to a single book-length study of the genre as it reappeared and proliferated in England during the Evangelical Revival. So from a biography of an individual, I turned to a biography of a genre.

My sense that conversion narrative was widespread and germane to the period—not merely a residue of the spirit-drenched universe of the seventeenth century, or a sectarian backwater in the forward current of secular enlightenment—was confirmed by my research. Spiritual autobiographies that took evangelical conversion as their leading theme were numerous in the period (and more so as the century advanced) and such narratives were spoken or written by people from all walks of life. I had little trouble finding a wealth of examples in manuscripts and printed books from a variety of sources. The very sites that are so problematic in discourse today, such as race, class, and gender, appeared together in this genre, as black Nova Scotians, women servants in Scotland, and London apprentices wrote about their conversion experiences alongside university educated clergy. To be sure there were variations on a theme, but a theme there was. The resurgence of conversion narrative in the eighteenth century was as a phenomenon as germane to the period as the Gin Craze of the 1730s or the rise in the price of wheat in the 1750s, and the study of conversion narrative therefore holds much promise for a better understanding of religion and culture in the early modern period.

It seemed to me, therefore, that this was an important story to tell. In my generation many scholars have come to reflect upon, and some to worry about, the modernist identity; the sense of self, that is, which is organized as a narrative of individual achievement. As I studied these evangelical narratives, I found that they bore witness to a religious understanding that was only ever a vector of the Enlightenment, and that did not succumb to the pathological elision of community, contingency, or faith that is typical of the modernist autobiography. The genre of conversion narrative is thus not only widespread and comprehensive of several traditions in the eighteenth century; it is also a potentially illuminating site for understanding the modern identity and its alternatives.

This book is a kind of minority report on self-identity in the early modern period. In order to tell this story and to point up something of the significance of a genre that could be, like any genre, hackneyed and clichéd in certain cases, I have chosen to trace the emergence of the genre in the seventeenth century in the Introduction and Ch. 1, and to show it over against some of its foils in the late eighteenth and early nineteenth centuries in Ch. 10. These chapters form the bookends of my study and help to show something of the significance of this cultural phenomenon: namely, that on the cusp of the modern period, thousands of women and men went through the travail of evangelical conversion and turned to a certain kind of spiritual autobiography to make sense of their experience, and, indeed, to make sense of their lives. While I do not think that many of the conditions under which they made their response to the evangel continue to exist any longer in the West today, I do think that human nature remains much the same and that these early evangelicals offered an important alternative to the project of self-construction typical of the modern period—one that points to the enduring significance of the message of the New Testament about Jesus Christ.

Given the wide variety of sources I have used, I should make a few notes here about usage. I have modernized the text of manuscript sources as little as possible except to expand silently the standard contractions, suspensions, and abbreviations, such as 'y^r' ('your') or 'H^{ond} S^r' ('Honoured Sir'). I have also modernized antiquated letter forms found in manuscript sources (and a few sixteenth- and seventeenth-century printed sources), such as 'y' (for the thorn) or the consonantal 'i' and 'u'. I have also minimally emended punctuation by introducing a comma or stop for readability where the spacing and appearance of the (largely unpunctuated) handwritten text seemed to warrant this. But, otherwise, I have tried to keep closely to the orthography and capitalization of the manuscripts, since this communicates something of the literacy and education of the authors in many cases. I have avoided intruding *sic* except where absolutely essential to avoid misunderstanding. Scripture quotations are taken from the Authorized Version. For printed works, London is the place of publication unless otherwise indicated.

The illustration that appears as a frontispiece is 'Whitefield preaching in Moorfields, A.D. 1742' by the historical painter Eyre Crowe (1824–1910), a pupil of Paul Delaroche. The painting appeared in the summer exhibition of the Royal Academy in 1865 (no. 559) and an engraving was published in the *Illustrated London News* on 22 July 1865. The subject is drawn from Whitefield's own account of his preaching in Moorfields in letters written on 11 and 15 May 1742, and I describe the incident in Ch. 2 below. The painting shows Whitefield preaching, a woman (with her child) at the bottom of the scene responding in earnest prayer, and notes being passed to Whitefield 'from persons brought under spiritual concern'. This triangle of gospel proclamation, conversion, and personal narrative nicely captures what this book is about. In particular, the woman in the scene and the notes being received could stand for many of the subjects and stories recounted in Ch. 4.

In a study of autobiography, I should say something about my voice in this book. I have written most of what follows in the third person, though I have not hesitated to use the first person (singular or, more often, plural, meaning 'you the reader and I') where it seemed appropriate. My desire has been to place my subjects in the foreground, and much of what is in these pages is an effort at careful historical reconstruction. Still, I am aware that I am also selecting, arranging, highlighting, and speaking through my subjects all along. As I say in the theoretical introduction at the beginning of the book, my aim has been to strike a balance between listening and criticism. And although this is not a work of sustained cultural critique or religious apologetic, I do suggest in the closing pages that the subjects of this book ought to be taken seriously, and that their experience is relevant to contemporary concerns. These early modern evangelicals speak to us of the hope and sanity of an identity that is found not in the resources of the self alone, but, as St Paul so often said, 'in Christ'. Increasingly, I find hope in this and in the words of Paul to the Colossians: 'For you died, and your life is now hidden with Christ in God. When Christ, who is your life, appears, then you also will appear with him in glory' (Col. 3: 3–4).

The modernist autobiography all too often omits the contribution of others to the making of one's life. I hope I am aware of something at least of the debt I owe in my life to numerous people in the writing of this book. The archives and antiquarian sources listed in my bibliography will indicate my indebtedness to many curators and librarians, but I would like particularly to thank Gareth Lloyd at the John Rylands Library for putting me on to the Early Methodist volume of letters to Charles Wesley, which I have depended upon extensively in writing Ch. 4, and the staff of the Upper Reading Room at the Bodleian Library in Oxford for their kindness, expertise, and even their indulgence, many times allowing me something more than my allotted ten books at a time. I made several visits to work in the libraries at Princeton, and Bill Harris, librarian for archives and special collections at Princeton Theological Seminary, made these visits especially efficient and enjoyable. His present to me of an eighteenth-century bust of John Wesley, from his own collection, was an act of surprising largesse such as one rarely experiences.

I have been fortunate in having had several hard-working, skilled gradu-ate assistants among whom I should especially thank Donovan Poulin, Chad Wriglesworth, and Julianne Kvernmo. I am sure none of them wishes ever to transcribe another manuscript of early modern, unpunctuated handwrit-ing, to see another microfilm of an eighteenth-century book, or to try the patience of yet another interlibrary loan clerk. Yet they did all such tasks, and more, with cheerfulness, and became great friends to me during this project. I am grateful too to have had the benefit of Karen Wuest's careful editing of my manuscript before it went off to the publisher.

There are a number of scholars whose work has stimulated my own thinking or provided a framework for my own enquiries, but as I went through my footnotes I was surprised to find how often the name Reginald Ward came up in particular. There were very few alleyways I explored that Professor Ward had not arrived at first and mapped sagaciously. Likewise, Richard Heitzenrater's exacting textual scholarship and thoughtful inter-pretation of John Wesley proved a source of continual insight and inspir-ation. Not least, I feel indebted to these scholars for their magisterial work on the new critical edition of Wesley's journal and diaries.

Other scholars generously agreed to read and critique my work at various stages. Mark Noll and John Walsh were a rich fund of advice from begin-ning to end of this project, and I am immensely grateful to them both. They also, along with Catherine Brekus, read the typescript, caught embarrassing errors, and offered helpful criticism that has made this a better book than it would have been otherwise. Richard Heitzenrater, Michael Haykin, Colin Podmore, Jim Packer, and Maxine Hancock offered specialist advice on sections of the book as well. In the end, however, I have to take responsi-bility, like an autobiographer, for what I have written.

Because this project was written over a number of years, I have had the opportunity to present aspects of my work in progress and to receive stimulating feedback in various settings, including an eighteenth-century studies conference at the University of Saskatchewan, a seminar of the North Atlantic Missiology Project at Cambridge (with Brian Stanley), a conference at the University of St Andrews (with Deryck Lovegrove), a seminar at Duke University of the Young Scholars in American Religion programme (with Grant Wacker), and a seminar at the Institute for Histor-ical Research, Senate House, London (with Mark Smith and John Wolffe). Some of the work I presented in these settings was later published, and I have drawn upon parts of three articles in particular, incorporating these in this book. Chapter 8 includes an edited version of 'The Olney Autobiographers: English Conversion Narrative in the Mid-Eighteenth Century', *Journal of Ecclesiastical History* 49 (1998), 61–84, reprinted with the permission of Cambridge University Press. Chapter 10 incorporates selections from 'Pat-terns of Conversion in Early Evangelical History and Overseas Mission

Experience', in Brian Stanley (ed.), *Christian Missions and the Enlightenment* (Grand Rapids, Mich., 2001), and this appears by the kind permission of Eerdmans Publishing Company. This same chapter also includes revised excerpts from 'Reshaping Individualism: The Private Christian, Eighteenth-Century Religion and the Enlightenment', in Deryck Lovegrove (ed.), *The Rise of the Laity in Evangelical Protestantism* (London, 2002), 67–84, and permission for this has been kindly given by Routledge.

The research for this book would not have been possible without the generous support of the Social Sciences and Humanities Research Council of Canada, who provided a faculty research grant (1995–8) and a post-doctoral fellowship (1995–7), the Pew Evangelical Scholars Program, who also provided major research funding in 1995, and a Lilly Small Grant from the Association of Theological Schools in 1999.

Most of all, however, it is my family that has lived with this book the longest and the most closely. Our third child, Samuel, was born when his father began this project, and he and his brother Matthew and sister Bethany have been a source of encouragement more than they know. Bethany even stepped in at the end to act as my research assistant, chasing down a few stray articles and books for me. (At 13 years of age, she must be the youngest faculty assistant to hold a library card at the University of British Columbia.) For now my children will probably use this book to press flowers, yet I think they are learning something about conversion already, and something of the truths contained in the epigraphs for this book (from Psalms 19 and 80). I am married to Carolyn, and she has been an insightful conversation partner and critic throughout my research and writing, and, to borrow a phrase beloved of John Wesley, she has been in this, as in all things, a 'means of grace' to me. To her this book is dedicated.

D.B.H.

24 May 2004
The Commemoration of John and Charles Wesley

Contents

Abbreviations

AM	*Arminian Magazine*
CWJ	*Journal of the Rev. Charles Wesley*, ed. Thomas Jackson, 2 vols. (1849)
EMP	Thomas Jackson (ed.), *Lives of Early Methodist Preachers,* 6 vols. (4th edn., 1871; repr. in 3 vols., Stoke-on-Trent, 1998)
EMV	Early Methodist Volume, John Rylands Library, Manchester
GWJ	*George Whitefield's Journals* (5th edn., Edinburgh, 1960)
GWL	*Letters of George Whitefield for the Period 1734–1742* (Edinburgh, 1976)
JWL	*Letters of John Wesley*, ed. John Telford, 8 vols. (1931)
McCulloch MSS	William McCulloch, 'Examinations of persons under spiritual concern at Cambuslang, during the Revival in 1741–42', 2 vols., bound MSS, New College, Edinburgh
MCH	Moravian Church House, London
MM	*Methodist Magazine*
Tyerman, *GW*	Luke Tyerman, *The Life of the Rev. George Whitefield,* 2 vols. (1876)
Tyerman, *JW*	Luke Tyerman, *The Life and Times of the Rev. John Wesley,* 3 vols. (1876)
Wesley, *Works* (BE)	*The Bicentennial Edition of the Works of John Wesley* (Nashville, Tenn., 1976–)
WJE	*Works of Jonathan Edwards* (New Haven, Conn., 1957–)
WV	John Telford (ed.), *Wesley's Veterans,* 7 vols. (1912–14)

The law of the LORD is perfect, converting the soul.

Psalm 19: 7

Turn us again, O God; show the light of thy countenance, and we shall be whole.

Psalm 80: 3 (Book of Common Prayer)

Introduction

From twelve at night till two it was my turn to stand sentinel at a
dangerous post . . . As soon as I was alone, I kneeled down, and determined not to rise, but to continue crying and wrestling with God, till
He had mercy on me. How long I was in that agony I cannot tell: but
as I looked up to heaven, I saw the clouds open exceeding bright, and
I saw Jesus hanging on the cross. At the same moment these words were
applied to my heart, 'Thy sins are forgiven thee.' My chains fell off; my
heart was free. All guilt was gone, and my soul was filled with unutter-
able peace. I loved God and all mankind, and the fear of death and hell
was vanished away. I was filled with wonder and astonishment.[1]

THIS was how Sampson Staniforth (1720–99) described his conversion as a
25-year-old soldier in the English army, while stationed in the Low Countries at the height of the War of the Austrian Succession. Staniforth was
converted in a Methodist revival that began among the soldiers after
the Battle of Dettingen in 1743. Discharged from the army in 1748, he
became a lay preacher under John Wesley, and later, at 62 years of age,
he wrote up an account of his life for Wesley's *Arminian Magazine*. This
quotation is an excerpt from that larger account.

Staniforth was quite clear that this conversion experience was the defining moment of his life, and he structured his entire narrative around it,
announcing, in his first paragraph, 'I shall, first, speak of my life from the
time of my birth, till I was about twenty-five years old: and, Secondly, from
the time that God called me, to the present time.'[2] Everything that preceded
his conversion was prologue; everything that followed was epilogue. Staniforth's evangelical conversion was not an experience on the periphery of
his life: conversion went to the heart of his identity and he proclaimed this
in a new ordering of his life's story.

This book is concerned with the proliferation of conversion narratives
such as Staniforth's during the period of early Evangelical Revival in
England from the mid-1730s until the mid-1780s—from the origins of
Methodism to the rise of the Clapham Sect. For precision we could define

---

[1] *AM* 6 (1783), 72.
[2] Ibid. 13.

this period as the fifty years between the conversion of George Whitefield in 1735 and that of William Wilberforce in 1785. Again, the period under survey corresponds roughly to the years during which John Wesley flourished, from his Aldersgate experience in 1738 until his death in 1791. The purview of this study extends well beyond such precise periodization and narrow geographical limits, however, since the questions we should like to ask of Sampson Staniforth will take us necessarily back to the roots of the early modern period and forward to the expansion of the evangelical impulse in foreign mission enterprise overseas in the early nineteenth century.

The approach taken in this book is therefore to set the subject of eighteenth-century evangelical conversion narrative within a broad chronological frame, beginning with the rise of the genre in the mid-seventeenth century and ending with the 'fall' of the genre in the non-Western context of some early nineteenth-century missionary enterprises.[3] The aim of painting within such a large frame is to allow the reader to view the genre whole as it appeared in the eighteenth century and to explore the conditions in general under which people turn to spiritual autobiography. Between these two poles the main body of the book traces the development of conversion narrative in England in the period of the Evangelical Revival as the genre appeared in different communities and representative writings. For completeness, it was necessary also to include a chapter on the Cambuslang Revival in Scotland. The result is a provisional typology of conversion and evangelical self-identity as it differed among the Arminian and perfectionist followers of Wesley, the Moravians under the influence of 'stillness', the moderate Calvinists in the Church of England, the confessional Calvinists in Scotland, the Particular Baptists who were just moving away from high Calvinism, and others. The chapters are organized to present a roughly chronological development of the genre alongside the growth of the evangelical movement itself, and also to allow for an exploration of the different forms of expression among leaders and laypeople, women and men, and Western and non-Western peoples. While I refer to other national contexts (such as Wales, Scotland, Ireland, New England and the colonies, and Germany) and make comparisons, my focus is chiefly upon England, and there remains more work to be done to place this genre more fully in its transatlantic and cross-cultural setting in the eighteenth century. Nevertheless, my concluding chapter argues that by being on the trailing edge of

---

[3] I put the term 'fall' in scare quotes here to make clear that I am not speaking of a diachronic pattern of 'rise and fall' in the early modern period, since the genre clearly persists and thrives into the nineteenth century and beyond. However, the case studies I have chosen in Ch. 10, to conclude my study, do set off the early modern episode in the history of conversion narrative as distinctive in important ways.

Christendom and the leading edge of modernity, England provided the right conditions for evangelical conversion narrative to revive and flourish in the mid-eighteenth century.[4]

In the balance of this introduction two sorts of context are provided for the chapters that follow: the first theoretical and the second historical. In the first instance we will situate evangelical conversion narrative within a multi-disciplinary discussion and highlight a number of significant issues raised by any serious consideration of the genre. In the second, we will set the stage for the rise of the genre in the early modern period by surveying forms of spiritual autobiography during the long Christian centuries when conversion narrative of the sort written by Sampson Staniforth did not exist.

THEORETICAL QUESTIONS AND CONCERNS

Discussions of conversion and spiritual autobiography face two opposite dangers. On the one hand there is the danger of naivety. Because an autobiography is first-hand testimony, it often appears as innocent factual reporting: the history of a life by the one who lived it. No doubt most of those who read Sampson Staniforth's serialized autobiography in the *Arminian Magazine* in 1783 accepted it at face value without worrying about the relationship between the life represented in the text and the life lived in the flesh. It is only when such commonsensical readings are contested that this naivety is challenged, and we realize again how creative and significant is the act of interpretation in selecting, arranging, and presenting events—even the events of one's own life.

The awareness of self-writing as a creative act of self-interpretation introduces the other, opposite danger that surfaces in discussions of conversion and spiritual autobiography, namely, a theoretical preoccupation or even solipsism. The danger here is often one of proportion, since literary or social-scientific theory can so easily crowd the foreground and obscure, rather than enlighten, the historical subject. In its most extreme form, a massive inverted pyramid of theory rests on a tiny point of historical matter. This is not meant to imply a call to return to hermeneutical naivety. Commonsensical readings of sources invariably contain assumptions that

---

[4] I use the term 'Christendom' here, and throughout my discussion, to refer not principally to the receding territory of Christian Europe that was under threat from the Ottoman Turks in the East, but rather to the receding *ideal* of a united Christian society with a ubiquitous and distinctively Christian culture, an ideal that was more or less realized at different times and in different places, but that was supremely the product of the high Middle Ages. The ideal of the fully confessional state and the fully territorial church goes hand in hand with the consciousness of Christianity as something assumed rather than chosen. The ideal or *mentalité* of Christendom, in this sense, is captured nicely in the title of Peter Berger's classic study on the social reality of religion, *The Sacred Canopy* (New York, 1967).

lie unexposed until a self-consciously theoretical interpretation illuminates previously hidden insights. The knife cuts both ways, though, since these new insights are just as quickly naturalized until contested once more.

However, as one finds when reading out-of-date monographs, time has a way of exposing both naivety and overly theorized writing. In a way both errors appear as a form of naivety after the passing of a certain amount of time. Paul Ricœur proposes a hermeneutic that balances trust and suspicion in the movement from first naivety, through critique, to a post-critical second naivety.[5] Accordingly, although I do not pretend to be able to transcend my own standpoint, or to be able to expose all of my assumptions, my goal is to steer somehow between these two dangers (too much trust, or too much suspicion) by engaging both in listening and in some critique. I want as nearly as possible to hear Sampson Staniforth with respect and on his own terms. To that end the bulk of my research has involved close reading of the archival and antiquarian sources themselves. But the questions and analysis I have brought to bear on these sources has also been informed by a number of important issues raised in contemporary discussions.

What are some of these issues? I would like to define five concepts that figure largely in any analysis of a story such as Staniforth's: autobiography, narrative, identity, conversion, and gospel. Conversion narrative is certainly patient of study from many angles. Indeed, the literature that bears on these concepts includes, at least, autobiographical and narrative theory, literary criticism, moral philosophy, psychology of conversion, sociology of conversion, anthropology, and theology. While not providing anything like an exhaustive theoretical prolegomena to the genre of conversion narrative, these five terms none the less help to focus some of the issues involved in analysing these particular sort of texts.

Autobiography

At the close of the fourth century St Augustine wrote his *Confessions*, a remarkably precocious spiritual autobiography without precedent in the ancient world. Augustine's autobiography was unlike any of the models provided by ancient biographers, such as Plutarch, whose 'lives' were by and large the *res gestae* or 'great deeds' of famous men. The *Confessions* was in a literal sense *sui generis*. Augustine was also precocious enough to reflect upon what he was doing by writing a spiritual autobiography. In Books 10 and 11 he turned from his narrative to consider the nature of time, change, memory, and identity. He wondered what the relationship was between himself in the present and himself in the past as a child and a young man and an adult. These are the classic questions of autobiographical theory, and Augustine found it hard going. He knew it had something to do with the

---

[5] Paul Ricœur, *The Rule of Metaphor*, trans. R. Czerney (Toronto, Ont., 1977), 318.

memory, but he was exasperated and wrote, 'Who is to carry the research beyond this point? . . . O Lord, I am working hard in this field, and the field of my labours is my own self. I have become a problem to myself.'[6] Anyone who has pondered long over the nature of autobiography will have some sympathy with Augustine.

Literary historians and theorists have discussed issues similar to those raised by Augustine and have recognized with him that autobiography has a hermeneutical significance transcending its appearance as a factual narrative about myself. James Olney asks three simple questions that are central to autobiographical theory: 'What do we mean by the self, or himself (*autos*)? What do we mean by life (*bios*)? What significance do we impute to the act of writing (*graphe*)—what is the significance and the effect of transforming life, or *a* life into a text?'[7] Like Augustine, Olney is asking about the relationship between myself as author, myself as subject, and myself as portrayed in a literary text. Georges Gusdorf's landmark essay, 'Conditions and Limits of Autobiography' (1956), argues that the significance of autobiography lies precisely in the fact that it raises these questions. This complexity is its 'anthropological prerogative' as a genre:

It is one of the means to self-knowledge thanks to the fact that it recomposes and interprets a life in its totality. An examination of consciousness limited to the present moment will give me only a fragmentary cutting from my personal being without the guarantee that it will continue. In recounting my history I take the longest path, but this path that goes round my life leads me the more surely from me to myself.[8]

The shift in that last phrase from the personal pronoun to the reflexive pronoun is significant. Gusdorf concludes that autobiography 'obliges me to situate what I am in the perspective of what I have been'.[9] At one level an autobiography simply promises to retrace the history of a life, but at a deeper level it is always an apologetic of the individual. Autobiography is one of the ways to answer the question of what my life *means*. The link, therefore, between autobiography and 'identity' (discussed below) is close.

More recent scholarship has built upon Gusdorf's arguments and stressed the importance of autobiography as one of the defining cultural practices of the modern period. For example, Michael Mascuch has expounded the formal relationship of autobiography to the *individualist* self-identity—the

---

[6] Augustine, *Confessions*, trans. R. S. Pine-Coffin (1961), 222.

[7] James Olney, 'Autobiography and the Cultural Moment: A Thematic, Historical, and Bibliographical Introduction', in James Olney (ed.), *Autobiography: Essays Theoretical and Critical* (Princeton, 1980), 6.

[8] Georges Gusdorf, 'Conditions and Limits of Autobiography', in Olney (ed.), *Autobiography*, 38.

[9] Ibid.

way, that is, in which autobiography has been a medium for displaying myself as the unique product of my own choices: 'the trope of the author as the hero and originator of his heroism'.[10] Modern autobiography thus has many parallels to the modern novel, a genre that emerges in this same period as something distinct from 'romance', with a narrative of a fictional but realistic experience in which the everyday life of the individual is meaningful and significant.[11]

In the analysis that follows, I hope to show that the evangelical conversion narrative represents an alternative version of modern self-identity, one that overlaps in some ways with the modern autobiographical identity, but one that also qualifies the notion of self-fashioning. Autobiographical theory helps us to identify the larger significance of the evangelical narratives in the chapters that follow. Evangelical conversion narratives are more than 'sources' for scholarly historical reconstruction. They are also acts of self-interpretation, or in Gusdorf's words, they are 'the parable of consciousness in quest of its own truth'.[12]

Narrative

We refer to Sampson Staniforth's account of his life not only as an autobiography but also as a narrative. Autobiography is a particular, specialized case of narrative literature. Or to put it the other way around, autobiography takes the form and assumes the disciplines of narrative writing more generally. While there are many ways to tell a story, the overall shape of a narrative often points beyond itself to some larger principle of meaningfulness: 'The moral of the story is . . .' This is much more than a facile point. For example, in Aristotle's *Poetics*, he identifies the plot (*mythos*) as the first principle or the soul of tragedy. The most important characteristic of a plot, according to Aristotle, is its wholeness or completeness, and a narrative whole is 'that which has a beginning, middle, and end'. 'Well constructed plots,' says Aristotle, 'should neither begin nor end at arbitrary points,' since this would be to destroy any sense of wholeness. Especially satisfying plots include complex elements of unexpected (but uncontrived) reversals and discoveries. But what Aristotle deplored was a merely 'episodic' plot governed by no overarching principle and without any larger probability or necessity.[13] In the field of autobiography, it is the title 'memoir' that often signals an episodic and anecdotal retelling of one's life. In contrast, conver-

---

[10] Michael Mascuch, *Origins of the Individualist Self* (Cambridge, 1997), 23.

[11] See further Michael McKeon, *Origins of the English Novel, 1600–1740* (Baltimore, Md., 1987), 20–2, who locates the origins of the novel in the 1740s in the midst of a crisis over questions of truth and virtue seminal to modern identity.

[12] Gusdorf, 'Conditions and Limits', 44.

[13] Aristotle, *Poetics*, Loeb Classical Library (1995), 55, 63.

sion narratives such as Sampson Staniforth's are highly emplotted and have a strongly etched beginning, middle, and end, and a sense of wholeness.

An author may use all manner of devices to create suspense or other effects for the reader, or to frame certain episodes as particularly significant. But to distinguish between the actual events and the emplotting of these events is to highlight the question of moral significance. By what principle do I select these particular events from my past for retelling, and to what end do I arrange them thus and so? Aristotle's temporal syntax of beginning–middle–end is also a moral structure. The narrator discerns the progress of the protagonist from an original situation through a moral transformation to a final situation. Considering conversion accounts as narratives, then, reminds us to look not only at the episodic level of the story but also at the emplotted level, the intelligible whole that governs the sequence of events in any story. Part of the task of this book is to render explicit this narrative structure in evangelical autobiographies.

Charles Taylor in his *Sources of the Self* (1992) argues that when we make statements of strong evaluation, we make an implicit appeal to the 'incomparably higher' or 'the good'. But this also implies a narrative understanding of ourselves:

In order to make sense of our lives, in order to have an identity, we need an orientation to the good, which means some sense of qualitative discrimination, of the incomparably higher. Now we see that this sense of the good has to be woven into my understanding of my life as an unfolding story. But this is to state another basic condition of making sense of ourselves, that we grasp our lives in a *narrative* . . . our lives exist also in this space of questions, which only a coherent narrative can answer. In order to have a sense of who we are, we have to have a notion of how we have become, and of where we are going. [14]

Again, the concept of narrative invariably introduces the issue of moral ends or 'orientation to the good'. It is therefore important to ask not just literary but also moral questions of the evangelical conversion narrative. What is the moral centre that gives significance to the sequence of events in these stories? What do these stories imply is the 'incomparably higher' or 'strongly valued goods' by which the subjects orient themselves in narrative space?

On the whole, what these evangelical narratives point to as the great desideratum of human life is the recovery of right relationship with God. This is sometimes expressed in terms of the restoration of the image of God, sometimes in terms of legal righteousness, sometimes in terms of freedom from bondage. But throughout, their narratives are preoccupied with the moral law, both as something that prepares a person for conversion and as something that guides the believer afterwards. From this arose all the fury of

[14] Charles Taylor, *Sources of the Self* (Cambridge, 1992), 47.

the evangelicals' debates about legalism and antinomianism. What was at stake were the very ends sought in their lives and in their narratives. Narrative wholeness in Aristotle's sense corresponds quite literally in their case to what these writers understood to be spiritual and moral wholeness.

Moreover, the narrative shape of these evangelical stories was clearly provided by the larger story of salvation history in the Bible. As in the case of Augustine, the Bible's account of fall from innocence and return provided a structure and many topoi for these spiritual autobiographies. It is sometimes assumed that the modern or bourgeois form of autobiography is characterized by its rejection of such ready-made universal patterns— concerned with the wholly immanent meaning of each unique life as the product of unique choices. Yet, while such forms of autobiography may reject the interpretative patterns provided by Christian theological concepts such as providence, law, and the order of salvation, the bourgeois narrative still surely represents another ready-made pattern, albeit an unacknow-ledged one. Often the implied goods are written in letters too large to read, since they are the typically modern ones of success in career and success in relationships—what Charles Taylor nicely summarizes as the goods of 'production and reproduction'. The modernist autobiography, too, has its own underlying scripts. There is an inescapably analogical pattern to narrative.

Identity

This analogical element introduces the concept of 'identity', which is so closely related to autobiography and narrative. The concept of identity ('this is that') underlines the metaphorical nature of self-description. Martin Heidegger argued that all understanding has an *as-* or *like*-structure, in the sense that we can only answer the question, 'What is this?' by saying that it is *like* something else, by positing an identity between this and that.[15] In the context of spiritual autobiography the term 'identity' is usually shorthand for 'self-identity' or 'narrative self-identity'. To identify oneself is therefore to answer the question, 'Who are you?' or, in the context of autobiography, 'Who am I?' These questions invite an answer in the form, 'I am *like* . . .' this or that; that is, by positing an identity between myself and something else. Telling my story is one way of doing this: I am the sort of person about whom such a story could be told.

In Aristotelian terms, this is to mark the close relation of plot (*mythos*) to character (*ethos*). Character, according to Aristotle, is 'that which reveals moral choice—that is, when otherwise unclear, what kinds of things an agent chooses or rejects', or again, it is 'that in virtue of which we ascribe

[15] Martin Heidegger, *Being and Time*, trans. J. Macquarrie and E. Robinson (New York, 1962), 188–95.

certain qualities to the agents'.[16] Character therefore emerges only tempor-
ally as patterns of choice are established, and a narrative simply rehearses this
pattern of moral agency. Moreover, the moral centre implied in various
ways by the narrative measures the character of the protagonist. While in
most stories the reader is called upon to distinguish between the character of
the author narrating the story and the protagonist, in autobiography the two
are the same. In autobiography it is not only the patterns of action portrayed
in the story (*mythos*) that reveal the moral qualities (*ethos*) of the subject, but
also the patterns of narration. We ascribe certain qualities not only to
characters in a story, but also to the writer (judicious, conceited, clever,
sloppy, affected, etc.) based on cues in the text itself. This leads to a double
evaluation of character in an autobiography, as the reader looks for a
consistency of character in both the writer and the protagonist.

'Identity' has a semantic range that overlaps with 'self', 'ego', 'I', and
'subject' in moral philosophy and related discussions. Friedrich Nietzsche
sharply critiqued René Descartes's assumption of a thinking subject—the
cogito—as nothing more than 'a grammatical custom which sets an agent to
every action'. In a linguistic turn followed in later theory, Nietzsche thus
defined the subject solely in terms of discourse. Again, he argued, '*Subject*: this
is the term we apply to our belief in an *entity* underlying all the different
moments of the most intense sensations of reality: we regard this belief as the
effect of a cause.' Rather, he continued, ' "Subject" is the fiction which
would fain make us believe that several similar states were the effect of one
substratum: but we it was who first *created* the "similarity" of these states; the
similising and adjusting of them is the *fact*—*not* their similarity (on the contrary, this ought rather to be denied).'[17] With Nietzsche then, as in much
contemporary discussion, 'I' am not revealed in speaking, but instead 'I'
constitute myself through discourse. Identity is constructed rather than given.

But Nietzsche's recognition that identity is constituted in language, and
that language is used to express power, need not imply that the self is only a
linguistic site for ideological conflict. These same insights allow one to
acknowledge that self-understanding is negotiated socially in the context
of the other. Identity is both constructed by myself and bestowed by the
other. Charles Taylor puts it this way, 'The question Who? is asked to place
someone as a potential interlocutor in a society of interlocutors . . . To be
someone who qualifies as a potential object of this question is to be such an
interlocutor among others, someone with one's own standpoint or one's
own role, who can speak for him/herself.'[18] The concept of 'interlocution'

---

[16] Aristotle, *Poetics*, 49, 53.

[17] Friedrich Nietzsche, *The Will to Power*, trans. A. M. Ludovici (New York, 1964),
ii. 14–15.

[18] Taylor, *Sources of the Self*, 29.

expresses many of the same insights that are found in Nietzsche and neo-Nietzschean theory, but in this case these insights are constructive. Indeed, to answer the question 'Who?' is to know where you stand, and you can only know where you stand by having a basic framework, a moral topography, even if this is unacknowledged. I answer the question 'Who?' meaningfully when I locate myself with reference to some concept of what is good. To understand that anything predicated of the word 'I' is predicated in the context of interlocution is to move on from the potential solipsism of discourse as mere constructivism to an acknowledgement of the inevitable moral structure implied by the speaking self.

Evangelical spiritual autobiography represents one attempt on the part of early modern people to answer the question 'Who am I?' with a narrative. Again, Taylor writes, 'The full definition of someone's identity thus usually involves not only his stand on moral and spiritual matters but also some reference to a defining community.'[19] Attention to the concept of identity allows us, then, to examine the ways in which evangelical narrative identity was negotiated and to what end. Was it constructed privately or bestowed socially? What does it mean that some subjects understood their identities to be bestowed supernaturally? How exactly was a man or woman's autobiography reconstructed through the travail of conversion and reception into evangelical communities? How far were these new identities contested? And how does the evangelical narrative identity compare with the other 'scripts' circulating in the wider culture? Many of these questions recur throughout the pages that follow, and, indeed, keen questions about individual identity were being asked in the period itself.

Conversion

Most of the subjects in this book found their deepest identities in their religious experience. And they typically answered the question 'Who am I?' by telling the stories of their conversions. The central image and etymological root of the word 'conversion' is 'turning', and its semantic field is wide. Consequently, conversion appears as a polyvalent term that depends much upon its context for its meaning. Turning from what to what? Converting from what to what? When linked with the term 'gospel' or 'evangelical' (discussed below) conversion is immediately freighted with theological meaning deriving from the Christian tradition. Conversion has come to have a much wider reference, however, in the behavioural sciences. The subject of extensive investigation within psychology, sociology, and anthropology in particular, religious conversion has been interpreted within diverse theories of the person, society, and culture.

---

[19] Taylor, *Sources of the Self*, 36.

William James's *Varieties of Religious Experience* (1902) was a pioneering work in this respect. James distinguished between the 'existential' and 'spiritual' analysis of religious texts and confined himself to the former—that is, to the phenomenon of religious experience as observable human behaviour. James was less interested in routine religious behaviour than in mysticism, and particularly the physical and psychic phenomena (visions, locutions, photisms, automatisms, etc.) that sometimes appear in accounts of climactic religious experience. He approached such accounts by carefully bracketing out the question of the supernatural or biological origins of religious experience and established instead a pragmatic standard of evaluation: 'In the end it had to come to our empiricist criterion: By their fruits ye shall know them, not by their roots.'[20] Regardless of the religious content of the experiences of believers, what mattered at the end of the day to James were the practical consequences. While such 'strong evaluation' calls for a more explicit articulation of moral sources—the implied good in the notion of 'fruits' and 'practical consequences'—James's attempt to study conversion as a scientist was precedent-setting. Indeed, the significance of James's work lies less in his particular theory of the healthy-minded person who is born once versus the sin-sick soul who must be twice-born, or his distinction between a voluntary type of conversion and that characterized by self-surrender, or his observation of similar psychological patterns that recur in mystical experience, than in his strictly phenomenological approach whereby religious experience is interpreted without reference to theology. Effectively, James used a psychodynamic theory of the person as his frame of reference, and in much of his analysis he was fascinated with the possibilities of marginal and subliminal consciousness. This allowed him, for example, to argue that even sudden conversions may be located in longer processes in which unconscious influences play a large part.

If William James's *Varieties of Religious Experience* was a pioneering work in the social-scientific study of conversion at the beginning of the twentieth century, then Lewis Rambo's study *Understanding Religious Conversion* (1993) stands as an impressive synthesis of findings from across a wide range of disciplines near the end of the century. Rambo presents a theory of religious conversion organized according to a sequential stage model to convey the way in which conversion is a process of change over a period of time. A life crisis provokes a quest and this moves one from one's immediate context into an encounter with advocates for the new belief system; interaction with these advocates leads the potential convert into a deeper exploration of the new option; then the process is consummated through some form of commitment, and any number of consequences follow from this, some of which emerge right away, and others of which emerge over

---

[20] William James, *The Varieties of Religious Experience* (2nd edn., 1902), 20.

time. This model is essentially heuristic, and Rambo acknowledges that it is principally a way to organize the complex data gathered in the social-scientific study of conversion. Individuals may loop back and forth through these stages, and any individual's conversion is always more complex than could ever be captured in a simple stage model.[21]

As observed in Ch. 1, the Puritans were pioneers in analysing the stages of religious conversion, and a keen sense of some such process was present for the majority of the subjects of this book. For the most part, we shall let them tell us how they understood the process of conversion, rather than impose a model upon their experience. However, the definitions and distinctions in Rambo's work suggest several lines of enquiry for our study. To take one isolated example from his work, Rambo analyses conversion in terms of the relative magnitude of social and cultural change necessary for someone to be considered a convert, ranging from apostasy (or unconversion) to tradition transition (full proselyte conversion). In other words, he asks how far one must go to be converted. Between these poles of unconversion and full conversion he identifies three more nuanced magnitudes of conversion: intensification, affiliation, and institutional transition.[22] This sort of analysis prompts us to distinguish, in the context of the eighteenth century, between the conversion to evangelical commitment of baptized nominal Anglicans under the preaching of John Wesley, and the proselyte conversion of some Delawares from a Native American religion to Christianity under the ministry of David Brainerd. In sociological terms, not all conversions cover the same distance.

It would be possible to analyse evangelical conversion narrative in a similar way in terms of various theories of the person, society, and culture, or to draw upon one particular theory from many put forward in the behavioural sciences, such as Anthony Wallace's revitalization thesis (anthropology), or Max Weber's theory of the routinization of charisma (sociology), or Erik Erikson's psycho-social theory of adolescent identity formation (psychology). Indeed, these theories and others have proven their heuristic value and been employed as a framework for historical explanation in certain settings. However, my approach to conversion in the pages that follow is to hover more closely over the sources. If conversion is contextual, as we noted above, then historical and textual analysis can offer a particular answer to the question, 'Turning from what to what?' That is not to suggest that one can explain historical texts in the absence of theory, but if we are interested in particular cases and limited generalization, then our use of scientific theories of conversion will necessarily be much more occasional

[21] Lewis Rambo, *Understanding Religious Conversion* (New Haven, Conn., 1993), 16–17, 165–70.
[22] Ibid. 12–14.

and eclectic. This book remains principally a historical study concerned with the appearance of a particular phenomenon in a given time and place. We want to know what is distinctive of early modern English spiritual autobiography, not principally what it is that might illustrate universal patterns observed with (as it were) the patient on the couch. Our methods are not those of clinical observation or survey research. What we have to do with are literary traces of historical events, evidence that must be weighed and assessed to reconstruct a plausible historical picture. So although our approach will be informed by the psychology, sociology, and anthropology of conversion, our interests will nevertheless be primarily hermeneutical.

Gospel (Evangelical)

The word 'gospel' introduces the theological domain for understanding evangelical conversion. Gospel is the noun for which 'evangelical' is the corresponding adjective: evangelical conversion narrative. The root 'evangel' derives from Greek and was translated in Old English by the word *gōdspel* or gospel. The close lexical connection between gospel and evangelical was perhaps more readily recognized in the sixteenth century, when William Tyndale wrote famously in a revised prologue to his translation of the New Testament, 'Evangelion (that we call the gospel) is a Greek word; and signifieth good, merry, glad and joyful tidings, that maketh a man's heart glad, and maketh him sing, dance, and leap for joy.'[23] It was this gospel message, as understood by the leaders of the Evangelical Revival, that contained the call to conversion.

What was this gospel that stimulated and defined the sort of conversion experienced by the subjects of this book? The sources for early evangelical understandings of the gospel were many, but the principal source remained the New Testament itself, filtered through the theology of the magisterial Reformation. The gospel and conversion are closely linked in the pages of the New Testament in terms of divine call and human response. In the synoptic Gospels the good news (*evangelion*) of Jesus commences with John the Baptist's call for conversion (*metanoia*) as preparation for the kingdom (Mark 1: 1–4). This was very much in the tradition of the repeated call of the Hebrew prophets since the eighth century BC for Israel to return to God. Again, at the beginning of Jesus' preaching, the announcement of good news is followed by a call to conversion: 'The kingdom of God is near. Repent (*metanoeite*) and believe the good news (*evangelio*)!' (Mark 1: 15). In the ministry of the apostle Paul likewise, conversion follows the proclamation of gospel. In 1 Thessalonians 1: 4–10, for example, the gospel (*evangelion*) was received by the Thessalonians as a word of spiritual power (1: 5),

---

[23] William Tyndale, 'A Pathway into the Holy Scripture', *Doctrinal Treatises*, ed. Henry Walter (Cambridge, 1848), 8.

and they turned (*epestrepsate*) from idols to serve the living and true God. Here we have both the turning from and turning to.

How did the subjects of this book understand the word 'gospel' which they read in such biblical texts? If eighteenth-century converts used the term 'evangelical' seldom, they often spoke of the gospel and pressed 'gospel' into service as an adjective, so that there were gospel preachers and gospel sermons and gospel conversations. And this gospel was linked, as in the New Testament, to the call to conversion. The word 'gospel' thus highlights the kerygmatic 'preached' character of theology; the gospel represents a word about God which is of the nature of a message that invites a response. Gospel in this sense precedes theological reflection, recalling the remark of Charles Williams that the early church did theology in such time as they had left over from coming into existence.[24]

In the context of the eighteenth-century revival, this gospel was understood through the Protestant Reformation. Luther described the gospel in terms almost identical to those of Tyndale, but added, 'The gospel, then, is nothing but the preaching about Christ, Son of God and of David, true God and man, who by his death and resurrection has overcome for us the sin, death, and hell of all men who believe in him.' Luther highlighted the character of the gospel as promise rather than law. Moreover, as a message the gospel specified the hearer: 'The preaching of the gospel is nothing else than Christ coming to us, or we being brought to him.'[25] Calvin described the gospel in similar terms as 'the proclamation of the grace manifested in Christ'.[26]

When eighteenth-century evangelicals spoke of the gospel, however, they most often equated it more narrowly with the Reformers' teaching about atonement and justification by faith. Charles Wesley's hymns on redemption, for example, amply illustrate this theme: 'Come sinners to the gospel feast' invites the sinner to Christ, declaring,

> Ye all are freely justified,
> Ye all may live—for Christ hath died.

Again the eighth stanza sets forth a tableau of the crucifixion:

> See him set forth before your eyes,
> That precious, bleeding sacrifice!
> His offered benefits embrace,
> And freely now be saved by grace.[27]

---

[24] Charles Williams, *The Descent of the Dove* (New York, 1956), 1.

[25] *Martin Luther's Basic Theological Writings*, ed. T. F. Lull (Minneapolis, Minn., 1989), 108, 113, 115.

[26] John Calvin, *Institutes of the Christian Religion*, ed. J. T. McNeill, trans. F. L. Battles (Philadelphia, 1960), ii. 425.

[27] Wesley, *Works* (BE), vii. 81–2.

This understanding of gospel is what has led David Bebbington to describe evangelicals as 'crucicentric'.[28]

The subjects of this book would on the whole have equally valued such theological inheritance from the Reformation and would have agreed that the gospel was epitomized in the divine promise of forgiveness offered to the sinner by virtue of Christ's atoning death. Increasingly through the seventeenth and eighteenth centuries, however, there was debate about the anthropocentric and theocentric poles of such a gospel. While all agreed that the main existential problem addressed by the gospel was the problem of guilt and the threat of divine judgment, debate centred upon the way in which one could construe the relationship between human and divine agency in salvation. This was wider than simply an academic debate about Calvinist and Arminian perspectives on predestination, since it is evident in the lives of the subjects of this book that close theological distinctions went to the heart of their identities.

The seventeenth century witnessed a significant anthropocentric turn as theology increasingly concerned itself with the sequencing of salvation and mapped this understanding onto experience as an order of conversion. At its most fundamental level this order identified a progress from law to promise (or 'gospel' in the narrow sense), which corresponded to the psychological states of conviction and relief. The theological certainty of a coming divine judgment provoked moral seriousness, introspection, and a psychological travail of conscience, and the gospel presented the only God-given solution for the relief of conscience. This became a matter of serious scrutiny at a theological and psychological level from at least the mid-seventeenth century, so that by the time of the Evangelical Revival there was not only a venerable tradition of 'gospel', but also many variations on its themes.

Questions raised by the concept of gospel govern much of the analysis of Chs. 3–9 as we distinguish sub-genres of conversion narrative across the spectrum of evangelical belief and practice in the eighteenth century. For example, how exactly did this gospel shape the narrative identity of the many converts in the revival? How did it provide the theory that ordered their experience? How did the variations in theological understanding among the partisans of the revival issue in different narrative forms? Or again, how did this gospel continue to inform their identities after the crisis of initial conversion? The answers to these questions reveal that theology was as often expressed in first-person narrative as it was in third-person propositions.

These five terms, then, will recur throughout the discussion that follows: autobiography, narrative, identity, conversion, and gospel (evangelical). The theoretical literature that bears on these concepts sharpens our

---

[28] David W. Bebbington, *Evangelicalism in Modern Britain* (1989), 14–17.

investigation. *Autobiography* is not naive reporting but an apologetic of the self. *Narrative* has a structure that points inevitably beyond itself to higher moral ends that give it meaning. *Identity* also requires a larger framework (an *as*-structure) and is thus negotiated through language within a particular community. *Conversion* is polyvalent and demands a close scrutiny of context (personal, social, cultural, and religious) to determine the nature of the change and the stages involved. And, finally, *gospel* (evangelical) connotes a particular theological field with the potential to integrate Protestant biblical theology with the construction of religious identity at a profoundly personal level.

Distant Antecedents: Spiritual Autobiography and the Christian Tradition

In addition to the theoretical questions raised by the study of conversion narrative, there are important historical questions. One might well ask, for example, whether conversion narrative is a genre that has been constant since the New Testament, present whenever and wherever Christian communities have existed, and whether there are, therefore, pre-modern precedents for the evangelical narratives recorded in this book. Some have claimed a long pedigree for the evangelical pattern of climactic conversion. In the nineteenth century, Matthew Arnold claimed that the conversion of Sampson Staniforth was of 'precisely the same order' as the conversion of St Paul.[29] Evangelicals themselves have sometimes similarly linked the apostle Paul, Augustine, Luther, and Wesley in a tradition of crisis conversion.[30] Yet for all the similarities at one level, the Damascus road encounter, the child's voice in the garden at Milan, the tower experience at Wittenberg, and the strangely warmed heart at Aldersgate Street took place in very different religious and cultural contexts.

The importance of these different contexts is something brought out in modern scholarship. In a landmark essay in 1961 Krister Stendahl critiqued the view that St Paul's conversion was identical with the evangelical pattern of conversion in which relief for a plagued conscience is found through the message of justification by faith. Stendahl argued that the plagued conscience is instead the product of centuries of penitential discipline in the West and should not be read back into the apostle's experience on the

---

[29] Matthew Arnold, *St. Paul and Protestantism* (1892), 36. William James linked the Nova Scotian evangelical Henry Alline with Augustine as similar cases of sin-sick souls who were 'twice-born'. (James, *Varieties of Religious Experience*, 166–75.)

[30] See e.g. Henry Pickering, *Twice-Born Men* (1934). Erik Routley refers to Paul, Augustine, and Wesley as 'classic conversions' in his *Conversion* (Philadelphia, 1960), 19–23. On readings of John Wesley's conversion, see Randy L. Maddox, 'Aldersgate: A Tradition History', in Randy L. Maddox (ed.), *Aldersgate Reconsidered* (Nashville, 1990), 133–46.

Damascus road—an experience that is better understood in its context as something like the calling of a Hebrew prophet through a vision at noonday prayer.[31] Since Stendahl, several competing interpretations of the apostle's Damascus road experience have appeared, but the consensus has been that 'the research of the last few decades has demonstrated the tendentious and misleading nature of more traditional portraits of Paul's Damascus road experience as a cathartic resolution of a guilty soul or the renunciation of Jewish "legalism" '.[32] Again, Henry Chadwick argues that the form of Augustine's narrative in the *Confessions* is indebted to the Neoplatonic pattern of the ascent of the soul. Augustine's quest was to achieve union with the God from whom all beauty, truth, and goodness derives, and his crisis of conversion was the crisis of a philosopher who could see the nature of the good life in ascetic self-denial and contemplation, but who had not the moral power to achieve it.[33] And Marilyn Harran contends that Luther's conversion should not be telescoped into a climactic experience in the tower, but should be interpreted as the culminating insight of a biblical scholar, wrestling with close exegesis of Scripture.[34] Clearly, context matters when it comes to conversion. It is safe to say that however much evangelicals owed to the theology of Paul, Augustine, and Luther, not many of the conversions in the eighteenth century owed much to Palestinian Judaism or Plotinus, or came as a result of a fine syntactical decision about a genitive ('righteousness of God') in the first chapter of Romans.

Autobiography and the Renaissance

In order to appreciate something of the novelty of the genre as it appears in the early modern period, we need to come at it from behind, setting its rise within a larger account of the rise of autobiography itself. Here the Renaissance was the decisive period. William Matthews began his exhaustive bibliography of British autobiography, saying,

In English, there are few medieval autobiographies and the effective beginnings of the modern form are to be sought in the religious lives of the sixteenth and seventeenth centuries, testimonials of sin and conversion and endeavours in behalf of the true belief by Baptists, Catholics, Presbyterians, Congregationalists, Muggletonians, and, most of all, Quakers. Autobiographies of worldly experience, the

---

[31] Krister Stendahl, 'The Apostle Paul and the Introspective Conscience of the West', in Krister Stendahl (ed.), *Paul Among the Jews and Gentiles and Other Essays* (1976), 78–96.

[32] Larry W. Hurtado, 'Convert, Apostate or Apostle to the Nations: The "Conversion" of Paul in Recent Scholarship', *Studies in Religion* 22 (1993), 283–4; cf. Richard Longnecker (ed.), *The Road from Damascus* (Grand Rapids, Mich., 1997).

[33] Henry Chadwick, Introduction to Augustine, *Confessions* (Oxford, 1991), pp. ix–xxviii; and id., *Augustine* (Oxford, 1986), 66–74. See also Peter Brown, *Augustine of Hippo: A Biography* (Berkeley, Calif., 1969), 158–81.

[34] Marilyn J. Harran, *Luther on Conversion* (Ithaca, NY, 1983), 185.

accounts of military life, travel and exploration, scholarly and scientific labors, political activities, begin in the same period although they are less common than the religious.[35]

In this analysis Matthews identifies some of the typical forms of autobiography. 'Testimonials of sin and conversion' points to the conversion narrative; 'endeavours in behalf of the true belief' specifies the apologia form; and 'autobiographies of worldly experience' identifies the tradition of *res gestae*, the record of great deeds by worthy men. Yet all of these are but 'the beginnings of the modern form' which will emerge later as the retrospective autobiography of individual self-expression.[36]

Conversion narrative thus emerged as part of a larger cultural turn towards autobiographical writing in the Renaissance, but how do we account for this autobiographical turn? One way this question has been addressed is through the Burckhardtian tradition of scholarship, which identified autobiography as an expression of Renaissance individualism, part of a linear development of 'the ascent of man'. It was in 1860 that Jacob Burckhardt wrote his famous *Civilization of the Renaissance in Italy*, tracing the rise of individualism in Italian culture. In a famous passage, Burckhardt painted a picture of the contrast between the Middle Ages and the Renaissance:

In the Middle Ages both sides of human consciousness—that which was turned within as that which was turned without—lay dreaming or half awake beneath a common veil. The veil was woven of faith, illusion, and childish prepossession, through which the world and history were seen clad in strange hues. Man was conscious of himself only as a member of a race, people, party, family, or corporation—only through some general category. In Italy this veil first melted into air . . . man became a spiritual *individual*, and recognized himself as such.[37]

According to Burckhardt, autobiography was simply one literary form of the new self-consciousness that appeared in Italy in the fourteenth century and then spread elsewhere.[38] Other expressions of this impulse were seen in painting and sculpture with the increasing popularity of portraiture and self-portraiture, and, indeed, the artist taking himself as a subject was the essence of this Burckhardtian individualism. Benvenuto Cellini's vain and unblushing *Life* in the sixteenth century was perhaps the fullest example of this

---

[35] William Matthews, *British Autobiography: An Annotated Bibliography of British Autobiographies Published or Written Before 1951* (Berkeley, Calif., 1955), p. vii.

[36] Cf. Michael Mascuch's comment that modern autobiography was first popularized in Protestant countries, and that among them England was especially precocious (Mascuch, *Origins of the Individualist Self*, 23). See also Wayne Shumaker, *English Autobiography: Its Emergence, Materials, and Form* (Berkeley, Calif., 1954), 5.

[37] Jacob Burckhardt, *The Civilization of the Renaissance in Italy* (New York, 1958), i. 143.

[38] Ibid. ii. 328–33.

artistic self-fashioning that arose in the Renaissance. For Burckhardt all this was but a cloud the size of a man's fist on the horizon: the modern West developed as a matter of course from these origins.

This account of the rise of individualism and the appearance of autobiography in the Renaissance was for long the standard view, but it has been criticized both for specific historical claims and for its grand narrative of the 'ascent of man'. Peter Burke, for example, raises three problems. Geographically, there are Japanese autobiographies from the eleventh century and Chinese portraiture in the seventeenth century, and other non-Western examples, that call into question the uniqueness of self-consciousness and autobiographical practice as something peculiarly occidental. Sociologically, the tiny minority of literate, upper-class males, usually Italian, that are drawn upon to tell the standard story of the rise of individualism raises the question of how far this story may be applied to lower orders of society or to women. And chronologically, there is evidence of individualism in the Middle Ages, especially from the twelfth century onwards, just as there is also evidence of identity shaped by kinship, guild, city, and so on well into the early modern period.[39]

Moreover the so-called 'revolt of the medievalists' refers to the sizeable scholarly literature that, in reaction to Burckhardt, has claimed for the twelfth century a renaissance to contend with that of the fourteenth and fifteenth centuries in Italy. One theme in this literature is precisely the 'discovery of the individual'.[40] The 'rise of individualism' is, in fact, a story often told. This dawn of individual self-consciousness has been located variously in the Athens of Pericles with the beginning of philosophy and Socrates' costly defiance of traditional society; in Christianity with its linear view of history, reaching classic expression in Augustine's *Confessions* and *City of God* in the late antique period; in the twelfth-century, epitomized in Abelard's *Historia Calamitatum*; in the fourteenth century, not only in Italian humanism, but also in the defeat of realism by nominalism in Ockham and others; in the sixteenth century with the Protestant conscience symbolized

---

[39] Peter Burke, 'Representations of the Self from Petrarch to Descartes', in Roy Porter (ed.), *Rewriting the Self: Histories from the Renaissance to the Present* (1997), 17–18. Alan Macfarlane, *The Origins of English Individualism* (New York, 1979), also takes exception to traditional portraits of the rise of the individual, arguing, controversially, that economic individualism was not a modern development: 'The majority of ordinary people in England from at least the thirteenth century were rampant individualists, highly mobile both geographically and socially, economically "rational," market-oriented and acquisitive, ego-centred in kinship and social life' (163).

[40] Wallace Ferguson, *The Renaissance in Historical Thought: Five Centuries of Interpretation* (Boston, 1948), 329–85; Charles Homer Haskins, *The Renaissance of the Twelfth Century* (Cambridge, Mass., 1927); Robert Benson and Giles Constable (eds.), *Renaissance and Renewal in the Twelfth Century* (Cambridge, Mass., 1982; repr. Toronto, Ont. 1991), 263–95. See also Colin Morris, *The Discovery of the Individual, 1050–1200* (New York, 1972).

in Luther's stand at the Diet of Worms, or again, in the Reformers' doctrine of the priesthood of all believers; in the seventeenth century in the Cartesian *cogito*; in the rise of science, the rise of capitalism, the rise of the nation-state with its bureaucracies, and the rise of Romanticism—and so on. The rise of individualism is clearly not a simple story.

The Burckhardtian tradition thus appears as a kind of Whig interpretation of the rise of individualism.[41] Critique of this tradition has made the story of the rise of individualism a richer and more complex one. We need to pay more attention to context and be aware that overlapping and multiple identities have thrived in different times and places, and under various conditions. There is no simple, diachronic story of the ascent of 'Western man'. Heightened individual self-consciousness may appear at various times and in various places if the right conditions obtain.

But the question remains, what *were* the conditions in the early modern period that fostered such individualism—and with it the heightened interest in autobiography in literature? One necessary condition for the emergence and popularization of written autobiography may certainly be found in the rising rates of literacy during these years. It was in the Renaissance that print first became a common part of everyday life, and this both reflected and stimulated a parallel growth in education and literacy.[42] Moreover, David Cressy claims that by the end of the Stuart period, 'The English had achieved a level of literacy unknown in the past and unmatched elsewhere in early modern Europe.'[43] From the evidence of signatures and marks, levels of literacy increased even further by the Hanoverian period. This is not to imply that people who used to speak their autobiographies (and therefore left no historical trace), now simply wrote them down. The cultural change signalled by literacy is something more profound. There is anthropological significance itself to increased numbers of people reading and writing, since these are practices engaged in privately for the most part, and this itself suggests a more introspective mode of being.[44] Writing is not

---

[41] 'The "Whig interpretation" focuses attention on those lines of development in the past which seem to culminate in present arrangements. This allows it, first, to justify present values (concerning those arrangements) by showing their historical rootedness, and, second, to read those values (once allegedly made tenable) back into the past to condemn the forces which are held to have inhibited the earlier emergence of modern practices.' J. C. D. Clark, *English Society, 1688–1832* (Cambridge, 1985), 11–12.

[42] Lawrence Stone, 'The Educational Revolution in England, 1560–1640', *Past and Present* 28 (1964), 41–80.

[43] David Cressy, *Literacy and the Social Order* (Cambridge, 1980), 176–7; cf. Roger Chartier, 'The Practical Impact of Writing', in Philippe Ariès and Georges Duby (eds.), *A History of Private Life* (Cambridge, Mass., 1989), iii. 112–15.

[44] See further, ibid. iii. 111–59. 'The spread of literacy, the widespread circulation of written materials, whether in printed or manuscript form, and the increasingly common practice of silent reading, which fostered a solitary and private relation between the reader

always linked to introspection, nor does introspection invariably require the practices of a literate society, but in seventeenth-century England writing and reading appeared together as a part of a greater recognition of interiority. Indeed, Philippe Ariès describes England as 'the birthplace of privacy' in this period.[45]

Yet, heightened literacy is insufficient of itself to account for the autobiographical turn. To literacy must be added other factors to account for the rise of the sort of individual self-consciousness evident in popular autobiography. For example, in the sixteenth and seventeenth centuries more people were living in cities, and just as scholars have been keen to correlate religious dissent with urban locations during the Reformation, so also it is evident that the diversity of the city fostered a sense of individual choice. As economic relations were based increasingly on cash and trade, rather than upon land, this likewise represented a greater commercial individualism. Increased travel, exploration, and communication also took the individual out of his or her primordial community and encouraged self-consciousness through the experience of difference.

Science and technology likewise contributed to the disengaging of the subject from nature as human beings sought to observe and control their environment, not by participation in divinely given forms of being that rendered the world intelligible, but by a special epistemology that sharply divided the inner state of the observer from the outward world of appearances. The picture of the detached observer is reinforced by the increased application of technology to organize the world according to human desires. Time was organized by the clock; space by the compass. Even so simple an invention as the Venetian silver-backed mirror, which replaced the burnished metal plates of the Middle Ages, played a role in fostering more detailed and accurate self-reflection. It was the Venetian mirror, for example, that allowed Rembrandt to paint his own self-portrait time and again.[46]

Developments in literacy, urbanization, mercantilism, travel, exploration, communication, science and related epistemologies, technology, art, and other areas devolved more weight upon the individual as a creative volitional agent who stood apart from his or her native surroundings and community. As a result, more men and women felt like Thomas Traherne when he claimed, 'A secret self I had enclos'd within,' or like Michel de

and his book, were crucial changes, which redrew the boundary between the inner life and life in the community. Between 1500 and 1800 man's altered relation to the written word helped to create a new private sphere into which the individual could retreat, seeking refuge from the community' (ibid. iii. 111).

[45] Philippe Ariès, Introduction to Ariès and Duby (eds.), *History of Private Life*, iii. 5.

[46] Gusdorf, 'Conditions and Limits', 33.

Montaigne when he spoke of a room of one's own behind the shop 'wherein we must go alone to ourselves'.[47] But the arrows point in both directions, and individualism was perhaps as much expressed through, as it was fostered by, these social conditions. In any case, it is clear that before 1500 there were precious few autobiographies in Europe; that after 1500 a few Renaissance examples appear; and that after 1600 the stream becomes a river and autobiographical practice is firmly established and increasingly popular—indeed, one of the central features of the 'modern' way of life. In this latter development—the popularization of autobiography—England played an important role, and for this, as Matthews suggests, the religious impulse was critical.

Spiritual Autobiography

We have begun our account of conversion narrative with the rise of greater individual self-consciousness and autobiographical practice under certain specific conditions in the Renaissance. It remains now to consider whether there are more explicitly religious sources for modern spiritual autobiography.

It is perhaps surprising that Augustine's magisterial example in the late-fourth century of what could be done with the confessional form of religious autobiography was so little imitated in the Christian centuries that followed. In the early Middle Ages the new situation north of the Alps, with the entry of the barbarian tribes into Christianity, certainly created a vastly different sort of conversion from the experience of private interiority in Augustine. The difference is epitomized in the contrast between the *Confessions* of Augustine and the *Confession* of St Patrick, despite the fact that these two autobiographies were separated by no more than a century. Augustine wrote at the end of one Christian civilization; Patrick wrote at the beginning of another. Augustine wrote about an inward journey prompted by keen theological questions; Patrick's account was principally of his outward vocation as a charismatic missionary, and he wrote in part to correct false accusations and misrepresentations about his mission. Indeed, Patrick's *Confession* is something of a foundation legend for Irish Christianity,[48] and in this sense it is similar to the royal conversion narratives of Clovis of the Franks in the fifth century, Ethelbert of Kent in the sixth century, and Edwin of Northumbria in the seventh century.[49] In the national conversions of early medieval Europe, right up to the conver-

---

[47] Thomas Traherne, *Selected Poems and Prose*, ed. Alan Bradford (1991), 31; Michel de Montaigne, *The Essayes*, trans. J. Florio (1904), 287.

[48] *The Works of St. Patrick*, trans. Ludwig Bieler (New York, 1953), 21–40; cf. Georg Misch, *A History of Autobiography in Antiquity*, trans. E.W. Dickes (1950), 678–81.

[49] Richard Fletcher, *The Barbarian Conversion* (New York, 1997), 97–129.

sion of the Lithuanians in the fourteenth century, there is little that we would recognize as spiritual autobiography. Somehow, the conditions and questions that would prompt an answer in the form of a retrospective interpretation of one's life from a religious perspective did not arise.

If early medieval converts were, so to speak, not Christian enough to write a conversion narrative like Augustine's, later medieval spiritual autobiographers, as they appeared beginning in the eleventh and twelfth centuries, were, on the contrary, too Christian. Christendom had become so englobing that conversion could no longer be the proselyte experience of conversion from paganism that it was for early medieval Christians, and as it still was for Augustine. Indeed, the word *conversio* came to denote not principally the transition from pagan to Christian, but the passage of a Christian into the life of a religious. Bernard of Clairvaux's sermon, 'On Conversion', preached at Paris in 1140 was, for example, a powerful piece of rhetoric that led more than twenty men to offer themselves to the Cistercian order.[50]

Thus, the first conscious imitations of Augustine's *Confessions* appeared in the eleventh century with the German monk Othloh and in the twelfth century with the *De Vita Sua* of Guibert de Nogent.[51] Guibert's memoirs have been described as the first comprehensive medieval autobiography, treating the course of the author's life from birth onwards.[52] Guibert was preoccupied in this book with his recurring struggles with sin and his repeated recoveries by the grace of God, but the 'conversion' he recounted was really his decision to take up the religious life of a monk at the monastery of Saint Germer. He had lived a rowdy and irreverent life, and his mother arranged for him to be received into the monastery. When he visited, he found his first longings for the monastic life: 'You are my witness, O Lord, you who had arranged all this ahead of time, that the moment I entered the church of that monastery and saw the monks sitting side by side, there welled up within me at the sight of this spectacle such a yearning for the monastic life that my fervour could not be abated nor my soul find its peace until its prayer was granted.' After trying to resist this inner goading for some time, he said, 'I went back to the abbot . . . I fell at his feet and tearfully implored him to receive me, sinner that I was.' And he received his habit the next day.[53] Conversion for Guibert meant becoming a monk, and

---

[50] Bernard of Clairvaux, *Sermons on Conversion*, trans. Marie-Bernard Saïd (Kalamazoo, Mich., 1981), 11–79.

[51] Shumaker, *English Autobiography*, 13; Morris, *Discovery of the Individual*, 79–86. *A Monk's Confession: The Memoirs of Guibert of Nogent*, trans. P. J. Archambault (University Park, Penn., 1996).

[52] Ibid. pp. xxii–xxiii.

[53] Ibid. 48, 49.

his conversion narrative was structured accordingly. The garden in Milan was exchanged for a cloister at Saint Germer.

However, within monastic theology, this understanding of *conversio*, which for Bernard and Guibert still meant a conversion of the heart, was further developed so that conversion came to denote not just the taking of vows, but also the perfection of one's life in God—that for which one took vows in the first place. As the last chapter of the Rule of Saint Benedict put it, the monk was to strive from *initium conversationis* to *perfectionem conversationis*. In consequence, spiritual autobiography in the Middle Ages was typically structured less by the experience of becoming a Christian—or even becoming a monk—than by the pursuit of compunction and final beatitude itself.

This was true inside and outside the cloister. For the fourteenth-century Italian laymen Petrarch and Dante, spiritual autobiography was cast in the form of allegory. The pursuit of spirituality involved the 'affirmative way' of courtly love, celebrating and yet transcending the unconsummated love of a woman—Dante's love for Beatrice and Petrarch's for Laura. This earthly desire became an allegory of the love between a person and God—a God for whom one longs but whom one cannot finally reach. In Dante's autobiographical work, *The New Life*, he recounted how his love for Beatrice led after her death to a spiritual vision, one that would reach its climax in the *Divine Comedy*.[54] Petrarch was greatly influenced by Augustine's *Confessions* and his autobiographical *Secretum* was a dialogue with Augustine over whether or not to withdraw from the world. In this and in his letters, we learn of how he climbed Mont Ventoux and how this ascent became another allegory of spiritual pilgrimage and the longing for the summit of the blessed life.[55]

In contrast to these most learned and world-affirming fourteenth-century poets is the anchorite Julian of Norwich some decades later. But the themes that shaped Julian's autobiographical writing likewise dealt with 'the summit of the blessed life', for it was of spiritual ecstasy that she wrote in her *Showings*, seeking to understand the visions she experienced in her early thirties.[56] Julian's contemporary, the laywoman Margery Kempe, likewise

---

[54] Dante Alighieri, *The New Life*, trans. C. E. Norton (Boston, 1909). Cf. James Collins, *Pilgrim in Love: An Introduction to Dante and His Spirituality* (Chicago, 1984), 19–33.

[55] *Petrarch's Secret*, trans. W. H. Draper (1911; repr., Norwood, Penn., 1975); cf. his letter to Father Dionigi De Roberti of Borgo San Sepolcro, dated 26 April 1336 (*fam.* iv. 1), describing his ascent of Mont Ventoux in *Letters from Petrarch*, trans. M. Bishop (Bloomington, Ind., 1966).

[56] Cf. also the experience of Margaret Ebner who was a religious for many years before she was provoked to more seriousness in her spiritual life by a severe illness that began to afflict her in the year 1312. The illness and suffering lasted for at least thirteen years, but through this she was brought to greater spiritual resignation, and her sense of God's love and consolation increased. In 1335 she had a profound mystical experience, her heart grasped by an ineffable divine power, and this led to ecstatic speech. Thus, even within the monastic life, one could be 'converted'. The preoccupation here is also, however, with final conversion

wrote of her vision of Christ and her attempt to live a contemplative life in the midst of foreign travel and pilgrimage.[57] If these writings by Dante and Petrarch, and Julian of Norwich and Margery Kempe, can be considered conversion narratives—and in one sense, of course, they are—then they are conversion narratives of a very different kind from those that emerged in the later Protestant tradition. Like the later spiritual autobiographies these late-medieval examples were occasioned variously by concerns confessional, apologetic, hortatory, and doxological, but in narrative terms they were shaped most profoundly by the desire for final conversion rather than the experience of initial conversion.

The Reformation and Conversion Narrative

While we have autobiographical writings from Ignatius Loyola and Teresa of Avila in the sixteenth century, it is noteworthy that the Protestant magisterial reformers did not, as a rule, write their spiritual memoirs or the narrative of their initial conversion experiences. The reformers wrote tracts, treatises, and catechisms, but they did not write spiritual autobiographies. We have to go to an autobiographical fragment written in 1545 in the prologue to the Wittenberg edition of Luther's Latin writings to find his famous 'tower experience'.[58] Luther described his spiritual breakthrough as something that occurred while studying the book of Romans. He recalled the sense of personal guilt under which he laboured, saying, 'Though I lived as a monk without reproach, I felt that I was a sinner before God with an extremely disturbed conscience.' As he meditated on the meaning of the 'righteousness of God' in Romans 1 he came to understand this in a new way as the righteousness by which God mercifully justifies the sinner by faith. Luther recalled the effect this had on him: 'Here I felt that I was altogether born again and had entered paradise itself through open gates.'[59] Many scholars now argue that Luther, looking back as an old man, telescoped a much longer process of growing insight into that alleged breakthrough some twenty years earlier, and that it may be misleading to construe it as his 'conversion'.[60] And in any case, it is a fragment only.

Our knowledge of John Calvin's conversion is even more slight, and it comes likewise from a document written at a much later stage in his life. At a distance of some twenty-five years Calvin wrote about his 'sudden

and beatitude. See further, *Margaret Ebner: Major Works*, trans. L. P. Hindsley (New York, 1993).

[57] Margery Kempe, *The Book of Margery Kempe*, trans. B. Windeatt (1994).

[58] Heiko A. Oberman, *Luther: Man between God and the Devil*, trans. E. Walliser-Schwarzbart (New Haven, Conn., 1989), 164–6; Harran, *Luther on Conversion*, 174–88.

[59] Martin Luther, 'Preface to the Complete Edition of Luther's Latin Writings, 1545', trans. L. W. Spitz, Sen., *Luther's Works* (Philadelphia, 1960), xxxiv. 336–7.

[60] See further Harran, *Luther on Conversion*, 189–93.

conversion', but again, to find this reference you have to search carefully through the Preface to his *Psalms Commentary* (1557) to find the passing reference.[61] Calvin wrote, 'When I was too firmly addicted to the papal superstitions to be drawn easily out of such a deep mire, by a sudden conversion He brought my mind (already more rigid than suited my age) to submission.'[62] This was a cryptic allusion in the course of a short description of his timid beginnings as a reformer, amid much trouble and persecution. The reference has occasioned much debate as to what exactly Calvin meant by a 'sudden conversion' (*subita conversio*) to 'submission' (*docilitas*). But Calvin's interest in spiritual autobiography itself was clearly accidental. His reflections were called forth by his desire to demonstrate how the Psalms were of comfort to those in a situation similar to David. Neither Luther nor Calvin offered anything that could be taken as a true precedent for the sorts of spiritual autobiographies examined in this book.

The same may be said about the Reformation as a whole. Judith Pollmann writes, 'There is a peculiar gap in the long tradition of the conversion narrative. The tens of thousands of Europeans who in the course of the sixteenth century turned to Protestantism left very few accounts of their experiences of conversion.'[63] Hence, we may speak of the evangelical conversion narrative in the eighteenth century, or the Puritan conversion narrative in the seventeenth century, but there is no genre of sixteenth-century Reformation conversion narrative.[64] As a reason for this lacuna Pollmann reminds us of the enormous effort of the Reformers to emphasize the antiquity of their doctrines, rather than the novelty of their ways. Innovation was widely unacceptable and to distance oneself from one's past life was perceived as a sin against filial piety. Typically, the Reformers spoke not of changes in their personalities but of learning old truths and unlearning bad habits.[65] For the Reformers conversion was understood

---

[61] On Calvin's conversion see Peter Wilcox, 'Restoration, Reformation and the Progress of the Kingdom of Christ: Evangelisation in the Thought and Practice of John Calvin, 1555–1564', D.Phil. thesis (Oxford, 1993), 177–209; id., 'Conversion in the Thought and Experience of John Calvin', *Anvil* 14 (1997), 113–28.

[62] *Calvin: Commentaries*, trans. and ed. J. Haroutunian and L. P. Smith (Philadelphia, 1958), 52.

[63] Judith Pollmann, 'A Different Road to God: the Protestant Experience of Conversion in the Sixteenth Century', in Peter van der Veer (ed.), *Conversion to Modernities* (New York, 1996), 47–8.

[64] Cf. the comments of W. R. Ward, *The Protestant Evangelical Awakening* (Cambridge, 1992), 2: 'The movements of renewal and revival of the eighteenth century sought their legitimation in the hand of God in history; their characteristic achievement was not, like the Reformers of the sixteenth century, to offer a confession of faith for public discussion, but to accumulate archives which would support their understanding of history.'

[65] Pollmann, 'Different Road to God', 52–4.

principally as a continuous and lifelong process of learning faith within the context of the church, often described as a school.[66]

While the secular autobiography followed its own course during this period as a memoir of outward achievements, the first forms of specifically religious autobiography among Protestants in the sixteenth and seventeenth centuries took the form of religious apologia, or narratives of suffering and martyrdom, reflecting the religious and political strife of the period.[67] Conversion figured in passing in these narratives, but it was not the central theme that it would become in the seventeenth century.

For example, Theodore Beza, Calvin's successor in Geneva, included an account of his conversion in the preface to his *Confessio Christianae Fidei*:

Behold [God] inflicted a very serious illness on me, so that I almost despaired of my life. What should I do in this wretched state, when nothing stood before my eyes beyond the horrific judgment of a just God? After endless torments of mind and body, God, taking pity on his fugitive slave, so consoled me that I no longer doubted that I had been granted forgiveness. Thus in tears I cursed myself, I sought forgiveness and I renewed my vow to openly embrace His true worship and finally I dedicated myself wholly to Him. And so it came about that the image of death placed before me in earnest aroused in me the slumbering and buried desire for the true life, and that this disease for me was the beginning of true health . . . And as soon as I could leave my bed, having severed all my ties and gathered my possessions, I once and for all abandoned my country, parents and friends to follow Christ, and together with my wife I retired into voluntary exile in Geneva.[68]

The experience Beza recalls here occurred in 1548 and was first written up in a letter to a friend in 1560, but Judith Pollmann argues that this 'conversion narrative' was an exception in the sixteenth century. Moreover, Beza's account was written not for doxological or hortatory motives per se, nor certainly for the celebration of individuality that appeared in Cellini, but rather for wholly apologetic reasons. Beza had been accused by his Catholic adversaries of having lived an unrighteous life as a young man. This narrative was offered as an explanation of the contrast between his past shortcomings and his present status.[69] It was *apologia* not *confessio*. The same was true of Hugues Sureau, a French Calvinist minister who converted to Catholicism and was pressed by officials to write a confession. A year later he reconverted to Calvinism. He therefore wrote a new conversion

---

[66] David C. Steinmetz, 'Reformation and Conversion', *Theology Today* 35 (1978), 30.

[67] For a description of the memoir or impersonal autobiography as distinct from spiritual autobiography in this period, see Donald A. Stauffer, *English Biography Before 1700* (Cambridge, Mass., 1930), 175–216.

[68] Quoted in Pollmann, 'Different Road to God', 49–50.

[69] Ibid.

narrative to explain his decision and to recant his earlier confession. Again it was the apologetic motive which was to the fore.[70]

The same could be said of the account we have of the conversion of the Anabaptist Menno Simons (1496–1561). Menno's account of his experience was not written and published as a stand-alone spiritual autobiography, but occurred in the course of his *Reply to Gellius Faber* (1554). This *Reply* was a formal response to a bitter attack on the Anabaptists in the Netherlands. Because Faber implied that Menno had received his doctrine from the notorious sect at Münster, and because Menno and his followers would therefore be associated with the revolutionary violence, polygamy, and other excesses of Münster, he felt he had to respond. But again, his reluctance to do so was profound: 'And so I am forced briefly to explain the transaction, of which I would otherwise, for the sake of modesty, remain silent; namely, how I came to the knowledge of my Lord and Saviour Jesus Christ.'[71] Again, he implored his readers 'for God's sake . . . that they will not think hard of me for it, nor consider it as vain boasting that I tell it here'.[72] Moreover, when he told of his conversion, he emphasized the truths he had learned, how God had given him a 'new mind' and the courage to live by these convictions.[73] At the end of his narrative (which was clearly set off by this inclusio) he again entreated his readers to accept his 'forced confession' and he pleaded again the exigency of the slanders to which he was compelled to respond.

For the most part sixteenth-century religious autobiographies were fragmentary and unpublished, collected and printed only posthumously. *The Bloody Theater, or, Martyrs' Mirror* is, for example, a collection of accounts of Anabaptist suffering compiled from various chronicles, memorials, and testimonies by Thieleman J. van Braght, and originally published in Dutch in 1660. The English edition is a large volume of closely printed text, laid out in double columns, over a thousand pages of which recount the details of Anabaptist martyrdoms during the sixteenth century. Most of the documents drawn upon in these accounts were official court records and letters written by the martyrs while in prison awaiting execution. The letters were typically cast in the distinctive form of a spiritual last will and testament, and most included a confession of faith and strongly worded admonition to the faithful who remained—exhorting family members and church

---

[70] Pollmann, 'Different Road to God', 50–1.

[71] *The Complete Writings of Menno Simons*, ed. J. C. Wenger, trans. L. Verduin (Kitchener, Ont., 1984), 667.

[72] Ibid. 668.

[73] Menno summarizes his conversion thus: 'And so you see, my reader, in this way the merciful Lord through the liberal goodness of His abounding grace took notice of me, a poor sinner, stirred in my heart the outset, produced in me a new mind, humbled me in His fear, taught me to know myself in part, turned me from the way of death and graciously called me into the narrow pathway of life and the communion of His saints.' Ibid. 671.

members to stand firm. The autobiographical narrative was typically limited to an account of the arrest, trial, and imprisonment, and there was almost no extended religious autobiography as such. The Anabaptist martyrs, like the magisterial Reformers, did not feel the need to offer up a religious narrative of their lives as a whole.

One exception to this appears in the account of Joriaen Simons, an Anabaptist weaver and bookseller, who was burned at the stake as a heretic at Haarlem in Holland on 26 April 1557. Simons was martyred in the persecution that followed the rise to power of Phillip II as king of Spain and his attempt to stamp out Protestantism in his dominions in the Netherlands. While in prison Simons wrote a 'testament' to leave behind for his young son, and in this he recounted some details of his own spiritual autobiography. His narrative has the shape of conversion, with its contrast between his life before and after choosing to follow Christ. He commenced his account, saying, 'The beginning of my life was unprofitable, proud, puffed-up, drunken, selfish, deceitful, and full of all manner of idolatry. And when I attained maturity, and began to be my own master, I sought nothing but what pleased my flesh, an indolent and luxurious life.' He added that he was greedy and referred cryptically to how he sought to 'bring my neighbor's daughter to a fall'. He continued, introducing his change of life, 'But, my dear child, when I betook myself to the Scriptures, and searched and perused them, I found that my life tended to eternal death, yea, that the everlasting woe was hanging over me, and that the fiery pool which burns with brimstone and pitch was prepared for me.' Simons evaluated his life and determined it was better 'to suffer affliction with the people of God for a little while, than to live in every luxury with the world, which will perish. Thus I abandoned my ease, voluntarily and uncompelled, and entered upon the narrow way, to follow Christ, my Head, well knowing that if I should follow Him unto the end, I should not walk in darkness.' He concluded this brief narrative by returning to his present situation in prison: 'Now, when I had partly forsaken and cast from me the old damnable practices, and wanted to be a new divine creature, and to lead a pious, penitent, godly life, I was immediately, like all the pious that had been before me, hated, yea, imprisoned in Haarlem, in St. John's gate.'[74]

Thus, within the larger form of 'last will and testament', Simons offered a spare and unembellished conversion narrative as part of an admonition that he hoped his son would read when old enough to understand such matters. The narrative recounted outward actions only, and can be contrasted with later Puritan and Pietist narratives by the complete absence of any sense of moral or spiritual inability, or any indication of a troubled conscience. Moreover, the

---

[74] Thieleman J. van Braght (ed.), *The Bloody Theater, or, Martyrs' Mirror*, trans. J. F. Sohm (Scottsdale, Penn., 1987), 565.

piety was that of the *imitatio Christi*, not of the penal, substitutionary atonement. He exhorted his son that he could escape the impending wrath of God 'in no better way than by looking to Jesus Christ, the Son of the Almighty and eternal Father, who is the Head and Pattern of all believers', and he warned him to avoid the 'sects' of the Lutherans and Zwinglians. He concluded by urging his son to a costly obedience, saying, 'You must be born again, and converted, if you would enter the kingdom of God.' The language is similar to that of later evangelicals, but the piety is very different.

John Foxe's *Acts and Monuments* was first published in English in 1563, and this also drew upon autobiographical documents. Like the Anabaptists' *Martyrs' Mirror* it was compiled to extol the heroic faith of martyrs, though its chief focus was on the English Protestants who were martyred under Queen Mary. And just as the *Martyrs' Mirror* was written with apologetic intentions—to defend Anabaptists and denounce Roman Catholic and Protestant persecutors—so also Foxe's *Acts and Monuments* was designed as a polemic for English Protestantism and a demonstration of Papist tyranny. It is impossible to understand the documents in these collections outside the context of intense religious polemic fostered by the determined efforts of state bureaucracies to enforce uniformity and achieve the ideals of a purely confessional state.

In all of this, however, was the beginning of a kind of spiritual autobiography, though, as in the case of the *Martyrs' Mirror*, the examples are very few. One comes from a letter recorded by John Foxe, written originally by Thomas Bilney (*c*.1495–1531) to Cuthbert Tunstall, Bishop of London, in 1527. The letter included an eloquent conversion narrative of sorts, but the occasion that called forth Bilney's personal narrative was emphatically adversarial. Indeed, the letter formed part of the legal records of Bilney's trial for heresy before the bishop, who was acting on behalf of Cardinal Wolsey. In this letter Bilney explained how he procured a Latin edition of Erasmus's New Testament because of his interest in Erasmus's Latin style. But upon his very first reading he was struck by the 'sweet and comfortable' sentence in 1 Timothy 1: 15: 'It is a true saying, and worthy of all men to be embraced, that Christ Jesus came into the world to save sinners; of whom I am the chief and principal.' Bilney described what passed within him: 'This one sentence, through God's instruction and inward working, which I did not then perceive, did so exhilarate my heart, being before wounded with the guilt of my sins, and being almost in despair, that immediately I felt a marvellous comfort and quietness, insomuch "that my bruised bones leaped for joy".'[75] These were early days in the reform movement and

---

[75] *The Acts and Monuments of John Foxe* (New York, 1965), iv. 635. See also John F. Davis, 'The Trials of Thomas Bylney and the English Reformation', *Historical Journal* 24 (1981), 775–90.

Lutheran ideas had only just begun to penetrate into England. Condemned as a heretic, Bilney was burned at the stake under Henry VIII three years before the Act of Supremacy. But this passing autobiographical reference anticipates the most significant formal element of conversion narrative that will later emerge among the Puritans: namely, conviction under the law ('wounded with the guilt of my sins') and relief under the promises of the gospel ('a marvellous comfort and quietness'). The larger document, and collection of documents, forms an apologia for an accused Protestant or Lollard, but within this is a more private psychological narrative of conversion.

Throughout the Tudor period and well into the early Stuart period in England, conversion was understood as a matter of true belief and allegiance to the true institutional church, whether that be the Roman Catholic Church or the Church of England. Yet, conversion was also understood, within this framework, as a matter of inward faith and personal salvation. Michael Questier argues that the political and religious motives for conversion in this period were in constant tension in the minds of individual converts: 'Conversion refers primarily to the way in which sinful man is made regenerate by grace. Nevertheless, the theology of conversion raises certain imperatives about the sort of Church to which the regenerate man should adhere. This promotes the second type of conversion, namely between ecclesiastical institutions, which takes on a political character.'[76] The state could demand, and often achieve, politico-ecclesiastical obedience, but the innermost religious beliefs of people could not be ignored. Clergymen on both sides of the religious divide sought to influence proselytes towards a deeper sense of conversion, one that transcended politico-ecclesiastical boundaries. Catholics were not satisfied with mere recusancy; Protestants were not happy with mere conformity. Both Jesuit and Puritan evangelists aimed for an ecclesiastical obedience that issued from a deeper conversion from sin to grace.[77]

Writing in the seventeenth century, Richard Baxter reflected a similar insight in his comments on conversion in his memoirs. First he recognized the category of proselyte conversion in which people turn to 'the profession of Christianity' from outside the Christian religion altogether. He was astonished to think that 'so small a part of the World hath the Profession of Christianity, in comparison of Heathens, Mahometans and other Infidels'. But then he made a further distinction, astonished also that 'among professed Christians there are so few that are saved from gross Delusions, and have but any competent Knowledge'. This distinction between 'gross

---

[76] Michael C. Questier, *Conversion, Politics and Religion in England, 1580–1625* (Cambridge, 1996), 3–4.
[77] Ibid. 168–202.

delusions' and 'competent knowledge' went to the heart of politico-ecclesiastical attempts at reformation. But Baxter's astonishment went one step further, as he expressed his wonder that among those with competent knowledge 'there are so few that are seriously Religious, and truly set their hearts on Heaven'.[78] Like peeling back the layers of an onion, Baxter's analysis at last reached the innermost sense of conversion, the conversion of the heart. It was this concept of inward conversion in the seventeenth century that provided the theological framework for the emergence of conversion narrative as a truly popular genre.

What then does this historical survey tell us? In short, the Renaissance made people more aware of themselves as individuals, and the church made them more aware of themselves as sinners. These two conditions were necessary for the emergence of evangelical conversion narrative as a popular genre. With the fracturing of Christendom in the confessional strife of the Reformation the question of allegiance to true church and true faith became acute. In this apologetic situation there appeared a new narrative of conversion based upon the teaching of the Reformers, one which emphasized the beginning of the Christian life in an individual's first experience of repentance and faith, in contrast to the monastic and mystical preoccupations of medieval spiritual autobiography. To state a theme to which we shall return, evangelical conversion narrative thus appeared on the trailing edge of Christendom and the leading edge of modernity.

[78] Richard Baxter, *Reliquiae Baxterianae* (1696), 131.

I

Early Modern Origins: The Rise of Popular Conversion Narrative

IN 1657 the English Puritans Thomas Goodwin and Philip Nye complained about the Catholic understanding of conversion, saying, 'But that first great and *saving Work of Conversion*; which is the foundation of all true *piety*, the great and numerous volumns [*sic*] of their most devout writers are usually silent therein. Yea they eminently appropriate the *word Conversion* and *thing* itself, unto a man that *renounceth* a *Secular life*, and entereth into *Religious orders* . . .' In contrast, Goodwin and Nye looked back over the previous century and claimed,

It hath been one of the Glories of the *Protestant Religion*, that it revived the Doctrine of *Saving Conversion*, And of the *new creature* brought forth thereby . . . But in a more eminent manner, God hath cast the honour hereof upon the Ministers and Preachers of this Nation, who are renowned abroad for their more accurate search into, and discoveries hereof.[1]

According to Goodwin and Nye, then, English Protestants were renowned in the late sixteenth and seventeenth centuries for their analysis of conversion.

How did this come about? With the accession of Elizabeth I in 1558 and the Protestant settlement enacted through legislation in the early years of her reign, England was increasingly a Protestant country. The Puritans— 'the hotter sort of Protestants' as they were described in a contemporary tract—arose as a party within this Protestant establishment and wished it to be more Protestant yet. England was but 'halfly reformed' and they wanted to see a purer church. Included among their number were many English clergy who had been exiles in Geneva and elsewhere on the Continent during the reign of Queen Mary, and who therefore brought back to England a vivid picture of what a fully reformed church might look like. Galvanized in the 1560s as a party during the Vestiarian controversy over 'popish' remnants in worship, such as copes and surplices, they became a powerful voice for reform through pulpit and press. Under the leadership of

---

[1] Introduction to Thomas Hooker, *The Application of Redemption . . . Printed from the Author's Papers . . . by Thomas Goodwin, and Philip Nye* (1657), n.p.

Thomas Cartwright it seemed for a period that their aims were limited to a more pure liturgy and a presbyterian form of polity, but the movement outlasted the failure of these ecclesiastical objectives. So, for example, while controversy swirled around the head of Richard Greenham, he, like many others, set himself principally 'to stir up the heart, and to quicken affections to embrace true godlinesse'.[2]

For all the feathering out of the movement into various sects and factions in the Elizabethan and early Stuart periods, there was a distinctive vein of 'experimental piety' that was grounded in Calvinism and that drew upon a long tradition of English practical divinity, exemplified in earlier divines such as the Marian martyrs John Hooper and John Bradford. This piety was evident during the reign of Elizabeth, for example, in a 'spiritual brotherhood' of Puritan ministers who eschewed controversy in favour of promoting practical godliness. Many of these men were later described by Richard Baxter as 'affectionate practical English writers'; many were also associated with Cambridge, including Richard Greenham, William Perkins, Richard Rogers, John Dod, and others.[3] This is not the place to follow the fortunes of Puritanism through all its variations in the turbulent politics of the late sixteenth and seventeenth centuries.[4] However, the political context for conversion shifted during these decades, so that conversion was framed at an ecclesiastical level, not principally in terms of Catholic versus Protestant (though this was always still thinkable), but in terms of internal Protestant schism. Yet notwithstanding these ecclesiastical tensions, preachers remained vitally concerned with personal salvific questions, not only with those of polity. Although the unregenerate person was seen by Puritans as papistical for his presumed dependence upon works righteousness, the Puritan understanding of conversion stressed the transformation of the individual by grace, a transformation that took place through the agency of a gospel ministry and which only thus contributed to establishing a more pure church and godly commonwealth. With such concerns, Puritan teaching and practice during these years formed a matrix within which spiritual autobiography would eventually flourish.

---

[2] Henry Holland, 'Preface to the Reader' in *The Workes of Richard Greenham* (1605).

[3] See further, Paul R. Schaefer, 'The Spiritual Brotherhood on the Habits of the Heart: Cambridge Protestants and the Doctrine of Sanctification from William Perkins to Thomas Shepard', D.Phil. thesis (Oxford, 1994).

[4] See further, William Haller, *The Rise of Puritanism* (1938; repr. New York, 1957); Marshall Mason Knappen, *Tudor Puritanism* (Chicago, 1939); Peter Lake, *Moderate Puritans and the Elizabethan Church* (Cambridge, 1982); Patrick Collinson, *The Elizabethan Puritan Movement* (Oxford, 1990).

THE PURITAN CONVERSION NARRATIVE

William Perkins and the Theory of Conversion

The Puritans fostered spiritual autobiography in part by their stress upon religious experience. As Goodwin and Nye implied, the Elizabethan Puritans built upon the doctrinal insights of the magisterial Reformers to develop a more applied theology of conversion. This development culminated in the work of William Perkins (1558–1602), who uniquely combined Continental Reformed theology with the indigenous tradition of English practical divinity and preaching.[5] Indeed, Perkins's widely read *Armilla Aurea* (1590) is an early example of the Puritan theology that would provide the structure of countless autobiographies in the seventeenth century and beyond. The *Golden Chain*, as it was called in English, was a comprehensive theology laid out according to the Reformed order of salvation: from God's decrees in eternity through their temporal realization in effectual calling, justification, sanctification, and glorification, to life eternal and the final glory of God—and the parallel realization of God's decrees in an order of damnation. Like other federal theologians, Perkins included a chart which summarized all this 'for them which cannot read'. His work went through fifteen editions in twenty years, and the 'golden chain' became a common trope among Puritans. For example, two generations later Thomas Manton wrote, 'There is a golden chain, the chain of salvation, which is carried on from link to link, till the purposes of eternal grace do end in the possession of eternal glory.'[6] For Puritans salvation had its own proper syntax. And by the late sixteenth century this syntax had been carefully parsed.

The practical concern that motivated Perkins in this still scholastic formation of theology is evident throughout his treatise. For example, he begins his work on the *Golden Chain* by emphasizing that theology is 'the science of living blessedly forever' and that such blessedness arises from the knowledge of God and of ourselves—the doctrine of double knowledge, with which Calvin also begins his *Institutes*.[7] Again, in chs. 30 and 31 Perkins expounds the proper uses of the law and gospel. The first use of the law is 'to lay open sinne and make it knowne'. Perkins apostrophizes to the reader, 'If therefore, thou desirest seriously eternal life, first take a narrow examination of thy selfe and the course of thy life by the square of God's law: then set before thine eyes the curse that is due unto sinne, that thus bewailing thy misery, & despairing utterly of thine owne power, to attaine everlasting happiness, thou maiest renounce thy selfe and be provoked to seeke and sue

---

[5] Lynn Baird Tipson, Jr., 'The Development of a Puritan understanding of conversion', Ph.D. thesis (Yale, 1972), 189–261; Norman Pettit, *The Heart Prepared: Grace and Conversion in Puritan Spiritual Life* (2nd edn., Middletown, Conn., 1989), 62–5.

[6] Thomas Manton, *Works* (1870), v. 202.

[7] William Perkins, *Works* (1626), i. 11.

unto Christ Jesus.'[8] Effectively, Perkins takes Calvin's first use of the law and applies it to the reader with precision in a close personal address. The use of the gospel follows, which he describes vividly as 'the instrument, and, as it were, the conduit pipe of the holy Ghost, to fashion and derive faith into the soule'.[9] This understanding of the relationship between law and the gospel was a foundation for the Puritan conversion experience. Perkins concludes his treatise by explaining how the doctrine of predestination is to be applied through self-examination, whereby each person ought to seek to discern the twin signs of election in his or her life: the inward testimony of the Spirit and the outward evidence of sanctification.

Such a searching and practical application of the Reformed scheme of salvation to the individual led to an unusual degree of introspection on the part of those who took it seriously. With the 'golden chain' schema, Perkins provided a complete theory of conversion that one could compare with one's own experience.[10] His stress upon the *ordo salutis*, the relationship between law and gospel in salvation, and the importance of self-examination and coming to assurance would shape conversion narrative for generations to come.

The introspective piety that such self-examination encouraged was also reflected in the detailed elaboration of Puritan casuistry to deal with cases of conscience. Puritan preachers were described as physicians of the soul, and they produced a voluminous literature which bore this out—a growing number of books of pastoralia and manuals, culminating in the seventeenth century in paranetic works such as Richard Baxter's monumental *Christian Directory*. In all of this the Puritans fostered a religious culture that stressed the importance of 'experimental knowledge' and the need to correlate experience with biblical theology. Vavasor Powell described spiritual experience in precisely these terms of inner and outer correlation: 'the inward sense and feeling, of what is outwardly read and heard'. Again, he claimed that experience was like salt to fresh meat: 'it seasons brain-knowledge'.[11]

William Perkins's *Cases of Conscience* (1606) was one important early casuistical manual. In this work Perkins proposed and answered practical questions that bore on the spiritual and moral life. There are few better examples of the way in which Puritans applied the sort of discursive soteriology in the *Golden Chain* intimately to the souls of their parishioners. If in the *Golden Chain* we hear the Puritan preacher in the pulpit, in *Cases of Conscience*

---

[8] William Perkins, *Works* (1626), i. 69.

[9] Ibid. i. 70.

[10] For a detailed discussion of the order of salvation in Puritan theology, see John von Rohr, *The Covenant of Grace in Puritan Thought* (Atlanta, 1986), 87–112; Dewey D. Wallace, Jr., *Puritans and Predestination* (Chapel Hill, NC, 1982).

[11] Vavasor Powell, 'Epistle to the Sober and Spirituall Readers of this Booke', prefixed to *Spirituall Experiences, of Sundry Beleevers* (1653), n.p.

we hear the Puritan pastor in his study. Near the beginning of the book, Perkins introduces his subject: 'Of the first maine question touching man. I. Question. *What must a man doe, that he may come into Gods favour, and be saved.*' Perkins identified ten divine actions in God's 'first grace'. Although the question Perkins set himself is phrased in terms of 'what must a man doe', his exposition is given in terms of what God does; thus God gives (1) the means of grace, especially preaching, and with this some inward or outward hardship, (2) knowledge of the law, (3) insight into one's own particular sins, and (4) legal fear of punishment and hell, leading to despair of salvation. These first four are preliminary stages ('workes of preparation') and do not necessarily lead to saving faith. Among God's elect, however, there follows the special operation of saving grace leading to further stages in the order of redemption. The remaining actions of God's grace are (5) to stir up the mind to consider seriously the promises of the gospel, (6) to kindle in the heart some sparks of faith,[12] (7) to test faith with doubt, despair, and distrust, (8) to quiet the conscience and give assurance of final salvation, (9) to stir the heart to a new evangelical sorrow for sin and evangelical repentance,[13] and (10) to give the capacity for a new obedience.[14] Since Edmund Morgan's *Visible Saints* (1963), it has been common to refer to this pattern as the 'morphology of conversion', and scholars have offered various reconstructions of the pattern.[15]

Here then was a map for the spiritual geography of the soul. Perkins provided the detailed religious terms for an individual to describe his or her own sense of spiritual inwardness, and to understand how this interiority changed through time and in the midst of crisis. The 'map' offered guidance not only for how to describe the present and past experience of inwardness, but also for how to act ('what a man must doe') in anticipation of the future—even when that 'acting' involved a passive sort of waiting and trusting. There was a definite teleology to divine grace, and knowing this allowed one to orient oneself in narrative space. This ability to define one's own sense of inner space was all the more important with the heightened self-consciousness that appeared in the Renaissance, as traced in the last chapter. In this sense, then, Perkins proposed and outlined a distinctive and

---

[12] Of this stage Perkins says, 'Now at the same instant, when God beginnes to kindle in the heart any sparkes of faith, then also hee justifies the sinner, and withall beginnes the worke of sanctification.' William Perkins, *Works* (1613), ii. 13.

[13] Perkins adds, 'Though this repentance bee one of the last in order, yet it shewes itself first: as when a candle is brought into a roome, wee first see the light before we see the candle, and yet the candle must needes bee, before the light can be.' Ibid.

[14] Ibid. This morphology comes from Perkins's *First Booke of the Cases of Conscience*, ch. 5. Perkins also deals with this question in a sermon, *A Case of Conscience, the Greatest that Ever Was; How a Man May Know Whether He Be the Childe of God or No* (1592); see further, Haller, *Rise of Puritanism*, 155.

[15] Edmund S. Morgan, *Visible Saints* (New York, 1963), 68–9.

lucid Puritan form of 'narrative identity': if a believer could discern these stages in her life, correlating outward and inward experience, then she would possess a well-ordered and integrated sense of herself—who she was, where she had come from, and where she was going.

Richard Kilby and the Beginnings of Puritan Conversion Narrative

How does the sort of theology in the *Golden Chain* and the casuistry of *Cases of Conscience*, with its 'morphology of conversion', pass over into narrative itself? One of the earliest examples of the genre of Puritan conversion narrative appeared with Richard Kilby's *The Burthen of a Loaden Conscience* (1608) and its sequel *Hallelu-iah: Praise Yee the Lord, for the Unburthening of a Loaden Conscience* (1614). In these works Kilby did not refer directly to Perkins or to other Puritan authors as sources for his beliefs and practices, but he did identify himself as a Puritan, and his piety clearly reflected the focus upon self-examination that was characteristic of Puritan devotional manuals published since the 1580s.

Richard Kilby (or Kilbye, d. 1617) was raised in Warwickshire just after the vestments controversy and during the period when many Puritans such as Thomas Cartwright were sharply criticizing the Elizabethan Church, arguing that it should be more presbyterian in form and discipline. A religiously observant youth, he was taught the Lord's Prayer and the Creed and participated knowledgeably in the divine office on Sundays. In this sense, he was one of the successes of the Protestant Reformation, which had directed so much energy into programmes of elementary catechism at a parish level. Later, however, Kilby remembered only the inadequacy of catechism, since he had then learned only 'outward religion' and his heart was still 'farre from God'.[16] Educated at Gloucester Hall, Oxford, and Emmanuel College, Cambridge, he became a schoolmaster in Kent before entering the ministry in 1595 and serving various curacies in Kent and Derbyshire.[17] Yet his biography illustrates the way in which the concept of an ecclesiastical conversion to the true church overlapped with the concept of personal regeneration by divine grace during this period. For though he was raised within the Elizabethan Church of England, Kilby was at one point received into the Church of Rome by a seminary priest, only to become afterwards a zealous Puritan. 'I do often wonder at my selfe,' wrote Kilby, 'how fervent I was, first a Protestant, then a Roman Catholike, afterward a Precisian.'[18] In an aside to the reader, he correlates ecclesiastical

---

[16] Richard Kilby, *Hallelu-iah. Praise yee the Lord. For the Unburthening of a Loaden Conscience. By his Grace in Iesus Christ, Vouchsafed unto the Worst Sinner of all the World* (1632), 36.

[17] *Alum. Cant.* and *Alum. Oxon.* Note that this is not the same Richard Kilbye (d. 1620) who was one of the translators of the Authorized Version.

[18] Richard Kilby, *The Burthen of a Loaden Conscience: or, The Miserie of Sinne: Set Forth by the Confession of a Miserable Sinner* (Cambridge, 1616), 9.

conversion with evangelical conversion, saying to those who are complacent and whose faith is nominal, 'I can tell you what religion is the fittest for
you; even that which you call the old religion: for that will so furnish you
with outward works and ceremonies, that you shall not dreame of meddling
with your heart.'[19] The equation of true church and true faith thus had its
corollary for Kilby in false church and false faith.

Like many later evangelicals, Kilby experienced profound spiritual crisis
after he was already ordained, when he came to the conviction that he was
not himself truly converted to God. He wrote of this crisis in *The Burthen of
a Loaden Conscience*. It is clear that the practice of spiritual self-examination
itself heightened Kilby's sense of individuality. In an apostrophe at the
beginning of the book, Kilby urged the printer to change nothing he had
written to make him look any better than he was, such as by changing 'I am'
into 'I was'. He continued, 'It is very needfull for a man to know what he is.
I know none but my selfe: I judge none but my selfe: I intreate others to
give me leave to judge my selfe, because I fear the judgement of God.'[20]
The intensity of his self-consciousness in the thrice repeated 'my selfe' was
thus 'needfull' precisely because of his tender conscience before God and his
awareness of judgment to come. This is a good example of the religious
sources of individuation. As we noted in the last chapter, the conditions for
narratable conversion include both this sense of selfhood and the conviction
that one's central existential problem is guilt and the corresponding judgment of God.

Moreover, in this early example of Puritan spiritual autobiography, all the
seams between self-examination and narrative show through clearly. Indeed, it is something of a hybrid or transitional genre: part self-examination
and confession, part biblical exposition, part sermonic exhortation, and part
factual narrative. A printer's horizontal rule divides the book into sections,
roughly corresponding to the Ten Commandments taken in canonical
order. Generally, Kilby takes one of the commandments and examines
himself by it, which occasions a short autobiographical narrative, as in the
case of the commandment, 'Thou shalt not steal,' about which Kilby writes:
'I have beene a theefe many waies; when I was a child, I remember I was
given to steale apples, and afterward I purloined divers things, yea monie
from my father and mother.' Though he evidently shared Augustine's
fondness for forbidden orchards (a recurring topos in Puritan spiritual
autobiography), it was the occasion of self-examination according to the
law that led to narrative ('when I was a child, I remember . . . '). Then follow
several paragraphs of direct exhortation to the reader, often signalled by the
vocative, as when in this section Kilby turns to the reader, saying, 'O ye

[19] Kilby, *Unburthening*, 37.
[20] Kilby, 'To the Printer' in *Burthen of a Loaden Conscience*.

people of God, for Christs sake be carefull to keep your selves true, and just. Doe not so much as get a pinne with an evill conscience.'[21] Often he gives additional scriptural proofs or exposition with numbered points, forming something like short sermons embedded in the text. But then he concludes most sections with an exemplary prayer, such as in the section on keeping the sabbath holy, where he prays for the reader, saying, 'Our blessed Lord God for Jesus Christs sake, vouchsafe to give you grace, that you may rest in him, which is the right keeping of the Sabbath daie.' The desire to instruct and warn the reader is thus paramount and always in the foreground.

The ordering of Kilby's book is not explicitly a narrative structure of situation—transformation—situation. It is ordered rather as an 'examen of conscience'. This practice was emphasized in devotional manuals such as Richard Rogers's popular *Seven Treatises* (1603). Rogers sought to persuade the reader to practise a 'daily direction' or rule of life that began with the admonition, 'that everie day wee should be humbled for our sins as through due examination of our lives by the law of God we shall see them'.[22] Kilby's practice can also be considered a personal appropriation of what was rehearsed liturgically whenever the Ten Commandments were read to the congregation in the service of Holy Communion according to the Prayer Book. According to the liturgy the congregation would respond finally by asking God to 'write all these thy laws in our hearts'. This prayer was one Kilby took to heart and extended over the space of ninety-six printed pages octavo.

In the midst of Kilby's examen of conscience and his various exhortations to the reader, we find short passages of autobiographical narration, yet there is little of the larger narrative syntax of what Aristotle called *mythos*—or beginning, middle, and end. There are points at which Kilby seems about to tell his story for its own sake, but then he returns to self-examination or exhortation. Significantly, the syntax of conversion itself is found in the symbolic space between this volume and its sequel, between *The Burthen of a Loaden Conscience* and *Hallelu-iah! Praise Yee the Lord, for the Unburthening of a Loaden Conscience*. This second book opens, 'Now I beginne. It pleased the good Lord God to unburthen my conscience by repentance, and beliefe in Jesus Christ, whereunto with verie much adoe I was brought by the knowledge of Gods word, and the consideration of mine owne very miserable and most dangerous estate.'[23]

For Kilby, conversion began just as Perkins said it did—namely, with some inward or outward hardship combined with a knowledge of God's word. Kilby wrote, 'Yet it pleased the Lord first by little and little to stablish

[21] Kilby, *Burthen of a Loaden Conscience*. 61.
[22] Quoted in M. M. Knappen (ed.), *Two Elizabethan Puritan Diaries* (Chicago, 1933), 7.
[23] Kilby, *Unburthening*, 2.

my wavering judgement, and then to let mee runne my selfe into many outward dangers, and divers bodily diseases, that so at last I might bee broken from sinne.'[24] Indeed, he was twice arraigned before a justice for popery and lost his curacy at Southfleet for unwittingly offending the bishop. (It was after these hardships that he wrote his *Burthen of a Loaden Conscience*.) But then from the summer of 1612 he began to suffer excruciating pain from kidney stones and fits of colic, and this renewed his spiritual earnestness.[25] There is a labyrinthine quality to his narrative—as with many later Puritan and evangelical narratives—so that just when it seems to the reader that Kilby has arrived at peace of heart and his conscience has been finally relieved, again he describes another layer of sin and descends into another period of lamentation and doubting. In due course, however, Kilby did come to experience faith and repentance. The bulk of the second volume is a diary of his illness and his spiritual reflections in the midst of intense pain.[26] Much as Richard Rogers had advised, he made for himself a rule of life of daily repentance based upon God's law and the promises in the gospel. He was led gradually, as Perkins had suggested was the norm, from legal fear to evangelical faith. As Perkins also claimed to be the general case, this faith was tested by doubts and temptations, until his conscience was gradually quieted and a new evangelical sorrow for sin predominated. Kilby concluded that 'true repentance, and right faith doe ease, and lighten a loaden conscience'. For he came to recognize that though it was impossible for him to put off his sin, he could pray in faith, 'Yea, but thy sonne hath told us, that all things are possible with thee,' and he began to focus not just upon the law of God, but also upon his promises. Finally, he arrived at full resignation, saying, 'To thy mercy and good pleasure I wholly betake my selfe, through Jesus Christ. Amen. Amen.'[27] Thus Kilby discovered a new peace which 'succoured and sustained' him in his attacks of the kidney stone. Notwithstanding the melancholy and seriousness that suffused his whole account, he emerged from the travail of conversion 'unburthened'.

Popular Forms: The Commonwealth and the Gathered Churches

Kilby's account was still a rare example of the Puritan autobiography that would appear in larger numbers later in the seventeenth century. It would in

---

[24] Ibid. 44.

[25] In the preface to a later edition of the first book, penned on 27 November 1613, he claimed that his conscience was now unburdened and that he would write about that shortly. But in the second book he confessed that when he wrote this, 'I was farre short of being unburthened.' Ibid. 53.

[26] There is a close parallel here to the posthumously published *Private Thoughts* (York, 1795) of the later evangelical Thomas Adam of Winteringham, who also suffered much from 'the stone'.

[27] Kilby, *Unburthening*, 142.

fact take a whole generation for conversion narrative to appear in print as a popular form in England. And after 1640 it would be chiefly members of the gathered churches, heirs of the Elizabethan Puritans, who would write their spiritual autobiographies.[28] Owen Watkins has shown how spiritual autobiography emerged as the result of specific characteristics in the Puritan way of life that looked back to Perkins's generation. Persistent emphasis from pulpit and press on the application of doctrine to experience, on the internal spiritual warfare of the soul, and on the importance of self-examination, all within the context of a well-defined scheme of regeneration, fostered widespread religious concern at a personal level. The typical literary expression of this concern was at first the confessional diary. This passed over into actual autobiography with the rise to prominence of the radical Puritans during the Commonwealth period, when a growing interest in biographies of pious men, an upsurge in religious innovation, and a stress on personal testimony in the reception of new members by the gathered churches all contributed to the emergence of the personal conversion narrative.[29]

In these ways Puritan culture continued to incubate a conversionist piety in the first half of the seventeenth century, though very few conversion narratives were published in England between Kilby's second book in 1614 and the early 1650s. One can only speculate about the reasons for this. Certainly, the perennial concern about the dangers of vanity remained, and most of the spiritual autobiographies extant from this period go to great lengths to defend publication as something other than self-promotion. Thus Kilby asks the reader 'to beleeve that I in making and putting forth this booke intended the glorie of my Saviour, the good of Christened people, and the hurt of no creature'.[30] However, the small number of examples of Puritan autobiography until the mid-seventeenth century also had much to do with how hazardous it was to expose oneself in print as a Puritan during this period, which corresponded roughly with the rise to power of William Laud and the intensified harassment of Puritans under Charles I.[31] By royal prerogative the monarch exercised an undefined but real power to censor

---

[28] I am using the phrase 'gathered church' to include both separatists and non-separatists who adhered to congregationalist polity, including Baptists and Independents. In this sense it would include both Robert Browne and Henry Jacob. Cf. Michael R. Watts, *The Dissenters* (Oxford, 1978), i. 94–9.

[29] Owen Watkins, *The Puritan Experience* (1972), 66; cf. Tom Webster, 'Writing to Redundancy: Approaches to Spiritual Journals and Early Modern Spirituality', *The Historical Journal*, 39 (1996), 33–56.

[30] Kilby, *Unburthening*, 1.

[31] In an earlier period, even for Kilby, such exposure had its risks in a time of controversy, and he noted that his *Burthen of a Loaden Conscience* was not received well, even by 'manie precise folks'. Ibid. 53.

publications that were critical of political or religious authorities. Indeed, the term 'crop-ears' was used for opponents of Charles I who lost their ears as penalty for expressing critical views. The collapse of this censorship in the Civil War was spectacular. The Thomason Tracts that line the shelves of the British Library, collected by the prescient bookseller George Thomason during these years, bear massive witness to this sudden unrestrained flood of print. The attempt of the presbyterian party in Parliament to reintroduce order through book licensing in 1643 was not able to contain the more radical sectaries. Dissent once expressed was not to be so easily silenced.[32]

Still, it was not until the end of the Civil War that conversion narratives began to appear in greater number in print, singly and in collections of spiritual experience. The radical Puritans of the Commonwealth were the first to publish their spiritual experiences, and in this, the historical moment was significant. These were the apocalyptic days of the Parliament's war against the Irish Catholic royalists (1649–52), followed by the 'rule of the saints' in the Barebone's Parliament (1653) and the early Protectorate. This was the political high water mark for the gathered churches and the political situation meant that eschatological expectations were aroused for many of Christ's imminent return, and of a special outpouring of the Spirit in the last days as Christ set up his millennial rule of the saints on earth in a 'fifth monarchy'. Spiritual autobiography now appeared as an expression of an altogether more radical religious voluntarism. The sobriety of Richard Kilby's narrative was replaced by a new confidence that the times were epochal, and there was a corresponding upsurge in religious innovation and experimentation. Oliver Cromwell claimed that England was a nation 'at the edge of the promises'.[33] John Milton declared that 'God is decreeing to begin some new and great period in his Church, ev'n to the reforming of Reformation it self.'[34] Vavasor Powell testified that Jesus Christ had 'manifestly appeared to his people (especially of late yeares)'. Samuel Petto observed that it seemed to be the work of 'this Generation' to declare God's works through their spiritual experiences.[35] The potent combination of unprecedented political turmoil with eschatological hopes and charismatic experience—at a time when the press could no longer be restrained—meant that conversion narratives were no longer merely conceived or spoken or privately written: they were also published.[36]

---

[32] Haller, *Rise of Puritanism*, 326, 364–77.

[33] Crawford Gibben, *The Puritan Millennium* (Dublin, 2000), 150.

[34] Ibid. 130.

[35] Powell, 'Epistle', prefixed to *Spirituall Experiences*, n.p. [sig. A2]; Samuel Petto, 'Epistle to the Reader', prefixed to *Roses from Sharon* (1654), n.p.

[36] The eschatological context is stressed in Gibben, *Puritan Millennium*. The charismatic element is emphasized by Geoffrey Nuttall, *Visible Saints* (Oxford, 1957), 111–12. Nuttall

The forms of spiritual autobiography that appeared in the mid-seventeenth century reflected this interpretation of the times as portentous. In addition to the narratives of 'orthodox Puritans', whose testimonies owed something to the sort of experimental Calvinism evident in Perkins, there was a small number of self-proclaimed and sometimes antinomian prophets who appeared during the Commonwealth, and who wrote of their spiritual experiences, such as Lodowicke Muggleton (1609–98), who helped to found the sect of Muggletonians and who claimed to be one of the two witnesses of the Spirit referred to in the eleventh chapter of the book of Revelation.[37] Muggleton's revelations were received in 1651–2, and with William Reeve, he published an account of his commission as a prophet in 1652. His own spiritual autobiography appeared posthumously. As Owen Watkins writes, these prophets 'were emphatically not ordinary converts, but men marked out by God to be a "sign and wonder" to their generation'.[38] Yet, they illustrate well the impetus given to spiritual autobiography by eschatological fervour.

Quaker testimonies and journals, recounting the writer's discovery of the 'inner light' or 'convincement', likewise first appeared in print during the Commonwealth. George Fox began preaching and gathering followers to form the Society of Friends in 1648. Although Fox's *Journal* was not published until 1694, after his death, he encouraged the practice of keeping records of experiences and suffering. Quaker autobiographical tracts began appearing already in 1654 as a development of the 'proclamation tract', which gave warning or made appeal to a particular group or situation.[39] Richard Hubberthorne, for example, published his *True Testimony of Obedience to the Heavenly Call* in 1654, just two years after the spiritual struggle that led to his convincement. The goal of these testimonies was to persuade the outsider of the reality of the experience narrated and to edify the convinced Friend. Although such Quaker testimonies owed much to orthodox Puritanism, and though they tell a story of conversion, the authority to which the writers appealed was not the Bible, but rather the personal experience of 'the inner Light' or 'the seed of God'. Their doctrine of original innocence and supernatural illumination, together with their

writes, 'At a deeper level, we may again observe the charismatic assumptions behind these exercises. The Holy Spirit who has brought men into a saving experience of Christ will also enable them to bear witness to it . . . Joy is a prime element in Christian experience, and joy is expansive and self-communicating' (111).

[37] *The Acts of the Witnesses of the Spirit . . . By Lodowick Muggleton: One of the Two Witnesses, and True Prophets of the Only High, Immortal, Glorious God, Christ Jesus. Left by Him to be Publish'd After's Death* (1699).

[38] Watkins, *Puritan Experience*, 144.

[39] Hugh Barbour and Arthur O. Roberts (eds.), *Early Quaker Writings, 1650–1700* (Grand Rapids, Mich., 1973), 27–32, 568.

rejection of the usual means of grace, not only distinguished the movement from the main body of Puritans, but also fostered a different sort of spiritual autobiography. The typical pattern of Quaker autobiography involved recounting an increasing dissatisfaction with orthodox Puritan teaching, a time of ineffectual seeking for true religion amongst various contemporary sects, and then, finally, the experience of submission to the inward light.[40]

Though the spiritual autobiography of the antinomian prophets and the Quakers owed much to the heart-searching introspective piety of early Puritanism, and though both forms have their counterpart in the eighteenth century, it was the narratives of the Calvinistic Puritans that established the conventions that would inform the later evangelical conversion narrative. Examples of such Calvinistic narratives also appeared in print during the Commonwealth, and many of these writers shared with other contemporary spiritual autobiographers the sense that they were living through 'some new and great period' in salvation history.

A number of these accounts of spiritual experience appeared almost simultaneously, edited by the ministers of Independent congregations. In 1653 two substantial collections of experiences appeared. *Spirituall Experiences of Sundry Beleevers* (most likely edited by the London Independent Henry Walker) contained sixty-one accounts 'wherein is wonderfully declared Gods severall workings in the various conditions of his chosen ones'. The Fifth Monarchist John Rogers published *Ohel or Beth-shemesh: A Tabernacle for the Sun* the same year, and it included thirty-eight testimonies from members of his Dublin congregation. Rogers came across the collection from Walker's church while he was working on his own, so it is evident that these works originated independently. A further small collection of spiritual experiences was published the following year by the Independent Samuel Petto in *Roses from Sharon or Sweet Experiences Reached out by Christ to Some of his Beloved Ones in this Wildernes*. Taken together, these three collections alone brought more than a hundred narratives before the public, most of them by laypeople. There were also single narratives published at this same time. For example, the Baptist Jane Turner published her *Choice Experiences of the Kind Dealings of God before, in, and after Conversion* in 1653. The following year the Baptist prophetess Anna Trapnel published her *Legacy for Saints; being several Experiences of the Dealings of God with Anna Trapnel, in, and after her Conversion*.

The table of contents in Walker's collection ('A Table of the Conversions of the severall Persons expressed in this Booke') gives an indication of the variety of spiritual experiences recorded and the centrality of conversion to

---

[40] Watkins, *Puritan Experience*, 162. See also Mary Cochran Grimes, 'Saving Grace Among Puritans and Quakers: A Study of 17th and 18th Century Conversion Experiences', *Quaker History* 72 (1983), 3–26; Howard H. Brinton, *Quaker Journals* (Wallingford, Penn., 1972).

the narratives. It includes, for example, 'T. A. Converted after three yeares terrour upon his Conscience, and then rowling himselfe on Christ,' and, 'A. L. By being driven through afflictions to goe to the meetings of godly people,' and 'L. P. By thoughts touching a childe in her wombe, when Satan tempted her to destroy her selfe.' Each of these seem to imply that conversion was occasioned, in Perkins's terms, by some outward or inward affliction, but there were a few whose conversion was begun otherwise, as, for example, 'F. D. By longing for Jesus Christ.'

The 'Experiences of M. W.' may stand as one illustration of the narratives in this collection. M.W. had lived in Ireland in relative prosperity and without much concern for the salvation of her soul. Upon moving to Liverpool some nine years before writing her narrative, she was brought under sharp conviction by hearing a sermon by one Mr Tompson. After sorrowing for her sins for a time and visiting ministers and other godly people, she found some comfort for her soul. But no sooner had this happened than crisis struck. 'For the Enemy took Liverpoole', she writes, 'and killed my Husband, and a childe, both before my face, and stript, and wounded me, and a childe of five yeares old; and it was thought I could not live.'[41] Understandably, she felt near despair. She sought to comfort herself with the promises of God. 'I was assured,' she continues, 'with much joy, that the Lord would bring me to himselfe, and in this confidence did rejoyce with my wounded Childe, and a little daughter, in a Barn where we were put, having gotten a peece of an old Bible; and then and since I have found much setlednesse [*sic*] in my faith from severall Promises of the Lord, revealed in his holy Word,' and she proceeds to list three passages (John 15: 7; Matt. 5: 6; Matt. 11: 28) and to describe the comfort she has derived from them.[42] She concludes with nine 'comfortable inferences' that testify to her love for God and her faith, such as that she readily rejoices in the ordinances and that her affections are drawn out after the people of God. This ten-page narrative provided an account of her spiritual experience that enabled the church to judge her suitability for admission to membership.

With the publication of a number of such accounts, it is evident that the conversion narrative form that had appeared so tentatively in Richard Kilby had by 1654 become something more widespread and popular. It had also become the provenance of the gathered churches. Almost all these narratives were written to fulfil the requirement that candidates for admission to the church had to offer not only a profession of orthodox belief but also evidence of personal saving faith. Thus John Rogers explained the practice of his English congregation in Dublin, saying that the church 'takes in Members, and of their Admission, upon clear Testimony'. This 'testimony'

---

[41] *Spirituall Experiences*, 11.
[42] Ibid. 12–14.

was threefold: the testimony of the congregation who raised no objections, the personal testimony of others who could vouch for the candidate, and the testimony of the candidate himself or herself. Of this latter testimony from the candidate, Rogers explained that 'the person to be admitted, being desired for the Churches satisfaction, to make an account of his faith, and of the work of grace upon his heart, he does so'. Indeed, it was to illustrate and adorn his exposition of church polity that Rogers then offered a number of specimens of such testimonies, under the chapter heading, 'Everyone to be admitted, gives out some experimental evidences of the work of grace upon his soul (for the Church to judge of) whereby he (or she) is convinced that he is regenerate, and received of God, which is proved and approved by about forty examples of worth.'[43] Thus many of the narratives in Rogers's collection begin or end with a direct appeal for admission to the church. Elizabeth Avery began, 'In this society I see much of God, and have a great desire to be one with you.' Humphrey Mills concluded, 'And being much refreshed by your Meetings and Members, I desire to be one with you in Christ.'[44]

Walker's collection was also presented with a similar, if less prominent, concern to illustrate the practice of gathered church ecclesiology. The narratives in his collection were given at 'severall solemne meetings and conferences' set up for this purpose. The second impression of Walker's collection included an appendix that made the occasion of these meetings more clear. The appendix is entitled, 'The Practice of the Gathered Churches in the City of London, and other parts of England', and it describes the manner of establishing a new congregational church. Part of the process involved a meeting to hear each other's spiritual experience: 'They then each of them, one after another, give an account of their faith and experiences of the grace of God by his spirit wrought in them.'[45]

These narratives cannot be understood apart from their context in an interpretative community. This is true of all narratives, but it is the more easily observed in the case of these Commonwealth churches. Just as the testimonies or 'confessions' recorded by Thomas Shepard from the members of his church at Cambridge, Massachusetts, during the years 1635–48 reflected the shared experience of the members of immigration to America, and, for many, a shared disappointment in the contrast between their original ideals and the harsh realities of the new world, so also many of the narratives from John Rogers's congregation in Dublin communicated a

---

[43] John Rogers, *Ohel or Beth-shemesh. A Tabernacle for the Sun: or Irenicum Evangelicum. An Idea of Church Discipline, In the Theorick and Practick Parts . . . Published for the Benefit of all Gathered Churches, More Especially in England, Ireland, and Scotland* (1653), ii. 286, 290, 354.

[44] Ibid. 401, 410.

[45] Appendix to *Spirituall Experiences*, n.p. [sig. U4].

sense of the spiritual solace found in Christ after the sufferings endured during the Irish rebellion in 1641.[46]

More profoundly, these narratives were shaped by the theology of the local minister.[47] Rogers and Walker presented edited versions of the experiences given by the members of their churches, and we may be sure that many of the emendations and elisions were theological. But even were this not so, these narratives certainly reflected the local teaching and discipline of the ministers to which the writers were subject. Michael Watts notes the different theologies of conversion held by Rogers and Walker: 'For Rogers conversion was the ultimate religious experience, the decisive victory over sin, the final release from the bonds of legal religion. For Walker conversion was a crucial, but not final, battle in the continuing warfare against sin and doubt; the enemy was defeated but not annihilated.'[48] The source of the more climactic view of conversion in Rogers's collection was his own radical eschatology. Rogers believed that the deposition of the House of Stuart would lead to the 'fifth monarchy' with the imminent inauguration of the millennial reign of Christ on earth. Several of the narratives in his collection reflect these themes. For example, Elizabeth Avery's conversion involved her finding that she was 'under the opening of the fifth seal, and very near the sixth' in the book of Revelation.[49] As Crawford Gibben writes, 'The conversion narratives of his people—and their subsequent experiences of Edenic bliss—were to be the ultimate justification of his millenarian ministry.'[50]

Notwithstanding the variety of these narratives in terms of local experience and theology, there was a recognizable continuity with the applied theology of conversion in Perkins and other Elizabethan Puritans, most strikingly in the concern with introspection and assurance and in the consistent application of law and gospel to govern the narrative of conversion from a psychological state of anxiety or despair to one of peace and joy (whether expressed in relative or absolute terms). The new feature of these Commonwealth narratives was their occasion in the admission requirement of gathered churches that candidates provide 'experimental' evidence of a work of divine grace in their lives.

It is not possible to say with certainty when gathered churches in England first introduced this new requirement, or which churches were the first to do so, but the stimulus it gave to spiritual autobiography was enormous.

[46] Cf. Patricia Caldwell, *The Puritan Conversion Narrative* (Cambridge, 1983), 26–35, 75–80, 150–1.

[47] Cf. Charles Lloyd Cohen, *God's Caress: The Psychology of the Puritan Religious Experience* (Oxford, 1986), 213 n.

[48] Watts, *The Dissenters*, i. 177.

[49] Rogers, *Ohel and Beth-shemesh*, 405.

[50] Gibben, *Puritan Millennium*, 158.

The timing of the publication of these narratives in England certainly had to do with the new confidence of the gathered churches in the Commonwealth and a greater liberty of the press. But how long had gathered churches been practising this admission test, and thereby fostering a culture of spiritual autobiography? This remains a matter of some debate. Our focus has been upon the situation in England (and an English congregation in Dublin), but Edmund Morgan suggested that it was in New England that the Congregationalist churches first began to require the membership test that Rogers described in the English context.[51] Morgan argued that this practice probably emerged under the ministry of John Cotton in about 1634, and that the English congregations who later developed similar tests did so based on the precedent in New England.[52] It is difficult to be certain. It is at least possible that the practice arose on both sides of the Atlantic at about the same time— sometime in the 1630s—in response to similar concerns. Calvin had argued that the visible church was always a mixed body, comprised of the elect and the non-elect. The ideal of the gathered churches on both sides of the Atlantic in the 1630s and 1640s was to attempt to make the visible church a more accurate spiritual approximation of the invisible church. This movement towards what we might call a more 'realized ecclesiology' was certainly stimulated by the quasi-utopian hopes for a more pure church that

---

[51] Morgan, *Visible Saints*, 65–6; cf. Caldwell, *Puritan Conversion Narrative*, 45–79. The development of spiritual autobiography in early America has been the subject of much study since Morgan, treated e.g. in Norman Pettit, *The Heart Prepared: Grace and Conversion in Puritan Spiritual Life* (New Haven, Conn., 1966); Daniel B. Shea, Jr., *Spiritual Autobiography in Early America* (Princeton, 1968); William K. B. Stoever, '*A Faire and Easie Way to Heaven*': *Covenant Theology and Antinomianism in Early Massachusetts* (Middletown, Conn., 1978); Charles E. Hambrick-Stowe, *The Practice of Piety: Puritan Devotional Disciplines in Seventeenth-Century New England* (Chapel Hill, NC, 1982).

[52] Morgan, *Visible Saints*, 65–6: 'My contention is that the practice came, not from Plymouth to Massachusetts as initially supposed, nor from England or Holland as presently assumed, but that it originated in Massachusetts among the nonseparating Puritans there and spread from Massachusetts to Plymouth, Connecticut, New Haven, and back to England.' Patrica Caldwell extended the arguments of Morgan in her study, *The Puritan Conversion Narrative* (1983) by comparing and contrasting the narratives of first-generation New England Puritans, recorded by Thomas Shepard in his congregation at Cambridge, Massachusetts, with the narratives recorded by Rogers in Dublin and Walker in London. Shepard had recorded fifty-one 'confessions' of persons applying for membership at Cambridge between about 1638 and 1645. She argued that the New England narratives were a distinctive form of American expression shaped by the experience of immigration, especially with the recurring contrast in these accounts between the dreams and reality of the new world. And she argued that the 'American' narratives were often more open-ended and ambiguous than the English parallels. Her analysis demonstrates helpfully the way in which the conversion narrative form, from the beginning, was adaptable to expression in terms of a wide range of experiences, from the Civil War in England to the experience of disillusioned immigration in New England. The principal source for conversion narrative in New England is *Thomas Shepard's 'Confessions'*, ed. George Selement and Bruce C. Wooley (Boston, 1981).

characterized the ideals both of the Puritans who emigrated and of many who lived through the Interregnum. The mechanism for this more radical ecclesiology was, in any case, the admission test of personal testimony. By developing this practice the mid-seventeenth-century Puritans in the gathered churches established an autobiographical religious culture that included both clergy and laypeople, and that would have far-ranging consequences.

Later Puritanism

In the second half of the seventeenth century the theology of conversion was expounded in a growing number of works of practical theology, such as Richard Baxter's *Treatise on Conversion* (1657), *Directions and Persuasions to a Sound Conversion* (1658), and *Call to the Unconverted* (1658), or Joseph Alleine's *Alarme to the Unconverted* (1672). These last two were reprinted often, but Puritan teaching about conversion was by no means limited to such evangelistic tracts; it was also embodied in a large number of treatises and sermons on sin, Christology, faith, the covenant of grace, and hypocrisy.[53] Thus, the theology of conversion expounded by Perkins in the late sixteenth century had by the late seventeenth century spawned a whole literature, which was widely read by English Nonconformists well into the eighteenth century, and was read also by many of the early evangelicals.

We have observed how the order of conversion that was expounded by Perkins in the Elizabethan church, and evident in Richard Kilby's autobiography during the Jacobean period, was adapted and popularized in the oral relations given by candidates for admission to the gathered churches during the Commonwealth. This practice of oral testimony spread widely among Independents and Baptists after the Restoration. With the persecution of Nonconformists under the Clarendon Code, the spiritual autobiographies of these believers acquired a new rhetorical edge in the imperative to defend one's beliefs and to encourage the faithful. Conversion narratives from the Restoration period thus came to overlap the literature of apologetic and to share some of the qualities of earlier narratives of suffering by persecuted Quakers and Continental Anabaptists. For many later Nonconformists in the eighteenth century, this period represented the heroic age in their movement, against which they measured the 'decay of the Dissenting interest' in their own day.

One of the most famous and enduring Puritan spiritual autobiographies from this period is John Bunyan's *Grace Abounding to the Chief of Sinners* (1666). His narrative reflects the embattled situation of Nonconformists, as it was written during the time of his imprisonment in the Bedford gaol for

---

[53] J. I. Packer, 'The Puritan View of Preaching the Gospel', in *Among God's Giants: The Puritan Vision of the Christian Life* (Eastbourne, 1991), 219.

preaching without a licence. Along with his *Pilgrim's Progress* (1678 and 1684), it helped to establish the form of the conversion narrative, for in it we see a narrative pattern that corresponded closely to the Puritan preaching of law and gospel.[54] Bunyan begins by recounting his parentage, dreams, serious religious thoughts, an escape from a poisonous snake, and other episodes from his childhood, concluding, 'Here . . . were Judgements and Mercy, but neither of them did awaken my soul to Righteousness.'[55] He describes his initial 'awakening' under a sermon at Elstow church and 'some outward Reformation' in his behaviour, particularly in the matter of refraining from sports on the sabbath and from cavorting with others and bell-ringing. Then at Bedford he heard a small group of poor women 'talking about the things of God' and, he says, 'me thought that they spake as if joy did make them speak'. This made Bunyan question his own spiritual sincerity, and soon he decided he must, in his words, 'put myself upon the tryal, whether I had Faith or no'. This led to a season of intensive introspection and spiritual doubt, including one period of despair that lasted two years. His experience of relief under the promises of the gospel came as a bolt out of the blue:

But one day, as I was passing in the field, and that too with some dashes on my Conscience . . . suddenly this sentence fell upon my Soul, *Thy righteousness is in Heaven*; and methought withall, I saw with the eyes of my Soul, Jesus Christ at God's right hand . . . Now did my chains fall off my legs indeed, I was loosed from my affliction and irons, my temptations also fled away.[56]

This experience is the climax of Bunyan's autobiography, and it is parallel to the scene in *Pilgrim's Progress* where the burden of guilt rolls off Christian's back at the sight of the cross. The last third of *Grace Abounding* is devoted to his entrance into the ministry, its course, and his imprisonment under the penal legislation of the Clarendon Code in the 1660s.

   Bunyan's narrative is a good illustration of the pattern of conversion that became well established among the Puritans. These accounts typically begin with serious religious impressions in childhood, followed by a descent into 'worldliness' and hardness of heart, followed by an awakening or pricking of religious conscience, and then a period of self-exertion and attempted moral

---

[54] In his introduction to Bunyan's *Grace Abounding*, Roger Sharrock describes how a pattern could be observed in the autobiography of Puritan ministers. This pattern is similar to Perkins's scheme, but here the stages are compressed into five and translated into more narrative terms: (1) Early providential mercies and opportunities, (2) Unregenerate life: sin and resistance to the Gospel, (3) Conversion (often initiated by an 'awakening' sermon), (4) Vocation to preach the Gospel, and (5) Account of the course of ministry. Roger Sharrock, Introduction to John Bunyan, *Grace Abounding to the Chief of Sinners* (Oxford, 1962), p. xxix.

[55] Bunyan, *Grace Abounding*, 8.

[56] Ibid. 72.

rectitude, which only aggravates the conscience and ends in self-despair. This self-despair, paradoxically, leads to the possibility of experiencing a divinely wrought repentance and the free gift of justification in Christ. Forgiveness of sins comes, thus, as a climax and a psychological release from guilt, and ideally introduces a life of service to God predicated on gratitude for undeserved mercy. Notwithstanding the false starts and self-doubts, and the ups and downs of the convert, this narrative pattern emerged with remarkable consistency in the spiritual autobiographies of the Puritans and Nonconformists in the seventeenth century.

Still there were many variations on the theme, and this pattern invited unique application and interpretation by different individuals. Ironically, the most clear witness to this pattern comes from Richard Baxter's posthumously published *Reliquiae Baxterianae* (1691), in which he identifies the pattern by its exceptional absence in his own case. When he was 15 he was awakened by reading a spiritual book, but he adds the gloss, 'Yet whether sincere Conversion began *now*, or *before*, or *after*, I was never able to this day to know.'[57] He describes his own spiritual formation and his anxiety lest all the moral progress in his life be but the result of education and not of true regeneration. Among the sources of this perplexity, Baxter recalls, 'I could not distinctly trace the workings of the Spirit upon my heart in that method which Mr. *Bolton*, Mr. *Hooker*, Mr. *Rogers* and other Divines describe! Nor knew the Time of my Conversion, being wrought on by the forementioned Degrees.'[58] In time, Baxter resolved his doubts, recognizing signs in his life of genuine spirituality wrought by God's grace. He came to a profound conclusion, writing, 'But I understood at last that God breaketh not all Mens hearts alike.'[59] In Baxter's case, then, we see the generic model of conversion narrative just as clearly as in Bunyan, but it is identified by negation.

Conversion Narrative: Beyond the English Puritans

With only a few qualifications, we can say that conversion narrative first appeared as a popular genre in the mid-seventeenth century in England and New England. We must at once add, however, that this was part of a larger post-Reformation experiential tradition that F. Ernest Stoeffler calls 'evangelical pietism', which was international in scope.[60] Although spiritual

---

[57] Richard Baxter, *Reliquiae Baxterianae* (1696), 3.

[58] Ibid. 6.

[59] Ibid. 7.

[60] F. Ernst Stoeffler, *The Rise of Evangelical Pietism* (Leiden, 1971). See also Ted A. Campbell, *The Religion of the Heart: A Study of European Religious Life in the Seventeenth and Eighteenth Centuries* (Columbia, SC, 1991); Menna Prestwich, *International Calvinism, 1541–1715* (Oxford, 1985).

autobiography flourished among Protestants in England, there were significant parallels in other parts of Britain and in Europe and America. For
example, the conversion of the Scots Covenanter James Fraser of Brea
(1638–98) was not published until 1738, but it recounts his ecstatic conversion in about 1657.[61] Likewise, the Welsh evangelist Vavasor Powell
(1617–70) wrote a nineteen-page autobiographical account of his conversion that owed much to the writings of Elizabethan Puritans such as Richard
Sibbes and William Perkins, and this narrative was prefixed to *The Life and
Death of Mr. Vavasor Powell* (1671).

New England calls for special mention. Jerald Brauer has placed the
accent less upon the immigrant experience as the distinctive element in
these conversion accounts and more upon the different social and political
contexts in England and New England over time. He sees little to distinguish the experience recorded in a Puritan narrative such as that of Richard
Mather (1596–1669) from the experience in a later evangelical narrative
such as that of David Brainerd (1718–47). 'The structure of the conversion
experience appears identical in Puritanism in both England and New
England and in the Great Awakening as the first phase of Revivalism.'[62]
Although the narratives themselves were surprisingly similar, the role and
consequences of conversion differed in changed contexts. Thus conversion
functioned within English Puritanism as part of an ideal to transform the
church and nation, and complete the Reformation. In early New England,
in contrast, conversion was the bedrock on which the church and state
rested. Then, in England after the great ejection of Puritan ministers under
the Act of Uniformity in 1662, and in New England with the adoption
of the half-way covenant in the same year, conversion often became a
statement of dissent from the majority culture. Brauer summarizes this
difference:

Whereas in New England Puritanism prior to the Great Awakening, conversion
was the means whereby the purity of the church and the stability of the state were
to be maintained, in both England and the Great Awakening conversion became
the religious source to express an intense dissatisfaction with the religious and social
status quo. In one case the role of conversion was to be a legitimating and
solidifying force; in the other two cases conversion was the religious resource for
profound criticism of the piety and practice of an established society.[63]

Finally, however, Brauer argues that the trajectory of Puritan conversion
narrative favoured the growth of subjectivity, so that by the revivals of the

---

[61] James Fraser, *Memoirs of the Life of the Very Reverend Mr. James Fraser of Brea* (Edinburgh,
1738).
[62] Jerald C. Brauer, 'Conversion: From Puritanism to Revivalism', *Journal of Religion* 58
(1978), 232–3.
[63] Ibid. 238–9.

eighteenth century there was a discernible shift away from the centrality of the Reformation, the covenantal community, or the godly commonwealth, and conversion increasingly existed almost wholly for its own sake, with the focus now upon the converted individual.

What was the case in England? Brauer passes over the Nonconformists in England during the Restoration and its aftermath (1660–89) and during the period that followed the Glorious Revolution that brought a new toleration from the state (1689–*c*.1730).[64] This latter period has sometimes been dubbed the 'tunnel period' between Puritanism and the Evangelical Revival. Yet it is among the pious Dissenters of these years that we find important, immediate antecedents to the spiritual autobiographies of Wesley and the early evangelicals. It is often assumed that once toleration was declared, Nonconformist piety grew moribund in the early eighteenth century, sunk in rationalism and moralism, and that the material prosperity of these years was matched by spiritual decline. The anti-trinitarianism evident in the debates at Salters' Hall in 1719 certainly represented a departure from orthodoxy. Although Strickland Gough and Philip Doddridge disagreed in print in 1730 about the reasons for the decay in the 'Dissenting Interest', they agreed that there was a loss of zeal. As Gough put it, 'Everyone is sensible it gradually declines, yet no one has endeavour'd to recover it.'[65] This decay was borne out in membership figures, but as Geoffrey Nuttall points out, 'There were always others whose faith was warm and expansive and the mainspring of their living. These were Evangelicals before the Revival.'[66] For example, Joseph Williams (1692–1755) was a layman and a Dissenter, a merchant from Kidderminster. His autobiographical papers were not published until the nineteenth century, but they reveal a warm evangelical piety during the very period when it is presumed that Nonconformity was at its lowest ebb spiritually.[67] Just as Jonathan Edwards in his *Personal Narrative* recalled a sense of divine glory upon hearing the words of the doxology ('Now unto Him immortal invisible . . . '), so also Williams described 'a lively sense of invisible things' that led him to draw up a personal covenant and consecrate himself to God in September 1710, and then to be admitted to communion the following

---

[64] Nonconformity during these years is surveyed in Watts, *Dissenters*, i. 221–393.

[65] Strickland Gough, *An Enquiry into the Causes of Decay of the Dissenting Interest* (2nd edn., 1730), 3. Cf. Philip Doddridge, 'Free Thoughts on the Most Probable Means of Reviving the Dissenting Interest', in *The Works of Philip Doddridge* (1804), v. 383–412. Doddridge notes in particular the observation of Bp. Gilbert Burnet some years earlier that even then the character and numbers of Dissenters had begun to decline (ibid. 387).

[66] Geoffrey G. Nuttall, 'Methodism and the Older Dissent: Some Perspectives', *United Reformed Church Historical Society Journal* 2 (1981), 261.

[67] Joseph Williams, *Enlarged Series of Extracts from the Diary, Meditations and Letters*, ed. Benjamin Hanbury (1815).

March. When revival came in the 1730s, Williams welcomed it, and he was well acquainted with Charles Wesley, Howell Harris, Lady Huntingdon, George Whitefield, Samuel Walker, and other leading figures in the Evangelical Revival.

This experimental vein of piety that looked backed to the Puritans thus also anticipated the evangelicals. Moreover, the conversion narrative form persisted in the declarations of spiritual experience that continued to be expected of prospective members in the Congregationalist and Baptist churches. A few of these declarations made it into print. For example, the Baptist Charles Doe edited *A Collection of Experience of the Work of Grace: (never before Printed) or the Spirit of God working upon the Souls of several Persons* (1700) that included three narratives intended (as the subtitle goes on to say) to 'convince the unregenerate that there is indeed such a thing as the working of the Spirit of God upon the soul'. All three narratives dated from the turn of the century and bore witness to the enormous influence of Bunyan, whose works were mentioned by name in two of the narratives. Doe himself was a part-time bookseller (as well as a combmaker) who specialized in the works of Bunyan, claiming to have sold about 3,000 of his books.[68] The spiritual autobiographies published by Doe represent a continuation of the genre for which Bunyan set a precedent in *Grace Abounding*.

One of the narratives comes from an apprentice named Will Devenport. He had been brought up strictly in the Church of England, but was in his adolescence addicted to swearing, lying, sabbath-breaking, and coarse jesting. When his conscience was pricked by a religious lecture, he immediately made every effort to reform his ways, yet this did not bring any lasting peace of mind. Employing an analogy that would later be made infamous by Jonathan Edwards, Davenport wrote,

One day, as I was walking by my self, and considering of my Estate, me thoughts I saw my self hang over a bottomless Pit by a small Cobweb, and every blast of Wind did so shake me, that I was amazed I was not dropt long before: so from this time *I began to see that my Estate was not safe*, and that I still wanted something as to my eternal Salvation, but knew not what; and this put me to be earnest and importunate with God, and likewise stirs up my great Adversary... who now tempts me to Despair and make away with my self.[69]

The shift to the historic present in the last two clauses is a signal that the narrative is now rushing on to its climax. A woman who was a Dissenter

---

[68] When Doe was himself in anxiety about his faith, he was comforted to think that he 'was not less a Christian than him that Mr. *John Bunyan*, in his *Progress*, calls Christian, that went to *Mount Sinai* to be helpt off with his heavy Burthen'. Charles Doe, (ed.), *A Collection of Experience of the Work of Grace* (1700), 39.

[69] Ibid. 3.

now spoke to him about 'free grace' and 'justification'. He found something touch him 'from above' so that he was made to attend to her words as if they were sent straight from God. After some struggle with unbelief, he was comforted by the words in Scripture, 'My beloved is mine and I am his', and this led him into a state of spiritual rapture.

This narrative once again contains the formal elements of conversion narrative that we observed earlier in Bunyan and to which Baxter pointed indirectly by marking their peculiar absence in his case. Original innocence is followed by habitual sin; awakening of conscience is followed by attempted reform. The awareness of the extent of the law and judgment leads to self-despair; the appropriation by faith of the promises of the gospel leads to evangelical joy. Unlike Bunyan's narrative, however, Devenport's account is occasioned, like those of John Rogers's congregation in Dublin, by his desire to be admitted as a member of a gathered church. His narrative concludes with his request to join the church. At the bottom of the page, the comment is added: 'He was Baptized (or Dipt) and admitted a Member.'[70] The second narrative in Doe's collection likewise constitutes a formal application to join a Baptist church. An anonymous apprentice thought his own experience was of little account and was ashamed to speak before the church, but 'the Lord brought somethings to my mind, that it was accepted by the Church'.[71] He too was baptized afterwards.

There were not many collections of conversion narratives published in the early eighteenth century, but it was precisely this sort of writing that would reappear with vigour in a new context during the 1730s and 1740s in the Evangelical Revival.[72] That this was still a controversial oral and written genre in 1700 is evident not only from the reticence and anxiety of the writers, but also from the reception of the printed collection itself. Doe's work is rare, but the copy in the Bodleian Library at Oxford is heavily annotated by a critical hand. The critic was clearly Anglican and considered Doe to be stepping beyond his station as a combmaker to publish this sort of piece, and he implies that Doe's motive must have been only to make money. 'Pray Sir,' scribbled the critic at one point, 'did you get more by selling these books than making combs?' Again, overleaf from the title page,

---

[70] Charles Doe, (ed.), *A Collection of Experience of the Work of Grace* (1700), 8.

[71] Ibid. 19.

[72] Another influential collection that was much reprinted in the early eighteenth century was James Janeway, *A Token for Children* (1671), which contained thirteen 'exact' accounts of 'the conversion, holy and exemplary lives, and joyful deaths of several young children' (taken from the subtitle). The preface exhorts parents and children to use these 'examples' to stir up similar piety, and a series of catechetical questions are proposed, such as, 'But tell me, my dear Children, and tell me truly, Do you do as these Children did? did you ever see your miserable state by Nature?' etc.

this critic asked sardonically, '*Query.* Whether all the anabaptists about town are not bound in Conscience to buy of our Author Charles Doe comb-maker all the combs that they have occasion to use to drie and set in order their locks when they first arise from plunging.' The anonymous critic is disapproving of all this as something Anabaptist and sectarian, but he or she clearly had concerns based upon social class as well. In the marginator's mind, the collection was contemptible for being vulgar and crudely popu-list. Moreover, the anxiety about self-display that concerned autobio-graphers throughout the early modern period resurfaces here. Doe himself pleaded on the title page that the collection was 'Published, Not to Applaud the Persons, but for the Comfort of Saints'. But the critical reader was unconvinced and added the marginal retort: 'A very good opinion Thou hast of thine own works.'

The early evangelicals in the 1730s inherited the genre of conversion narrative not just from the Puritans and their Nonconformist descendants, but also from Continental Pietists and their descendants, though conversion narratives appeared in German-speaking lands somewhat later than in England. In the late seventeenth century, after the disorder and disillusion-ment of the Thirty Years War, Pietism emerged as a renewal movement in Germany, whose aim was to renew Lutheranism by returning to Luther's teachings about the priesthood of all believers and the necessity of practical piety. Although more radical anti-establishment forms of Pietism devel-oped, the movement was initially concerned to supplement the focus upon institutions and doctrinal rectitude that predominated within Lutheran orthodoxy. The key figure in early Lutheran Pietism was Philipp Jakob Spener (1635–1705) and the programme for Pietism was laid out in his influential *Pia Desideria: or Heartfelt Desires for a God-Pleasing Improvement of the True Protestant Church* (1675). That there are many points of similarity in the concerns of Pietism and Puritanism is not accidental, since the movements were distinct but by no means independent of one another. W. R. Ward claims that Puritan literature enjoyed an unparalleled prestige in Protestant Europe during these years and was translated into Dutch, German, and other European languages with increasing frequency. Accord-ing to one calculation, nearly 700 English religious works, among which devotional writings predominated, were translated into German between 1600 and 1750, running into some 1,700 editions and reprintings. By the end of the seventeenth century Bunyan had a large Dutch readership and was already regarded as a hero within Protestant Germany. He was but one of many Puritan authors read on the Continent. Lewis Bayly's *Practice of Piety*, which was such an important influence upon Bunyan himself, was likewise significant for stimulating the early Pietist leaders in Germany.[73]

---

[73] W. R. Ward, *The Protestant Evangelical Awakening* (Cambridge, 1992), 10–13, 48.

This Puritan influence within Pietism is important to stress, since it has sometimes been made to appear that the later influence of Pietism upon the experience of conversion among English evangelicals was something alien, somehow isolated from indigenous religious traditions.

How then did conversion function within Pietism and what autobiographical forms emerged? Spener himself wrote an autobiography, but it was little more than a continuation of the memoir form with a general confession of sin at the conclusion.[74] A new stress upon personal conversion appeared in the next generation of Pietists under the leadership of August Hermann Francke (1663–1727). If Bunyan's *Grace Abounding* was the *locus classicus* for the Puritan genre, then Francke's *Vita* in the late seventeenth century had a similar place within Pietism. Well educated in philosophy, theology, and languages, Francke became a lecturer at Leipzig in 1685, and it was there in his early twenties that he began to experience spiritual anxiety over the worldliness of his heart. Such anxiety, he says, 'drove my heart as a stormy sea now to one side, now to the other, even though I often presented an external joyousness before others'.[75] He became more earnest about that state of his soul but found himself profoundly powerless in moral and spiritual matters. He began to make some progress, and this was noted by his friends, but was still in 'semi-darkness'. Moving to Lünenberg, he was called upon to preach a sermon and this provoked a crisis, for he wished to preach on the nature of true belief in John 20: 31 but found that he did not have such a faith himself. He described his condition as one of dread, sorrow, mental agitation, and much weeping. The evening before he was to preach, he cried out to God once more:

He immediately heard me. My doubt vanished as quickly as one turns one's hand; I was assured in my heart of the grace of God in Christ Jesus and I knew God not only as God but as my Father. All sadness and unrest of heart was taken away at once, and I was immediately overwhelmed as with a stream of joy...I arose a completely different person from the one who had knelt down.[76]

Lest there be any question about the decisiveness of this experience, Francke marks its significance a few paragraphs later, saying, 'This is the period to which I can point as that of my true conversion. From this time on my Christianity had a place to stand.'[77]

Francke not only testified to such a conversion experience, but he also taught this pattern of conversion in his many writings. It was really a version of the Puritan morphology: conviction of sin under the law, despair and fear

---

[74] W. R. Ward, Introduction to Wesley, *Works* (BE), xviii. 13–14.

[75] Peter C. Erb (ed.), *Pietists: Selected Writings* (1983), 100.

[76] Ibid. 105.

[77] Ibid. 106.

of divine judgment, the desire for redemption, struggle in prayer, and then a breakthrough to faith, followed by real sanctification and continued vigilance in self-examination.[78] The crisis at the centre of all this became a distinctive feature of Pietist conversion. God's grace comes at certain specified moments or 'hours of grace' during which the inward penitential struggle (*Busskampf*) is followed by a sudden breakthrough (*Durchbruch*). Through Francke's leadership of the movement at Halle, this pattern was spread and widely emulated in diaries and autobiographies. The Moravians who made contact with John Wesley in the 1730s were still operating within this Pietist understanding of conversion, the framework established by Francke, though Zinzendorf later moved Moravianism away from the *Busskampf*.[79]

FROM AUGUSTINE'S *CONFESSIONS* TO WESLEY'S *JOURNAL*

We have brought our account of the rise of conversion narrative to the point where we can now see the streams that fed into the Evangelical Revival: a native tradition of Puritan and Nonconformist spiritual autobiography and teaching about conversion, related traditions in British and American piety, and Continental Pietism. The emergence of popular conversion narrative in these antecedent traditions of piety took place within the larger phenomenon of an autobiographical turn in the early modern period and the rise of heightened self-determination, introspection, and individuality. But it drew also on very specific religious and theological sources. In particular, conversion narrative was predicated on what Krister Stendahl called the 'introspective conscience' of the West. From the penitential of Finian in the seventh century to the *Busskampf* of Pietism a thousand years later, there was a deeply rooted sense within Western European Christianity that the fundamental human predicament was one of conscience, guilt, and divine judgment.[80] With the englobing rituals of Christendom in the Middle Ages, spiritual autobiography was preoccupied with final conversion: compunction and beatitude. The Catholic ascetical theology of mortification and vivification, which formed an essential part of

[78] Ward, *Protestant Evangelical Awakening*, 61; id., Introduction to Wesley, *Works* (BE), xviii. 14.

[79] John Wesley's debt to Francke appears in the fact that he published an abridged translation of Francke's *Nicodemus: or, a Treatise on the Fear of Man* in his *Christian Library*. This was a treatise that urged the reader to exercise a real and courageous, rather than a merely formal faith.

[80] The cultural history of the Western conscience is traced in Jean Delumeau, *Sin and Fear: The Emergence of a Western Guilt Culture, 13th–18th Centuries*, trans. E. Nicholson (New York, 1990).

the progress of the Christian from beginner to proficient to perfect, was later recast within Protestant theology. Mortification and vivification still formed an essential part of sanctification, as for example in Calvin's *Institutes*, but much more attention was devoted, especially among the English Puritans, to a related understanding of law and gospel in the beginnings of Christian experience in non-sacramental personal regeneration. Puritan pastoral theology taught that the first use of the law was to intensify the pangs of introspective conscience on the part of the unregenerate, in fact to lead them to despair. The crisis this induced was the centre of all the various 'morphologies' of conversion that appeared during the seventeenth and eighteenth centuries among Puritans, Pietists, and evangelicals of various sorts. And this was reflected first in diaries and then in the full expression of narrative identity, the self-interpretation of the entirety of one's life in terms of conversion. James Fraser of Brea, who wrote one of the earliest of such works, stated, 'A Man's whole Life is but a Conversion.'[81] It was the unique convergence among Protestants of heightened individualism and heightened guilt, of self-consciousness and conscience, that led to the emergence of the new literary genre of conversion narrative. The formal occasion for such an oral narrative appeared in the requirement of the gathered churches for evidence of personal conversion, a requirement that emerged in the mid-seventeenth century and then became widely adopted. Still, throughout the seventeenth century and well into the eighteenth, a special motive to publish spiritual autobiography was required—especially specimens from ordinary folk without any social standing—and this motive was most often found in the need to defend oneself or the sense that the times were epochal or indeed apocalyptic. It remains to see how the genre fared in the eighteenth century, for the very term 'revival' in the Evangelical Revival alerts us to the renewal of historical forms of expression in a new context.

---

[81] *Memoirs of James Fraser*, 91.

2

The Revival of Conversion Narrative: Evangelical Awakening in the Eighteenth Century

ON 12 October 1737, when Isaac Watts and John Guyse introduced Jonathan Edwards with a preface to the London edition of his *Faithful Narrative of the Surprising Work of God in the Conversion of Many Hundred Souls*, they mentioned the 'friendly correspondence' they maintained with their brethren in New England, and how by this means they learned now and then about instances of conversion. They welcomed the news of revival in Massachusetts, but on the whole, they regarded the times as unpropitious for conversion: 'There has been a great and just complaint for many years among the ministers and churches in Old England, and in New . . . that the work of conversion goes on very slowly.'[1] How soon all this would change. Already, at the same time that Watts and Guyse were writing these words, the newly ordained George Whitefield, 22 years of age, was in London preaching about nine times a week to crowded congregations, growing in popularity, and finding himself remarked upon in the newspapers. Within eighteen months he would be back in London preaching on the New Birth to thousands in the open air. A few years more and the spiritual awakening would appear to be general on both sides of the Atlantic.

Indeed, a new episode in the history of spiritual autobiography opened in the late 1730s with the advent of transatlantic evangelical revival. As the title of Edwards's book suggests, the distinguishing characteristic of this revival or 'work' in all its manifestations was the increased incidence of conversion. As Frank Lambert puts it, 'When scores of men and women came under "conviction" for their sins and seemed to undergo "conversion," the revivalists declared the existence of revival.'[2] Although the conception of conversion varied among the partisans of revival, there was a discernible continuity in the evangelical experience that recalled Puritan teaching and

---

[1] *WJE* iv. 131. Cf. the similar commentary on the times by John Willison in Scotland: 'The Work of Conviction and Conversion hath been rare, the Golden Showers of the Spirit have been restrained, the Pangs of the New Birth little experienced, and few Sons and Daughters born to God, in respect of former Times.' *The Christian History . . . for the Year 1743* (Boston, 1743), no. 11.

[2] Frank Lambert, *Inventing the 'Great Awakening'* (Princeton, 1999), 6.

practice.[3] Now, however, conversions began to appear in clusters, amidst great religious excitement, and these clusters were linked through news, letter writing, and itinerancy. Contemporaries soon felt that they were witnessing a surprising work of God of great proportions, a quickening of religious life taking place across the North Atlantic world. In the early 1740s evangelicals in different places concluded that they were experiencing nothing less than a worldwide effusion of the Holy Spirit. During this initial phase of the evangelical movement hopes ran high, and to many on both sides of the Atlantic it appeared that the pentecostal outpouring of the Holy Spirit upon all nations had come at last. Above all, the contemporaneity and extent of revival, both geographically and numerically, seemed to set the period apart from earlier seasons of divine grace. Within this context, narratives of conversion by men and women, leaders and laypeople, published and unpublished, began to multiply.[4]

INTERNATIONAL EVANGELICAL REVIVAL

Evangelical spiritual autobiography in the eighteenth century must be seen therefore within the context of contemporary testimony to the increased numbers of conversions across a wide area in the 1730s and 1740s. During this period the major evangelists, such as George Whitefield, John Wesley,

---

[3] This did not go unnoticed at the time. A hostile critic of Whitefield and Wesley wrote in the *Weekly Miscellany*, 15 December 1739, deploring 'the Practices of our modern *Puritans*, called *Methodists*'.

[4] The analysis in this chapter does not directly address Jon Butler's provocative criticism of the Great Awakening in America as an 'interpretive fiction' or John Kent's parallel complaint about 'the myth of the so-called evangelical revival' in England. Principally, it seems to me, these writers are concerned that the religious and political consequences of revival in the period have been overstated. Butler argues that revival in eighteenth-century America was 'erratic, heterogeneous, and politically benign', and Kent equates 'evangelical revival' narrowly with Wesleyanism and interprets it as simply one more case of the perennial recrudescence of primary religion with its 'basic belief in intrusive supernatural power' (Jon Butler, 'Enthusiasm Described and Decried: The Great Awakening as Interpretive Fiction', *Journal of American History* 69 (1982), 325; John Kent, *Wesley and the Wesleyans* (Cambridge, 2002), 7). However, despite their provocative language of 'fiction' and 'myth', neither of these historians deny that participants themselves in eighteenth-century revivals often described their own experience in terms of larger solidarities that were transnational and transdenominational. Although they might not have referred to this solidarity as the 'Great Awakening' or as the 'Evangelical Revival', they did typically describe it as a single 'work' of God. For keen analysis of the international breadth of the eighteenth-century revival, see W. R. Ward, *The Protestant Evangelical Awakening* (Cambridge, 1992), and Michael J. Crawford, *Seasons of Grace* (New York, 1991). For an analysis of the whole idea of a coherent, interconnected revival as something 'invented' in the eighteenth century (and in the eighteenth-century sense of the term, wherein 'invention' involved both discovery and promotion, especially in the media), see Lambert, *Inventing the 'Great Awakening'*.

and Jonathan Edwards, all wrote with a keen sense of a revival going on around them. In 1742 Whitefield wrote, 'I believe there is such a work begun, as neither we nor our fathers have heard of. The beginnings are amazing; how unspeakably glorious will the end be!' and he continued with a review of the awakening he had observed in New England, Scotland, Wales, and England.[5] Jonathan Edwards wrote to Scotland in 1743, saying, 'We live in a day wherein God is doing marvellous things; in that respect we are distinguished from former generations', and he expected this to only increase: 'What has now been doing is the forerunner of something vastly greater, more pure, and more extensive.'[6] In 1745 Wesley asked his opposers, 'In what age has such a work been wrought, considering the *swiftness* as well as the *extent* of it?' and he answered his own question, saying, not since the time of Constantine.[7] A few years later he wrote, 'Many sinners are saved from their sins at this day, in London . . . in many other parts of England; in Wales, in Ireland, in Scotland; upon the continent of Europe; in Asia and in America. This I term a *great work of God*; so great as I have not read of for several ages.'[8]

Evidence for the contemporaneity and extent of the revival may also be found among the writings of some of its lesser-known figures, demonstrating how the sense of a worldwide stirring reached beyond the leaders to be felt even by men of little influence in the larger movement. Joseph Humphreys (1720–?), for example, was a young man training at a Dissenting academy who was drawn into the Methodist revival through the open-air preaching of Whitefield in London. During this period when Methodism was undivided, he also became acquainted with the Wesleys and assisted them in London, Bristol, and Kingswood. By 1741 he had become a lay Methodist exhorter for Whitefield, and he focused his labours on Bristol and Gloucestershire.[9] When John Cennick—also at this time associated with Whitefield and the Calvinistic wing of the revival—published a hymnbook at Bristol in 1743, it included a hymn written by Humphreys entitled,

---

[5] Tyerman, *GW* i. 553, quoting a letter written by Whitefield from London, 6 April 1742. John Erskine of Edinburgh wrote a pamphlet in the same year with the title, *Signs of the Times Considered, or the High Probability that the Present Appearances in New England, and the West of Scotland, are a Prelude of the Glorious Things Promised to the Church in the Latter Ages.*

[6] *WJE* iv. 539–40.

[7] Wesley, *Works* (BE), xi. 276.

[8] Ibid. 374. John Willison similarly identified revival in Scotland as part of one international work of God, wherein God appeared 'first in *America,* through the *British* Colonies there; then in *Britain* itself, and particularly in several Parts of the West of *Scotland*'. The 'extraordinary Work' in Jonathan Edwards's parish was, he claimed, 'of the same Kind with that at *Cambuslang,* and other Places about', *Christian History* (Boston, 1743), no. 11.

[9] Geoffrey Nuttall, 'George Whitefield's "Curate": Gloucestershire Dissent and the Revival', *Journal of Ecclesiastical History* 27 (1976), 377–81; Wesley, *Works* (BE), xix. 152 n.; Tyerman, *JW* i. 346, 402; Tyerman, *GW* i. 223–7.

'Of Intercession and Thanksgiving for the Progress of the Gospel in various Parts of the World'.[10] In all the tumult of the early years of Methodism, this hymn is remarkable evidence that already, at an early date, a layman of little consequence was privy to international intelligence about revival and understood his local experience of renewal to be a part of one global, latter-day work of God's Spirit.

Expressed as a prayer of thanksgiving in twelve stanzas, this hymn is set in the exuberant trochaic metre (77.77 D) of many of Charles Wesley's festival hymns, such as 'Hark! the Herald Angels Sing'. While it is decidedly not to be compared with the poetic merit of the best of Charles Wesley's verse, Humphreys's hymn is none the less of great historical interest. It serves well to introduce the eighteenth-century Evangelical Revival by setting it in its international context. A grand tour of God's work in the world, the hymn begins in stanza 4 with Europe:

> 4   Thanks, with many thousand Tears,
>   That Thy Church'es Labourers
>   Ev'ry where such Blessings meet;
>   For this Grace we kiss Thy Feet.
>   Many in these latter Days
>   Have experienc'd JESU's Grace:
>   Souls in *Europe*, not a few,
>   Find the Gospel-tidings true.

It is not clear from the passing reference to Europe how much Humphreys knew about the revivals that had occurred not only at Herrnhut in Upper Lusatia, with the quasi-pentecostal communion service that gave rise to the Renewed Moravian Brethren in 1727, but also in and around Habsburg lands among Protestant minorities in Silesia, Bohemia, Moravia, and Salzburg; in the Bernese Oberland, the Wetterau, the Lower Rhine, and the United Provinces; and far away in the Baltic, among Swedish prisoners of war in Russia, and elsewhere.[11] He does recognize, however, that the souls touched by revival in Europe are 'not a few'. The phrase 'latter days' signals the eschatological interpretation he gives to these revivals, as a fulfilment of

---

[10] John Cennick, *Sacred Hymns For the Use of Religious Societies. Generally composed in Dialogues,* part 2 (Bristol, 1743), 89–92. This hymnbook was published before Cennick joined the Moravians, while he was still identified with Whitefield and Calvinistic Methodism.

[11] Revival in central and eastern Europe in the early eighteenth century is described in Ward, *Protestant Evangelical Awakening,* 54–115. News of European revival was available in England through tracts such as *Praise out of the Mouth of Babes: or, a Particular Account of some Extraordinary Pious Motions and Devout Exercises, Observ'd of Late in Many Children in Silesia* (1708), or August Hermann Francke, *Pietas Hallensis: Or a Publick Demonstration of the Footsteps of a Divine Being yet in the World: in an Historical Narration of the Orphan-House, and Other Charitable Institutions, at Glaucha near Hall in Saxony* (1705).

the promised outpouring of divine grace in Joel 2: 28. Four years before this hymn was published Jonathan Edwards had already made the link between the revival and eschatology for his congregation in New England in a series of sermons later published as *A History of the Work of Redemption*.[12]

When Humphreys turns to Britain in particular, he picks out the key sites of revival activity, including the London–Bristol–Newcastle triangle of early Methodism, the Wiltshire connexion of John Cennick, the scene of his own labours in Bristol and Gloucestershire, the revival in Wales under Howell Harris and Daniel Rowland, and the Yorkshire circuit built up by Benjamin Ingham:

> 5 *Britains* Isle has catch'd the Flame;
> Many know and love the LAMB:
> Both in *England* and in *Wales*,
> And in *Scotland*, Grace prevails:
>   *London, Wilts*, and *Glou'stershire*,
> Feel our SAVIOUR very dear:
> *Bristol* Sinners seek the LORD,
>   And in *Kingswood* he's ador'd.
>
> 6 And a few Sheep, here and there,
> Are belov'd in *Oxfordshire*:
> At *Newcastle*, and near *York*,
> We are told GOD is at Work:
>   And on many Sinners Hearts,
> Who're unknown, in various Parts;
> By whatever Means he will,
> We are bound to thank him still.

When Humphreys turns his attention to Scotland, he picks up on the 'Cambuslang Wark' in the parish of William McCulloch, a revival that Whitefield had helped to ignite in 1742 and that soon spread widely to other Scottish communities, including Muthill, north-east of Glasgow, and Kilsyth, thirty miles further distant, where the minister was James Robe:

> 7 And our Shepherd's Arm infolds
> *Edinburgh* and *Glasgow* Souls:
> *Muthel, Kilsyth, Cambuslang*,
> Late of JESU's Love have sang.
>   Carry on Thy Work with Pow'r,
> Ev'ry Day and ev'ry Hour:
> Still let thousands in the *North*
> Know the great Redeemer's Worth.

Humphreys was also aware of the work of the Moravians, and particularly of their foreign missionary enterprise. Moreover, he knew of the theological

---

[12] Cf. also John Erskine, *The Signs of the Times Considered* (Edinburgh, 1742).

controversy over quietism ('stillness') that had led to an open breach between Wesley and Moravians in 1740, and thus he betrays some doubts about their theology:

> 8 Many *Germans* walk with GOD,
>   Thro' the Virtue of CHRIST's Blood;
>   Self deny, the Cross take up:
>   They, no doubt, with CHRIST shall sup.
>   What they know not, teach them, LORD;
>   Surely they do love Thy Word:
>   To the World by them make known
>   What for Sinners thou hast done.

When he reaches America, he is effusive as he thinks of Whitefield's orphanage in Georgia and of Whitefield's triumphant preaching tour in 1740 through the South, the Middle Colonies, and especially New England:

> 9 Likewise in *America*
>   Shines the glorious Gospel-day:
>   Fair it rises to our Sight;
>   Jesu, make it Thy Delight.
>   *Pennsylvania* had been blest
>   With an Evangelick Feast:
>   On *South-Carolina* too
>   CHRIST distills His heav'nly Dew.
>
> 10 LORD, be praised for Thy Work
>   In the *Jersey's* and *New York*;
>   And in ev'ry other Place
>   Where appears the SAVIOUR's Grace.
>   O defend the *Orphan-house*;
>   Lo, it stands amidst its Foes:
>   Hear our Cries, the Children bless,
>   Father of the fatherless.
>
> 11 Thousand *Negroes* praise Thy Name;
>   And *New England*'s in a Flame;
>   Triumphs in Thy Mercy's Power:
>   JESU, call ten thousand more!

The idea of African-Americans responding to the gospel under Whitefield's ministry turns Humphreys's thoughts in the last half of this stanza again to the Moravian missions abroad, which began with the West Indies in 1732, but also included Greenland in 1733 and South Africa in 1736:

> And we hear the *Hottentot*
> By our LORD is not forgot:
> And that *Greenland*'s frozen Soil
> Now's become His Cross's Spoil.

Humphreys's knowledge of international evangelical activity here is certainly remarkable—almost as remarkable as the rhyme '*Hottentot*...not forgot'.[13]

He concludes again on an eschatological note, with the ingathering of the nations in the apocalyptic kingdom, and his hopes are expressed in terms of the Moravian-influenced piety of the melting heart and contemplation of the suffering Lamb of God:

> 12   LORD, we're hearing frequently
>   How Thy Kingdom makes its Way:
>   When the Tidings reach our Ears,
>   We could almost melt in Tears.
>   Still let more receive Thy Name,
>   O Thou crucified LAMB:
>   Out of ev'ry Land and Place,
>   Bring forth some redeem'd by Grace.

This last line brings us back to the experience of conversion that Humphreys celebrates in this hymn. In all, the hymn provides a comprehensive overview of the transatlantic evangelical awakening in early 1743. Humphreys does not mention Cornwall, since Wesley and his lay preachers would begin their important work there only in mid-1743. And early Cornish evangelicals in the Church of England, such as Samuel Walker of Truro, came to their evangelical convictions for the most part some years later as well. Likewise Humphreys does not mention Ireland, since Moravians would pioneer in the establishment of evangelical religious societies there only in 1745 under Benjamin LaTrobe and John Cennick, and Wesley would not follow until 1747. Notwithstanding these omissions, it is a remarkably complete survey. This international spiritual awakening was constituted at its most fundamental level by countless individual experiences of evangelical conversion. The literary trace of this awakening is to be found not only in the testimony of evangelical leaders such as Wesley, Whitefield, and Edwards, or in the hymnody of a little-known lay preacher, but also in the large number of published and unpublished conversion narratives from the period. All of this together bears witness to the reinvigoration of a Protestant form of spiritual autobiography under new conditions.

THE CONDITIONS OF THE AWAKENING: NEWS

What were these conditions? The third line of the final stanza, 'When the Tidings reach our Ears', bears passing witness to changes in the North

---

[13] Cf. Charles Wesley's journal entry for 15 April 1739, after waiting upon Count Zinzendorf: '[He] told us of six hundred Moors converted, two hundred Greenlanders, three hundred Hottentots.' *CWJ* i. 146–7.

Atlantic world that helped to create the conditions for the sort of international revival intelligence included in Humphreys's hymn. Until the eighteenth century, it would have been unlikely that such distant tidings would have reached the ears of a middling layman such as Humphreys, or that they would have reached him so quickly. The modernity of the eighteenth century, not only with its more rapid forms of transportation and communication, but also with its religious cross-currents, did much to break down the insularity of local, parochial religious experience and connect the most humble believer with far-distant events.

So how did Joseph Humphreys become so remarkably well informed? His knowledge of the progress of revival in remote regions was due in part to innovations in the religious press in the eighteenth century to which evangelicals themselves contributed significantly. Newspapers and weekly periodicals began to flourish in the early decades of the eighteenth century, after the loosening of press censorship in 1695. Weekly reviews, such as the *Tatler* (started 1709) and the *Spectator* (started 1711), appealed to a growing reading public, though these essay-periodicals were superseded by the 'magazine' genre (incorporating a greater variety of content) with the publication of the *Gentleman's Magazine* in 1731. About the same time William Webster began publishing the *Weekly Miscellany* (1732–41), which though not called a 'magazine' also contained a range of pieces, including orthodox Anglican essays on religion, morals, and government, notices of books, and general news. All of these were polite and improving publications, and they shared an Augustan climate of moralism; all shared likewise the assumption of periodical publishing that what was current was of importance. With the advent of revival, these precedents in journalism were adapted to serve the evangelical ends.

Between 1741 and 1743 four major evangelical periodicals were established. Each depended heavily upon copy supplied by correspondents or lifted from each other, and each was chiefly under the editorial control of one person. In 1740 John Lewis, a London printer associated with Calvinistic Methodism, launched *The Christian's Amusement*, and this was taken over by Whitefield in 1741 and rechristened *The Weekly History*. At the end of that year William McCulloch established *The Glasgow Weekly History* in explicit imitation of Whitefield's London paper. Thomas Prince followed in Boston in 1743 with *The Christian History*, and James Robe in Edinburgh the same year with *The Christian Monthly History*.[14] The subtitles of all four magazines were almost identical, each promising an account or relation of 'the Progress of the Gospel at Home and Abroad'. This phrase is echoed in the title of Humphreys's hymn which was a prayer of intercession and

---

[14] See further Susan O'Brien, 'Eighteenth-Century Publishing Networks in the First Years of Transatlantic Evangelicalism', in M. A. Noll, D. W. Bebbington, and G. A. Rawlyk

thanksgiving 'For the Progress of the Gospel in various Parts of the World'. The parallel is close enough in this and other ways to warrant thinking of the hymn as a versed outline of the contents of the magazines. What was the effect of all this news for the reader? A minister 'in the country' who had been reading *The Weekly History* in February 1742 commented on its contents: 'If Conversion-work is a Miracle . . . what must such Numbers of Conversions be? When a little one becomes a Thousand, and a small one a mighty Nation, who will doubt, it is the Lord that hastens it?'[15] The news of conversion in the magazines had led this reader to infer that God's hand was at work in his own times.

Tidings of revival almost certainly reached Humphreys's ears through the evangelical periodical press, but these magazines themselves were dependent upon the extensive network of communication 'at home and abroad' built up by the evangelical leaders through travel and familiar correspondence.[16] Some 80 per cent of the content of McCulloch's *Glasgow Weekly History* was made up of letters, and this was not unusual for these magazines. The London-based *Weekly History* depended not only upon news and letters from Whitefield, but also upon reports from circuit preachers in England and Wales.[17] Indeed, Humphreys was himself a major contributor to the periodical.[18] Through Humphreys's itinerancy in southern England, and through his personal contact with the Wesleys and Whitefield in London and Bristol, John Cennick in Wiltshire, and Howell Harris in Wales, he was also kept well informed. Perhaps he participated in some of the Methodist 'letter days' as well, meetings where news from abroad or accounts of spiritual experience were read out in a society meeting for general edification. He certainly corresponded with Harris between 1742 and 1745, and also with the Wesleys and other leaders, in the course of his ministry. In this, he was an example of how even a minor, provincial figure in the awakening could be well informed if he was connected to the larger evangelical network through travel, personal contacts, correspondence, and the magazines.

(eds.), *Evangelicalism: Comparative Studies of Popular Protestantism in North America, the British Isles, and Beyond, 1700–1990* (New York, 1994), 48–51, and Frank Lambert, *'Pedlar in Divinity': George Whitefield and the Transatlantic Revivals, 1737–1770* (Princeton, 1994), 69–75. See also Joseph L. Altholz, *The Religious Press in Britain, 1760–1900* (New York, 1989), 8–9. W. R. Ward further describes the circulation of religious news in Europe and abroad in *Protestant Evangelical Awakening*, 1–10.

[15] *Weekly History* (London, 1740–2), no. 46.

[16] Thomas Jackson notes, 'The Wesleys and Mr. Whitefield were all in the habit of reading in their religious meetings extracts from the letters of their correspondents, relative to the progress of the Gospel in various parts of the world.' *CWJ* i. 285 n.

[17] O'Brien, 'Eighteenth-Century Publishing', 49.

[18] Tyerman, *JW* i. 346. See e.g. *Weekly History*, nos. 42 and 45.

The evangelical experience, illustrated in the case of Joseph Humphreys, represents an expansion of the Puritan experience in the seventeenth century. The eighteenth-century experience was distinguished in part by the extensive connectedness of local revival to revival elsewhere, to a world that transcended the local milieu of parish, denomination, or sect.[19] For example, in the absence of a regular religious periodical or its equivalent, it is unlikely that the participants in the Six-Mile-Water Revival in County Antrim, Ireland in the 1620s ('a bright and hot sun-blink of the gospel'), though that revival spread throughout Ulster and western Scotland, were able to see their experience in anything near as broad a contemporary context as Humphreys did his.[20] International travel and correspondence in the 1620s were more constrained, even for the elite, and religious pamphleteering had not yet evolved into the periodical. How different the situation was a century later when revival returned to Scotland. The 24-year-old Janet Jackson, daughter of a weaver in Cambuslang, took pleasure in reading the *Weekly History* in 1741, just months before her own conversion and the general awakening in the parish. She mentioned the magazine by name in the course of her own conversion narrative.[21] Her younger sister, Elizabeth, likewise recalled hearing William McCulloch read from the magazine, and she remembered how she was emotionally stirred, 'especially on observing how much good others were getting, while I was let alone'.[22] Two daughters of a weaver in a small Scottish parish were thus made anxious about conversion by reading about contemporary revival in far-distant lands, and when revival came to Cambuslang, they knew it to be part of one interconnected, divine work in their generation.

What were the implications of this enlarged network of religious intelligence in the eighteenth-century Atlantic world? On the one hand, the flow of information from distant quarters had the effect of stimulating parallel religious activity elsewhere. John Wesley's first *Journal* illustrates this well, since it was on ship and in remote Georgia in 1736 that Wesley, an English clergyman, was provoked to spiritual anxiety by the questions of believers whose religious fervour had originated deep in central Europe.

---

[19] Cf. Frank Lambert's comment: 'Seventeenth-century divines had largely conceived of their audiences as private bodies, defined by parish, sect, or denomination. With the introduction of inexpensive popular print, especially newspapers, evangelicals could now think of addressing a new, much broader public. Indeed the word *public* assumed new meaning.' Lambert, '*Pedlar in Divinity*', 7.

[20] Scots–Irish revivalism was nevertheless an important precedent for eighteenth-century revival in Scotland and the mid-Atlantic colonies in North America. See further, Marilyn J. Westerkamp, *Triumph of the Laity: Scots-Irish Piety and the Great Awakening, 1625–1760* (New York, 1988).

[21] McCulloch MSS i. 21.

[22] Ibid. i. 103.

Moreover, the occasion for revival needed no longer to be local. What Jonathan Edwards wrote in his study some three-and-a-half thousand miles away profoundly influenced what happened in London or Glasgow several months later. Within a year John Wesley was reading the account and exclaiming, 'Surely "this is the Lord's doing and it is marvellous in our eyes".'[23] This was a formative time for Wesley and for Methodism, and Edwards's *Faithful Narrative* contributed to the discovery of his own mission to convert the English nation.

What began for Edwards as a private correspondence became significant internationally because it answered the hopes of many across the North Atlantic world. For Edwards, it was an unintended consequence of writing a private letter to another minister to explain how he preached justification by faith and witnessed local revival. But as Edwards's narrative was taken out of his hands and thrown to the larger winds of North Atlantic culture, his story was reified in print and became, in modern parlance, a media event. As his narrative was read aloud to congregations and serialized in the revival magazines, it inspired ministers such as Wesley and laypeople such as Humphreys to hope that such an experience could be duplicated among themselves. The much reprinted *Faithful Narrative* stimulated ebullient expectations on the part of readers. As Clarence Goen shrewdly observes, 'During the awakening of 1734–35 Edwards faithfully pursued his pastoral work with reverent wonder, for . . . his surprise was genuine. But when he gave his narrative to the world, the simple fact is that no revival could ever be a surprise again.'[24]

The effect of such an international network of revival intelligence was not only, however, to excite emulation but also to foster new interpretations of religious experience altogether. If seventeenth-century calf-bound theological treatises appealed to the authority of tradition, reason, and exegesis, then eighteenth-century letters and magazines reflected an appeal to experience and a new confidence about discerning the hand of God in history. Moreover, the context of conversion was no longer only the parishioner in his or her local community of faith, but the individual as a member of the broader public, even when that 'public' was one created in part through new patterns of communication, such as 'public' preaching and the magazines. Just as the marketplace could be imagined as something larger than one's local village market, something international in scope, so also the sphere of God's work in the world could be likewise pictured as something that transcended local experience. The distinctive polity of Methodist

---

[23] Wesley, *Works* (BE), xix. 16.

[24] *WJE* iv. 27. See further, Bruce Hindmarsh, 'The Reception of Jonathan Edwards by Early Evangelicals in England', in D. W. Kling and D. A. Sweeney (eds.), *Jonathan Edwards at Home and Abroad* (Columbia, SC, 2003), 201–21.

connexionalism also represented a wide community, with which converts could identify, and this contrasted sharply with the decentralized parish system of the Established Church.[25] Moreover, there was a sense in Humphreys's hymn that the news of individual conversions, taken in aggregate, pointed to the present as a culminating episode in salvation history: 'Many in these latter Days | Have experience'd JESU's Grace.' We noted in the last chapter that the appearance of conversion narrative in print in the 1650s owed something to the rule of the saints under Cromwell and the sense on the part of Fifth Monarchists and others that England was a nation 'at the edge of the promises'. So also now in the 1730s and 1740s, conversion narrative was revived in the midst of similar expectations, though the context was now broader. John Wesley, George Whitefield, and Jonathan Edwards each speculated that the revival was an eschatological outpouring of the Spirit. Wesley and Whitefield wondered if the spiritual life and gifts of the early church were being restored—particularly the perceptible experience of the Holy Spirit—and Edwards speculated at the height of revivalistic optimism in 1743 that the millennial kingdom would appear in America.[26] Millennialism, charismata, and revival have often appeared side by side in the course of history, but the web of international religious news available in the eighteenth century heightened expectations with an up-to-the-minute sense of contemporaneity. In an unprecedented way revival was now concentrated in time and extended in space.

Within a decade this eschatological and pentecostal stage of the revival had passed, and none of the revival magazines lasted beyond 1748. Wesley concluded that the kingdom of God did not generally come, after all, 'with observation', but that it would 'silently increase wherever it is set up, and spread from heart to heart, from house to house'.[27] Indeed, this seemed to be the case. The evangelical movement continued to grow in numbers, sophistication, and confidence, and there were clusters of revival activity and raised expectations, but the sense of a great international pentecost had passed. Nevertheless, the itinerancy, letter-writing, and periodical publishing of the early evangelicals had promoted conversion and made it public in a new way, making the experience of conversion itself the central identifying trait of a new evangelical movement.

THE CONDITIONS OF THE AWAKENING: MOVEMENT

The other important condition of revival in the eighteenth century, closely related to the rapid dissemination of news, was the more extensive move-

---

[25] An important observation made by John Walsh in personal correspondence.

[26] Nathan O. Hatch and Harry S. Stout (eds.), *Jonathan Edwards and the American Experience* (New York, 1988), 29, 131–41.

[27] Wesley, *Works* (BE), ii. 493, cf. 530.

ment of people, goods, and ideas in the period generally. John Walsh writes, 'In its inception evangelicalism was very much a *movement*; it was marked by mobility, excitement, restlessness, experimentation, fluidity, and controversy.'[28]

This characteristic of evangelical religion was grounded in the material conditions of eighteenth-century life, since it became more efficient to travel or move goods as the century progressed. For example, transatlantic shipping became more reliable and serviceable with more ships sailing, and doing so on a more regular schedule. More than twice as many ships were plying colonial ports at mid-century than were at its beginning.[29] This was significant for the early evangelicals, since they depended upon the British merchant marine for the exchange of news and to evangelize abroad. John Wesley's career as a missionary in Georgia was a near disaster, but the voyage nevertheless exposed him to religious influences that would be critical to his formation as an evangelical leader. Whitefield, the 'Grand Itinerant', was the ocean-going traveller par excellence, crossing the Atlantic thirteen times in little more than thirty years. His ministry followed closely on the larger expansion of Atlantic maritime activity.

In Britain itself a national road network, achieved in part through turnpike trusts, was one of the major achievements of the period. John Wesley was critical of 'the vile imposition' of turnpike tolls, but few could have taxed and tested the road infrastructure of Britain more thoroughly than he. He was a shrewd observer of improvements. On 15 June 1770 in North Yorkshire, he noted, 'I was agreeably surprised to find the whole road from Thirsk to Stokesley, which used to be extremely bad, better than most turnpikes.' Roads had been similarly improved, he commented, without turnpikes, 'for several hundred miles in Scotland and throughout all Connaught in Ireland'.[30] Wesley did much of his travelling on horseback, but he also made use from time to time of a coach or chaise or, more rarely, the post-chaise or mail-coach. The continuous, regular, and largely punctual itinerancy of Wesley and of the other evangelists and Methodist lay preachers evolved alongside an unprecedented boom in road-building and improvement in Britain.[31]

Many contemporaries observed that the roads led to improved communications, and that this was one of the great changes of their lifetime. As Paul Langford puts it, 'A new age of speed had dawned.'[32] Travel times dropped

---

[28] John Walsh, ' "Methodism" and the Origins of English-Speaking Evangelicalism', in Noll, Rawlyk, and Bebbington (eds.), *Evangelicalism*, 23.

[29] Lambert, *'Pedlar in Divinity'*, 28.

[30] Wesley, *Works* (BE), xxii. 233.

[31] W. R. Ward, 'John Wesley, Traveller', in *Faith and Faction* (1993), 249–63.

[32] Paul Langford, *A Polite and Commercial People: England, 1727–1783* (Oxford, 1990), 404.

off sharply over the course of the century, and traffic increased apace. Some lamented that this led to the spread of immorality and the breakdown of local social control. Others, such as Arthur Young, celebrated the 'general impetus given to circulation; new people—new ideas—new exertions—fresh activity to every branch of industry'.[33] By the Regency period, a visitor to England could comment, 'Nobody is a provincial in this country. You meet nowhere with those persons who never were out of their native place, and whose habits are wholly local.'[34] The sense among evangelicals of a general work of God that included but also transcended the local experience of revival was in part predicated on these new communication patterns.

One practical implication was that mail delivery also became more swift and reliable, though it could still be expensive. During the mid-eighteenth century a correspondent who wrote from London to someone in another major city on Monday could receive an answer by Friday. After mail coaches were introduced in 1784, the answer might be received by Wednesday.[35] The Augustan period has been described as 'the great age of the personal letter',[36] and religious leaders of all sorts accumulated large archives of correspondence. However, even in an age of letter writers, the evangelicals, like the Pietists, were noteworthy as particularly energetic and frequent letter writers. August Hermann Francke had some 5,000 correspondents. John Wesley's case was similar.[37] The voluminous correspondence of the evangelicals was the paper parallel to their restless itinerancy, and this too was certainly shaped in part by the new efficiencies of travel and communication.

But the impulse to correspond was still religious. Letters played a crucial role in disseminating religious news. They also served a practical purpose. For example, Whitefield typically received invitations to preach and set up his itinerary by correspondence, so that when he arrived at his destination, he could preach 'by appointment', as he so often recorded in his journal. Word of mouth and the local press then attracted the crowds. But letters were also important as a means of pastoral care. After a full day of preaching, exhorting, and counselling, Whitefield would often stay up past midnight answering his correspondents and addressing their spiritual concerns. On

---

[33] Quoted in Roy Porter, *English Society in the Eighteenth Century* (1990), 193.

[34] Quoted ibid. 39.

[35] Wesley, *Works* (BE), xxv. 24.

[36] See further, Howard Anderson and Irvin Ehrenpreis, 'The Familiar Letter in the Eighteenth Century: Some Generalizations', in H. Anderson, P. B. Daghlian, and I. Ehrenpreis (eds.), *The Familiar Letter in the Eighteenth Century* (Lawrence, Kan., 1966), 269–82.

[37] For the new edition of Wesley's *Works*, the editors intend to include about 1,600 correspondents but note that his total correspondents certainly reached several times this number. Wesley, *Works* (BE), xxv. 28–30.

2 April 1739 Whitefield left Bristol after preaching to thousands and then toured Wales and the West Country. When he reached Gloucester seven days later he found a 'great packet of letters, giving me an account of the success of the Gospel in different parts'. Two days later he returned to Gloucester to find some thirty letters waiting for him from friends in Bristol 'whose hearts God hath been pleased to bless'.[38] He spent the next morning answering these 'dear correspondents', counselling them through letters. Even a resident evangelical clergyman such as John Newton was in the 1790s always working from a stack of fifty or sixty unanswered letters—most of these letters from enquirers looking for some sort of spiritual direction through the post. The use of letters by evangelicals in these ways augmented their face-to-face ministry and provided one more means of stimulating and directing revival and counselling those in spiritual concern. In an artless way, such letters often passed over easily into spiritual autobiography. A large proportion of extant conversion narratives from the eighteenth century were written in the course of such familiar correspondence, or they began this way and were only later revised for the press.

Improvements in shipping, roads, and communication, and the related growth in efficiency in postal service were all important factors in stimulating a larger traffic of ideas, people, and goods, and evangelicals were at the forefront of the flux and excitement that this created. These factors also contributed to economic expansion, as did the development of hundreds more miles of navigable inland waterways. Just as the roads increased the efficiency of moving people and parcels, canals allowed raw materials—especially coal—to be moved easily and cheaply to distant markets and manufacturing centres. New canals also introduced demographic change as the population of these manufacturing centres, such as Birmingham, Manchester, Leeds, and Sheffield, mushroomed. Agricultural reform led to the decline of the open-field village under enclosure acts during the second half of the century, and this too accelerated the movement of people from country to town. In consequence, the proportion of Englishmen living in an urban centre approximately doubled over the century. London itself grew from half a million to nearly 900,000 inhabitants. Just as cities fostered religious dissent during the Reformation by offering greater scope for anonymity, freedom from the social control of local elites, and exposure to diverse viewpoints, so also the accelerated pace of urban growth in the eighteenth century provided a setting congenial to religious experimentation.

Many of Methodism's converts were artisans who had recently arrived in these growing cities or market towns. The swelling population of such centres contributed to the crowds that thronged in the thousands to hear Whitefield and Wesley at Moorfields and Blackheath in London, or at

---

[38] *GWJ* 249.

Baptist Mills and Rose Green in Bristol. Thousands also gathered in the parish of Cambuslang in 1742 from all over western Scotland, and the proximity of Cambuslang to Glasgow (only five miles away) meant that a large proportion of those at Cambuslang were also city dwellers. Philadelphia, New York, and Boston were likewise the places of Whitefield's most concentrated ministry in the American colonies. Indeed, most of the places listed in Joseph Humphreys's hymn were growing towns and cities, or nearby such centres. Although the Evangelical Revival was not only an urban phenomenon, and many converts were garnered in remote parishes and scattered villages, the enlarged social intercourse and commercial exchange of the city and market town supplied one more source for the mobility and fluidity that characterized evangelicalism.[39]

Improvements in transportation and communication and the growth of urban centres were closely related to the remarkable expansion of the Atlantic economy as a whole during the eighteenth century. Market analogies were common in spiritual literature since the seventeenth century, but the link between spiritual autobiography and commerce is more than literary. Economic relations profoundly shaped self-understanding then as now. Within a client–patron economy it was always more plausible to see religion as part of the natural order of things, and deference might more naturally be expected (if not always granted) to clergy in the Established Church as much as to landed gentry in society. By contrast, within a market economy it was more natural to see religion as a matter of individual choice, and the logic of the vendor–customer relationship was more egalitarian and governed by suasion.

Historians have coined the term 'consumer revolution' to describe the dramatic expansion of the marketplace during the eighteenth century in Britain and America.[40] As real incomes rose early in the century and the price of commodities such as sugar and tea dropped, and as more manufactured goods were available and credit was extended more widely, men and women of all ranks in Britain and the colonies spent more on a wider range of material comforts beyond bare necessities. This growth in consumption, and the threat it implied to traditional relations, helps to explain the clerical

---

[39] I am indebted to John Walsh for drawing my attention to the fact that local landholding patterns were often the key to receptivity to evangelical preaching in rural areas. Estate parishes, where the ownership of the land was concentrated in the hands of a small number of gentry, constituted a 'dependency system' and were much more resistant to evangelical influence than were the large, open parishes, characterized by pastoral agriculture and which had a larger number of small freeholders. Evangelical preachers had marked success *both* in the 'modern' environment of the city and in certain pockets of very traditional rural English society. See further, Alan D. Gilbert, *Religion and Society in Industrial England* (1976), 97–110.

[40] Neil McKendrick, John Brewer, and J. H. Plumb (eds.), *The Birth of a Consumer Society: The Commercialization of Eighteenth-Century England* (Bloomington, 1982).

jeremiads against luxury and the moral satires created by Augustan poets and painters in this period.

These economic changes occurred at the same time as the emergence of evangelical revival in Britain and America, and it has been argued that George Whitefield's success was due in part to his adaptation of new commercial strategies, characteristic of the consumer revolution, to evangelism.[41] Whitefield not only used the new print media to good effect to stimulate demand, much as a merchant would use advertising, but he also preached in the open air, competing with public entertainments in the marketplace. Lest we think of Moorfields as a pastoral scene reminiscent of Constable's *Hay Wain,* a letter from 1742 describes the scene in Whitefield's own words. All the agents of the devil were there, he maintained, including 'drummers, trumpeters, merry andrews, masters of puppet shows, exhibiters of wild beasts, players, &c. &c. all busy entertaining their respective auditories . . . My pulpit was fixed on the opposite side, and immediately, to their great mortification, they found the number of their attendants sadly lessened.'[42] In the evening the entertainers came to complain that they had taken several pounds less that day than usual, and they sought to disrupt Whitefield's preaching by slashing at him with a long whip and beating a drum. Whitefield's elastic round numbers are problematic (he claimed to have preached to more than twenty thousand), but he clearly preached to a vast audience. While he preached, or afterwards, his hearers would pass him notes, and he said he received more than a thousand that day, that some 350 persons were awakened, and that this was the beginning of the Moorfield's Tabernacle society.

This is but an extreme example of what was characteristic of the preaching of the early Methodist evangelists. These were not scholar-preachers or gentleman-parsons, agents of a religious monopoly addressing a parish congregation of the Established Church, supported by law and custom. Rather, these were popular preachers who openly competed for the willing attention of individuals in public spaces, preaching in the market or on the common or from the court house steps. And they did so just at the time when changing patterns of consumption introduced a new level of choice into Anglo-American society. Depending upon moral suasion alone, and directing their message to the individual conscience and will, these sermons found their mark. The common refrain of the hearers was that this message seemed to be new, since it addressed them as individuals as never before. Margaret Austin was one of those who heard Whitefield at Moorfields in 1739, and she wrote, 'Though I went to Church as often as I could, I never

[41] See especially, Harry S. Stout, *The Divine Dramatist: George Whitefield and the Rise of Modern Evangelicalism* (Grand Rapids, Mich., 1991), and Lambert, *'Pedlar in Divinity'.*
[42] *Letters of George Whitefield for the Period 1734–1742* (Edinburgh, 1976), 385

was struck in such a manner as then.'[43] Austin's conversion narrative was shaped in part by its setting, and by her hearing a religious message that was adapted for a mobile, more voluntaristic society.

Along with material and economic conditions, the politics of eighteenth-century Europe set large numbers of people on the move. The Westphalia settlements of the mid-seventeenth century were an uneasy détente after the Thirty Years War (1618–48) on the Continent, and certain regions did not come under its provisions. Religious tensions were interwoven with commercial, nationalist, and dynastic aspirations and continued to incite conflict between states well into the next century. During the period about which Joseph Humphreys wrote, these conflicts involved the English, for example, in the Jacobite scares of 1715 and 1745 and the War of the Austrian Succession (1739–48). Among the English soldiers who saw military action on the Continent were numbers who were converted in Methodist-like revivals among the troops and who formed religious societies. War had dislocated these soldiers from their homes, introduced them to new temptations, and placed them in near-death situations that prompted serious religious reflection. Some, such as John Haime and Sampson Staniforth, went on to serve as lay preachers under Wesley.

As a further consequence of the political tensions in the aftermath of the Westphalia settlements, there were ethnic minorities and religious constituencies left without toleration, such as the Protestant Salzburghers whose religion was proscribed in the archdiocese. Waves of religious refugees travelled the length and breadth of the North Atlantic world in response to the policies of modern state bureaucracies. There was a movement from regions of oppression to those of toleration, or to regions short of labour that actively recruited immigrants. These restless minorities helped to catalyse revival in Britain and America, and elsewhere.[44] One of the reasons that Joseph Humphreys knew so much about revival in lands he had never visited was due to the breakdown of national insularity that this movement fostered, increasing contact between the English and foreign Protestants. The most important group thus set on the move were the Moravians, who began as an eclectic collection of religious refugees on Count Zinzendorf's estate in Saxony, and then, under the impetus of revival, took up a mission to the church universal. Humphreys had direct contact with German Moravians, as he says in his hymn, in '*London, Wilts,* and *Glou'stershire*'. No doubt he also heard of the Salzburghers and others from the Wesley brothers and Whitefield, whose travels to America and whose religious leadership in London had brought them into contact with Continental Protestants.

[43] Margaret Austin to Charles Wesley, MS letter, 19 May 1740, EMV.

[44] Ward, *Protestant Evangelical Awakening*, 3–10; id., *Christianity under the Ancien Régime* (Cambridge, 1999), 1–33, 105–46; id., 'Power and Piety: the Origins of Religious Revival in the Early Eighteenth Century', in *Faith and Faction*, 75–93.

One of the most serious problems of the early modern world was how religious differences were to be related to the confessional state and the territorial church. The exposure to difference, hastened by increased travel, communication, and trade, could lead in a number of directions. It could lead to retrenchment with the shoring up of the apparatus of confessional politics and the efforts to secure compliance with orthodoxy through proselytization and penal legislation, such as occurred in England earlier under the Clarendon Code. It could also lead to a retreat from religion altogether into secular rationalism as occurred with many Enlightenment thinkers. In a more mild form of retreat, impatience with religious strife could lead to 'indifferentism' or various forms of latitudinarianism. Or again, it could lead to a new focus on experience, especially to various forms of 'inward religion' or popular revival, as men and women sought to bolster religious feeling in the absence of traditional supports and to bear witness to a spiritual ecumenicity that transcended the differences in external forms between various religious traditions. Because religious pluralism was in some sense now permanent, and because religious warfare proved futile, some or all of these reactions occurred in most areas of Europe.

The constitutional situation in England after the Act of Toleration in 1689 created a situation that was more favourable to religious minorities than most *ancien régime* states, and indeed, most English citizens in the eighteenth century were proud of their advanced 'religious liberty'. If Salzburg was a region of 'high pressure', England was a region of relatively low pressure, and colonies such as Pennsylvania were regions of extremely low pressure. And the movement from high pressure systems to low pressure systems created its own religious turbulence, if only the internal disturbance of John Wesley wondering why he did not *know* that he was a child of God in the way that August Gottlieb Spangenberg and the German-speaking settlers in Georgia did.

In sum, material, economic, and political conditions in the eighteenth century led to an unprecedented level of *movement* of people, goods, and ideas. The most important implication of this for evangelical revival is that this sort of exchange dislocated people and exposed them to differences, and to new opportunities and threats, while also underlining their sense of insecurity in the modern world. Religious experience became, therefore, far more voluntary and self-conscious, and far less a matter of custom or givenness, as women and men were presented with alternatives. In this context the turn to spiritual autobiography played a crucial role by allowing believers to negotiate an identity that could no longer be merely assumed. This places the renewal of spiritual autobiography among evangelicals squarely in the early modern world, alongside the sort of material and social developments that constitute modernity as a whole.

Thus, the experience of conversion among the eighteenth-century evangelicals can be distinguished from the earlier Puritan experience, in part, by the new social space it inhabited, a space defined by an accelerated and continuous traffic in commodities and news. According to Jürgen Habermas, it was precisely conditions of this sort that allowed for the emergence of a bourgeois public sphere during this period, the sphere where 'private people come together as a public'. The evangelical autobiographers who wrote about their conversion experiences contributed to the 'audience-oriented subjectivity' that was altogether characteristic of this new public sphere.[45] We shall return to these themes at the conclusion of this book.

Conversion Narrative

It remains the case, however, despite all these predisposing conditions, that the international Protestant awakening of the eighteenth century was constituted chiefly by the repeated experience of evangelical conversion, and that there was an irreducibly religious element in this experience that was in continuity with seventeenth-century Puritanism and related traditions. What preceded the awakening of general spiritual concern on the part of large numbers of people in eighteenth-century England, and the appearance of conversions not singly, here and there, but in large concentrations, was the comparatively isolated, but remarkably parallel conversions of a handful of leaders during a short period of time. The following chapter will examine the path-breaking journals of the Methodist evangelists, serial accounts of their ministries in which were embedded set-piece narratives of their own conversions and those of others. But it is worth ending this chapter with the less well-known figure with whom we began—Joseph Humphreys—since Humphreys's experience illustrates how the larger evangelical revival, about which he wrote in his hymn, was itself constituted by individual conversion experiences, and how these experiences so often compelled converts to retell their life's story from the beginning, even venturing sometimes to do so in print before an anonymous public.

In addition to a few pamphlets and his hymn on the worldwide progress of the gospel, Joseph Humphreys published a conversion narrative in 1742 entitled, *Joseph Humphreys's Experience of the Work of Grace upon his Heart*. We have record of John Wesley reading it in 1790, but the work itself is extremely rare.[46] A tract of forty-four pages, it sold for two pence and

---

[45] Jürgen Habermas, *The Structural Transformation of the Public Sphere*, trans. T. Burger with F. Lawrence (Cambridge, Mass., 1991), 1–67.

[46] Humphreys's *Experience* is not listed in the *English Short Title Catalogue*. The copy I consulted is in the rare book collection at the Speer Library, Princeton Theological Seminary, New Jersey. I am grateful for the generous assistance of William Harris and David Stewart in my research at Princeton.

was printed at Bristol by Felix Farley, who was closely associated with John Wesley, and was sold in London by the bookseller John Lewis, who was closely associated with Whitefield.[47] Humphreys, like so many Dissenters and later evangelicals, kept a private diary, and perhaps also further 'private memoirs' (unless this was the same document) that went back about seven years. These he maintained as an aid to devotion only 'for my own private advantage'. To go beyond this and enter into print in the eighteenth century, especially with a work of autobiography, still required some public justification. Humphreys did not appeal to apologetic motives, as Wesley did with the first number of his *Journal*, nor did he plead the importunity of friends or privileged access to information in the public interest. His declared motives were wholly hortatory and doxological: 'Knowing the experiences of others have often been blest, and believing it to be my duty to tell what the LORD hath done for my soul, I thought it might not be amiss to take this way of publishing it: which peradventure may be *useful* to some, and a *satisfaction* to others.'[48] Humphreys did not write with a long retrospective view of his life either. He was only 21 years of age, and it was little more than two years since he had undergone the climactic spiritual experiences of his narrative. He wrote out of the fullness of his heart. As he put it, 'I have as *plainly* and as *simply* spoke what I have *felt* in my soul, as ever I spoke in my life-time what I *felt* in my body.'[49] As a writer he imposed more order on his experience than many of the early Methodist laypeople, whose experiences have been preserved mainly in unpublished letters, but less order than most of the early Methodist lay preachers, whose narratives were written at a relatively late date and then edited by Wesley.

The first half of Humphreys's narrative reads like a typical account of a pious Dissenter—something that could have been written at any time between 1690 and 1730, between the Act of Toleration and the rise of Methodism. Born in 1720, Joseph was the son of Asher Humphreys, a Dissenting minister who was instrumental in gathering 'and converting' his own congregation at Burford. Joseph was consequently exposed to many religious influences in his childhood. He could recount 'early impressions' made upon his conscience by books, dreams, and sermons. Between 10 and

---

[47] Joseph Humphreys also published two sermons in 1744 which bear further witness to his concern for conversion: *A Discourse on the Parable or Story of Dives and Lazarus . . . Design'd for Those who are Convinc'd of the Way of Truth, to Lend or Give to Such of their unconvinc'd Friends or Relations who will not Come to Hear the Word of Life* (Bristol, 1744), and *Our Lord's Grace to the Thief upon the Cross . . . now Publish'd for a Pattern of Mercy to the Chief of Sinners, and Especially Condemn'd Malefactors, who shall hereafter Believe on Jesus Christ to Life Everlasting* (Bristol, 1744). He also published an apologetic tract in question-and-answer format: *An Answer to Everyman That Asketh a Reason of the Hope that is in us* (2nd edn., Bristol, 1744).

[48] *Joseph Humphreys's Experience of the Work of Grace upon his Heart* (Bristol, 1742), 2.

[49] Ibid.

13 years of age he was at a local grammar school, and it was there that he began to experience a divided conscience as he oscillated between serious spiritual resolve and wrongdoing. In common with many of the early evangelicals, and in a tradition that went back among Dissenters to the model provided by the ejected minister Joseph Alleine, Humphreys made a solemn personal covenant with God, 'promising therein to take the Lord for my God, and that I would be his child: and wherein I had done wickedly, I would do so no more'.[50] But as so many others found, all of this was only to intensify his distress. He became strict in his devotional exercises, morning and night, and fancied himself converted. He remembered, 'how I would often stand before the looking-glass in my chamber, beholding myself, and admiring what a *grave countenance* and *solid look* I now had'—a good reminder that when godly Dissenters in the seventeenth and eighteenth centuries spoke of becoming 'serious', they meant it.[51] At the same time, however, Humphreys was entering early adolescence and behaving in a way that left him overwhelmed with guilt. His father died when he was 12 and he was sent to London to train for the ministry at a Dissenting academy. His inward distress continued, and though he could understand the atonement, he did not know what it was to have Christ's righteousness 'experimentally imputed'. His convictions began to diminish by degrees, and his conscience to be quieted, notwithstanding the guilty pleasure he found, like Bunyan earlier, in games and coarse jesting.

During this period Deism was at the height of its appeal in England, and most of the early evangelicals entertained intellectual doubts about Christianity at some point or other. The Dissenting academies were pioneers in the teaching of science and modern philosophy, and many fostered a spirit of free enquiry that went hand in hand with the quest for 'rational religion'.[52] Humphreys himself soon 'began to query, whether religion was not all a cheat', and he determined 'to think freely for myself'.[53] But for all this, he had many returns of guilt and spiritual concern.

The academy moved to Deptford when Humphreys was 14, and he came under the direction of the Independent minister Abraham Taylor. Here his spiritual conflict moved towards a crisis. He catalogued his sins of 'self conceit, lust, envy, and...unforgiving temper'. His adolescent sexual awareness was a source of particular distress to him: 'With regard to uncleanness, I strove against it, but seldom could get the victory. I was brought so far now, as generally to hate the thing that I did...and the

---

[50] *Joseph Humphreys's Experience,* 4. Cf. Nuttall, 'Methodism and the Older Dissent', 267–8.
[51] *Joseph Humphreys's Experience,* 4.
[52] Gordon Rupp, *Religion in England: 1688–1791* (Oxford, 1986), 172–9.
[53] *Joseph Humphreys's Experience,* 8.

practice became odious to me.'[54] He thought often of death and the seriousness of striving against sin. Like John Cennick, he entertained a secret fantasy of escaping to the Continent to join a Catholic monastery, where in anonymity he could make a full confession of his sins and find absolution.

As his convictions waxed and waned, he grew convinced that he needed something more, a deeper spiritual life and inward power over sin. He resolved to be more serious than ever. He presented himself to be received into membership at John Guyse's Independent Church in London, thinking that the grace conveyed in the sacrament would strengthen him against temptation. His verdict on his condition was that God had begun a work upon his soul, 'but all this while I had not seen my *heart*; neither was the clear knowledge of Christ discover'd to me'.[55] Although he was examined prior to being received into membership, and enquiries were made about his spiritual experiences, his doctrinal views, and his manner of life, he found the examination 'lax and superficial', as had become typical in the Independent churches. However, by this point he had recovered his 'historical faith' and was little troubled by Deism. He was an orthodox Calvinist.

He quotes from his diary to show that he was becoming more acquainted with his heart, and that he had begun to experience God's grace. Yet he was in the conflicted state of mind described by William James as the 'divided self'. Indeed, he was a textbook case, ashamed, he says, 'to think what different personages I wore', and vexed 'because I was not all of a piece'.[56] He began to see his need for help from beyond himself, for some 'supernatural inward principle', for a 'real interest' in Christ and a 'sensible application' to his soul of the benefits of the atonement. So he began to meet with a few other students in a small religious society to pray and tell each other of their experiences one evening a week. It was in this condition that he came to hear from the chambermaid about a woman who died full of faith and assurance, certain that her sins were all forgiven. 'Her flame of love catch'd me,' wrote Humphreys. 'I went home, and those words were applied to me with great power, *There is now therefore no condemnation to them which are in* CHRIST JESUS.'[57] This experience of a text of Scripture being made personal ('applied to me') recurred frequently in evangelical conversions. Humphreys went to sacrament and came home 'melted down' with love, with an inward certainty that he was united to Christ.

Thus far Humphreys's experience was within the framework of orthodox Dissent, and he appears as a fine example of what Geoffrey Nuttall termed 'evangelicals before the revival'.[58] Like the pious Dissenter Joseph Williams, Humphreys welcomed the revival when it came. Within two months of this conversion experience, he was enticed by all the talk about Whitefield to go

---

[54] Ibid. 10.   [55] Ibid. 15.   [56] Ibid. 18.   [57] Ibid. 20.
[58] Nuttall, 'Methodism and the Older Dissent', 261.

and hear him on Kennington Common (about three miles from Deptford) on 2 May 1739. This was the beginning of an intimate association with Methodism in its early, formative period.

Humphreys liked what he heard of Whitefield ('I felt the power of the Lord to be with him') and was impressed by the seriousness and tears of the crowds. He returned several times. He could not rest until he made Whitefield's acquaintance, and finally he was able to have dinner with him and Howell Harris at a pub on Blackheath. During the summer he travelled to Cirencester to have a further interview with Whitefield. And in August he set up a society for Whitefield's converts at Deptford. Several hundred came and at first Humphreys would read Whitefield's sermons to them, but soon he was himself preaching extempore. Whitefield left for America in August 1739 and at the end of September John Wesley visited the society. However, Abraham Taylor, tutor of the Deptford Dissenting academy, was clearly not impressed with Humphreys's fascination with Methodism. Samuel Brewer, one of Humphreys's fellow pupils, had gone off to see Whitefield, for which he received corporal punishment.[59] O Christmas Day 1739, Humphreys was expelled from the academy.

He transferred to John Eames's Dissenting academy at Moorfields early in 1740 and threw himself into the Methodist work with vigour. The previous summer he had met Mrs Fox at Oxford, a woman who hosted a Methodist society there and whose name frequently recurs in Wesley's journal and diary. She spoke of her own spiritual experience and inspired Humphreys to seek after 'real power' against sin, beyond the pardon he had already received. Now he got to know some Moravians, who spoke to him of the 'witness of the Spirit', and he also read Thomas Goodwin's *Lectures on Ephesians* on the same subject, and these combined influences—Moravian and Puritan—drove him to seek a further experience of God: 'I now wanted Christ form'd in me, as well as Christ given for me,' or, again, 'I now groaned after a new nature, as before I had after pardon.'[60]

In a paragraph that forms the high point of his narrative and runs over three pages, Humphreys describes how he experienced this new inner witness of the Spirit in April 1740 at Wapping under the preaching of Charles Wesley. The italicized personal pronouns *me, my,* or *mine* recur thirteen times in this paragraph, as Humphreys rhapsodizes over the union with Christ he experienced that night. Was this the same as what John Wesley referred to—especially after about 1760—as an experience of 'entire sanctification' or being 'perfected in love'? Humphreys was not theologic-

---

[59] 'Life of the Rev. Samuel Brewer', *Evangelical Magazine* 5 (1797), 5–18. For Abraham Taylor, see Geoffrey Nuttall, 'Northamptonshire and the Modern Question: A Turning-Point in Eighteenth-Century Dissent', *Journal of Theological Studies* NS 16 (1965), 101–23.

[60] *Joseph Humphreys's Experience*, 27.

ally precise. He described what he felt in the language of regeneration, liberty of soul, and the witness, sealing, or receiving of the Holy Spirit. As many converts have put it, he said, 'I was brought as it were into a new world . . . I found myself born again.'[61] In the year that followed he lived on the cusp of this heightened spiritual awareness, and in his narrative he recounts not only his continual moment-by-moment sensible experience of the presence of God, but also such phenomena as a photism at midday, coming from just above the sun ('a ray of the eternal God beaming into my soul'), and a direct revelation by the Holy Spirit of the eternal godhead of Christ—a experience that took place over the course of an afternoon. He was 'swimming in an ocean of love' and he found he had a new power over sin and a new compulsion and authority to preach. He found that under his preaching, as at Bristol and London at the same time under the preaching of the Wesley brothers, there were scenes of shaking, convulsions, and crying aloud.

For eight days he came under the influence of a woman at Deptford, 'something like the french prophetesses', who had an 'unaccountable power' over him. The Camisards, or French Prophets as they came to be known in England, were a radical faction of Huguenots who responded to persecution in France with ecstatic prophecy, accompanied by swooning, contortions, and other bodily phenomena. Some had emigrated to England and were present on the fringes of Methodism, disturbing some of their outdoor meetings, and drawing away some of their followers.[62] Perhaps Humphreys was more vulnerable to the allure of this woman in his more animated religious state, but this was a passing distraction, as was his temporary consideration of the appeal of some of the Moravians to leave off preaching and be 'still'.

In September he began to preach for Wesley at the Foundery and, in October, to assist him at Bristol and Kingswood. But during the first half of 1741 the 'Free Grace' controversy between Wesley and Whitefield over predestination was coming to a crisis. In March John Cennick withdrew from Wesley with a secession of Methodist followers at Kingswood, and at the end of the month Whitefield published a riposte to Wesley's earlier anti-Calvinist sermon, 'Free Grace'. Humphreys seceded shortly afterwards and joined Whitefield formally in May. In August he resettled at Bristol and made it his base for itinerant preaching in the West Country. This was his situation in 1742 when he published his *Experience*.

Thus it was that Humphreys recounted his formation as an orthodox Calvinist Dissenter, and his entry into Methodism. In essence he had two

---

[61] Ibid. 30.

[62] See further Ann Taves, *Fits, Trances, & Visions: Experiencing Religion and Explaining Experience from Wesley to James* (Princeton, 1999), 15–16.

climatic experiences: an experience of pardon for sin (4 March 1739) and the witness of the Holy Spirit (April 1740). But beyond this, Humphreys illustrates the wide range of experiences that were possible for a young person with a tender conscience in the early period of the Evangelical Revival. The movement and flux described earlier in general terms as social conditions of eighteenth-century England were present in Humphreys's experience not only in his travel and correspondence, but also in his exposure in a concentrated period of time to orthodox Dissent, Deism, Calvinistic Methodism, Arminian Methodism, Wesleyan perfectionism, Moravian stillness, and the ecstasies of the French Prophets. By the last page of his narrative, he had come to a more Calvinistic interpretation of his 'second blessing' experience under Charles Wesley's preaching. His experience of spiritual rapture was now interpreted as a revelation of God's eternal decree and his electing love, and it was something he could look back upon as 'the day of my espousals'. He had repudiated Wesleyan perfectionism and now saw perfection only as the distant goal of the Calvinist *ordo*.

Joseph Humphreys did not experience his own evangelical conversion as a parishioner under a godly Puritan ministry in a village tightly bound to the land and the local elites, a village with perhaps minimal contact with the wider world; rather, a distinguishing feature of his experience was his exposure to religious diversity. This troubled him as a young man, and he wrote, 'I was for joining the Papists, Church-people, and Dissenters of all denominations in *one*; I was for reconciling the Arians, Socinians, Arminians, and Calvinists altogether; I would have had them lay aside all disputable points, and harmonize in those things wherein they were all agreed.'[63] This latitudinarian sentiment was not uncommon in the early eighteenth century, and it was often based on just such a disturbing personal exposure to the competing claims of separate religious traditions. In consequence Humphreys made a number of shifts and realignments of his beliefs over the course of his life.

The problem with writing an autobiography at age 21, however, is that one is left with much to live up to. Humphreys's spiritual odyssey was by no means over in 1742. Indeed, conversion had become something of a habit for Humphreys. Sometime around 1744 he turned his back on the Methodists, and he fetched up at Bradford-upon-Avon in 1748 as a Dissenting minister. John Wesley wrote that Humphreys was ordained a Presbyterian, but in the end conformed and became a Anglican clergyman (probably in 1751). Howell Harris reported in 1762 that Humphreys was 'now fallen asleep' and preached 'dead morality and doctrine only as a Church minister'. As Wesley put it, Humphreys now 'scoffed at inward religion'. Thus he not only left behind his association with the Methodist movement, but he also

---

[63] *Joseph Humphreys's Experience*, 13.

repudiated his evangelical conversion. Indeed, he described his *Experience* as 'one of the foolish things I wrote in the time of my madness!'[64]

So, in addition to the wide range of evangelical experiences that were possible in 1739 and the early 1740s, there was also the possibility of unconversion. Clearly, there was much involved in discovering, constructing, and negotiating religious experience in the eighteenth century. Humphreys's half-dozen changes in religious affiliation and conviction within his short lifetime reflect the tumult of the times, recalling some of the religious experimentation of the Interregnum. At many times and places in *ancien régime* states in Europe, such switching would have involved enormous social disruption or would have incurred civic penalties if not state persecution. But under the conditions in England at the time, Humphreys was able to move about and experiment. His story illustrates how plastic religious identity had become by the mid-eighteenth century.

Notwithstanding the instability of Humphreys's identity and his later movements, it is clear that between 1742 and 1744—when he wrote this narrative, his hymn, and other evangelical tracts—the experience of evangelical conversion was not merely one experience among others. It was seen to have tremendous explanatory power and compelled him to retell his story from the beginning, such that this became the turning point of his life. In this Humphreys was representative of a whole host of women and men from the period whose conversions combined to constitute what many regarded as an unprecedented spiritual awakening. How they described this experience in their own words is the subject of the balance of this book.

[64] Wesley, *Works* (BE), xxiv. 186.

3

The Early Methodist Journalists: George Whitefield and John Wesley

B Y the end of the eighteenth century there was a recognizable evangelical party in the Church of England, a large body of Methodists of various sorts, and a significant number of English Moravians. There was also a new, more visibly evangelistic bloc of Dissenters in England. None of this existed in 1735. It was achieved through the conversion to evangelical faith and practice of large numbers of people over the course of the last two-thirds of the century. The evangelical mission that produced this substantial following, significantly changing the religious topography of England, was preceded by the conversion of a small but influential number of men and women, who were subsequently drawn into an overlapping campaign to convert the nation.[1] The first converts created this new religious movement; the later converts joined it. As Wesley recalled, 'Just at this time . . . two or three clergymen of the Church of England began vehemently to "call sinners to repentance". In two or three years they had sounded the alarm to the utmost borders of the land.'[2] Wesley's 'two or three' narrows the movement too much in its origins, but he captures well the sense that a new movement had spread across the country.

The revival during this early period can be described as 'Methodist' (with or without the scare quotes), since the term was in general use for those associated with revival, whether or not they were followers of Wesley, Whitefield, Howell Harris, or the Countess of Huntingdon. The term Methodist certainly did not describe a religious denomination. A good number of the regular 'Gospel clergy', though not directly linked with any of the societies in connexion with the 'Methodist' leaders, were also willing (though sometimes reluctantly) to own the label Methodist.[3] They

---

[1] John Walsh, 'Origins of the Evangelical Revival', in G. V. Bennett and J. D. Walsh (eds.), *Essays in Modern English Church History in Memory of Norman Sykes* (Oxford, 1966), 132–62.

[2] Wesley, *Works* (BE), xi. 274.

[3] See e.g. John Newton, *Works* (1808–9), v. 507, 571; vi. 271. Even in 1787, Newton confessed to Wilberforce that 'the term [Methodist] is indiscriminately applied to all who profess the doctrines of the Reformation' (Newton to Wilberforce, MS letter, 1 Nov. 1787, Add. Wilberforce Papers, c. 49, Bodleian Library, Oxford).

recognized that they shared in a common religious movement and the distinctive experience they shared was that of conversion. Most of the leaders also shared a common preoccupation with recording this experience in first-person narrative. Indeed, the wide range of autobiographical records of the early Methodist leaders during these years, published and unpublished, constitutes one of the most significant literary traces of this religious movement. In the course of these personal writings, which were typically set down for purposes other than confessional autobiography, the familiar Puritan-Pietist genre of conversion narrative resurfaced.

THE CONVERSION OF THE EARLY 'METHODIST' LEADERS

Thus, in the last half of the 1730s we find a number of similar conversion experiences on record. George Whitefield and Howell Harris were converted in 1735. About two years later there followed the conversions of John Cennick and Benjamin Ingham, who would exercise significant leadership among the Methodists and then later among the Moravians. James Hutton and the Wesley brothers were converted in 1738, and the conversion of the Countess of Huntingdon followed within another year or so. Several clergy were converted in the 1740s, such as William Grimshaw of Haworth, Thomas Adam of Winteringham, and Samuel Walker of Truro. The mariner John Newton, who would later be ordained Vicar of Olney, was converted at sea in 1748. The experience of conversion for these influential leaders can be described as parallel, for there was remarkable similarity in the way that each passed through a crisis of moral and spiritual insufficiency that led to the brink of despair, before the crisis was resolved by an intense experience of spontaneous spiritual joy. As John Cennick claimed, the change made at conversion was real, 'for then all those fears, jealousies, and uneasiness which generally, if not always, precedes it in the upright and sincere, are brought to an end'.[4]

This was, for example, the experience of Howell Harris between 30 March 1735, when his conscience began to be troubled as he contemplated his own spiritual state in preparation for Holy Communion, and 18 June the same year, when he suddenly felt his heart melt like wax during private prayer, his soul filled with the assurance that he was loved as a child of God.[5] The experience was not always pinpointed to the day, as it was for Harris, or to the minute, as it was for John Wesley (at 'about a quarter to nine' on 24 May 1738), but there was typically a marked contrast drawn between one's spiritual state before and after conversion. John Berridge was one of the

---

[4] John Cennick, *The New Birth* (1788), 12.
[5] *A Brief Account of the Life of Howell Harris, Esq; Extracted from Papers Written by Himself* (Trevecka, 1791), 10–15.

most colourful clergymen of the Evangelical Revival. The epitaph that he composed for his own gravestone is perhaps one of the shortest evangelical conversion narratives on record, and it marked the crisis of conversion in his life in stark terms:

> Here lie the earthly remains of John Berridge
> Late Vicar of Everton,
> And an itinerant servant of Jesus Christ,
> Who loved his master and his work,
> And after running on his errands many years
> Was called up to wait on him above.
> Reader
> Art thou born again?
> No salvation without a new birth!
> I was born in sin, February 1716.
> Remained ignorant of my fallen state till 1730.
> Lived proudly on faith and works for salvation till 1754.
> Was admitted to Everton vicarage, 1755.
> Fled to Jesus alone for refuge, 1756.
> Fell asleep in Christ, January 22, 1793.[6]

This climactic understanding of conversion ('Fled to Jesus alone for refuge') marked almost all the early evangelical leaders. Yet not all evangelicals would agree that regeneration was generally a psychologically perceptible experience, for in theological terms, this often depended upon whether one believed that assurance (the perceptible element) was of the essence of saving faith (the salvific element). But just as Richard Baxter's experience was the exception that proved the rule in the seventeenth century, so also in the eighteenth century—and particularly in the early phase of the Revival— the momentous conversion experiences of the early leaders were soon seen as exemplary, the great desideratum of the awakened sinner. Thus William Grimshaw, for example, claimed that justification, assurance of forgiveness, union with Christ, and hope of eternal life were all things that a man or woman could experience directly: 'All this they *experience* and *feel* in the Heart, not daring (as counting it the most shameful Enthusiasm, and the grossest Presumption) to call themselves *Christians*, before they clearly feel these Things *in them*. But so soon as they *feel* this, then they are sure, but not before this, that they are *Christians*.'[7]

Yet, however similar the experience of conversion among the early leaders, the vast majority were converted in relative isolation from each other. Harris wrote that he was a 'total stranger to all controversies about

---

[6] L. E. Elliott-Binns, *The Early Evangelicals* (1953), 279.

[7] William Grimshaw, *An Answer to a Sermon Lately Published against the Methodists by the Rev. Mr George White* (Preston, 1749), 28–9.

religion' and that he had neither seen nor heard of anyone who had a 'saving knowledge of God in Christ'.[8] And though Berridge's conversion occurred much later, he declared 'I was no Methodist at all, for I had no sort of acquaintance with them.'[9] Notwithstanding John Wesley's tendency to describe the rise of 'Methodism' in terms of his own spiritual biography, there were in fact few early evangelical clergy who could trace their spiritual genealogy directly to him. The way in which the early leaders of the Evangelical Revival were converted was thus different than the pattern among Puritan preachers a century earlier, where it is often possible to trace spiritual lineage like a family tree. For example, in less than two decades Paul Baynes (d. 1617) converted Richard Sibbes (1577–1635), who converted John Cotton (1584–1652), who converted John Preston (1587–1628).[10] The pattern among the early evangelicals, however, was less like a virus gradually spreading from one person to another than like the spontaneous appearance of similar symptoms amongst widely separated individuals at more or less the same time.

The consequence of the shared experience of conversion on the part of these leaders was that they discovered a common mission. This was, for example, what occurred when on 8 March 1739 George Whitefield and Howell Harris met in person for the first time at Cardiff. Whitefield and Harris spent the evening 'telling one another what God had done for our souls'. Immediately, Whitefield's heart was drawn to Harris, and a 'divine and strong sympathy' was felt between them.[11] Their stories bound them to one another. As would happen so often in the Evangelical Revival, narrative communities formed round shared, spoken experience. In consequence of this encounter, Whitefield and Harris put their heads together and made plans—'such measures as seemed most conducive to promote the common interest of our Lord'.[12] Thus, out of all the chaos of the 1730s and early 1740s there emerged a religious movement that, notwithstanding its internal divisions, was united in the aim of converting the nation to

---

[8] *Brief Account of Howell Harris*, 17.

[9] John Berridge, *Works*, ed. R. Whittingham (1838), 359.

[10] William Haller, *The Rise of Puritanism* (New York, 1957), 66–71; cf. Paul R. Schaefer, 'The Spiritual Brotherhood on the Habits of the Heart: Cambridge Protestants and the Doctrine of Sanctification from William Perkins to Thomas Shepard', D.Phil. thesis (Oxford, 1994). Later, in the lives of Wesley's lay preachers we may sometimes observe something like a chain of conversions. For example, William Hunter experienced 'perfection' under the preaching of Thomas Olivers who had himself been converted under the preaching of Whitefield. *WV* i. 205; iv. 178.

[11] *GWJ* 229–30. Whitefield had already written to Harris on 20 Dec. 1738, saying, 'Why, should not we tell one another, what God has done, for our Souls?' *Brief Account of Howell Harris*, 111.

[12] *GWJ* 230. Cf. Richard Evans, 'The Relations of George Whitefield and Howell Harris, Fathers of Calvinistic Methodism', *Church History* 30 (1961), 179–90.

evangelical faith and practice through local and itinerant preaching, publishing, hymn-singing, testimony, and all the disciplines of the religious society.

THE JOURNAL FORM

How did these early leaders, who were thus converted and mobilized in evangelism, speak and write about their own conversion experiences? The most influential figures in the 1730s and 1740s were arguably George Whitefield and John Wesley, but here we encounter the enormous importance of the journal form in the early years of the revival. The conversion narratives of Whitefield and Wesley did not appear in print as stand-alone spiritual autobiographies, but rather as set pieces within the serial publication of their journals. Moreover, in neither case were their conversion narratives offered as introductions or autobiographical prefaces to their journals; rather, their accounts of their conversions appeared as later instalments in a publication programme already underway.

The word 'journal' derives from the Old French word for 'daily', much as the word 'diary' derives from the Latin equivalent. Both English words retained this adjectival (or adverbial) sense in English into the seventeenth century, a sense maintained now only in our use of the related word 'diurnal' to describe something that occurs by day. By the time of the Evangelical Revival the terms were long familiar as substantives to denote different forms of 'day-books'. Although the terms overlapped, 'journal' was more often used for public records; 'diary' for the more private observations of an individual. This distinction did not always hold, however, since 'diary' could be used of printed almanacs or professional day-books, and 'journal' could certainly be used of a book containing very personal entries. But for the evangelical leaders the diary was typically the more private document.

The spiritual diary of the seventeenth century is the first and most important precedent for the evangelical diaries. As observed in Ch. 1, self-examination and related forms of introspection emerged as significant devotional practices among English Protestants about the middle of the reign of Elizabeth in the context of new forms of personal discipline associated with experimental Calvinism.[13] Devotional manuals such as Richard Rogers's, *Seven Treatises* (1603) devoted a great deal of attention to the examen of conscience as 'a reckoning to the Lord at the end of every day', and he himself kept a detailed spiritual diary.[14] In the middle of the

---

[13] See further, Tom Webster, 'Writing to Redundancy: Approaches to Spiritual Journals and Early Modern Spirituality', *The Historical Journal* 39 (1996), 33–56.

[14] Richard Rogers, *Seven Treatises* (1603), 399–404; M. M. Knappen (ed.), *Two Elizabethan Puritan Diaries* (Gloucester, Mass., 1966).

seventeenth century, Isaac Ambrose, a leading Puritan divine, likewise advocated self-examination in *Media: the Middle Things* (1649) as one of the 'means, duties, ordinances, both secret, private and publike, for continuance and increase of a godly life', and he explicitly added directions for the practice of keeping a diary or day-book or register (he uses all three terms) as a useful way to do this. In the diary the Christian was able to observe 'something of God to his soul, and of his soul to God'. Ambrose began keeping such a diary in 1641 and provided several excerpts for the reader from January 1641 to May 1649.[15] A few years later John Beadle introduced his *Journal or Diary of a Thankful Christian* (1656) by explaining that his practice of diary-keeping was something more like a treasury of praise. Just as Israel recorded the mighty acts of God, so might a Christian keep 'a rich treasury of experience'. And for this, one must needs 'keep a constant Diary . . . of all Gods gracious dealings with them'. There were in fact three leaves that one ought to read daily to make up this diary: 'the black leaf of thy own and other sins . . . the white leaf of Gods goodnesse . . . the red leaf of Gods judgments felt'.[16]

Notwithstanding these religious motives for diary-keeping in the seventeenth century, there were still many secular analogies to be drawn upon in contemporary practice:

We have our State Diurnals, relating to Nationall affairs. Tradesmen keep their shop books. Merchants their Accompt books. Lawyers have their books of presidents. Physitians their Experiments. Some wary husbands have kept a Diary of dayly disbursements. Travellers a Journall of all they have seen, and hath befallen them in their way. A Christian that would be exact hath more need, and may reap much more good by such a Journall as this.[17]

Similar analogies were available in the eighteenth century, but the devotional desire for exactness expressed here ('a Christian that would be exact') corresponds especially well to the contemporary characterization of Puritan piety as 'Precisian'. The diary was a technology well suited to this spiritual ideal of precision. As Richard Rogers had said earlier when accused of being too precise, 'O sir, . . . *I serve a precise God.*'[18]

There were, of course, examples of private diary-keeping motivated by concerns other than those of piety. Samuel Pepys kept his remarkably detailed diary of public and private life from 1659 to 1669 (though the early Methodists would have had no knowledge of it since it was deciphered

---

[15] Isaac Ambrose, *Media: the Middle Things* (1649), 69–85.

[16] John Beadle, *The Journal or Diary of a Thankful Christian* (1656), from the unpaginated Epistle Dedicatory by Beadle and the essay 'To the Reader' by John Fuller.

[17] John Fuller, 'To the Reader'.

[18] Giles Firmin, *The Real Christian* (1670), 67.

and published only in the nineteenth century).[19] Pepys's daily discipline and observant eye have their parallel in the diaries of some of the Puritans and later evangelicals (particularly Wesley), but the humanist and sometimes dissolute ethos of Pepys's diary was worlds away from the intensity of devotion in these more religious figures.

The seventeenth-century confessional diary was thus the key antecedent for the evangelical diaries. In the 1650s Beadle could speak of diary-keeping as an uncommon practice that ought to be more widely observed, but when in 1662 Richard Baxter referred in passing to reading one's diary or 'Book of Heart Accounts' he seemed to assume this was a fairly standard exercise.[20] By the 1730s diary-keeping was an established practice among a number of groups, from the Nonconformist descendants of the Puritans, to the Anglicans of the holy living tradition, to the various proponents of 'inward religion'.

The early Methodist evangelists not only kept confessional diaries as an aid to devotion, like the Puritans, but they also wrote and published journals in order to stimulate, direct, and defend the growing evangelical movement and to legitimate their own leadership. The parallels for this practice in the wider culture were many. Published works that advertised themselves as journals in the first half the eighteenth century fall into several categories, and these works represent an expansion of the list of analogies given in Beadle's book earlier. Most numerous were the many official registers of the votes and deliberations of public bodies, especially colonial legislatures.[21] A growing body of periodical publications that came on the scene during this period also described themselves as journals. Residents of London who read Whitefield's journals would also be aware of such serials as *The London Journal* or the satirical *Grub-Street Journal*, and the evangelicals were sometimes taken notice of in similar newspapers.[22] These journals were distinguished from the monthly magazines by being more current and closer to the 'diurnal', published daily or weekly. The early evangelical initiatives in periodical publication were also sometimes referred to in passing as journals.[23] It had also long been common to use the term 'journal' in financial book-keeping, where the wastebook was a merchant's daily record of all transactions, which anyone could use, kept out for easy access, and the

---

[19] Claire Tomalin, *Samuel Pepys: The Unequalled Self* (2002), 80–92, 381–5.

[20] Richard Baxter, *The Mischiefs of Self-Ignorance and the Benefits of Self-Acquaintance* (1662), 304.

[21] See e.g. *The Journal of the Honourable House of Representatives, of His Majesty's Province of the Massachusetts-Bay in New England Begun and Held at Boston, in the County of Suffolk, on Wednesday the Thirtieth Day of May, Annoque Domini, 1739* (Boston, 1739).

[22] James T. Hillhouse, *The Grub-Street Journal* (Durham, NC, 1928), 3–46.

[23] In a letter dated 20 Aug. 1740, William Seward refers to the papers published by John Lewis as 'journals'. *The Christian's Amusement*, no. 1 (1740), 3.

journal was more exact ('expressed accomptantly') and was to be used only by one trained in accounting. But like the wastebook it was organized *de diem in diem*.[24]

These uses of the term 'journal' were relatively impersonal, but they retain vividly the sense of reporting accurately, and with a view to public accountability, the contemporary observations of an eyewitness. The journal form was reserved for history written as it happens—diurnal history. There were also published journals that were more personal and that originated in private observations. The military journal of an officer might be of interest to the public and published to give a lively on-the-spot report of a battle or campaign, as, for example, in the case of *An Exact and Full Account of the Siege of Barcelona, By way of Journal, from the 2nd of April to the 11th of May, 1706, containing many particulars never yet published . . . By an Officer who was in the Place all the time* (1706).[25] Narratives of Britons taken captive overseas were likewise popular and were sometimes presented in the form of journals, as in the case of *Madagascar: or, Robert Drury's Journal During Fifteen Years Captivity on that Island* (1729). As Linda Colley has remarked, such journals supplied readers in the eighteenth century with the sort of information and analysis provided today by anthropologists and ethnographers.[26] The journal form here provided the quality of present tense narration ('This day we . . .' or 'This morning we . . .'), rather than a retrospective sense of distant recollection. Accurate and timely reporting were also of the essence in scientific and medical reports, and so these were sometimes also identified as journals.[27]

While all these journal forms retained the notions of precision, contemporaneity, and accountability, and by so doing bore witness to the preoccupations of the age with firsthand experience, the voyage or travel journal was the closest secular analogue to the journals of John Wesley and George

[24] John Hawkins, *Clavis Commercii; or, the Key of Commerce: Shewing, the True Method of Keeping Merchants Books . . . With a Practical Waste-Book, Journal and Ledger* (1718), 3–4.

[25] See also e.g. George Lumle, *A Journal of the Squadron, under the Command of Nicholas Haddock, Esq; Rear Admiral of the Red, &c. from Spithead to Mahon: Introduced with Impartial Thoughts, upon the Past and Present State of our Affairs* (1739).

[26] Linda Colley, *Captives: Britain, Empire and the World, 1600–1850* (2002), 13–17; cf. Joe Snader, *Caught between Worlds: British Captivity Narratives in Fact and Fiction* (Lexington, Ky., 2000). Jonathan Edwards's relative John Williams was taken captive in an Indian raid in 1704 in Deerfield, Massachusetts, and he wrote a captivity narrative upon his release, *The Redeemed Captive, Returning to Zion* (Boston, 1707), that was a 'classic of its kind' and was reprinted in America many times before the end of the century. It was not, however, reprinted in London, and the British were, on the whole, less aware of the captivity panics in North America (ibid. 153). See also George Marsden, *Jonathan Edwards: A Life* (New Haven, 2003), 14–17.

[27] See e.g. *The Secret Patient's Diary: also the Gout and Weakness Diaries. Being each a Practical Journal or Scheme* (1725).

Whitefield. Francis Bacon had earlier recommended that those who travel on land or sea should keep journals.[28] By the early eighteenth century, journals of voyages in particular were much in demand. There was, for example, *A voyage to the South Sea, and round the world . . . Containing a journal of all memorable transactions . . . By Capt. Edward Cooke* (1712), which was introduced with this claim: 'As to the Journal itself, the Reader may be assur'd it was exactly kept all the Time we were Aboard, and that I cannot presume to impose any Thing beyond the Strictness of Truth.' Evidently this was the next best thing to being there. Some of these voyage journals were businesslike accounts; others were more picaresque.[29] Then there also were accounts of castaways such as Alexander Selkirk, a story that inspired Daniel Defoe's *Robinson Crusoe* (1719).[30] Indeed, Daniel Defoe used the conceit of such a journal to narrate the first portion of Robinson Crusoe's adventures once he was settled on his island—until Crusoe runs out of ink. It was an effective literary technique to give vividness and verisimilitude to the story.[31] In 1739 George Whitefield's friend, the bookseller James Hutton, published one of these dramatic voyage journals under the title, *An Exact Account of the Wonderful Preservation of a Gentlewoman from Shipwrack, Coming from Altona to England. Taken from Her Own Journal* (1739). This sixteen-page pamphlet recorded the firsthand account of a woman on her way from Hamburg to London, who was shipwrecked on 14 October 1735

---

[28] Francis Bacon, 'Of Travel', *The Essays* (1701), 46.

[29] A businesslike account is found in Philémon de La Motte, *Several Voyages to Barbary. Containing an Historical and Geographical Account of the Country . . . With a Journal of the Late Siege and Surrender of Oran . . . by Captain Henry Boyde* (1736). A more picaresque account appears in Adrian van Broeck, *The Life and Adventures of Capt. John Avery, the Famous English Pirate, (Rais'd from a Cabbin-Boy, to a King) Now in Possession of Madagascar . . . Written by a Person who made his Escape from thence, and Faithfully Extracted from his Journal* (1709).

[30] The account of Selkirk was printed in Captain Edward Cooke, *A Voyage to the South Sea* (1712), and also in Captain Woodes Rogers, *Cruising Voyage Round the World* (1718). See further James Sutherland, *Defoe* (1937), 240. Other castaway accounts include the popular journal of a Jan Svilt, a Dutch sailor abandoned on Ascension island as punishment for alleged sodomy: *An Authentick Relation of the Many Hardships and Sufferings of a Dutch Sailor, Who was put on shore on the Uninhabited Isle of Ascension . . . Taken from the Original Journal, found . . . by some Sailors . . . in January 1725/6* (1728); cf. Captain Mawson, *The Just Vengeance of Heaven Exemplify'd. In a Journal Lately Found by Captain Mawson . . . All Wrote with his Own Hand, and Found Lying near the Skeleton* (1730). See also Peter Agnos, *The Queer Dutchman Castaway on Ascension* (New York, 1978).

[31] Cf. Daniel Defoe, *A Journal of the Plague Year, Being Observations or Memories of the most Remarkable Occurrences, as well Publick as Private, which Happened in London During the Last Great Visitation in 1665*, ed. Louis Lanada (1969), in which Defoe likewise uses the journal form to give verisimilitude to the plot. Defoe also owed a debt to the seventeenth-century tradition of spiritual autobiography, since, as G. A. Starr has argued, this literary tradition offered him a principle of narrative coherence that could be taken up into fiction. See G. A. Starr, *Defoe and Spiritual Autobiography* (New York, 1971).

and nearly drowned in the sea before being rescued by an English captain and taken safely to Whitby. It was set out with careful attention to chronology, and the latter part (after her rescue) appears as a series of daily journal entries. The narrative itself was rehearsed as 'an instance of the especial Providence of Almighty God' and, in the words of the publisher, it offered an example of 'living Faith, and an entire Trust in God'.[32] The same year that Hutton published this piece, he also published three journals by Whitefield. The journal form was much in demand.

Whitefield's first journal was published by Hutton in 1738. Notwithstanding its spiritual concerns, this initial autobiographical venture by Whitefield was decidedly in the genre of the voyage journal, and it was published as such: *A Journal of a Voyage from London to Savannah in Georgia. In Two Parts. Part I. From London to Gibraltar. Part II. From Gibraltar to Savannah.* A popular publication, Hutton's version went through four editions in 1738 alone. In addition to descriptions of his evangelical ministry, Whitefield captured the feeling of being on ship with references to small details that gave the reader the vicarious thrill of going to sea: a poor soldier tied neck and heels for mutinous words, a near collision with a careless East India ship, waves as high as mountains crashing on the quarter deck, the sailors catching a dolphin, waterspouts making a calm sea boil like a pot, and the colony of Gibraltar pictured in terms of its physical and social geography. Such vivid description closely paralleled other voyage journals, such as Cooke's *Voyage to the South Sea* (1712).[33] The domestic appetite for such nautical 'journalism' was insatiable.

The lesser-known William Seward (1711–40) was an intimate of many of those involved in early Methodism, and he too travelled to America and kept a journal, part of which was published in 1740. Converted some six

---

[32] *An Exact Account of the Wonderful Preservation of a Gentlewoman from Shipwrack* (1739), 16.

[33] A comparison of Edward Cooke's *Voyage to the South Sea* (1712) with Whitefield's travel journals demonstrates many ways in which the latter shares in the ethos of the former. Just as Whitefield described vividly the catching of a dolphin, so also Cooke's journal reported catching two large dolphins near St Vincent, about three months into the voyage (ibid. 19 cf. 28–9). Likewise, Cooke recounted a violent storm in January near the Falkland Islands in 1709, in which his ship took on much water and, he said, 'we expected the Ship would sink every Moment' (ibid. 32). After describing the havoc, he concluded, 'but God in his Mercy deliver'd us from this and many other Dangers' (ibid. 33). A general providence was acknowledged, but not, as evangelicals would have said, 'improved'. Again, just as Whitefield described a sailor who was disciplined, so Cooke described how two men tried to desert, but got lost and frightened, and then begged to be taken back on board. He explained how they were confined in irons, whipped, and then set at liberty (ibid. 21–2). Perhaps Whitefield's descriptions of the colony at Gibraltar most closely approximated the ethos of Cooke's published journal, with its many detailed observations on the places visited, such as Cooke's ch. 6, 'The Description of Chile, its Extent, Boundaries, Soil, Seasons, Immense Wealth, Fertility, Prodigious Mountains, Rivers, Fishes, Birds, Beasts, Plants, etc.' (ibid. 60) and ch. 7, 'Of the People of Chile, their Disposition, Customs, Bravery, Manner of Fighting, Habit, Food, Houses, Marriages, Funerals, Way of Reckoning, etc.' (ibid. 72).

months after John Wesley in 1738, Seward became Whitefield's devoted travelling companion and business manager in England and America, writing up most of the accounts of Whitefield's preaching in 1739 for the newspapers.[34] Seward knew Whitefield's *Journals* well—five of these had already been published and many reprinted before Seward went to print in 1740. (Wesley's first *Journal* had also already been published in May.) It was in July that Seward ventured forth with his *Journal of a Voyage from Savannah to Philadelphia, and from Philadelphia to England*. Like Whitefield, he gave the reader the feeling of being at sea, noting for example the sighting of an iceberg and of penguins, and the catching of a shark. Indeed, his calling to travel overseas with Whitefield was the occasion for him to begin a journal in the first place. Thus he remarked that he had kept a journal 'from the Time I went abroad', or since he went on board the *Elizabeth* in 1739 bound for America. His published journal, however, commenced in April 1740 as he was preparing to return to England on business, thus offering a kind of sequel to Whitefield's last public offering. Seward instructed the reader to read Whitefield's last journal before reading his own, in order to learn about the rise and progress of the 'great work' now happening in America. Seward's journal was full of the spiritual exuberance of the revival scenes he had recently witnessed. He reassured the reader, however, that his own journal overlapped with Whitefield's for only two weeks, and that his journal was 'as different as might be from Mr. Whitefield's'. He even pleaded that he had avoided looking into Whitefield's journal to make sure of this. Seward also informed the reader that he left a 'very long and particular' journal in Georgia that could be published in due course if there were demand. And he mentioned that he had thoughts of publishing an account of his conversion too, if there were a call for it. None of this was to be, though, since that November he died from a head injury incurred in anti-Methodist mob violence in Wales. Thus he left two journals extant in manuscript.[35] Even in these few short years, however, Seward had clearly learned from Whitefield the rhetorical force of first-person testimony, and how great was the public interest in nautical journalism.

As if according to script, John Wesley's first autobiographical publication was also a voyage journal, *An Extract of the Rev. Mr. John Wesley's Journal From his Embarking for Georgia to his Return to London*, published in Bristol in 1740.[36] Wesley had kept a manuscript voyage journal and a journal of his

---

[34] Seward frequently noted, for example, 'Wrote Paragraphs for the News, where our Brother was to preach and had preached.' William Seward, *Journal of a Voyage from Savannah to Philadelphia, and from Philadelphia to England* (1740), 10 cf. 16–17.

[35] One is preserved at the John Rylands Library, Manchester, and the other at the University College of North Wales.

[36] Some years later the former sea captain John Newton would also emerge as a public figure among evangelicals through an autobiography which was both a spectacular account

Georgia ministry in addition to his diary, and he sent 'journal letters' to his family and friends. For example, he sent a journal letter to James Hutton (as did Whitefield later) to be read with others gathered at his house in Westminster who were interested in the mission to Georgia; he also sent a journal letter to his friend, the bookseller Charles Rivington.[37] Whether or not Wesley had ideas at this stage of this material being published (having sent journals to two booksellers), his journal was soon, in his brother's words, 'in every one's hands'.[38] The gap between manuscript and print culture in the eighteenth century was not nearly as wide as it is today, and in a very real sense Wesley was 'publishing' his journal well before it was printed.

The distinction here between Wesley's manuscript diary and his manuscript journals is significant.[39] The journals were distinguished from the diaries precisely by the fact that they dealt with a voyage and with foreign travel. Though he later wrote occasional journal letters or wrote up preliminary drafts for the published journals, he did not continue to keep a separate running journal, in addition to his diary, after the Georgia mission. These early manuscript journals were distinguished from his diary from the start, not as some document intermediate between the diary and the published journals, but as journals of his travel overseas. The shared conventions of any genre emerge out of shared conditions and occasions, and so, like any traveller wanting to keep a record of his experiences in order to communicate with those left behind, Wesley used his journals as the basis both for the letters he wrote to friends and relatives and for his later published 'extract'. In this, the occasion and reception of Whitefield's and Wesley's first journals were not unlike the earlier Jesuit relations from New France.[40] They were not only voyage journals; they were also missionary letters.

Wesley may have intended from an early date to publish the journals of his voyage and Georgia mission, but the intervening crisis of the Sophy Hopkey affair, made public in England by an affidavit sworn by Captain Robert Williams at Bristol in 1740, meant that Wesley needed to use the occasion to defend himself, and the journal became an immediate way to do that.[41] Still, notwithstanding this urgent apologetic occasion, the first

---

of his maritime adventures and a conversion narrative: *An Authentic Narrative of Some Remarkable and Interesting Particulars in the Life of* ******* (1764).

[37] Daniel Benham, *Memoirs of James Hutton* (1856), 12–13.

[38] *CWJ* i. 57.

[39] See further, Heitzenrater, Editorial Introduction to Appendix: MS Journals and Diaries, Wesley, *Works* (BE), xviii. 299–310.

[40] See e.g. S. R. Mealing, *The Jesuit Relations and Allied Documents: A Selection* (Toronto, Ont., 1963), 16–21.

[41] In Georgia, Wesley became fond of Sophy Hopkey, but when he delayed or failed to communicate his intentions clearly, she made a hasty marriage to William Williamson.

published journal of John Wesley originated and was first intended for the public, much like George Whitefield's first journal, as a religious version of the familiar voyage or travel journal genre. It remains to see how the conversion narratives of these two influential figures appeared in the course of this novel publication programme.

George Whitefield

Whitefield's first *Journal* had traced his voyage from London to Georgia and covered roughly the first half of 1738. His second *Journal* appeared early the next year and continued from his arrival in Georgia until his return to London at the end of 1738. This second *Journal* also included a preface in which Whitefield explained that 'the Journals already published were printed without my knowledge'.[42] Whitefield was alluding here to the row that broke out between the booksellers Thomas Cooper and James Hutton over publication rights, a row that spilled over into the pages of the *Daily Advertiser* during the first week of August 1738. Eventually, Hutton was able to negotiate to obtain exclusive rights from Cooper, for a price. Whitefield's *Journals* were clearly controversial best-sellers. Indeed, within three years Hutton had done handsomely as Whitefield's publisher, having made 'several hundreds' by him. The *Journals* attracted criticism too, not only in the newspapers, but also in tracts such as *Remarks on the Reverend Mr. Whitefield's Journal*, signed by T.G. and complaining of Whitefield raising 'Expectations of these new Tokens of the Spirit, *Pangs, Feelings*, and the like'.[43] The author claimed that he had had esteemed Whitefield and admired his zeal—until his first *Journal* was published.[44] The *Journal* seemed to set up Whitefield's piety as a standard for the religious societies in London, and this could only lead them into error, making religion a matter of 'Perturbations of Mind, Possessions of God, Extatic Flights, and Supernatural Impulses'.[45] Nevertheless, consumer demand for Whitefield's *Journals* continued strong, and Hutton published four editions of the first before the end of the year. Though he had occasioned controversy, Whitefield also received letters that made him think that God had blessed this initial *Journal*.

Wesley banned her from Holy Communion, and this led to formal charges being laid against him by the grand jury in Savannah. It was the culmination of the opposition to his ministry in Georgia, and it finally drove him out of the colony altogether. The affair can be traced in Wesley, *Works* (BE), xviii. 183–93 and 365 ff. *passim*.

[42] *GWJ* 154.

[43] T. Gib, *Remarks on the Reverend Mr. Whitefield's Journal* [Signed T.G.] (1738), 7; cf. Tyerman, GW i. 151–2.

[44] Gib, *Remarks*, 8.

[45] Ibid. 2.

Given the 'importunity of friends', he was therefore willing to venture publishing a sequel.

Whitefield thus entered print as an autobiographer through the accidental publication of his voyage journal. But why did he write this journal in the first place? He had kept a private confessional diary after the 'exacter' manner of other 'Oxford Methodists' in 1735 and 1736, but this new voyage journal was something different from the beginning—more outward-looking and concerned with mission.[46] It was in fact intended from the first for a public, if not necessarily for printed publication. It was a 'journal letter' (like Wesley's earlier) for the religious society in London that was centred at the home of the Revd John Hutton, father of James Hutton, the publisher. Thus it began, 'My dear Friends', and offered up an 'account of what God has done for my soul since I left England' as something done 'according to your request'.[47] As we have observed, this was an altogether typical occasion for a voyage journal. What could not perhaps have been predicted was how strong would be the demand for Whitefield's account. It was during the last four months of 1737, just before he left for Georgia, that Whitefield had become a popular sensation in London and the West Country, and that he was first taken notice of in the newspapers. It is a witness to just how popular he had become that a reading public were so eager to purchase, at sixpence a copy, every available impression of his *Journal*.

Much has been made of Whitefield's relationship to the press and to the marketplace, and the older view of him as a latter-day Puritan has been challenged by a revised picture of him as a proto-modern figure, an anticipation of revivalism and media evangelism.[48] Certainly the expansion of the press and the reification of his popularity through print contributed to creating a public personality for Whitefield, and this contributed to his notoriety. But whether or not Whitefield himself was conscious of the

---

[46] Whitefield's confessional diary was in the coded system used by other Oxford Methodists. His diary for 1736, and a fragment of his diary from 1735, are extant. See *Diary of an Oxford Methodist, Benjamin Ingham, 1733–1734*, ed. Richard P. Heitzenrater (Durham, NC, 1985), 4. Whitefield refers to his 'diary' in his *Short Account, GWJ* 53, 55.

[47] *GWJ* 97; cf. Part II, p. 128: 'My Dear Friends,' etc., referring to his correspondents' solicitude towards him.

[48] The traditional view is reflected in Arnold Dallimore, *George Whitefield* (Edinburgh, 1990), and Michael Haykin (ed.), *The Revived Puritan: The Spirituality of George Whitefield* (Dundas, Ont., 2000); the view of Whitefield as proto-modern is advanced by Frank Lambert who refers to the preacher as 'a full-fledged forerunner to evangelists like Charles Grandison Finney and Billy Graham' ('Pedlar in Divinity: George Whitefield and the Great Awakening, 1737–1745', *Journal of American History* 77 (1990), 813), and also by Harry Stout who sees Whitefield's mode of revivalism as something that would 'transcend media and embrace television and characterize evangelicalism into the twentieth century' ('George Whitefield in Three Countries', in Mark Noll, David Bebbington, and George Rawlyk (eds.), *Evangelicalism* (New York, 1994), 69).

media as a force to be strategically manipulated, he certainly was confident
that he was seeing the present, unique work of the Holy Spirit all around
him. He interpreted the groundswell of spiritual interest that he was witnessing in eschatological terms.[49] On 1 January 1739, during the hiatus
between the publication of his first and second *Journals*, Whitefield was
present at the love-feast at Fetter Lane, where the whole night was spent
praying and singing. This was the night when, in John Wesley's words, at
'about three in the morning... the power of God came mightily upon us,
insomuch that many cried out for exceeding joy, and many fell to the
ground'.[50] After they had recovered a little, they broke out spontaneously
in the Te Deum. And most of the next day (from seven in the morning until
three in the afternoon) Whitefield spent counselling men and women who
had come to him longing for salvation.[51] The Wesleys had been converted,
the Moravian Brethren appeared to be restoring 'primitive Christianity', the
Spirit had fallen in a New Year's pentecost, and the masses were crying out
for salvation. Is it any wonder that Whitefield felt able, even at 24 years of
age, to continue in print as a 'journalist'. It was precisely this sense of the
present work of the Holy Spirit that sufficiently overcame modesty to allow
spiritual autobiography to flourish among Fifth Monarchists and others in
the mid-seventeenth century. So it was again, as England appeared to be
once more a nation 'at the edge of the promises'.

Whitefield's first *Journal* was not, however, introspective or retrospective
autobiography; it was not, that is, a narrative designed to tell his own
spiritual story in terms of a beginning, middle, and end. As a voyage journal,
it began with his departure from London and ended with his arrival at
Savannah. Within this frame was another more important story, a narrative
of the expansion of the work of God that had begun in London, a story of
how God used this young evangelist to call sinners to repentance. The
Journal therefore contained embedded narratives of conversions, such as that
of a 'young gentleman' on board the ship who was converted on 26 March
1738 in the midst of a fever. 'His convictions were strong,' noted Whitefield, and 'a thorough renovation begun in his heart'.[52] Again two days later,
he recorded the observation, 'Many marks of a sound conversion appear in
several on board,' and he added the apostrophe to his correspondents in
London, 'Surely, my friends, your prayers are heard.'[53] Conversion narratives thus helped to tell his story of the present work of the Spirit.

---

[49] He did not, however, interpret the revival as millennial, as some were doing. *GWL*
50–1.
[50] Wesley, *Works* (BE), xix. 29.
[51] *GWJ* 196.
[52] Ibid. 143–4.
[53] Ibid. 145.

Yet, most of the *Journal* was a journal in the older sense of the word: an itinerary. On a given day he read prayers, catechized the children, visited the sick, composed a sermon, read Bishop Patrick's *Prayers*, etc. This particular and detailed sense of his life, day to day, was of interest to his friends and followers. Everything that he did was set down as exemplary. Against this background or fabric of day-to-day entries in his journal the advance of the kingdom of God was expounded in terms of his observations of the work of God among the soldiers at Gibraltar, or the sailors on board, and so on. The reader gained the pleasure of going to sea, the pleasure of experiencing something of another's life day to day, and the pleasure of witnessing the expansion of God's work through the conversion of sinners. The genre was well suited both to Whitefield's evangelical intentions and to the interests of the reading public in the 1730s and 1740s.

The second *Journal* continued in much the same vein, but by the third and fourth *Journals*, Whitefield had found his voice as an evangelist. While still structured round his travels, these accounts were much more clearly narratives of his evangelical ministry. Though he had been preaching the New Birth earlier, he was, he says, 'not so clear in it as afterwards'.[54] His third and fourth *Journals* covered essentially his time in London in the first half of 1739 and they were published immediately that same year while the events were still fresh in the public mind. They provided a raw and largely unedited spiritual history as it unfolded. This was the most remarkable year yet for Whitefield in terms of his popularity as a preacher.[55] At 24 years of age, he had thousands hanging on his every word. 'There is no end,' he wrote, 'of people coming and sending to me . . . What a great work as been wrought in the hearts of many within this twelvemonth. Now know I, that though thousands might come at first out of curiosity, yet God has prevented [preceded] and quickened them by His free grace.'[56] Accordingly, his *Journal* became an expansive account of his ministry, a record of his experience of being filled with the Holy Spirit and enabled to preach with spiritual authority. Thus he wrote, 'How has He filled and satisfied my soul! Now know I, that I did receive the Holy Ghost at imposition of hands, for I feel it as much as Elisha did when Elijah dropped his mantle. Nay, others see it also.'[57] His *Journals* in 1739 were self-published, though printed by James Hutton, and it is clear that he had a new charismatic self-confidence. On page after page he wrote how he 'felt the Spirit of God working in me'.[58]

---

[54] Ibid. 81.
[55] It was in this period, in May 1739, that Joseph Humphreys first heard Whitefield, and then sought him out.
[56] *GWJ* 195.
[57] Ibid. 206.
[58] Ibid. 210.

This sort of bold self-assertion drew opposition, of course, and in 1739 Whitefield provoked nearly fifty pamphlets for and against him.[59] But it also provides a clear example of the way that a vivid and present sense of the Holy Spirit overcame traditional autobiographical modesty. This was not missed by his critics, who quickly made the link between Whitefield and the Quakers. A writer in the *Weekly Miscellany* in 1740 remarked that the life of Jesus had been recorded by the Evangelists and the Acts of the Apostles by St Luke, 'but I do not know, that any one except *George Fox* and himself [Whitefield] did ever publish their own Journals'.[60]

Again, these *Journals* in 1739 contained accounts of conversion and reports of response to his preaching, such as when many came to him on 5 March to enquire about salvation.[61] At Bristol the following month, he wrote, 'Many sinners, I believe, have been effectually converted; numbers have come to me under convictions; and all the children of God have been exceedingly comforted.'[62] In addition there were small conversion narratives embedded in his text, such as that of Benjamin Seward or Joseph Periam or the anonymous tailor from Bretforton.[63] Whitefield's great theme was the New Birth, and he published a controversial sermon on the topic this same year.[64] As one critic described his preaching, 'Hark! Hark! he talks of a sensible new birth! Then, belike, he is in labour . . . He dilates himself, cries out,' and then after all this—'Well: he is, at last delivered; he has felt the new birth; and damns all that have not.'[65]

Whitefield was riding a wave of popularity in 1739 and was almost relieved when he finally embarked again for Georgia on board the *Elizabeth* in August. In the relative retirement on board, once again living 'a little by rule', he had time to reflect on all he had experienced. And one of the things he set himself to do in his cabin on board was to write his spiritual autobiography, 'an account of God's dealings with me from my infant days'.[66] This was a different sort of self-writing altogether, with a different sort of beginning, middle, and end. He had been wanting to do this for three years, and he finally wrote it in less than a fortnight in late August and early

[59] Tyerman, *GW* i. 283–5.

[60] *Weekly Miscellany*, 28 March 1740. Whitefield's *Journals* were often held up to ridicule and critique in the pages of the *Weekly Miscellany* in 1739–40. See e.g. the issues for 5 May, 18 and 25 Aug., 22 Sept., and 15 Dec. 1739. Cf. also the point-by-point critique in Zachary Grey, *The Quaker and Methodist Compared. In an Abstract of George Fox's Journal . . . And of the Reverend Mr. George Whitefield's Journals* (1740).

[61] *GWJ* 227.

[62] Ibid. 242.

[63] Ibid. 254–5, 266–71, 314–15.

[64] List of sermons in Tyerman *GW*, i. 294–6; cf. *GWJ* 236.

[65] *The Weekly Miscellany*, 21 July 1739, quoted in Tyerman, *GW* 279.

[66] *GWJ* 332.

September 1739. It appeared in print in 1740 as *A Short Account of God's Dealings with the Reverend Mr. George Whitefield: from his Infancy, to the Time of his Entering into Holy Orders*. This time the middle point of this narrative—between infancy and holy orders—was his conversion at Pembroke College in Oxford in 1735. After preaching about conversion to thousands, here now was his own conversion narrative.[67] This was no longer episodic autobiography, as in the *Journals*: this was emplotted autobiography.

In the introduction to this work he explained that since God had called him to public work, he thought that God's people would want to know how he was prepared for it. He identified many of the typical motives of spiritual autobiography—that he sought simply the glory of God, etc.—but he also mentioned explicitly the benefit he himself received from Christian biographies. Though some might have said he should let this be written after his death, he argued that it would do more good and be more credible if it came straight from the living author. He suggested this approach would be more candid and acknowledged flatly, 'I am not over cautious.'[68]

The outline of this plot is clear enough. As he tells the story, the chief obstacle to God's providential plan for his life was his own sinfulness, which became increasingly manifest as he grew up from infancy. This led to a crisis that was eventually resolved through an emotional evangelical conversion, an experience that set him ablaze with a new zeal to proclaim the gospel. Thus God's providence superintended this whole process to bring him to a place of public usefulness. Clearly, then, Whitefield's conversion narrative functions, in part, as an explanation of his sense of unique commission as a gospel preacher. And the conversion narrative is of the well-established Puritan-Pietist type, as we might expect, given his reading in his formative years of classic expositions of the Puritan morphology in works such as Joseph Alleine's *Alarm to the Unconverted* and Richard Baxter's *Call to the*

---

[67] Frank Lambert, *Inventing the 'Great Awakening'* (Princeton, 1999), 101, claims that Whitefield was the author of *A Faithful Narrative of the Life and Character of the Reverend Mr. Whitefield, B. D., From his Birth to the Present Time. Containing an Account of His Doctrine and Morals; His Motives for Going to Georgia, and His Travels through several Parts of England* (1739), and, moreover, that Whitefield sought to link this autobiography with Edwards's *Faithful Narrative* by using a similar title. This is mistaken. The 25-page tract was not autobiographical, but was published by a partisan supporter of Whitefield in the summer of 1739 in the midst of intense public controversy over his ministry. There is little in the tract that echoes Edwards's narrative. The special pleading of 'faithful' in the title was a recognition of the highly charged debate over Whitefield's ministry and the need to correct the many rumours and calumnies circulating about the evangelist. This was one of some forty-nine pamphlets published for and against Whitefield in the tumultuous year of 1739, q.v. Tyerman, *GW* i. 285. Internal evidence strongly suggests that William Seward was the writer of the tract, which includes details of Whitefield's childhood and college years that would not be published by Whitefield himself until the following year in his *Short Account*.

[68] *GWJ* 36.

Unconverted, or the exemplary *Holy Life and Triumphant Death of Mr. John Janeway.*[69]

Whitefield identified his childhood and adolescence as a period during which his innate sinfulness became more and more evident, as he began to lie, curse, steal, break the Sabbath, and indulge in worldly entertainment. 'Yet,' he wrote, 'I can recollect very early movings of the blessed Spirit upon my heart,' and 'some early convictions of sin'.[70] These 'drawings of God' began to fall off when he commenced grammar school. Some later examples of spiritual precociousness, including devotional reading and 'unspeakable raptures', were again qualified by the presence of an 'abominable secret sin'. Still, during the year before going up to university, when he was 17 years of age, he seemed again spiritually in earnest and religiously observant. Soon after arriving at Oxford he read William Law's *Serious Call to a Devout and Holy Life* (1728) and joined in the religious exercises of the 'Oxford Methodists' or 'Holy Club'. 'I now began,' he wrote, 'like them, to live by rule.'[71] It was under this regimen that he was, in evangelical parlance, 'awakened'; that is, his conscience was pricked by the realization of how extensive were the demands of God for holiness, and that the obligations of the law extended to one's every motive. Through Henry Scougal's *Life of God in the Soul of Man* (1677) he was introduced to the similar demands of 'inward religion', that 'true religion was union of the soul with God, and Christ formed within us'.[72] This insight, he claimed, caused a ray of divine light instantly to dart in upon his soul.

Whitefield especially marked off the next section of his narrative with the subtitle, 'A Brief and Summary Account of my Temptations', and this introduced the crisis that would lead to his evangelical conversion. As he sought after purity of intention in his spiritual life, he was increasingly regarded by those around him at Oxford as extreme in his devotion or even mad for his excessive fastidiousness. He reflected that Satan was trying to lead him into quietism as he withdrew from more and more social contact and religious exercises. He felt a palpable weight upon his chest and a sense of dread, and it seemed the devil was round every corner waiting to trouble him. After consulting with John Wesley as a spiritual director, he resumed some of his religious observances, and indeed, during Lent his mortifications left him emaciated and enervated. For the seven weeks following Easter 1735 he was ill and virtually confined to his rooms at Pembroke College, but he felt this was nevertheless a time of spiritual purging. He had felt this 'unspeakable pressure' on his body and soul for

---

[69] *GWJ* 62.
[70] Ibid. 38.
[71] Ibid. 47.
[72] Ibid.

nearly a year now, but it was all to come to crisis during the last week of May. In Whitefield's words:

One Day, perceiving an uncommon Drought, and a disagreeable Clamminess in my Mouth, and using Things to allay my Thirst, but in vain, it was suggested to me, that when Jesus Christ cried out, 'I thirst,' his Sufferings were near at an End. Upon which, I cast myself down on the Bed, crying out, I thirst! I thirst!—Soon after this, I found and felt in myself that I was delivered from the Burden that had so heavily oppressed me! The Spirit of Mourning was taken from me, and I knew what it was truly to rejoice in God my Saviour, and, for some Time, could not avoid singing Psalms wherever I was; but my Joy gradually became more settled, and, blessed be God, has abode and increased in my Soul (saving a few casual Intermissions) ever since![73]

After this experience he could say that he had 'now obtained mercy from God, and received the Spirit of Adoption in my heart'.[74] Whitefield soon recovered from his illness, but upon the advice of others he took six months out from university to return home to Gloucester to rest. The remaining pages of his *Short Account* narrate his recovery and his entry into holy orders at 21 years of age with renewed evangelical zeal. He sums up his account this way: 'Thus did God, by a variety of unforeseen acts of providence and grace, train me up for, and at length introduce me into, the service of His Church.'[75]

This narrative was more than a vindication of his public ministry, however. It was also clearly a mirror for the reader to hold up to herself. The final two paragraphs are addressed immediately to 'my dear reader' and laid out Whitefield's life for this sort of comparison: 'If thou art immersed in sin as I was . . . ', or, 'If He should lead thee through a longer wilderness than I have passed through . . . ', and so on. His final exhortation is a prayer-wish for the reader to 'experience the like and greater blessings'.[76] Whitefield the autobiographer was again Whitefield the preacher.

In all, it was a narrative not unlike John Bunyan's in its themes and even in its style, with, for example, its appeal to preternatural causes, its narration of direct diabolical temptation, and its frequent use of the passive voice ('It was suggested to me'). Unlike Bunyan and many other Puritan-Nonconformist narratives, however, Whitefield's spiritual crisis was not induced by a fear that he was not of the 'elect'. He would move increasingly in a Calvinist direction in his own theology, but the spiritual anxiety that prompted his conversion was induced in 1735 more by the high-church

---

[73] Ibid. 58; cf. pp. 48–9 in the original 1740 edn.

[74] *GWJ* 59.

[75] Ibid. 70.

[76] Ibid. 70–1.

piety of William Law and the 'holy living' tradition than by any introspective doubts that came with a high predestinarian theology.

   With this narrative in print, Whitefield returned to his episodic journalism. Two more *Journals* were published by Whitefield in 1741 (for a total of
seven).[77] But then he gave up the journalistic enterprise altogether. 'I have
not the freedom to continue writing a journal as usual,' he wrote to Gilbert
Tennent early in 1742. 'I shall proceed, for the future, in a more compendious way.'[78] By this he signalled that he would abandon the journal form
for the autobiography as something 'more compendious'; that is, shorter
and more comprehensive. All of this implies a return to the more emplotted
form of the *Short Account*. And in 1744 he did indeed write a continuation of
his autobiography, *A Further Account of God's Dealings with the Reverend
Mr. George Whitefield, from the Time of his Ordination to his Embarking for
Georgia*.[79] This piece filled in the chronological gaps in his life story. The
reader could now peruse his *Short Account* and his *Further Account*, and then
turn to his seven published *Journals*, and he or she would have a more or less
connected narrative from his infancy to March 1741, or the first twenty-six
years of his life. He had hoped then to write an epilogue that would bring
things up to date from the end of the *Journals* to 'this day' (1756).[80]

   Placing some 600 pages of autobiographical prose on public record while
still in one's twenties leaves plenty of time to repent one's mistakes. And
Whitefield did come to regret much of what he had written. In 1748, he
wrote of his rashness in too quickly and summarily giving the character of
certain people. He acknowledged that he often claimed to speak by the
Spirit of God when he was speaking merely in his own spirit, and that mixed
with 'wild fire'. 'I have likewise too much made inward impressions my rule
of acting,' he added, 'and too soon and too explicitly published what had
been better kept in longer, or told after my death'. He remained grateful to
God for any good done, especially given that he could now see what a 'poor
weak youth' he was, carried along by such a torrent of popularity and
controversy.[81] In a response to Bishop Lavington's attack on his autobio-

----

   [77] An American edition of the sixth journal reached the press in 1740. A further journal
was left in manuscript and was discovered and published in 1938.
   [78] *GWL* 366.
   [79] This account was written on board the *Willmington* in August or September 1744 (*GWJ*
511), but for some unspecified reason it was not published in England until 1747, after three
years had elapsed.
   [80] *GWJ* 31.
   [81] Quoted in Dallimore, *George Whitefield*, ii. 241. Whitefield also claimed in 1748 that he
had revised all his journals and planned to have a new edition issued. This new edition was
not published until 1756 (ibid. 241 n.). Whitefield's first biographer, John Gillies, was able to
quote from an unpublished autobiographical manuscript by Whitefield—distinct from any
published journals—that begins in 1737 and runs through to 1761, though after 1748, he says,
the account is 'very short and imperfect'. This manuscript is now lost. But given that the

graphical writings, he acknowledged likewise that his *Journals* were written 'in the very Heights of my first Popularity' and there was much to correct and mend.[82]

He finally made good on all this contrition in 1756, at 41 years of age, when he republished his whole autobiographical corpus (the two-part autobiography and the *Journals*) in a corrected and abridged version. Many passages that were 'justly exceptionable' were silently omitted. By comparing the originals with the 1756 edition, we can thus see two narrative identities for Whitefield: an ebullient and obstreperous young evangelist in the late 1730s and early 1740s, and a chastened and experienced evangelical minister in 1756. A few passages illustrate the change in how he viewed his own life and spiritual experience.

Whitefield began his narrative in 1740 by talking about the circumstances of his birth and the great hopes his mother had of him: 'This, with the circumstance of my being born in an inn, has been often of service to me in exciting my endeavours to make good my mother's expectations, and so follow the example of my dear Saviour, who was born in a manger belonging to an inn.'[83] All of this was deleted in the 1756 edition. This was one of those passages that Whitefield could look back on after sixteen years and recognize as presumptuous, given its Messianic overtones. Whitefield had been pilloried mercilessly by Bishop Lavington for this: 'Being born in an Inn;—makes him like Christ, who was not born in an Inn . . . From the Circumstance of the Sign of the Bell [i.e. the Bell Inn at Gloucester] he might more aptly have prophesied, that in Time he should become as sounding-Brass.'[84] Whitefield also revised the account of his conversion experience in his rooms at Oxford to avoid the Messianic allusion, 'I thirst'.[85] He likewise removed the statement, 'Satan seemed to have desired me in particular to sift me as wheat,' since this implied an identity between himself and St Peter.[86] As Whitefield had already confessed in 1748, 'Being fond of Scripture language I have often used a style

account is imperfect only after 1748, it is possible that this autobiographical manuscript was begun as a draft towards the intended revision of his journals, written in response to the criticisms that he began to take more seriously at about this time. John Gillies, *Memoirs of the Life of the Reverend George Whitefield* (1772), 17 n., 235 n.; cf. Gillies's remarks about this MS having been written 'after many years', ibid. 24, 50.

[82] George Whitefield, *Some Remarks on a Pamphlet Entitled, 'The Enthusiasm of Methodists and Papists Compar'd'* (1749), 34, quoted in Lambert, *'Pedlar in Divinity'*, 193.

[83] *GWJ* 37.

[84] George Lavington, *The Enthusiasm of Methodists and Papists Compared* (1754), ii. 27.

[85] *GWJ* 58; cf. the 1756 deletion of the Messianic statement 'and though Satan for some weeks had been biting my heel, God was pleased to show me that I should soon bruise his head'. Ibid. 56.

[86] Ibid. 51.

too apostolical.'[87] He also deleted or rewrote passages that had appeared to remove all human agency from the narrative and to make all his actions depend upon the agency of either God or the Devil in a sort of psycho-machy, implying that he had been entirely passive in this supernatural contest. In all, the convert in the narrative of 1756 was far less charismatic and spiritually exceptional than that of 1740.[88] Nevertheless, Whitefield would always mark his conversion as the great turning-point of his life. In an autobiographical passage in a sermon preached near the end of his life, he recalled, 'Whenever I go to Oxford, I cannot help running to the spot where Jesus Christ first revealed Himself to me, and gave me the new birth. . . . From that moment God has been carrying on His blessed work in my soul.'[89]

Thus, from writing a journal letter to his friends in London at 23 years of age, Whitefield's experiment in nautical-cum-religious journalism and autobiography gradually enlarged. He was soon caught up in the first wave of revival enthusiasm. As his popularity increased, he became more convinced that the Spirit of God was using his life in an unprecedented way to bring women and men to conversion, and he grew more confident in his self-writing. In due course, this led him to narrate his own conversion experience in a way that recalled Puritan precedents. A large readership sanctioned this self-identity as consumers, readers, and followers. It is also clear, however, that Whitefield's self-proclaimed identity did not go un-contested. Bishop Lavington thought that Whitefield was a 'papist', Zachary Grey compared him to a Quaker, and William Hogarth portrayed him as an 'enthusiast'. Similar charges appeared again and again in the pages of periodicals such as the *Weekly Miscellany* in 1739–41. That Whitefield's evangelical identity was thus contested in print—and that he himself felt able to revise his self-portrayal after some sixteen years had passed—suggests that evangelical conversion could never be pure fideism. Such a religious experience required rational justification and invited lifelong theological reflection. Though conversion might be experienced as an interior or private event, it was now occupying a significant public space.

---

[87] Dallimore, *George Whitefield*, ii. 241.

[88] Whitefield was not the only young evangelist to revise his understanding of this season of revival from the perspective of age and experience. Jonathan Edwards confessed in 1751 that he needed to revise his self-understanding in a similar way, and that he had unwittingly encouraged spiritual pride during the 'extraordinary awakening about sixteen years ago'. Looking back, he could say: 'One thing that has contributed to bring things to such a pass at Northampton, was my youth and want of more judgment and experience, in the time of that extraordinary awakening about sixteen years ago.' *WJE* iv. 565.

[89] Tyerman, *GW* i. 27.

JOHN WESLEY

While George Whitefield was the more famous evangelist in the early years of the revival, John Wesley soon dominated the movement in England by dint of his consistent and indefatigable labours not only as an itinerant preacher opening up new fields of ministry in places large and small, but also as a writer, organizational leader, apologist, publisher, keen theological interpreter, and catechist. Wesley has also come to dominate the historiography of the revival simply by outliving the other evangelists and submerging their reputations in a sea of printed paper. Wesley's chief literary monument was his *Journal*, published in twenty-one instalments ('extracts') between 1740 and 1791, and running to over a million printed words. Yet despite this wealth of testimony, Wesley remains an enigmatic figure, and he did not offer a univocal, retrospective interpretation of his life.

Wesley's conversion—his famous Aldersgate experience—does not appear in the first instalment of the *Journal*, even though that experience had indeed occurred before its publication in May 1740. Wesley narrated his conversion experience in the second *Journal*, published four months later at the end of September. Wesley came before the public first with a voyage journal of his career as a foreign missionary. It is unlikely that he envisaged an ongoing, serial publication programme at this stage, but he soon realized the potential of the form for defending and directing his ministry, and with the second *Journal* he established his own spiritual biography. The stage was then set for a narrative of the rise and progress of Methodism.

John Wesley's Record of His Life

The difficulty of interpreting John Wesley's life lies in part in the nature of the documents he left behind. He recorded his life in diaries, in manuscript journals and letters, in the printed *Journals* themselves, and in a few other apologetic pieces on the rise of Methodism.[90] What he recorded, however, were chiefly his actions and his observations, and he was little concerned with subjective autobiography for its own sake. Even when his gaze turned inward, it was still a clinical gaze. He tackled himself as a project or a problem and then sorted himself out. There is very little *confessio* in the whole of his written works. To interpret Wesley's narrative identity, and to evaluate the significance of evangelical conversion to his self-understanding, it is necessary to examine more closely the nature of the records he kept of his life.

---

[90] See e.g. *The Nature, Design, and General Rules of the United Societies* (1743); *Plain Account of the People Called Methodists* (1748); *A Short History of Methodism* (1765); *A Short History of the People Called Methodists* (1781); *Thoughts on Methodism* (1786). These tracts are included in vol. ix of Wesley, *Works* (BE).

Behind Wesley's massive public *Journal* was a remarkable private practice of disciplined, meticulous diary-keeping and self-examination. If the occasion of the published *Journal* was largely apologetic, the occasion of the diary was the desire for moral and spiritual betterment. At 21 years of age Wesley responded to the advice of Jeremy Taylor (1613–67) in his *Rule and Exercises of Holy Living* (1650) and began to keep a diary as an exercise in more exact management of his time. Wesley kept up this diary for the rest of his life—another nearly sixty-six years. Although several volumes are no longer extant (leaving a gap from 1741 to 1782), there remain more than two thousand pages of detailed entries. The transmission and transcription of these manuscript diaries is a complex story in itself, since the diaries were for many years not accessible to scholars and then, once available, found almost incomprehensible. Wesley used a coded system of entries including ciphers, abbreviations, symbols, number schemes, and shorthand—and he changed his method over time.[91] In 1969 Richard Heitzenrater found the key to Wesley's diary in the diary of another Oxford Methodist, Benjamin Ingham, and he edited the critical edition of these diaries for the Bicentennial Edition of the *Works of John Wesley*.[92]

It is clear then that Wesley had kept a disciplined diary for fifteen years before he published the first *Journal*. It is also clear that there was no continuous longer journal in manuscript form, from which Wesley took 'extracts' for his published *Journal*—some document supposedly intermediate between the diary and the *Journal*. The only manuscript journals were the voyage journal and Georgia journals, and the related journal letters he sent to friends from Georgia and that he occasionally wrote later.[93] Even these were not, however, the larger and more complete drafts that Wesley supposedly abridged for his first printed *Journal*. More properly, his 'extracts' were fresh compositions based upon his diary and other occasional papers.[94] The diaries may be distinguished from the *Journals* in a number of ways. As Heitzenrater says, 'There is no hindsight, no editorializing, no propaganda; they were not intended as reflective, apologetic, or narrative documents.'[95] Effectively, the diaries were a technology for self-improvement that

---

[91] Richard P. Heitzenrater, 'Wesley and His Diary', in John Stacey (ed.), *John Wesley: Contemporary Perspectives* (1988), 12–15; and id., *Mirror and Memory: Reflections on Early Methodism* (Nashville, Tenn., 1989), 66–8.

[92] Wesley, *Works* (BE), xviii–xxiv. The Oxford diaries are scheduled to appear in vol. xxxii.

[93] W. R. Ward, Introduction, Wesley, *Works* (BE), xviii. 89–91.

[94] Ibid. 81–93. Cf. *JWL* vii. 44: 'In Georgia I wrote three distinct Journals. Afterwards I extracted one from them all . . . omitting abundance of things which I judged would not profit.'

[95] Heitzenrater, Editorial Introduction to Appendix: MS Journals and Diaries, Wesley, *Works* (BE), xviii. 302, cf. Ward, Introduction, ibid. 37.

reflected the spiritual ideals of the Oxford Methodists. The diaries were also a spur to Wesley's memory for later reflection.

Wesley's various records of his conversation with August Gottlieb Spangenberg (1704–92) in Georgia in February 1736 offer a good example of the difference between Wesley's diary, his manuscript journal, and the printed *Journal*, and the different degrees of self-reflection present in each. The winter of 1735–6 was a critical time in Wesley's spiritual formation, when at the height of his ascetic idealism he met the Moravians on board the ship to Georgia. He found he was afraid in the midst of storm, while they were not. In conversation with Spangenberg after arriving in America, Wesley was asked whether he had sensible assurance, the inward witness of the Spirit. Wesley claimed that he did, but added the gloss in his first published *Journal*, 'I fear they were vain words.'[96] Yet the meaning of this conversation for Wesley's own spiritual pilgrimage had emerged only gradually.

This *Journal* was published in 1740, and his account of his meeting with Spangenberg on 7 February 1736 was therefore written up some four years after the event. What did Wesley write in his diary on the occasion itself? In fact, his conversation with Spangenberg had stretched over three days. It is worth quoting in full a longhand transcription of his diary entry on that Sunday:[97]

Sunday, February 8.

4.45 Dressed; (well); prayed. 5 Prayed; meditated; writ diary.	6 +
6 Meditated; dressed.	5
7 Necessary talk; breakfast.	5
8 Religious talk with Spangenberg (excellent man).	6
9 Necessary talk (religious). 9:30 Read Prayers.	6
10 Preached. 10.15 Meditated; read Patrick to them.	6
11 Patrick; religious talk. 11.30 Read Prayers, preached.	7
12 Sacrament. 12.30 Meditated.	6
1 Religious talk with Spangenberg of myself.	7
2.30 Meditated; prayed.	6
3 Dinner.	6
4 Read Prayers, expounded.	lively zeal 6
5 Meditated; prayed; sang; tea.	meditated fervently 7
6 Meditated; sang [supper?] with Spangenberg; Oglethorpe came.	7 +
7 With Oglethorpe, necessary talk; necessary talk (religious) with Spangenberg.	6
8 Necessary talk with Oglethorpe, etc.	6
9 Necessary talk; undressed. 9.45.	6

---

[96] Ibid. xviii. 146.

[97] Ibid. xviii. 352d. I have laid out the text in columnar form, after the manner of Wesley's 'exacter diary' during these years, rather than follow the paragraph form used in the published edition. I am grateful to Richard Heitzenrater for providing me with a photocopy of the original of Wesley's diary for this day.

Providence: Mr Spangenberg a wise man; advised me as to myself!
Grace: 7 rating four times [11 to noon, 1 to 2, 5 to 7 p.m.]; 6 eleven times [all but 6
to 8 a.m.]. + twice [5 to 6 a.m., 6 to 7 p.m.]. Meditated fervently [at 5 p.m.]; lively
zeal [4 to 5 p.m.]. Resolved: To follow Christ.

The form of his diary entry here is that of the 'exacter diary' of the
Oxford period—a telling indication that his piety also remained within the
framework of Oxford Methodism. Earlier he used a paragraph form of two
or three lines per day, and later he would revert to that practice, but here the
form of entry was columnar, with a notation for each hour of the day. The
second column, with the figures, recorded Wesley's 'temper of devotion' on
a scale of 1–9, and was summarized at the bottom of the page under the
heading 'Grace'. The cross symbol (+) was used to indicate contrition or
some positive spiritual virtue or blessing. On this day, he clearly regarded his
conversations with Spangenberg about his own spiritual condition (at 8 a.m.,
1 p.m., and 6–8 p.m.) as a special providential blessing, as indicated in his
summary at the foot of the entry.

This diary entry thus offers a picture of the moment when Wesley's ascetic
idealism was confronted with the comparative fideism of the Moravians.
Wesley was taking his spiritual pulse hourly and striving with might and
main after 'a devout and holy life'. The form of the diary illustrates vividly
its function within Wesley's spiritual life as a means of self-improvement.
On Tuesday, two days later, he was equally engaged in devotion and
Christian service, but he noted, 'A poor, careless, lukewarm day!'[98] Wesley
was keeping these records in order to push himself harder. And yet, on the
Sunday in question, Wesley's preoccupation with control was confronted
squarely by Spangenberg's comparatively acquiescent spirituality, advocat-
ing simple faith and divinely wrought assurance.

The next layer of reflection comes in Wesley's manuscript journal (the
voyage journal), which moved beyond the bare data of the diary and offered
a short paragraph that focused on Spangenberg. This recollection appears
very near the conclusion of the journal, since the journal ends with Wesley's
arrival in Georgia. Here it becomes clear that the act of selection itself is a
significant act of interpretation. Wesley could have commented on his early
morning meditations or his reading of Bishop Patrick's *Prayers,* but the
entire entry for 8 February reads thus:

I asked Mr. Spangenberg's advice with regard to myself. He told me he could say
nothing till he had asked me two or three . . . questions. 'Do you know yourself?
Do you know Jesus Christ? Have you the witness of the Spirit in your heart?' After
my answering these, he gave me several directions, which may the good God who
sent him enable me to follow.[99]

---

[98] Wesley, *Works* (BE), xviii. 355.
[99] Ibid. 352.

We do not yet have here the note of self-doubt of the printed *Journal* ('I fear they were vain words'), but it is none the less clear that Wesley approached Spangenberg for advice and considered him as something of a spiritual director.

There are thus at least three levels of reflexivity in Wesley's recollection of the conversation. There is the initial data recorded cryptically in the diary almost certainly on the day itself. Here there was no attempt at interpretation, though the recognition of the conversation as 'providential' points towards some sort of moral narrative beyond mere chronology. Then secondly, there is the recollection of the conversation itself given some weeks or months later in the manuscript journal of his voyage, a journal-cum-letter which now had an intended audience in London. Yet here again, there was little in the overall narrative to set apart this conversation as critical in Wesley's spiritual autobiography other than to point up his growing fascination with the Moravians.[100] Then, finally, there is the published *Journal* that was written up several years later—after Wesley's Aldersgate experience in May 1738, but before he had broken completely with the Moravians at Fetter Lane in London in July 1740. And here it is that we have at last the added gloss about Wesley's claim to the witness of the Spirit in 1736: 'I fear they were vain words.' This interpretative gloss functions within Wesley's spiritual autobiography to prepare the reader for Aldersgate, since it signals that his spiritual state in 1736 was one of inner anxiety, notwithstanding his self-discipline. If the diary was a *record* and the manuscript journal a *selection*, then the printed *Journal* was clearly a *narrative*. Wesley's sense of the significance of his conversation with Spangenberg was something that he discerned with increasing clarity only after the passing of a certain amount of time.[101]

The Apologetic Character of the Printed Journals

The *Journal*, as we have noted above, originated as the record of a missionary's voyage and his observations on life in a young and distant British colony. The immediate occasion of publication was, however, that Wesley found he needed to defend himself on a number of fronts. By 1740 he was a

---

[100] Indeed, even when Wesley records an account of Spangenberg's own spiritual pilgrimage (on 9 February), Wesley stresses his purity of intention and the apostolic simplicity of the Brethren, more than Spangenberg's progress through a definable evangelical conversion. Wesley, *Works* (BE), xviii. 353–4.

[101] The Aldersgate narrative is most clearly anticipated in Wesley's short review of his own spiritual state in a private memorandum on 24 January 1738, while on board ship returning to England from Georgia (about two years after his conversation with Spangenberg). Here it is clear that he has for some time felt 'tossed about by various winds of doctrine'. Wesley, *Works* (BE), xviii. 212 n.

public figure, and a controversial one, in England. The really significant wave of public criticism of Wesley began with his more aggressive preaching in 1739 and the revivals that followed. He was attacked in sermons, pamphlets, and periodicals—from the *Weekly Miscellany* newspaper in London to the polite pages of the *Gentleman's Magazine*.

Wesley was embroiled in at least five major public controversies by the time he published his first *Journal*. First, he was involved in a public dispute with Captain Williams over the Sophy Hopkey affair in Georgia and other colonial matters. All of this had become public in Bristol in March 1740. Secondly, he had been under attack since the days of Oxford Methodism for 'enthusiasm' of one kind or another. William Morgan, one of the original Oxford Methodists, died in the autumn of 1732, and it was widely believed that the rigorous asceticism of Wesley and his group had been the cause. A letter to the *Fog's Weekly Journal* that December made all this public, accusing 'this sect called Methodists' of an 'enthusiastic madness' that resulted in excessive melancholy. Elite clerical figures such as Joseph Butler, Bishop of Bristol, continued the charge of enthusiasm in 1739, but now the worry was over the report 'that many people fall into fits in your societies'.[102] Indeed, in 1739 and early 1740 Wesley played a leading role with Whitefield in provoking outcries and other demonstrations of religious excitement in London and Bristol. Moreover, Wesley seemed more determined in 1738–9, as he put it, 'to declare the whole counsel of God' at every opportunity, and consequently he noted at church after church in London that he had preached 'for the last time', such was the offence he caused.[103] Thirdly, rumours had begun that Wesley was a Papist, or even a Jesuit—organizing secret meetings and proselytizing by guile. These allegations would intensify over the next five years and lead to anti-Methodist riots, especially as fears mounted of a French invasion and the return of the Young Pretender. But already in 1739 at Bristol it was believed by many that Wesley was a Jesuit.[104]

If these first three disputes related to opposition from those outside the early Methodist movement, two further controversies came from within. In August 1739 Wesley published his sermon 'Free Grace', attacking Calvinism, and the controversy over predestination with Whitefield, which had remained largely private until then, became public and divisive. Fifth, Wesley's controversy with the Moravians over quietism ('stillness') began in this same year and would come to a head in July 1740 in London when he seceded from the Fetter Lane society to establish the Foundery society. (This

---

[102] Wesley, *Works* (BE), xix. 472.
[103] See e.g. ibid. xix. 28.
[104] Ibid. xix. 89; cf. the allegations against Whitefield in the *Weekly Miscellany*, 30 August 1740, in the course of which he was compared in detail to Ignatius Loyola.

secession occurred in the interval between the publication of his first and second *Journal*.)

Wesley was thus both a public and a controversial figure when he appeared in print as an autobiographer. This is important to remember when considering his conversion narrative. For all his personal disclosure, and even introspection, he revealed himself not with the temerity of the confessional, but with the dialectical forcefulness of the debating chamber. Even though his *Journal* was organized around his own travels, ministry, and encounters, its ethos was one of self-defence and moral suasion. Wesley was far from undressing for the public. He was not, like Rousseau, seeking to lay his psyche bare; nor was he, like Augustine, seeking to discern God's presence in his own soul by introspection. The *Journal* was shaped by Wesley's apologetic concerns. It was not therefore a subjective spiritual autobiography in any thoroughgoing sense, though it contained passages of reflexive narrative and self-interpretation.

Autobiographical Reflection in the Early Journals

That Wesley wrote in the midst of public controversy and with an eye to his opponents and the needs of his societies does not, however, suffice to explain—or to explain away—the autobiographical significance of the *Journal*. It remains true that the Wesley of the diary, seeking both self-knowledge and holiness, was present in the printed *Journal*. Wesley consistently appears as the detached observer, even of his own experience. For example, he sometimes records 'strange but true' events, with the disclaimer that he was offering simply a 'bare recital of those facts', nothing more.[105] Frederick Dryer has argued persuasively that Wesley's epistemology was empirical, after the manner of his age, and that this is the best way to make sense of his apparent eclecticism.[106]

From time to time Wesley turned this empirical gaze in upon himself and analysed his own spiritual state. He had most to say about his own formation in the first three *Journals*. These *Journals* were published in 1740 and 1742, and they rehearsed the period from 1735 to 1739. Each included at least one extended passage of autobiographical reflection, the most significant of which was the narrative of Wesley's Aldersgate experience on 24 May 1738 in the middle *Journal*.[107] The significance of each *Journal* in terms of

---

[105] Wesley, *Works* (BE), xix. 4.

[106] Frederick Dreyer, 'Faith and Experience in the Thought of John Wesley', *American Historical Review* 87 (1983), 12–30; id., *The Genesis of Methodism* (1999), 79–93.

[107] The principal autobiographical portions were recorded under 8–25 January 1738 in *Journal 1* (1740), Wesley, *Works* (BE), xviii. 208–16; 24 May 1738, *Journal 2* (1740), Wesley, *Works* (BE), xviii. 242–50; 16 December 1738 and 4 January 1739, *Journal 3* (1742), Wesley, *Works* (BE), xix. 16–19, 20, 22, 27–31.

Wesley's spiritual life and his ministry may be taken from the motto verses selected for the title page of each. The first *Journal* carried a motto from Rom. 9: 30–1:

What shall we say then?——That Israel which follow'd after the Law of Righteousness, hath not attained to the Law of Righteousness.——Wherefore? Because they sought it not by Faith, but as it were by the Works of the Law.

By analogy, then, Wesley considered his Georgia ministry to be a period of legal righteousness. In contrast, the second *Journal*, which narrated his return to England in early 1738, his 'conversion', and his travels in Germany, bore a motto from 1 Tim. 1: 16:

For this Cause I obtain'd Mercy, that in me first *Jesus Christ* might shew forth all Long-suffering, for a Pattern to them which should hereafter believe on Him to Life everlasting.

Here the analogy was provided by the conversion of St Paul. This was a favourite passage for evangelicals, and it highlighted the exemplary character of Wesley's conversion ('for a Pattern'). It also signalled that this *Journal* would treat his progress from legal righteousness to 'free grace'. The third *Journal* took up a new theme, offering an account of the beginnings of the Methodist societies in London and Bristol and the spectacular scenes of revival that accompanied Wesley's outdoor preaching. Accordingly, the motto was drawn from Acts 5: 38–9:

If this Counsel or this Work be of Men, it will come to nought; But if it be of *God*, ye cannot overthrow it; least haply ye be found even to fight against *God*.

Early evangelical leaders typically referred to seasons of religious concern as a 'work' of God, as in this motto, even more than they called it a 'revival'. This motto therefore implied an identity between the 'work' of Methodism and the expansion of the early church in the book of Acts. Thus, if Wesley was benighted Israel in the first *Journal*, and St Paul the convert in the second, he was in the third *Journal* a persecuted apostle, and 'Methodism' itself represented a new Pentecost.[108] Despite the episodic character of the *Journals* themselves, the larger periodization could not be more clear: Wesley moved from law to gospel to evangelical proclamation.

In fact, the narrative of Wesley's Aldersgate experience could be said to have begun with the gloss on his conversation with Spangenberg recorded in the first *Journal*, analysed above. That conversation was the point at which the concept of 'the witness of the Spirit' was first introduced by Wesley in the printed *Journals*, and his autobiographical summary at the conclusion of

---

[108] The fourth *Journal*, published in 1744, was the last to carry a motto. It was taken from Job 32: 16–17, 21–2, and suggested that Wesley's position in dispute with the Moravians and the Calvinists was like Job among his counsellors.

his return voyage to England ended on precisely this note, the last sentence being a quotation from Rom. 8: 16, arguing that the true believer possesses the Holy Spirit, who 'beareth witness with his spirit, that he is a child of God'.[109] Those are the very last words of the first *Journal*. The burden of the autobiographical summary that preceded this, beginning on 8 January 1738 and leading up to this conclusion, was that Wesley had discovered in Georgia that he did not possess true, saving faith—that he was no more converted to God than the Amerindians he went to evangelize. The *Journal* thus concluded on a plaintive note: 'I want that faith which none can have without knowing that he hath it.'[110]

Writing these words in 1740, Wesley portrayed himself at the end of his Georgia mission as a man who was awakened, but not yet converted to God. And, like Whitefield in his *Short Account*, Wesley explicitly presented his case as exemplary, saying that he spoke all this 'if haply some of those who still *dream* may *awake*, and see that as I am, so are they'.[111] Wesley added twelve rhetorical questions ('Are they read in *philosophy*? So was I,' etc.), and these questions make it abundantly clear that as he described his condition, he was writing as the representative or universal 'I'. Wesley the evangelical preacher in 1740 recounted Wesley the spiritual pilgrim in 1738 to the end that the reader, too, might seek that faith which is self-evidencing and empowering.

It is significant that the second *Journal* appeared only four months after the first. No subsequent *Journals* were printed so closely together, and most appeared at intervals of two or three years. The second *Journal* was unmistakably the sequel to the first. That the theme of this second *Journal* would be conversion is evident not only from the motto and from the incompleteness, or even the note of suspense, of the first *Journal*, but also from the manner in which Wesley's experience on 24 May 1738 is set off as momentous, and the fact that this second *Journal* concludes with no less than eleven specimen conversion narratives that Wesley recounts from interviews conducted at Herrnhut.[112]

How did Wesley flag his narrative on 24 May 1738 as momentous? First, he prefaced the account, saying, 'What occurred on Wednesday 24, I think best to relate at large.'[113] This was something that required a different sort of narrative than had been given hitherto in the *Journal*, and it required exposition at length and in full. Secondly, he gave his account in eighteen numbered paragraphs. This was unusual for Wesley unless he was constructing an argument, conducting a summary, or reviewing rules and resolutions.

---

[109] Wesley, *Works* (BE), xviii. 216.
[110] Ibid.
[111] Ibid. 214.
[112] Ibid. 273–97.
[113] Ibid. 242.

People do not generally tell stories in numbered paragraphs, and this is an important indication that Wesley was here raising his narrative from the episodic level to the emplotted level; that is, he was going to trace his development in periods to show how his present condition followed from prior influences and stages of growth. This was not then *res gestae* or chronicle, but logical arrangement. Indeed, it is likely that there was an earlier written source that Wesley was here incorporating into his *Journal.*[114] Paragraphs 1–12 are retrospective, paragraphs 13–14 narrate the events of the day in question, and paragraphs 15–18 form a denouement.[115]

The retrospective paragraphs follow a periodization that is familiar as the Puritan-Pietist pattern. His childhood (para. 1) was a time of relative innocence, and Wesley's belief in baptismal regeneration marked this all the more starkly so. However, sacramental regeneration could be, and was, forfeited as he fell into outward sin as a schoolboy at Charterhouse (para. 2). As a student at Christ Church, Oxford (para. 3), he was religiously observant but had as yet no grasp of inward religion. This came with his reading of Thomas à Kempis's *Imitation of Christ* during a period of increased religious seriousness as he prepared for ordination (para. 4). The quest for holiness, purity of intention, and Christian perfection, following the guidance of William Law, marked his life while a fellow at Lincoln College (paras. 5–6). The influence of mystical divinity was, he now realized, a dangerous detour (para. 7). Thus trusting in his own righteousness and experiencing no real spiritual comfort, he encountered the Moravian Brethren on board ship to Georgia, and though they pointed him towards a better way, he continued to rely upon his own spiritual efforts (para. 8). While in Georgia he was deeply frustrated and divided in his conscience, unable to live up to the standards of God's law, though he desired this earnestly (para. 9). His condition could be summarized as being 'under the law', and he as yet knew nothing of the 'witness of the Spirit' (para. 10). In England he met Peter Böhler and was persuaded that he had not true faith, and so he began to seek a new faith as the gift of God, an intensely personal faith that would bring with it its own conviction and moral power (paras. 11–12).

All of this was retrospective and designed to prepare the reader to see the autobiographical significance of what indeed took place on 24 May, or as Wesley wrote at the beginning of the account, 'premising what may make it the better understood'.[116] On the day itself, in this state of earnest seeking (and Wesley had said earlier that he had been in 'continual sorrow and heaviness of heart' these three days), he found that he thrice struck at

---

[114] Wesley, *Works* (BE), xviii. 242 n.

[115] Wesley's Aldersgate narrative, given thus in numbered paragraphs, is found ibid. 242–51.

[116] Ibid. 242.

random upon Scripture texts that spoke to his condition and seemed to portend his approaching salvation—twice privately and then in the anthem at St Paul's Cathedral (para. 13). Then followed the famous Aldersgate experience (para. 14):

In the evening I went very unwillingly to a society in Aldersgate Street, where one was reading Luther's Preface to the Epistle to the Romans. About a quarter before nine, while he was describing the change which God works in the heart through faith in Christ, I felt my heart strangely warmed. I felt I did trust in Christ, Christ alone for salvation, and an assurance was given me that he had taken away *my* sins, even *mine*, and saved *me* from the law of sin and death.[117]

This was clearly the climax of his narrative. The remaining paragraphs in the account form the denouement. As a consequence of this experience Wesley prayed for his enemies and 'testified openly to all there what I now felt in my heart' (para. 15). He experienced a heightened sensitivity to his inward spiritual and emotional states, and he found his experience tested by diabolical suggestions, temptations, and fears, though he was now able to conquer these by grace (paras. 15–18). This heightened sensibility was reflected in the diary entries that followed over the next week and a half, and then he was off for Germany. By 8 June 1738 he had returned to the former mode of the *Journal,* recording objectively his actions and observations as he travelled. His gaze had turned outwards once again.

So Wesley was converted. The autobiographical passages in the third *Journal* illustrate how fragile, however, was the narrative identity established through this account of his experience on 24 May 1738. Because Wesley had so privileged the sensible operation of the Holy Spirit on this occasion, he was put into a quandary when his religious feeling ebbed. On 14 October that same year he decided it was necessary to take time for 'considering my own state more deeply'.[118] He conducted an interrogation of himself according to a number of criteria. Was he a 'new creature', such as St Paul spoke of? Such a one has new judgements of himself. 'Thus, by the grace of God in Christ, I judge myself. Therefore I am in this respect a new creature.'[119] And so on, he continued, through a number of criteria. This was the Puritan 'practical syllogism' without the doctrine of election. He concluded his examination with the verdict,

Yet, upon the whole, although I have not yet that joy in the Holy Ghost, nor that love of God shed abroad in my heart, nor the full assurance of faith, nor the (proper) witness of the Spirit with my spirit that I am a child of God, much less am I, in the

---

[117] Ibid. 249–50.
[118] Ibid. xix. 16.
[119] Ibid. 16–17.

full and proper sense of the words, in Christ a new creature; I nevertheless trust that I have a measure of faith and am 'accepted in the Beloved'.[120]

Wesley had discovered that his religious emotions ('joy' and 'love') were evanescent, and that his direct perception of divine favour ('full assurance' and 'witness of the Spirit') was not constant. And so, he fell back upon ratiocination, but this could only provide a relative judgement ('upon the whole' and 'a measure of') that he was in fact a new creature in Christ.

Wesley returned to these criteria of self-examination two months later on 16 December. Curiously, he thinly concealed these reflections as the observations of a third party, saying, 'One who had examined himself . . . made the following observations on the state of his own soul.'[121] This third-party conceit only heightens the appearance of clinical observation, and the objective treatment of himself as one case study among many, and it offers one more specimen of his ideal of empirical observation, even when dealing with himself. But this time his interrogation focused upon his feelings, so he began, for example, contrasting his judgement with his emotions: 'I *judge* thus of myself. But I feel it not. Therefore there is in me still the old heart of stone.' Inference was evidently a poor substitute for directly sensible spiritual experience, and Wesley concludes, 'Herein manifestly appears that I am not a new creature.'[122] On 4 January 1739 Wesley again recorded the reflections of 'one who had the form of godliness many years', and here his judgement was most severe of all: 'I affirm, I am not a Christian now.' Why? Because he could not *feel* the fruits of the Spirit directly in the emotions of love, peace, joy, and so on.[123] Wesley made a similar judgement of his own condition in a letter to his brother Charles in 1766, in which he described himself as only an 'honest heathen' and a God-fearer. Again, the reason for this indictment was that he had only the evidence 'such as faintly shines from reason's ray', rather than the 'direct witness'.[124]

Wesley's position was made more clear in his *Principles of a Methodist* (1742) in reply to the anti-Methodist pamphlet of Josiah Tucker. To make his apologia Wesley trawled back through his second *Journal*, and through the Moravian testimonies at its conclusion, clarifying what he believed about conversion. From this it appears that he understood that the believer's justification produced an instantaneous peace with God that was invariably sensible, though this 'first sense of forgiveness'[125] was so mixed with fear

---

[120] Wesley, *Works* (BE), xix. 19.

[121] Ibid. 27.

[122] Ibid. 27–8.

[123] Ibid. 29–31; cf. xviii. 252 n.

[124] Richard P. Heitzenrater, *The Elusive Mr. Wesley* (Nashville, 1984), i. 198–200.

[125] Wesley, *Works* (BE), ix. 61. This phrase appears not only here in Wesley's *Principles of a Methodist* in a description of what is the general case of the believer, but also in Wesley's

and doubt that one could still say, 'But I dare not affirm I am a child of God.' Wesley added the comment, 'Many such instances I know at this day. I myself was one, for some time.' Wesley held, however, that there was a further experience of 'full assurance' in which all doubt and fear would be excluded.[126] The most plausible reading of Wesley's self-interpretation in 1742 (the year he wrote the third *Journal* and the reply to Tucker) is that after the heightened sensibility at Aldersgate had faded, he realized that he could make no apodictic claim to be a Christian. He could still make reasoned deductions about his probable state, and he could still look at the evidence of his spiritual emotions and perceptions, mixed and variable as they were, but the great desideratum of Wesley's life and ministry was the final perfection of the Christian, in which justification, sanctification, and full assurance were fused in a single experience or state of being. Initially it appears that Aldersgate bore the weight of all these hopes and expectations, but, as Richard Heitzenrater has argued, Wesley gradually separated out each of these elements and distinguished degrees of faith and stages in the *via salutis*.[127] In 1738 this was all still telescoped into one ideal. And in 1742 this was the only definition of Christian worthy of the name for Wesley. Thus, when he says, 'I am not a Christian,' we should probably understand him to mean, 'I will not arrogate the name Christian to such a one as I.' It is possible, of course, that Wesley was simply inconsistent in his beliefs and mercurial in his spiritual moods, but if so, it would be hard to account for his literary intentions in including this material in his *Journal* in 1742. Moreover, Wesley's reply to Josiah Tucker demonstrates that he was in earnest about establishing a defensible, consistent theology of experience.

The Place of Aldersgate in Wesley's Self-Understanding

It should be stressed, though, that these autobiographical portions, however celebrated, were the exception in the printed journals, and that the main narrative as a whole looks outwards and takes as its theme the progress of the kingdom and the 'gathering of the Methodist people'. In this sense the *Journal* consistently bears witness to Wesley's *ethos* as the main actor in the story, even while it does not provide a strong overarching *mythos* for his life. There is more action than syntax. Wesley spends little time, compared to Augustine, in pondering what his life *meant*. With the exception of these

---

personal recollection of Aldersgate on 4 January 1739, when he lamented, 'Indeed, what I might have been I know not, had I been faithful to the grace then given, when, expecting nothing less, I received such a *sense of the forgiveness of my sins* as till then I never knew.' Wesley, *Works* (BE), xix. 29 (italics added).

[126] Ibid. ix. 63.

[127] Richard P. Heitzenrater, 'Great Expectations: Aldersgate and the Evidences of Genuine Christianity', in Randy L. Maddox (ed.), *Aldersgate Reconsidered* (Nashville, 1990), 49–91.

few autobiographical set pieces, Wesley's record of his life in the *Journal* was not of his introspection but of his observation. In W. R. Ward's felicitous phrase the *Journal* was for the most part *res gestae christianae*.[128]

Was the Aldersgate narrative central to Wesley's life and his *Journal* taken as a whole? W. R. Ward thinks not: 'By keeping up the *Journal* to within a few months of his death Wesley reduced the conversion narrative to an insignificant proportion of a huge work running to a million words, of which the principal theme was his service to the Kingdom of God and the gathering of the Methodist people.'[129] In point of sheer volume, Ward is of course right. A keen observer of form, he is also right that the *Journal* was eclectic: part spiritual autobiography, part conversion narrative, part religious chronicle, part *res gestae*, part travel journal, part commonplace book, and part news journal. Yet the placement of Aldersgate in the *Journal* is significant, and it holds a central place in Wesley's transition from impression to expression, from formation to proclamation. The syntax of the first three *Journals*, illustrated above from the mottos on the title pages, is Law–Grace–Proclamation. We referred to this as the emplotted (rather than episodic) level of the narrative in these early *Journals*. Aldersgate forms the middle term in this sequence, and without it there really is no narrative syntax at all. When taken in narrative sequence, however, Aldersgate leads logically to the birth of Methodism. Wesley is first revitalized, and then he is able to exercise a new charisma of spiritual leadership in London and Bristol after his return from Germany.

One more piece of evidence helps to highlight the centrality of Aldersgate in Wesley's *Journal*. Wesley's second *Journal* closed with an account of his visit to Herrnhut, and, in what forms the longest part of this account, he reported 'the substance of several conversations' he had with Moravian converts. Thus, the same instalment of his *Journal* that recorded his Aldersgate experience concluded with eleven autobiographical conversion narratives parallel to his own. These narratives, like his own, rehearsed the converts' sense of their own inability to vanquish sin in their own strength. Christian David said, 'I did all I could to conquer sin; yet it profited not; I was still conquered by it,' and David Nitschmann confessed similarly, 'I continually strove; but was continually conquered.' Albinus Theodorus Feder complained, 'I was on the very brink of despair'; Wenzel Neisser lamented, 'I could not gain full victory over my sins'; and David Schneider admitted, 'Many sins got the dominion over me.'[130] These statements of acute spiritual inadequacy reinforced the picture Wesley had drawn of himself prior to Aldersgate. Like Wesley's own narrative, the converts'

---

[128] Ward, Introduction, Wesley, *Works* (BE), xviii. 39.
[129] Ibid. 41.
[130] Ibid. 274, 282, 284, 286, 287.

accounts went on to recount their experience of pardon for their sins. Christian David found the gospel of Christ came 'with power to my soul' and he found peace: 'I was assured *my* sins were forgiven.'[131] In this account, and in several others, Wesley called for the printer's italic type to emphasize the same personal pronoun that he had earlier stressed in his own autobiographical narrative, when he wrote of the assurance given him that Christ had taken away '*my* sins, even *mine*, and saved *me*'. Although there were differing views on assurance among the German converts, their language emphasized the climactic nature of conversion. 'Immediately my burden dropped off,' said Michael Linner, and 'in that hour' Nitschmann broke through to full assurance. 'In that moment' Wenzel Neisser laid hold of Christ as '*my* Saviour', and 'in that moment' Christoph Demuth was filled with peace and joy.[132] Even those who found assurance grow stronger only by degrees could still arrive, like David Schneider or Augustin Neisser, at a certainty that their sins were forgiven. Wesley's Aldersgate experience was, in a sense, reinscribed eleven times at the close of his second *Journal*. It was not an isolated or passing experience: it was a model.

Moreover, the Aldersgate account prefigured hundreds of shorter narratives that recurred in Wesley's record of his ministry in the *Journal* and the *Arminian Magazine*.[133] The expansion of Methodism recounted by Wesley was constituted precisely by the repeated occurrence of this or that person arriving at a perceptible experience of divine grace, whether in pardon for sin or through instantaneous sanctification. The experience that Wesley's ministry reproduced, as narrated in the *Journal* and elsewhere, was distinctively Aldersgate-like. The account given by Wesley in his second *Journal* on 24 May 1738 was undeniably therefore an evangelical conversion narrative that belongs within the family of narratives discussed in this book, including not only the various examples from the eighteenth-century revivals, but also the accounts we have from the antecedent Puritan and Pietist traditions. It remains, however, to ask whether Wesley's narrative was distinctive in certain ways, and whether his self-understanding changed in later years.[134]

---

[131] Ibid. 274.

[132] Ibid. 281, 283, 285, 289.

[133] See e.g. the entries s.v. 'conversion' in the index to *Journal of John Wesley*, ed. Nehemiah Curnock (1909–16), viii. 378.

[134] Methodist scholars in particular have been keenly interested in this question since it impinges so strongly on Methodist identity today. The 250th anniversary in 1988 provoked a renewed debate on the question. See Jean Miller Schmidt, '"Strangely Warmed": The Place of Aldersgate in the Methodist Canon', in Maddox (ed.), *Aldersgate Reconsidered*, 109–19. See also Kenneth J. Collins, 'Twentieth-Century Interpretations of John Wesley's Aldersgate Experience: Coherence or Confusion?' *Wesleyan Theological Journal* 24 (1989), 18–31; David L. Cubie, 'Placing Aldersgate in John Wesley's Order of Salvation', *Wesleyan Theological*

Wesley's Ethos as a Journalist

Because Wesley's *Journal* was a serial publication, his project of self-interpretation was, like George Whitefield's, ongoing. We have noted how theorists of autobiography speak of the *autos* (the authorial 'self'), the *bios* (the past life as 'subject'), and the *graphe* (the literary representation of the life).[135] In the case of Wesley's autobiography, we must picture these components set in motion, the pieces shifted and rearranged as time passes. One of the consequences of this change of perspective over time was significant revision on Wesley's part, despite his reluctance in dispute ever to admit that he had changed his views. Most noticeably, in the 1774 corrected edition of his earlier *Journals*, he added significant disclaimers to some of his remarks in 1740. For example, in 1740 he wrote of the period before Aldersgate, 'I who went to America to convert others, was never myself converted to God,' but then in 1774 he added the commentary, 'I am not sure of this.'[136] This is but one example of many parallel emendations in the 1774 and 1775 editions of his *Journal*, and it reflects his mature view that there were degrees of faith. He came to describe this as the difference between the faith of a servant, on the one hand, which is weak and subject to fear, and the faith of a son, on the other, which is full of confidence. There was thus more than one *autos*, a different one in 1774 than in 1740. As Wesley's views on assurance changed, so, subtly, did the shape of his narrative self-interpretation. Upon consideration, he flattened the curve into his Aldersgate crisis and allowed for degrees of faith on the part of a Christian.[137] This sort of revision is a unique feature of the journal form, and it emphasizes the essentially interpretative nature of self-writing, despite its initial plausibility as a self-evidencing factual narrative. The creative, reflective self intervenes between the experience of conversion and the conversion of that experience into text.

In retrospective autobiography this potential for autobiographical revision is concealed, since the author writes from one vantage point. In contrast, Isabel Rivers has noted how serialization emphasized that Wesley's quest was never complete.[138] With its ongoing publication, its complex

---

Journal 24 (1989), 32–53; Randy L. Maddox, 'Celebrating Wesley—When?' *Methodist History* 29 (1991), 63–75; Kenneth J. Collins, 'Other Thoughts on Aldersgate: Has the Conversionist Paradigm Collapsed?' *Methodist History* 30 (1991), 10–25; Randy L. Maddox, 'Continuing the Conversation', *Methodist History* 30 (1991), 235–41.

[135] James Olney, 'Autobiography and the Cultural Moment', in James Olney (ed.), *Autobiography: Essays Theoretical and Critical* (Princeton, NJ, 1980), 6.

[136] Wesley, *Works* (BE), xviii. 214.

[137] Heitzenrater, 'Great Expectations', 84–91.

[138] Isabel Rivers, '"Strangers and Pilgrims": Sources and Patterns of Methodist Narrative', in J. D. Hilson, M. M. B. Jones, and J. R. Watson (eds.), *Augustan Worlds* (Leicester, 1978), 194.

textual history, and its multiple recensions, Wesley's *Journal* was more open-ended. The journal form was particularly appropriate, therefore, to someone who was the leader or trailblazer of a movement, the first one to venture into uncharted territory, because it was a form equal to his hermeneutical intentions. Moreover, it suits what we know of Wesley's epistemology (outside his rhetorical posture in debate): that is, that he placed a premium on the careful observation of spiritual experience. He was particularly careful to observe cases of white-hot piety in which people seemed to come into some kind of direct contact with God and to be overwhelmed and transformed by that experience. As a result, his journal is also something like a social-scientific journal, as Wesley recorded his data, took down notes and probed various frontiers of religious knowledge along the way, and published his findings to the wider world.

THE ROLE OF THE JOURNAL IN EARLY METHODISM

The *Journals* of Whitefield and Wesley were enormously important for directing the course of the revival and stirring up similar experiences on the part of others. In February 1745 Whitefield met a minister near Boston who claimed that his *Journals* had been instrumental in his conversion.[139] Wesley and Whitefield both knew the mimetic power of personal testimony. Wesley included an account of the revival at Everton in his *Journal* in which the correspondent said, 'Nothing I can say makes so much impression on myself or others, as thus repeating my own conversion.'[140] Whitefield wrote likewise, 'Experience daily convinces devout souls, that nothing has a more immediate tendency to affect themselves . . . than an artless, humble narration of the many favours, spiritual or temporal, which they have received from him.'[141]

The most striking example of this comes from John Cennick, who recalled the deep impression such autobiographical narration made upon him: 'About the latter End of the Year 1738, one lent me a Part of Mr. *Whitefield's* Journal, to whom I was then a Stranger, and much against my Will I read it . . . But when I read the Place where he mentions the Woman, *who had been in the Pangs of New Birth*, my Heart cleav'd to him; believing him not unacquainted with that bitter Cup, the Dregs of which I had long been drinking.'[142] He immediately laid down the book and prayed that God would allow him to come to know Whitefield. When Whitefield returned from Georgia and Cennick heard he was in London, he

---

[139] *GWJ* 546.
[140] Wesley, *Works* (BE), xxi. 220.
[141] *GWJ* 74.
[142] *The Life of Mr. J. Cennick* (Bristol, 1745), 28.

walked all night to get there. They met together at Hutton's house the next morning, and Cennick said, 'I met my dear brother, and fell on his neck and kissed him.' They spent several days together and felt their communion to be 'sweet continually'.[143]

This then is another example of how powerfully an autobiographical text could function in the revival to stimulate parallel experience and allow the formation of a narrative community. Indeed, Cennick himself emerged as a powerful lay evangelist in his own right at Kingswood and then rural Gloucestershire and the West Country. True to form as another early Methodist preacher, he kept a journal[144] and in 1745 published a spiritual autobiography with an account of his conversion. (It was distributed by the usual Methodist booksellers, John Lewis and James Hutton.) And he too used his own conversion experience as an exemplum for others. Preaching in London in 1743, he apostrophized to the sin-sick hearer or reader, 'My dear Fellow-sinner, what I have been speaking as the Language of thy Heart, was a few Years ago the Language of my own . . . ' and then launched into personal testimony.[145] The laywoman Anne Beaker responded to this sort of preaching, and her conversion narrative, published by Cennick, added one more link in the chain.[146] Summing up this narrative culture, Cennick wrote, '[Saying] thus hath God done for my Soul, hath been blessed to me, and not to me only.'[147]

Wesley and Whitefield were not then the only early Methodist leaders to keep diaries or to publish journals. We noted above that William Seward published a voyage journal and Benjamin Ingham wrote a journal letter. Ingham was also an avid diarist.[148] The early Methodist preacher John Bennet likewise began a diary in 1742, which he later drew upon, like Cennick, to write an autobiography.[149] But the most remarkable diary for

---

[143] *The Life and Hymns of John Cennick,* ed. J. R. Broome (Harpenden, Herts, 1988), p. xxxix.

[144] *Extracts from the Journals of John Cennick,* ed. J. H. Cooper (Glengormley, Co. Antrim, 1996).

[145] John Cennick, *The Bloody Issue Healed* (1744), 10–11.

[146] John Cennick, *A Short Account of the Experience of Mrs. Anne Beaker* (1744). Cf. the remarkable conversion narrative, in verse, running to more than 66 quatrains of iambic pentameter, also published and endorsed by Cennick, *A Brief Account of God's Dealings with Edward Godwin. Written by Himself* (2nd corrected edn., Bristol, 1744). Godwin described his turning point thus: 'In this sad State I was; when Light broke in, | I felt the heavy Burden of my Sin | Immediate leave me, like a loosen'd Load, | And Faith was giv'n me in the Saviour's Blood.' (Ibid. 18.)

[147] Ibid. p. iii.

[148] *Diary of an Oxford Methodist,* ed. Heitzenrater.

[149] *Mirror of the Soul: The Diary of an Early Methodist Preacher, John Bennet (1714–1754),* ed. Simon Valentine (Werrington, Peterborough, 2002); Simon Valentine, *John Bennet and the Origins of Methodism and the Evangelical Revival in England* (1997), 5–11.

sheer bulk is that of Howell Harris, who began to keep a diary after his conversion in 1735. No less than 284 volumes are extant in manuscript.[150] Once Wesley began to gather lay preachers to assist him in the Methodist work, and to suggest at the first conference in 1744 that they should keep personal diaries, the pattern was set.[151] Several of these lay preachers, such as John Nelson, followed Wesley's lead and published their own *Journals*. Among the Moravians, too, the leaders kept ongoing diaries, which were distinct from the memoirs of the lay members.[152]

In summary, the early Methodist leaders may be distinguished in part not only by their experience but by the fact that they almost all *recorded* that experience. In W. R. Ward's words, 'The movements of renewal and revival of the eighteenth century sought their legitimation in the hand of God in history; their characteristic achievement was not, like the Reformers of the sixteenth century, to offer a confession of faith for public discussion, but to accumulate archives which would support their understanding.'[153] They did this, of course, through letters, but they also did so through a genre they discovered almost accidentally. The private diary for spiritual improvement became the public journal through the precedent of nautical journalism and the preoccupation of the public with journalism in various forms. The practice was so common among them, and unpublished manuscripts were spreading so widely, that General Oglethorpe could complain to Charles Wesley of 'the mischief of private journals'.[154] In today's terms, it was as if recordings of private conversations were being circulated—and stirring up strong feelings. In any case, the early Methodists soon discovered the journal to be a powerful instrument to defend and promote revival. It was a new or adapted form for a new movement, and serial publication was appropriate to the leaders of the movement whose religious experience was path-breaking and a model for others.

While the journal was the distinctive literary form for the autobiographical reflection of the early Methodist leaders, evangelical conversion was the distinctive content. Their own experience of conversion led to their calling as itinerant preachers of gospel, and in this calling they sought above all to reproduce authentic conversion among their hearers. Though different in form, the records of their lay followers suggest that they were successful.

[150] Geraint Tudur, *Howell Harris* (Cardiff, 2000), 1–12.

[151] *Mirror of the Soul*, 1.

[152] See e.g. Jacob Rogers's diary in Edwin Welch (ed.), *The Bedford Moravian Church in the Eighteenth Century* (Bedford, 1989), 55–74.

[153] Ward, *Protestant Evangelical Awakening*, 2.

[154] *CWJ* i. 66.

4

White-Hot Piety: The Early Methodist Laypeople

AUTOBIOGRAPHICAL practice (oral and literary) had an important place in the evangelical movement from the beginning, and there was a close relationship between the journals of the leaders and the experience of their followers. Lay converts responded very early with their own narratives, expressed in their own terms. Typically, however, they turned not to journals to give voice to their experience, but to oral testimony in band meetings or to familiar letters written to the very Methodist preachers whose message had first awakened and converted them. These lay narratives of conversion were thus written 'white hot' in the heat of experience and forged into evangelical shape largely under the oversight of their Methodist pastors.

LAY TESTIMONY: LETTERS TO CHARLES WESLEY

This surge of intense religious experience may be observed in a remarkable collection of lay narratives in manuscript. A little-known scrapbook at the John Rylands Library, Manchester, contains 151 items, most of which are letters to Charles Wesley. The provenance of the collection in its present form is not known, but the manuscripts date from 1738 up to a few weeks before Charles Wesley's death in 1788.[1] The archive includes forty-one conversion narratives, forty accounts of pious deaths, and nine reports of deathbed conversions (including two of dying malefactors). There are also ten accounts of illness or suffering, two third-person memoirs, and a few letters reporting what evangelicals often called remarkable or alarming providences (a gentlewoman who mysteriously burned to death in her chamber, the narrow escape of many at Newcastle from a flash flood, etc.). The balance of the collection consists of correspondence related largely to controversial issues in early Methodism such as the apocalyptic frenzy inspired by Thomas Maxfield and George Bell in 1762–3 and the schism that followed.

---

[1] Three items from the nineteenth century were added to the collection at a later date. Documents from the collection are cited in this chapter by name and date.

These manuscripts were almost certainly preserved by Charles Wesley himself over the course of his ministry, and the collection itself provides another example of the way in which evangelicals looked to discern the hand of God in history in their generation—not only through journals, but also through letters.[2] As Charles Wesley wrote in his own journal on one occasion: 'While the letters were reading, we had a glimpse of the felicity of God's chosen, and rejoiced in the gladness of his people, and gave thanks with his inheritance.'[3] The common theme among the letters is therefore of spiritual experience, and the preponderance of evangelical conversions and deaths, beginnings and endings, points to these as special loci for discerning evidence of the supernatural operation of the Holy Spirit in particular persons. God could likewise be seen to act in judgment or mercy in 'remarkable providences', just as his presence could be discerned in a special way among those who bore illness and suffering with pious resignation. John Prickard remembered Charles Wesley once saying, 'Young and healthy Christians are generally called to glorify God by being *active* in *doing* his will; but old and sick Christians in *suffering* it.'[4] In these several forms, then, it appears that Charles Wesley wished to document the work of God as he had witnessed it over the course of the fifty years between his conversion and his own death.

Conversion appears in this collection as a special case of the more general category of spiritual experience that Wesley wished to record and preserve. One indication that conversion narrative was thus a special case—and not just one form of spiritual experience among many—is the fact that Charles Wesley not only preserved the letters containing conversion accounts but also solicited them in the first place. Martha Jones wrote to him reluctantly in 1740, beginning, 'I should have been very glad if I had been excused from this task . . . [but] I knew it was my duty to obey you as my spiritual pastor.' James Hewitt in 1741 began, saying, 'Honoured Sir, In complyance with your Request I have Sent you the following Account.' Nathaniel Hurst likewise wrote about the same time, 'Reverend Sir, according to your Desiring I shall give an [account] how the Lord has Dealt with my soul.'[5] Charles Wesley thus had a leading role in initiating and superintending these lay autobiographies.

A further indication of the importance of these narratives as validation of the present work of the Spirit of God was that Charles Wesley referred to

---

[2] One of the letters, E. Bristow (12 Apr. 1740), EMV, is reproduced in *CWJ* i. 217–18. Its context suggests that Charles Wesley solicited these testimonies as evidence by which to oppose Moravian 'stillness' and to validate his own ministry.

[3] *CWJ* i. 285.

[4] *AM* 12 (1789), 182.

[5] Martha Jones (1 June 1740), James Hewitt [Nov. 1740], and Nathaniel Hurst [1741], EMV.

them specifically as 'seals to my ministry'. During this period, Charles was clearly an influential evangelist in his own right, and many converts placed him above his brother as a preacher and spiritual director. For his part, he gauged his own vocation by the response of those who heard him. On 20 May 1740, he wrote in his journal, 'The work of grace goes on in several that were with me to-day; and God still gives fresh seals to my ministry.'[6] Margaret Austin wrote to him about her spiritual experience at this same time, and her letter is annotated in the collection by another hand (presumably by Charles Wesley himself) at the bottom of the final page: 'Marg Austin's Experience: A Seal'.[7] Martha Claggett's letter in 1738 includes the similar annotation: 'one of the First Witnesses'.[8] Some years later, on 14 July 1745, Charles Wesley felt particular power in his preaching and remarked in his journal that God had 'set his seal' while he spoke. The entry in his journal the next day demonstrates the relationship that letters, such as those of Margaret Austin or Martha Claggett, bore to his sense of divine authority: 'The Lord comforted our hearts by the letters, and confirmed our faith, that the work he is now reviving shall never be destroyed.'[9] For Charles Wesley, then, letters of spiritual experience were considered an important validation of the Evangelical Revival in general and of his ministry in particular.

The result is that we have superb evidence in these letters for the character and formation of early Methodist autobiographical culture. Except for a handful of letters, the conversion accounts in the collection at the John Rylands Library were written between the years 1738 and 1741 by lay Methodists from London and Bristol. A little more than half the accounts are from women. Most of the writers appear to have been members of band meetings. The names of 'Sister Robinson' and 'Brother Edmunds' come up in a number of the London narratives, and these were likely the lay leaders of the respective women's and men's bands to which several of the converts belonged.[10] Of those whose age could be determined, most were in their twenties or early thirties when they were converted, though two women were clearly in their fifties. The occupation and social status of the letter writers is more difficult to discern, though two women were schoolmistresses and several of the men were apprentices to trades such as joinery. Martha Claggett, one of the women in her fifties, was described as a

[6] Cf. *CWJ* i. 270, 286, 401.

[7] Margaret Austin (19 May 1740), EMV.

[8] Martha Claggett (24 July 1738), EMV.

[9] *CWJ* i. 401.

[10] Wesley refers to a Mrs Robinson or Sister Robinson of London in his diary in 1739 and 1740, Wesley, *Works* (BE), xix. 372, 387, 425. John Edmunds (or 'Edmonds') recurs also in Wesley's journal and diary during this period, but in 1742 Edmunds appears as one of the founding members of the Moravian Congregation in London. Ibid., xix. 65n., 130–1; Daniel Benham, *Memoirs of James Hutton* (1856), 90.

gentlewoman. There is little evidence of the involvement of an amanuensis in any of these accounts, and the crude handwriting and uneven orthography of many letters points to these being the autographs of the converts themselves. Indeed, a few of the letters point to a very low level of literacy. Elizabeth Hinsome, for example, scored her paper with horizontal lines to guide her unsteady hand, wrote without any punctuation whatever, and had more than usual difficulty with spelling. Her spelling was often phonetic, so that 'forgiven' was written as 'for giveing', and the pronoun 'who' as the Welsh name 'huw'.[11] Elizabeth Sayce offers a good example of what can be lost in the transmission between different levels of literacy. She had evidently heard a preacher such as Charles Wesley quote the biblical text of Habakkuk 3: 2, 'O LORD, revive thy work in the midst of the years,' but what she wrote was that she had told her neighbours 'what a Strange Work the Lord was Reviving in the Midst of the Ears'.[12]

This collection thus has a special significance for the way in which it comprises the diverse testimony of women and men, those literate and barely literate, and persons of higher and lower ranks in society. These documents are also significant as sources for the genesis of the Evangelical Revival in England, since they are early and unedited sources from the period when the movement was first undivided and then experienced its initial partisan divisions in 1739 and 1740. With these narratives we are able to view the Evangelical Revival in its origins 'from below'. The voices of the preachers who would stand 'upon a little eminence' and address the crowds are heard in their journals and sermons; the voices of the hearers in the crowds who followed are heard in these letters. And because the letters were contemporary accounts written in the initial ardour of the experience, there is an immediacy and artlessness in these narratives that sets them apart from the more carefully circumscribed conversion accounts in the published journals of the leaders or the retrospective memoirs of the lay preachers published during the 1780s in the *Arminian Magazine*.

Charismatic Joy

The first and most important observation to be made from this collection of lay manuscripts is that they illustrate the profoundly charismatic nature of the early revival, when all seemed to walk in a cloud of wonders. These women and men had a keen sense that God had conferred his favour upon them in a direct, immediate way, beyond anything that they deserved, and as a result these letters are marked by a note of spontaneous joy. Margaret Austin exclaimed, 'I had Such Joy that I could Scarce forbear Speaking' out

[11] Elizabeth Hinsome (25 May 1740), EMV.

[12] Elizabeth Sayce [May 1742], EMV; cf. Jonathan Barry and Kenneth Morgan (eds.), *Reformation and Revival in Eighteenth-Century Bristol* (Bristol, 1994), 95.

loud in the meeting. The rushing parataxis of Elizabeth Hinsome's style bears its own witness to her similar fervour when she wrote, 'I trembeld and should have fell done but the peopel heald me up and I was out of my senses but the lord a wakened me with peace be unto you your sins are for giveing you. I went home full of joye not knowing ware to bestow my self . . . I am lost in wonder when I see what god has done for my soul.' Maria Price was a burdened soul who wrote of the relief she experienced through conversion: 'I as planly felt a burden taken off my heart as I could feel one took of[f] my back . . . I trembled so with joy and Cried.'[13] Thomas Cooper was similarly effusive: 'I felt my heart hopen within me and like a fountain of water run from it and in that moment I felt such Love, peace, and joy past all expresen. We Sang a him [and] I thought I was out of the bodey with the angels in heaven for I was so full of joy I Could not express my Selves.' Samuel Webb claimed that for three months running he experienced what he called 'a Glowing and Bigness in my Brest'. When Joseph Carter described his conversion, it was in kinetic terms: 'I burst out a Crying, and Laughing, and Dancing, and Jumping about the Room.'[14] The spontaneous, ecstatic quality of the converts' joy was often described as inexpressible or uncontainable, beyond the normal boundaries of speech and experience. There was often an unspoken allusion in their writings to the phrase 'joy unspeakable and full of glory' from 1 Peter 1: 8—a favourite text in the revival, and one that Jonathan Edwards would use as a basis for his treatise on the *Religious Affections*.

Most of these examples come from the early awakenings, about 1738–41, but one of the most intensely ecstatic accounts derives from the perfectionist revival in 1762. John Walsh was a lay Methodist who described his experience to Charles Wesley upon hearing a few lines of a hymn: 'I felt a Palpitation at the bottom of my Stomach, and a small giddyness in my Head; the Lord also gave me his peace at the Same time.' But this was not all: 'In a few Minutes, the Spirit of the Lord so abundantly filled me that I sat down in an Elbow chair, prayed silently for an entire deliverance from the power of Sin, breathed short, and panted in the multitude of Peace from 7 o'Clock till 1/4 past 8.' He felt he might be about to die suddenly, so overpowering was the experience, but it was delightful too, and he did not want it to stop. He described it as having an electric intensity: 'I felt as if Lightning, or a slower etherial Flame, had been penetrating and rolling thro every Atom of my Body.' In the end, he walked about the room rejoicing, with his body feeling so light 'that I might choose whether to walk or fly'.[15]

---

[13] Margaret Austin (19 May 1740), Elizabeth Hinsome (25 May 1740), and Maria Price (18 May 1740), EMV.

[14] Thomas Cooper [1741], Samuel Webb [Nov. 1741], and Joseph Carter [Nov. 1741], EMV.

[15] John Walsh (11 Aug. 1762), EMV.

Walsh referred to this as his 'unaccountable experience'. Though not all the experiences of the early lay Methodist had this level of intensity, most shared a keen sense that spiritual joy had come to them spontaneously and immediately.

The Novelty of the Medium: The New Evangelical Homiletic

These narratives expressed a common experience of spontaneous joy, but this experience was itself part of a new religious self-understanding. Indeed, novelty is a key note in these narratives. The converts wrote again and again that what they heard from the early Methodist leaders was new to them, an unprecedented message communicated in unprecedented ways. Most of those who wrote to Charles Wesley first encountered the novelty of Methodism through the preaching of George Whitefield in 1739, before his second voyage to America, and particularly through his outdoor preaching, which began at the end of April. Margaret Austin first heard Whitefield preach in London when his popularity was waxing in January 1739. She also went to hear him in Moorfields. She could remember the sermons distinctly and remarked, 'Though I went to Church as often as I Could I never was struck in such a manner as then.' Martha Jones heard Whitefield four times before he left for Georgia, and this prompted a new sense of spiritual anxiety for her. As a result, she said, 'The preaching in the churches afforded me no comfort.'[16]

For many of the converts, hearing Whitefield marked the beginning of their spiritual history. Elizabeth Hinsome's letter to Charles Wesley began abruptly, 'I was a Pharisee but god was plest to convince me by hearing Mr Witfeald sermon, that I may know him and the power of his resurrection.' Ann Martin claimed that God used Whitefield as 'the first Instrument' in drawing her to Christ. Sarah Middleton likewise spoke of hearing Whitefield as a spiritual initiation. She expressed her thanks to God for 'first drawing me to hear Mr Whitefeld' and remarked that she 'could not keep from hearing him where ever he went'. Sarah Barber confessed the same sense of calling: 'The Lord was pleased to Call me first by the ministry of Mr Whitefield.' Nathaniel Hurst chose to begin his narrative, saying, 'When first the Lord sent Mr. Whitfield out into the fields I went to hear him in moorfields.'[17] Hearing Whitefield was, in his case, literally the start of his spiritual narrative.

One of the most consistent traces that Whitefield's spectacular preaching left in the written testimonies of laypeople was the vividness with which they recollected his sermons. The most remarkable sermon recollections in

[16] Margaret Austin (19 May 1740) and Martha Jones (1 June 1740) EMV.
[17] Elizabeth Hinsome (25 May 1740), Ann Martin [1740], Sarah Middleton (25 May 1740), Sarah Barber [May 1740], and Nathaniel Hurst [1741], EMV.

these letters came from Mary Ramsay, a schoolmistress who wrote to Charles Wesley about a year after first hearing Whitefield on 2 June 1739 at Hackney. A full two pages of her narrative consists of a sermon diary. She was a true Whitefield devotee and heard him thirteen times during the summer of 1739 in various locations about London, mostly south of the Thames. Moreover, she went to hear him and the other field preachers even though this cost her the respect of her acquaintances and meant that several withdrew their children from her school. It may be that she kept a diary, and that this underlying document provided the structure for her conversion narrative as a series of sermon reports. But the impact of the sermons was none the less for that, and she was no mere stenographer. 'I would go home in a Great hurry with a Great Deal of the Sermons in my head,' she claimed, 'So that I Could repeat half or Sometimes three-quarters of the Discourse.'[18]

The field preaching of Whitefield and others was clearly a novelty and a powerful attraction for many of these early converts. Sarah Barber had missed hearing him the first time at Moorfields, when he preached in the open air, and so, she said, 'My Curiosity was the Stronger to return.' Mary Ramsay said that she 'very much admired him' and when a finely dressed gentleman standing beside her began to heckle Whitefield on one occasion, she cut him off sharply and told him to his face that he was an infidel. In between sermons she had a 'Longing Desire' to hear him again.[19] Some of this was sheer spectacle, as Whitefield's critics liked to point out. Zachary Grey claimed, 'I have heard of an *old Woman*, who tho' out of the Reach of his Voice, seem'd to be much affected with Mr. *Whitefield's* preaching. A *Gentleman* who stood next to her, told her, He could not hear one Word, and ask'd her, if she could. No, Sir, said she, *But see what a heavenly Wag he has with his Head*. Another was moved by his *heavenly Leer*, as she called it.'[20] It was not, however, only the women who were attracted to Whitefield. The lay preacher Thomas Olivers was first awakened by Whitefield, and his devotion was complete: 'The love I had for Mr. Whitefield was inexpressible. I used to follow him as he walked the streets, and could scarce refrain from kissing the very prints of his feet.'[21]

And yet, as the detailed sermon reports in these lay narratives indicate, there was much more to this religious phenomenon in 1739 than histrionics from the preacher and frenzy or gawking on the part of the followers. It is possible to overstate the modernity of Whitefield's theatrical rhetoric and its adaptability to a mobile consumer society, for the evidence of these letters

[18] Mary Ramsay (4 June 1740), EMV.
[19] Sarah Barber [May 1740] and Mary Ramsay (4 June 1740), EMV.
[20] Zachary Grey, *The Quaker and Methodist Compared* (London, 1740), 94 n.
[21] *AM* 2 (1779), 85.

is that converts heard a profoundly doctrinal message. Consistently, these converts wrote not only about the novelty of the medium but also of the message. They remarked that they were surprised to learn that 'going to church and sacrament' and 'doing no harm' did not fulfil their religious obligations. This is why we find the recurring trope of 'Pharisee' as a description of their state before they encountered this shattering message. Sarah Middleton told Charles Wesley that she 'used to rest in going to church and Sacrament but now I do not rest upon them but upon Christ Jesus my Lord and My God'. Joan Webb likewise claimed to have always sought to live a sober life: 'I kept to my church and Sacrament every Sunday.' But after hearing some of the Methodist preachers, her self-evaluation changed, and she wrote, '[I] was fully convinced that I did not Love God.'[22]

In 1738 and 1739 Charles Wesley preached his sermon on the 'three states' at least twenty-one times.[23] In this sermon he identified three clearly demarcated possibilities for the hearer. One was either in a state of sin and death, in the state of 'an imperfect life', or in a state of true spiritual health and vigour: 'The first is a state of rest and acquiescence in sin; the second is a state of contention; the third is a state of victory.'[24] In the course of describing those in the first state, Wesley stressed that both the brazenly sinful and those with 'a little outward religion' were alike but 'baptised heathens'.[25] Thus it was that the laywoman Sarah Middleton looked back upon her life before conversion with disgust: 'We went to church and Did all the outward things [but] we were but baptised heathens.'[26]

It is important to bear in mind that most of the lay converts who wrote to Charles Wesley had a religious upbringing and a sense of at least nominal adherence to the Established Church.[27] When Charles Wesley addressed his hearers, he could speak to them about 'the moment of our baptism', and assume that they were all baptized and therefore formally Christian.[28] James Hewitt claimed that he was nearly 21 years of age before he had any solid thoughts of God or religion, but this was exceptional. Most of the converts were more like Nathaniel Hurst, who spoke of having had 'a form of

---

[22] Sarah Middleton (25 May 1740) and Joan Webb [May 1742], EMV.

[23] The sermon was based upon 1 John 3: 14: 'We know that we have passed from death unto life, because we love the brethren. He that loveth not his brother abideth in death.' *The Sermons of Charles Wesley*, ed. Kenneth G. C. Newport (Oxford, 2001), 130–51.

[24] Ibid. 134.

[25] Ibid. 136.

[26] Sarah Middleton (25 May 1740), EMV.

[27] Mary Ramsay had a religious upbringing but appears to have been Huguenot, referring to her first communion at 15 years of age in 'the French Church'. Ramsay (4 June 1740), EMV.

[28] *Sermons of Charles Wesley*, 135.

Godliness', or Thomas Cooper and Taverner Wallis, who remembered
'drawings' of God in their youth.[29] Moreover, most of the conversion
narratives written to Charles Wesley point to a high view of the sacrament,
and many found their first religious concern aroused by the need to prepare
properly for devout reception. As Hurst put it, '[I] did not dare to come to it
without prepareing my self.'[30] Fragments of text from the Prayer Book
occasionally find their way into the language of the converts, as when Mary
Ramsay asked Charles Wesley to 'Pray that the Lord would Cleans my heart
by the inspirations of his holy Spirit,' or when Thomas Cooper recalled
hearing a still small voice echoing the 'words of comfort' from Matt. 11: 28
and 1 Tim. 1: 15.[31] Several attended and communicated at St Lawrence
Jewry in the heart of the city, and at least one layman was involved in a religious society nearby in Miles Lane. Notwithstanding the post-conversion
rhetoric, pouring scorn upon the preconversion faith as something nominal,
many of these laypeople were far from irreligious before they became
Methodist. This is how Martha Jones described her upbringing:

I was brought up in all the outward duties of religion. At the age of fourteen I was
confirmed and solicited by my parents to receive the holy Sacrament. My father
had taken care to provide me books of instruction, the authors of wich [*sic*] were, as
he called them sound churchmen. Thus I went on for some time and thought
I should be saved for these things.[32]

As a Methodist convert, she of course looked back on this period of her life
as one in which she had only a 'shadow of goodness' and 'the form of
godliness'. But in that shadowy morality and formal piety were embedded a
great many assumptions and anxieties that would be, as it were, at the
fingertips of the Methodist clergy, and that would allow these laypeople
to be prime candidates for evangelical conversion. As Haddon Wilmer
expressed it, 'The common background of thought was, humanly speaking,
evangelicalism's most powerful instrument of evangelism. It created the
need for the Evangel.'[33]

W. M. Jacob concludes his study of lay religion in the period by saying,
'The Church of England in the first half of the eighteenth century was a
communal Church to which the greater part of the population actively
adhered, and it was a Church in which the laity played a full part.'[34] But the

---

[29] James Hewitt [Nov. 1741], Nathaniel Hurst [1741], Thomas Cooper [1741], and
Taverner Wallis [Nov. 1741], EMV.

[30] Nathaniel Hurst [1741], EMV.

[31] Mary Ramsay (4 June 1740) and Thomas Cooper [1741], EMV.

[32] Martha Jones (1 June 1740), EMV.

[33] Haddon Willmer, 'Evangelicalism, 1785–1835', unpublished Hulsean Prize Essay
(Cambridge, 1962), 20.

[34] W. M. Jacob, *Lay People and Religion in the Early Eighteenth Century* (Cambridge,
1996), 227.

keynote in Jacob's analysis is the notion of a 'communal Church' and a form of lay piety he describes as adherence. This, however, was exactly the religious condition that Whitefield and the other early Methodist evangelists pointedly challenged by their preaching in 1738 and afterward. From their perspective, to be only an adherent was to be an 'almost Christian'.

The Novelty of the Message: 'The Spirituality and Extent of the Law'

What the lay converts heard as a novelty in the preaching of the Methodist clergy was the idea that the demands of God's law were much more stringent than they ever imagined. William Turner said, after reading the discourses of the evangelical clergyman William Romaine, 'I had been shewn the spirituality of the Law.' Joseph Carter likewise had become 'more and more convinced of the Spirituality of Religion but could not find it in my self'. Sarah Middleton heard John Wesley preach on 10 September 1739 from Acts 16: 3: 'What must I do to be saved?' She recalled, 'He explained the ten Commandments which wounded me so much that I was hardly able to stand under him for I thought I had kept them ... from my youth up, but hearing them explained I felt I had broke all of them, so that I could take no rest night nor day by reason of that load of sin which I felt within me.' She went on to explain that the law had now come to her 'in a spiritual meaning'. James Hewitt likewise discovered that he had violated every command of God, except perhaps murder, but even that 'in the Spiritual Sence a thousand times'.[35] This was a personal appropriation of the doctrine of 'the spirituality and extent of the law' as preached by the Methodist evangelists. God's moral scrutiny and judgment extended beyond religious observance and public moral propriety. It extended to one's thoughts and intentions and to every sphere of endeavour, public and private, sacred and secular. Whitefield's preaching, and that of the Wesleys, seemed to name and call into being a new sense of interiority for these converts, a new space of moral and spiritual agency.

These laypeople found this to be a novel and upsetting message. It awakened them to the extent of their religious obligations and made them more serious about their spiritual condition, especially when this declaration of God's law was coupled with the sanctions of traditional eschatology. From the testimony of the lay converts, it is evident that Whitefield did not always expound the idea of original sin in a particularly delicate or polite manner. Mary Ramsay vividly remembered him saying that his hearers were half beasts and half devils. Margaret Austin took this to heart: 'I was really half a beast and half a Devill.' This was a devastating conclusion for these laypeople, since this left their consciences exposed to the full terror of divine

---

[35] William Turner (9 March 1756), Joseph Carter [Nov. 1741], Sarah Middleton (25 May 1740), and James Hewitt [Nov. 1741], EMV.

wrath and judgment. As Charles Wesley told his hearers in one of his sermons, 'You must own and feel yourselves to be utterly lost without Christ, to be lost, undone and damned forever.'[36] Indeed, nothing better illustrates how widespread were the Christian assumptions that prevailed in eighteenth-century English society than the fact that religiously observant laypeople were so quick to feel the guilt of their sins under evangelical preaching and then to fear that they would be damned to a literal hell. Nathaniel Hurst said, 'I used to think that the ground whereon I stood was hot under me which made me almost to tremble and to think if the ground should open and swallow me up I should perish forever.' Mary Ramsay worried when she went to bed at night, 'lest I should never awake. I felt the pangs of hell and misery very plain.' Elizabeth Sayce likewise claimed, 'When I went to Bed I feared I should be in Hell before the Morning.' Such a conviction of sin and judgment was for many converts completely absorbing. 'I saw nothing but hell and Damnation before me,' wrote Sarah Barber. Sarah Middleton related this same conviction directly to her wounded conscience: 'I felt my self so vile that I thought hell was ready to swallow me up.'[37]

This was the first surprise recounted in these lay narratives: the converts' discovery that devout adherence to the public observances of the Church of England and conventional moral rectitude were no better than hypocrisy. This alarming message of the early Methodist preachers introduced a new period of anxiety that upset the religious status quo. As Mary Thomas put it in 1742, 'When I went to Church I seldom found any thing there that disturbed me except it was being there to[o] Long but when I came to hear Mr John Wesley I found nothing but discontent in my mind.'[38] So often the convert used the metaphor of being woken from a deep sleep to describe his or her experience, so much so that to be 'awakened' became a cliché. This was the initial pricking of conscience, the very beginning of the process of disturbance that evangelicals hoped would lead to conversion, the travail that would end in new birth. Joanna Barber's husband began an account of his wife's pious death in a letter to Charles Wesley in 1752, saying,

When She was first awakened itt was under your Brother ministry that very Sabbath day that he Preached att St Giles in the fields, and such an awakening that I have seldom seen for the Lord in that hour gave her such a sight of her self had nott the people been very thick She must a sunk down to the Ground. In a few days after the Lord Convinced her of unbelife and sett her sins in araye before her face in such a manner that indeed She Could truly say the Burthen of them was

---

[36] *Sermons of Charles Wesley*, 145.

[37] Margaret Austin (19 May 1740), Nathaniel Hurst [1741], Mary Ramsay (4 June 1740), Elizabeth Sayce [May 1742], Sarah Barber [May 1740], and Sarah Middleton (25 May 1740), EMV.

[38] Mary Thomas (24 May 1742), EMV.

intolerable. She Laboured under the Burden of her Sins for near Two years before She found deliverance.[39]

In the case of Joanna Barber, then, her awakening introduced a significantly prolonged period of soul-struggle before her conscience was finally put to rest. For her, as for these other converts, this new understanding demanded a new narrative, one that would recount the whole of life in such a way as to take account of this profound crisis of conscience and its ultimate resolution.

The Novelty of the Message: Knowing One's Sins Forgiven

In addition to the message of the 'spirituality and extent of the law' which awakened their consciences, these lay Methodists identified a further theological idea that struck them, on first hearing, as unprecedented—an idea, moreover, that held out hope for the resolution of this crisis. This was the novel suggestion that one could know with certainty that one's sins were forgiven. Thomas Cooper worried about making this claim, saying, 'I thought I should speack blasfemey if I should say my sins were forgiven mee.' He claimed that Charles Wesley had told them 'they must feel their Sins forgiven them in this Life or they never would in the Life to Come', and that Wesley had followed this up by reading from the Church of England Homilies on the subject of faith. Cooper reflected, 'I thought it Comfortable doctrin but Strange doctrin to me for I never heard such beforer.' Elizabeth Sayce wrote, 'I thought we might receive Forgiveness of Sins but not in Such a manner as to know and feel it applied.'[40] This was exactly how the lay preacher Thomas Hanson remembered his state of mind before encountering Methodism: 'I thought God did forgive men their sin; but that none could know it for himself.'[41] Martha Jones remarked of the doctrine, 'I had never heard of any such thing,' and S. Ibison commented likewise, 'I was a stranger to the Doctreing for I had [never heard] anything Like this.' Joan Webb was so worried about whether it could be true that she turned to *sortes Biblicae*, opening the Scriptures at random to see if she could find confirmation of this new doctrine. After reading a chapter in the epistles of John, she was fully convinced and decided she would 'wait Gods time'. Brother Lambertson's daughter was dying in 1755 and desperately hoping to break through to a certainty that her sins were forgiven before she passed away. She argued with three friends about this, and they claimed there was 'no such thing as knowing ones Sins forgiven' and they worried she was going to make herself more ill. In the end she did win through to a

---

[39] 'Joanna Barber's Death' [Feb. 1742], EMV.
[40] Thomas Cooper [1741] and Elizabeth Sayce [May 1742], EMV.
[41] *AM* 3 (1780), 479.

direct sensible experience of spiritual joy before she died, and in the narrative this clearly functioned to seal her case in the dispute.[42]

The same experiences were repeated in the north of England. The Methodist lay preacher John Nelson frequently commented upon the scandal it caused in Yorkshire to claim to know your sins forgiven. His own relatives said 'they never heard of such a thing in their lives'. When Nelson told them that he knew these things by direct experience, he recalled, 'they begged I would not tell any one that my sins were forgiven; for no one would believe me; and they should be ashamed to show their faces in the street.'[43] Examples could be multiplied, but these are sufficient to demonstrate what a novelty it was in the 1730s and 1740s for laypeople in the Church of England to be told that they could directly experience forgiveness for their sins and have their consciences at rest before God. Here too the evangelists named and called forth new perceptions of interiority and agency in their hearers.

The 'spirituality of the law' and the knowledge of 'forgiveness of sins' were thus two novel ideas that went to work to shape these lay narratives not only in their sense of the beginning and end of conversion, but also as two poles between which the convert would oscillate. Since at least Thomas Bilney and William Perkins in the sixteenth century, these ideas in various forms had played a crucial role in the conversion and narrative identity of many English Protestants. Now, some two centuries later, in the popular piety and familiar correspondence of lay Methodists, these embers revived and glowed again white hot.

INDIVIDUATION AND MIMESIS: LAY NARRATIVE CULTURE

What sort of narrative identity, or sense of self, was reflected in these letters? The lay narratives written for Charles Wesley bear witness both to a new sense of individuation, as converts repeatedly testified to their discovery that all of this was 'for me', and to a keen sense of community, as converts likewise found themselves united to new relationships, larger stories, and shared practices. The result is that these lay narratives appear both individual and mimetic, since in them we hear both the individual voice and the voice of the community.[44]

---

[42] Martha Jones (1 June 1740), S. Ibison (23 May 1740), Joan Webb [May 1742], and 'An Account of Brother Lambertson's Daughter' [1755], EMV.

[43] *WV* iii. 38.

[44] This dialectic between the individual and the community is central also to the changes in English prose fiction that take place at precisely this same time, as the novel emerges as something distinct in readers' minds from 'romance' or 'history'. See further, John Richetti (ed.), *The Cambridge Companion to the Eighteenth-Century Novel* (Cambridge, 1996), 1–8.

Individuation: The Unique Voice

The first way in which the narratives witnessed to a keen sense of individuation was in the response of the converts to evangelical preaching. Many contemporaries remarked on Whitefield's ability to create a vivid tableau out of the Scriptural narratives and to place his hearers in the story as living actors. Most of Whitefield's published sermons have a literary quality that obscures this vividness, but those sermons that were published from live transcriptions communicate something more of this sense of personal address. Whitefield's sermon on Saul's conversion, preached in Glasgow on 12 September 1741, was 'taken from his mouth and published at the earnest desire of many of the hearers' almost immediately after the event as a forty-page tract. On this occasion, Whitefield's rhetorical strategy was clear. The high priest who sent Saul to persecute the Christians in Damascus was equated with unconverted ministers in the present; the followers of 'the Way' in the Book of Acts were 'supposed enthusiasts'; Ananias was an awakened, experienced Christian who knew what to do with Saul; Saul's vision on the Damascus Road was his awakening of conscience; his period of three days' darkness was his evangelical humiliation; his recovery of sight under Ananias's prayers was his New Birth; Paul's companions were 'mere hearers'; the believers at Damascus whom he joined were like a Methodist band meeting, and so on. In this way Whitefield brought the scriptural narrative to life in eighteenth-century Glasgow. 'Ah my dear Friends,' he implored, 'this must be done to you as well as to *Saul* . . . God must speak to you by Name, God must reach your Heart in particular, ye must be brought to see the Evil of Sin, and to cry out after *Jesus Christ*.'[45]

For the laypeople who wrote to Charles Wesley, this sort of preaching did indeed 'speak to them by Name'. Margaret Austin had been abused and abandoned by her husband, left with two children to care for, and yet when she went and heard Whitefield preach on 'the Rich man of the Gospel, how he had Laid up treasures on Earth but none in heaven', she knew on the spot, 'I was that Person.' She added that though she had no worldly treasure, she had 'a great Deal in Desire'. It is testimony to the power of Whitefield's preaching performances that he could leave an utterly destitute single mother convinced that she was a rich young ruler. This letter was written more than a year after the event, and yet she remembered his sermon vividly. Like Mary Ramsay, she also reported in detail on other sermons. As she followed Whitefield, Charles and John Wesley, and the other young Methodist preachers, and listened to them preach, she found herself personally addressed in every sermon: *she* was the rich man who went empty away, *she* was the proud Pharisee, *she* was at the foot of the cross watching

---

[45] George Whitefield, *Saul's Conversion: A Lecture, Preached on . . . September 12th, 1741, in the High-Church-Yard of Glasgow* (Glasgow, 1741), 14.

the soldiers pierce the bleeding side of Christ. 'I Saw my Self to be a Lost undone Sinner,' she said after one sermon. Again, on another occasion her response was that 'the Lord Saw fit to Lett me See my Self'.[46]

This sense of personal, individual address was so strong that many converts thought the preacher was singling them out—even reading their minds. When the collier Samuel Tippett heard Whitefield upon Hanham Mount at Kingswood—where Whitefield had observed white gutters made by tears on the coal-blackened faces of the miners as he spoke—he claimed Whitefield 'described my wretched condition as exactly as if he had known me in most thoughts'.[47] 'I thought it was all spake to me,' was how one woman responded to a sermon John Wesley preached. When Thomas Cooper heard Wesley, he felt condemned for his sins and damned on the spot: 'I thought I was the person he made his discorse upon for he tould mee all that every [sic] I did. I . . . was so ashamed of my selves.' When Charles Wesley preached on the woman of Samaria and adultery, Samuel Webb felt so exposed that it was all he could do not to make a disturbance before the sermon was over. Sister Macham reluctantly went to hear John Wesley because of the pleading of a friend. After the sermon she accused the friend of having 'told Mr Wesley all her life'. When he assured her that he had done no such thing, she knew that 'God had directed the word to her'.[48] Similarly, when the lay preacher Thomas Mitchell was preaching in Heptonstall, a butcher was so cut to the heart by his message that 'he went home and beat his wife', said Mitchell, 'because he thought she had told me all his sinful ways'.[49] Such testimony points to the new way in which these converts felt personally confronted by Methodist preaching that applied the law of God to the whole of their lives, public and private, outward and inward. In direct contrast to 'going to Church and Sacrament', where they might confess their 'manifold sins and wickedness' in recitation of the general confession, these laypeople found their sins and guilt exposed in an acutely individual way.

The dislocation that was a feature of demographic change in the eighteenth century further contributed to the sense of some of these converts that they were individuals, seeking to find a new way in the world at some distance from their families and communities of origin. For example, Thomas Cooper—the man who thought Wesley told him all he ever did—was a layman who kept up a respectable life of church attendance and moral rectitude while an apprentice in the country, but then he moved

---

[46] Margaret Austin (19 May 1740), EMV.

[47] Gillies, *Memoirs of Whitefield*, 38; Barry and Morgan (eds.), *Reformation and Revival in Bristol*, 122.

[48] S. Ibison (23 May 1740), Thomas Cooper [1741], Samuel Webb (20 Nov. 1741), and 'Account of Sister Macham' [1765], EMV.

[49] *WV* i. 182.

to London and got into a bad crowd and, as he put it, 'Spent a Deal of my time in horing, drincking, dansing, plays, and such vice as youth is prone to.' Moving from the morally reinforcing structures of a village apprentice-ship to life in an anonymous city had been unsettling, and he and an acquaintance confided to each other at a local pub that their consciences were troubled. The same was true of William Turner, a 25-year-old joiner who came to London and worked day and night only to find that his master went broke. He 'had no friend living, and away from all old acquaintance in a strange place, thought I must seek happiness from God'. He began reading William Romaine, found he was not right with God, and then was set at liberty under Charles Wesley's preaching. Joseph Carter was another ap-prentice who met a Methodist layman at the White Horse Ale House in Little Britain Street in London. They struck up a conversation about the Wesley brothers ('this new religion'), and Carter folded his arms and protested that he believed all the Articles of Religion, the Bible, and the Creeds. The Methodist apprentice asked if he had this faith in his heart, not just his head. Then he recommended an old Puritan book, and as Carter recalled, 'bid me Consider on't'.[50] The result was again that Carter felt deeply singled out, and his 'reigning sin' of adultery was exposed and he was soon on the path to personal conversion. For Maria Price, her sense of being personally identified by Charles Wesley's preaching led to intense self-despising. She stacked up the adjectives, describing herself as 'a dark dead stony hearted damned unbeleveing pharisee'.[51]

Though painful, the message of the Methodist preachers seemed for these laypeople to make sense of their uniquely personal histories and experi-ences. Consequently, they did not simply recount commonplaces that could have been true of anyone. They often recalled tiny narrative details—utterly trivial episodes in their individual experiences that were now worthy of repetition since they helped to tell the story of conversion. Joseph Carter told how 'one Saturday night being in a Barbers Shope, the Barber said he had been to hear a Sermon Preached before all the Religious societies in London'. As readers, we can almost hear the scissors snipping and see the locks of hair on the floor. Carter moved naturally into dialogue as he continued to recount their conversation and to tell how this had led him to encounter James Hutton and other early evangelicals.[52] William Barber, another lay Methodist, explained in his narrative how he and his wife were becoming more serious about their spiritual state, and how they had begun preparing themselves to receive the sacrament, when a crucial spiritual

---

[50] The book was Thomas Wilcox, *Choice Drop of Honey from the Rock Christ* (1690).

[51] Thomas Cooper [1741], William Turner (9 Mar. 1756), Joseph Carter [Nov. 1741], and Maria Price (18 May 1740), EMV.

[52] Joseph Carter [Nov. 1741], EMV.

obstacle arose that had to do with getting dressed on Sunday morning: 'The Enemy of our Souls begune to sett himself in array against us by endevering to keep us from going, for Something being amiss with my stockings I was to putt on, words arose between us, butt the Enemy did nott gett his desier of us, for we disapointed him of his hope for in the name of the Lord we went.'[53] One small victory for God's side.

These passing details—the Barber Shop on Saturday night, the worn-through stockings on Sunday morning before church—were unique to the persons involved. Whatever the formal and generic elements of conversion narrative were as they knew it, their individuality was far from being overpowered by a series of universal tropes or standard topoi. On the contrary, their experiences called out a down-to-earth verisimilitude that compares with the narrative techniques being explored by Daniel Defoe, Samuel Richardson, and other novelists who emerged during in this period.[54]

A strong sense of individuation can be seen, further, in the way the experience of conversion was uniquely refracted in the lives of women. First of all, it is clear that these women were not writing their narratives in the midst of some splendid Cartesian isolation. Mary Maddern closed her letter with an apology, saying, 'I beg you Sir [to forgive] the incorrectness of this, as I am obliged to writ Sirronded with Children.' Other women who wrote to Charles Wesley spoke of their physical suffering as women, including two cases of breast cancer, one of an ulcer in the womb, and one of extreme fear of pain in childbirth. Moreover, many of these women encountered Methodism after having been abused or forsaken by their husbands. Martha Claggett's husband became violent to her after she began following the Methodists. Both Margaret Austin and Joan Webb had been abandoned by their husbands. As the latter put it starkly, 'I was in Great trouble.' When Webb realized that she did not love God as she ought, she related this immediately to her trouble with her husband, saying, 'I was So grieved with the thoughts of not Loveing God that my other troble abated.' Sister Macham was married at 20, but her husband was 'Quite unconcerned about his salvation', and after following him in breaking the Sabbath, her conscience gave her no rest—indeed, her guilt made her suicidal for a period. It was only when her husband was away at sea that she was able to go and hear 'the field Preaching'. When her husband died in the West Indies and left her alone with one child, his relatives helped take care of them, until Macham joined the Foundery society, at which point his

---

[53] William Barber [1741], EMV.

[54] The relationship between individuality and idealization in spiritual autobiography and the importance of these themes for the 'rise of the novel' is discussed in G. A. Starr, *Defoe and Spiritual Autobiography* (New York, 1971), 3–50; see also the discussion in Ian Watt, *The Rise of the Novel* (Berkeley, Calif., 1957), 74–85.

family abandoned her completely.[55] Clearly, then, all these women heard the gospel message of the Methodist clergy, not in a vacuum, but in great extremity.[56]

As these women encountered Methodism and experienced conversion, they did not find that their unique experiences as women were somehow suppressed by the dominant narrative, transmitted as it was through the male Methodist clergy. On the contrary, their experiences as women were specified and called out into a personal story. Margaret Austin, whose narrative we have encountered at various points already, began with a concession that as far back as she could remember she had had a problem with pride, and more than anything, she nursed her reputation in the community. 'But,' she wrote, 'marrying when young and having a Cruel husband, that brought Down my pride very much'. Near the beginning of 1739 her husband walked out on her and left her with two children. At this same time, she heard Whitefield, John and Charles Wesley, William Delamotte, and other preachers, finding herself in every sermon. When she came under conviction for her sin, the people around her tried to extend sympathy to her, but like many abused persons, she responded, 'Methought I had rather they had Beat me, for I Deserved no pity.' The crucial moment came when another Methodist woman, Sister Robinson, came alongside her. 'She bestowed much pity on me, prayed and Comforted me very much. I told her my State and She told me how She had received faith under the ministry and by the Prayers of you Sir.' Sister Robinson wrote a note on her behalf to introduce her to John Wesley, but when he said nothing and took no notice of Austin, she was again in despair of finding the mercy of God. She desparately wanted to join the bands, and when she was finally admitted, she found great comfort 'hearing the other[s] tell the State of my their [*sic*] Souls'. This emboldened her 'to Speak of the State of mine'. Sister Robinson continued to pray with her and sing hymns with her, and finally Austin broke through to joy.[57]

For Margaret Austin the travail of evangelical conversion did not suppress her gender, but instead it drew out her experience as a woman and allowed her to find solidarity in her suffering with other women. Indeed, some literary historians find the origins of 'gendered identity' in precisely such texts, as women discovered the literary space to express their own concerns

---

[55] Mary Maddern (29 June 1762), Martha Claggett (24 July 1738), Margaret Austin (19 May 1740), Joan Webb [May 1742], and 'Account of Sister Macham' [1765].

[56] Cf. also the marriage troubles of Sarah Ryan and Sarah Crosby recounted in *AM* 2 (1779), 296–310, and *MM* 29 (1806), 422. Mary Fletcher (née Bosanquet) tells of her struggle with her father when she sought to follow the Methodists. Henry Moore (ed.), *The Life of Mrs. Mary Fletcher* (6th edn., 1824), 29–35.

[57] Margaret Austin (19 May 1740), EMV.

in a male-dominated culture.[58] Within Methodism Margaret Austin found a social space in which to speak of her abuse and abandonment, and a religious space in which to experience empathy, redemption, and even happiness ('such Joy that I could Scarce forbear speaking'). The women's band became like another family for her, and the kinship language ('Sister Robinson') is a telling indication of this.[59] Indeed, Margaret Austin's account underscores the importance of the lay leadership of women and the women's bands in early Methodist conversion. If the Methodist clergy were physicians of the soul, then Sister Robinson was an influential midwife.

Moreover, in telling their stories of conversion, these women most often recounted the decisive influence of a woman's text or experience in Scripture. The most common of these was the declaration of Christ, 'Daughter, be of good cheer, thy sins are forgiven thee.' Margaret Austin heard these words three times over one May morning in 1740 just as she awoke. She knew immediately that this meant old things were passing away and all things were becoming new. Sarah Middleton and Grace Murray also experienced these words as a direct, divine locution, and Joanna Mussell and Mary Thomas recorded these lines as a turning point in their experience. Mrs Platt of Oxford drew upon the underlying biblical pericope for this text when she wrote, 'It was said unto me, if I could but tutch but the Hem of his Garment I should be hole.'[60] The text was in fact a conflation of the words Christ spoke to the man with a palsy, 'Son, be of good cheer; thy sins are forgiven thee' (Matt. 9: 2 and par.) with the words Christ spoke to the woman with the issue of blood, 'Daughter, be of good comfort, thy faith hath made thee whole' (Matt. 9: 22 and par.).[61] Whether this conflation originated with Charles Wesley or with the women who heard him, it is a

---

[58] On the relationship between gender and religious ideology raised in such narratives, see Felicity A. Nussbaum, *The Autobiographical Subject: Gender and Ideology in Eighteenth-Century England* (Baltimore, 1989), 154–77; Martha Tomhave Blauvelt and Rosemary Skinner Keller, 'Women and Revivalism: The Puritan and Wesleyan Traditions', in Rosemary Radford Ruether and Rosemary Skinner Keller (eds.), *Women and Religion in America* (San Francisco, 1983), ii. 316–67. Virginia Lieson Brereton continues the story into the nineteenth and twentieth centuries in *From Sin to Salvation: Stories of Women's Conversions, 1800 to the Present* (Bloomington, 1991).

[59] Martha Claggett (whose story is recounted in the next chapter) likewise found that in telling her story of conversion she was also telling of her experience as a woman, especially as she told of her fear of childbirth and her guilt for having seriously contemplated the abortion of an unborn child.

[60] Margaret Austin (19 May 1740), Sarah Middleton (15 May 1740), 'Account of Joanna Mussell' [1762], Mary Thomas (24 May 1742), Mrs. Platt (20 Sept. 1738), EMV; Grace Murray's experience of this text appears in *CWJ* i. 224.

[61] It is evident from Charles Wesley's journal that this was a common conflation of the biblical texts when speaking of a woman's experience of divine grace. See the entries for 28 Sept. and 3 Oct. 1739 in *CWJ* i. 182, 185. In contrast, E. Bristow recalled hearing the lines

further indication that the message of conversion within early Methodism was specified and adapted to address women directly.[62]

If any of these women ventured across to Whitefield's Tabernacle in London on a Thursday evening in October 1743, they would have heard John Cennick preach a sermon on this same text. Cennick used the woman in the Gospels as an analogy of coming to Christ with a 'bloody issue' of sin that cannot be staunched. He focused especially on the poor and those who were great sinners with sore consciences, and urged them to 'touch' Jesus. The analogy of the woman touching Jesus led him to describe faith in similarly sensate terms:

Some indeed teach that we may be forgiven, and yet not know it; and healed, and yet we not be sensible of it; but such Doctrine is dangerous, and tends to make Men easy where they are . . . Do not you so learn *Christ*. Let none here rest till they know they have clos'd with *Jesus*, till you can say, with full Assurance of Faith, That you *have touched him; and till Jesus* bears witness in your Hearts, that Virtue is gone out of his Wound, to heal you. This woman *felt in her Body that she was healed of her Plague.* So you may know and feel in yourselves, even while you are in these Bodies, that your Souls are healed of the Plague of Sin.[63]

The witness of the women who wrote to Charles Wesley was that such preaching, based upon a woman's experience, was persuasive.

Some women identified with other biblical figures. Ann Martin identified with Mary, speaking the words as her own, 'The power of the most highest Overshaw'd me.' E. Bristow likewise identified with Mary, applying to herself the words of the Magnificat, 'He regards the low Estate of his handmaid.' Margaret Jenkins wrote that after her conversion, 'I praised the Lord in the words of the Virgin Mary.' Mary Ramsay began her letter with a different biblical exemplar, saying, 'With the woman of Samaria, I May Say, Come See a man that told me all that ever I did in my Life.'[64] As they drew on such biblical analogues, the early Methodist laywomen were clearly hearing the message of the Methodist clergy in their own terms as women. They were hearing that this gospel message was for them and specified them and their concerns uniquely.

---

more exactly as they appear in Matt. 9: 22, without conflation. E. Bristow (12 Apr. 1740), EMV.

[62] In Charles Wesley's *Journal* he recorded a visit with Ms Hanney in 1739, and noted: 'From the time of her turning to God, her husband has used her most inhumanly. Yesterday he beat her, and drove her out of doors, following her with imprecations and threatenings to murder her, if ever she returned. When she was cast out, Jesus found her, and said unto her by his Spirit, "Be of good cheer, thy sins are forgiven thee." She continued all the night in joy unspeakable, and can now with confidence call God her Father.' *CWJ* i. 182.

[63] John Cennick, *The Bloody Issue Healed* (1744), 13.

[64] Ann Martin [1740], E. Bristow (12 Apr. 1740), and Mary Ramsay (4 June 1740). Margaret Jenkins's account is given in *AM* 1 (1778), 228.

Whether male apprentices or single mothers, the Methodist lay converts never tired of exclaiming that the gospel was 'for me' or 'mine'. Martha Jones was sitting at home one evening when she finally believed her sins were forgiven and that 'Christ died for me and his righteousness was imputed to me.' Catherine Gilbert wrote to Charles Wesley to tell him what God had done 'for Me and in Me'. When Sarah Barber seemed to see Christ bleeding on the cross, she said, 'I was astonished and Stood amazed to think it was for me.' The preaching of the early Methodists was such that it stirred up hopes that ran ahead of the personal experiences of the converts, so that Mary Ramsay wrote, '[I] was in Great Expectation that the Lord had still something in store for me.' James Hewitt described his new insight into salvation in variations on prepositional phrases and the first-person singular pronoun: 'God Soon Showed Me it was to have Something Done in Me and for Me which Could Not be Done by Me.' Joseph Carter underlined the key prepositions in his letter when he wrote, 'I plainly see that all the work that hath been done already, hath been done *for* me; but now I am fully persuaded that it must be wrought *in* me.'[65] Again, the converts often used phrases of Scripture as their own to express this sense of strongly individuated salvation. Most often the convert borrowed the words of St Paul in Galatians 2: 20, recounting the Christ 'who loved me and gave himself for me', or the exclamation of Thomas in John 20: 28: 'My Lord and my God'. Indeed, Martha Claggett, whose story is told in the next chapter, borrowed both lines to make clear her sense of newly discovered personal faith in Christ.[66]

Mimesis: The Communal Narrative

For most of these converts, the sense of being an individual before God was reinforced by their experience of Methodism, since their conversion experience distinguished them uniquely and gave them their own voice and their own history. Yet, at the same time, these narratives bear witness to the ways in which the convert felt connected through Methodism to a shared experience with others and to larger, unitary patterns of belief and practice. If the converts in the early Evangelical Revival appear as individualists of a sort, they were also communitarians of a sort.

Repeatedly in these narratives, attention is drawn to the small, intimate group meetings—the band and society. This is true of the accounts in manuscript, and it is also true of some of the later published narratives. Thomas Olivers, who had heard some Methodist preaching at Bristol, soon found himself in deep spiritual concern for his soul. He was fascinated and

---

[65] Martha Jones (1 June 1740), Catherine Gilbert [1740], Sarah Barber [May 1740], Mary Ramsay (4 June 1740), James Hewitt [Nov. 1741], and Joseph Carter [Nov. 1741], EMV.
[66] Martha Claggett (24 July 1738), EMV.

attracted by the intimacy and fellowship the Methodists seemed to share, and so he stalked them secretly, following them to their meetings and eavesdropping on them. As they sang their hymns, he would be outside crying; when they came out, he would follow them at a distance, still listening, sometimes following them for over two miles. He knew they had something he wanted.[67] Margaret Austin felt similarly attracted to these meetings, saying, 'I had a strong Desire to get into the Bands.'[68] The kinship language we have noted above ('Sister Robinson', 'Brother Edmunds', and 'Dear Father in God') is a further indication of the close bonds between members of the early Methodist communities. For many of the Methodists who were dislocated through employment or domestic troubles, Methodism offered the family that they missed or had never had. Notwithstanding the intensely individual language in these narratives, conversion was not experienced in isolation. The trope of new birth stood not only for new life, but also for the discovery of a new family of brothers and sisters.

In certain forms of gathered church polity that emerged in the seventeenth century, conversion had functioned as an admission test. Among the early Methodists, however, men and women joined the bands as seekers, and they shared not just the experience of joy in salvation, but also the experience of sorrowing after it. Mary Maddern met with John Wesley and recalled, 'He advised Me to Meet a Band wich I did for sumtime before I found any relife from that deep distress of Soul.' For the most part, the new members of the bands were just grateful to find they were not alone in their spiritual concerns. When Joan Webb joined a band and heard that others shared the same temptations, she claimed that this experience 'greatly Strengthened me'. Sarah Barber was at first refused entry to the bands, but when finally admitted as a member, she said, 'The band was of great Service to me, for I never went away without Some Comforts.' In the band meeting itself, Elizabeth Halfpenny 'received an Extraordinary measure of the Love of God'.[69]

These intimate communities were but one of many 'means of grace'— religious practices in which one could engage that were known to be conduits of divine blessing. The sense of these shared experiences as 'means of grace' points away from individualism, since these were given things, received and not constructed. Members were to 'wait on God in the means of grace' and to 'use and not abuse' the means. This was something very different than the modern language of self-fashioning or creative agency. The language of 'means' became controversial in the early Revival

---

[67] *AM* 2 (1779), 85–6.
[68] Margaret Austin (19 May 1740), EMV.
[69] Mary Maddern (29 June 1762), Joan Webb [May 1742], Sarah Barber [May 1740], and Elizabeth Halfpenny [May 1742], EMV.

as tension mounted between the Methodists and Moravians over precisely these questions of agency, and some of those influenced by the 'stillness' doctrine retreated into quietism and eschewed any talk of means. Nevertheless, from the evidence of the letters, it is plain that a number of shared practices ('means') characterized the communities in which men and women were led to evangelical conversion.

In addition to hearing sermons, attending band meetings, and receiving the sacrament, the accounts of laypeople frequently witness to the importance of hymn singing. This is further evidence for the importance of community and shared experience in fostering Methodist conversion, for hymns were not lyric poetry but communal song. Mary Ramsay was one of many who remembered the lines of certain hymns word for word and included them in her account. She wrote of her experience in 1739, saying, 'Another thing that workt in me was some words of that hymn Called Christ the friend of Sinners.' She then cited two lines of the hymn: 'His bleeding heart will make you room, | His open side shall take you in.'[70] The influence of hymns extended beyond the singing that took place in meetings. John Henderson hinted at the emotional immediacy of hymns when he wrote, 'Hymns are the chief of my Reading, for they may be felt without Study.' Martha Claggett confessed somewhat sheepishly, 'I was delighted with Singing Hymns when I was sure no one heard me.' Elizabeth Halfpenny found some encouragement for her heavy-burdened soul when two Methodists sang with her at breakfast. In the collection of letters to Charles Wesley are two accounts of the conversions of condemned criminals on different occasions, and both record the malefactors singing hymns after their conversions and on their way to the gallows.[71]

For some of the lay converts, a hymn occasioned the breakthrough in their spiritual experience. Thomas Middleton went to the Foundery and found that the hymns and preaching seemed to be directed at him, adding that the hymn at communion 'reached my very Heart'. Elizabeth Downs described an experience like an electric shock during a hymn that mentioned the cross: 'I felt as itt were a change as I thought inward and outward. My heart fluttered as though itt would have tore out of my body. I seemed as though I had been Convulsed.'[72]

For some converts the hymn-singing of the Methodists contributed to a sense of holiness in the society meetings. Thomas Tennant wrote, 'I was

---

[70] This is the hymn that begins, 'Where shall my wondering soul begin?' Wesley, *Works* (BE), vii. 116–17, and the lines quoted are from st. 6.

[71] Mary Ramsay (4 June 1740), John Henderson [May 1787], Martha Claggett (24 July 1738), Elizabeth Halfpenny [May 1742], J. Bults (14 Apr. 1743), and 'Concerning Malefactors' [Apr. 1771], EMV.

[72] Thomas Middleton (8 Oct. 1743) and Elizabeth Downs (13 Apr. 1742), EMV. See further the examples of hymn-inspired conversions in *WV* v. 233 and vi. 58.

glad indeed when one asked me to go to a meeting of Christian friends; but when I came to the door, and heard them singing, I had such an idea both of their goodness, and of my own unworthiness, that I durst not presume to go in.'[73] The lay preacher Duncan Wright wrote about a remarkable episode in Wexford. A Roman Catholic adversary had hidden in a sack in a barn where Methodists were meeting, planning to let in the mob in due course, but during the singing he was touched. 'He thought it a thousand pities... to disturb them while singing.' Soon, Wright continued, 'the power of God did so confound him, that he roared out with might and main. And not having power to get out of the sack, lay bawling and screaming. At last one ventured to see what was the matter, and helping him out, brought him up, confessing his sins, and crying for mercy: which was the beginning of a lasting work in his soul.'[74] Hymns were clearly a potent means of conversion, and one of the most significant ways that individuals were drawn into a whole narrative culture of conversion.

Preaching, band meetings, and hymn-singing did much to catechize men and women about conversion, but the form of conversion itself was learned by example. That there was a close relationship between the autobiographical constructions of the leaders in their journals and the experiences of their lay followers is abundantly clear from the lay narratives. Martha Jones read Whitefield's *Short Account*, which included his conversion narrative, and remarked that this had much more effect upon her than his sermons. 'The piety of the young preacher made a deep impression,' she recalled. Sarah Barber heard Charles Wesley read from his journal, and during his prayers afterwards she recalled, 'I saw my Saviour Bleeding on the Cross and... I was astonished and Stood amazed to think it was for me. I heard the voice saying, This I do for my own Sake.'[75] Margaret Austin also heard Charles Wesley read from his journal (perhaps on the same occasion) and she had a premonition that her own conversion was near: 'When you was Reading your Journal and Said the Same Spirit that raised Jesus from the Dead Shall quicken Thy Dead body, then I felt that Christ would finish what he had begun.' Austin returned to hear Charles Wesley again on the following Monday: 'We heard another of your Journals: and that Day two year year [*sic*] you said you had received remission of Sins, and in your Prayers I found great Comfort.' When Austin continued with her account and described her own conversion, it followed the pattern of Charles Wesley's experience, as she heard a voice that sealed her pardon just as he had two years earlier. 'The next morning: as I was arising the voice of the Lord Said to me, Thy Sins are forgiven, twice-over. I heard a third time, Daughter be of good

[73] *AM* 2 (1779), 471.
[74] *AM* 4 (1781), 474.
[75] Martha Jones [1742] and Sarah Barber [May 1740], EMV.

Cheer thy Sins are forgiven thee. Then I felt old things passing away and all things becoming new.'[76]

Thus, Charles Wesley read from his journals at least twice to members of the society, and this provoked at least two mimetic conversions. Both experienced, as he did in his own conversion, a biblical locution—words heard, or recollected vividly, that confirmed that their sins were forgiven. And on the day referred to by Austin, Charles Wesley included a short account of her experience in his journal—another vindication of his ministry.[77] The Wesley brothers had written their journals in part as models for their people, and so it proved. Sarah Barber and Margaret Austin were empowered to believe that they could be forgiven after hearing Charles read from his journal.[78] They, in turn, wrote accounts of their experience in letters to him, completing the hermeneutical circle.

To appreciate properly the force of this modelling of conversion by the early Methodist clergy, one must understand the exalted status these figures had in the minds of their followers. The lay converts who wrote to Charles Wesley showed remarkable deference to him. Though he was at this time barely 30 years old, he was addressed with reverence that was almost sacerdotal. In the minds of his converts he was not only a popular preacher with a self-evident charismatic authority, but he also possessed the traditional authority of the Church of England and its ministry. Thomas Middleton began his letter to Charles Wesley, saying, 'You are my Father, my Counsellor, and my Guide.' Margaret Austin, Mary Jane Ramsay, and Sarah Barber all addressed Charles Wesley as their 'Reverend Father' or 'Father in God' and concluded their letters by subscribing themselves 'your young babe in Christ'. This was in part simply the ebullience of the convert, and an extension of the metaphor of new birth, but the language also denoted their submission to him as a spiritual director. Thus Martha Jones spoke on behalf of her whole band, acknowledging their 'desire to be obedient to you in all things knowing that ye are set over us in and by the lord'. Some of these converts felt that Charles Wesley had a unique charism. S. Ibison was convinced that she would be set at liberty if only she could receive the sacrament from his hands. But Margaret Austin's attachment to the young evangelist was the strongest of all. Under her signature she wrote: 'Awakened by the Reverend Mr Whitefield: Convicted by the Reverend Mr Jn Wesley: Converted by the Reverend Mr Charles: for the truth of whose

---

[76] Margaret Austin (19 May 1740), EMV.

[77] *CWJ* i. 207.

[78] Charles Wesley recorded reading to the bands from his journals on 24 June 1740 and 12 Apr. 1741 (*CWJ* i. 243, 267), and he did so in part for apologetic reasons: to oppose the Moravian practice of stillness. Sarah Barber also remembered hearing his journals, writing in May 1740 that 'Sister Robinson told me you gave her Leave to bring us to hear your Journals for which I have Reason to Praise God.' Sarah Barber [May 1740], EMV.

Doctrine in the Strength of the Lord I am Ready to Lay down my Life.'[79] The partisan implications of this loyalty are telling, as is the implied morphology of conversion, but her language also bears witness to the piety of self-abandonment and yearning that predominated in the early 1740s, particularly among the women's bands in London. On 5 April 1740 Charles Wesley noted in his journal: 'Margaret Austin tells me, she has longed for my coming as a child for the breast.'[80] It is precisely this sort of deference and affectionate attachment that fostered a mimetic religious culture, so that, again, Austin wrote to Wesley, 'I received your words as coming from [my Saviour's] mouth; and with the eye of faith I again saw my pardon, written in his blood.'[81]

James Hutton had a different interpretation of this sort of relationship. He wrote to Count Zinzendorf in 1740, saying, 'J.W. and C. Wesley, both of them, are dangerous snares to many young women; several are in love with them. I wish they were once married to some good sisters, but I would not give them one of my sisters, if I had many.'[82] The Wesleys and Whitefield were unmarried and young, and several of the women in the bands were undoubtedly infatuated with them, and this certainly added an additional motive on the part of some of the women to emulate the piety of the Methodist clergy. But it would be well not to overstate Hutton's point, since he was himself harbouring a serious partisan animus against the Wesleys at this time, and the evidence of the letters written by the converts, male and female, points to a whole range of influences that contributed to their spiritual experiences.

Among these influences was not only the example of admired leaders, but also the spoken testimony of other laypeople. The expansive joy of the convert so often and so easily passed over into narrative. S. Ibison, for example, recorded how conversion led to an irrepressible urge to speak: 'I was fild with Love as well as Joy. I prayed for all and I wept to see so many Dead people in the streets. I Could hardly get home without telling them so.' This sort of straight-from-the-heart testimony was influential. When John Cennick spoke of his own experience, Samuel Tippett responded in kind: 'Then my heart was broken.' For William Barber it was a lay testimony that was the 'first instrument' that drew his soul out of darkness: 'Our Brother Cooper...happyly Comeing to work where I was and having opportunity, he began to tell me what the Lord had done for his soull. I Readaly Received his saying.' Elizabeth Downs was amazed and

---

[79] Thomas Middleton (8 Oct. 1743), Martha Jones (1 June 1740), and Margaret Austin (19 May 1740), EMV.

[80] *CWJ* i. 207.

[81] Ibid.

[82] Benham, *James Hutton*, 47.

actually feared for herself when, as she remembered, 'One of the Society came to me with Great joy telling what the Lord had done for her.'[83] When John Valton was in deep crisis, sorrowing after conversion in March 1764, he met someone who could sympathize with him, and this likewise made all the difference. 'He related his experience, which very much agreed with mine, while groping the way to peace of conscience, as it were, over a dark mountain. We spent the evening in very profitable conversation, and closed with singing and prayer. I never, in all my life, enjoyed such happiness as this evening afforded me.' Two years later, Valton met a Mrs Smitton who related a similar experience when sharing not the sorrows, but the joys of conversion: 'Under such testimonies I catch a flame from the celestial altar, which glows with hallowing influence. What, shall one member be blessed, and all the others not rejoice?'[84] Even after Joseph Humphreys had parted ways theologically with the Wesleys, such testimony continued to transcend theological disagreements. To Charles Wesley, he acknowledged their differences, but urged, 'At present let us go on, simply declaring to others what the Lord hath done for our souls.'[85] Clearly, personal narrative was one of the most important shared practices of the religious culture of Methodism. These shared practices and this common religious culture were as central to the identity of the early Methodist converts as their new sense of individuality.

WHITE-HOT PIETY

The most striking characteristic of the lay narratives in manuscript, when compared with the published journals of the clergy and the later memoirs of the lay preachers, is the raw, unedited intensity of the religious experiences. It is significant that these accounts were written as familiar letters. The accounts were typically short, with the handwriting covering two sides of a quarto sheet or less (though there were a few writers who reached for a second sheet). And the accounts were occasional and ad hoc, responding in an unpremeditated way to the request of a pastor for more information about an episode in the writer's life. As letters, these accounts were also written and intended for a known and familiar audience of one. Consequently, such narratives reflected much more clearly a moment in the life rather than the summing up of a life. With a few exceptions we know little of the future history of these converts, whether they lived to fulfil the expectations of their narratives, or whether their lives took a different

---

[83] S. Ibison (23 May 1740), William Barber [1741], and Elizabeth Downs (13 Apr. 1742), EMV. For Samuel Tippett, see Barry and Morgan (eds.), *Reformation and Revival in Bristol*, 122.

[84] *WV* vi. 11, 38.

[85] Joseph Humphreys (3 Dec. 1741), EMV.

direction. There is something very punctual about these documents, unlike the serial autobiographies of the leaders and the life-englobing memoirs of the lay preachers.

This is not, however, simply a matter of the form of the familiar letter. These accounts of conversion are generally open and untidy, without a strong or imposed morphology. They are cyclical and labyrinthine, intense but often incomplete. William James described raw sense perception as a 'blooming, buzzing confusion' until ordered by categories of the mind.[86] The Methodist lay narratives are much closer to the 'blooming, buzzing confusion' of the Evangelical Revival than many of the other autobiographical documents that derive from the period. Very few of the writers could have been aware in any meaningful sense that they were writing in a literary genre. In so far as they picked up a sense of narrative convention—a principle of selection and omission—they did so in the immediate discourse of the Methodist community: through preaching, singing, and testimony. Through these communal practices they learned what was commonly expected in religious experience, and what was common became, in literary terms, conventional. (Conventional, in this sense, does not of course mean monotonous or dull, any more than the literary conventions of poetry constrain creativity.) Thus, ultimately, these conventions were lived out. In expectation of conversion, evangelical discourse acted like a map, identifying the sort of terrain one might cross and the sort of destination one might arrive at if one chose to venture out, waiting upon God in the means of grace. Changing metaphors, this discourse acted like a magnet that could draw from memory certain spiritually charged episodes in one's past life, and assign significance to them. Uniquely, we are able, in these letters, to look in on the experience of conversion in the Evangelical Revival before it gets tidied up, placed in due order, and fixed in memory and text. Perhaps Charles Wesley even solicited these accounts to that end—that as a pastor he could help his people make better sense of their experience.

What is therefore foregrounded in these accounts, more than others, is the overwhelming expectation of the converts that the experience of God, and especially a climactic sense of sins forgiven, would arise spontaneously. The expectation was not that one would achieve that great desideratum of assurance of salvation through volition or by ratiocination. There was no direction in which one could apply the will other than in 'waiting in the means of grace'—a waiting on tiptoes in the hopes that maybe now, maybe this time, I shall experience a direct intuition of my acceptance in the Beloved. And there was no simple act of rational introspection by which one could deduce one's own conversion. These laymen and laywomen would, as it were, hold their souls up to the light of God like a mirror and

---

[86] William James, *Writings, 1902–1910*, ed. Bruce Kuklick (New York, 1987), 1008.

hope against hope to see a spontaneous, uncontrived reflection there. As one of John Cennick's hymns expressed this:

> If e'er I would my *Saviour* find,
>   I to my Heart repair:
> If e'er I want to know his Mind,
>   I go and learn it there.[87]

The language of the converts was often, therefore, in the passive voice, and they very much felt themselves to be engaged in an act of discovery more than an act of construction.

However, because they thus privileged the direct and sensible experience of divine favour or disfavour, the converts in these narratives oscillated back and forth between joy and despair. There was rarely one simple passage from anxiety to relief. Conversion for these laypeople was an agonistic experience. Charles Wesley's sermon on the three states, preached so many times during the early years of the revival, emphasized 'striving' as the characteristic of the person who was awakened to spiritual things but remained suspended between spiritual death and spiritual life, between acquiescence in sin and victory over sin. People in this middle state were 'striving to enter in at the strait gate', and were those who 'labour after the renewal of their souls', only to find themselves caught in a cycle of repentance and moral failure. They sometimes thought themselves in that state of 'the glorious liberty of the sons of God', but were deluded about 'what they call their conversion'. About such a person, Charles Wesley wrote, 'He treads the same dreadful round of sin, repenting and sinning again. His comfort is withdrawn, his peace is lost: he pray[s], resolves and strives, but all in vain; the more he labours, the less he prevails; the more he struggles, the faster he is bound.'[88]

In the lay narratives we can observe this dialectical experience, repeated over and over again, and taken up and transposed into new keys in other contexts. For example, between March and September 1739, Elisabeth Hinsome experienced first an awakening of conscience ('I know myself a damd sinner') and then a conversion ('I went home full of joye'). From the published accounts of early evangelical conversions, such as that of Sampson Staniforth—who so clearly made this sort of event the turning point in his life—we might expect that this was the *terminus ad quem* of her narrative, and that what followed would be a denouement. In Aristotelian terms, we have already had a beginning, middle, and end—situation, transformation, situation. But, on the contrary, as Elisabeth Hinsome's narrative continues, we find that this experience of anxiety and relief is repeated, and as readers

---

[87] John Cennick, *Sacred Hymns For the Use of Religious Societies* (1764), part iii, hymn 5.
[88] *Sermons of Charles Wesley*, 139.

we are left wondering, like peeling back layers of an onion, whether we have yet reached the core of her conversion. Only a day after her first 'conversion' she lost her feeling of joy. As so often in these accounts, this was experienced as preternatural psychomachy: 'Satan came in and told me I had lost christ and I mite as well hang my self.' She expressed her longing for a return of spiritual joy eloquently: 'I was ready to cry out with mary, they have taken a way my lord and I know not ware they have laid him.' And, sure enough, she had an intimation that her comforts would return, and under the public prayers of Charles Wesley, 'the lord came a gane to my soul with pwoer [*sic*]'. This was round two, but it was not the end. A week later the whole cycle was repeated again. It is often the word 'again' in these narratives that signals the reinscribing of this pattern, as when Taverner Wallis wrote during one of these many cycles, 'I fell again,' or 'I was again restored to his favour.'[89]

More than a century before, William Perkins had written of the seventh stage in the process of conversion as one in which faith was tested by doubt, despair, and distrust. The difference in the testing of conversion for these later converts was that they regarded their religious feelings so entirely as the locus of this testing and presented themselves as so keenly sensible to the evocation of despair or joy. The very evanescence of these emotional states meant that conversion itself did not appear nearly as linear a process among the lay Methodists as it did in Perkins's analysis. Conversion was, in the 1740s, an unstable compound.

This also meant that the travail of conversion, and the testing and temptation that accompanied it, typically involved a kind of vertigo, as the subjects often really could not locate themselves in spiritual space. What did their feelings mean? Were they forgiven, or were they under the just and eternal condemnation of God? This situation led to the oft-repeated confession that the writers thought they were going mad or were tempted, like Hinsome, to kill themselves.[90] Thomas Cooper wrote, 'Now the devil tempted me to go and hang myself.' Elizabeth Downs confessed, 'I could bee Glad to quitt myself of the world but I so dreaded the torments of Hell,' and again, 'I could have dispatched myself.' Sister Macham locked herself in her bedchamber with a knife, but was prevented from killing herself by her husband.[91] This sort of nervous desperation was a corollary of the unresolved oscillation between fear and hope that was so characteristic of these

---

[89] Elizabeth Hinsome (25 May 1740), EMV.

[90] Concerns about madness and suicide in conversion narratives are discussed further in Ch. 8 in the context of William Cowper's autobiography.

[91] Thomas Cooper [1741], Elizabeth Downs (13 Apr. 1742), and 'Account of Sister Macham' [1765], EMV; cf. the similar accounts of temptation to suicide in the narratives of the lay preachers John Valton, Robert Wilkinson, John Prickard, and Thomas Payne. *WV* i. 14; v. 231; iii. 230; *EMP* (1998), i. 441.

narratives. Conversion was experienced on the cusp of a very heightened emotional sensibility.

As Taverner Wallis, Elisabeth Hinsome, and Ann Martin talked about this sort of experience, each of them alluded in different ways to the biblical exodus from Egypt, the sojourn in the wilderness, and the promise of Canaan. The trope of post-conversion testing as a 'wilderness state' was in fact the subject of one of John Wesley's sermons (dated variously as either 1751 or 1760). Wesley's text was, 'Ye now have sorrow: But I will see you again, and your heart shall rejoice, and your joy no man taketh from you' (John 16: 22). When, however, Wesley discussed the reasons for the believer's loss of faith, love, joy, peace, and power, he made no concession to temperament, illness, or the transitory nature of emotion. Without question, he argued, the normal state of the believer is happiness. Wesley distanced himself from the notion in Catholic spiritual theology that God himself sometimes withdraws from the believer and that a 'dark night' experience is in any way necessary or normative: 'He never *deserts* us, as some speak; it is we only that *desert* him.'[92] The only reasons Wesley allowed that a believer might not be happy are sin, ignorance, or temptation. Understandably, then, this eudaemonistic teaching—that spiritual happiness could be largely equated with the spiritual good—was mirrored in the lay narratives in their intense preoccupation with various states of joy and sorrow.

Wesley's sermon allows us to revisit the relationship of the Methodist leaders to the laity in general terms. In Jonathan Edwards's *Treatise Concerning Religious Affections* he analysed the relationship between the sort of white-hot piety we have seen in the early Methodist lay narratives of conversion and the gradual development of order, plot, or, as he put it, 'a scheme':

A scheme of what is necessary, and according to a rule already received and established by common opinion, has a vast (though to many a very insensible) influence in forming persons' notions of the steps and method of their own experiences. I know very well what their way is, for I have had much opportunity to observe it. Very much, at first, their experiences appear like a confused chaos... but then those passages of their experience are picked out, that have most of the appearance of such particular steps that are insisted on; and these are dwelt upon in the thoughts, and these are told of from time to time in the relation they give: these parts grow brighter and brighter in their view; and others, being neglected, grow more and more obscure: and what they have experienced is insensibly strained to bring all into an exact conformity to the scheme that is established.[93]

---

[92] Wesley, *Works* (BE), ii. 208.
[93] *WJE* ii. 162.

What Edwards referred to as a rule 'received and established by common opinion' that 'insensibly strained' the experience of his parishioners was something in the early Methodist context that was provided by the leaders through their own example in their journals and through the interpretative culture they superintended. Such influence and such culture supplied the principles by which one selected, arranged, and explained the events of one's life. This 'insensible straining' of experience had, however, only just begun in these lay testimonies. In the *Lebensläufe* of the Moravians, the 'Experiences' of the Cambuslang converts, and the memoirs of the early Methodist lay preachers we shall be able to see an evangelical *ordo* increasingly drawn out in narrative form.

5

'Poor Sinnership': Moravian Narrative Culture

FROM the embryonic evangelical movement in 1738–9 there arose discrete evangelical communities, and these communities were distinguished in part by the autobiographical narratives they fostered and preserved. The breach between Wesley and Whitefield over Calvinism began in 1739 and became common knowledge in 1741, when Wesley publicly tore up Whitefield's open letter on predestination. Soon lay followers such as Joseph Humphreys and John Cennick were choosing sides. In July 1740 Wesley led a secession from the pro-Moravian Fetter Lane Society over the issue of 'stillness', and this second breach soon became permanent despite various attempts to heal the division. The Fetter Lane Society itself was reorganized and settled as a Moravian congregation on 30 October 1742. According to estimates based upon Moravian sources, the Moravians were by 1748 overseeing between 5,000 and 6,000 souls, while Wesley's followers amounted to some 12,000 and Whitefield's to 20,000 (before John Cennick seceded with his societies).[1]

Each of these souls also had a story to tell. Indeed, the narrative culture that emerged among English Moravians out of the original undivided revival movement in the 1730s bore witness to a different view of conversion. Consequently, among the Moravian laity we are able to observe a sub-genre of the evangelical conversion narrative, one in which soul-distress under the preaching of the law was replaced by the ideal of self-abandonment and childlike trust in the love of the bleeding Saviour.

THE MORAVIANS AND THE EVANGELICAL REVIVAL

Notwithstanding the importance of the Moravians to the English revival, they did not arrive in England with a missionary strategy, seeking to acquire converts or establish a church. Soon after the quasi-pentecostal experience

---

[1] Colin Podmore, *The Moravian Church in England, 1728–1760* (Oxford, 1998), 120. Numbers would change dramatically by the end of the century with the growth of Methodism and New Dissent. See Alan D. Gilbert, *Religion and Society in Industrial England* (1976), 23–48; Robert Currie, Lee S. Horsley, and Alan D. Gilbert, *Churches and Churchgoers: Patterns of Church Growth in the British Isles Since 1700* (Oxford, 1977), 23–4; Michael R. Watts, *The Dissenters* (Oxford, 1995), ii. 22–9.

among the eastern European refugees at Herrnhut in Upper Lusatia, the event that gave birth to the Renewed Unitas Fratrum or Moravian Church in 1727, members made contact with Protestants in England. As Colin Podmore has argued, their motivation throughout the next decade was to establish ecumenical relations and facilitate the settlement of some Moravians in the new colony of Georgia. The role they came to play in the network of religious societies in London was thus unplanned, but that role was significant and out of all proportion to their numbers.[2]

During 1738–40 a new religious society was formed at Fetter Lane in London, a society that would prove the matrix for both Methodism and the English Moravian Church. The Fetter Lane Society and figures such as Peter Böhler have already appeared in our account of the Methodist leaders and laity during the revival in 1739. According to Wesley's version of events, recorded especially in his fourth *Journal*, he was the co-founder of the society with Peter Böhler but the Moravians took over in his absence, introducing a dangerously quietist theology, and for this reason he led the secession in July 1740. This story looks different from the point of view of Moravian writers.[3] According to Moravian sources Wesley's leadership role in the society was not as central as he made it appear. Instead, it was Böhler who helped form bands and introduced Moravian discipline at Fetter Lane at the request of members, so that the society was already 'pro-Moravian' during the heyday of revival in early 1739. Although the Moravians had not sought influence they increasingly gained it as English men and women— many of them 'awakened' by Whitefield's preaching—turned to them for spiritual guidance. What Wesley decried as 'stillness' on the part of Moravian leadership in 1740, the Moravians themselves regarded as an appropriate pastoral response to the problem of English 'enthusiasm' run amok. Philipp Heinrich Molther, whom Wesley pilloried as the key culprit in the affair, wrote a letter from London back to Herrnhaag in which he described his shock at finding convulsions, crying out, and groaning happening in the meetings at Fetter Lane. It was enough to 'bring one out in a cold sweat', he said.[4] The Moravians were concerned that the Wesleys and Whitefield were working their converts up into a lather by insisting upon a protracted crisis of conscience under the law as the necessary prelude to the experience of grace. After looking at the evidence from Wesley and from Moravian sources, Colin Podmore says, 'It is no longer possible to decide whether Molther had disturbed the confidence of those who were suggestible, or whether he had responded as he felt appropriate to the pastoral situation he found.'[5] Notwithstanding this uncertainty over the extremity of Methodist frenzy, on the one hand, and the extremity of Molther's

---

[2] Podmore, *Moravian Church*, 5–119.   [3] Ibid. 59–65.
[4] Quoted ibid. 59.   [5] Ibid. 64.

doctrine of 'stillness', on the other, it is clear that two narrative cultures of conversion had formed very early in the revival. The critical issue dividing these cultures concerned the extent to which contrition under the law was a necessary preparation for authentic conversion.

Zinzendorf's Rejection of the Pietist Busskampf

Notwithstanding Zinzendorf's enormous debt to Pietism, his own spiritual experience was at odds with the Pietist expectation modelled in the auto-biography of August Hermann Francke that conversion necessarily involved first a painful struggle (*Busskampf*) and then a breakthrough to consolation (*Durchbruch*). On the Franckean model, one was to experience deep contrition until convinced of the justice of his or her own damnation, since it was in the midst of this despair that true faith was born. The Count, on the contrary, had a spiritually precocious childhood, and his religious sensibilities had deepened over time as he grew older, particularly when as a young man at Dusseldorf in 1719 he was emotionally stirred upon contemplating Domenico Feti's painting, *Ecce Homo* ('Behold the Man'), a picture of Christ presented by Pilate after his scourging. The painting bore the inscription, 'This I have suffered for you but what have you done for me?' Zinzendorf was moved by this question. But this experience was no *Busskampf*. Indeed, he came to reject the Pietist stress upon a fixed method of conversion: 'The penitential struggle (*Busskampf*) is mostly a chimera, an imaginary illness, a self-induced sickness.'[6] The Franckean scheme was legalistic 'methodism', and he detested any such statement of general principles about the way conversion must or must not happen. Such Pietist reasoning about conversion was 'pedantic, scholastic, fanatical or even nonsensical'.[7] 'No rules nor Bounds', he said, 'can be prescribed to our Saviour in the Humiliation and Conversion of Sinners.'[8] What Zinzendorf advocated instead was a more cheerful, contemplative spirituality in which one's gaze was directed away from interior states towards the concrete and sensual apprehension of Christ suffering on the cross—something more like his own experience at Dusseldorf. The *Busskampf* was replaced with an understanding of salvation in which no legal preparation was necessary, but only a childlike trust and radical identification with the love of the dying Jesus.[9] 'The ordinary Method of our Saviour', claimed Zinzendorf, 'is not to prescribe Souls a long Preparation and Form of Repentance, but it costs him *oftentimes but one*

---

[6] Quoted in W. R. Ward, *The Protestant Evangelical Awakening* (Cambridge, 1992), 137; cf. id., *Faith and Faction* (1993), 99.

[7] Ward, *Protestant Evangelical Awakening*, 137.

[8] Nicolaus Ludwig Zinzendorf, *Sixteen Discourses on the Redemption of Man by the Death of Christ* (1740), 32.

[9] Peter Erb, Introduction to *Pietists: Selected Writings* (1983), 9, 21; Frederick Dreyer, *The Genesis of Methodism* (Bethlehem, Penn., 1999), 37–44.

Word, and Grace is present and takes away all Sins.'[10] Conversion could in fact be something quick, happy, even cavalier. Evidently the Moravians in America even boasted they could 'make a Christian in three days'.[11]

Again, the timing of this European dispute between Zinzendorf and the Hallensian Pietists is significant for the English revival. The rift occurred on the eve of significant Moravian contact with English Methodists. In 1733 August Gottlieb Spangenberg was dismissed from his post at the Orphan House and University at Halle largely because of his association with Zinzendorf. And according to Frederick Dreyer it was about this same time that Zinzendorf privately rejected the *Busskampf* and adopted his more contemplative, atonement-centred view of conversion.[12] Moreover, Dreyer claims that Zinzendorf did not publicly teach this new doctrine until 1738 and that it did not become formal Moravian teaching until 1740—the year of the Fetter Lane schism involving Wesley. On this reading of events, Wesley was responding to a change within Moravianism itself regarding the doctrine of salvation. Dreyer argues that early Moravianism—the Moravianism that formed Wesley—taught the necessity of the classic penitential struggle characteristic of Pietism. When Zinzendorf moved away from this understanding of conversion, however, the *Busskampf* came to be seen as legalistic.[13] As we shall see below, this division over the question of how one was to understand the role of the law in preparing the sinner's heart for conversion left its mark in the personal conversion narratives of lay Moravians, distinguishing their spiritual autobiographies from those of the Methodists.

Methodist Conversion as 'Legal'

As a result of this Continental background, the Moravians in London in the 1740s easily interpreted early Methodism as Hallensian Pietism redivivus. Here was another dangerously anthropocentric and legalistic spirituality, and thus they sought by their teaching and pastoral efforts to pacify the situation. There were two different views of conversion increasingly circulating among partisans of the revival, and this is borne out in the

---

[10] Zinzendorf, *Sixteen Discourses*, 32.

[11] Ward, *Protestant Evangelical Awakening*, 136n.

[12] Dreyer, *Genesis of Methodism*, 41; cf. Craig D. Atwood, 'Blood, Sex, and Death: Life and Liturgy in Zinzendorf's Bethlehem', Ph.D. thesis (Princeton Theological Seminary, 1995), 22, who places Zinzendorf's break with Pietism in the 1720s.

[13] Dreyer, *Genesis of Methodism*, 40–54. In redressing an imbalance in Methodist historiography, which has not sufficiently appreciated the Continental and Moravian influence upon Wesley, Dreyer overstates his case in the other direction, saying e.g. 'Methodism as a finished and developed system owes little to its background in England. Deriving from German Pietism, it originated in Saxony and came to England by way of Georgia' (ibid. 110). As the previous chapters of this book have tried to argue, however, Wesley was influenced by a range of sources, including several indigenous influences. The *Busskampf* was arguably well established in Puritanism before it appeared in Pietism.

narratives of the laity. In a manuscript memoir in the London Moravian archives Peter Syms, a butcher by trade, told how in 1736 (at about 20 years of age) he joined one of the religious societies in London and got to know Whitefield, the Wesleys, James Hutton, and others. During the 'genl. stirrings among the Souls at that time' he joined in with all 'who were for willing and Running, exercising themselves in all Religious Duties by Fasting, praying, Mortyifying and attending the Com[munio]n'. But then he encountered the zealous preaching of the Moravians Molther, Böhler, Spangenberg, and Toltschig. He thought they had 'more knowledge and experience of the Real matter than I could meet with among other Religious Teachers'. Apparently, these teachers advocated Zinzendorf's more contemplative doctrine of atonement, since Syms wrote, 'My Ideas and course was now altered from seeking Salvation as it were by works of the Law, to an earnest desire to obtain it alone through faith in the Blood of Jesus the all sufficient atonement for Sinner's guilt.' He found that the breakthrough came not by striving but by yielding, and thus he quoted a stanza from a Moravian hymn:

> Strive I to make my own Self poor
> I get much pain and nothing more
> Strive I in comforts to be great
> Instead of Joy I mis'ry meet.

The keyword negated in these lines is the word 'strive'. Rather than in striving, it was in casting himself at the Saviour's feet that Syms experienced 'the Manifesting of his love to me'.[14] Syms stuck by the Moravians when Wesley seceded from Fetter Lane in 1740 and went on in 1742 to become one of the founding members of the London Moravian Congregation. But here in the first-person memoir of an English butcher were recapitulated the very theological issues at stake between Zinzendorf and Halle in the 1730s.

Susannah or 'Suky' Claggett appears frequently in Charles Wesley's *Journal* and he was on intimate terms with several members of her family in 1739 and 1740. Her story provides a further illustration of this fault line between the culture of conversion in Methodism and Moravianism. Four days after John Wesley's Aldersgate experience, Charles met with Susannah and sensed that she was 'under the work of God'. He 'asked, urged, believed that she believed'. While she was trembling and in tears, he 'consulted the oracle for her' and they came up with a series of texts by *sortes Biblicae* that led her through a conversion experience: 'She now openly professed her faith, and increased in confidence every moment.'[15] According to Moravian records

---

[14] Peter Syms (b. 1716), memoir, MCH.

[15] *CWJ* i. 97–8. There were two 'Miss Claggetts' with whom Charles had contact during this period, Susannah (the younger) and Elizabeth or 'Betsy' (the older). There was also a third unnamed younger sister, mentioned in passing in October. I take it that this account

she was probably no more than about 15 or 16 years of age at this point, and, indeed, she did go on with most of her family to join the Moravians. She died among them at 79 years of age and the Moravian archives include her ten-page autobiographical memoir written (or at least concluded) late in life, with a posthumous commentary by a third-party continuator, as was typical of these *Lebensläufe*. In this memoir we get a different version of what happened to Susannah while under the direction of Charles Wesley. She wrote of 'a great awakening' that took place in London and 'drew us all together in a wonderful manner', adding the commentary, 'but our course was very legal'. She came increasingly under the influence of Molther, Böhler, and other Moravians, and then she met Zinzendorf himself. 'In a blessed Meeting kept by the dear Count Zinzendorf, I had an amazing stroke upon my heart, as if stabbed to the quick by the sword of the spirit.' Lest the reader be confused about what kind of conversion this was, she continued, 'This was a new awakening of an evangelical kind, differing entirely from the former, which was legal: now I was in a quite particular leading of the holy Spirit.—I felt my deep depravity, but not with fright and terror. Floods of tears streamed from my eyes, and in a tender godly sorrow and contrition my heart was day and night sighing soft for the Beloved.'[16] Her conversion was clearly of the Moravian type ('sighing soft for the Beloved') and not of the Methodist-Pietist sort ('with fright and terror').

The issue of whether one needed to go through an agony of conscience before being truly converted became a point of dispute between Methodists and Moravians during the stillness controversy in 1740. The Wesleys were regarded by Moravians such as James Hutton as 'legal' for their insistence upon this preliminary work of travail—their emphasis upon the 'spirituality of the law' noted in the last chapter. Like the earlier debate in New England over 'preparationism' in conversion, the issue was now construed as one of legalism versus antinomianism. Certainly, John Wesley believed in the preparatory work of the law. He urged the lay preacher Joseph Cownley in 1750,

Let the law always prepare for the gospel. I scarce ever spoke more earnestly here of the love of God in Christ than last night; but it was after I had been tearing the unawakened in pieces. Go thou and do likewise. It is true the love of God in Christ alone feeds his children; but even they are to be guided as well as fed—yea, and often physicked too: and the bulk of our hearers must be purged before they are fed; else we only feed the disease. Beware of all honey.[17]

above relates to Susannah Claggett, since Betsy's conversion was told to Charles by Susannah a month later (*CWJ* i. 112–13). Of the Claggett daughters in the Moravian records, only Susannah and Betsy were old enough in 1738 to be the subjects of Charles's journal entries.

[16] Susannah Claggett (*c.*1723–*c.*1802), memoir, MCH.
[17] *JWL* iii. 34.

That the early lay members of the undivided society had come to regard the soul struggle of the awakened sinner as *de rigueur* is clear from Mary Thomas's eavesdropping on a conversation: 'Two young women sat behind me and telling how they was and how they had cryd out such a time and what an agony they had been in before they had received forgiveness, and they said that those that did not feel those agonies, that they deceived themselves.'[18] The result was that Mary Thomas herself began to doubt her justification. It was this sort of anxiety that the Moravian teaching about conversion challenged.

The divergence between Moravian and Methodist in their understanding of conversion involved not only a difference regarding the place of the law in inducing a psychological crisis preparatory to conversion, but also extended to the issue of how far one might take any initiative to use means towards one's own conversion—means such as going to church, hearing sermons, praying, and taking the sacrament. How far was one to remain 'still'? The debate about 'stillness' is writ large in many of the lay narratives in both the Moravian and Methodist archives. In 1741 William Barber recalled how worried he was when his wife came home from a band meeting and reported that Molther had said, 'the Sacrament was onely for such as was in such a state as She described to me'. He was uneasy since he knew he was not in that spiritual state. Elizabeth Hinsome stayed away from church and sacrament until her mother asked her to go, and then she was too ashamed not to. Taverner Wallis heard Richard Viney 'speak ag[ains]t the means' and claimed this led him 'back into the World, and into Sin'. Thomas Cooper claimed he was challenged by the 'German bretheren' to go to bed without prayer and to cease praying altogether for a fortnight to prove that he was not trusting in his own works. Many of his acquaintances, he said, left off prayer and going to the sacrament and were now almost as bad as if they had never been awakened. Samuel Webb, however, went to Fetter Lane twice a week and 'heard them Preach their Still Doctrine', but for his part he did not think they were saying anything more than that you ought not to trust that routine religious practices could in any way merit salvation.[19]

This testimony comes from letters written to Charles Wesley during a period roughly contemporary with the events recorded, and it signals again that doctrinal debate will lead to separate narrative cultures at a popular level. John and Charles Wesley soon entered the lists against the Moravians in print, to follow up and defend the secession from Fetter Lane, and much of what they had to say was collected and reprinted in a pamphlet entitled,

[18] Mary Thomas (24 May 1742), EMV.
[19] William Barber [1741], Elizabeth Hinsome (25 May 1740), Taverner Wallis (24 Nov. 1741), Thomas Cooper [1741], and Samuel Webb (20 Nov. 1741), EMV.

Short View of the Difference Between the Moravian Brethren, Lately in England, and the Reverend Mr. John and Charles Wesley (1748). The pamphlet included six anti-Moravian hymns by Charles, and these rounded out the Methodist objections to Moravian views of conversion and stillness. For example, the hymn, 'For those that are turned out of the way', includes the provocative stanza (addressing God),

> In vain, till Thou the Power bestow
>   The double Pow'r of quic'ning Grace,
> And make the *Happy Sinners* know
>   Their Tempter with his Angel-Face,
> Who leads them Captive at his Will
> Captive—but *Happy Sinners* still.

Picking up the vogue diction among Moravians of being 'happy sinners', Charles Wesley makes the phrase ironic here, since the final word of the stanza is a double entendre, meaning that the Moravians are not only still, but they are still happily sinning. Stillness was for the Wesleys a diabolical doctrine, and so the imperative rings out in another hymn: 'Never more our Duty leave, | When Satan cries, *be still!*' With their differences thus aired in private letters and in public rhetoric, Methodists and Moravians would increasingly go their separate ways.

Consequently, during the 1740s Moravian and Methodist relations blew hot and cold. Wesley and Whitefield remained attracted, even enchanted, by Moravian piety but ultimately kept their distance because of insurmountable doctrinal disagreements. None the less, there were serious attempts at rapprochement, and Whitefield even proposed a full union of his Association with the Moravians in 1742. These attempts at reunion failed not only because of doctrinal differences, but also because of personality clashes and the increasingly distinct identities of the personal connexions formed by the Methodists. It would be wrong, however, to give the impression of Methodism and Moravianism as two entirely separate spheres, especially in these early years. The lay preacher John Cennick, for example, was a member of the Fetter Lane society, who worked with Wesley until 1741 and Whitefield until 1745, before joining the Moravians entirely, taking several societies in Wiltshire with him and prompting many other individual Methodists to follow suit. Benjamin Ingham had done similarly with his own societies in the north a few years earlier. There were two cultures of conversion, but there was also plenty of traffic between them.

MORAVIAN ORGANIZATION, DISCIPLINE, AND RECORDED EXPERIENCE

From this beginning, Moravian organization expanded rapidly in England. In 1742 the Moravian leadership began to establish formal congregations as a recognition of their obligation to provide pastoral oversight to those who had come to them for direction. From personal relationships formed during the lengthy delays in London, while Moravians were en route to Georgia, there developed an unsought influence upon the religious societies. As Wesley and Whitefield withdrew and formed their own connexions, the Moravians came to supervise a diaspora of their own cells within the Church of England. Zinzendorf believed that his wider international, interconfessional *Brüdergemeine*, or Church of the United Brethren, was neither a visible church alongside other confessions, nor a supra–church comprising all others. It was, rather, an experimental fellowship that made visible the unity of the children of God hidden among the world's various churches.[20] As Craig Atwood writes, the *Gemeine* was, for Zinzendorf, 'distinct from a congregation or a religion or a church'. It was an extension of Spener's concept of the *ecclesiola*, a place 'where a group of likeminded individuals motivated by the love of Christ establish a community of love within the established church... and spend their time together not in speculating on divine mysteries or developing novel doctrines, but simply in mutual exhortation and edification'.[21]

The forms of community life for English Moravians evolved over time.[22] The society, whose members were still dependent upon the local parish church for sacraments, consisted of women and men who were not members of the Moravian Church itself. Moravian influence in England began with pastoral oversight of such societies, and these societies were the nucleus of early Methodism as well. Society members often longed for a closer connection to the Moravian Church, however, and from 1742 (when the first Moravian congregations in England were established) they could apply for membership in a congregation. The congregation was the formal ecclesiastical body, whose members received the sacraments and came under the episcopal order and discipline of the Moravian Church. There were different types of congregations, and members moved among them. Zinzendorf's 'pilgrim congregation' was a mobile congregation that gave leadership to the church. 'Town congregations' were formed in places such as London and Bedford. And there were also 'house congregations' such as at Lamb's Inn (Broadoaks). Modelled upon Herrnhaag, the settlement was, however, the ideal for the Moravian congregation—in effect, a Protestant monastery with members of both sexes, single and married, in all stations of life. The congregation formed in Bethlehem, Pennsylvania most thoroughly realized this ideal of a residential economic and spiritual community. Yet even many

---

[20] Podmore, *Moravian Church*, 162.

[21] Atwood, 'Blood, Sex, and Death', 33 n.

[22] Edwin Welch (ed.), Introduction to *The Bedford Moravian Church in the Eighteenth Century* (Bedford, 1989), 10.

of the town congregations developed patterns of more intensive communal life, as was the case, for example, in London, where a number of Moravians moved to community houses nearby the chapel. The commitment to community life among Moravians was thus reflected in a variety of forms, but this commitment was fervent. As Craig Atwood writes, 'The Moravian demand for absolute devotion to Christ was also a demand for devotion to the community that Christ had created.'[23]

The first formal Moravian congregations in England were formed out of the Fetter Lane society in London in 1742. The Bedford Congregation followed in 1745, and another eight congregations were established in Britain by 1755. Fulneck in Yorkshire was the first settlement, founded in 1744, and most of the settlements that followed were likewise established in rural areas, including Ockbrook in Derbyshire, and Fairfield near Manchester. The organization of Moravian community life in town congregations and rural settlements was elaborate. Although there was some variation in practice, the life of the congregation included a system of separately organized divisions of the community ('choirs') for the pastoral care of single men, single women, married couples, and widows and widowers; ordered economic arrangements; a highly structured liturgical life; and a series of committees and offices of leadership.[24] All this was further integrated into the larger provincial and general synodical structure of the international Moravian Church through further committees, visitation, and a remarkably comprehensive system of reporting and exchanging records.

Within this elaborate Moravian discipline record-keeping and spiritual biography played a key role. Like other evangelicals on both sides of the Atlantic, Moravians believed that God was working among them in their own times, and that it was important to record what was happening in diaries, letters, memoirs, and even the minutes of committee meetings. This was analogous to Methodism but much more highly organized, as is evident from even a brief survey of the British Provincial archive. Zinzendorf adapted the *Hausarchiv* of a German aristocrat, as had earlier Pietists, to serve evangelical purposes.[25] But the sheer bulk of this archive is significant not as the reflection of some sort of mundane denominational bureaucracy, but for the spiritual sense its writers and readers had that this archive was the very record of salvation history. Moreover, Zinzendorf believed that the individual's radical identification with Christ made his or her life a symbol or re-presentation of Christ's own life and death. It is within this context

---

[23] Craig D. Atwood, 'Sleeping in the Arms of Christ: Sanctifying Sexuality in the Eighteenth-Century Moravian Church', *Journal of the History of Sexuality* 8 (1997), 27.

[24] See further, Podmore, *Moravian Church*, 136–58.

[25] Ibid. 3.

that we must see the archives, and especially the spiritual autobiographies of the early English Moravians.

In the Moravian archives the distinction already observed in Methodism—between leaders who kept journals and diaries, and followers who wrote ad hoc narratives of spiritual experience—holds true, but in the case of the Moravians these documents were part of a consistent ecclesiastical discipline. The minister of each congregation kept a 'congregation diary' that recorded events in the local Moravian life and in the larger community, and like the Methodist journals, these diaries were abstracted and reproduced for distribution to other congregations. For the Bedford Congregation, three of the original four diaries of ministers have survived—one of these in the summarized form in which it was read aloud at a watch night service.[26] The 'congregation diary' was thus the central record, but it was also a model for all aspects of congregational life. At Moravian Church House in London, for example, in addition to the forty-one volumes of the congregation diary for the Fetter Lane Congregation (1742–1928), the shelves are lined with multiple volumes of the 'Elders' Conference Minutes', the 'Daily Helpers' Conference Minutes', 'Chapel Servants' Conference Minutes', 'Minute Book of the Committee of Wardens', 'Congregational Council Minutes', and another seven 'sundry single volumes'—all this for Fetter Lane alone. To this congregational level of record-keeping may be added records at a supra-congregational level in the minutes and resolutions of General and Provincial Synods, and at a sub-congregational or individual level in the hundreds of unbound manuscripts of personal letters of application to the congregation for membership or confirmation, or the memoirs of members.

The last of these—the Moravian memoirs—were a distinctive form of evangelical spiritual autobiography.[27] These were variously called memoirs, memorials, personalia, lives, relations, or simply 'course of life' as a direct English translation of the German *Lebenslauf* or Latin *curriculum vitae*. Hundreds of these accounts are preserved in England in the archives at Moravian Church House in London, the University of Bristol, the Bedfordshire Record Office, and in the archives that remain *in situ* at Fulneck, Ockbrook, and elsewhere. A selection of records from these archives, and from the archives of the Moravian community at Bethlehem, Pennsylvania, has been published.[28]

---

[26] Welch (ed.), *Bedford Moravian Church*, 12, 22–74.

[27] See further, Katherine M. Faull (ed.), Introduction to *Moravian Women's Memoirs* (Syracuse, NY, 1997), pp. xxxi–xl; ead., 'The American *Lebenslauf*: Women's Autobiography in Eighteenth-Century Moravian Bethlehem', *Yearbook of German-American Studies* 27 (1992), 23–48; Beverly Prior Smaby, *The Transformation of Moravian Bethlehem* (Philadelphia, Penn., 1988), 125–80; Ward, Introduction to Wesley, *Works* (BE), xviii. 17–20.

[28] J. Barry and K. Morgan (eds.), *Reformation and Revival in Eighteenth-Century Bristol* (Bristol, 1994); Welch (ed.), *Bedford Moravian Church*; Faull (ed.), *Moravian Women's Memoirs*.

How did these archives originate? As W. R. Ward has described, it was part of Moravian and Methodist practice from the beginning to expect members of bands to be open and frank with each other and to speak of their spiritual experience. Uniquely, however, the Moravians not only received these accounts of religious experience, but they collected them and bound them in books. After 1760, during the post-Zinzendorf era, many of these volumes were destroyed as part of the effort to purge the church of its early excesses. Nevertheless, by the middle of the century various forms of spiritual autobiography had evolved, and the practice of life-writing was well established.[29] The international synod in 1764, and those that followed, would issue particular instructions about the practice of collecting and preserving memoirs. Unlike the Methodist accounts by laypeople, which were solicited ad hoc by Charles Wesley, the Moravian *Lebensläufe* were formally required of members. The General Synod passed a resolution that obliged the Elders' conference of every congregation to send in a monthly summary of 'the most remarkable occurences in that Cong:n; of Child:n who were born . . . of those who are gone to our Sav:r and especially also the Course of Grace in their Cong:n. Is there a peculiar, remarkable life of a departed Brother or Sister? The same is to be added.'[30] The General Synod also regulated these narratives, and its resolutions included the admonition: 'that the courses of Life of our Brn and Srs ought in particular to be without flattery and strictly true'.[31] There was evidently a concern that obituaries in particular might not tell the whole story. But then again, the Synod had to add that it did not always want the whole story, especially if the whole story included details that were indiscreet and ought not to be communicated more widely. This was true even at the congregational level. 'The Labourer in the Religions should make *prudent* use of the Accounts which they receive,' the Synod instructed, adding that 'the Readers in the Cong:ns should read every Accounts [*sic*] previous at home before they are communicated to the Congregation'.[32]

At both congregational and synodical levels of governance, there was a delicate balance that Moravian leaders were seeking to achieve, a balance between candour and editorial control: 'With regard to the *Personalia* or lives of those who are gone home, the Synod is forced to repeat very earnestly . . . that they may not appear as painted or ornamented, nor to[o] much good said therein, but that everything be laid out openly and honestly according to simple truth.' Yet this concern for frankness had limits, one of which was, as it were, the inviolability of the confessional: 'But this does not

---

[29] Ward, Introduction to Wesley, *Works* (BE), xviii. 17–19.

[30] Minutes of the General Synod at Marienborn, 1 July–17 Sept. 1769, MCH 184.

[31] Resolutions of the General Synod at Marienborn, 2 July–22 Aug. 1764, MCH 34.

[32] Harmony of the Synods of 1764, 1769, 1775, and 1782, vol. 2, MCH ch. xxi.

mean, that such faults also of the deceased, which perhaps are only known to their Choir Labourers, are to be uncovered and openly mentioned for this must by no means be done.' The Synod was also aware of the danger that Moravian narrative could easily become hackneyed, and so it continued with an exhortation to local biographers, 'Those who draw up these lives, are also to be put in mind, not to tie themselves to certain forms, but express themselves simply and naturally.' But the final instruction was that the best solution of all was to make sure that everyone wrote his or her own narrative: 'At the same time the Synod again desires the Brothers and Sisters heartily, that everyone would if possible, write down something of their own course of grace or dictate it to somebody rather than leaving things to be drawn up by others, as the relation drawn up by the person themselves, is quite another thing and of more effect than when drawn up by a stranger.'[33] In the best of all possible worlds, every Moravian was to be a spiritual autobiographer.

MORAVIAN SPIRITUAL AUTOBIOGRAPHY

How then did spiritual autobiography in general, and evangelical conversion narrative in particular, appear among English-speaking Moravians as the movement developed its own life apart from Methodism in the 1740s and afterward? Moravian conversion narratives differed from the Methodist narratives associated with the followers of George Whitefield and John and Charles Wesley in three principal ways: they were more quietist and less agonistic; they were more preoccupied with devotion to the bodily suffering of Christ than with monitoring inner emotional states, a devotion that passed over into responding to Christ as a wounded lover and bridegroom; and their narratives were more shaped by liturgical rhythms, stressing the importance of formal ecclesiastical rites such as admission, confirmation, first communion, and funerals, than were their Methodist counterparts. These emphases looked back to Zinzendorf's own formation and his distinctive theology, and to the importance for Zinzendorf of the medieval mystical tradition, mediated to him through his reading and his friendships with Catholic clergy, such as the bishop of Paris, Cardinal Noailles.[34] Indeed, just as the Wesleys supervised a narrative culture within Methodism that bore the impress of their own theology, so also Zinzendorf's beliefs and example were defining for Moravian laypeople.

Self-Abandoning Quietism

The quietism that Wesley called 'stillness' in the 1740s was reflected in the Moravian memoirs not in an antinomian rejection of church ordinances and

---

[33] Harmony of the Synods of 1764, 1769, 1775, and 1782, vol. 2, MCH ch. xxi.
[34] Ward, *Faith and Faction*, 114–15; Faul (ed.), *Moravian Women's Memoirs*, p. xxii.

spiritual disciplines, as the Methodists feared, but in a whole ethos of self-yielding, self-abasing resignation to the will of God and the will of the community. This was held up as the great ideal of the spiritual life, and thus the characteristic Moravian diction in these narratives involved the author describing himself or herself as a 'poor sinner' or 'sinner-like'. Here at a popular level in the narratives of London artisans, servants, and merchants was the spiritual language—albeit often clichéd and unrefined—of Madame Guyon, François Fenelon, and Jean-Pierre de Caussade. Zinzendorf had led several discussions about Guyon's writings at Herrnhut, and though he did not seek to promote them, he was influenced by her theology and that of other mystics to redefine his own understanding of faith as a matter of religious feeling and direct spiritual perception. Instead of a struggle, conversion involved looking to Christ and yielding to him as one's all. For Zinzendorf this implied an ideal of childlikeness and simplicity. Thus he wrote, 'Here one must do nothing but quietly attend the Voice of the Lord, when he comes to approach the Heart with his Power, with his Fire, with his Drawings, and with his Spirit.'[35] This was reflected in the language of the Moravian converts. Susannah Claggett wrote, 'I rejoice in this, that I am nothing, *He is all!*' Peter Syms described how 'the H. Spirit compelled me to cast my Seolf with all my Misery and Darkness at our Saviour's Feet scarce expecting that Mercy for such a wretched Creature was to be obtained', and added, 'I find cause for deep abasement.' Sarah Verney spoke the vernacular when she wrote that Christ 'gave me grace to be truly a sinner before him . . . I cannot express in words how ashamed I was, and truly abased before him.' Ever afterwards, she noted, 'I kept more sinnerlikely to him.'[36]

Applications for membership were also occasions for self-writing and this seemed particularly to call out expressions of longing to be as nothing before God. 'Never did I feel my Self so exceeding Poor good for nothing weak Creature as I am at Present,' wrote John West. Thomas Lateward's application for membership was likewise abject, but when he wrote to offer himself to organize a school for the Moravian children in London, the quietist ideals came through most clearly. He communicated his desires but then added a long caveat, saying that what he wanted most of all was 'to have no will of my own, for I find my own will to be so hurtful in many things that I hope I shall gladly give it up, to be drowned in our Dear Saviour's Blood'.[37]

Moravian autobiographers also expressed a strong longing to be enfolded in the community itself. Notwithstanding their high membership standards,

---

[35] Zinzendorf, *Sixteen Discourses*, 29.

[36] Susannah Claggett, Peter Syms, and Sarah Verney (1758–95), memoirs, MCH.

[37] John West (n.d.) and Thomas Lateward (8 Nov. 1742), letters of application, 1740s, MCH.

the Moravian Church held great appeal for many English men and women. Converts often felt that this international community of believers, with its primitive discipline and profound *koinonia*, represented the true church of Christ, under his direct rule. Here at last, you could be sure you had found Mother Church. Thomas Lateward wanted to be 'admitted into the Number of his Witnesses and Pilgrim's to go through the World', and added, 'I kiss and embrace heartily the whole Church.' Olaus Backer wrote in his application that he had 'a great desire to belong to you'. He wanted to be part of the 'Sinner flok' and to be received in Christ's church, 'which is his Bride upon earth'.[38] The Moravian Church was seen as a refuge, and their reputation for pastoral care, extending to guidance about marriage and sex, drew many. In the Moravians, English converts found a disciplined, settled community, a safe haven in the midst of the world's troubles, a place where within intimate small groups they could unburden their souls with complete honesty, and where within worship they could express themselves with emotional intensity. Consequently, once they had tasted something of Moravian worship and community life, they longed for more. Susannah Claggett had 'a powerful and irresistible call to be a Member... It was extremely important to me to be united to this part of the Bride of Christ.' Susannah Duree's writing was unsteady and her spelling rough and phonetic, but she, too, longed for closer union with the Moravians: 'The prayers Days has Beane a great Blesin to my hart wich makes me long to get Kuite neare to my Saver Children that I may portake of those Blesin wich thay in joy.' Mary Lewis confessed, 'I feell such a feloship when I am with you and so much coldness wen I am from you that I want to be closer to you.' Thomas and Mary Lidington applied together, saying, 'We are poor and helpless and stand in need of your Care and wachfulness and So we Committ our selvs unto you to do what is best.' John and Mary Lindstrum almost quivered with desire, 'Longing and Thirsting to be Joined, to our Dear Lambs Church in a more Cloesser Connection'. Thomas and Martha Babair picked out the metaphor that underlies many of the applications, namely, the desire to be home, out of the cold: 'I am colder by being in the open Air, than if I was in the House.' Some such spiritual *Sehnsucht* seems to be present in most of these applications. Finally, Thomas Everitt combined the longing to submit wholly to Christ and to surrender wholly to the community in the language of 'the sifting time' when he spoke of joining the church as being 'Ingrafted or rather Inoculated into that Cavity the Side Hole that so I may partake more freely and plentifully of that Sap of Life'.[39]

[38] Thomas Lateward (n.d.), and Olaus Backer (n.d.), letters of application, 1740s, MCH.
[39] Susannah Claggett, memoir; Susannah Duree (3 May [n.y.]), Mary Lewis (20 July 1745), Thomas and Mary Lidington (9 Apr. 1749), John and Mary Lindstrum (19 Apr. 1756), Thomas and Martha Barbair, and Thomas Everitt (14 Aug. 1748), letters of application, 1740s, MCH; see also the similar sentiments expressed by Marie Miner in Bethlehem, Penn.,

The longing for effacement and to be as nothing appears here and there in other evangelical conversion narratives and spiritual autobiographies in this period but never with this consistency and intensity, and typically it appears only momentarily at the point of self-despairing faith that marks the transition between legal humiliation under the law and evangelical humiliation under the gospel promises. The Moravian memoirs idealize and sustain this surrender rather than the agonistic struggle in their account of conversion.

Devotion to the Corporeal Suffering of Christ

In addition to this note of self-yielding quietism, the Moravian narratives are characterized by the vivid devotion of the writers to the bodily suffering and wounds of Christ. If their quietism recalls Madame Guyon and others, then this corporeality seems a popular Protestant version of the Sacred Heart of Jesus piety seen in the Middle Ages in writers such as Bonaventure or Julian of Norwich, and such as was widely and popularly revived in seventeenth-century Catholicism and, to a lesser degree, in the Lutheran hymns of Paul Gerhard. But this emphasis came to the lay Moravians not from such distant sources, but from the Christology of Zinzendorf himself. As Craig Atwood claims, 'The many strands of his heart religion came together when he discovered the power of wounds theology.'[40] The *Busskampf* was not something that the convert needed to suffer, as the Pietists taught. Rather, Jesus himself endured the *Busskampf* on behalf of all women and men. Therefore the suffering of Christ uniquely evoked a response of love from those who contemplated it devoutly. 'In [Christ's] Gospel or the Doctrine of his Blood, Cross, Death and Passion . . . he has made such an Impression', wrote Zinzendorf, 'that whosoever sees his Saviour once upon the Cross, and in Spirit espies him in that Posture, wherein he bled himself to Death, he has obtain'd Something, which neither the World nor Satan, neither Prosperity nor Adversity, neither Friend nor Foe can deprive him of.'[41] Again, 'the blessed Effect of the Blood of the Lamb . . . makes the Heart melt in a Moment'.[42]

Moreover, for Zinzendorf, the sufferings of Christ were not to be contemplated abstractly, but were to be known through a particular devotion to his wounds. Like a Roman Catholic with a rosary, the Moravian was to count one wound after another.[43] Yet the supreme wound, above all others, was the side wound of Christ, since this was a symbolic passage

---

in Faull (ed.), *Moravian Women's Memoirs*, p. xxvii. On the 'sifting time', see further Craig Atwood, 'Zinzendorf's 1749 Reprimand to the *Brüdergemeine*', *Transactions of the Moravian Historical Society* 29 (1996), 59–84.

[40] Atwood, 'Blood, Sex, and Death', 93.
[41] Zinzendorf, *Sixteen Discourses*, 77.
[42] Ibid. 80.
[43] Atwood, 'Blood, Sex, and Death', 98.

through which individuals must pass in order to enter into union with the heart of God. The side hole was baptismal and Eucharistic. It was a birth canal and a place of retreat, a place of healing and of salvation, the origin of the church and the portal of paradise. In the 1740s, this would be expressed supremely in the popular Moravian 'Litany of the Wounds of the Husband', which addresses in turn the 'worthy wounds', the 'covenant wounds', the 'mysterious wounds', the 'glistening wounds', the 'cavernous wounds', the 'purple wounds', the 'juicy wounds', and so on, in twenty-three antiphonal cadences.[44] Craig Atwood sums up Zinzendorf's distinctive 'blood and wounds' theology thus: 'This Christology may appear bizarre to those outside his circle, but it had a powerful effect on his followers. They entered the mental world of Zinzendorf. They longed to become Christ's lovers lying in his dead arms. Their communities were truly born out of the side of Christ. Zinzendorf's theology, especially his wounds theology, cannot be divorced from the communal mission of the *Brüdergemeine*.'[45]

Just how true this is may be seen in the personal testimonies of lay Moravians in the London archive. The Moravian Sarah Verney recounted the moment of her conversion and how she sighed, 'O that I would but believe,' and continued, 'No sooner had this sigh burst from my heart, but it was as if our Saviour appeared before me in his Corpse's figure, and assured me that it was on account of my sins that He had suffered and dy'd.'[46] Olaus Backer described Christ's wounds as having become 'Dearer and dearer to me, because I want them so much, and his Blood which come out of his wounds is powerful.' Often the applicant for membership wrote, like Grace Lowe, of a desire 'that I may Love his Sides hole more and more very day and hour', or, like Elizabeth Lighton, that 'I am very happy and cheerful in the Side hole.'[47] This too was the language often used by the Moravian autobiographer in the approach of death. Elizabeth Berill's dying wish was that Christ 'would take her into his wounds', and Ann Okely's biographer commented that her last desire was to have a vision like that of Sarah Verney: 'The Summit of her Wishes was, that he might appear to her in his Death's Form and Agony in that Clearness and Rightness of Faith she had in Part experienced, and had heard of in others.' This was in fact the experience of one Sister Rogers at Bedford. She died at 36 years of age, but a fortnight before her death she was able to 'read her election in Nailprints of the Saviour on the Cross of whom she begg'd a Pardon with many tears'. The scribe closes her narrative with the benediction, 'Gloria Pleura' (Glory

---

[44] Craig Atwood, 'Zinzendorf's "Litany of the Wounds"', *Lutheran Quarterly* 11 (1997), 206–8.

[45] Ibid. 107.

[46] Sarah Verney, memoir, MCH.

[47] Olaus Backer, Grace Lowe (n.d.), Elizabeth Lighton (n.d.), letters of application, 1740s, MCH.

to the Side Wound).[48] A final example of Moravian corporeality comes from the letter of application of the barely literate Susannah Duree, already quoted in part above. She again spelled out her aspirated vowels and wrote the words as they sounded right to her ear, expressing her desire simply 'to give my self Kuite up to my Deare Saver So that I may get In to Is Deare Sidhole and to a Bide theare for hever To hall he tarnety I can not find Rest any weare hels wich makes me wich to Sink kuite in to that Deare Sidhole thow I am so un faithful'.[49]

Many other evangelical autobiographers, such as the Methodist Sampson Staniforth, described their conversion vividly in terms of an apprehension of the atonement, and sometimes the language became sensual or visionary. But the language of blood and crucifixion was, more often than not, the language of signification and symbol rather than of realistic portraiture. John Wesley's preaching of the atonement certainly had affinities with that of Zinzendorf, and in 1744 he even published an *Extract of Count Zinzendorf's Discourses on the Redemption of Man by the Death of Christ*. But a close comparison of Wesley's extracts with the full text of the 1740s edition of Zinzendorf's sermons is telling. For example, in Zinzendorf's second discourse he wrote that 'he that understands the Mystery of the Cross and the Wounds of Christ, can never want Comfort and Relief', but in Wesley's abridgement he silently omits the phrase, 'and the Wounds of Christ'.[50] In contrast, the Moravian autobiographers dwelt upon the wounds of Christ in their imaginations. Comparatively, they were scene painters, providing a baroque tableau of human suffering and pity. This was precisely the language used by Martha Hussey to describe her conversion under Spangenberg. She had not found peace of heart under Whitefield or the other preachers, but Spangenberg 'painted a picture before my eyes of the dear Saviour in His whole martyrdom'.[51]

For other evangelical autobiographers the blood of Christ or the cross was often a metonym for the atonement—a sign substituted for the thing signified. Isaac Watts was perhaps the most reserved and carefully controlled in this respect. His hymn, 'When I survey the wondrous Cross', was first published in 1707 but was widely sung by the evangelicals during the revival. But the adoration of the cross in this hymn is very different from what we see among the Moravians. When he wrote, 'See from his Head, his Hands, his Feet, | Sorrow and Love flow mingled down', he removed at a distance from the

---

[48] Welch (ed.), *Bedford Moravian Church*, 213, 221, 211–12. The phrase, 'Gloria Pleura', comes from the Litany of the Wounds. See further, Atwood, 'Zinzendorf's "Litany of the Wounds"', 189–214.

[49] Susannah Duree, letters of application, 1740s, MCH.

[50] Zinzendorf, *Sixteen Discourses*, 31; cf. *Extract of Count Zinzendorf's Discourses . . . by John Wesley*, 10.

[51] Faull (ed.), *Moravian Women's Memoirs*, 98.

scene, chastely substituting 'sorrow and love' for the actual blood. Even when he wrote of Christ's 'dying Crimson like a Robe' spreading 'o'er his Body on the Tree', it was 'crimson' rather than blood, keeping the reader or singer in the realm of signification rather than gory imagery.[52] In complete contrast to Watts is this eighteenth-century Moravian hymn:

> Dearest Lamb, thy Wounds so blessed
> Are a bottomless Abyss!
> For a Host quite numberless
> Of now healthy, and of diseased,
> Do from them drink their Salvation.
> No true Witness upon Earth,
> But craves in that wounded Heart
> Deep to fix his Habitation.
> Happy, Happy, Happy are,
> Who in the *Hole of the Pit*, whence they digged were, bury'd are![53]

There are much more delicate examples of Moravian hymnody treating the theme of the crucifixion, such as Zinzendorf's, 'Jesu, thy Blood and Righteousness', freely translated by John Wesley.[54] Moreover, Charles Wesley himself could sound like the Moravians at times, and his Eucharistic hymns could paint vivid pictures of Christ in agony, but again it was the Moravians who sustained this sort of devotion most consistently and intensely. In an age of sensibility and sentiment, this exquisite crossing of grief and joy, suffering and happiness, represented something of a Moravian aesthetic. The subject contemplates the exquisite sufferings of Jesus on her behalf and responds with tender feelings of pity; she feels herself small and as nothing before such grandeur and magnanimity; she desires to lose herself, to be absorbed in the vision she contemplates. Zinzendorf's response to Feti's *Ecce Homo* seems, therefore, paradigmatic for the sort of piety we see in his followers.

Moravian Bridal Mysticism

In several of the women's narratives this devotion to the corporeal suffering of Christ passes over into a bridal mysticism that is also reminiscent of earlier centuries of Christian spirituality, recalling the writings of Bernard of Clairvaux, Catherine of Siena, or Teresa of Avila.[55] Here the language of love, courtship, marriage, and union—taken from the Song of Solomon

---

[52] See further, the insightful reading of this hymn in J. R. Watson, *The English Hymn* (Oxford, 1999), 160–70.

[53] *A Collection of Hymns . . . Designed Chiefly for the Use of the Congregations in Union with the Brethren's Church* (1754), 26.

[54] Wesley, *Works* (BE), vii. 309–11.

[55] Cf. the observation of W. R. Ward, that Zinzendorf's poetry 'combined a sort of Bernardine Christ-mysticism and the contemplation of the sufferings of the Saviour with an impulse to conversion'. Ward, *Faith and Faction*, 114.

and New Testament texts describing the church as the bride of Christ—is borrowed by the autobiographer and made her own. It was altogether typical of medieval hermeneutics that the allegory of the church as the spouse of Christ became the trope of the individual soul as his bride. In the late 1730s Zinzendorf took up this image of Christ as the bridegroom of the soul and made it central not only to his understanding of salvation, but also to his whole understanding of human sexuality.[56] In 1747 he wrote, 'The complete religion, the chief religion, the one that most properly merits the name religion, is marriage, the marriage of the soul.'[57]

This was also the language of the English-speaking Moravian autobiographers. Benigma Zahm referred in her narrative to Christ as 'my Friend and Lover' and 'the Bridegroom of my soul', and at her first communion she was 'His faithful handmaiden'.[58] Likewise Marie Elizabeth Kunz was accepted into the Moravian congregation at Bethlehem, Pennsylvania at 16 or 17 years of age; when she received first communion, the scribe referred to her partaking of 'the flesh and blood of the Bridegroom of her soul'. Then in her own words, she described her reception of another sacrament five years later, saying, 'As I was actually enjoying it I could hardly remember whether I was still here or already in the marriage hall.' Again, during Passion week the next year she was so overwhelmed with contemplating Christ's suffering that she expressed her longing 'to keep my soul and body chaste until I reached His arms and embrace'.[59]

To these examples from Pennsylvania may be added further instances from the London congregation. We have already taken notice of Susannah Claggett's memoir and her migration from the Methodists to the Moravians. Susannah was from an upper-middle-class family in London, and the language of her narrative was much more sophisticated and refined than that of her namesake, Susannah Duree, whose grammar, diction, and imagery was comparatively raw and crude. Yet, Susannah Claggett's narrative is also significant for its use of bridal imagery. This is all the more poignant in her case, since she wrote immediately after ending a courtship which, as she described it, forced her to choose between her suitor and Christ. 'A Religious person who had a great regard for me solicited me with great importunity to become his partner for life,' she said, adding, 'I was strongly attached to him.' Then while sitting alone in her room she seemed to hear Christ speak to her 'as if I had heard His voice with my outward ear', saying, 'Give up that person; or give me up.' In the next paragraph she related her conversion in a meeting with Zinzendorf—that new awakening 'of an

---

[56] Atwood, 'Sleeping in the Arms of Christ', 33–9.
[57] Quoted ibid. 34.
[58] Faull (ed.), *Moravian Women's Memoirs*, 20–1.
[59] Ibid. 58.

evangelical kind' that made her Methodist experience seem 'legal'. This conversion left her 'sighing soft for the Beloved' and she described the 'pure delight' she experienced then in nuptial terms: 'The Covenant was sealed, and the knot was tied,' and she was 'ravished by his winning charms' so that she compared herself to Mary Magdalene kissing his feet ('his thro' pierced Foot got many a Magdalene Salute'). When out on a solitary walk she experienced a further divine revelation: 'My gracious Redeemer revealed Himself to me as my Eternal Bridegroom who had betrothed me unto Himself for ever.' From this spiritual betrothal she continued her narrative with a more contracted account of joining the Moravians, keeping Classes for the Single Sisters Choir and taking up the office of Deaconess. She closed her narrative by expressing a desire for heaven in bridal language: 'I long to be fully prepared in the bridal dress of His righteousness, for the marriage feast above.'[60]

Martha Barham (*c.*1760–86) was also from a well-to-do family, the daughter of the Bedford Moravian Foster Barham, who owned extensive plantations in Jamaica. Her narrative, extracted in the archives of the London congregation, is a very moving spiritual diary kept from when she was about 18 years old until just before her death seven years later. The diary, unlike the narrative of Susannah Claggett, gives little indication of her outward life and remains almost wholly introspective and confessional. The London extract began in 1781 with her first communion, and her language mirrored that of the matrimonial vows in the Book of Common Prayer: 'I . . . gave myself entirely to him, for better, for worse, for richer for poorer, in sickness and health, till death shall convey me into his dear arms and bosom.' Again and again she borrowed the words of the lover and the beloved in the Song of Songs: 'My beloved is mine and I am his.' She wrote like a latter-day Cistercian with her longing for union with Christ and her expressions of pain and compunction at the awareness of her spiritual poverty. She described her spiritual failures as 'adulterous' and she dared not go to communion unprepared, since this would be to go to the 'marriage supper without a wedding garment'. When she sinned, she grieved at having hurt her 'Bridegroom' after having been united to him by the closest ties, even as 'one spirit flesh and bone with thee'. As consolation and desolation alternated, she turned to the language of lovers' games in the Canticle: 'My beloved had again withdrawn himself . . . nothing afforded me any joy, because my best love was gone.' She was led into a period of profound spiritual desolation, and through this she experienced a greater humiliation and saw her need for a more simple and unquestioning contemplation of Christ as her bleeding saviour. She identified with Mary,

---

[60] Susannah Claggett, memoir, MCH.

the sister of Lazarus, longing to sit at the feet of Jesus and hear his words only. Her heart cleaved to Christ throughout this desolation, and then in 1785, just as her spiritual desolation became yet more acute, she experienced a sealing of her heart, with 'many love-tokens' and a sense of Christ 'embracing me in a very particular manner whenever I wept before him'. Finally, she was consoled, not in ecstasy, but with a great peace of heart.[61]

Her use of Mary, the sister of Lazarus, as a narrative model for herself was appropriate, since Mary is the traditional trope for the contemplative life, over against Martha, who represents the active life. Evangelicals were fond of using Jesus' words concerning Mary ('one thing is needful') to point out the necessity of wholehearted devotion to Christ, but in the case of Susannah Claggett and Martha Barham, this looks remarkably like two young Protestant women taking vows of celibacy, renouncing the world, and taking up the conventual life in a spiritual wedding to Christ as Bridegroom.[62] Again, this language appears elsewhere in evangelical spiritual autobiography, but for the Moravians, the language of spousal union was more intense and sustained.[63]

The Importance of Moravian Liturgy

Finally, the Moravian autobiographies were not only more quietist and more corporeal in their devotion (both in terms of Christ as victim and Christ as spouse), but they were also more deeply marked by liturgical rhythms than their Methodist counterparts. Moravian liturgical life repeatedly provided occasion for members to speak or write about their own spiritual experiences. Applying for membership, confirmation, admission to Holy Communion, or reception into one of the choirs (Single Sisters, Single Brothers, Married Choir, etc.) was an occasion for devotional

---

[61] Martha Barham (*c.*1760–86), memoir, MCH. An abridged and edited version of Barham's account appears in *AM* 9 (1786), 603–7, 653–5.

[62] On the experience of Moravian women in particular see further, Beverly Prior Smaby, 'Female Piety Among Eighteenth Century Moravians', *Pennsylvania History* 64 (1997), 151–67; Peter Vogt, 'A Voice for Themselves: Women as Participants in Congregational Discourse in the Eighteenth-Century Moravian Movement', in Beverly Mayne Kienzle and Pamela J. Walker (eds.), *Women Preachers and Prophets Through Two Millennia of Christianity* (Berkeley, Calif., 1998), 227–47; and Madge Dresser, 'Sisters and Brethren: Power, Propriety and Gender among the Bristol Moravians, 1746–1833', *Social History* 21 (1996), 304–29.

[63] Catherine Cameron's account of her spiritual experience during the Cambuslang revival was, for example, expressed vividly in terms of the language of the Song of Songs, as were the experiences of Margaret Borland, Sarah Gilchrist, Daniel McLarty, and John Parker. Many of these were inspired by Whitefield's sermon, 'Thy Maker is thy Husband'. See further, McCulloch MSS, i. 320, 323–6, ii. 141, 163, 541, 680. See also the analysis in Leigh Eric Schmidt, *Holy Fairs* (Princeton, 1989), 158–68. The phrase, 'Thy Maker is thy Husband', is from Isaiah 54: 5 and was often used by Zinzendorf to sum up his own theology. Atwood, 'Sleeping in the Arms of Jesus', 34.

self-examination and self-expression before the community.[64] But it was particularly in anticipation of the ending of one's worshipping life that Moravians had recourse to life-writing, since the *Lebenslauf* was written above all as something to be read out or excerpted at one's own funeral. In 1747 Zinzendorf decided that the memoir of the deceased should be read out at the service of song (*Singstunde*) on the day of burial as a way for the deceased individual to bid farewell to the rest of the community.[65] It is no wonder that W. R. Ward writes, 'No one had come nearer to institutionalizing the personal confession than the Moravians.'[66]

In the Moravian community, then, both beginnings and endings were cause for spiritual autobiography. Zinzendorf's creativity as a liturgist has been noted by scholars such as Colin Podmore, who comments that Zinzendorf understood the whole of life to be liturgical, Sundays and workdays, waking and sleeping.[67] All of this gave opportunity for the deepening of personal piety. Zinzendorf provided a cradle-to-grave narrative culture, and this was reflected after his death in the constitutional documents of the church, the so-called 'Brotherly Agreements' of 1776 and 1777 in England. The Brotherly Agreement for the London Congregation explained the reasons for the careful ordering of their life together: 'The primary view of all congregation regulations must refer to the human heart . . . that the labour upon souls . . . may be facilitated.' The whole structure of Moravian life together was to the end that 'a vital knowledge of Jesus Christ . . . be implanted in the hearts of congregation members'.[68] Moravian autobiographies were not only called forth by ecclesiastical occasions, but such occasions were also often highlighted in the narratives themselves. A Methodist such as Margaret Austin might have referred to the importance of joining a band meeting, but the Moravian conversion accounts invariably culminated in admission to the congregation itself (as we have seen above). And the continuing spiritual autobiography, as in the case of Martha Barham, was often structured around the liturgical events in the congregation such as Holy Communion, or the Single Sisters' Quarter Hour, the *Singstunde*, and so on. Thus Mary Rogers, after writing of her awakening, her reception into the Moravian community in Bedford, and her entry into the Single Sisters' Choir, wrote of some of the Quarter Hour meetings kept by Ludolf Ernst Schlicht with the sisters and of one in particular during which

---

[64] The ritual life of the Moravian Church is described in Atwood, 'Blood, Sex, and Death', 164–84.

[65] Faull (ed.), *Moravian Women's Memoirs*, p. xxxii.

[66] Ward, Introduction to Wesley, *Works* (BE), xviii. 17.

[67] Podmore, *Moravian Church*, 144.

[68] *The Brotherly Agreement and Declaration Touching the Rules and Orders of the Brethren's Congregation at London* (1776), 7–8.

she finally experienced peace with God after years of anxiety.[69] The memoir of Hannah Nelson of Bristol was likewise ordered around such meetings and their impression upon her, and she concluded, 'The Congregation and Choir-Opportunities were always dear to me.'[70] Elizabeth Berrill of Bedford wrote likewise, 'Papa's Choir Quarter-Hours are so much to me that I cannot express what I feel.'[71]

Not surprisingly, then, elements of the formal liturgy, and especially of Moravian hymns, were frequently echoed in the lay memoirs. Upon Peter Syms's deathbed, he was reported to have sung 'many beautiful liturgie verses with his attendants'.[72] Ann Okely reportedly loved the Moravian liturgies, especially that to 'the Head is full of Bruises'.[73] But even more than a liturgical cadence here and there, hymn texts were ubiquitous in these memoirs. We observed something similar in the early Methodist narratives, but for the Moravians hymns were again tied uniquely to liturgical rhythms. For Zinzendorf the service of singing was more important than the preaching service, second only to the Communion. Singing bracketed all the major liturgical services, and hymns were carefully chosen for the occasion at hand. At the monthly *Gemeintag*, for example, letters from abroad would be read, or someone would read a journal letter from Zinzendorf or another labourer, or a diary from another congregation might be read for information and edification. But as the Bethlehem diary attests, individually selected hymns were chosen and sung throughout the meeting as quasi-liturgical responses to what was heard, and as a means of intercessory prayer, invoking God's aid or blessing upon this or that person. A letter might be read, and then, as the diary of the meeting records, a hymn would be sung 'with him in mind'.[74] After hearing about missionary work among the Indians, the congregation sang, 'Keep them in mind | As toil they find, O Saviour.' In 1742 a letter from Peter Böhler's sister was read out, giving an account of her conversion at Herrnhaag, and in response the congregation at Bethlehem sang, 'Let the sweat of Jesus' face', etc.[75] Hymns truly punctuated the whole of Moravian life and were made personal and applied as responses to particular community narratives. It is no surprise, then, to find that most Moravian autobiographies quote hymns directly or indirectly—in fact, this is so common that we must regard it as a convention of the genre in this context. Typically, hymns were chosen for the high points of the narrative,

---

[69] Mary Rogers (b. 1722), memoir, MCH.

[70] Barry and Morgan (eds.), *Reformation and Revival in Bristol*, 121.

[71] Welch (ed.), *Bedford Moravian Church*, 212.

[72] Peter Syms, memoir, MCH.

[73] Welch (ed.), *Bedford Moravian Church*, 220.

[74] See e.g. Kenneth G. Hamilton (ed.), *The Bethlehem Diary*, i. *1742–1744* (Bethlehem, Penn., 1971), 44–5, 71.

[75] Ibid. 96–7.

especially the moment of conversion, or to conclude the account. For example, Susannah Duree wrote these lines below her signature at the bottom of the page:

> to the Lamb Let me ever cleave
> and in thy holy wounds believe
> and live in peace and take my fell [*sic*]
> and be as happy as I will

Then she added the ingenuous postscript: 'this vears came very frech in to my mind as I was riten'.[76] At the other end of the social scale, Susannah Claggett's account was filled with hymn quotations from front to back, including several of her own compositions at the close of her narrative. Hymnic fragments are but one more example of the close connection of Moravian personalia to the rhythms of Moravian worship.

In all, the Moravian autobiographers in the middle of the eighteenth century witnessed to an ideal self-abasing resignation to Christ and to the community, the desire to be as nothing and to have no will. When Hannah Syms recorded her prayer-wish for the Saviour 'to preserve me from *Self*', she spoke for all these writers of their desire not to promote the self but to deconstruct it.[77] This was not, however, a desire for abstract dissolution or a philosophical rejection of individuality, but was instead something reflexive, a response to a *particular* vision of Christ in his humanity as the wounded *Heiland*, whose agonies were all 'for me', or Christ as the Friend and Bridegroom whose words of love are addressed 'to me'. There was a sensibility in these narratives that had to do with the religious use of the imagination—a sensibility not uncommon, as we have noted in passing, in medieval traditions of meditative piety and later movements of spirituality. Above all, however, these distinctive themes in Moravian lay narrative reflected the teaching of Zinzendorf himself. If the early Methodist narratives represented an agonistic struggle that ended in victory or a travail that ended in new birth, these Moravian narratives represented a more receptive and meditative religious consciousness and an appeal to more tender feelings. The Methodist narratives were ascetic; the Moravian accounts, aesthetic.

THE CASE OF MARTHA CLAGGETT

As Methodist and Moravian divided over doctrine and practice, so their community life fostered different sorts of spiritual experience and interpretations of that experience. This in due course resulted in different autobiographical storylines, as the narrators sought alternative explanations for the

---

[76] Susannah Duree, letters of application, 1740s, MCH.
[77] Hannah Syms (d. 1789), memoir, MCH.

way in which present states had arisen out of prior life conditions. It is rare to find this sort of subtle divergence in autobiographical culture reflected so clearly in separately preserved caches of documents. From the undivided Fetter Lane society, the nerve-centre of the undivided revival in the late 1730s, Wesley led his secession in 1740. If the collection of letters written to Charles Wesley preserves the narratives on one side of the dispute, then the archive of the Moravian Fetter Lane Congregation in London preserves the narratives on the other side. And we have autobiographical documents in both collections that are roughly contemporary with the division. Indeed, there are a few names that appear in both archives, since some of the laity vacillated in their allegiance or simply maintained multiple loyalties to various groups in the early revival. Others migrated from one community to another. For example, the Kingswood collier Samuel Tippett was awakened by the preaching of Whitefield in 1739 and then organized into a band that was connected first to Wesley, then to Whitefield, and then to the Moravians.[78]

One of the women whose narrative appears in both archives is Martha Claggett (1691–1773), the mother of Susannah.[79] We mentioned her in passing in the previous chapter, but the manuscript evidence, together with the entries in the journals of the Wesley brothers, points to the importance of Martha Claggett as an influential figure in the Evangelical Revival in her own right, someone who ought to be recognized along with Lady Huntingdon, Anna Nitschmann, and Mary Fletcher as one of the women leaders in the movement. Moreover, a closer examination of her life and autobiography will illustrate further the ways in which narrative identity changes from one context to another. In the Methodist archive she appears as a soul awakened and converted in the midst of extremity through the ministry of Charles Wesley. In the Moravian archive, Charles Wesley drops out of the story entirely, and she appears as a religiously precocious child, like Zinzendorf, whose later soul travail was slight or misguided, and who found spiritual comfort chiefly through the ministrations of Peter Böhler.

From the extant records we know that Martha Claggett was born in Yorkshire in 1691 to a respectable family, that she was sent away to school and then at about 22 years of age married Wyseman Claggett, who had an estate at Broadoaks in Essex and a residence in London near Fetter Lane.[80]

---

[78] Barry and Morgan (eds.), *Reformation and Revival in Bristol*, 123.

[79] Martha Claggett (24 July 1738), EMV.

[80] The biographical details of Martha Claggett's life may be reconstructed from a number of sources. Scattered references to her in the Fetter Lane Congregation archive may be traced in 'Extracts from the London Archives of the United Brethren' [1850], bound MSS, i. 231, and E. Seymour Cooper, 'Analytical Index to the first and second volumes of the London Congregation Diary', bound typescript (1904–7), 29–32. See also *CWJ*, passim, and Daniel Benham, *Memoirs of James Hutton* (1856), 93, 96–7, 100n.

She was 46 years old in 1738 when her daughters first made contact with Charles Wesley. According to Charles Wesley's *Journal*, it was on 29 June 1738—a little more than a month after Charles's own conversion and while he was flush with evangelical zeal—that he received the news that not only Susannah, but also her sister Elizabeth had received faith. Moreover, Susannah had brought an invitation from her mother, Martha, for Charles to visit. He 'sought the oracle' and was directed by a random Scripture passage to go to her. She had had some worries about him being an enthusiast, but he read a sermon to her and this seemed to mollify her. He prayed, and then prayed again with more fervency, and then prayed again a third time even more strongly, ratcheting up the pressure. 'I *knew* that she believed. I believed for her,' he wrote. 'At first she said she must not presume to say she believed; but grew more and more confirmed. I left her,' he concluded, 'in confidence God would soon clear up His own work in her soul, beyond all doubt or contradiction.'[81] Two days later he met with her again and counselled her. She seemed pleased to learn that 'a person might have faith, and have it long obscured by worldly cares, yet not lost'.[82]

On 24 July 1738 (exactly two months after John Wesley's Aldersgate experience) Martha Claggett wrote an eight-page spiritual autobiography, which appears alongside letters written to Charles Wesley preserved in the scrapbook at the John Rylands Library. It is one of the first lay conversion narratives from the Evangelical Revival. It is dated and identified as Mrs Claggett, but the manuscript bears neither the salutation nor formal closing of a familiar letter.[83] It begins with the words, 'In my infancy . . .' and carries on with an autobiographical narrative that ends on the night of 1 July, just after her second encounter with Charles Wesley. It seems therefore that Martha Claggett was writing more-or-less consciously in the genre of autobiography, and not simply writing a letter.

The story she tells is deeply personal. As a child she was quite often left alone and would spend her time poring over the pages of a tall leather-bound Bible with woodcut illustrations. Her parents, worried she was becoming too introspective, sent her off to boarding school to develop polite manners. She learned to dance and took great pleasure in what she called 'the vanities of the world', and soon her religious seriousness was forgotten. She was dangerously ill for two years as a young teenager and her condition was beyond the help of doctors. She prayed in desperation and made a remarkable recovery, and took this as a direct, divine intervention. Soon, however, she forgot this experience, since she was packed off to

---

[81] *CWJ* i. 112–13.

[82] Ibid. 114.

[83] Martha Claggett (24 July 1738), EMV. Quotations from Martha Claggett in the following three paragraphs are taken from this source.

London once more 'to improve her vanity'. Then at 22 she was married and found herself entirely preoccupied with her new role. Her greatest trouble, though, had to do with childbirth. This is how she put it: 'I had uncommon sufferings in Child bearing which kept me in continual fear. The enemy took advantage of my weakness and when I had conceived of my fifth child [he tempted] me to use some means to disappoint God's providence in bringing it to perfection, and that way free myself from the pain I so much dreaded.' In other words, she was seriously considering how she could devise a secret abortion. 'Sometimes', she reasoned with herself, 'I thought it would be Murder. He [the devil] answered No, that yet there was no Life.' In the end she did not go through with the abortion, and it was this child, a daughter, who would prove the most encouragement to her over the years and who would be 'Instrumental to the bringing about of my own Salvation'. This suggests that the daughter she nearly aborted was in fact Susannah, the one who would introduce her to Charles Wesley.

That would be some years later. In the meantime she had more suffering to endure. A brother she loved died in spiritual anguish, and Martha tells how she spiralled down into depression, her condition compounded by a run of serious fevers. She sank into spiritual despair and toyed with suicide. She had another six children and her pain in childbirth seemed to get worse with each one, not to mention the growing cares of the household. In her own words:

I knew not what to do, having none to guide me till God sent Mr Whitefield amongst us. He told me of Original Sin and man's fallen estate. This by sorrowful experience I had proved to be true. He talked of a new Birth and Change of Nature, which I thought I had understood, but Since find I did not. I was pleased with his conversation and was delighted with singing hymns, when I was sure no one heard me.

Whitefield again, as for so many, was an initial catalyst. She thought maybe she was becoming a new creature, but then quickly found she was mistaken. And she described her state in terms of the agony so typical of Methodism: 'My Sins which for Some time lay concealed, attacked me again with greater force than ever. I prayed, resolved, Strove, but all in Vain, the impetuous torrent Soon Prevailed notwithstanding my feeble Resistance.' This storm and striving seemed to increase and even affect her physical health.

It was at this point that her narrative begins to overlap what we find in the entries in Charles Wesley's *Journal*. Susannah and Elizabeth began to speak to their mother of 'free grace', and this seemed to make an impact on her. But then, after talking with a friend, she began to worry that her daughters were mixed up with a set of enthusiasts. The daughters were saying that they *knew* their sins were forgiven, and she was anxious that they might be merely self-deceived. On 29 June 1738 Charles Wesley visited her and spoke of Christ's love for her in particular. It was St Peter's Day, and she thought how appropriate it was that Charles, like the angel who opened the prison door for Peter in Acts 12, should bid her to rise up quickly. He told her, she recalled, 'that if I would only Believe I might that moment receive the Attonem't'. They spent most of the afternoon in prayer and singing, and one wonders if they might have sung these lines from the hymn 'Free Grace', which Charles would publish the following year,

> Long my imprisoned spirit lay,
>   Fast bound in sin and nature's night.
> Thine eye diffused a quick'ning ray;
>   I woke; the dungeon flamed with light.
> My chains fell off, my heart was free,
> I rose, went forth, and followed thee.[84]

But even after all this—and all of Charles's fervent attempts to believe for her—she still was not sure. She felt so unworthy. Charles's second visit a few days later affected her more than before, and she felt as though Christ was perhaps smiling on her. She started practising saying, '*My* Lord and *My* God'. After Wesley left she went to bed that night strangely peaceful. Then, between three and four in the morning she woke up suddenly, 'in such joy as I never felt before, my Heart overflowed with the love of God, the Spirit bearing witness that I was the Child of God, and I could not keep joining the immortal choir in their hallelujahs'. This, however, is where her manuscript breaks off. And if this was all we had, we might think that her conversion narrative was over. Travail under the law was followed by relief under the gospel.

But that was not the end of the story. Throughout the summer and the autumn, Charles Wesley saw Martha Claggett and her daughters almost every day. He records in his *Journal* in September and October that Martha was being 'much threatened by her husband' and that he had become 'very violent' towards her. She was near despair and hanging on to her faith by a thread. Charles began to intervene and made some progress with Mr Claggett, and indeed was soon gathering large crowds ('near a thousand sinners') at their estate at Broadoaks.[85]

There are hints, though, that trouble was brewing. In April 1739, while Zinzendorf was in London, Charles felt he needed to warn the Claggetts against schism. The last entry in his *Journal* concerning the Claggett family was on 5 April 1740, when the stillness crisis was approaching its zenith. He was preaching at a meeting among many of the 'still ones', and he noted his

[84] Wesley, *Works* (BE), vii. 322–3.
[85] *CWJ* i. 130, 132, 134.

resolve 'not to converse with such of our misled, misleading brethren as I love best; particularly... M. Claggetts'.[86]

Here is where we must cross the street, as it were, and pick up the story in the archives of the Moravian Fetter Lane Congregation in London. Martha Claggett died in 1773, at 81 years of age, and her *Lebenslauf* was written by her daughter Susannah and recorded in the Congregation Diary.[87] If typical practice was followed, this would have been based upon Martha's own oral or written testimony. From this narrative we learn that Martha Claggett came under the influence of Peter Böhler in 1739 and was 'evangelically awakened', and this is offered up as a contrast to her previous experience— 'distress about her salvation' and 'many pious resolutions in a legal way' and 'striving... all to no purpose'.[88] Indeed, nothing is mentioned in this narrative of Charles Wesley at all, or any kind of conversion under his ministry. Rather, under Böhler's exposition of the parable of the prodigal son, Martha felt 'her Soul was melted down' and the words pierced her heart powerfully. Susannah copied out a hymn that her mother had used to express herself on this occasion, and it is full of tenderness: 'The voice of my Beloved sounds...' and 'Gently he draws my heart along', etc.[89]

Then when Molther came to England, she was again 'fired with tender Love and attachment to our Saviour'. She remained 'in meltedness as a poor Sinner at the feet of her bleeding Lover, of whom she was fond with a sinnerlike and bridal affection'.[90] Soon she was writing hymns, and one written about this time was published in later years in the official Moravian hymnbook. The first stanza expresses the sort of quietist piety we have already observed in other Moravian memoirs:

> Dear Lamb, in me fulfil
> Whatever is thy Will;
> I willingly resign
> Myself, and all that's mine,
> Into thy precious Wounds,
> Where rest and peace abounds.[91]

At some point in 1739–40 her husband also joined the Moravians, but he died soon afterwards and she was thus a widow when the London Congregation was settled in 1742. She made over the estate at Broadoaks to the

---

[86] Ibid. i. 208.

[87] Fetter Lane Congregation Diary, vol. 18 (1 Jan. 1772–31 May 1773), bound MS, MCH 125–31.

[88] Ibid. 126.

[89] Ibid. 127–8.

[90] Ibid. 128.

[91] Martha Claggett wrote this hymn shortly before her husband died. It was printed as no. 86 in *A Collection of Hymns... Designed Chiefly for the Use of the Congregations in Union with the Brethren's Church*, ii. 60.

church (though this was contested legally by one of her sons), and it was rechristened Lamb's Inn and became a Children's Oeconomy or school. She was not only one of the founding members of the London Congregation, but she was appointed Eldress—the highest office a woman could hold. Four of her daughters and one servant were also members of the congregation. Within a month she travelled to Yorkshire to be blessed in her office by Zinzendorf and the Pilgrim Congregation. Having rehearsed the main milestones of Martha Claggett's spiritual autobiography, up to her entry into formal leadership of the Moravian Church, Susannah's account passes more quickly over the following three decades of her mother's service in the church, rushing on to recount her last illness and pious death.

Thus, in Martha Claggett's case, we may observe not only her transition from one religious context to another, but also the subtle differences between the Methodist and Moravian views of conversion and the different formative influences these two religious cultures exerted on her narrative. The Martha Claggett of Charles Wesley's *Journal*, and the woman whose fragmentary memoir from 1738 was preserved among his papers, was a typical Methodist convert, and her story was one of the characteristic agonistic–ecstatic conversions of early Methodism—a sin-sick soul who travailed under the law, bewailing her past sins, until at last she broke through to hallelujahs in the night. The Martha Claggett of the Fetter Lane Congregation Diary, whose larger memoir was taken up and recounted by her daughter, appears instead as a typical Moravian convert whose experience was marked by a more contemplative vision of the wounded *Heiland*, the bleeding Lover, to whom she yielded her soul even as she submitted her life and her goods to the Moravian discipline, and lived out her days within the liturgical rhythms of their common life. There could be no better example of the similarities and differences that emerged in evangelical autobiography in the eighteenth century as the result of the separation of the followers of Wesley and the followers of Zinzendorf.

6

'The Word Came in With Power': Conversions at Cambuslang

THE story of lay conversion is more difficult to trace for the Calvinistic wing of the Evangelical Revival than for the followers of Wesley or the Moravians. The supporters of Whitefield in England were less well organized, and many were later absorbed into Dissent, and an archive of lay conversion narratives from the 1740s, comparable with the Wesleyan and Moravian records, does not seem to have been preserved.[1] However, by moving beyond the geographic limits of England it is possible to trace a contemporary narrative response to Calvinistic preaching—including the preaching of Whitefield—among a number of Presbyterians in south-western Scotland who were subjects of the well-documented 'Cambuslang Wark'.

Five miles south-east of Glasgow, Cambuslang was a small parish of less than a thousand people, a parish that does not appear on many maps of Scotland even in the eighteenth century. It became the unlikely epicentre of a revival that climaxed in the summer of 1742 with two outdoor communion services at which Whitefield preached, the second of which attracted crowds estimated at more than thirty thousand. The crowds were, by any measure, significantly larger than the population of Glasgow itself in the 1740s. The revival spread to Kilsyth, about nine miles north-east of Cambuslang, and to Muthil in southern Perthshire, and soon reports of awakenings were heard from other communities in Scotland as well. Through the evangelical magazines and other pamphlets the news of this revival spread further still, and before long the tiny parish of Cambuslang was the subject of international attention and a model for revival in the evangelical world, alongside Northampton, Massachusetts. Jonathan Edwards was aware of the revival already in 1742 and wrote of 'the glorious work of God' at Cambuslang, which 'we have since understood has spread into many other towns and parishes in that part of Scotland',[2] John Wesley also noted in his *Journal* 'what God wrought in Scotland' at Cambuslang and Kilsyth.[3]

---

[1] I could find nothing e.g. among the papers of Lady Huntingdon and Trevecka College in the archive at Westminster College, Cambridge.

[2] *WJE* iv. 539.

[3] Wesley, *Works* (BE), xx. 315.

Whitefield's first visit to Scotland during the late summer of 1741 and his preaching in Glasgow that September did much to quicken spiritual concern for many from Cambuslang and the surrounding area. The following January William McCulloch, the minister at Cambuslang, received a petition signed by about ninety heads of families, asking him to provide a weekly lecture, which he happily set up on Thursdays. Societies for prayer had existed in the parish for some years, but their meetings now became more earnest and they met for the three evenings prior to the Thursday lecture on 18 February 1742. On this evening a number of the hearers came under 'soul distress', their consciences awakened to the seriousness of their sins, and many began to cry out in their agony. Following the lecture, a crowd of about fifty women and men under spiritual anxiety sought the minister's counsel at his house. Throughout that spring the pattern continued, with heart-searching sermons followed up with emotional displays and long queues at the manse. James Robe, the minister at Kilsyth and an early publicist of the revival, estimated that there were more than three hundred conversions in the first twelve weeks. Many more were to follow.

Whitefield's preaching in Glasgow in September 1741 and McCulloch's evening lecture in February 1742 figure largely in the narratives of converts as markers for the beginning of the Cambuslang work. But increasingly people were drawn from farther afield to see for themselves what was happening in the parish and to participate in the revival. When Whitefield revisited Scotland in June 1742, he came directly from the experience of preaching outdoors to thousands at Moorfields and elsewhere in London. Soon these scenes were repeated in Scotland, and he claimed that some twenty thousand turned out at Glasgow to hear him. The return of the communion season, along with the return of Whitefield to Cambuslang, enlarged the numbers there in the summer of 1742. On 6 July Whitefield arrived at midday, but still had time to preach three times and witness emotional scenes that night that, as he said, 'far out-did all that I ever saw in *America*'.[4] Whitefield continued to preach before, during, and after the communion at Cambuslang to crowds he again estimated at twenty thousand. McCulloch thought more than five hundred were converted. After the sacrament was over, Whitefield preached from the text that had meant so much to Zinzendorf, namely, Isaiah 54: 5, 'Thy Maker is thy Husband.' It was a sermon long remembered by those who heard it. Whitefield's spectacular ministry in Cambuslang in the summer of 1742 ensured the wider dissemination of revival throughout south-western Scotland. The 'Cambuslang Wark', like the Connecticut Valley Revival of 1734–5, spread well beyond the parish to the surrounding area, and it became news.

[4] *GWL* 405.

THE MCCULLOCH MANUSCRIPTS

William McCulloch recorded the case histories of more than one hundred women and men who were the subjects of the revival, and these spiritual narratives are extant in manuscript in two quarto volumes of more than six hundred pages each at the library of New College in Edinburgh.[5] The accounts were taken down for the most part in McCulloch's own hand, based on interviews he had with the converts within approximately one or two years of the 1742 revival. Some narratives were written down as late as 1748. The collection is as rich as its textual history is complex. Scholars since the nineteenth century have variously reported the total number of accounts at anywhere between 105 and 110, and this discrepancy reflects the condition of the archive, which includes fragments and repetitions, and which has been reordered according to different pagination and indexing schemes more than once in its history. However, the important feature of the material organization of the archive is that the forty-six cases in the first volume, unlike those in the second, were prepared for publication, with passages marked for deletion or emendation by four clerical editors, who had been solicited by McCulloch for this purpose, and this provides a unique opportunity to see clerical and lay perspectives on religious experience side by side. In the end McCulloch did not publish the accounts he so carefully collected, but a century later the minister Duncan Macfarlan abridged and paraphrased eleven narratives from the first volume and twelve from the second for his *Revivals of the Eighteenth Century, Particularly at Cambuslang* (1845). Aiming to inspire readers to hunger after revival themselves, Macfarlan's account was part of a tradition of evangelical historiography that the Cambuslang revival itself helped to create, and which looked back to James Robe's contemporary revival narratives and the broader evangelical historiography of John Gillies, a minister from Glasgow who was also present at Cambuslang.[6]

The last three decades of the twentieth century saw the McCulloch manuscripts used afresh by historians for various purposes: to give a sympathetic but more source-critical account of the Cambuslang Revival,[7] to

---

[5] The actual number of case histories has been reported variously as 105 (Macfarlan), 106 (Fawcett), 110 (Smout), and 108 (Schmidt).

[6] James Robe, *A Short Narrative of the Extraordinary Work at Cambuslang* (Glasgow, 1742); id., *A Faithful Narrative of the Extraordinary Work of the Spirit of God, at Kilsyth* (Glasgow, 1742); id., *Narratives of the Extraordinary Work of the Spirit of God, at Cambuslang, Kilsyth, &c* (Glasgow, 1790); id., *The Christian Monthly History* (Edinburgh, Nov. 1743 to Jan. 1746). John Gillies, who also preached at Cambuslang during the revival, published a landmark work in evangelical revival historiography, *Historical Collections Relating to Remarkable Periods of the Success of the Gospel* (Glasgow, 1754).

[7] Arthur Fawcett, *The Cambuslang Revival* (Edinburgh, 1971).

assess levels of literacy and popular education in the period,[8] to relate
putative social change to religious ideology,[9] and to demonstrate continuities and discontinuities in religious ritual, especially in relation to the
communion season, in Scottish communities at home and abroad since
the seventeenth century.[10] For our purposes, the McCulloch manuscripts
offer a superb opportunity to observe the emergence of spiritual autobiography in a third archive of lay narratives from the early 1740s, one which
contrasts nicely with the materials collected by Charles Wesley and with the
personalia in the London Moravian records. In this new context at Cambuslang the genre of conversion narrative appears within a well-established
tradition of biblical literacy, orthodox Calvinism, and communal piety,
including disciplined presbyteral oversight.

The Occasion of McCulloch's Case Histories

Very few, if any, of the manuscripts in McCulloch's collection are autographs. In a letter in 1751 McCulloch explained that perhaps a quarter of the
'persevering subjects' of the revival in 1742 gave him 'very particular
accounts of God's dealings with their souls', and he acted as amanuensis:
'I set down very many of these from their own mouths, always in their own
sense, and very much also in their own words.'[11] Thus, T. C. Smout nicely
describes this collection as 'Scotland's first oral history project'.[12] The result
is that we are one step removed from the voices of the converts themselves.
Alongside the voice of the convert, we hear the understated but ever-
present voice of McCulloch himself as interlocutor, asking the questions
that largely structure each narrative, giving it its beginning, middle, and end.
Like the anthropologist who subtly changes the group she studies by virtue
of her presence among them and the questions she asks, McCulloch's
influence on these narratives was formative.

---

[8] T. C. Smout, 'Born Again at Cambuslang: New Evidence on Popular Religion and
Literacy in Eighteenth-Century Scotland', *Past and Present* 97 (1982), 114–27.

[9] Ned Landsman, 'Evangelists and Their Hearers: Popular Interpretation of Revivalist
Preaching in Eighteenth-Century Scotland', *Journal of British Studies* 28 (1989), 120–49.

[10] Marilyn J. Westerkamp, *Triumph of the Laity* (New York, 1988); Leigh Eric Schmidt,
Holy Fairs (Princeton, 1989); Michael J. Crawford, *Seasons of Grace* (New York, 1991). See
also W. R. Ward, *The Protestant Evangelical Awakening* (Cambridge, 1992), 329–39.

[11] John Gillies (ed.), *Historical Collections Relating to Remarkable Periods of the Success of the
Gospel* (rev. edn. 1845; repr., Edinburgh, 1981), 461. Given McCulloch's editorial involvement, the Cambuslang manuscripts compare with the narratives taken down in the 1650s by
the ministers Thomas Sheppard in Cambridge, Massachusetts and John Rogers in Dublin
(examined in Ch. 1, above). The difference is that in those earlier cases the collected
narratives furnished part of the requirements for admission to membership, but for McCulloch this was not an issue.

[12] Smout, 'Born Again', 115.

This may be seen, for example, in the occasion of these narratives, which were prompted by McCulloch's initiative and did not arise principally from some inner necessity on the part of the converts. These case histories were called forth not simply by the ebullience of the convert who must say what God has done for his soul, or by an act of incorporation or application for membership, but rather by McCulloch's desire to discern, document, promote, and defend the present work of the Spirit. This discernment and documentation was necessary in the first instance in order for him to offer spiritual counsel as pastor to the troubled souls who called on him. It was also necessary so that he could form a judgement about the events at Cambuslang as a work of God, and then provide a body of evidence upon which he could draw to promote it among friends and defend it before critics. Not for nothing are the manuscripts described as *examinations* by the nineteenth-century archivist. (The volumes are entitled, 'Examinations of persons under spiritual concern at Cambuslang, during the Revival in 1741–42'.) Indeed, the manuscripts can aptly be compared to medical examinations, except of course that McCulloch was seeking to diagnose the condition of the soul rather than the body.

An observer commented on McCulloch's clinical practice at the height of the revival. After the sermon ended, McCulloch would talk with those that were 'under convictions' at the Manse, 'where he takes down in Writ the names of the new ones, with their Designations, Place of Abode, Time and Manner of their being seiz'd'.[13] James Robe did the same at Kilsyth and showed himself to be a journalist like Wesley and Whitefield, recording spiritual history as it unfolded—literally, 'diurnally'. He was quite pleased with his method, saying, 'I have kept a book, wherein, from day to day, I wrote down whatever was the most material in the exercise of the distressed ... An index I kept brought me soon to the part of the book where the person's case was recorded. I had then a full view of their case.' This had the advantage, he claimed, of allowing him to pick up with his parishioners where they had left off, knowing 'what progress their convictions had made'.[14] With due care and caution, he would then make a judgement concerning whether one was truly brought out of a state of nature into a state or grace or not. In all, he sounded very much like a spiritual midwife, assessing true and false labour, monitoring the progress of the soul's travail, and then finally witnessing the new birth.[15] He cited examples from these

---

[13] *A Short Account of the Remarkable Conversions at Cambuslang in a Letter from a Gentleman in the West-Country to his Friend at Edinburgh* (Glasgow, 1742), 5.

[14] Gillies (ed.), *Historical Collections* (1981), 450

[15] Cf. the Gentleman, quoted above, who noted the link between a woman's labour pains and the travail of new birth. He reported that 'several Women who have born Children, say, *They suffer'd more bodily Pain when under these Convictions than ever they did in Child-bearing*'. *A Short Account of the Remarkable Conversions at Cambuslang*, 6–7.

case histories in his account of the revival at Kilsyth. One of the ends served by these narratives—perhaps the principal end—was clearly pastoral.

Thus McCulloch and James Robe used the journal as an aid to spiritual discernment and direction. However, they and the other publicists-cum-historians of revival in Scotland were also motivated, as were evangelicals elsewhere, to document the present work of the Spirit of God as something exemplary in order to stimulate and spread revival further. They also needed evidence by which they could defend their movement, particularly with respect to the displays of emotion and the outcries of the converts. This need to provide an apologia for the movement gave McCulloch's 'Examinations' and the various published 'Attestations' an almost legal character—as though these conversion narratives were part of a brief prepared for a courtroom.

Contested Experience: Case History as Apologia

Heated criticism of Cambuslang came from the wider society, and this was reflected both at the level of pamphlet warfare and at the level of lay autobiography. There was, for example, the contemporary tract, *A Short Account of the Remarkable Conversions at Cambuslang in a Letter from a Gentleman in the West-Country to his Friend at Edinburgh* (1742), which was critical of the paroxysms and group hysterics, the rapid conversions, late night meetings, and immodest behaviour of the converts. But what perhaps troubled this gentleman the most was the offence to social propriety, the way in which laypeople were praying and exhorting in public and 'country people' were neglecting their necessary duties and their masters' business. Such opposition was described also in the narratives collected by McCulloch. John Wier was a tenant farmer whose gentleman-landlord 'arreisted' (legally seized and took over) his crop at harvest and turned him out of his land for his association with Cambuslang and Whitefield, complaining that whenever Wier went off to Cambuslang, he could not work the next day. Moreover, Whitefield was a 'mountebank' and 'damned rascal' who was 'putting all the People Mad'.[16] If Wier could read his catechism, the landlord felt, that was all the religion he needed, and he added 'that if we would stay more at home at our work and go less to Camb. to hear that Damned Rascal, and get our brains cracked we might pay our rent better, and work better' (i. 311). The marginalia provided by the ministers who edited these accounts makes it clear that they were sensitive to such criticisms.[17]

---

[16] McCulloch MSS i. 310. Subsequent quotations from McCulloch's 'Examinations' are cited in the text by volume and page number.

[17] This entire passage from Wier's account above was flagged for deletion by all four clerical marginators, as was a later biblical passage that came to Wier's mind ('Behold the Lilies they toil not'), which was clearly in danger of being understood as sanctioning a weak work ethic (i. 312; cf. i. 313).

Yet the most intense opposition to Cambuslang came neither from the wider society nor from the national church, but from other evangelicals, since evangelicals in Scotland, as in England, were divided. Just as the Moravians and Methodists offered rival interpretations of conversion, so also there were evangelical partisans in Scotland who took different views of Cambuslang. Evangelical identity was contested in England by 'stillness'; it was contested in Scotland by secession. Led by Ebenezer Erskine (1680–1754), the Secession of 1733 was the first major schism in the Church of Scotland, and it was provoked by concerns over the Erastian character of the national church, and particularly over the vexed question of patronage and the imposition of ministers on unwilling parishes. By the time Whitefield was preparing to make his first trip to Scotland the Secession Church (or 'Associate Presbytery') was firmly entrenched. Something of the evangelical piety of the Seceders may be inferred from their writings and their correspondence with other evangelicals, and from the fact that Ralph Erskine, the younger brother of Ebenezer, warmly invited Whitefield to come to Scotland and was at first willing to go up into the pulpit with him. But very soon the lines hardened, and Whitefield was asked to preach only for them, for 'they were the Lord's people'. Ideally, the Seceders felt, he would also sign the Solemn League and Covenant as proof that he was really and truly Reformed. When Whitefield responded that, on the contrary, he would preach to those who were *not* the Lord's people since their need was surely greater, and what is more, he would happily preach for the Pope if offered his pulpit, he did not endear himself to his new Secessionist friends. As he wrote to a friend in New York, with a certain amount of bathos, 'Soon after this, the company broke up.'[18]

Indeed, soon after this Whitefield found himself the subject of criticism and outright vitriol at the hands of the Associate Presbytery. When revival came to Cambuslang, under the aegis of the corrupt Church of Scotland, the Secession Church could not accept it. They preached against it and on 15 July 1742 declared a solemn public fast to repent of the 'strong delusions' and goings on at Cambuslang and the 'fond reception' given to Whitefield. Before long there was a pamphlet war between defenders and critics of Cambuslang.

There is plenty of evidence here, too, from the testimony of the converts that this public division also caused private anxiety. Just as the issues over 'stillness' came to be worked out in first-person narrative by rank-and-file Methodists and Moravians, so also the converts at Cambuslang told their stories in terms of the temptation to secede or not. For example, when George Tassie was converted at Cambuslang this also involved a conversion in his attitude to schism. The Seceders had been using Psalm 118: 22 ('The

[18] *GWL* 308.

stone which the Builders refused, the same is become the head of the Corner') to refer to the national church's rejection of Christ. Now, however, Tassie saw the verse differently. 'This I knew the Seceders had used to apply to others: But now in the View I got of it, I saw it belonged to themselves' (i. 149). For Janet Tennant, it was not quite so clear-cut. She was sitting on the brae before a sermon at Cambuslang and heard the man next to her say that the Seceders were 'calling all this work at Camb. a Delusion' and preaching against it. 'This put me into so great confusion,' she said, 'that I could give little heed to what was said' (ii. 12). Her conversion involved a kind of disorientation, hovering between two evangelical options, the Secession Church or Cambuslang.[19]

CONVERSION NARRATIVE AT CAMBUSLANG

Given the controversy that Cambuslang excited, McCulloch conducted his interviews with the 'persevering subjects' of the revival with apologetic aims, as well as with a pastoral desire to discern accurately the condition of those under spiritual concern. What then did he find? Principally, the spiritual autobiographies he recorded shared a common narrative structure, displayed a profoundly experiential biblicism, and bore witness to robustly Calvinistic convictions.

Narrative Structure: Conviction and Conversion

Unlike many later evangelical conversion narratives, these case histories focus on a quite narrow slice of autobiographical history. Typically there is one paragraph treating early religious education and preconversion piety, and then the subject proper is introduced: the process of awakening and relief—conviction and conversion—precipitated by the revival at Cambuslang in 1741–2. Then again, there is generally one paragraph at the conclusion of the narrative that provides the denouement in the form of the results or changes manifested in the present life of the convert.[20] On the whole, there is relatively little secular detail, except in passing. A woman might say,

---

[19] W. R. Ward argues that the secession contributed to the revival in three ways: (1) by increasing anxieties in the establishment, (2) by turning in on itself and therefore leading others to search for another way, and (3) by making fresh appeals to outside forces including Whitefield, the Leicester House circle, and the Moravians—all of which would open Scotland more significantly to interconfessional evangelicalism. Ward, *Protestant Evangelical Awakening*, 332–3.

[20] James Robe noted this pattern very early in the revival, saying that most of the converts could give 'a good Account of what they have felt in their Convictions and Humiliation for Sin, of the Way of their Relief by Faith... and of the Change they feel in the prevalent Inclinations and Dispositions of their Hearts'. Robe, *Short Narrative of the Work at Cambuslang*, 6.

'As I was at my wheel...', but this might be the only clue that she was involved in spinning and weaving. Most of these narratives were wholly preoccupied with interior states and formally religious experiences. The story of 'conviction and conversion' was traced in most cases not through the narration of the leadings of providence in family, relationships, work, and other preoccupations, but through the reporting of a series of sermons heard, sacramental occasions observed, and biblical texts recalled, and the way each of these affected the convert.

Is it possible to reconstruct from these narratives the sort of questions McCulloch asked of the converts? We get some kind of indication of his probable questions from the themes that recur (and the order in which they appear) and from a few tell-tale verbal cues in these narratives. The first question he asked must certainly have been whether they had learned to read the Bible and had learned their Shorter Catechism, since almost all the narratives record this information within the first few lines, and an index to the second volume likewise tracks this data. Then, McCulloch most likely questioned the converts concerning their life before their awakening, and whether they were observant in private and public religious duties. One indication of narrative convention in these accounts is the presence of several straightforward declarations that are placed in the negative. When Margaret Borland said, 'I never prayed any by my Self alone till I was about 14 years of age...' it is clear that she expected 'secret prayer' to be a standard item in the narration of childhood piety (ii. 535). Either she had internalized this convention, or McCulloch asked her about it directly. This was true also of William Ballie's declaration concerning his early years, 'I was not given to any gross outward vices' (i. 2). A narrative of all the things a convert did *not* do would make for a long autobiography. That these particular subjects were mentioned in this way strongly suggests that they were assimilated as narrative conventions.

Just as the early Methodist laypeople often described themselves in their preconversion state as Pharisees or hypocrites, so also these Cambuslang converts looked back on their preconversion piety as lacking something. James Kirkland said of his religious observance, 'I went these rounds thro' custom,' and he added that 'in all my former attendance on Duties, I cannot say that I ever felt the word of God come home with power' (i. 362). John Parker worried similarly, like Richard Baxter earlier, that his religious life was 'much owing to religious Education, the Example of others, and the force of natural Conscience'(ii. 662).

Again, it seems likely that McCulloch asked them to describe their evangelical awakening, since the Scots preposition 'anent' ('concerning' or 'with respect to') introduces the subject in several narratives, flagging this as another expected topos for discussion. Thus, when William Ballie said, 'Anent the Means of My own effectual awakning...' (i. 4), he was clearly conscious that this was 'the next subject' to be treated. With this first awakening of conscience came typically a fear of hell, and this was followed in due course by a more evangelical shame for having offended God.[21] Charles Cunningham explained, 'At first it was chiefly the fears of Hell that startled me, but afterwards . . . of sin as dishonouring to God' (ii. 412). Some converts referred to having discovered not just sin in general but then also their 'particular' sins. William Ballie saw his 'original sin' and then his 'actual transgressions' which included his unmortified 'heart's lusts'. From this discovery of the depth of sin was born a self-despairing faith in Christ. 'I was now resolved with a distrust of myself,' said Ballie, and from this time he was 'enabled to plead with a more than ordinary earnestness' (i. 4–5). The expectation that the narrative would proceed from the onset of convictions to relief from this spiritual anguish is reflected in Bethea Davies's words (as she again flagged the convention with the word, 'first') when she said, 'The first Outgate I got [from] my soul-distress was . . .' (ii. 362).

This process of 'conviction and conversion' was not a simple passage from darkness to light, and the process could be as labyrinthine and cyclical for these converts as it was for many of the Methodists and Moravians. John Aiken described his spiritual life during these years as consisting of 'many ups and down' (i. 466) and William Jameson said likewise, 'I may sum up my then exercises of Spirit in this, That I spent my life between hope and fear' (i. 495). And yet the great desire was that this oscillation between hope and fear would be resolved in a new steady spiritual state. John Parker used a striking metaphor to express this, saying, 'My heart is just like the mariner's needle, which though it may be jogged to the one side and the other; yet it is never quiet till it point to the North Pole; so neither does my poor heart ever settle or rest, till it fix on God in Christ, and find rest in him' (ii. 680).

Finally, McCulloch almost certainly ended each interview by asking the Edwardsian question about the abiding transformation in the convert's character as a result of these spiritual experiences. William Ballie signalled the convention not with 'anent' this time, but with the signposting phrase, 'as to'. He concluded his narrative with the words, 'And now as to the Ordinary bent of my desires since my first effectual awakning . . .' (i. 8).

On the whole this is a the same pattern that we have observed already in many Puritan, Pietist, and evangelical narratives: early religious piety but hardening of heart, awakening of conscience, consolation through the gospel, and a changed life thereafter. The core beliefs to which this pattern bore witness were expressed in John Wesley's summary of essential Methodist doctrines upon which all should agree: original sin, justification by

---

[21] Again, it was noted if the convert did *not* feel a fear of hell. George Tassie recorded that he trembled, 'but I had not at that time a great dread of hell' (i. 145); cf. the similar expression of Sarah Gilchrist (ii. 139).

faith, and holiness of heart and life.[22] James Robe put it the same way, saying that the work at Cambuslang was carried on 'under the Influence of the great and substantial Doctrines of Christianity', and that ministers pressed home 'the Necessity of Repentance . . . of Faith . . . and of Holiness'.[23]

This framework was present in the narratives at Cambuslang in part because of the sort of questions McCulloch asked. The question therefore remains, If the converts had been given free rein, might they have begun or ended differently or taken other detours as they told their stories? Perhaps. But there is good evidence that they did in fact internalize this framework, since this was the whole thrust of the preaching and counselling they received in the first place. Janet Jackson implied as much when she recalled that McCulloch preached on 'Effectual Calling, and the general parts and steps of it', and added what was her own response: 'My heart was melted down under a sense of the mercy of God, while I was made to see the general parts and steps of that work on my own soul' (i. 35). The Reformed *ordo*, expounded from the pulpit, became the very order by which she traced her own interior states. Clearly these lay parishioners at Cambuslang were well educated in the theory of conversion.

One final example of how these converts were catechized into the doctrine of conversion that so manifestly structured their narratives comes from the height of the revival in 1742. Archibald Bell was one of those who went to the hall of the manse after a sermon one Saturday evening. He reported that McCulloch gave a short exhortation, 'dividing these present into several sorts, "these that had got convictions, and these that had got none; or never had any; or none that had come to a good issue" and speaking to these several sorts, he shewed the necessity of Convictions, in order to Conversion, and the necessity of Conversion, in order to being fitted for Communion with God' (i. 401). It was not untypical for a Puritan sermon, or one by an evangelical preacher, to close with a peroration that applied the message to 'several types of hearers', but here McCulloch actually did this division of his hearers bodily: the convicted, the unconvicted, the never-convicted, and the half-convicted. And according to Bell he then summarized the expected stages of a work of God in the soul with three words: conviction, conversion, and communion. The homiletical habit of alliteration had evidently followed him into the hall of the manse. These three stages would also structure the narratives he later recorded. As a body of conversion narratives, the McCulloch manuscripts are far more consistently structured in this way than the more ad hoc narratives in the Methodist and Moravian archives.

---

[22] *JWL* iv. 237.
[23] Robe, *Short Narrative of the Work at Cambuslang*, 8.

Part of what made these conversions at Cambuslang so controversial was the appearance of various physical and psychological manifestations, such as those that accompanied the early revival in London, Bristol, Newcastle, mid-Wales, and New England. These manifestations presented a particular interpretative challenge, as many wondered what they could mean. George Tassie heard James Robe exhort people to cry out to God to help them, and he came under great concern and was 'seized with trembling and shaking of my body' (i. 145). Elizabeth Dykes said on another occasion, 'I felt a power strike me to the ground' (i. 209).[24] Others reported dreams, visions, locutions, and, for one woman at least, preternatural smells. Almost certainly McCulloch asked each of the converts about whether they had experienced anything of this sort, since numbers felt they needed to say, like John Aiken, 'I never cry'd out in publick nor had I any visions or swarfs [swoonings]' (i. 464), or to add a gloss like James Kirkland, 'Yet I never fell into swarfing or fainting' (i. 364). Isobel Provan was worried she was going to cry out in a meeting, and she held her throat so tightly that she nearly strangled herself.

But these phenomena almost invariably followed the same stages of conversion noted already, and were usually patient of interpretation as physical signs of 'conviction and conversion'. One trembled or swooned because of terror of hell or shame for sin. As George Tassie observed, 'It was the terrors of the Law, set home upon their Consciences, that made them so to cry out' (i. 148). This was how Whitefield himself understood such phenomena: they were 'extraordinary things, proceeding generally from soul-distress'.[25] Once this soul-distress was removed, one often cried out with joy because overcome with the relief of sins forgiven and a sense of intimacy with God. Thus Sarah Gilchrist observed at Cambuslang 'many persons there crying and fainting and swooning in their agonies', and this made her, like others, question the depth of her own sense of sin. She also heard of 'the many Sweet Outgates, and ravishing joys that many were getting', and this too made her long for more of a sense of her 'interest in Christ' (ii. 139). The picture of 23-year-old Sarah Gilchrist watching displays of spiritual agony and ecstasy and rather wishing that this could be her experience, too, suggests that there was more than one way to be catechized in the stages of conversion.

Experiential Biblicism

Thus far the Cambuslang narratives look very much like what we have witnessed elsewhere in the evangelical tradition, except that they are more

---

[24] In Duncan Macfarlan's nineteenth-century edition of the narrative, this passage is made more respectable: 'I was unable to stand.' Duncan Macfarlan, *The Revivals of the Eighteenth Century, Particularly at Cambuslang* (1845; repr., Glasgow, 1988), 143.

[25] George Whitefield, *Works*, ed. John Gillies (1771), iv. 160.

consistently structured according to what Edwards called a 'scheme... received and established by common opinion'.[26] Yet there are certain characteristics that stand out as exceptional in the accounts from Cambuslang and that deserve further attention. First among these is the remarkable biblical literacy and intense preoccupation of converts with memorable texts of Scripture as conduits of spiritual power.

The high level of biblical literacy among the Cambuslang converts confirms the observations of foreign observers about Scotland more generally. Daniel Defoe noted in 1707 that in Scotland 'if you shut your eyes when the minister names any text of Scripture, you shall hear a little rustling noise over the whole place, made by turning the leaves of the Bible'.[27] Whitefield observed the same phenomenon when he preached in Scotland in 1741, and he stressed also how surprising this was: 'After I had done prayer, and named my text, the rustling made by opening the bibles all at once, quite surprised me: a scene, I never was witness to before.'[28] Because it was important to McCulloch to record details about the literacy of the converts, we know that virtually all of them could read, and, in the context that usually meant reading the Bible in particular.[29] In the index to the second volume, we find repeated entries that appear similar to this one, in the case of Jean Wark: 'Put to school when a Child, taught to read Bibl.'[30] One of the few that struggled to read was 23-year-old Margaret Borland, who was ashamed that she could not read better. She overcame this handicap, she said, 'by following the minister with my eye on the Bible, as he read that portion of Scripture he was going to Lecture on', and when she was awakened during the revival, she would frequently return home after the sermon, take out her Bible, and read the text over again for herself (ii. 535, 537).[31] Sarah Gilchrist was at first worried that Cambuslang was filled with a 'Quaker Spirit' with all the trembling and talk of an immediate sense of God's presence, but then she was reassured 'seeing them make so much use of their Bibles, and looking out places there by which they had got relief' (ii. 137). One consequence of all this biblical literacy is that when these subjects turned autobiographers, their conversion narratives were easily woven out of a skein of Scriptural quotations. Their minds were already well stocked. Indeed, hardly a page can be turned in the McCulloch

---

[26] *WJE* ii. 162.

[27] Quoted in Fawcett, *Cambuslang Revival*, 81.

[28] *GWL* 305.

[29] Smout claims that they could all read, though John Willison does refer to some subjects of the revival who could not. Smout, 'Born Again', 121; cf. Robe, *Short Narrative of the Work at Cambuslang*, 13.

[30] McCulloch MSS, index appended to vol. i, but in fact giving details of the narrators recorded in vol. ii.

[31] Cf. Smout, 'Born Again', 126.

manuscripts without coming across a text from the Bible, usually given verbatim.

Yet the Cambuslang converts used Scripture quite differently on the whole from the way in which their learned ministers handled the sacred text, at least in public discourse. Seldom did the lay narrators interpret biblical texts by formal reasoning or apply texts to their own lives by any extended ratiocination, as George Whitefield did even in his most histrionic preaching. Instead, in these lay narratives, biblical texts were recalled to mind, often spontaneously, as words of immediate spiritual power. And typically these texts were short, one or two sentences; they were not read in biblical context but atomized and made to function as aphorisms.[32] Such treatment released the texts to function freely and powerfully in the context of one's own life. Once Sarah Gilchrist was convinced that the Cambuslang converts were not Quakers and were soundly biblical, she found soon enough what other converts reported, namely, that words of Scripture were 'brought to my mind with greater power than anything ever I had met with' (ii. 142). In the terminology of speech–act theory, these biblical texts were not locutionary acts, or statements of fact, but perlocutionary acts, or words used to bring about an effect by being repeated. The key trope that signalled this was the often repeated phrase, 'That word came into my mind with power . . . ' This was not the descriptive word but the effective word.

Janet Jackson is a case in point. In her narrative of twenty-two pages quarto she quoted more than thirty Scripture passages, not including allusions or biblical diction which was simply folded into her own first-person discourse. She remembered some texts from sermons preached, but most, she claimed, came spontaneously to mind and brought with them great conviction. She commented on this phenomenon explicitly: 'When I was kept from My nights rest, some sentences from Scripture would have come unto My mind with sweetness; and I was frequently made to bless the Lord that such comforting and supporting words to people in trouble are in the Bible' (i. 23).[33] And so, for example, as she was entering the church, she remembered, 'That word (in Ps: 51. 17) came into My Mind with great Power, "A Broken and a Contrite heart I Lord thou wilt not despise."'[34] Or as she was spinning at her wheel, 'That word came into My Mind with power and supported Me Much (in Ps 102. 17 in metre), "The prayer of

---

[32] The use of Scripture in these accounts compares—though it is a far distant analogue—with the hermeneutics of the Egyptian desert fathers recounted in Douglas Burton-Christie, *The Word in the Desert* (New York, 1993), 107–77.

[33] Several of the narrators use the perfect tense ('would have') of 'will' instead of the simple past ('would') in this sort of construction. The sense is not conditional but habitual (i.e. 'used to' or 'tended to'), as in the sentence, 'You *would* do that!'

[34] The quotation itself is displayed as two lines of poetry in the manuscript, since the quotation was from the metrical Psalter.

The Destitute | He surely will regard"' (i. 24–5).[35] Upon waking one morning, she recalled, 'These words (in Acts 16. 31) struck My heart with great Power, "Believe on the Lord Jesus Christ and thou shalt be saved"' (i. 29).

That this experience was associated uniquely with the awakened soul is apparent from the remarks of several converts, such as Bethea Davie that she 'never felt the word of God coming home with the power of God to my heart till I came to Camb. in the Spring 1742' (ii. 361), or James Kirkland that he never 'felt the word of God come home with power . . . till about the Middle of April 1742' (i. 362).[36] The word that came home so powerfully was most often a word of promise or comfort, but not always. Elizabeth Dykes said 'the first time I felt the word come with ane awakning convincing power' was when McCulloch preached on the text, 'He that believeth not on the Son is condemned already.' She knew 'this word was just to me, for that I was condemned already, and with that I felt a power strike me to the ground' (i. 208–9). But whether it was a word of comfort or conviction, or a word heard in a sermon or spontaneously recalled, it has to be taken as one of the key features of these narratives and of this revival that converts so often felt texts penetrating their hearts with such apparently self-evidencing spiritual power. There were variations on how this was expressed. 'The word came into my heart,' Archibald Bell said simply (i. 404), but James Tenant expressed it, 'These words were strongly impressed on my Mind' (i. 426), and Mary Mitchell rose to a higher ecstasy, saying, 'That word came unto me with a powerful, ravishing heart overcoming delight' (i. 98). John Aiken reported, 'That word came into my Mind, with great life and power' (i. 464), but Catherine Cameron made this even more vivid when she said, 'These words were darted into My Mind' (i. 328–9). The image of the arrow is exchanged for one of a bell for Charles Cunningham, who said that a particular text 'came home with a knell to my heart' (ii. 412). Andrew Faulds contrasted this sort of experience with his preconversion state when he used to hear the word preached and 'it came in at the one ear and went out at the other' (ii. 319). Likewise George Tassie recalled that though he had learned to read the Bible as a young person, he 'understood nothing of the spirituality of the Scriptures' and 'could never make application of what I read to my self' (i. 144). John Parker, in contrast, found that the word instead left an impression like a hammer: 'These words came with a dint on my heart' (ii. 664). This, then, is what the converts meant by the word 'coming home'. As with the Methodist followers of Charles Wesley, the 'spirituality' of the Bible referred to the way in which it addressed not simply one's outward behaviour before men, but also one's inward condition. Thus George Tassie found in June 1742 that everything was changed:

[35] The parenthetical scriptural references appear to be provided by McCulloch.
[36] Cf. Daniel McLarty, ii. 159, 163.

the word that had gone in one ear and out the other now 'came home with power to my soul' (i. 144).

The way in which the word of God was impressed on these lay converts indicates that their experience of conversion was not simply a matter of following the patterns that were laid down for them by their ministers. Like the early Methodist converts, their experience was both mimetic and unique. On the one hand, there were common narrative structures and a defined morphology of conversion, but, on the other hand, these women and men found themselves individuated and addressed in ways that seemed to specify them uniquely. Janet Jackson recalled that while McCulloch was speaking, 'All the time of that sermon he was preaching at Me as directly and distinctly as if he had named me before the Congregation' (i. 21). When he made his application, she thought, 'This was exactly My case' (i. 26). Listening to a sermon, James Kirkland likewise found, 'I thought I was the person' (i. 365). Isobel Provan thought, 'I was just the Person pointed at' (ii. 203). The consequence of this was that William Jameson could describe his religion before conversion as a matter of custom and 'the Example of others . . . I cannot say it was my own choise' (i. 492), but by the end of his narrative, he said, instead, 'By the grace of God, I have made choise of him' (i. 495). The experience of Scripture as a 'word come home with power' conveyed to these converts, in a new way, the living reality of God, but it also gave them a new sense of themselves that quickly passed over into self-expression. Elizabeth Jackson found her voice as an evangelist, speaking, as it were, through her tears: 'I could not forbear bursting out into tears, breaking out before all in the house to speak in commendation of Christ . . . and many Neighbours about flocking in I continued to speak on that subject with great freedom, for a considerable time.' It was not that she was a particularly loquacious or histrionic person by nature, for she wrote, 'I was before this time ashamed to open my mouth and speak anything almost before others. But now I thought if a whole Congregation had been present, I could not have been able to hold my peace before them all' (i. 106–7). Jean Ronald, too, 'got some liberty to tell my Case to some Ministers and private Christians', and on another occasion, on her way home, she said, 'I was not able to contain myself, But was obldiged to discover to some of my Friends, how it was with me' (i. 454, 452). William Ballie was asked to be God's mouthpiece among some laypeople in a barn, and he said, 'I fell a sweating through fear and shame,' but he ventured and 'found great liberty and heart enlargement in it' (i. 8). This pattern recurs over and over in these narratives. The convert feels personally addressed by the word of God, and he or she cannot help but speak to others.[37] A new

---

[37] For some converts, as with some of the lay Methodists and Moravians, this led them to express themselves in verse. George Tassie gave his account of what God had done for his

sense of interiority leads to a new expansiveness and boldness in self-expression. The underlying metaphors of 'not able to contain myself' and 'liberty and heart enlargement' all suggest that the self has become larger and has been set free from previous constraints.

Often the biblical texts remembered and quoted were fragments of metrical psalms. Whereas the Methodists and Moravians could hardly fail to incorporate a stanza of a hymn into their narratives, the Cambuslang converts remained Calvinistic psalm-singers. But like their fellow evangelicals in England, they cherished the sacred words they experienced in communal song, and these words found their way into their stories. As Alexander Biswell remembered, when he first approached Cambuslang: 'Before I got near I heard the 45th Psalm and was greatly melted and warmed' (i. 120). A royal wedding psalm, readily interpreted like the Song of Songs as the marriage between Christ and the soul, Psalm 45 also touched Mary Mitchell's heart. She came under such conviction during the singing of this psalm in the kirk that she could not continue. In fact, she wept through the whole sermon that followed. Later on in her narrative, after her conversion, she wrote of her delight in 'singing of Psalms of which I could never get enough' (i. 97, 100). Isobel Provan also 'fell a trembling' during worship, when certain 'Lines of the 6th Psalm [were] a giving out to be sung' (ii. 205). For Catherine Cameron the singing of Psalms seemed 'like the Melody of Heaven' (i. 318), and John Parker said that it was 'particularly the Psalms' that God 'impressed on my Spirit' (ii. 672). Psalms were thus a special case of the word coming home with power, one that compares with the English experience of hymns.

Although the public use of Scripture by the ministers associated with the Cambuslang revival was governed by rational exposition and application, there is evidence that the end they sought was precisely that these texts would become 'effective' in the lives of their hearers. When Margaret Borland went to the manse at Cambuslang, she heard James Robe 'telling some persons there under Concern, That when God was pleased to send in a word with the Power of his Spirit into their hearts; and to comfort them, they should not doubt and disbelieve' (ii. 543). This is a clue to the use of Scripture by the lay converts, since according to Robe it would appear that the phrase 'the word came home with power' is a metonym for 'the word came home with the power of the Spirit'. As the Shorter Catechism put it, 'The Spirit of God makes the reading, but especially the preaching of the word, an effectual means of convincing and converting sinners.'[38] The

---

soul in a poem that began: 'Lord thou didst make the glittering skies so clear | Yet I've been here this 40 & near a Year: | Yet did not see till that time came | That Thou didst shine at Cambuslang' (i. 152).

[38] Thomas F. Torrance, *The School of Faith: The Catechisms of the Reformed Church* (1959), 275. See also the discussion of the office of Christ as Prophet, whereby he reveals himself 'by His Word and Spirit'. Ibid. 266.

power of the word for these converts was the heart-convicting power of the Spirit. The way that Scripture came home to the hearers at Cambuslang delighted not only James Robe, but also John Willison, one of the ministers who 'attested' to the work in an appendix to the first published narrative of the revival and who later read and annotated the first volume of McCulloch's case histories. Willison wrote, 'All the Comfort and Relief they got from Trouble, still came to them, by some promise or word of Scripture cast into their Minds, and it was pleasant to hear them mention the great variety of these Words up and down the Bible.'[39]

For the most part, then, it seemed that the ministers approved and in fact stimulated this piety of the 'powerful word'. For a few of the converts, however, their use of Scripture passed over from the personal application of the word to their own spiritual needs, to something more prophetic, and when this happened, it raised some clerical eyebrows. The narrative of Alexander Biswell, for example, employed a charismatic hermeneutic, by which he applied texts to what he saw happening 'here and now' at Cambuslang, just as the apostle Peter did at Pentecost in Jerusalem when he said, 'This is that' spoken of by the prophet Joel (Acts 2: 16). When the text from Genesis 1—'The Spirit of God moved upon the face of waters'—came into his mind with power and light, he interpreted this creation text in terms of Scotland in 1742—'that the Spirit of the Lord had been moving upon the face of the waters of the Sanctuary at Camb.' (i. 120). A little later, on his way to Cambuslang, he found a jumble of texts impressed upon his mind, including the words in Judges 13: 18, 'It is secret,' and the words, 'Shall I do this great work and hide from my servant that which I do?' (a misquotation of Genesis 18: 17). Again, a 'this-is-that' insight followed: 'This great work I understood to be the great work of the Spirit of the Lord at Camb.' (i. 122).[40] Bisland soon began to feel that he could discern which biblical locutions were from God and which were diabolical by the manner in which the texts came into his consciousness. God-sent words came with 'sweetness and love and melting of heart' or gave him a keener sense of his own sins, but Satanic counterfeits came with unrelenting ferocity, 'with a fierceness and violence . . . pressed so furiously upon me' (i. 124). The high point of prophetic intuition in his narrative came when he began to see the import of those earlier words, 'it is secret'. One morning in June 1743 he awoke with two Bible passages leaping to mind from Psalm 18 and Genesis, texts having to do with David's victory over Saul and the destruction of Pharaoh and his hosts in the Red Sea. Bisland immediately turned to his

---

[39] Robe, *Short Narrative of the Extraordinary Work at Cambuslang*, 12–13.

[40] If this was a misquotation of Gen. 18: 17, then Bisland's choice of text is ironic, since the great thing Yahweh was hiding from his servant Abraham in this text was his intention to destroy Sodom.

wife and said, 'Surely the Lord has been . . . giving some great deliverance to our armies abroad.' Within an hour they heard the bells ringing to an-nounce the spectacular victory of the outnumbered British over the French at the Battle of Dettingen. This was all the confirmation he needed that he had been given a 'secret' from God. This, once again, was that.

All of this was too much for the clergymen McCulloch had solicited to edit and comment on the manuscripts. Each of the passages I have quoted from Bisland were flagged by at least two of the ministers for deletion. Alexander Webster struck the largest number of lines, but Thomas Ogilvie flagged this last passage having to do with Bisland's premonition of the victory of the British as something he would be 'very sorry to see in Print' (i. 130–1). Indeed at the conclusion of Bisland's narrative, Ogilvie wrote candidly, but not without charity, 'I think this Person should be cautioned (as no doubt he has been) about not being heasty in regarding every Impression on his Mind, or Occasional thoughts, as if they were all from the Lord's Spirit. He seems to need Advice much in this way, though indeed there are many excellent and uncommon things in his Case. The same Caution has also doubtless been given to others' (i. 142). It was acceptable for the word to come home with power if it led to 'conviction and conversion', but not if this was in fact mere suggestibility or if it led to grandiose prophecy.

The word that came home with power was thus central to these narra-tives, even though this led to extremes that discomfited the ministers. Recent studies have rightly stressed the importance of the communion season in Scottish piety and have interpreted the 'Cambuslang Wark' largely in terms of cyclical sacramental piety.[41] However, the Bible-saturated character of these narratives and the preoccupation of the converts with texts of Scripture, snatches of metrical psalms, and sermons seems to have been even more defining for these autobiographers. It would probably be best, though, not to see these in opposition. Indeed, there is a Reformed tradition, which looks back to Augustine, by which the elements of the Lord's Supper are themselves seen as 'visible words', or as John Willison, one of the editors of the McCulloch manuscripts, put it, 'visible Gospel'.[42]

---

[41] See Leigh Schmidt, *Holy Fairs*, 119, 121, who argues for the centrality of the commu-nion season in the piety of the narrators in the McCulloch manuscripts. Schmidt offers a close reading of Catherine Cameron's account as an example of someone for whom the Lord's Supper represented 'a high point in the rhythm of her piety'. Indeed, it 'wholly dominated her piety'. As Michael Crawford, *Seasons of Grace,* 217–22, has pointed out, however, a 'season of grace' was a distinct category in the minds of the pastors and people, something that referred to a wider spiritual quickening or revival, distinct from (though incorporating) the return of the communion season, but depending even more significantly upon preach-ing. Thus the converts themselves periodized the onset of the revival not in terms of the communions in 1742, but in terms of Whitefield's arrival in Glasgow in the autumn of 1741 and the awakening under McCulloch's preaching in February 1742.

[42] Schmidt, *Holy Fairs*, 69.

Surrounded as the communion table was by preparation sermons, the action sermon, and thanksgiving sermons, it is surely right to see even the bread and the wine also as 'words come home with power'.

Reformed Theology

The case histories recorded by McCulloch not only have a clearly structured pattern of conversion and a dynamic biblical textuality, but they also are marked by a debt to orthodox Calvinism in both the content and form of the accounts.

This may be witnessed, for example, in the importance placed on the Shorter Catechism by most of the converts, and according to the index in the second volume over 80 per cent had learned their catechism.[43] Elizabeth Dykes was 16 years old and wrote, 'I also got the Shorter Catechism by heart and have so still' (i. 208). Archibald Bell was older, 38 years of age, and yet he could echo Dykes almost exactly, saying that he had got the whole of the catechism by heart, 'and have it to this day' (i. 398). Although 41-year-old George Tassie retained the catechism only 'in good measure', the language of the catechism crept into his narrative. He concluded his account by echoing the first answer of the Westminster Shorter Catechism. Now that he was converted the 'great and chief End' he had habitually in view was 'the glory of God' (i. 152). Jean Ronald experienced a period of 'deadness and darkness' and she recovered 'by means of that passage in the Shorter Catechism, "The Spirit of God Maketh the reading..."', and she proceeded to quote the whole answer to Question 89 of the catechism, 'How is the word made effectual for salvation?' At the close of her narrative, she too could say, 'Now my chief end is to Glorify God, and to Enjoy him for ever' (i. 437, 459). But the most outstanding example of the role the catechism could play in one's spiritual autobiography came with Thomas Barclay, who in his soul's distress was advised by a friend to look over his Shorter Catechism. He turned for comfort to Question 31, 'What is effectual calling?' and went on reading up to Question 87, 'What is repentance unto life?' He internalized all this, saying, 'I found what had before been a dead letter, was accompanied with something of life to me,' and this led him to 'some measure of Joy' (i. 351). There were not perhaps many people in the eighteenth century whose conversion was begun between Questions 31 and 87 of the Shorter Catechism, but Barclay shows how deep an education in the Westminster standards could go and how this, when kindled by revival, could help to shape a conversion.

Consequently, the language of confessional Calvinism recurs throughout these narratives. There is little anti-Arminian rhetoric such as we might expect to find in New England or among the Methodists, where Calvinism

---

[43] Smout, 'Born Again', 124.

was more hotly contested, but there are indications none the less that Calvinism had formed the outlook of Cambuslang converts. For example, both Elizabeth Dykes and George Tassie tip their hats to orthodoxy and the doctrine of the limited atonement when they refer to Christ's dying love for 'perishing Elect Sinners' (i. 216, 146).[44] For Sarah Gilchrist, this was the way in which her soul's struggle was framed. She worried about her state and whether her sorrow for sin and the desire of her heart to close with Christ were sufficient, 'whether this was a Saving and thorow work, and if God had accepted of me'. Her 'interest in Christ' was something settled by God himself, but she needed to get clarity about it. 'I was thereupon made to plead more earnestly than ever, that he would clear up to me my Interest in Christ; and he was pleased to give me clear and satisfying views of the Covenant of Redemption, wherein a certain Select number were given to Christ to be redeemed and saved by him, and that I was among that number' (ii. 136). The very language of her conversion had to do not with the subjective ground of her conversion in her own will or own faith, but rather with its objective ground in the finished work of Christ. What she needed and was given was a 'view' of this salvation, as accomplished for the elect, and her stake in it.

To the language of election may be added the recurring reference of these converts to the 'offices' of Christ. Questions 23–6 of the Shorter Catechism expound the Reformed teaching about how Christ accomplishes redemption by executing the offices of prophet, priest, and king—the one who teaches, mediates, and rules over his people. It is the exception for these narratives not to say something like what Elizabeth Jackson reported, 'I was enabled to close with him in all his offices' (i. 107).[45] William Jameson was even more emphatic. He had discovered Christ 'in all his Offices, as a Prophet to teach and instruct me; a Priest, to attone, and intercede, for me; and as a King to rule in and over me' (i. 495). This theology was made personal, just as the biblical texts were, since the converts used various terms to express their relation to Christ in these roles. They 'received', 'embraced', 'accepted', and above all 'closed' with Christ in all his offices.

The concept of covenant is essential to orthodox Calvinism, and it is no surprise to find that the Cambuslang autobiographers speak often of the covenant of grace or covenant of redemption, and that they stress not the bilateral obligations of the covenant but its unilateral aspect as deriving from

---

[44] Cf. Alexander Biswell's similar reference in passing to the salvation won by Christ for 'his Elect' by his death (i. 129).

[45] See also, for further examples, George Tassie (i. 146), Elizabeth Dykes (i. 211), James Kirkland (i. 367), James Tenant (i. 429), Alexander Biswell (i. 119), Catherine Cameron (i. 321, 335, and 342), Archibald Smith (ii. 444), Margaret Borland (ii. 143), Sarah Gilchrist (ii. 143), and John Parker (ii. 667).

the unconditioned grace of God. Archibald Bell was no mean exponent of
Reformed theology when he concluded his narrative, saying that in times
of fear or doubt he would look to some word of promise 'that the Covenant, I hope he had made with me, is a well ordered, sure and everlasting
Covenant; and that Christ the surety of the New Covenant, has undertaken
both for the debt and duty of his people in that Covenant' (i. 406). As John
von Rohr has written of the orthodox Calvinism of the Puritans, 'The
conditional covenant is employed for purposes that are themselves absolute . . . The covenant is conditional, but for the elect the fulfilment of its
conditions is guaranteed. The covenant is also absolute.'[46] This subtlety was
clearly not lost on Archibald Bell, but when other narrators slipped up, then
the clerical marginators were there to help out. James Kirkland did not get
the balance right in his speaking of the covenant. He said he was going to
'retire from the world and set about the duty of Personal covenanting with
God', but Thomas Gillespie flagged those last four words and suggested he
might do better to put it, 'taking hold of God's covenant' (i. 363). Catherine
Cameron said, 'I thought I got My Covenant renewed,' but this did not get
past Gillespie either, and he offered the alternative, 'I thought I got my
Interest in God's Covenant cleared up' (i. 335). This was not just circumlocution, or it was circumlocution with a theological aim: *soli Deo gloria*.

These Calvinistic theological subjects—election, the offices of Christ, the
covenant—featured in the narratives alongside the order of salvation, which
could be seen in the very structure of the accounts. Yet an even more
telling, if subtle, indication of the Reformed ethos of Cambuslang is the
syntactical habit of the narrators to resort to the passive voice when talking
about their spiritual experiences. The principle of *soli Deo gloria* was so
deeply imbibed that converts really could not speak about their response to
God without putting it in the passive. Helen Finlay did not just weep and
mourn but 'was made to weep and mourn' (ii. 58). Bethea Davies did not
just cry out in a meeting but 'was made sometimes to cry out' (ii. 361).
Alexander Bisland 'was made to believe'; John Wier 'was made to rejoice';
Charles Cunningham 'was made to rely' on Christ; Jean Ronald 'was
enabled to receive and rest upon him'; and Elizabeth Dykes 'was made to
see' the corruption of her own nature (i. 120; i. 314; ii. 414; i. 454; i. 210).
The qualifying of wilful action became even more pronounced if one
ventured to speak about moral resolution. William Ballie 'was in some
measure strengthened to resolve upon new obedience in dependence on
his grace' (i. 7). The verbal hedges 'in some measure' and 'in dependence'
have been added to the passive construction to make sure that divine agency
is not in any way compromised. This habit of language also constituted a
conversion aesthetic. When William Jameson said, 'I felt deep impressions

---

[46] John von Rohr, *The Covenant of Grace in Puritan Thought* (Atlanta, Ga., 1986), 123.

of the infinite distance and disproportion betwixt Christ and my soul,' he gave voice to the Calvinist sublime that lay behind this repeated use of the passive voice.[47] This sort of construction appears occasionally in other evangelical narratives, but not with this intensity and consistency. The doctrine of predestination became a matter of grammatical custom for the hearers at Cambuslang, and their use of this 'Presbyterian passive' distinguishes their accounts from the others we have examined south of the Tweed. [48]

Calvinism also subtly distinguishes these narratives through the role of doubt in one's spiritual progress. Whereas most of the Methodist followers of John and Charles Wesley looked largely to the evidence of their feelings to discern their spiritual state—and took this evidence at face value as John Wesley did at Aldersgate and at least twice thereafter in his third *Journal*—the Cambuslang converts used the evidence of their feelings as part of a broader calculus to determine whether they were in a state of grace. For many lay Methodists it was sufficient to look for psychological evidence of conversion as a subjective work ('the witness of the Spirit'), but for these Calvinists the psychological evidence had to be augmented by other evidence of election as an objective work. In this they were much closer to William Perkins's morphology of conversion, which involved, as an expected part of the conversion process, a period during which faith was tested by 'doubting, despair, and distrust'.[49] The subjects of the Cambuslang work spoke of this as 'doubts and fears' and 'damps and doubtings'. They heard many sermons from their ministers about 'evidences' and 'marks' and the danger of being deceived about one's state, and their response was to examine themselves. After one such sermon, which identified one of the distinguishing marks of true conversion as the curbing of the very first impulses towards sin in the heart, William Ballie said, 'I having examined

---

[47] This Calvinist sublime appears in Sarah Gilchrist in language that sounds remarkably Edwardsean. She said that upon closing with Christ she found a beam of heavenly light—she did not know quite how to put this—shining into her heart or mind, for a little while, 'giving me the most ravishing discoveries of the transcendent Glory and Excellency and amiableness of Christ in his Person as God–Man, and in all his offices of Grace, and his perfect suitableness to all my wants and desires' (ii. 143). It is almost as though she had been reading the second of the signs in the *Religious Affections*, about which Edwards says, 'The first objective ground of gracious affections, is the transcendently excellent and amiable nature of divine things, as they are in themselves; not any conceived relation they bear to self, or self-interest.' *WJE* ii. 240.

[48] Although some historians of women's religious experience, such as Catherine A. Brekus, *Strangers and Pilgrims* (Chapel Hill, 1998), 39, have observed in certain contexts that women tended to use the passive voice more often than men, I did not find this to be true in the Cambuslang narratives. In the accounts that I read, Calvinism, more than gender, generally determined the extent to which a subject portrayed herself or himself as a passive recipient of God's grace.

[49] William Perkins, *Works* (1613), ii. 13.

my self by this mark ... my doubting about the reality of a saving Change upon my mind went off' (i. 6). Again, after Dr Alexander Webster preached following the second communion at Cambuslang on the marks of those who belonged to Christ, Ballie recalled, 'I got liberty to apply these marks with much clearness; which afforded me a great deal of comfort' (i. 8). Being able to interpret the evidence was all the more important with an approaching communion season since such a season provoked worries about worthy reception. On the fast day before the second communion, Elizabeth Jackson responded to the sermon, saying, 'I ... was helped to apply the marks of Believers then given to myself' (i. 109). In a paragraph narrating his experience between his conversion and the first communion at Cambuslang, George Tassie mentioned three sermons, to each of which he responded by examining himself, adding comments such as, 'I had the satisfaction, to find several of the marks agreeing to myself' (i. 149–50). Catherine Cameron spoke of 'applying the marks' to herself four times in as many pages in her account (i. 322–36).

The outcome was not, however, always one of settled assurance. Elizabeth Jackson concluded her narrative with the summary, 'When I reflect on the workings of my heart, for more than a twelve month past, I find that the Ordinary and Chief bent of it is after Christ,' but she added, 'I cannot pretend to a stated assurance, that I am in a gracious state' (i. 110). Neither could Elizabeth Dykes: 'And now to this day; I cannot say that I have ane assurance of heaven; but I desire to lay the stress of my salvation on Christ and his own righteousness ... but I dare not say much for fear of presumption' (i. 216). Indeed, McCulloch had preached on the danger of presumptuous sins, and James Kirkland accordingly examined himself and thought he was guilty of them all (i. 365–6). Jean Ronald, too, for all her experiences at Cambuslang, concluded, 'I cannot say indeed I have attained to ane unshaken assurance of My interest in Christ' (i. 459).

If David Bebbington is right, and evangelicalism in the eighteenth century differed from Puritanism by virtue of a more robust doctrine of assurance—that 'Evangelicals believed it to be general, normally given at conversion and the result of simple acceptance of the gift of God'—then these Cambuslang converts were much closer to their Scottish forebears, who joined with the English Puritan divines to write the Westminster standards, which included the acknowledgement that assurance was rare, late, and the fruit of struggle. [50]

This is perhaps what we should expect, since the revival in south-western Scotland took place, unlike the English Evangelical Revival, within a much more clearly defined tradition of theology and piety. Unlike the English revival, which was preceded by the parallel but unrelated conversions of a

---

[50] D. W. Bebbington, *Evangelicalism in Modern Britain* (1989), 43–4.

number of ministers, many of whom then later turned to Calvinism to make sense of their experience of 'Free Grace', the revival at Cambuslang occurred within a tightly nucleated community in which the whole parish, land, and nation could be seen in terms of a long tradition of Scots-Calvinist piety. This inherited tradition was of course contested between evangelicals and moderates, as between evangelicals within the national church and Seceders without, but the sense of community cohesion and theological continuity with the past in the McCulloch manuscripts contrasts sharply with the situation in England.

The title of a forty-page tract published in Edinburgh in 1742 communicates what was at stake: *An Apology for the Presbyterians of Scotland who are the Hearers of The Reverend Mr. George Whitefield, Shewing that their Keeping Communion with Him, in the Ordinances of the Gospel, Stands Justified by the Principles and Practice of the Church of Scotland from the Reformation to this Day, Especially by the Westminster Confession of Faith and Solemn League and Covenant.* Indeed, the anonymous author claimed that if Presbyterians from the period of the Reformation or the Restoration were alive now, 'they would hear and embrace Mr. Whitefield's Ministry just as we do'.[51] Evangelical conversion in Scotland was not only about religious experience, but also about how the past related to the present, and who were the true heirs of the Reformation and the Covenanters.

The appearance of conversion in clusters within a defined community, where pastors and people together participated in revival, differed from the situation in London or even Bristol, where converts were clearly gathered out of the wider society into distinct Methodist cells. Here Cambuslang compares less with Methodism than with other parish-based revivals such as at Northampton, Massachusetts in 1734–5, or Everton in Bedfordshire under John Berridge in 1758, or Olney in Buckinghamshire under John Newton in the 1760s.[52] But in these latter two contexts, even allowing for the strength of Dissent in the English Midlands, there was nothing like the Calvinist heritage at Cambuslang. Just as Jonathan Edwards could speak of revival in Northampton, for all its novelty, as in continuity with the five previous 'harvests' under Solomon Stoddard when there had been an

---

[51] *An Apology for the Presbyterians of Scotland*, 29.

[52] The parallels to Everton under John Berridge are particularly noteworthy. Both were local, parish phenomena that attracted larger attention, and both focused upon the sermons in the church and counselling in the rectory or manse afterwards, and both involved intense physical and psychic manifestations of terror and joy in a concentrated period of time. The experience of Elizabeth Dykes, being unable to stand and carried into the manse (i. 208–17), or Janet McAlpin, who tells of folks walking back and forth to the manse, staying up all night, falling under conviction while walking home, etc. (ii. 258)—all this compares well with Elizabeth Blackwell's letter, quoted in Wesley's *Journal*, giving an account of the revival at Everton. Wesley, *Works* (BE), xxi. 195–200.

'extraordinary success ... in the conversion of many souls',[53] so also James
Robe argued that the revival that began at Cambuslang was in continuity
with the Six-Mile-Water revival in Ireland and the revivals in Shotts and
Stewarton in the west of Scotland in the 1620s. The Seceders also claimed
this same pedigree.[54]

EDITORIAL CONCERNS: SOCIAL CONTROL OR SPIRITUAL DIRECTION?

In all the lay conversion narratives we have examined in England and
Scotland there has been a close relationship between pastors and people,
and the leaders generally provided the theological scheme for the emplotting of one's life in religious terms. In the English context the leaders also
provided many biographical role models, published and unpublished, which
helped to foster a narrative culture. The Moravians also closely superintended this culture by incorporating self-writing into an elaborate ecclesiastical discipline. The approach of the clergy who stimulated and
monitored the revival at Cambuslang was, in contrast, fittingly Presbyterian,

---

[53] *WJE* iv. 145–6, cf. 190: 'The work that has now been wrought on souls is evidently the
same that was wrought in my venerable predecessor's days.'

[54] Westerkamp, *Triumph of the Laity*, 119, 132. Westerkamp argues likewise for the
continuity of piety at Cambuslang, and indeed among the Seceders, with Scots-Irish popular
piety more generally. Both were 'products of the revered, reformed Protestant ethos ...
Popular, emotional participation had always been a part of this tradition. From the public
acceptance of John Knox through the Six-Mile-Water Revival and the suppressed conventicles to the signings of the Solemn League and Covenant, the laity sought active participation in their church's rituals. Ideology was far less important, although basic adherence to the
tenets of Calvinism was required. What was firmly at the center of this tradition was
the ritualized experience of community conversion. The 1630 revivals, the activities of the
Remonstrators, the conventiclers, and now the Seceders all worked toward a pure, renewed
community of God. Even the Cambuslang revivalists, enjoying the individual conversion
experience prescribed by Whitefield, realized their true goal in the communions.' Ibid. 135.

Schmidt pushes the continuities back further, into pre-Reformation piety, arguing that the
atmosphere of the communion was that of a 'holy fair' with piety and impiety, devotion and
diversion, both present together. Religious agony and ecstasy existed side by side with
impiety and immorality in a carnival atmosphere until bourgeoisification finally took over
in early nineteenth-century America. With respect to Cambuslang, Schmidt makes his case
by conflating the revival with the communion season, and augmenting this with cases of
discipline in church records. The revival narratives provide evidence of religious ecstasy and
an intensity of sacramental piety, and the discipline proceedings provide evidence of
drunkenness, sexual dalliance, cursing, and blasphemy. However, I am not sure that all of
these sources can be so tightly correlated: revival, communion, and the cases of discipline.
Only one of the cases of discipline, for example, comes from Cambuslang, and it is late
(1744), and none of the others come from the period of the revival (1741–2). The examples
given from Cambuslang—those whose 'devotions had never quite worked'—Thomas Foster
and David Logan (the old soldier) are not representative of the collection as a whole. See
Schmidt, *Holy Fairs*, 115–68.

since a large role was accorded to authorized ministers acting in a collegial and consultative way to maintain discipline.

The ministers collaborated first of all in the ministry of preaching and spiritual counselling during the revival at Cambuslang. McCulloch provided a list of the ministers who preached at the second sacrament in 1742 and it includes not only McCulloch and Whitefield but also another nine ministers. McCulloch adds that more than twenty-four ministers were present on the last day.[55] Repeatedly in the lay narratives the names of ministers other than McCulloch come up at Cambuslang—ministers preaching in the kirk or on the brae or exhorting at the manse—and the laity themselves were also mobile and went to neighbouring parishes or to Glasgow to hear evangelical preaching or participate in a sacramental occasion.

Not only did the ministers thus act in concert to stimulate conversion, but they also monitored how this religious experience would be expressed. This is apparent first in the solicitation and publication of numbers of 'attestations' printed alongside James Robe's account of the revival. He provided an 'attestation of the facts' of his narrative from McCulloch, and then another nine attestations of the facts of the narrative 'relating to the Fruits of this Work'. These were letters that McCulloch himself solicited from various people who had travelled to visit Cambuslang—all, of course, ministers. Both Robe and McCulloch also later published testimony from their respective Kirk Sessions to attest to the perseverance of the converts in the faith and the abiding good results of the revival; these documents too were signed by duly authorized elders and heritors of the parishes.[56] The presence of all these attestations in the revival narratives associated with Cambuslang give the impression of an ecclesiastical court. All in all, it was a very Presbyterian way to have a revival.

This presbyteral approach to superintending the work of God at Cambuslang can be seen above all in the fact that McCulloch consulted respected ministers to edit the lay narratives he collected and to advise him on the prospect of publication. In the manuscript narratives each clerical editor indicated the passages that concerned him by scoring the passage in the margin and adding the first and last letter of his surname. So, for example, Thomas Gillespie would score a passage with G——E, written vertically in the margin against the offending text, which was also sometimes further indicated with square brackets. Various footnotes were also added. The four clerical marginators were Thomas Gillespie of Carnock (one of the later

---

[55] McCulloch, 'An Account of the Second Sacrament at Cambuslang', in Robe, *Narratives of the Work at Cambuslang, Kilsyth, &c* (1790), 35.
[56] Gillies (ed.), *Historical Collections* (1981), 451–2, 458, 462.

founders of the Relief Church), Dr Alexander Webster of Edinburgh, James Ogilvie of Aberdeen, and the devotional writer John Willison of Dundee.

We have already observed some of the clerical emendations to the lay narratives. They did not, for example, appreciate Alexander Bisland's charismatic hermeneutic or his self-important prophecies and worried he was too suggestible; they were also careful to safeguard the prerogatives of divine agency where narrators seemed a little too wilful; and they did not want to give ground to those who complained that the revival drew labourers away from their work. Well aware of the criticisms that were circulating concerning the revival, the ministers were also careful with passages that described the converts crying out in meetings. After the minister spoke of Christ riding forth on the white horse of the Apocalypse in the triumph of the gospel, Janet Jackson was so overcome with joy that she stood up and 'cry'd out aloud, That Christ had glorify'd himself, and would glorify himself again, in my Redemption'. Gillespie flagged this and wrote, 'Though this Passage is Good this liable to be abused' (i. 18). Webster agreed. But when James Tenant spoke of his own unworthiness and the greatness of God's mercy, and how he was so overcome with this that he cried out before the congregation, 'O Lord I will bless and praise thy Name,' this seemed a little more acceptable. Gillespie said that if they were going to publish any of these instances of crying out, then this one was the best. Ogilvie concurred but thought they could just as well mention joy without including the bits about crying out (i. 434). They were less concerned with the impropriety of the outbursts, however, than that to publish these would be to give ammunition to the critics and justify the charge of enthusiasm.

Other emendations suggest clerical concerns not only over potential misunderstanding by the public, or misrepresentation by the Seceders, but also over the authenticity of the religious experiences themselves. When Jean Ronald had a Scripture passage impressed upon her mind while she was sleeping, Gillespie struck the passage and noted, 'What Passes in Sleep should be Overlooked' (i. 455). The editors were concerned that the converts use Scripture with care. It was not enough to have words come home with power, or to find comfort, if the convert was not brought to place her faith in Christ. Thus Gillespie wrote (and Webster noted his agreement) under a passage in Elizabeth Jackson's account, 'Here she seems to take Comfort Without having believed in Christ and to think the Impression of Scripture on the Mind Simply is Intimation of his Love' (i. 106). Was this a concern only that the public might misconstrue the passage, or was it more a concern that Elizabeth Jackson needed further spiritual direction? In this case the latter issue seems more to the fore, though it would also have been reason to hold back this passage from publication. The same was also true of the section noted by Gillespie in

Jean Ronald's narrative, where a biblical text was, to his mind, misapplied, giving him cause to drop the whole passage (i. 430). Scripture was not to be abused.

As Leigh Schmidt comments, however, the auditory and visionary experiences of some of the converts troubled the ministers most, and they rarely failed to mark a passage where the narrator reported hearing things or seeing things if this was not qualified by the clause, 'it seemed to me', or some close equivalent. When the word came home with power, this was acceptable, but if the word came home with 'power and light', it usually was not. Jean Hay said, 'I had my Eyes Shutt when these words came all the three lines; but after the Third line, when this marvellous light shone into my heart, I opened My Eyes, to see if it might be the light of the Sun' (i. 271). This photism was far too corporeal. Webster marked it, and Willison wrote, 'This woman's case may be passed by and not published' (ibid.). At the conclusion of James Jack's account the ministerial commentary was more fulsome: 'There is something Visionary in this mans experiences,' wrote Webster, and Willison agreed, adding that he thought it should not be published. Gillespie said that he got tired of scoring so many passages for deletion and so gave it up, but he emphatically did not think this account should see the light of day. Moreover, he added, there was 'not the Humility, and Self Denial, one Would Wish and Expect, where Extraordinary Attainments are pretended Which Obliged me to speak in Stronger Terms than I Enclined' (i. 497). Ogilvie noted his agreement. The combination of the visionary with seeming Christian immaturity was too much: a full four votes against. Even when Catherine Cameron claimed that one night she saw 'as it were' Christ standing with outstretched arms ready to receive her, Ogilvie and Gillespie expressed concerns, saying that this at least needed to be explained. Perhaps they were worried that the vision of Christ's embrace at night might be taken as erotic, but given that they let this sort of thing go elsewhere, it may simply be that this was another concern about dreams.

The auditory was likewise highlighted by the clergy as a worry. Anne Wyke claimed that while alone and in distress she heard that single word, 'Hear'. It was 'as it were spoken to me, by somebody in the room'. Again this was too immediate and bodily an experience and so it was marked for deletion (i. 48). Something of what the clergy were looking for instead may be seen in their suggested emendations to the sentence, 'The Lord signify'd to me that He would visit us yet again,' in Mary Lap's account. Willison thought she perhaps meant something more like, 'It was impressed on my mind,' and Gillespie proposed the alternative, 'the Lord Caused me hope that he would . . . ' (i. 15). Vivid religious consciousness was welcomed, but not miracles in the world of sense. The ministers were perhaps particularly sensitive to this issue since Catherine Jackson, one of the early Cambuslang converts, had been taken to tell her story to James Fisher, a leading Secession minister. In the course of telling her story, she spoke of seeing Christ 'with her bodily eyes', which was later seized upon by the Seceders to discredit the revival (ii. 288).[57] When the public fast was declared by the Seceders in the summer of 1742, it was on account of strong delusions at Cambuslang, and these included 'visions and revelations'.[58]

And yet the ministers were concerned most of all with discerning evidence of spiritual and moral transformation. Thus James Ogilvie wrote at the bottom of several of the case histories that he would have liked to see more of this or that one's experiences. To Janet Reed's account he appended the note, 'If this desireable Person has attained to a further Establishment, and more of Joy and Peace in Believing, I humbly think it should be observed, the Means of it recorded' (i. 92). He also wrote below A. Roger's narrative, 'I should be glade this Persons after-Experiences since this were added. The World knows or hears perhaps too little of a Christian's progress, though this appears to me one of the most useful parts of the Lord's Work with them and the most edifying to others' (i. 175). Intense spiritual experience in the midst of revival was fine and good, but the really important thing was lasting change.

With its combination of lay narrative and clerical interlocution, the archive accumulated by McCulloch is indeed a rich resource for historians, and several interpretations have been offered of the relationship between pastors and people during the revival at Cambuslang. Ned Landsman contends most forcefully that there was a cleavage between ministers and laypeople, where the converts at Cambuslang 'forged a concept of conversion that diverged dramatically from that prescribed by the preachers'.[59] The laity saw conversion in psychological terms; the ministers viewed it in doctrinal terms.[60] A century earlier, ministers and their hearers were closer to one another, but now social fragmentation had led to the revival not of a whole community but only a segment of it. Landsman argues that the Cambuslang revival was heavily weighted toward lay leadership and participation from a new weaver community, with master weavers as key spiritual counsellors, and with the revival reinforcing their own group identity and moral discipline.[61] Although Landsman is certainly right about the significance of lay leaders and lay agency in the revival, the number of weavers involved in the revival was far fewer than he reckoned,

---

[57] The pagination here jumps in the MS from p. 277 to p. 288. See further, with respect to this episode, Landsman, 'Evangelists and Their Hearers', 139; *Short Account of the Remarkable Conversions*, 12.

[58] Fawcett, *Cambuslang Revival*, 189.

[59] Landsman, 'Evangelists and Their Hearers', 132.

[60] Ibid. 142.

[61] Ibid. 141.

and the idea that the revival followed along a new social fault line in the community does not hold up to close scrutiny.[62]

Marilyn Westerkamp argues that the Cambuslang revival was all about the laity but not, as Landsman claims, about one segment of the community. For Westerkamp the revival, as indeed the Secession movement itself, represented the 'triumph of the laity', since it was they who demanded a communal, emotional piety over against what was offered by the moderatist, rationalizing elites in the church. Both the Secession and the revival were products of a 'revered, reformed Protestant ethos', and 'popular, emotional participation had always been a part of this tradition'. From John Knox to the revivals in Ireland and western Scotland in the 1620s and the suppressed conventicles to the Solemn League and Covenant— through all of this there was a 'ritualized experience of community conversion' which assumed the basic tenets of Calvinism but was not fervently ideological.[63] In effect, Westerkamp argues for a demand-side, rather than a supply-side, view of the religious economy in Scotland in the 1740s.

Michael Crawford suggests that the relationship between pastors and people was more mutual, and that the influence flowed both ways. He observes that the lay initiative seen at Cambuslang was often encouraged by the evangelical clergy, and that people and pastors shared very similar views on conversion, on the wisdom of not trusting too much in imaginary visions and voices, and on the priority of Scripture in Christian experience. On the one hand, the ministers influenced the people: 'The guiding hand of the preacher was evident not only in each of the stages leading to conversion, but also in the ways the laity verbalized their joyful, intimate communion with the Savior after conversion.'[64] On the other hand, the people influenced the ministers: 'The laity's reports of their spiritual exercises shaped the revivalists' understanding of the workings of grace in a community during an outpouring of the Holy Spirit'; that is, the very concept of revival, or a 'season of grace' in a community, was something the laity gave to their ministers.[65]

Finally, Leigh Schmidt offers a nuanced description of the mental worlds of clergy and laity at Cambuslang based upon an examination of some fresh sources, including kirk session records and devotional manuals, such as those written by John Willison. He argues that notwithstanding 'a lingering gap between pastors and some of their people', and even though the clergy clearly 'failed to mould lay piety as fully as they would have liked', none the less 'it would be precipitous to draw a sharp line between pastors and the

---

[62] Crawford, *Seasons of Grace*, 201–22.
[63] Westerkamp, *Triumph of the Laity*, 135.
[64] Crawford, *Seasons of Grace*, 213.
[65] Ibid. 222.

people'.[66] With regard to visionary and auditory experience, for example, 'ministers relied upon distinctions that were not interiorized by a large number of their communicants. Even so the gap between pastors and people on this point was hardly unbridgeable. Ministerial expression often blurred the distinctions, and lay experience elaborated upon, as much as controverted, pastoral diction and devotion.'[67]

It seems to me that Schmidt is right to see the relationship between lay and clerical piety as overlapping substantially, but not, of course, entirely. While acknowledging the imbalance of power between pastors and people, one does not need to assume that this was a movement riven by ideological conflict. To presume that the ministers were social elites using ideas as a means of social control or that conversion was all about the bourgeoisification of a proto-industrial guild would be to import assumptions of class conflict into a setting where they are not warranted. The ministers did have some preoccupations that differed from those of the laity, but these had to do principally with their calling *qua* ministers. Their aims were not social control through ideology, but Christian maturity through spiritual direction. And in this they had the support of the majority of the laity. The people sought spiritual guidance and the pastors welcomed genuine religious experience.

Several of the lay narrators commented explicitly on their desire for spiritual counsel. As Jean Ronald said, 'I went to one of the Ministers . . . to direct and assist Me, as to my soul concerns' (i. 458). This is why they so often went to the manse at Cambuslang, just as Whitefield's hearers would often queue outside his residence the day after he had preached. And this is why James Robe needed his journal to record and keep straight the spiritual experiences he was hearing about and the souls he was advising. The same was true across the breadth of the revival, from Jonathan Edwards's study in Northampton, Massachusetts to the rectory at Everton where John Berridge met with people in spiritual distress. Yet the importance of lay leadership should be noted even here, for converts also spoke about turning to elders and to acquaintances for advice. Bethea Davie, when vexed in spirit, said 'I . . . sent for an Elder to speak with him as to my soul's case' (i. 361). And Archibald Smith said he would often be 'conferring with this and the other Person that I thought knew something of serious Religion from Experience, to see what they thought of my case, and get directions and advice' (ii. 444).

The concerns expressed by the clerical editors of the McCulloch manuscripts and the nature of the questions McCulloch asked the converts—in so far as we can reconstruct them—suggest that the clergy were preoccupied

---

[66] Schmidt, *Holy Fairs*, 153, 147, 151.
[67] Ibid. 153.

with how they would pastor the people as a whole (including influencing the movement through publication), and how they would monitor and direct individuals toward lasting transformation. As a collegium, the Presbyterian leaders at Cambuslang were feeling their way, much like the Moravian and Methodist leaders, toward criteria and methods to canalize the fervour of intense conversionist piety into wise channels.

Their aims, as evidenced in the clerical marginalia, overlapped with the programme of Jonathan Edwards in Massachusetts, with his succession of works on revival and religious experience from the *Faithful Narrative* (1737) to the *Distinguishing Marks* (1741) to *Some Thoughts Concerning Revival* (1743) to his definitive work, *The Religious Affections* (1746). McCulloch, Robe, Gillespie, and Willison avidly corresponded with Edwards. McCulloch read the *Faithful Narrative* from the pulpit; John Willison claimed that the work described by Edwards in the *Distinguishing Marks* was 'of the same kind with that at *Cambuslang*'; and Gillespie confessed that the *Distinguishing Marks* and *Some Thoughts Concerning Revival* were 'peculiarly agreeable to me'.[68] Indeed, Christopher Mitchell argues that Edwards helped these Scottish friends to 'redefine Scottish evangelical Calvinism by adapting it from its didactic/catechizing function within a godly commonwealth, to a more mission-oriented role where the faith of the individual became prominent'.[69] In his pastoral work and his writing Edwards was seeking, like his Scottish correspondents, to discern and direct the work of God in 'the conversion of many souls', and he, like them, had recourse to case histories, including Abigail Hutchinson, Phoebe Bartlett, and his own wife, Sarah Edwards.[70] For Edwards, as for McCulloch and the other clerical marignators of the Cambuslang narratives, soliciting, editing, and publishing spiritual autobiography was part of the task of pastoring, promoting, and defending the 'work' of God in their generation.

These concerns were not, however, unique to the Calvinist internationale. They were shared by Wesley, too, whose very different theological agenda was pursued in the pages of the *Arminian Magazine*, where he first began publishing the autobiographies of his Methodist lay preachers. Soon there were Arminian case histories to match those collected by Edwards in Northampton, and McCulloch and Robe in Scotland.

---

[68] Christopher Mitchell, 'Jonathan Edwards's Scottish Connection', in David W. Kling and Douglas A. Sweeney (eds.), *Jonathan Edwards at Home and Abroad* (Columbia, SC, 2003), 230, 232.

[69] Ibid. 223.

[70] *WJE* iv. 191–205, 331–41.

7

'A Nail Fixed in a Sure Place': The Lives of the Early Methodist Preachers

'THE people of Scotland . . . have from their earliest years, been accustomed to hear the leading truths of the gospel, mixed with Calvinism, constantly preached, so that the truths are become quite familiar to them.' So wrote John Pawson (1737–1806), one of three Methodist itinerants that John Wesley ordained for work in Scotland in 1785, and so we observed of the converts of the revival at Cambuslang in 1742. But to Pawson's mind this simply made the Scots downright intractable when it came to true Christian experience. 'The life and power of godliness, is in a very low state in that country,' he lamented, adding, 'I am fully satisfied that it requires a far higher degree of the divine influence, generally speaking, to awaken a Scotchman out of the dead sleep of sin than an Englishman.'[1] Pawson was in Scotland for two years, seeking to make inroads on behalf of Methodism, but he found it hard going. He certainly did not witness anything like what McCulloch did under his preaching in Lanarkshire, and his own views of evangelical conversion were shaped by a different theological agenda.

Pawson wrote these observations on Scotland in his own spiritual autobiography, *An Account of the Lord's Gracious Dealings with J. Pawson, Minister of the Gospel* (1801). This narrative was not written 'white hot' within days of his conversion, as were most of the lay narratives written in letters to Charles Wesley in the early 1740s, nor was it written as part of a programme of serial publication of his autobiography, as were the journals of John Wesley and George Whitefield. Instead, it was written with a long retrospective view of his life, more than four decades after his conversion, and well after the initial euphoria of the Evangelical Revival had passed. He had written a shorter account of his life in 1779 for the second volume of the *Arminian Magazine*, but even this took a much longer view of his religious life than anything we have witnessed thus far in the Evangelical Revival. By 1779 the evangelical conversion narrative was an established genre, and Pawson was responding, like other Methodist lay preachers, to John Wesley's request that he give an account of his life in print. The autobiographies

---

[1] *WV* iv. 63.

of lay preachers such as Pawson thus form another significant body of evangelical spiritual autobiography from the eighteenth century.

The most distinctive feature of these narratives, and the invariable narrative convention that links them to the other accounts of evangelical experience in the eighteenth century, was the detailed rehearsal of the subject's conversion. In the case of John Pawson, the story of his conversion was a family story, especially since he had to overcome his father's opposition to Methodism. His parents were devout members of the Church of England in Yorkshire, and he was taught to avoid sin and to be regular in observance of 'church and sacrament', but in all of this there was nothing of the 'power of godliness'.[2] In 1758, in his late adolescence, he read two sermons by Henry Crook, the evangelical Anglican minister at Leeds, and these made him see something of his need of salvation. Shortly afterwards he sought out the Methodists and attended their meetings, though this was in defiance of his father. He read some of the classic seventeenth-century works on conversion by John Bunyan and Joseph Alleine, and his conscience began to trouble him more acutely. His father, however, was ready to disown him for having joined the 'despised Methodists' and thought him incorrigible. Finally Pawson struck a bargain with his father. If his father would attend three Methodist sermons and then show him from the Bible how they were erroneous, he would never return to another meeting. But of course his father came under conviction and was soon found one Sunday morning out in the stable, where no one could hear him, crying out to God, roaring, and trembling. The whole family, eight persons in all, joined the Methodist society, and then one by one they were brought to a similar awakening of conscience. There must not have been much privacy in the Pawson house, since the family had recourse again to the farm buildings to give vent to their souls' agony. Pawson went to the barn one day, 'wept, prayed, and roared aloud', and sought God for mercy only to find to his surprise that his brother was there doing the same thing. His father and mother heard all the noise and came to see what was the matter, only to be followed by his sister and her husband. 'We were now six in number, all in the same state of mind, and in the deepest distress.'[3] Then, on 16 March 1760, at a Methodist prayer meeting on Sunday morning, Pawson, along with several others, finally found relief. People were crying out round him, and he was on his knees in the middle of the room, praying for soul deliverance. Like the Cambuslang converts, Pawson heard a word of Scripture that he felt was addressed to him personally: 'Thou art Mine' (Isa. 43: 1). 'In a moment I was perfectly delivered from all my guilty fears; my deep sorrow, my extreme distress, was entirely gone. The peace of God flowed into my conscience, and the love of

---

[2] Ibid. 1, 3.   [3] Ibid. 20.

God was shed abroad in my heart abundantly; my whole soul was filled with serious, sacred, heavenly joy; yea, I triumphed in the God of my salvation.'[4]

Although this conversion account resembles the lay narratives from the 1740s, it was written relatively late in Pawson's life and was the fruit of a longer remembering. It was clearly rehearsed in terms of how one thing led to another, from his earliest days, to bring him and his family to the point of conversion. Hortatory asides to the reader and theological apostrophe made it clear that this experience was (to use a Methodist topos) 'a nail fixed in a sure place'.[5] Its place in his memory was immovable. He demonstrated this further by signposting significant events along the way with phrases such as, 'The time of my deliverance now drew near,' or adding reflective commentary such as, 'The change in my mind was so extraordinary, that I never could doubt of my acceptance with God through Christ to this day.'[6] The prepositional phrase, 'to this day', recurs, signalling to the reader that Pawson's present state in life arose as a matter of course from prior conditions. This is the syntax of a retrospective consciousness, and it differs markedly from the punctual identity of the lay converts in the 1740s or the serial identity of the Methodist leaders who continued to publish and revise their journals over time.

Six weeks after Pawson's conversion he experienced the 'witness of the Spirit' during a class meeting and claimed to have an abiding communion with God thereafter. Before long the whole family found conversion. A further narrative of the pious death of his father, later in his account, completed the theme of the redemption of the family who had at first opposed him. Pawson continued his story with his call to preach, and then his autobiography was structured largely as an account of his various circuits, punctuated by Methodist conferences, of which he attended more than forty.

Seen thus in bare outline, the autobiography of an early Methodist lay preacher seems to be a conversion narrative followed by the curriculum vitae or itinerary of an evangelist. Although it does appear at times that two genres have been thus stitched together, and the seam left showing, it is also clear that for these preachers it was the dynamic of conversion that led as a matter of course to speaking of 'what God has done for my soul'.[7] As Pawson put it, 'Having found salvation myself, I felt an intense desire that others should enjoy the same unspeakable blessing.'[8] Proclamation was a

---

[4] *WV* iv. 24.

[5] The phrase is from Isa. 22: 23 and was used e.g. by Robert Roberts and Thomas Walsh for words that make a lasting impression on the heart. *WV* iv. 236; v. 67.

[6] Ibid. iv. 22, 24

[7] The tension between confessional and professional autobiography among Pietists is discussed in Ward, Introduction to Wesley, *Works* (BE), xviii. 14–23.

[8] *WV* iv. 25

part of the logic of conversion. Thomas Jackson noted that when these men offered themselves to Wesley to serve him as 'sons in the gospel', Wesley requested from each of them a 'written account of his early life, including the time and circumstances of his conversion, and the manner in which he was led to preach the Gospel'.[9] This then determined the shape of these narratives and linked them to the earlier seventeenth-century genre, which was so amply represented in the reading that Wesley required of his preachers and published for them in his own *Christian Library*. The plot of each preacher's narrative drove first towards the crisis of a guilty conscience and its relief under faith in the promises of God, then drove towards the second crisis of spiritual vocation and the decision to forsake all to preach the gospel. If you look up any of the preachers in the index to John Telford's edition of the lives, there are typically only three sub-entries: 'conversion', 'enters itinerancy', and 'other'.

The spiritual autobiographies of the early Methodist preachers were for the most part memoirs of a substantial portion of their lives, interpreted in terms of evangelical conversion. By the late 1770s evangelicals such as Pawson were no longer feeling their way into a genre; they were writing within a tradition. Within the body of spiritual autobiography penned by these preachers in the last decades of the eighteenth century, conversion had become not only a matter of Christian initiation, but also of ongoing Christian experience and identity. As Arminians, they believed that one might need to renew one's conversion. And in their accounts of entering the ministry, their experiences of Christian perfection, and even in their deathbed utterances recorded by others, their narratives imitated the structure of conversion itself as an agony of travail and relief. In one sense, these Methodists were born again and again.

THE *ARMINIAN MAGAZINE* AND THE NOVELTY OF
CONTEMPORARY BIOGRAPHY

The provocatively named *Arminian Magazine* began in 1778 as an organ of Wesleyan Methodism 'consisting of Extracts and Original Treatises on Universal Redemption'. Just in case this was not enough for anyone to place the periodical theologically, the first article in the first issue was a 'Life of Arminius'. This was a conscious effort to challenge the periodicals of the evangelical Calvinists: *The Gospel Magazine*, begun in 1766, and the *Spiritual Magazine*, begun in 1761. As Wesley put it, 'The deadly poison has for many years been spread through England, chiefly by means of those pestilent declamations of the *Gospel* and *Spiritual Magazine*. Whatever is designed for an antidote to this poison must be spread in the same manner.' Wesley

---

[9] Thomas Jackson, Introduction to *EMP* i. 11.

was conscious of the growing number of evangelical Calvinists. Thousands were already poisoned, he said, and were now twice dead. So, 'I fight them with their own weapons. I oppose magazine to magazine.'[10] The magazine was thus from its very beginning set in an adversarial context in which questions about conversion and spiritual experience were highly contested.

The fourfold plan of the *Arminian Magazine* was to illustrate 'universal redemption' through doctrinal essays, extracts of holy lives, verse, and 'accounts and letters, containing the experience of pious persons, the greatest part of whom are still alive'.[11] The 'extracts of holy lives' referred to posthumous biography, such as the life of Arminius, but the way the last item was described points to the boldness of the agenda Wesley set by aiming to publish not just posthumous biography, but up-to-the-minute living autobiography ('persons . . . who[m] are still alive'). 'Nothing of the kind has appeared before,' wrote Wesley.[12]

After ten monthly instalments, which included biographies of Arminius and Luther and other historical figures, Wesley published the first contemporary autobiography, as he had promised. It was the life of the lay preacher Peter Jaco (1728–81), appearing with an engraving of his portrait in the issue for November 1778. Jaco's account was written as a letter to John Wesley, beginning, 'Rev. and Dear Sir, I am sorry I cannot comply with your Desire so effectually as I could wish; having left the Papers containing the Particulars of God's Dealings with me, some hundred Miles off. At present I can only give you some Circumstances as they occur to my Memory,' and so it continued for another five pages.[13] Evidently he was already a practised autobiographer (given the papers he mentioned), and perhaps this was why Wesley called upon him for this first 'living' memoir, but it was certainly Wesley's explicit request that drew Jaco into print. The inclusion of an engraving of Jaco's portrait was also significant. Engravings were very popular with the reading public in the eighteenth century, and an anonymous correspondent had written to Wesley in June about the magazine, complaining, among other things, that there were no pictures. Wesley heeded the criticism and included the engraving to embellish the account, the first of the engravings to appear in the magazine.[14] The appearance of a graphic image of this lay preacher in what was otherwise a sea of unrelieved text would certainly have fastened the reader's attention on this part of the magazine.

---

[10] *JWL* vi. 295   [11] *AM* I (1778), vi.   [12] *JWL* vi. 295

[13] *AM* I (1778), 541.

[14] An engraving of Wesley's own portrait was the frontispiece to this first volume of the *Arminian Magazine*, but this page would probably have been published only after all the numbers for the year had been completed and ready for binding. On the novelty of portraiture engravings of living writers, see Michael Mascuch, *Origins of the Individualist Self* (Cambridge, 1997), 50.

It would be easy today to fail to appreciate how radical it was for Wesley to publish autobiographies of living authors and to provide vivid iconic representations of the subjects. Indeed, an enormous row erupted in 1783 among the evangelical Calvinists over precisely this issue, and it illustrates some of what was at stake when contemporary spiritual biographies or autobiographies, such as that of Jaco, were reified through print and portraiture and made public through distribution to a large readership. Alexander Hogg (fl. 1778–1819) was a London printer whose ecclesiastical commitments were loose at best. He claimed not to attend 'statedly' any one meeting, chapel, or church, but that he watched over his moral behaviour and attended services when and where he thought proper.[15] However, he had a shrewd eye for business opportunities, and he saw the potential there was to exploit the growing market for religious periodical publication. In July 1783 he published the first issue of the *New Spiritual Magazine*, presenting it as a successor to the *Spiritual Magazine* and the *Gospel Magazine*, the latter of which he claimed had degenerated through neglect. He noted that it was in direct opposition to the *Gospel Magazine* that 'the Arminian Goliath stepped forth', alluding to Wesley's magazine that was now into its sixth year of publication. The *New Spiritual Magazine* would in contrast be established on moderately Calvinistic grounds.[16] In the middle of August 1783 Hogg circulated a proposal to more than a hundred 'gospel ministers', inviting them to send in pieces for the new magazine, giving notice of his intention to publish portraits and memoirs of living ministers, and soliciting biographies for this purpose. Hogg recognized that this would be good for sales, and he pleaded the precedent of the *Arminian Magazine* and other common magazines for this practice. Contemporary religious biography was clearly a hot commodity.[17]

However, it was later reported that a number of ministers thought this circular had intentionally misled them, making it seem that several ministers had already endorsed the magazine. One of the ministers on the list was the Independent Thomas Towle (1723–1806), who never bothered to respond to Hogg's circular but found that the magazine nevertheless announced it would soon be publishing his portrait and biography. He was incensed. In August he came down to Hogg's shop and had a blazing row with him. According to Hogg, Towle spat out angry words, vulgarities, and threats, and their argument drew a crowd on the street. A month later an advertisement

---

[15] *A Familiar Letter of Reproof and Humiliation to the Rev. Thomas Towle* (1785), p. xiii.

[16] *New Spiritual Magazine* 1 (1783), pp. v, viii. Hogg was also publisher of the *New Christian Magazine* (1782–6), designed to appeal to a churchly and more highbrow readership, and he obtained the patronage of a number of bishops for the magazine. He presented it as 'undertaken by a Society of Clergymen of the Diocese of London'.

[17] *Familiar Letter of Reproof*, pp. v–viii.

appeared in the London morning and evening papers with the names of twenty-seven ministers disclaiming any association with the *New Spiritual Magazine* and complaining about the liberty taken to use their names and make them appear to be its patrons. Hogg was furious with these men for the injury they would do to his reputation, and he blamed Towle for the advertisement. He thought all these ministers were hypocrites and claimed that three had already sat for portraits or agreed to do so. He was still going to publish these 'living' biographies with their portraits, but he was also going to get even with Towle and the rest of the 'advertising parsons'.[18]

Although in October 1783 Hogg told his readers that he would not be publishing Towle's life or other contemporary biographies, because it was just too controversial, he recanted within a year and resumed his programme of biographies of living ministers.[19] At the same time, though, he published a series of 'squibbs, satires, lampoons, advertisements, rebuffes, epitaphs, epistles, epigrams, acrostics, caricatures, anecdotes, songs, etc.' against Towle and the other ministers.[20] All of a sudden the public reputation that Towle had been guarding so carefully was under attack. Hogg published a set of satirical pieces about 'Tommy Dishclout', playing on the homonym of his last name ('towel'). First his preaching was ridiculed:

> Now straining high in tone, now very low,
> He drawls forth dry remarks to those below;
> And squee——zes out his wo——rds for gen——eral use,
> As bar-maids squeeze and press out Lemon-juice.

But then the satire became more personal yet:

> Tommy's a minister, don't think it odd,
> Ordain'd to preach by man, but not by God;
> Without a grain of grace within his soul,
> Lost to all charms, but of the flowing bowl,
> E'en such a worthless wretch, is Parson T——.[21]

Hogg was embittered because of the damage Towle had done to the cause of religion and 'to private property', and he claimed to have lost over a thousand pounds on account of Towle. In fact, Hogg was now encountering serious competition, since an alternative magazine, the *Theological Miscellany*—a magazine he criticized as insipid and half-Arminian—had begun publication in 1784.[22] He blamed Towle for this new magazine, and early in

---

[18] *Familiar Letter of Reproof*, pp. ix–xix.   [19] *New Spiritual Magazine* 1 (1783), 153.

[20] *A Miscellaneous Collection of Satirical Pieces . . . Respecting the Extraordinary, Unprecedented and Scandalous Conduct of Master Tommy Dishclout . . .* (1785), 18.

[21] Ibid. 7–8.

[22] Ibid. 9–10. The *Theological Miscellany*'s first editor was Charles DeCoetlogon (1746–1820), a well-heeled evangelical Anglican clergyman. The magazine appealed to the same

1784 announced his intention to wind down the *New Spiritual Magazine* within another year. The correspondence that ran in the magazine suggests that the publication of the biographies and portraits of living ministers continued up to the end to be a delicate matter and to raise concerns.

What this controversy demonstrates forcefully is that the publishing of contemporary religious biography or autobiography was a radical step, and that it powerfully established one's reputation—for good or ill. It also points vividly to the way in which print and portraiture (or, more properly, mass-produced engravings) reified one's life, and even turned it into a potentially lucrative commodity upon which entrepreneurial publishers might well trade. The fluid life became fixed in print, and the public consumption of that life as a product further fixed the narrative identity of the subject in public discourse. It was one thing to speak to fellow believers of what God had done for your soul; it was another thing to write about this in a familiar letter to a minister; but it was something else yet to offer up your 'life' for printed publication. Once your life was published, it was hard to take it back and revise it. Wesley and Whitefield had been able to do this to some extent through the medium of the serialized journal under their control, yet the later in one's life such a narrative appeared, the more difficult it was to make such revisions.

THE LIVES OF THE EARLY METHODIST PREACHERS

The lives of the early Methodist preachers thus represented a progression of conversion narrative from the oral and manuscript culture of lay autobiography to the public culture of the printed page. However, among the evangelicals, such as John Pawson, who wrote their spiritual autobiographies in the late eighteenth century, it was still the hortatory and doxological motives that were to the fore, and Hogg's concerns about property and profit were not what prompted them to write about themselves. John Wesley invited his preachers to submit accounts of their lives for publication because their lives would be exemplary and would bear witness to 'universal redemption'. Nevertheless, the controversy that erupted over the *New Spiritual Magazine* helps us to appreciate what a revolutionary agenda Wesley set for the *Arminian Magazine* when he first published Jaco's account in 1778. As late as 1799 John Pawson had to defend the propriety of publishing autobiographies or biographies of living preachers, since as he

constituency as the *Gospel Magazine* and the constituency aimed at by the *New Spiritual Magazine*, and had some of the same contributors, such as the Baptist, John Ryland, jun. But it clearly set a higher standard for itself as something more polite and respectable than the *New Spiritual Magazine*, seeking 'all the pleasing recommendations of elegance, purity, and strength of diction', etc. The editor was also well aware of the controversial nature of publishing the writings of living authors. *Theological Miscellany* 1 (1784), p. xv.

said, 'some of our brethren object to this, and tell us, that it will be soon enough to publish their experience and manner of life when they have finished their warfare ... lest they should fall away from their steadfast-ness.'[23] Heedless of such concerns, Wesley continued to publish contemporary lives, however, and John Pawson's narrative was among another ten accounts of travelling preachers printed in the second year of the magazine. Thus began a significant programme of periodical publication of religious autobiography from 1778 to 1811, as lives and portraits of lay Methodist itinerants appeared in successive issues of the *Arminian Magazine* (and its successor after 1798, the *Methodist Magazine*). As one later writer said, 'For a Methodist a place in the Magazine was something like a niche in the Abbey for a statesman or a poet.'[24] This observation points to what we have referred to as the reification of the genre. Through publication, the narratives were set in stone.

Some autobiographies by lay preachers had a publishing history independent of the *Arminian Magazine* or beyond it. For example, the life of Silas Told (1711–79) was published as a stand-alone book, and Wesley later abridged it for the *Arminian Magazine*.[25] The lives of Thomas Walsh (*c.*1730–59) and John Nelson (1707–74) were also independently published.[26] Likewise, some autobiographies first published in the *Arminian Magazine* were later separately printed as books, sometimes in enlarged editions, as was the case for John Pawson, John Haime (1710–84), Thomas Mitchell (1726–84), Thomas Taylor (1738–1816), and others.[27] There were also lay preachers, such as Joseph Humphreys and John Cennick, who had once been in connexion with Wesley but left, and who published their own autobiographies.[28] The *Arminian Magazine* was still the chief vehicle for the publication of the preachers' lives, but clearly the lay preachers of the Evangelical Revival formed a group who were exceptionally articulate about their religious experience.

---

[23] *EMP* ii. 247.

[24] John Telford, *The Life of John Wesley* (New York, 1898), 326–7.

[25] *An Account of the Life, and Dealings of God with Silas Told* (1786); *AM* 10 (1787), 72 ff.

[26] Wesley had a hand in these narratives, even though they were not printed in the *Arminian Magazine*. He added his endorsement to James Morgan, *The Life and Death of Mr. Thomas Walsh, Composed in Great Part from the Accounts Left by Himself* (1762 [1763]), and later revised and reprinted the work himself. He likewise reprinted *The Case of John Nelson, Written by Himself* (1745), and would also revise *An Extract of J. Nelson's Journal* (Bristol, 1767) in subsequent editions.

[27] *A Short Account of God's Dealings with Mr. John Haime* (1785); *A Short Account of the Life of Mr. Thomas Mitchell* (1781); Thomas Taylor, *Redeeming Grace Displayed to the Chief of Sinners* (York, 1780).

[28] *The Life of Mr. J. Cennick* (2nd edn., 1745); *Joseph Humphreys's Experience of the Work of Grace upon his Heart* (Bristol, 1742). See also *Some Particulars of the Life and Experience of Nicholas Manners* (York, 1785).

The Lives of the Early Methodist Women Preachers

The *Arminian Magazine* included a large number of accounts of women's spiritual experience, including autobiographical writing. According to Margaret Jones's calculations, 40 per cent of the biographical and autobiographical material published in the *Arminian Magazine* while John Wesley was editor related to women.[29] Yet most of the women's autobiographical writing appeared in the form of occasional correspondence with Wesley, much like the earlier letters preserved in manuscript by Charles Wesley. As editor, John trawled through his collection of letters and made selections which he then prepared for the magazine. The women's narratives were not commissioned by Wesley in the way the lives of his lay preachers were. For example, an account of the conversion of an early Bristol Methodist, Margaret Jenkins, was included in the 'letters' section of the magazine in its first volume in 1778. It belongs very much to the sort of 'white hot' narratives of conversion we have already observed, accounts written within a year or so of the spiritual experiences they recount. However, this short narrative was written by Jenkins as a letter to Wesley in 1743—thirty-five years before its publication in the magazine. In fact, Wesley added a note after the narrative, 'I insert this Letter, chiefly for the Benefit of her Daughters. God grant, they may tread in their Mother's Steps!'[30] This was not, like Pawson's account and the lives of the preachers, a long retrospective autobiography. This was still a moment in the life, rather than the summing up of the life of a Methodist convert. And there was, of course, no picture included of Jenkins, nor of any of the women who appeared in the magazine.

The first autobiography by a woman was a fifteen-page account of Sarah Ryan (1724–68), published in the magazine in 1779 as 'a good substitute' for another account that was for some reason deemed inadvisable to print.[31] Although published posthumously, this was Ryan's own spiritual autobiography, written in 1760. It was no doubt included in the magazine because Ryan had been an intimate, if controversial, correspondent of Wesley's, whose spirituality he highly respected.[32] A domestic servant with a chequered history, her spiritual experiences were spectacular and visionary, but she was introduced as 'a Woman of long and deep experience'. Wesley also

---

[29] Margaret Jones, 'From "The State of My Soul" to "Exalted Piety": Women's Voices in the Arminian Magazine/Methodist Magazine, 1778–1821', in R. N. Swanson (ed.), *Gender and Christian Religion* (Woodbridge, Suffolk, 1998), 275.

[30] *AM* 1 (1778), 228–30.

[31] *AM* 2 (1779), 296–310.

[32] Wesley's relationship with Ryan, a domestic servant and 'repentant Magdalen', was ostensibly the cause of the separation between him and his wife. Ryan, whom W. R. Ward calls 'a devout bigamist twice over', was married to three men, all of whom were still alive when she entered into Wesley's confidence and was appointed as his housekeeper at Bristol and Kingswood. Wesley, *Works* (BE), xxii. 69 n.

included eleven of her letters to him and eight of his to her in the 1782 volume of the magazine, letters which he likewise regarded as demonstrating a 'deep, and strong, unaffected Piety'.[33] Later Methodist historians were not quite so sure.[34]

Sarah Ryan was closely associated with Sarah Crosby (1729–1804) and Mary Fletcher (née Bosanquet, 1739–1815), some the first women preachers in Methodism, both of whom began to move beyond short exhortations and to preach from biblical texts in the early 1760s. On 31 December 1771, Sarah Crosby made this entry in her diary in the form of a prayer:

> Thou has enabled me, from the first of last January to the fourth of this month, (December,) to ride 960 miles, to keep 220 public meetings, at many of which some hundreds of precious souls were present, about 600 private meetings, and to write an 116 letters, many of them long ones: besides many, many conversations with souls in private.[35]

She clearly had no problem keeping pace with the men. Many other women would join the ranks of Crosby and Fletcher by the end of the century, and their call to preach was slowly recognized by Wesley as an 'extraordinary call'.[36] Was there therefore a body of printed autobiography by these female preachers like that of the authorized lives of Wesley's male preachers?

Although many of these women appeared in the *Arminian Magazine* as correspondents, there was in fact no genre comparable to the lives of the male preachers in the magazine. Wesley valued women's spiritual experience and, on the whole, treated that experience as having an authority equal to that of a man; women were also among his most trusted correspondents when it came to spiritual matters. But his views on women's preaching developed over time, and he permitted women's preaching only on a case-by-case basis. To Grace Walton and Sarah Crosby, Wesley wrote, advising them to stick to exhortation, 'but keep as far from what is called preaching as you can'.[37] But in 1771 he acknowledged that Mary Bosanquet possessed an 'extraordinary call' and he even compared this to the calling of the unordained male lay preachers and to the whole work of Methodism itself, which was nothing less than 'an extraordinary dispensation' of God's providence.[38] Women preachers, like lay preachers, and like Methodism itself, were an exception, not a rule.[39] Desperate times called for desperate

---

[33] See further, Jones, 'Women's Voices', 278; Paul Wesley Chilcote, *John Wesley and the Women Preachers of Early Methodism* (Metuchen, NJ, 1991), 124–30.

[34] Tyerman, *JW* ii. 285–8.

[35] *MM* 29 (1806), 567.

[36] Chilcote, *Wesley and Women Preachers*, 141–81.

[37] *JWL* v. 130; cf. iv. 164.

[38] *JWL* v. 257.

[39] See Wesley's comments to this effect, distinguishing Methodism from the Quakers, in his letter to Sarah Crosby, *JWL* vi. 290.

measures. And if ministry derived from charism rather than office, then as so often in the history of the church, space was opened for gifted women to exercise those gifts if they manifestly had them. Still, Wesley reserved the right to permit or forbid in particular cases. He forbade women's preaching at Grimsby in 1780, but he authorized Sarah Mallett to preach in 1787 and even gave her practical pointers in 1789.[40]

Although Wesley allowed for such deviations from Anglican church order, and more so as he grew older, his reasoning seems to have been prudential rather than strictly theological. His theological concern was certainly for a 'universal salvation' that extended to all, bestowing dignity on the spiritual experience of those without power and without a significant voice in society, including women and the poor. But why did he stop short of the full endorsement of women's preaching alongside that of men? It seems that Wesley's views were based in part on what seemed possible and expedient on the ground, rather than simply on what could be defended in terms of first principles.

Accounts of the lives of women preachers would not, then, be privileged in the *Arminian Magazine* in the same way as the accounts of Wesley's authorized male preachers. Although by the 1770s some women were preaching regularly to hundreds, their lives were not commissioned for the magazine. It is clear that many of the women kept diaries or wrote accounts of their lives, like the male preachers, but these were mostly published posthumously, late in the period, and through the intermediary of a male editor.[41] One exception was Sarah Mallett, whose autobiography appeared in the magazine in 1788 but whose account dramatically emphasized a woman's call to preach as something extraordinary, since her call to preach came through fits and trances. She had felt strongly impressed to 'call sinners to repentance' but thought herself unsuited to the task. She then had a premonition that she would be compelled to do so with or without her will. In December 1785 she began to fall into fits and trances ('looking like one dead') during which she would speak, and on Christmas Day she began to preach during one of these fits on the text, Rev. 3: 20. She continued to preach during each following fit, and soon drew as many as two hundred to hear these remarkable sermons delivered in an altered state of consciousness.[42]

Notwithstanding this exception, during Wesley's lifetime the readers of the *Arminian Magazine* would have been hard pressed even to know that

[40] *JWL* vii. 9; viii. 190; Zechariah Taft, *Biographical Sketches of the Lives and Public Ministry of Various Holy Women* (1825; repr. Peterborough, 1992), i. 84.

[41] Many of these biographies were later published in the two-volume work by Taft, *Holy Women*.

[42] *AM* 11 (1788), 91–3, 130–3, 185–8, 238–42; Wesley, *Works* (BE), xxiii. 426–7. Cf. the account of the 'sleeping preacher' Rachel Baker in Ann Taves, *Fits, Trances, & Visions* (Princeton, 1999), 137.

there were women preachers, never mind that they wrote autobiographies like those of the male preachers. When their posthumously published lives are examined, however, it is clear that though the women had unique concerns, they also shared with the male preachers a sense of narrative identity shaped by the experience of conversion both as an experience of Christian initiation and as a pattern for ongoing Christian life; that is, they too wrote retrospective autobiographies that took evangelical conversion as a theme. Despite the fact, then, that Wesley privileged the lives of his male preachers in print, some of these women's lives may be drawn upon, alongside those of the men, to illustrate the way in which conversion was taken up as the theme of one's whole life.

Women's narratives thus appeared within Methodism in oral, written, and published form, but on a different timetable, and a gender hierarchy was still preserved when it came to lay preaching.[43] Under Wesley, women had been allowed a limited role in the ministry of the word, and some of their posthumous lives appeared in the magazine in the transitional period between Wesley's death in 1791 and the editorship of Joseph Benson in 1804. Then there was a shift in the gender culture of Methodism in the early nineteenth century, and the contributions of women to the *Methodist Magazine* (successor to the *Arminian Magazine* in 1798) were far fewer and more stereotyped.[44] Margaret Jones notes that there were no structured autobiographies by women after 1804, under Benson's editorship, and women's voices were progressively edited out between 1804 and 1821.[45] At least one woman preacher's autobiography, that of Elizabeth Collett (née Tonkin), was explicitly rejected 'lest it should be a precedent to young females in the Connexion'. Obituary notices of other women preachers passed over this aspect of their ministry in silence.[46]

John Wesley's Authority in the Lives of his Lay Preachers

By Wesley's death in 1791 the *Arminian Magazine* had an annual circulation of 7,000, though as always in the eighteenth century its readership would

---

[43] Cf. Felicity A. Nussbaum, *The Autobiographical Subject* (Baltimore, 1989), 176.

[44] Jones, 'Women's Voices', 280, 283.

[45] Ibid. 284–5. Catherine Brekus examines the emergence of female preaching in the 1740s in New England (and a little later in the South) in the egalitarian context of fervent revival, but traces a similar decline in the public acceptance of the ministry of these women as revival fires cooled and churches and their leaders pursued respectability. The tradition appears to have died out by the mid-1750s in the North and the 1770s in the South. The result was that when female preaching revived in later episodes in American history, the earlier stories had been forgotten. There was a tradition of female preaching in early America, but it was a 'broken and disconnected tradition'. Catherine Brekus, *Strangers and Pilgrims: Female Preaching in America, 1740–1845* (Chapel Hill, NC, 1998), 1–67, 339–41.

[46] Leslie F. Church, *More about the Early Methodist People* (1949), 156, 171.

have been much larger. Wesley's aims had been to set before his readers candid illustrations of 'experimental and practical religion' from their own contemporaries. But soon this generation passed from the scene, and the filial piety of a new generation of Methodists canonized 'their venerable fathers who now sleep in Jesus'.[47] Many of the accounts of the male lay preachers that had been first published in the magazine were gathered together and published by Thomas Jackson in multiple volumes as *The Lives of the Early Methodist Preachers* (1837–8). Successive editions augmented the collection until there were forty-one narratives in print, and thirty-six of these were again reprinted with additional notes by John Telford and retitled, *Wesley's Veterans* (1912–14).[48] Zechariah Taft also published a two-volume collection, *Biographical Sketches of the Lives and Public Ministry of Various Holy Women* (1825) which contained accounts of many of the women preachers of Methodism, though this was privately printed and not an authorized Methodist publication. Within a generation or two, however, the religious experience of pious persons 'who[m] are still alive' was turned back into posthumous biography to serve the needs of later Methodists, just as the Cambuslang narratives were published in the mid-nineteenth century for a later generation of evangelical Presbyterians.[49] Moreover, it should be emphasized that Jackson and Telford reprinted only a selection of the male preachers' lives published in the *Arminian Magazine*, and there were several that were passed over for various reasons. For example, the account of John Atlay (b. 1736) was the second of the preachers' autobiographies in the magazine, printed in 1778, but in the 1780s Atlay had a dispute with Wesley and became a troublemaker for the whole connexion; eventually he tried to try to set up his own circuit in the north-east of England and was accused by John Pawson of outright heresy.[50] Neither Jackson nor Telford felt any need to keep *that* particular memory alive.

If these autobiographies were thus destined for canonization in the nineteenth century, they had their genesis in the eighteenth century in a preoccupation with recorded experience that was altogether typical of the Evangelical Revival. Many of the preachers had kept diaries or journals like Wesley and Whitefield, and they used these for sources, as Jaco implied he would have done if he had not been separated from his papers. For example,

[47] Jackson, Introduction to *EMP* i. 24.

[48] There were four editions of Jackson's *Lives of Early Methodist Preachers*: 1837–38 (3 vols.); 1846 (2 vols.); 1865 (6 vols.); and 1871 (6 vols.). This last edition is the one commonly cited; it has been reprinted in 3 vols. by Tentmaker Publications, Stoke-on-Trent, 1998. The Jackson and Telford editions are compared in F. F. Bretherton, '"Early Methodist Preachers" and "Wesley's Veterans" ', *Proceedings of the Wesley Historical Society* 22 (1940), 102–5.

[49] Cf. Telford, Introduction to *WV* i. 8: 'Their heroic constancy and devotion were never more needed at home and abroad.'

[50] *AM* 1 (1778), 577 ff.; Tyerman, *JW* iii. 552–9.

John Valton (1740–94) accumulated a six-volume journal of his religious experience before entering the ministry, and after becoming a preacher his journaling continued, so that he was able to recount his early years as a story and then narrate his conversion and later itinerancy in terms of dated entries, similar to Wesley's own *Journal*. His narrative was published in the *Arminian Magazine* in 1783–4, and this was enlarged by editors in later reprintings with further additions from his journal.[51] For many of these lay preachers, the narrative of their itinerant years betrays some such underlying source. The posthumous lives of women preachers, such as Sarah Crosby and Mary Fletcher, likewise drew upon the detailed diaries they had kept, diaries that recorded their own spiritual experiences and kept a record of their ministries. These diaries were part confessional and part professional.[52]

Notwithstanding such sources, the narratives of the lay preachers were moulded above all by Wesley himself. In the case of the male preachers, he both called for them to be written and then edited what they wrote. On 9 February 1780 Wesley added a postscript to his letter to Valton, saying, 'Why should you not give me a short account of the life of John Valton!'[53] When Wesley wrote to Valton two years later, it is clear not only that Valton had begun but that Wesley was closely supervising the project. 'Be not afraid of writing too much; I can easily leave out what can be spared,' he generously offered.[54] Thomas Payne was pleased that Wesley should have a hand in his narrative in this way. He concluded his account, saying, 'Dear Sir, blot out or keep in just what you please of this narrative.'[55] Wesley offered practical advice too. To Valton, he wrote 'You should take care never to write long at a time, and always write standing; never on any account leaning on your stomach.'[56] The itinerant preacher wrote his life very much in an itinerant mode—in snatches, and without pausing to sit down. More importantly, Wesley recognized that Valton's account would provide an important contribution to the whole œuvre of religious experience that he wished to have before his readers, since Valton had been 'a long way through the wilderness'. Others God had led through a shorter and smoother way, but by different ways God could lead people to the same place. Valton's case history was one of the means by which Wesley could communicate this theological point effectively. Just as McCulloch and

[51] *AM* 6 (1783), 404–7, 459–64, 514–21, 574–9, 635–8, and *AM* 7 (1784), 13–19, 69–75, 127–32, 182–6, 241–3.

[52] *MM* 29 (1806), 418–23, 465–73, 517–21, 563–8, 610–17; Henry Moore (ed.), *The Life of Mrs. Mary Fletcher* (New York, 1848).

[53] *JWL* vi. 380; vii. 17, 35, 44. Wesley added an almost identical postscript to a letter to Christopher Hopper a week later (ibid.).

[54] Ibid. vii. 100–1.

[55] *EMP* i. 445.

[56] *JWL* vii. 101.

Robe drew on conversion narratives to communicate to the public something of the way in which God worked, so also Wesley was using the religious experience of his preachers to catechize the readers of the *Arminian Magazine*.

The lives of the early Methodist preachers thus have a coherence that derives not only from Wesley's explicit influence as commissioning editor and copy editor, but also from his wider superintendence over their lives and their work within Methodism. These are narratives of religious experience, but they are also narratives of a guild, analogous to a craft guild with the strong group identity and discipline that this implies. In fact, most of the preachers had begun their working lives as skilled labourers of one sort or another—small craftsmen, tradesman, or artisans—and many had known (or chafed against) the discipline of a long apprenticeship. Among them were former builders, bakers, printers, clothiers, and a quarter of those whose lives were republished by Jackson were also ex-soldiers.[57] Wesley effectively moulded these converts into a cohesive company of preachers with their own culture, where he was the master preacher and they were his apprentices. When Thomas Rankin left his trade to begin preaching, he paid 'very particular attention to the manner of Mr. Wesley' and of Thomas Maxfield. 'As I had them for a pattern, I endeavoured to tread in their steps.'[58]

Isabel Rivers has demonstrated how thorough Wesley's influence was on his preachers, and how the preacher's written lives were the product of a unique literary subculture deriving from Methodist organization and discipline. In addition to a shared itinerant vocation, the preachers' whole literary environment—what they read and what they wrote—was under Wesley's strict supervision.[59] At one Methodist conference, for example, Wesley asked what could be done to revive the work where it had decayed. The answer: 'Let every Preacher read carefully over the "Life of David Brainerd." Let us be followers of him as he was of Christ, in absolute self-devotion.'[60] John Valton took this sort of exhortation to heart, read Brainerd's life, and saw himself on every page.[61] Through Wesley's *Journal* and his other publications, through the *Arminian Magazine* itself, and perhaps above all through some fifty books he reprinted inexpensively in the *Christian Library*, he provided a nearly complete literary environment for his preachers. Thomas Hanson was altogether typical, when after his

---

[57] Telford, Introduction to *WV* i. 7; Michael Watts, *The Dissenters* (Oxford, 1978), i. 408.

[58] *WV* vi. 155

[59] Isabel Rivers, '"Strangers and Pilgrims": Sources and Patterns of Methodist Narrative', in J. D. Hilson, M. M. B. Jones, and J. R. Watson (eds.), *Augustan Worlds* (Leicester, 1978), 192–6.

[60] *The Works of John Wesley*, ed. Thomas Jackson (3rd edn., 1872; repr., Grand Rapids, Mich., 1984), viii. 328.

[61] *WV* vi. 55

conversion, he said, 'I read the chief part of the Christian library, with Mr. Wesley's works that were then published.'[62] Among these publications there was a preponderance of religious biography of exemplary value, including illustrations of Christian perfection. It is clear too from Wesley's correspondence with women preachers, not only that he closely supervised their activities and acted as their spiritual director, but also that he guided their reading. To Sarah Mallet he wrote apologizing that his *Notes on the Old Testament* was virtually out of print, but he added, 'Any other books are at your service. I want to forward you in all useful knowledge.'[63]

Not only did Wesley thus supervise what his preachers read, he also supervised what they wrote. They were not allowed the right of free publication. Among twenty-one 'smaller advices' for preachers, the Large Minutes included the warning, 'Print nothing without my approbation.'[64] Here was a powerful culture of moral and literary discipline. Rivers argues that the preachers' autobiographies were, in consequence, 'the product of Wesley's disciplinary, educational, and editorial control of his preachers' lives, reading habits, and style'.[65] Consequently, this body of evangelical spiritual autobiography uniquely reflects themes in Wesleyan theology and ministry and adds a further sub-genre to our survey of conversion narrative in the eighteenth century.

CONVERSION AS LEITMOTIF

For the early Methodist preachers, often writing late in life or at least at some distance from their first spiritual awakening, the whole of their lives had now become explicable in terms of conversion. They invariably re-hearsed their own early formation, spiritual decline, awakening, and con-version as the centrepiece in their autobiographies. For some, like Sampson Staniforth, conversion explicitly divided life into two halves: before and after. But conversion also became a leitmotif for the whole of these auto-biographies, and this appears in their uniquely Arminian perspective on conversion, their call to the ministry, their experience of perfection, and even their own deaths, as narrated by others.

Arminian Conversion

Given the polemical nature of periodical publishing among evangelicals in the 1780s, along with Wesley's stated aims for the *Arminian Magazine*, it

---

[62] *AM* 3 (1780), 481; cf. Thomas Rankin, who could say much the same (*WV* vi. 148).

[63] *JWL* viii. 108; cf. 77: 'My Dear Sister, Let me know any time what books you wish to have, and I will order them to be sent to you.'

[64] *Works of John Wesley*, ed. Jackson, viii. 317.

[65] Rivers, 'Strangers and Pilgrims', 195.

comes as no surprise to find that one of the themes in the lives of Wesley's lay preachers was anti-Calvinism. Thomas Payne (1741–83) was unusual among the early Methodist preachers for his background as a Particular Baptist or 'Particular Anabaptist' as he called himself. While he gave much credit to his parents as pious and devout, his narrative was strongly shaped by his anti-Calvinist polemic. It was the story of his emancipation from the 'unchangeable decree'. When at sea and about to be attacked by a French frigate, he said, 'I was troubled at first, knowing I was not fit to die; but I soon comforted myself with the unchangeable decree.' When a man was lost overboard, he wrote, 'This alarmed me a little: but then I thought, "It was decreed," and was easy again.'[66] The point he was stressing was that Calvinism had led him to irresponsible acquiescence in fate. This even delayed his conversion: 'But I was a strong Calvinist, and that kept me from the blessing a long time, waiting for the irresistible call, and thinking it horrid presumption to venture upon Christ, till God compelled me by His almighty arm.'[67] However, an unidentified German book inspired him to take the kingdom of heaven 'by violence', to 'strive to enter' the narrow gate, and to venture everything on Christ. Stationed on the island of St Helena, and with two 'serious' companions, he found a quiet spot and set about 'wrestling for Christian liberty'. Joy broke through, and he narrated this as his conversion experience, an experience that involved repudiating fatalism and fortifying his will. When Calvinism again threw him into doubting, he 'lost the witness of the Spirit'. What was the answer? Again, said Payne, 'I then found that I must strive, not only to gain, but to hold fast, the witness of the Spirit.' He renewed his repentance, and soon found himself without any further doubts. The language of his conversion was thus all about resolve, striving, violence, and the vigorous exertion of his will. Seven paragraphs later he noted that he had read Wesley, John Fletcher, and Walter Sellon and was 'entirely delivered from the whole hypothesis of absolute predestination'.[68] For Thomas Payne, therefore, spiritual conversion could not be separated from his theological conversion from Calvinism to Arminianism. Likewise, Thomas Taylor concluded his autobiography with an account of his 'commencing what is called an Arminian'.[69]

Benjamin Rhodes's autobiography, printed in 1779, was one of the early accounts in the *Arminian Magazine,* and he likewise conflated his conversion with his deliverance from Calvinism, but in his case this theological emancipation came in a form altogether typical of the means of evangelical conversion generally: a text was impressed on his mind. He dreamed of reading a passage of Scripture that put the matter to rest, but when he woke

---

[66] *AM* 4 (1781), 582   [67] Ibid. 584.   [68] Ibid. 585, 640.
[69] *AM* 3 (1780), 440. His autobiography was also published in an expanded version, *Redeeming Grace Displayed to the Chief of Sinners* (York, 1780); cf. *WV* vii. 7–126.

in the morning he could not remember the words. He cracked open his Bible and found the text immediately—2 Pet. 3: 9, a passage that promises that God is 'not willing that any should perish, but that all should come to repentance'. 'Such light and conviction attended the words', said Rhodes, 'as removed every doubt.'[70] Sarah Crosby also had 'reasonings about predestination' but, she recalled, 'God applied this verse to my soul by the Spirit', and she quoted some lines of a hymn. As so often in the case of initial conversion, this was persuasive: 'Since that time I have had no doubt but grace is free for all.'[71] A similar experience of conversion away from Calvinism was related by John Nelson, Robert Wilkinson, Thomas Taylor, Jonathan Maskew, and John Prickard.[72] All of this served Wesley's apologetic intentions well, as he sought to provide 'living witnesses' to universal redemption and to provide an antidote to the 'deadly poison' of Calvinism that was spread by the *Gospel Magazine* and its surrogates.

This polemical ethos was evident also in many of the comments made in passing in these narratives. Sarah Mallett recorded the temptation she encountered not long after her conversion to believe 'once in grace always in grace', but this was truly a temptation, since she confessed she only wanted to believe this because 'I had a darling sin, which I wanted to keep and go to heaven.'[73] The doctrine of final perseverance was clearly pernicious. Some, like John Nelson, recorded dialogues with Calvinist interlocutors, debates in which the Arminian preacher always had the last word and trumped his opponent.[74] Others stressed the inevitable antinomianism that followed upon Calvinist beliefs. John Pritchard reported that in 1772 at Norwich, where a Calvinist row had erupted, he needed to expose antinomianism and deal with incorrigible hearers who were 'enraged against personal holiness' and who once even ran down the gallery stairs like madmen crying 'False doctrine! False doctrine!' when they heard holiness preached.[75] John Haime confirmed what was often alleged—that antinomian theology led to antinomian behaviour—when he described one such preacher in the army who was guilty of lying and frequently drunk 'twice a day'.[76] As Thomas Taylor tersely summarized one man's career, 'He first turned Calvinist, and then to nothing.' Staffordshire could likewise be

---

[70] *AM* 2 (1779), 363.   [71] *MM* 29 (1806), 466.

[72] *WV* i. 43–4 (Nelson), iii. 368 (Wilkinson), iii. 42 (Taylor), ii. 398 (Maskew), and ii. 369 (Prickard).

[73] *AM* 11 (1788), 185.

[74] Nelson reported at least four such disputes (*WV* i. 100–2, 165–71); cf. John Murlin's disputes with Calvinistic Baptists in *AM* 2 (1779), 532.

[75] *AM* 8 (1785), 622.

[76] *AM* 3 (1780), 263. *WV* i. 35–6; cf. William Black's encounter with the radical New Light antinomians in Nova Scotia. *EMP* iii. 183 ff., and G. A. Rawlyk, *The Canada Fire: Radical Evangelicalism in British North America* (Kingston, Ont., 1994), 19–32.

written off, since 'Calvinism, Antinomianism, and downright Ranterism' had laid it waste.[77] These sorts of anti-Calvinist asides contributed to an Arminian plot-line in the printed lives of Wesley's Methodist preachers.

This was not, however, just *parti pris* on the part of these Arminian autobiographers. The high Calvinist Independent hymnwriter Joseph Hart (1712–68) regularly denounced the teaching of Wesley and wrote a tract against him at the height of the early revival. Wesley had published his 'Free Grace' sermon attacking the Calvinism of Whitefield, and Hart entered the dispute with *Remarks on the Unreasonableness of Religion; being Remarks and Animadversions on the Rev. John Wesley's Sermon on Rom. viii. 32* (1741). Yet from his later autobiography, published as a preface to his *Hymns* in 1759, we learn not only that Hart was at this time a *doctrinal* antinomian, believing that the law did not apply to the believer, but also that he was a *practising* antinomian. 'Rushing impetuously into Notions beyond my Experience, I hasted to make myself a Christian by mere Doctrine,' he confessed, and the spiritual liberty he claimed 'soon grew to *Libertinism*; in which I took large progressive Strides, and advanced to a dreadful Height, both in Principle and in Practice'. He felt at liberty to sin: 'Not to dwell on Particulars, I shall only say ... that I committed all Uncleanness with Greediness.'[78] It was only in about 1751 that he began to reform his moral behaviour, and not until 1757 that he was converted through the influence of the Moravians. He went on to become the celebrated minister at Jewin Street in London, and as an Independent hymnwriter was second only to Isaac Watts in popularity. But it was against the example of figures such as the early Joseph Hart that the lives of Wesley's preachers were presented to the public.

However, the Arminian ethos of the lives of the early Methodist preachers was evident not only in their polemic and in their various accounts of theological emancipation from Calvinism; it was also evident in the way they spoke of conversion itself as something that could be lost and renewed. When they broke through their travail of conscience and experienced assurance of salvation, this assurance typically came in the form of the inward witness of the Spirit. This assurance was neither of eternal justification, nor of an interest in God's eternal covenant, nor of final perseverance; it was an assurance only of present pardon. Unlike the self-examination of the Cambuslang converts, with their preoccupation with objective 'marks' and 'evidence', Wesley's lay preachers depended far more on a direct sensible perception of their acceptance with God.[79] Wesley also

---

[77] *AM* 3 (1780), 441; *WV* vii. 46.

[78] Joseph Hart, *Hymns ... With a Preface, Containing a Brief and Summary Account of the Author's Experience* (1759), vii.

[79] See e.g. the experience of John Pawson (*WV* iv. 26).

wrote about certain marks which distinguished the witness of the Spirit (conjoined to the witness of the believer's spirit) from mere presumption, but even so his position was profoundly intuitionist: ' "How may one who has the real witness in himself distinguish it from presumption?" How, I pray, do you distinguish day from night? . . . Do you not immediately and directly perceive that difference, provided your senses are rightly disposed?' This was true also, concluded Wesley, in the spiritual realm. The real witness is 'immediately and directly perceived'.[80] This view of assurance was amply illustrated in the lives of the preachers.[81] John Haime experienced spiritual anxiety after his conversion and this was resolved not through self-examination but through something he directly felt and experienced. The 'full witness from the Spirit' was a change that he sensed 'through my soul and body'.[82] Thomas Payne contrasted the Calvinist experience with that of the Wesleyan Arminian. He recalled that when he first was converted, and still operating on Calvinist assumptions, he believed, 'I must *doubt* of my Justification, which those wretched Casuists lay down, as one great mark of sincerity.' Believing this, he said, 'I lost the witness of the Spirit.'[83] He thus learned that one was not to be perplexed by 'reasonings'.

Moreover, because grace was not indefectible, conversion was not necessarily once and for all. Thomas Taylor concluded his narrative of release from Calvinism with the statement, 'I am firmly persuaded a man may make shipwreck of faith and a good conscience.'[84] And as if to prove it George Shadford recounted the tragic, sudden death of a backslider in Cornwall. Yet this event allowed others to renew their conversions: 'Some backsliders, who were acquainted with him, were stirred up to return to him, from whom they had revolted.'[85] This possibility of decay and renewal was also experienced in regard to Wesleyan perfection. After an experience Richard Rodda described as having emptied him of every evil, he worried that he had lost 'the blessing'. Not only that, he said, he 'had hard work to retain what I had received even in Justification'.[86] It was possible to slide back two steps, to double-backslide, as it were.

---

[80] Wesley, *Works* (BE), i. 282. And yet, though the witness of the Spirit was thus directly perceived, it was not to be separated from Christlike virtue. To Sarah Crosby Wesley wrote, 'Neither must the *witness* supersede the fruits, nor the fruits the witness of the Spirit.' *JWL* vii. 18.

[81] *WV* I. 55.

[82] *AM* 3 (1780), 311.

[83] *AM* 4 (1781), 585.

[84] *AM* 3 (1780), 441.

[85] *AM* 13 (1790), 236.

[86] *AM* 7 (1784), 356.

While the Calvinist converts doubted their 'interest in Christ' and their assurance waxed and waned with their feelings as surely as did the Methodists' assurance, the early Methodist preachers did not speak of their salvation as a finished work that they needed to discern, but as a present work they needed to experience. Thus, Robert Roberts joined a Methodist society and found peace with God six weeks later, only to be dejected and cast down again and to worry that he had deceived himself. This anguish, as for so many of the Calvinists, lasted a long time—nine months in his case. When his unbelief and doubt were finally overturned, this new 'gracious manifestation' was very much like a second conversion.[87] Thomas Hanson was likewise decisively converted on 16 July 1757 only to feel anger a few days later and lose his assurance, so much so that he was 'ready to choose strangling'. But he cast himself on Christ once more, and 'peace, love, and joy returned in a moment'. After two years, this erosion and renewal of sensible communion with God was repeated once more.[88] The phenomenon of consolation and desolation was parallel to that experienced by Calvinist converts, but the interpretation was different.

John Valton's case was similar. He was converted in March 1764: 'My heart swelled, and my eyes so overflowed, that I left the house; a spark of celestial fire now kindled in my breast, which dispelled the gloom, melted the rock, and diffused divine love through all my heart.' But in November he wrote, 'I have been much tempted to doubt of the pardoning love of God which I received while in London. Because it was not incontestably clear, I feared it was not really the case; and that my comforts were only the drawings of the Father.' A few weeks later he was able to believe again. Significantly, Valton thought he might have been in the 'wilderness state described in Mr. Wesley's sermon', and acknowledged that not everyone passed through the wilderness to the promised land.[89] As observed in Ch. 4 above, the sermon referred to by Valton (variously dated at 1751 or 1760) was one in which Wesley explained the reasons for the loss of love, joy, and peace that so many experienced after conversion. He identified the possible causes of this 'wilderness state' as outright sin, simple ignorance, or overwhelming temptation, but stressed that God does not withdraw from us; it is always we who withdraw from him. For Wesley, one might well need to be 'renewed by repentance' and 'again washed by faith'.[90] Indeed, one could be converted again and again.

Call to the Ministry as Conversion

If conversion was in principle repeatable or capable of being renewed for the early Methodist lay preachers, so also their call to the ministry followed

---

[87] *WV* ii. 240–4. [88] *AM* 3 (1780), 481–2. [89] *WV* vi. 12, 22.
[90] Wesley, *Works* (BE), ii. 217.

from the new-found joy of their conversion and was narrated very much in the manner of their initial conversion as a matter of travail and relief. Moreover, as a final proof of their call to ministry these lay preachers looked to see their own conversion replicated among their hearers.

First, the call to preach flowed directly from the dynamic of conversion itself. There was a progression from praying and giving testimony in band or class, to exhortation (speaking to a group for perhaps five minutes, but without 'taking a text' of Scripture), to formal preaching itself, at first locally and then as a travelling evangelist.[91] Thomas Rankin wrote after his conversion, 'I felt such love to the souls of my fellow creatures that I longed to tell everyone what God had done for my soul.' Then he began to pray in class meetings, and then, he said, 'Thoughts arose in my mind that I ought wholly to dedicated myself to God in preaching the gospel.'[92] Robert Roberts was converted, worked through his doubts and fears, and then, as he recalled, 'I gave a word of exhortation' to various class meetings and then, notwithstanding opposition, 'It was strongly impressed upon my mind that I was called to preach the gospel.'[93] The stitching together of the conversion narrative genre with the genre of ministerial itinerary was accomplished through the logic of conversion itself; the two halves of the narrative were connected as cause and effect.

The women lay preachers also followed a path from conversion through testimony and exhortation to 'taking a text', but because this latter decision required extraordinary justification, the call to preach usually flowed not only from the dynamic of conversion but also from an overwhelming experience of further sanctification.[94] When Hannah Harrison sought and received 'full sanctification' she responded with the rhetorical question, 'Must I hide this light under a bushel?'[95] As soon as 'all darkness was dispersed' for Sarah Mallett and her soul set at liberty, she said, 'It was imprest on my mind, to speak in public for God.'[96] Once Sarah Crosby was 'overwhelmed with the power of God', she heard these words from Christ: 'Feed my sheep.'[97] After Ann Gilbert was 'filled with the divine presence' and scarcely knew whether she was in the body or out of it, she felt God answering the cry of her heart with the words, 'Thou are holy,—thou art sanctified,—thou art cleansed from sin.' The very next paragraph of her

---

[91] This progression can be seen clearly, e.g. in the case of William Ashman. *AM* 13 (1790), 462–3.

[92] *WV* vi. 130 (repr. of an account in *MM* 1811); cf. *AM* 2 (1779), 192.

[93] *WV* iv. 245.

[94] Cf. the similar dynamic in female preaching in early nineteenth-century America, discussed in Brekus, *Strangers and Pilgrims*, 162–93.

[95] *MM* 25 (1802), 321.

[96] *AM* 11 (1788), 187–8

[97] *MM* 29 (1806), 470.

narrative continued, 'One blessed fruit of the work which God had wrought in me, was a more than usual concern for the salvation of poor sinners. I would have done or suffered any thing on their account, if I might have been the instrument of their conversion.' So it proved. When a preacher failed to show up, she took the floor, and soon 'many were convinced of sin, some of whom continue steadfast to this day'.[98] Some of the male preachers likewise found their call to preach following such an experience of sanctification, but for most of them the calling to preach came first. In part, this may also reflect the fact that the women preachers entered into their ministries in the 1760s during the perfectionist revivals in Methodism, whereas many of the male itinerants began preaching earlier.

Not only did the call to preach derive from the dynamic of conversion (or sometimes sanctification), but also it resembled the experience of conversion itself in many respects. The gospel message was heard as novel, like something the convert had never heard before, and the first thoughts of preaching often came likewise with the sense that this was something extraordinary. 'Nothing', said William Ashman, 'but the mighty power of God could cause me to do this.'[99] It was a 'miracle' like conversion was a miracle. John Furz was in a meeting and found himself called upon to speak. 'I had no thought of exhorting or preaching to this hour. But now the power of God came upon me, and enabled me to speak from an experimental knowledge, of freedom from condemnation.'[100] The tongue was loosed just as the heart had been earlier. John Prickard described his initial consideration of preaching in terms that could have been used of the witness of the Spirit. A friend urged him to begin to preach, and he confessed that he had felt an inclination to do so, 'yet I could not say assuredly that it was from God . . . I durst not, till I was sure I was called of God'.[101] The words 'assuredly' and 'sure' recall the quest for assurance of salvation in the narratives of conversion, but in this context the assurance sought was that of the inward call of God to preach.[102] Just as the awakened sinner doubted that his sins could really be forgiven, so Matthias Joyce experienced a 'damp' when he thought of preaching: 'I was ready to conclude it could never be, that such a vile creature should be chosen to labour in the vineyard of the Lord.'[103] When Thomas Hanby thought of his initial call to preach it was with an 'anxious mind'.[104] John Allen was in 'fear and trembling' while seeking to discern his call.[105] The convicted soul might 'wait on God in the

---

[98] *AM* 18 (1795), 44.   [99] *AM* 13 (1790), 463.   [100] *AM* 5 (1782), 519.
[101] *AM* 11 (1788), 626.
[102] A similar experience of inward call and testing was narrated by Prickard later with respect to missionary service. *AM* 12 (1789), 15–16.
[103] *AM* 9 (1786), 532.
[104] *AM* 3 (1780), 513.
[105] *AM* 2 (1779), 637.

means of grace' and mourn while seeking after conversion, but the would-be preacher's travail came through 'preaching on trial'. Conversion was not achieved through education, and neither was one qualified to preach principally by book learning. John Prickard 'consented to make a trial' and set off not in the duly authorized channels of education and ordination, but along the path of 'experimental knowledge' to see if God 'owned' him while he preached, if he was 'enlarged' and fluent when he spoke extempore. On the first trial, he felt the power of God and said, 'He gave me utterance, and many were comforted greatly.' But as no one was explicitly awakened or justified, he went home certain that he was not called. Urged on by his friends, however, he tried again, and this time things went better.[106] The breakthrough to certainty of one's call to preach, when it came, was attended with a joy like that of conversion. Matthias Joyce remembered what it felt like while he was preaching: 'I was so filled with joy, that it was as if I had got upon the wings of an eagle, and was soaring to endless day.'[107]

Conversion first led these autobiographers to preach, and then their call to preach was experienced like a conversion, and then finally their preaching resulted in new conversions. Above all, the call to preach was confirmed—as it was for Charles Wesley—by finding 'seals' to one's ministry; that is, by finding women and men brought under conviction or carried through to conversion under the word preached. Joyce worried that he did not have 'many seals of my ministry', and so he prayed harder and preached more fervently. 'However, nothing would satisfy me, but hearing the people roar under the sermon, from a sense of their misery; and, on the other hand, shouting for joy, through a sense of pardoning love.'[108] Because this did not happen, or at least not with the drama he had hoped, he was about ready to give it over. But then he heard some of the testimonies at class meetings and love-feasts, and this reassured him that he was doing some good. Thomas Rankin narrated a very similar experience when he began to preach: 'I had been led to think, if I really was called of God to preach, the divine power would attend the word in a very remarkable manner, in the conviction and conversion of sinners.' And he gave a clue regarding where this expectation came from, adding, 'This arose from reading Messrs. Wesley's and Whitefield's *Journals*, as also in hearing Mr. Whitefield myself.'[109] For Thomas Lee the test of whether he was called to be a travelling preacher was whether or not he could break new ground spiritually. He set

---

[106] *AM* 11 (1788), 626–7; cf. William Hunter's similar doubts and their resolution through making an experiment of preaching (*AM* 2 [1779], 592).
[107] *AM* 9 (1786), 534.
[108] Ibid.
[109] *WV* vi. 146.

out to places where no one had yet preached, thinking that 'if God would own me here, and raise up a people for himself, I shall know he hath sent me'. Again, he referred to this as looking for God to 'set his seal' to his ministry. He passed the test: 'A Society was quickly raised. Many sinners were convinced, and several of them truly converted to God.'[110] This same test of evangelical usefulness was evidently applied by the women who had to defend their extraordinary call to preach. The Cornish preacher Ann Gilbert felt God had satisfied her about her calling 'by owning my poor labours in the conversion of many sinners'.[111] Moreover she was said to have defended her call to preach before one who wished to silence her by saying, 'If Mr.——, can produce more converts than I, I will give it up.'[112]

This understanding of the call to preach did indeed come from Wesley himself. In answer to the question of how to discern who was moved by the Spirit to preach, Wesley proposed that such candidates must first know for themselves the pardoning love of God, that they must, secondly, have some manifest 'gifts and grace' for the work, including 'utterance', and that, thirdly, they must have fruit. This last test he put this way: 'Are any truly convinced of sin and converted to God by their preaching?'[113] Thomas Hanby wrote his autobiography as a letter to Wesley, and his narration of his call to the ministry appears almost as if a direct response to this question. He preached on trial, and two people received a sense of pardon. 'This, dear Sir, was my beginning, and, what I looked upon as my Call from God.'[114] Hanby's own conversion had reached fruition and been reproduced in others.

The subsequent itinerary of the early Methodist preacher, as narrated in these autobiographies, had several themes, but the chief concerns were the continued conversion of hearers and the rigours of the itinerant life as the preacher faced privation, temptation, suffering, and persecution. Most included, for example, episodes of persecution and mob violence that were interpreted in apostolic terms as opposition to the gospel on the part of the spiritually blind.[115] All of this teased out themes implicit in the call to ministry. The life of itinerancy, thus narrated, was the final proof that the inward call of God was genuine, even though it may have come to a humble tradesman with few of the normal qualifications for the ordained ministry.

---

[110] *AM* 3 (1780), 28–9.
[111] *AM* 18 (1795), 45.
[112] Quoted in Chilcote, *Wesley and Women Preachers*, 146.
[113] Jackson, Introduction to *EMP* i. 12–13.
[114] *AM* 3 (1780), 545.
[115] See e.g. the narratives of Thomas Mitchell and Thomas Lee in *WV* i. 175–96; iii. 198–219. Cf. John Walsh, 'Methodism and the Mob in the Eighteenth Century', in G. J. Cumming and Derek Baker (eds.), *Popular Belief and Practice* (Cambridge, 1972), 213–27.

The desire expressed by Richard Rodda 'to live and die a Methodist preacher' was entirely typical of all these autobiographies.[116] They understood their lives in retrospect and prospect in terms of this calling to preach, a calling that was itself understood principally in terms of conversion.

Entire Sanctification as Conversion

The experience of entire sanctification was often narrated as a further conversion, comparable with the earlier experience of justification and parallel in form. This experience was still theologically distinct, since the justification that was psychologically perceptible as pardon was always anterior to the sanctification that might come later as an equally perceptible, climactic purgation of sin. But the two experiences were analogous in form and expression. As Wesley said, 'I have continually testified in private and in public that we are sanctified, as well as justified, by faith . . . Exactly as we are justified by faith, so are we sanctified by faith.'[117]

Like the experience of initial awakening, the convert on the path to entire sanctification began with a sense of something painfully lacking and felt a need to seek wholeheartedly after this missing spiritual reality. So Richard Whatcoat wrote, 'I soon found, that though I was justified freely, yet I was not wholly sanctified. This brought me into a deep concern, and confirmed my resolution . . .' And like that first conversion, this second conversion involved travail. Whatcoat spoke of 'many sharp and painful conflicts' and of 'wrestling with God' before he was suddenly 'stripped of all but love' and 'rejoicing evermore'.[118] Robert Wilkinson similarly understood his need for sanctification in terms of something missing in his initial conversion, or justification. At Weardale in 1767 a Methodist preacher urged the members of the bands to seek the 'second blessing'. Wilkinson was there and he thought that if anyone needed it, he did, but because he had 'been justified only a few months', he did not think he could receive it. Then again, he reasoned that God was not limited by time. 'No sooner did that thought pass through my heart than the power of God seized me. I found I could not resist, and therefore turned my self over upon the seat . . . But as I was coming to myself I found such an emptying, and then such a heaven of love springing up in my soul, as I had never felt before.'[119] Both of these autobiographers described the period preceding this experience as one of anxiety, and both also wrote of the experience as having come with the same climactic spontaneity as their conversion.

In form, then, this appeared as a second conversion. If for Robert Wilkinson, this was a 'second blessing', for William Hunter it was a 'greater salvation'. Hunter completed his narrative for an issue of the *Arminian*

---

[116] *AM* 7 (1784), 468.   [117] Wesley, *Works* (BE), ii. 163.
[118] *AM* 4 (1781), 192.   [119] *AM* 5 (1782), 237.

Magazine in 1779, and then he wrote to Wesley a further letter, remembering that he had more to tell. Perhaps Wesley himself had asked him to say something about his experience of perfection, since Hunter signalled this subject as something expected: 'As touching that greater salvation, being saved from inbred sin, I shall simply relate what I know of the dealings of God with me in this respect.'[120] This was clearly a sequel to his earlier narrative of conversion. His first letter dealt with his justification, his second with his sanctification. After his justification he became aware of his need for a 'far greater change in my nature than I had yet experienced'. Though Calvinists had said that sin necessarily remained in believers until death, Hunter wanted to be decisively saved from all sin. He began to seek this with all his heart, and he had an experience not unlike that of Wilkinson and Whatcoat:

[God] gave me to experience such a measure of His grace as I never knew before: a great measure of heavenly light and divine power spread through all my soul: I found unbelief taken away out of my heart: my soul was filled with such faith as I never felt before: my love to Christ was like fire, and I had such views of him, as my life, my portion, my all, as swallowed me up; and oh! how I longed to be with him! A change passed upon all the powers of my soul, and I felt a great increase of holy and heavenly tempers. I may say, with humility, it was as though I was emptied of all evil, and filled with heaven and God.[121]

Most of this could as easily have been written by a convert after 'justification', but here it was Hunter's narrative of his 'sanctification'. 'From the time the Lord gave me to experience this grace', he said, 'I became an advocate for the glorious doctrine of Christian perfection.' Hunter concluded this perfectionist addendum to his conversion narrative with a kind of personal creed in which he outlined his conviction that God first justifies the sinner 'in a moment' and then to the one who grows in grace, faithful in a few things, God shows there to be a 'state of greater liberty' and 'this too is generally given in a moment'.[122] To Hunter, the experience was further along from conversion, but it was clearly analogous to it.

  Both conversion and the experience of perfection could also be *in extremis*. Charles Wesley's conversion occurred while he was ill and thought he might be dying. John Furz recounted his experience of being perfected in love when he, too, was ill and all his friends considered him to be dying, with plans being made for his funeral sermon. 'Mean time the cry of my heart was, "Lord, sanctify me now or never." In that instant I felt the mighty power of his sanctifying Spirit. It came down into my soul as a refining fire, purifying and cleansing from all unrighteousness. And from that instant I began to recover.' He reflected on how his slowness to understand

---

[120] *AM* 2 (1779), 594.   [121] Ibid. 596.   [122] Ibid. 597.

God's sanctifying work was akin to his previous misapprehension that justification was progressive: 'I had the same conceptions of Sanctification that I had before of Justification. I preached it as a slow, gradual work. And while I did so, I gained no ground . . . But now, glory be to God, I feel no anger, no pride, no self-will: old things are passed away. All things are become new.'[123]

This last allusion to 2 Corinthians 5: 17, or the trope of new creation generally, recurs in accounts of conversion and provides another link between conversion and perfection. George Shadford found that he was 'in Christ a new creature, old things were done away, and all things become new', but he was speaking of his initial conversion in 1762.[124] Likewise Richard Rodda used the language, 'every heart present appeared like melting wax before the fire', to describe his response and that of others to the outpouring of the Spirit in sanctification, but this was the same trope used by others for their response to the power of God in conversion. Thomas Walsh expressed his experience of conversion in nearly identical words, saying, 'My heart melted like wax before the fire.'[125] The rhetoric of conversion did double service for the rhetoric of perfection.

For these Methodists, conversion seemed at first self-authenticating and indubitable, but doubts and worries often crept in during the days that followed, and converts experienced a post-conversion 'wilderness state'. This was true too for perfection. John Valton had an overwhelming experience in prayer that seemed self-evidently, as he said, to have 'destroyed my sin, and made me holy'. But three days later Valton confided his misgivings to his diary, 'Various doubts have crossed my mind to-day whether the work which the Lord has wrought in me be real.'[126] Jasper Robinson's autobiography was highly abbreviated, and the style staccato, such that the structure of it comes through all the more clearly. He became a 'serious professor' in 1759, was converted under John Wesley in 1760, received 'a large effusion of the Holy Spirit' in 1763, and again felt a 'blessed change' in his heart in 1765. This experience was lost, renewed, and lost again. In 1770 he once more received a blessing and lost it through unbelief. These were a lot of 'conversions' for one short paragraph. In the next two paragraphs, he covered his itinerary as a travelling preacher from 1776 to 1782, and then he provided a diary of his experience of full sanctification in April 1783. This last experience of blessing—his fifth—was narrated in more detail than what had come before and was characterized less by rapture than by entire resignation.[127] But still, his narrative illustrates the way in which for the

---

[123] *AM* 5 (1782), 638–9.
[124] *AM* 13 (1790), 128.
[125] *AM* 7 (1784), 353; *WV* v. 26.
[126] *WV* vi. 43; cf. *AM* 6 (1783), 576–8.
[127] *AM* 13 (1790), 575–9, 630–6.

follower of Wesley there was always something more of conversion to be had as the years went by.

Death as the Final Conversion

The sense that a pious death was the consummation of evangelical conversion was so strong that the later editors of the lives of the Methodist lay preachers felt compelled to append to each narrative, wherever possible, an account of the subject's final end, drawn in most cases from letters and obituaries already published in the *Arminian* or *Methodist Magazine*. Henry Rack nicely refers to these as 'Evangelical Endings'.[128] Indeed, a vivid awareness of the awesomeness of death often provoked spiritual seriousness in the first place and began an individual on the path to conversion. Sarah Crosby recalled how, at age 17, 'while sitting alone, I was struck, as I thought with *death*; being seized with a cold trembling from head to foot'. Her response was to cry out to God: 'I directly fell on my knees, and prayed to the Lord to forgive my sins, and save my soul.'[129] Many of the early Methodist preachers had been engaged in dangerous occupations that made them keenly aware of death. While Thomas Payne was at sea, he said, 'We had men killed continually.' Half the army and half the inhabitants on the island of St Helena did not live out half their days, which Payne said, 'gave me very serious thoughts of the uncertainty of human life'.[130] The ex-soldiers John Haime and Sampson Staniforth likewise were converted on the eve of the battle of Dettingen in 1743, and then saw an awakening among the men of their regiment who had witnessed the bloodshed of that engagement. Richard Rodda was a tin miner in Cornwall who recounted several dramatic life-threatening incidents as he and his fellow miners tunnelled more than two hundred feet underground and then out under the ocean. In 1759, when 240 feet underground, he nearly drowned in eighteen feet of water; another time he was knocked over by a falling stone and fell twelve feet onto his back; still later he fell through a mound of tailings and escaped suffocation by falling right through into the pit below. And then finally, and most remarkably, while thirty feet down in a shaft he felt an impulse to kneel and pray, only to find that the shaft began to collapse and boulders fell all around him, such that they formed a wall and a roof over his head. He was preserved without injury in a way which would have been impossible had he been in any other posture but kneeling at his prayers.[131] These sorts of episodes were narrated as 'providential deliverances' but they also provoked

---

[128] Henry D. Rack, 'Evangelical Endings: Death-Beds in Evangelical Biography', *Bulletin of the John Rylands University Library of Manchester* 74 (1992), 39–56.

[129] *MM* 29 (1806), 419.

[130] *AM* 4 (1781), 583.

[131] *AM* 7 (1784), 357–8.

religious seriousness. Yet the encounter with death could be much less dramatic than this and still have the same effect. John Prickard was 20 years old when his cousin died of consumption as a repentant and hopeful Christian. 'This extraordinary death of so near a relation,' he said, 'was a loud call to all the house, and to me in particular.' He went to church and heard a sermon on the theme of the day of judgment, and it landed on a tender place. 'I was cut to the heart,' he said, and even afterwards 'the day of judgement still stared me in the face'.[132]

Death was thus an eschatological reality that provoked conversion. And Wesley duly recorded numbers of accounts of 'happy deaths' in his *Journal* and in the pages of the *Arminian Magazine*, knowing the spiritual impact made by such accounts. For example, John Nelson wrote a letter to John Wesley in February 1748 (published in the *Arminian Magazine* in 1778) recounting how the Christian death of Brother William Holmes had led to an awakening throughout the region. At the moment William Holmes died, his brother Robert was in bed some miles away and groaning under conviction for sin. He heard a voice telling him, 'Believe on the Lord Jesus, and thou shalt be saved,' and the voice was none other than his brother's whom he did not know to be dying. He had a vision likewise of his brother William present with him in his room. Robert was left 'rejoicing in God'. Clearly, death was an awe-inspiring occasion filled with spiritual significance and power.[133]

If an immediate consciousness of death was thus significant at the beginning of conversion, and if conversion was in some sense a response to the eschatological threat it represented, then it should come as no surprise that the final coda to the evangelical conversion narrative was often an account of how the convert was finally enabled to vanquish death by the grace of God. The devotional literature on the art of 'holy dying', or *ars moriendi*, first appeared in the fifteenth century and continued in various forms among Catholics and Protestants well into the eighteenth century. There was a particularly strong Jesuit and Puritan tradition in the seventeenth century. Whereas the Catholic tradition emphasized that the state of the soul was determined at the moment of death, the Protestant tradition—witnessed in a work such as William Perkins, *Salve for a Sicke Man* (1595)—stressed more the art of living so as to reach a blessed end. Indeed, at the very beginning of his published *Journal*, Wesley referred to reading a classic work in this tradition, Jeremy Taylor's *Rules for Holy Living and Dying*.[134]

While this tradition may have been waning generally in the eighteenth century, 'dying well' continued to be important to evangelicals.[135] As late as 1816, when the lay preacher Thomas Taylor died at 78 years of age—the

---

[132] *AM* 11 (1788), 460–1.   [133] *AM* 1 (1778), 529–30.
[134] John Valton also read this same book (*WV* vi. 23–4).
[135] Rack, 'Evangelical Endings', 39.

longest-serving preacher in the connexion besides Wesley himself—the *Methodist Magazine* lamented that his 'death was so sudden that he experienced little or nothing of the formality of dying'.[136] There was an understood 'formality' to death for the evangelicals. Henry Rack argues that the evangelical Anglicans of the period, moderate Calvinists generally, stressed human helplessness and entire dependence upon grace in the hour of death, but Methodists more often emphasized the evidence of their feelings and sought a direct assurance of their salvation at the end.[137] As they had lived, so they died. Neither were these deathbed narratives the sentimental accounts of 'going home' that would be more common in the nineteenth century, since for eighteenth-century Methodists the eschatological realities of judgment and damnation remained stark possibilities to the end. The importance of dying well may also be seen in several of Charles Wesley's hymns, which constitute a kind of *ars moriendi* tradition in verse. In the *Collection of Hymns for the Use of the People Called Methodists* (1780) there is a section, 'Describing Death', which included Charles Wesley's encomium 'Ah, lovely appearance of death!' and other hymns. He also wrote a two-part 'Dying Malefactor's Prayer' and other hymns for the dying and mourning, such as 'Happy soul, thy days are ended', with its lines:

> Struggle through thy latest passion
> To thy dear Redeemer's breast,
> To his uttermost salvation,
> To his everlasting rest.[138]

One was to 'struggle through'. Likewise Isaac Watts's life and exemplary death were recorded in the *Arminian Magazine*, and Methodists regularly sang his hymn, 'I'll praise my maker while I've breath', which continues with the lines, 'And when my voice is lost in death, | Praise shall employ my nobler powers'.[139] This was the hymn that John Wesley sang just moments before he died.

The accounts of happy deaths were not as common in the first few years of the *Arminian Magazine* as they became after about 1782, when such accounts appeared with increasing frequency. This reflected Wesley's decision to publish more posthumous material, accounts of 'those real Christians who ... have lately finished their course with joy'.[140] This probably also

---

[136] *WV* vii. 123; cf. Robert Roberts, whose death was lamented by his biographer in part because he died speechless, unable to give the customary testimony and admonitions to the family and onlookers (*WV* iv. 249).

[137] Rack, 'Evangelical Endings', 47.

[138] *A Collection of Hymns for the Use of the People Called Methodists ... With a New Supplement* (1877), 777. The hymn originally appeared in *Hymns and Sacred Poems* (1749), under the heading, 'For one departing'.

[139] Wesley, *Works* (BE), vii. 349–50.

[140] *AM* 4 (1781), p. v.

reflected the ageing of the movement generally, as the first generation of preachers and Methodist faithful reached the end of their course. By the late eighteenth century the conventions were well established. In 1799 John Pawson sent the *Methodist Magazine* an account of the death of John Murlin, with a prologue in which he also reflected on the genre. He was sure that readers had appreciated the accounts in the magazine of the lives of the preachers, since these demonstrated that these men were not only ministers but also 'witnesses'. Pawson claimed that few had given cause for shame after their lives were published, and that most were able 'with their last breath, to bear witness to the truth which, through life, they had published in His name'.[141] The twice-repeated word 'witness', with all its juridical connotations, indicates something of the concern that governed these deathbed narratives. Like the earlier accounts of Anabaptist martyrs of the sixteenth century, the narrative of the death of a Methodist was the 'last will and testament' of the convert and carried a special authority as the seal of the integrity of that life—in the double sense of the life lived and the life written. This was precisely what Pawson was leading up to with this prologue. He reminded the reader that John Murlin's life and ministry had been recorded earlier in the *Magazine* in 1779. Pawson's task was to show how Murlin had fulfilled what had been predicated earlier—how he had finished well.[142] For the writer narrating the moment of death, the common refrain was, as in the case of William Hunter, 'Thus died, as he had lived, Mr. William Hunter . . .'[143] The death sealed the life. Just as the early Christian apologists had appealed to the example of their martyrs, so also John Gaulter claimed in his conclusion to the life of Jonathan Maskew, 'It is no small honour to the cause in which we are engaged that most of our brethren have met death, not only with unshaken fortitude, but with the most lively prospects of the fruition of heaven.'[144]

Two years before his death Thomas Walsh disputed with John Fletcher about the manner of a Christian's death. Fletcher argued that even a strong believer might die in the midst of tremendous conflicts for reasons inscrutable to us, but Walsh disagreed publicly and 'with some degree of warmth'.[145] How painful, then, that in his own dying hour Walsh was 'in the utmost extremity of spiritual distress' and 'but few degrees removed from despair of his salvation'.[146] He found peace just before the end, but this whole episode caused a sensation among the Methodists. This was not the way a Methodist exemplar was to die.

---

[141] *EMP* ii. 246–7.
[142] Cf. also Pawson's letter giving an account of the death of Thomas Hanby (*WV* ii. 75–7).
[143] *WV* iv. 186.   [144] *EMP* ii. 403.   [145] *WV* v. 191.   [146] *WV* v. 189.

Effectively the deathbed was to be one's final pulpit, from which one could speak with a unique authority. John Pawson, who had written so many accounts of the 'happy deaths' of others, was well prepared for his own demise, and he used this last opportunity to the full. He took over a month to die and had time to write more than one 'final letter' to his friends and to the Conference, to exhort many of his visitors, and even baptize a child. And many were the dicta recorded for posterity at his bedside. Death was a sacred site, one of the places where time and eternity touched and where one might expect to witness the presence of the supernatural, both in diabolical temptation and in divine solace. Like other dying evangelicals, Pawson was granted a foretaste of heaven, a vision of the new Jerusalem. In one of his last letters he described the rapture and supreme delight he experienced while seeing 'the holy, happy spirits . . . worshipping at Emmanuel's feet, all ready to bid me welcome'. This vision of heaven included a final assurance of salvation: 'No clouds, no doubts, no fears,' he claimed. 'No; all was quietness, peace, and assurance for ever.'[147] Conversion had reached its final consummation, and Pawson was determined to proclaim it.

This dying ecstasy was certainly the ideal, but the form of the experience was often narrated like conversion itself as a struggle followed by victory, anxiety superseded by peace. And the devil might well show up, along with the angels. A few days before the lay preacher Hannah Harrison died, she wrote to a friend about her 'hard struggle'. Her biographer said, 'She had at times sore conflicts with the powers of darkness; but, through the Captain of her salvation, she came off victorious.'[148] The narrative of Robert Wilkinson's death on 8 December 1780 provides another example of this pattern. When he realized that he was dying he exhorted his wife to trust God, and he prayed for his family and his fellow spiritual labourers. But then followed his dying crisis: 'In the night season he had a severe conflict with Satan, and his spirit wrestled with God in prayer. Yea, he was in an agony, as he said afterwards. At last the tempter fled; and he seemed as if he was admitted to heaven, to converse with God, with angels and saints.'[149] Suddenly he woke his wife and told her he had been in heaven and seen the glory of God and been overwhelmed by the love of God. One ecstatic exclamation after another followed, and then he died in peace. It was the Methodist agonistic conversion all over again. But it was more than this too. As James Rogers described his experience of dying to his wife, it was 'hard work, my dear . . . good work, good work, once for all'.[150] As the consummation of conversion and the translation to glory, death represented the last agony, 'once for all'.

---

[147] *WV* iv. 89.   [148] *MM* 25 (1802), 366, 367.
[149] *WV* v. 239.   [150] *WV* v. 179.

Retrospective Autobiography and Conversion Narrative: The Growth of Genre

The different sense gained from a retrospective memoir, compared with Wesley's serialized life or with the immediate autobiographical reflections dashed off by a convert in an occasional letter, is clear from the final paragraph in Thomas Olivers's autobiography. After a lengthy narrative he concluded:

Upon the whole. When I consider how the providence of God provided for me in my infancy—Brought me up to the state of man—Preserved me from those evils which brought others to an untimely end—Directed my wandering steps to the means of my conversion—Cast my lot among His people—Called me to preach His word—Owned my preaching to the conversion of others—Stood by me in many trials—Brought me back, so often, from the brink of the grace—Healed my manifold backslidings... When I consider all these things, I must say, Surely Goodness and Mercy have followed me all the days of my life; and I hope to dwell in the house of the Lord for ever.[151]

The small phrase that begins this paragraph ('upon the whole') indicates the retrospective sense. Having a long view of his life and having had many years to reflect upon his conversion, he was able to sum up the meaning and pattern of the whole.

The lives of the early Methodist preachers thus represented a further stage in the growth of the genre of conversion narrative, a progression from the lay narratives examined in Ch. 4. Casting their minds back over their whole lives, their autobiographies took the longest path, 'the path that goes round my life ... [and] leads me from me to myself'.[152] Their autobiographies also represented a development from oral to written to printed narrative. Appearing in print was particularly important for establishing one's identity not just within an interpersonal milieu, but in the abstract public sphere. The act of mature retrospection and the act of printed publication together firmly established the religious identity of these writers 'like a nail fixed in a sure place'. The features of this religious identity included the concerns of the guild, as it were, but even more so, this identity was defined by conversion. The agony of travail and relief that marked the momentous beginning of their spiritual journey became the pattern for their later experience even as they devoted themselves to seeking the conversion of others.

---

[151] *AM* 3 (1780), 145–6.
[152] Gusdorf, 'Conditions and Limits', 38.

8

The Olney Autobiographers: Conversion Narrative and Personality

IN 1764 John Wesley wrote to forty or fifty clergymen in the Church of England, reminding them of the great work God had begun some years before, but lamenting that those who laboured in that work had become so quickly divided. He proposed a closer union of all who agreed on the essential points of original sin, justification by faith, and holiness of heart and life. Only three clergy even bothered to write back, however, and Wesley famously gave up on the others as a 'rope of sand'.[1] Although Wesley was unsuccessful in his attempt to unite the evangelical clergy with him in common cause, his letter does point to the growing number of evangelicals in the Church of England by the middle of the century. William Romaine was one of the early evangelical clergy and for a long time the only beneficed evangelical in London. He set aside a day each year to pray for other 'Gospel clergy', beginning with only twenty names on his list, but by 1795, the year he died, he was praying for five hundred.[2] For most of the century, these evangelical clergy—and the laypeople associated with them—remained only very loosely associated. There were clusters in Cornwall and Yorkshire, and evangelical clerical societies emerged locally here and there, but there was nothing like the organization or discipline of the Methodists, Moravians, or Scots Presbyterians.[3] For the most part these Anglican evangelicals connected with one another through letters and personal visits, along with an occasional exchange of pulpits. The chief issues that divided them from other evangelicals were church order (or 'regularity') and doctrine. Regular clergy, such as Samuel Walker of Truro,

---

[1] Wesley, *Works* (BE), xxi. 454–61; *JWL* iv. 235–9.

[2] John Walsh and Stephen Taylor, 'Introduction: The Church and Anglicanism in the "Long" Eighteenth Century', in John Walsh, Colin Haydon, and Stephen Taylor (eds.), *The Church of England, c.1689–c.1833* (Cambridge, 1993), 44.

[3] G. C. B. Davies, *The Early Cornish Evangelicals, 1735–1760* (1951); John Walsh, 'The Anglican Evangelicals in the Eighteenth Century', in Marcel Simon (ed.), *Aspects de L'Anglicanisme* (Paris, 1974), 87–102; id., 'The Yorkshire Evangelicals in the Eighteenth Century: With Special Reference to Methodism', Ph.D. thesis (Cambridge, 1956); L. E. Elliott-Binns, *The Early Evangelicals* (1953).

felt bound to the canons of the church and this included an obligation not to itinerate and thereby intrude in another man's parish. There were many who were irregular, such as William Grimshaw of Haworth, who was in close alliance with Wesley, or 'semi-regular', such as John Newton, who would go for the occasional 'gospel ramble' beyond his own parish, but for most of the evangelical clergy, some sort of commitment to Anglican order and parish ministry distinguished them from other evangelicals. Doctrinally, most were, like Henry Venn of Huddersfield, moderate Calvinists.[4] Given the opprobrium that attached to Calvinism generally, associated as it still was with the Commonwealth sects and the regicide, most of these evangelicals in the Church of England found their way to Calvinism slowly and only after their conversion experience. Thus John Newton wrote, 'I believe most persons who are truly alive to God, sooner or later meet with some pinches in their experience which constrain them to flee to those doctrines for relief, which perhaps they had formerly dreaded, if not abhorred . . . In this way I was made a Calvinist myself.' This statement could easily have been echoed by Henry Venn or John Berridge, who trod the same path to Calvinism.[5] Over the course of the century sufficient clergy and laity were attracted to this theology to rebuild a lasting Calvinistic tradition in the Church of England.[6]

Many of these moderate Calvinists in the Church of England were also autobiographers who recounted their conversions as the defining experiences of their lives. Consider the central religious crisis in the life of three such individuals. First, on 21 March 1748, in the belly of a ship in the dead of night, awakened by a raging North Atlantic storm that threatened to sweep all on board to a watery death, John Newton cries out to God for mercy. Second, at an insane asylum on 26 July 1764, William Cowper emerges from nearly a year of psychological derangement and repeated attempts at self-destruction, and, flinging himself into a window-seat in the parlour, he opens a Bible, reads, and falls into a spiritual reverie as a kind of divine light floods into his soul. And then third, after months of anxiety over his ineffectual pastoral ministry, and remorse over the levity with which he entered holy orders, Thomas Scott shuts himself up in his study with his Bible and the works of Richard Hooker and other Anglican divines, and by Christmas 1777 argues himself into evangelical conviction.

These crises of evangelical conversion were described by three Anglican evangelicals in the course of spiritual autobiographies written during the

---

[4] Charles J. Abbey and John H. Overton, *The English Church in the Eighteenth Century* (1878), ii. 185–6.

[5] John Venn, *Life and . . . Letters of the Late Rev. Henry Venn* (2nd edn., 1835), 29–32; *Works of John Berridge*, ed. Richard Whittingham (1838), 14–15.

[6] John Newton, *Works* (1808–9), vi. 279.

1760s and 1770s. During much of this period, John Newton (1725–1807), William Cowper (1731–1800), and Thomas Scott (1747–1821) lived near one another in the north-eastern corner of Buckinghamshire in the small market town of Olney and the neighbouring village of Weston Underwood. Newton and Scott were clergymen in the Church of England, and Cowper was a local gentleman-poet living on patronage. Like most evangelical Anglicans, they were each moderate Calvinists when they wrote their narratives. Newton's autobiography was published in 1764 under the title, *An Authentic Narrative of Some Remarkable and Interesting Particulars in the Life of* *******. Cowper's account was penned privately in 1767, with no intention of publication, but after he showed it to a few friends it began to circulate more and more widely in manuscript form, until it was finally published posthumously in rival editions in 1816.[7] Scott's *Force of Truth, an Authentic Narrative*, was written and published in 1779.

Newton and Cowper composed their accounts independently before moving to Olney, yet something about their lives attracted them to one another when the ink was barely dry on Cowper's manuscript. Newton also had an important influence upon the preservation, transmission, and perhaps even the revision of the manuscript Cowper brought with him to Olney.[8] Likewise, Newton and Cowper each had a hand in editing Scott's text some years later, and all three men used Joseph Johnson as their first publisher.[9] The important links between these three narratives are more profound, however, than their overlapping textual history. All three

---

[7] *Memoir of the Early Life of William Cowper* was published by R. Edwards; *Memoirs of the Most Remarkable and Interesting Parts of the Life of William Cowper, Esq., of the Inner Temple* was published by E. Cox & Son. See also the following note.

[8] Cowper's original holograph is lost, and published versions of his memoir have been based on various copies. Consequently, the textual history is complex. For the critical edition of Cowper's spiritual autobiography, *Letters and Prose Writings of William Cowper*, ed. James King and Charles Ryskamp (Oxford, 1979), i. 1–48, the editors used a transcript of Cowper's memoir copied by Maria F. Cowper in 1772. There is, however, an undated shorthand copy of Cowper's memoir extant, of which the editors were aware but which they described as 'in an unknown hand' and of doubtful authority. I have examined this shorthand MS, contained in an octavo copybook at Mills Memorial Library, McMaster University, Hamilton, Ontario, and the shorthand in fos. 1–38 may be confidently attributed to Newton. External evidence, such as the watermark, also links this copybook firmly to Newton's sermon notebooks during his Olney ministry. Newton's transcription of Cowper's narrative is an earlier copy of the original than the transcription made by Maria Cowper. The textual variants are not, however, substantial. See further the editors' introduction to *Letters and Prose of Cowper*, i. pp. xxiii–xxix; James King, 'Cowper's *Adelphi* Restored: the Excisions to Cowper's Narrative', *Review of English Studies* 30 (1979), 291–305; and Norma Russell, *A Bibliography of William Cowper to 1837* (Oxford, 1963), 189–201, 221–65.

[9] Newton refers to editing Scott's narrative on 2 Mar. 1779 in his MS diary, 1773–1805, Firestone Library, Princeton, NJ; Cowper's editorial intervention is mentioned in John Scott, *Life of the Rev. Thomas Scott* (6th edn., 1824), 127.

autobiographers became closely linked as Christian friends, maintained a common theological perspective, and engaged in similar Christian concerns. It is this kind of a shared world of associations that fosters common diction and familiar commonplaces in speech and writing, and this was reflected in the narratives written by Newton, Cowper, and Scott. While the lives of the early Methodist preachers might have possessed greater uniformity, deriving in large measure from the common vocation of the subjects and the strong editorial intervention of John Wesley, the Olney autobiographers were associated closely enough as friends to justify comparison, while being independent enough in other ways for that comparison to yield insights also into their individuality.

Newton and Scott were well educated, and Cowper was a distinguished man of letters. Accordingly, their autobiographies are characterized not only by an act of retrospection, but also by a degree of literary creativity that turned life into art. All autobiography turns life into text, and by so doing engages in an act of creativity, selecting certain events as significant, suppressing others, and arranging these in a meaningful order. What is thus true theoretically of all the autobiographies examined in this book, may be seen more explicitly in the case of the Olney autobiographers. Karl Weintraub draws attention to autobiography that clearly displays the developmental process by which 'an inner world of ideas unfolds by its own necessity': 'It seems wise to peel out of a widely varying genre of autobiographically colored writings that particular form in which an author undertakes to formulate a retrospective vision over a significant portion of his life, perceiving his life as a process of interaction with a co-existent world.' Moreover, Weintraub considers this form to be 'the essence of autobiography'.[10] Such an autobiographer may write with a model in mind, whether of the Homeric hero, or the ideal Roman *pater familias*, or the Stoic wise man, or the Christian saint, but 'the individual will always find room for his idiosyncrasies in the interstitial spaces of the basic components of his model.'[11] Although Weintraub generally laments the influence of models as something that stifles individuality, one can never really escape a model of some sort in autobiography, since identity inevitably must be understood in terms of the other. Indeed, against a model one may see one's uniqueness in a way that had not been noticed before. Certainly, in the autobiographies of Newton, Cowper, and Scott, their discovery and vivid display of personality occurred not despite the presence of a model, but because of it.

[10] Karl J. Weintraub, 'Autobiography and Historical Consciousness', *Critical Inquiry* 1 (1975), 831, 833–4.
[11] Ibid. 837

John Newton: Providence and Grace

Written some sixteen years after his crisis at sea, *The Authentic Narrative* (1764) was John Newton's first book of any significance.[12] Newton was an only child, born in 1725, and his recollections of his childhood were dominated by the memory of his pious, Dissenting mother who died when he was only 7. Though his father, a nominal Anglican and a captain in the merchant marine, took him on several voyages during his adolescence and sought to watch over his behaviour, Newton remembered that he oscillated between sinful indulgences and pangs of conscience. The anxiety of alternating between a good and a bad conscience did not end until late adolescence, when he drifted into Deism and abandoned religious moral restraints altogether.

His father attempted to set him up in business abroad, but romantic infatuation with a young family friend, Mary Catlett, caused Newton twice to evade his father's plans. Before another opportunity could be found, he was press-ganged into the navy in the tense days just before the Seven Years War. Newton soon went absent without leave, but he was caught, put in irons, whipped, degraded from office, and cast among the lowest rank of sailors back on the ship. Before very long, Newton was transferred to a merchant ship in the African slave trade. He described his behaviour in this new company as utterly abandoned, hinting at his own sexual profligacy. After six months trading, he determined to stay on the Guinea coast to work in the on-shore trade, hoping to make his fortune as a slave factor. But instead, during the next two years he suffered illness, starvation, exposure, and ridicule as his master used him poorly. Newton marked this point as the nadir of his spiritual journey.

In time, an English ship located and rescued Newton. Returning to England along the triangular Atlantic trade route via Brazil and Newfoundland, the ship encountered a North Atlantic storm. While the ship was splintering and filling fast with water, and with one man already swept overboard, Newton muttered his first prayer for mercy in many years. When the ordeal was over, he and most of the crew had survived the storm but were left with little food and water and a ship out of repair. Newton began to read the Bible and other religious books. By the time the ship at length reached Ireland, he considered himself no longer an 'infidel', if not yet a true believer. On shore, Newton made vows of obedience at the sacrament, but on his next voyage six months later he soon found himself

---

[12] John Newton, *Works*, i. 1–105. The most important biographies are Richard Cecil, *Memoirs of the Rev. John Newton* (1808); Josiah Bull, *John Newton of Olney and St Mary Woolnoth* (1868); Bernard Martin, *John Newton* (1950). See also my study, *John Newton and the English Evangelical Tradition* (Oxford, 1996). The discussion of Newton above is a summary of the fuller exposition, ibid. 13–48.

again unable to impose any moral restraint on his behaviour. Only a violent fever brought him to himself. Delirious, he crept to an isolated spot and cast himself before God in an act of surrender, trusting wholly in the atonement of Christ, and from that hour, he claimed, his peace and health were restored and the power of sin in his life destroyed.

From this point on, Newton increased gradually in his knowledge of the Christian faith. He soon became a master mariner and married Mary. Eventually, he met a fellow captain who acquainted him with the progress of evangelical revival in England. Consequently, when a convulsive fit led him to leave the maritime trade in 1754, Newton caught up for lost time, frequenting religious meetings in London. He got a job as a tide-surveyor in Liverpool about a year later. Once settled there, he pursued a course of private study in divinity. At the close of his narrative, he was still at Liverpool, eager to enter the ministry but as yet unable to achieve episcopal ordination. By the time the narrative was published, though, Newton was settled at Olney as a minister in the Church of England.

When Newton devoted three weeks early in 1763 to write up the story just recounted, he was not without literary models at hand. In the first place, there were the Scriptures. His diction was dominated by biblical idiom, and favourite scriptural phrases and tropes recurred at intervals. He often dropped biblical text directly into his running narrative in a kind of scissors-and-paste fashion, using the borrowed words as a part of his own first-person vocabulary. Thus, for example, when describing a cautionary dream he had on one occasion, he wrote that if his eyes could have been opened, he would have seen a contest in heaven: 'I should perhaps have seen likewise, that Jesus, whom I had persecuted and defied, rebuking the adversary, challenging me for his own, as a brand plucked out of the fire, and saying, "Deliver him from going down to the pit; I have found a ransom."'[13] This sentence was constructed by Newton entirely as a collocation of scriptural texts from the Authorized Version (Acts 9: 5; Zechariah 3: 1–2; Job 33: 24). Yet these texts were patched into the new semantic context and made to bear the internal weight of Newton's own narrative. He needed no vocabulary of his own.

Beyond vocabulary, the Scriptures also offered numerous biographical exempla. The sacred narrative which Newton most often compared to his own was the life of St Paul. Newton quarried almost every line of Pauline testimony for phrases that he could use to describe himself. He was 'the chief of sinners', 'in deaths oft', 'preaching the faith which he once destroyed', and so on. Newton drew on other analogues too. He was struck at various points with the way his case resembled the man delivered of an unclean spirit, or the prodigal, or the spared fig in the Gospels. At other key

---

[13] Newton, *Works*, i. 26.

points in his story he linked his narrative to the lives of Old Testament figures such as Jacob, Joseph, Sampson, David, and, of course, Jonah.

But the two loftiest analogues Newton employed were the history of Israel and the life of Christ. He began his autobiography by referring to the scene in Deuteronomy 8: 2, where Moses prophesied to the Israelite nation in the wilderness that there would come a happy day when their journey and warfare would be over, and when they would look back with pleasure on their present troubles. Newton claimed that these words could be taken in a 'spiritual sense' as addressed to all those who by faith must pass through this world (wilderness) to heaven (Canaan), drawing Israel explicitly into the centre of the bundle of sacred associations which he crowded into his narrative. When he described himself at the nadir of his spiritual declension in Africa as 'an outcast lying in [his] blood' (borrowing the metaphorical description of Israel in Ezekiel 16), he was simply extending into his narrative a figural use of Israel already made explicit in his introduction.

Newton was less explicit in linking his story with the life of Christ. Here the key phrase was from John 2: 4, where Christ says to his mother, 'Mine hour is not yet come.' Newton used this to dramatic effect by associating the words indirectly with his two years in Africa (again the low point in his narrative), saying, 'the Lord's hour of grace was not yet come'.[14] This had the effect of foreshadowing the central crisis of the narrative, for when he came to describe the storm of 1748, he announced, 'now *the Lord's time was come*'.[15] Implicitly, his crisis at sea was linked to the passion of Christ. In this way, Newton helped to establish the storm as the climax of his story and added a Messianic motif to the fugue of biblical tropes already resonating in the text.

These analogues point out the essentially figural interpretative structure of his autobiography. When Newton, on the first page of his narrative, spelled out that the history of Israel might be applied in a 'spiritual sense' to his own case, it appears as though he might be invoking some sort of *sensus allegoricus*, recalling medieval and patristic exegesis. Yet he elsewhere made explicit his commitment to the Reformation tradition of literal exegesis, allowing for typological interpretation only where the New Testament had already set an explicit precedent.[16] Divine revelation was in this context a historical phenomenon of promise and fulfilment, not an allegorical phenomenon of the abstract contemplated through the particular. Newton rejected allegory and identified his practice of figuration as one of 'accommodating' texts to illustrate doctrines made explicit elsewhere in Scripture.[17] However, this was licence enough to quarry a multitude of sacred symbols for his autobiography. The final effect was that his own life read as

[14] Ibid. 38.   [15] Ibid. 57, italics his.   [16] See e.g. Bull, *John Newton*, 231–2.
[17] Newton, *Works*, iv. 260–2.

an episode in salvation history, one small story embedded in the larger sequence of God's saving acts in history, parallel in structure to the biblical pattern of original prosperity, descent into humiliation, and return.[18]

Newton's autobiography should also be seen in the context of mid-eighteenth-century literature. The title itself gives some indication of its genre, pointing in two directions that relate respectively to the outward and inward aspects of his story. As regards the outward aspect, the key words *Authentic Narrative* and *remarkable experiences*, or their close synonyms, were often used in sensational tracts such as the sordid lives of criminals, tales of travellers in strange lands, or accounts of current catastrophes, all of which were in popular demand at the time of Newton's writing. There was, for example, *The **Remarkable** Life of James Smith, a Famous Young Highwayman, who was Executed at Surbiton Common . . . for a Robbery in Surrey. Containing a **True** and **Faithful Narrative** of all Robberies that he has, within a few Years, Committed . . . Written by Himself* (1756). Here, as in Newton's work and many others, the special pleading of *authentic* or *true and faithful narrative* is in proportion to the *remarkable* incidents that the title promises.[19] Newton's title also points in another direction, however, linking his autobiography in its religious aspect to contemporary revival and conversion narratives and providence literature. His *Authentic Narrative of Some Remarkable Particulars* nicely echoes Jonathan Edwards's **Faithful Narrative** *of the* **Surprising** *Work of God in the Conversion of Many Hundred Souls in Northampton* (1737) and James Robe's **Faithful Narrative** *of the* **Extraordinary** *Work of the Spirit of God, at Kilsyth* (1742). This same 'strange but true' construction can be found also in individual conversion narratives of the period.[20]

For all its adventure, it was this latter link to the evangelical conversion narrative, with its Nonconformist and Puritan antecedents, that was most important, for here was a native lives-of-the-saints tradition with which Newton was thoroughly acquainted from childhood. He had heard many times the public testimonies of would-be members of Independent Meetings, oral conversion narratives that anticipated his own. His introduction to the life of the London and Liverpool religious societies in the 1750s also

---

[18] Cf. Northrop Frye, *The Great Code* (1982), 198.

[19] Donald Stauffer, *The Art of Biography in Eighteenth-Century England* (Princeton, 1941), 218–19, picks up this strand in Newton's work and treats it with other contemporary lives under the heading, 'Lives of soldiers of fortune'. Newton's period on the Guinea Coast as 'the slave of slaves' also allows his account to be compared with other captivity narratives of the period. See further, Linda Colley, *Captives: Britain, Empire and the World, 1600–1850* (2002).

[20] The life of the Puritan John Flavel was reprinted e.g. as *A Saint Indeed: or, the Great Work of a Christian . . . to which is added, a **Faithful** and Succinct **Narrative** of some Late and **Wonderful** Sea-Deliverances* (Glasgow, 1754).

exposed him to a spoken culture of personal testimony. His reading likewise drew him into the Anglo-Calvinist tradition as he studied the writings of many famous Puritans and Nonconformists. *The Life of Colonel Gardiner* (1747) by Philip Doddridge was, for example, a highly significant pattern for Newton's narrative, mentioned often in his diary and referred to in his published autobiography.

The morphology of conversion was elaborated at great length by the sort of writers read by Newton during this period, and from this reading he learned that the progression from a 'legal call' to an 'evangelical call' in one's life simply reflected in experience the important link between law and gospel in theology. This twofold structure is evident in Newton's narrative. He carefully proscribed his description of his initial change of heart after the storm in 1748. Although he described himself as no longer a freethinking Deist, having now some right notions, and having given over the habit of swearing, he began the next paragraph with 'But' and added all the necessary concessions demonstrating this to have been only a 'legal' repentance, which left him still self-righteous. It is another eight pages before his 'evangelical' repentance is described, when he was prompted by a severe fever to acknowledge his own moral impotence and make his surrender to God.[21]

Newton did not consciously think of his conversion in generic terms. He wrote, 'We must not therefore make the experience of others, in all respects, a rule to ourselves, nor our own a rule to others ... As to myself, every part of my case has been extraordinary.—I have hardly met a single instance resembling it.'[22] Yet, as was true of Richard Baxter's earlier autobiography, the assumption that his case was extraordinary demanded that he possess a strong and clear sense of what was in fact ordinary. Indeed, the pattern of Newton's narrative was a pattern he discovered in the 1750s through his renewed acquaintance with orthodox Dissent, his introduction to Methodism, and his growing familiarity with Puritan practical divinity and Calvinistic orthodoxy.[23]

The *Authentic Narrative* comprised three interwoven plots of Newton's career, courtship, and conversion. In the first instance it was a 'rags-to-riches' story of a young man who had squandered all the greatest advantages and opportunities in commerce, who was consequently reduced to extremities of misery and want, but who was then beyond all expectation raised to respectable social status and given more than he could desire of the good things of life. It was also a tale of romance in which love at first sight

[21] Newton, *Works*, i. 66–77.   [22] Ibid. 74.
[23] For this pattern within Pietism see further, F. Ernest Stoeffler, *German Pietism During the Eighteenth Century* (Leiden 1973), 1–38; Ward, Introduction to Wesley, *Works* (BE), xviii. 1–36.

was followed by years of unrequited passion, crowned at long last by the happiness of marriage when all obstacles were finally overcome. And lastly, it was an evangelical narrative in which common grace in childhood was spurned, resulting in a course of hardened unbelief and wilful sin from which the protagonist recovered only through an act of divine mercy, leading in time to a new season of religious usefulness. Because the three plots concur in shape and correspond in chronological sequence, a narrative echo recurs through the work as a whole. As Owen Watkins observes, 'It is the ability to set up this kind of resonance between the inward and the outward that does most to give significance to the private events of a spiritual autobiography.'[24]

What unified the three-layered narrative was the central theme of a benign providence working out the salvation of the elect. Newton gave a concise statement of this grand motif in his introduction, after having explained the Israel typology. He claimed that Christians

> may collect indisputable proof that the wise and good providence of God watches over his people from the earliest moment of their life, over-rules and guards them through all their wanderings in a state of ignorance, leads them in a way that they know not, till at length his providence and grace concur in those events and impressions which bring them to the knowledge of him and themselves.[25]

Thus, a proleptic knowledge of the ultimate meaning of one's past was attainable by viewing scriptural patterns and biographical facts in a kind of stereoscopy. Providence and grace concurred: outward and inward experience came into focus.

WILLIAM COWPER: DESCENT INTO HELL

When the facts of William Cowper's life became widely known after his death, a fervent debate arose about whether evangelicalism, and Calvinism in particular, had contributed to his dementia. Newton's influence over Cowper was evaluated accordingly as either helpful or malign. The debate hardened almost immediately along confessional lines and studies of the poet reflected entrenched *parti pris* throughout the nineteenth century and well into the twentieth.[26] But for all this, the autobiographies of these two men have never been compared in literary terms.

---

[24] Owen Watkins, *The Puritan Experience* (New York, 1972), 66.

[25] Newton, *Works*, i. 7.

[26] See further, Lodwick Hartley, 'Cowper and the Evangelicals: Notes on Early Biographical Interpretations', *Proceedings of the Modern Languages Association* 65 (1950), 719–31; id., *William Cowper* (Chapel Hill, NC, 1960), 16–32. Of the more than thirty biographies of Cowper, the most important modern study is James King, *William Cowper* (Durham, NC, 1986); see also George Ella, *William Cowper* (Darlington, 1993).

If the locus of Newton's spiritual autobiography was his experience, the locus of Cowper's was his own psyche; if Newton's was a typological reading of the past, Cowper's was an emblematic one. It was not the salvific exodus motif that controlled Cowper's narrative, but rather the application to himself of an extraordinary occurrence in nature. He imbedded into his narrative the story of a sheepdog that wrests a sheep from the flock and forces it to the edge of a precipice. The dog stares down the trembling sheep for several minutes, nose to nose, until the sheep edges slowly away from the cliff and steals back towards the flock. This episode, which Cowper observed in person, he took as an allegory of his own case.[27] His autobiography was consequently controlled by this image of the knife's edge, the either/or, the precipice. He totters on the brink of suicide, he totters on the brink of hell; he totters on the brink of insanity, he totters on the brink of conversion.[28] This instability was only resolved in the closing pages of the narrative as Cowper provided a satisfying denouement to the crises of his mind and spirit, projecting hopefully into the future a life of spiritual and moral growth, infused with gratitude to God for his recovery as he began a new life in rural retirement among the pious Unwin family. However, all this was written from the perspective of 1767. Six years later this hard-won self-interpretation would be tragically and utterly undone with the onset of Cowper's third depression and the unremitting conviction of his own damnation.

For good reason, Cowper's narrative has frequently been read as part of a genre of 'stories of the insane'.[29] At the outset of his narrative, however, Cowper stated that his overall aim as an author was not to write an account of his mental suffering or a defence of his sanity, but 'a history of my heart so far as religion has been its object'. He located his autobiography squarely within the religious genre. From the beginning, therefore, he demonstrated his familiarity with the conventions of conversion narrative, such as the noting of 'serious impressions' in childhood.[30] He related a series of memorable episodes of religious conscience in his boyhood, such as the occasion when he was startled by a skull in a graveyard and made to think of his own mortality. As a schoolboy at Westminster his early seriousness about religion soon wore off, and Cowper noted, again conventionally, the growing hardness of his heart towards religion throughout his adolescence.

At 21, after being articled to a solicitor for three years, Cowper entered the Middle Temple. He set off this period as the crucial one: 'a most critical

---

[27] *Letters and Prose of Cowper*, i. 11–13.

[28] The closest parallel, in this respect, to Cowper's narrative is the life of John Haime (1710–84), *AM* 3 (1780), 207–17, 255–78, 307–13.

[29] See e.g. Roy Porter, *A Social History of Madness: Stories of the Insane* (1987).

[30] *Letters and Prose of Cowper*, i. 5.

season of my life upon which much depended'. The crisis that followed this announcement was his first bout of depression. Cowper described his condition vividly: 'Day and night I was upon the rack, lying down in horrors and rising in despair.'[31] The depression lasted for a year, but he interpreted this affliction in religious terms as a means employed by providence to lead him to recognize his own insufficiency and to force him to prayer.

A brief episode of happiness at the seaside was poisoned by Cowper's subsequent reflection that his sense of peace with God might be only a delusion. He wrote of this suggestion as a diabolic attack upon his soul by Satan himself, introducing a preoccupation with spiritual warfare that continued throughout his autobiography. Afterwards, Cowper described his life back in London as 'an uninterrupted course of sinful indulgence'. He still believed that the Scriptures were true, but this belief only afflicted him, since he increasingly discovered his mind and heart at odds. He tried not to think about damnation.

With little money, Cowper found himself wishing that the Clerk of Journals in the House of Lords would die, so that he himself might become a candidate for the post, which was in the gift of his uncle. But no sooner had he wished this, than he was stricken with remorse, overwhelmed with guilt for his murderous thoughts and his covetousness—all the more so, when the man did die, and Cowper was offered the post. When Cowper's right to the preferment was contested, he became terrified, since he would have to defend his right before the Bar of the House. Cowper described the psychological strain that followed under the metaphors of an execution and a darkening maritime storm. At the same time, he interpreted the crisis in theological terms as a 'means' employed by God to prepare him to receive the gospel.

As the crisis approached, Cowper railed against God but did not pray for help, believing he would not receive it. He made a comparison of his situation here to that of Saul at Endor—a powerful, if cryptic, typological reference, since Saul was the perfect scriptural illustration of a spiritual outcast who, as a subject of malign supernatural forces, was finally driven insane.[32] In the midst of this crisis, Cowper, like many other evangelicals, made a brief foray into the demanding spirituality of the *Whole Duty of Man* (1658), only to be driven further into spiritual despair. His anxiety was such that he wished for mental derangement as an escape from his dilemma, and he had a presentiment that this would indeed be the case.

With dramatic effect, Cowper introduced the 'great temptation' to which Satan and his minions had 'all the while been drawing' him:

---

[31] *Letters and Prose of Cowper*, i. 8.
[32] Cf. 1 Samuel 28: 8–25.

attempted suicide. Cowper was again a victim in the contest of the gods.[33] Fired by the passion of his remembered anguish, his evangelical diction was largely set aside, and he wrote vividly—almost with delight—describing his torments.

The story of Cowper's attempted suicide is well known. In November 1763, after unsuccessful attempts to poison himself, to throw himself into the Thames, and to stab himself with his penknife, he prepared a noose from his garter with which to hang himself. Reminding the reader of the story of the dog and sheep, he pointed out that he was *now* at the edge of the precipice.[34] He attached the garter to the top of the chamber door, and here hung long enough to lose consciousness and fall to the floor. Sometime afterwards Cowper sent for his uncle and told him of his suicide attempts and was accordingly relieved of his obligations to take up the parliamentary post. The external crisis was over.[35]

Cowper described this entire episode of his repeated attempts at suicide, a period of less than twenty-four hours, in lurid detail, minutely relating his physical and psychological symptoms at each stage. It was the centre of his narrative. The theological commentary that follows then tied the vivid psychological narrative back into the conventions of the conversion genre. Now, he began to feel a sense of conviction for his sin, particularly for having attempted to kill himself, and he grew afraid of God's wrath and of death and damnation. A strange sensation in his brain he took as an ominous signal from God that he had sinned against the Holy Ghost, and with this, Cowper tells us, he gave himself up to 'absolute despair'.

Cowper sent for his evangelical relation Martin Madan (1726–90), whom he thought of as an 'enthusiast' but whom he yet considered his last hope. Madan's doctrine of original sin offered some comfort to Cowper by placing all mankind on the same level. It made his case not, after all, unique. Madan then explained the hope held out in the gospel, but though Cowper wished he could believe, he did not feel he had the necessary faith. Then, just when it seemed that there might be some hope, he was again tormented by diabolical visions and voices that seemed to confirm his damnation. The next day he was seized by a 'stroke' which left him entirely deranged.

Cowper's brother sent him to St Albans to be under the care of Dr Nathaniel Cotton. Cowper did not go into detail about his psychological condition at St Alban's, but chose at this point instead to push to the fore the theological pattern he had all along been seeking to tease out of the

---

[33] On the interpretation of madness as 'psychomachy', see Roy Porter, *Mind-Forg'd Manacles* (1990), 60–81; on suicide as a diabolical temptation, see Michael MacDonald and Terence R. Murphy, *Sleepless Souls: Suicide in Early Modern England* (Oxford, 1990), 324.

[34] *Letters and Prose of Cowper*, i. 23.

[35] Ibid. 18–25.

narrative. The first eight months at the asylum were filled with religious delusions, but the whole he summed up tersely under the words: 'conviction of sin and despair of mercy'.[36] Then, one day he found his spirits brightened a little and something seemed to hint that there might yet be mercy for him. He woke the next morning free from despair for the first time. He commented that God was here preparing him for conversion, and then took the reader back two months to an episode in which, like Augustine, he had picked up a Bible on a bench in the garden and read a passage at random. It was the passage in the Gospels about Lazarus, and Cowper was moved as he contemplated Christ's mercy in raising Lazarus. This, he reflected, was 'an exact type' of the mercy that God was about to extend to him.[37]

Just as Cowper had foreshadowed his first depression and set off the suicidal crisis as key points in his narrative, and just as Newton prepared the reader for his own cry for mercy on the high seas, so also Cowper now used such signposting to set up expectations of his own climactic conversion: 'The happy period that was to strike off my fetters and to afford me a clear opening into the free mercy of the Blessed God in Jesus was now arrived.' Sitting by the window after breakfast, he picked up a Bible again and read from Rom. 3: 25 about Christ's atonement. Cowper writes, 'Immediately I received strength to believe it. Immediately the full beams of the sun of righteousness shone upon me. I saw the sufficiency of the atonement He had made, my pardon sealed in His blood, and all the fullness and completeness of my justification. In a moment I believed and received the Gospel.'[38] The repeated 'immediately' and 'in a moment' stress the spontaneity and freedom of Cowper's conversion experience. The moment of illumination is true to the evangelical type: a new quality of self-evidencing knowledge was imparted to him by supernatural agency, and the focus was upon justification through faith in the atoning death of Christ. The language also recalled a fine point of Anglo-Calvinist theology in Cowper's theologically loaded reference to the 'sufficiency' of the atonement.

Cowper described the spiritual glow of his feelings after this experience in language thick with scriptural and evangelical allusions. Equating his quiet ecstasy with the classic text of the eighteenth-century revivals, 1 Pet. 1: 8, he experienced 'joy unspeakable and full of glory'. He also claimed, in another theologically loaded phrase, that God gave him 'full assurance of faith at once',[39] an experience that would later be so completely undone. In June

---

[36] *Letters and Prose of Cowper*, i. 34.

[37] Ibid. 38–9.

[38] Ibid. 39.

[39] Cf. Hebrews 10: 22. Hermannus Witsius, an author admired by the Olney autobiographers, discussed 'full assurance' in Martin Madan (ed.), *A Treatise on Christian Faith, Extracted and Translated from the Latin of Hermannus Witsius* (1761), 38.

1765, Cowper left St Albans for Huntingdon, where for four months he experienced repeated moments of spiritually charged emotion, communing with God in rural seclusion, in church, and in solitude. Telescoping the account of his spiritual life since conversion, he wrote simply of 'long intervals of darkness interrupted by short returns of joy'. Yet he had great expectations for the future. He placed himself thus along the Calvinist *ordo*, between justification and glorification, at the place where the believer lives in patient hope of growth in grace.

It is no wonder that Cowper's memoir was the most private of the three examined here, remaining in manuscript form until after his death, since his autobiographical task was the most challenging, seeking to convince his readers that a religious conversion in the midst of insanity was not itself a delusion. We have observed already in Ch. 4 that the crisis of evangelical conversion often left converts wondering if they were losing their minds, and some were tempted to suicide, so profoundly was their sense of themselves challenged by the demands of the 'spirituality of the law'. Opponents of Methodism had already made much of the link between religious enthusiasm and madness. ''Tis but too notorious', wrote George Lavington, 'that the same enthusiasm...hath driven numbers of these unhappy creatures into direct madness and distraction, either of the moaping, or the raving kind; or both of them, by successive fits, or into the manifold symptoms of a delirium, and phrensy.'[40] It was frequently charged that Bethlem Hospital, near Wesley's Foundery and Whitefield's Moorfield's Tabernacle, was filled with Methodists.[41] In the same year that Cowper wrote his narrative, Nathaniel Lancaster published a mock epic, *Methodism Triumphant* (1767) which calls upon Mania, divine source of 'visions, raptures, and converting dreams | Awful Ebriety of New-Birth Grace', as the evangelical muse: 'Thee, MANIA, I invoke my pen to guide, | To fire my soul, and urge my bold career.'[42] Especially after Cowper's relapse into mental suffering in the 1770s, which included an unremitting sense of his own damnation, his evangelical friends must have been anxious lest Cowper's interpretation of madness as a heaven-sent means of grace to bring him to spiritual awakening might be seized upon as evidence that climactic conversions of the Methodistical type were essentially evanescent, the product of enthusiasm and a distempered mind.[43] Cowper's theme of

---

[40] George Lavington, *The Enthusiasm of Methodists and Papists Compared* (1754), iii. 10; cf. Erasmus Darwin, *Zoonomia* (1794), ii. 379, who includes *orca timor*, the fear of hell, in his taxonomy of systemic human disorders: 'Many theatric preachers among the Methodists successfully inspire this terror...the poor patients frequently committ suicide.'

[41] Albert M. Lyles, *Methodism Mocked* (1960), 109; cf. Porter, *Mind-Forg'd Manacles*, 33; id., *Stories of the Insane*, 93.

[42] Quoted in Lyles, *Methodism Mocked*, 42.

[43] Cf. Porter, *Stories of the Insane*, 29.

providential madness, together with his relapse, meant that his private story has continued to be vulnerable to such criticism. More recently, these same ambiguities have made it a convenient site for post-structuralist criticism.[44]

However, these readings of Cowper go against the grain of his narrative and fail to do justice to his professed religious self-understanding or his literary intentions in 1767. It has rarely been noted by literary critics that Cowper was writing within a clearly recognizable genre, with formal conventions and topoi as well defined in this case as in the didactic poetry he wrote. Even the sense that one was descending into madness and the urge to commit suicide were typical, if not universal, features of the evangelical genre of spiritual autobiography.[45] And as in Cowper's case, these were sometimes narrated in terms of a contest between God and the devil for the soul, including divine and diabolic locutions and visions.[46] In the second section of Jonathan Edwards's *Faithful Narrative of the Surprising Work of God* (1737), he expounded the common features in the great variety of conversions he witnessed. Edwards observed in passing that when a sinner's conscience was troubled but not yet comforted, and damnation was felt as a terrifying certainty, people of a melancholy temper sometimes descended into an irrational and irremediable despair. Indeed there had been one shocking suicide in his own town of Northampton from such causes.[47] Examples of the temptation that Edwards observed may be multiplied from the literature.[48]

What was unique about Cowper's narrative was that the descent into madness and the recovery of his senses was so *central* to his story, structurally

---

[44] See Felicity A. Nussbaum, 'Private Subjects in William Cowper's "Memoir"', in Paul Korshin (ed.), *The Age of Johnson* (New York, 1987), i. 307–26, who takes Cowper's narrative as a 'site' that registers various unresolved cultural tensions and rejects the assumption that the text is the expression of a liberal humanist self.

[45] Indeed, both Newton and Scott recorded temptations to suicide in their narratives: Newton, *Works*, i. 33; Scott, *Force of Truth*, 23.

[46] Cf. the case of the Methodist preacher Robert Wilkinson (1745–80), who, while under conviction for his sin, was in distress 'day and night' and worried that the devil lay waiting to devour him. 'For many nights he suggested, if I prayed, he would appear and tear me in pieces.' One evening, Wilkinson was tempted 'to put an end to a wretched life', and he confessed to a fellow Methodist that he was driven to 'distraction'. 'My neighbours said I was beside myself, for I could not rest in my bed. I often rose and wandered in the fields, weeping and bewailing my desperate state.' *AM* 5 (1782), 180–2. This kind of psychomachy is taken by Roy Porter as a phenomenon that belongs more properly in the gothic, late Renaissance worldview of the seventeenth century. However, it is surely an anachronism to refer to this vivid sense of the reality of supernatural powers as 'fundamentalist' when it occurs in the eighteenth century, as it does frequently, if not universally, in evangelical autobiography. See Porter, *Mind-Forg'd Manacles*, 66, 73, 80, 265, 279.

[47] *WJE* iv. 46–7; cf. George M. Marsden, *Jonathan Edwards* (New Haven, Conn., 2003),163–9.

[48] See e.g. the extensive citations in MacDonald, *Sleepless Souls*, 324.

parallel to the spiritual pattern of fall and redemption he was already narrating, that he believed and implied that God was the agent of his madness, that he narrated the actual experience of derangement so vividly, and, above all, that the spiritual sunshine he basked in, in 1767 proved to be but a brief respite in his mental suffering.

Thomas Scott: Books I Read and How They Changed My Mind

Twenty-two years younger than Newton, sixteen years the junior of Cowper, Thomas Scott was best known to nineteenth-century evangelicals for his massive commentary on the Scriptures, written in weekly instalments over the course of many years while he was a minister in London. Scott's autobiographical *Force of Truth* was written earlier, only about eighteen months after he had become a convinced evangelical and while he was still an obscure country curate, living near Newton and Cowper.[49]

Scott's autobiography was written against the backdrop of the Feathers Tavern Petition (1772) and the renewed controversy over the requirement of clerical subscription to the Thirty-Nine Articles that followed Francis Blackburne's *The Confessional, or a Full and Free Enquiry into the Right, Utility, and Success of Establishing Confessions of Faith and Doctrine in Protestant Churches* (1766). Earlier in the century, most Latitudinarians understood subscription as little more than a recognition of the duly established authority of the Church of England. Now, however, such arguments for subscription were increasingly regarded as casuistical, and the Articles treating the doctrine of the Trinity were taken more seriously, provoking a crisis of conscience on the part of clergymen such as Scott.[50] Theophilus Lindsey (1723–1808) wrote a narrative of his crisis of conscience and how it was resolved by leaving the church and becoming a Unitarian. In contrast, Scott wrote of how his crisis of conscience had led him to orthodoxy and indeed to Methodism.[51] Lindsey knew that a conscientious examination of the Articles could lead to such an outcome, since, as he recalled in his narrative,

---

[49] Thomas Scott, *The Force of Truth: An Authentic Narrative* (1779). Scott revised his narrative for the 1798 edn., reprinted in the first volume of id., *Theological Works* (Buckingham, 1805–8). See also, Scott, *Life of Thomas Scott*.

[50] See further, Martin Fitzpatrick, 'Latitudinarianism at the Parting of the Ways: A Suggestion', in Walsh, Haydon, and Taylor (eds.), *The Church of England*, 209–27; John Gascoigne, *Cambridge in the Age of Enlightenment* (Cambridge, 1989), 194–8; id., 'Anglican Latitudinarianism and Political Radicalism in the Late Eighteenth Century', *History* 71 (1986), 22–38; Abbey and Overton, *English Church in the Eighteenth Century*, i. 435–42; Leslie Stephen, *History of English Thought in the Eighteenth Century* (1876), i. 421–6.

[51] In many ways, Scott's narrative is parallel to that of Lindsey. See Theophilus Lindsey, *Apology* (1774), 202–25; id., *Sequel to the Apology* (1776), pp. v–xxiv.

'None but those called Methodists . . . preached in conformity to them.'[52] To Lindsey, then, only Methodists and Unitarians took the Articles seriously.

Like Lindsey's autobiographical section of his *Apology* (1774), Scott's narrative was rigorously controlled, not by chronology, but rather by his own strongly conceived interpretative plan. Concentrating on his theological development, he drew on his past selectively and made the narrative serve an apologetic purpose. Part of his literary strategy was to create the picture of a peculiarly reluctant convert: 'I considered myself to be a very singular instance of a very unlikely person, in an uncommon manner, being led on from one thing to another, to embrace a system of doctrine, which he once heartily despised.'[53] Intensely dialectical, Scott's narrative traced the progressive demolition of his arguments for unbelief and his reluctant capitulation to evangelical views as he was propelled by the sheer 'force of truth'. If Newton was concerned with experience, and Cowper with the inner workings of his own psyche, Scott was clearly interested in the rational intellect itself as the setting for the drama of conversion. For Scott there were to be no providential deliverances or near-death turning points, no demons or psychomachy, no flash insights from chance readings of Scripture, and above all, no signs of mental instability. Scott wrote reason's account of its own conversion.

His book is divided into three parts: the first and shortest section simply established his condition prior to the beginning of the 'great change' he was setting out to narrate; the second and longest part was the essence of the book and traced the history of the change in his religious views; the third part abandoned narrative altogether in order to make certain observations on his story in an apologetic epilogue.

With economy Scott developed the principal theme of Part I: total depravity and original sin, and the way he stifled his nascent consciousness of this condition by embracing heterodox theology. He dealt with his childhood and adolescence summarily, plunging the reader into the forward stream of his intellectual narrative. At sixteen his conscience was pricked when he began to prepare for his first communion. Then for about nine years, his religious and moral earnestness followed a cyclical pattern, like Newton's earlier, as his devotional discipline increased in expectation of each celebration of the sacrament, but fell off quickly afterwards. But just as his conscience was awakening, he was introduced to religious ideas that lulled it back to sleep. Scott recalled, 'A Socinian comment on the Scriptures came in my way, and I greedily drank the poison, because it quieted my fears, and flattered my abominable pride.'[54] The two specific doctrines

[52] Lindsey, *Apology*, 203.
[53] Scott, *Force of Truth*, 148.
[54] Ibid. 7–8.

he embraced were, first, that sin was 'small and tolerable' and, second, that final condemnation involved annihilation rather than eternal torment.

In one long periodic sentence, Scott described his entry into holy orders while in this condition of sin and heterodoxy:

After having concealed my real sentiments under the mask of general expressions; after having subscribed Articles directly contrary to my then belief; and after having blasphemously declared, in the presence of God, and of the congregation, in the most solemn manner, sealing it with the Lord's supper, that I judged myself to be inwardly moved by the Holy Ghost to take that office upon me (not knowing or believing that there was a Holy Ghost), on September the 20th, 1772, I was ordained a Deacon.[55]

The moral irony of Scott's situation is teased out masterfully by the very length of this sentence (which was even longer in a later revision), and by the bathos of its abrupt ending.

Part II of Scott's narrative opened in 1774 with an episode that pricked his conscience over the extent of his pastoral neglect. Two of his parishioners were dying and he had not bothered to visit them, yet he learned that Newton had, unsolicited, called on them several times. Scott resolved to do better. But his guilt was reinforced by reading Gilbert Burnet, whose posthumous conclusion to his *History of His Own Time* (1734) included a vigorous charge to the clergy to renounce all worldly ambition and live up to their high spiritual calling. Scott noted that Newton's example and Burnet's exhortation together 'increased the clamorous remonstrances of my conscience'.[56]

Burnet's *History* was the first of twenty-three books that Scott discussed in this middle and central part of his autobiography. Indeed, his narrative amounts almost to a bibliographic essay. Typically, Scott described how he met with a certain author, quoting or summarizing significant passages from the works concerned, and then explaining the influence on his own theological views.

First, however, Scott told how, with an overweening confidence in his intellectual capacities, he was eager during the first years of his curacy to provoke a dispute with one of the many local Calvinists. Newton became his target. After establishing some familiarity, Scott sought to draw him into an epistolary controversy. The correspondence lasted from May to December 1775, and Scott tried on every occasion to provoke, but Newton would not be drawn. Newton vexed Scott by treating him as a sincere enquirer and addressing each of his questions as a matter of earnest spiritual concern, rather than theological debate.[57] He acted more the part of a spiritual director than an intellectual combatant.

---

[55] Ibid. 14–15.   [56] Ibid. 27.
[57] Newton's side of the correspondence is preserved in his *Works*, i. 521–80.

Then, when an opportunity for preferment came Scott's way, he felt scruples over subscription, though he had carelessly subscribed twice before. But now his conscience would not allow it. When Scott was accosted by his friends with arguments to persuade him that he could and should subscribe, he dug in deeper. He dedicated himself to a disciplined intellectual investigation: to reject human authority altogether and to compare the offending Articles and Creed directly with the Scriptures. The passages of Scripture he encountered, however, all seemed to challenge his intellectual confidence; all seemed to demand an attitude of prayer, obedience, and humble dependence upon God as a prerequisite for knowing the truth. He therefore began to pray for right understanding. Scott's wide reading of Anglican pastoralia also made him painfully aware of the seriousness of his responsibility for the souls of his parish. This, he claimed, 'laid the foundation of all my subsequent conduct' and of his change in sentiments.[58]

Then began Scott's bibliographic slalom course. A book of evidential apologetics opened his mind and heart to the possibility that the gospel was a matter of divine revelation, and he began to reconsider the nature of the atonement. Samuel Clarke's *Scriptural Doctrine of the Trinity* (1712) lifted him one step back up the slippery slope he had earlier descended, as he now abandoned Socinianism for Arianism. William Law's *Serious Call* (1728) raised his ideal of holiness and persuaded him to make his own devotions more 'fervent and pertinent'. This prepared Scott for Richard Hooker's *Discourse of Justification* (1612), which convinced him that human obedience was inevitably flawed and that divine mercy was necessary in everything. Hooker's impeccable Anglican credentials also helped Scott to get over his remaining obstacles and eventually to accept the doctrine of justification by faith alone, in its entirety. After reading the Book of Homilies, he was astonished to find that 'that doctrine, which hitherto I had despised as novel, and methodistical, was the standard doctrine of the established church when that book was composed'.[59]

Throughout Scott's narrative there was this twin focus on conscience and theology, and conscience was always intimately related to his pastoral vocation. Now again, as he began to preach a stricter concept of the law, he found himself confronted by anxious enquirers, to whom he knew little what to say except to advise them to pray and study the Scriptures as he was doing. The pastoral context of Scott's doctrinal enquiries added an urgency to his deliberations.

Scott had a few more rungs to climb back to confessional orthodoxy, however. The doctrine of original sin he embraced after thinking over the third chapter of St John. Then, his esteem for Newton growing, he noticed the difference in their sentiments about the Trinity. Scott began to fear that

[58] Scott, *Force of Truth*, 57.   [59] Ibid. 88.

the weight of Christian tradition was against him, and after prayer and a fresh study of the relevant texts of Scripture, he acceded to a full Trinitarian position. In the end, he was convinced by the ancient argument that salvation by its very nature required a divine Saviour and Sanctifier. Finally, Scott read and reread James Hervey's popular *Theron and Aspasio* (1755), praying over passages he found hard to accept, but then accepting Hervey's presentation of imputed righteousness.[60]

In the conclusion of Part II, Scott described his acceptance of predestinarian ideas. Again, pastoral concerns were closely connected to intellectual deliberations, since Scott found himself with anxious and doubting enquirers for whom he had no comfort or counsel to give. Herman Witsius's *Oeconomy of the Covenants* showed him how the doctrine of election could be used to encourage people in this very situation.[61] Having before considered the doctrine pernicious, Scott now came to believe that it was a mystery, not to be plumbed by metaphysical argument, but to be accepted as a clear teaching of Scripture, universally maintained in the constitutional documents of the Reformation churches. By about Christmas 1777, Scott acknowledged that his system was incomplete without election, since once original sin was granted, and one believed that there was no possibility of initiative on the part of the sinner, then salvation had to begin with the initiative of God, who by his eternal nature did all things in accordance with his omniscience. Scott immediately began to use this doctrine in counselling distressed believers. The outline of Scott's system of doctrine was now complete.[62]

Part III of Scott's book defended his narrative to readers whom he supposed as hostile as he might once have been. He argued for the case that he was the most unlikely of converts. He claimed, moreover, that his conversion was contrary to his financial and social interests, was gradual and uninfluenced by

[60] On Hervey's *Theron and Aspasio* as an apologetic for evangelicalism, very different from Scott's, but likewise addressed to the intellectual elite, see Isabel Rivers, 'Shaftesburian Enthusiasm and the Evangelical Revival', in Jane Garnett and Colin Matthew (eds.), *Revival and Religion since 1700* (1993), 36–9.

[61] Witsius, whose work on the covenants was translated into English in 1763, was held in high regard by Newton as well. Newton, *Works*, v. 85.

[62] As a polemic for Calvinism, it may be significant Scott used the phrase 'Force of Truth' as a title for his book, since this phrase comes up in the famous (if doubtful) story that Petrus Bertius told of Arminius's first momentary conversion away from the high Calvinism of Beza in 1591: 'But while he [Arminius] was contriving a proper refutation, and had begun accurately to weigh the arguments on both sides, and to compare different passages of scripture together . . . he was conquered by the force of truth, and, at first, became a convert to the very opinions which he had been requested to combat and refute': 'Funeral Oration', *Works of James Arminius* (1825), i. 30; cf. Carl Bangs, *Arminius* (Nashville, 1971), 138–41. Arminius's life had been reprinted in the first number of Wesley's *Arminian Magazine* in 1778, the year just prior to the publication of Scott's narrative.

others, was based on reading authors of the highest reputation in the Established Church, and, above all, was stimulated by patient attention to prayer and the Scriptures.[63] He concluded by defending himself against the charge of 'enthusiasm', urging his critics to examine his case with candour.

The structure of Scott's autobiography is paramount, since its division between Parts I and II expressed the distinction, observed already in Newton, between nature and grace, law and gospel. Yet unlike Newton's account, which was grounded in scriptural typology, Scott's narrative was the story of 'how my mind changed' and was almost wholly devoid of remarkable incident. And unlike Cowper, Scott rehearsed the history of his mind as a seat of intellectual reasoning, not as a matrix of complex psychological motives. He was concerned chiefly with those factors that related to a determined theological method, not with the range of influences that derived from predisposing conditions. His account, like those of more liberal divines in the wake of the Feathers Tavern Petition, was therefore predicated in large part on his own intellectual virtue and theological disinterestedness.

Observed thus against contemporary apologetic literature, Scott's autobiography can be seen to share with many heterodox writers this element of rational self-vindication. But there is an important difference. Scott set out with an unshakeable confidence in his reason, before which he set an array of evidence to be weighed and evaluated, but his reason was gradually chastened by what it discovered. Aided by the Scriptures, he found that it was unreasonable to trust in corrupted reason, and he turned to prayer and the other 'means of grace'. In the end, he found that truth was not the abstract conclusion of a chain of ratiocination, but a personal God who stood self-revealed in the terrors of the law and the consolations of the gospel, and who by his Spirit quickened the conscience, engendered faith, and revivified the soul.

REASON AND UNREASON: GENRE AND PERSONALITY

After conversion, all three of these autobiographers reread their life histories in terms of Calvinism, as each author rehearsed the ways in which God

---

[63] Scott's experience was not unique. The anonymous, *Brief Memoir of the late Revd Wm Richardson* (1822), 10–11, quotes from a MS by Richardson: 'Truth forced itself upon me against my will, and I yielded to it with a very bad grace; for well I foresaw the consequences of adopting such a scheme of religion . . . I will not treat this subject at large. It will only be going over the same ground that is travelled in Scott's "Force of Truth", and the "Life of Mr. Milner" prefixed to his Sermons. When Mr. Scott's account of his religious experience came out, both Mr. Milner and I agreed that it would have suited us both, and that Mr. Scott might have presented his "Force of Truth" to either of us, and said: *"De te fabula narratur."'* Richardson's *Memoir* is prefixed to *Sermons by the Late Rev. William Richardson* (York, 1822), i. 1–71.

infallibly led him to saving faith. These autobiographies may be contrasted immediately, therefore, with those of Wesley's Methodists. For the followers of Wesley there was less of a sense of an invisible hand guiding them along a path, than of a series of agonistic crises where grace broke through after striving. In these Arminian autobiographies there was always the possibility of multiple peaks and valleys, particularly with the prospect after conversion of a further experience of instantaneous sanctifying grace, or, conversely, of the loss of grace altogether. The theology of the Olney autobiographers may be distinguished further by noting that in none of the three cases was their Calvinism of the 'high' variety of some of the Nonconformists from the region, who refrained from using moral suasion in preaching because of predestinarian convictions; nor was it 'moderate' in the way that some evangelicals would be moderate later in the century, regarding key distinctions in the doctrine of election as merely verbal. More theological than the latter, more pietistic than the former, Newton, Scott, and Cowper were strict but evangelical Calvinists.[64]

They did not stand in a long Calvinist tradition or understand themselves as exemplars of a covenant community or national heritage as was more typically the case in Scotland and New England. While they read federal theology, the concept of covenant was not the controlling idea of their own theology, and they rejected scholasticism as something 'now exploded as uncouth and obsolete'.[65] Rather than the covenant, it was the understanding of the Reformed order of salvation that gave structure to their narratives. They shared a common understanding of this *ordo*, which William Perkins had earlier called the 'golden chain' of predestination, calling, justification, sanctification, and glorification. In Newton's lecture notes at Olney, he commented on Rom. 8: 30: 'This verse contains the *golden chain* of salvation. The first and last link are in heaven, the two intermediate are let down upon earth,' and he proceeded to expound each link in a series of three lectures on this one verse alone. Thomas Scott likewise referred to the sequence in Rom. 8: 30 as 'this golden chain'.[66] This Reformed order of salvation was for them a kind of script by which they could interpret their

---

[64] In the language of their day, they believed in particular redemption but preached the free offer of the gospel. See e.g. Scott, *Theological Works*, ii. 569–630; Newton, *Works*, i. 162–71; iv. 184–97.

[65] Ibid. iv. 523.

[66] John Newton, 'Vol. 5. Lectures on Rom. ch. viii', MS notebook, no. 14, Cowper–Newton Museum, Olney (italics mine); Thomas Scott, *Commentary on the Holy Bible* (6th edn., 1823), iii. n.p. (comments on Rom. 8: 28–31). Cowper's theology can probably best be derived from the influence of Martin Madan as his chief source for evangelical theology up to *c*.1767. Madan's evangelical principles were similar to those of Newton and Cowper at this time. See Madan (ed.), *Treatise on Christian Faith*, and id., *A Scriptural Comment upon the Thirty-Nine Articles of the Church of England* (1772).

experience, comparing the empirical and temporal realities of life with the rational and eternal verities of theology.[67]

Likewise, they shared a doctrine of providence, whereby history was understood to be progressing in a straight line towards its intended goal under divine supervision. Within this providential order, they believed that God elected some to receive his mercy, and that he 'interposed' in the normal course of affairs to preserve these individuals for salvation and then to lead them towards repentance and faith. Their Calvinism thus provided a theoretical basis for spiritual biography. It provided a principle of selection in answer to the question of what was important in one's past life; and it offered a principle of arrangement in answer to the question of how one's story should be told and how the events related one to another. Calvinism was literary theory as well as a theological system.

The common pattern in each of these narratives was therefore very similar to the traditional morphology that derived from English Puritanism, such as was evident in John Bunyan's autobiography. The subject progressed from childhood religious impressions to adolescent anxiety about sin and damnation, and then there followed a degeneration into worldliness and a state of hardness of heart. Each author went on to relate the spiritually corrosive influence of Deist ideas and his ignorance of the leading themes of the gospel. As so often in all these narratives, conscience was painfully awakened as each was made aware of the unattainable ideal represented in God's moral law, but at first it was only a 'legal repentance' that followed—an attempt at personal reformation in one's own strength. Then followed a crisis of moral and spiritual insufficiency, the pivot upon which each conversion narrative turned. Each author came to learn that the gospel held forth a promise of God's gracious and complete forgiveness, but the personal hope awakened thereby was deferred. After a period of waiting, in which each one's helplessness was made plain, each made an 'evangelical repentance', renouncing self-sufficiency and casting himself on the mercy of God in Christ's atonement. Psychological relief accompanied this experience, and the subject bore witness to a transformed perspective on all of life, credited to having been inwardly regenerated by the Spirit of God. The narratives projected into the future the expectation that each would become slowly a more moral and spiritual person, dedicated to Christian service, and settled upon a trajectory that would climax (it may be supposed) in a pious death.

Despite this common pattern, the creative aspect of the evangelical autobiographer's task was hermeneutical: to read this pattern in the details of past experience, both inward and outward; to discern, as Newton put it,

---

[67] On Newton's Calvinism in particular, see further, Hindmarsh, *John Newton*, 49–82, 119–68.

how 'providence and grace concur'. In many of the examples of spiritual autobiography we have examined the subject gives very little sense of time and place, and the narrative is almost wholly spiritual. In others, for various reasons, there is very little sense of the unique personality of the writer. This was not the case for the three autobiographers examined here. Notwithstanding the common elements of their spiritual experience, they stand out from the page as vivid individuals. By reading their life-histories against this traditional morphology of conversion, each of these three autobiographers distinguished themselves as unique. As Linda Peterson observes, 'To write an autobiography, one must in some way violate the generic tradition or deviate from it and, in so doing, discover the self.'[68] In the autobiographies considered here, the authors established their own uniqueness—'discovered the self', as Peterson puts it—by developing the tradition of spiritual autobiography in novel ways.

Newton's method of interpretation was the most traditional, using biblical typology like his Puritan forebears as a way of incorporating his experience into a unitary pattern of salvation history. In contrast, Scott interpreted his life not typologically, but intellectually. The history of the workings of a mind and conscience, his autobiography portrayed him as the defeated party in a theological debate, forced by the weight of rational argument to yield to evangelical doctrine. While Cowper's autobiography included some of these elements of typology and intellectual dialectic, his story was above all the drama of his descent into and recovery from insanity by the extraordinary workings of providence.

Of the three, Cowper's narrative possessed the least conviction and interpretative control. While he sought like these others to announce to the world his conversion, and to proclaim his new evangelical self-perception, a nervous quality in his narrative undermines this profession.[69] Yet perhaps this is an easily wrought judgement, since we are inevitably aware, as he was not, that his religious terrors were only in remission at the conclusion of his autobiography. His evangelical friends continued to believe, even when he could not, that the person described in his narrative was his truest self.[70]

---

[68] Linda Peterson, 'Newman's *Apologia* and English Spiritual Autobiography', *Proceedings of the Modern Languages Association* 100 (1985), 304.

[69] After quoting one of Cowper's letters to Mrs Madan in the late 1760s, Morris Golden writes similarly, 'Perhaps I read this sort of letter (typical of his correspondence of this time) too subjectively, but it seems to me uneasy, unsure at bottom while it pretends to certainty.' Morris Golden, *In Search of Stability* (New York, 1960), 24. King, *William Cowper*, 81, concurs, but notes that Cowper achieves a greater confidence and narrative control in his account of his brother's death, *Adelphi*, which he appends to his own spiritual autobiography.

[70] This is a point that has been overlooked by several critics who have commented on Cowper's melancholy. Cowper's evangelical friends did not at all share his deranged

We might think of these three autobiographies as a triptych. It appears that Newton's story best fits the central panel, picking up as it does traditional Bunyanesque themes of spiritual autobiography, and setting these in eighteenth-century dress. In his autobiography the common pattern identified in Ch. 1 stands out most clearly. Scott and Cowper, occupying the panels on either side, provide the extremes that focus the attention back upon the centre. They are like foils or reverse images of each other, representing either side of that celebrated eighteenth-century dichotomy between reason and unreason. The first impression of the one is of swaggering intellectual confidence entering the lists against ignorance and folly; the first impression of the other is of a rapid descent into a psychological disarray. Yet these images are themselves transcended in the narratives. Upon closer examination, unreason becomes a kind of reason, as for Cowper sin is itself revealed as the one cosmic surd, and as the cosmopolitan culture of wit and refinement is found to be spiritually irrational. Likewise, reason becomes a kind of unreason, as for Scott rationalism is itself chastened by the truth. Each of the narratives folds back in upon the same theological ideas (cf. 1 Cor. 1: 18–31). Newton in the belly of the ship, Scott on the field of intellectual combat, and Cowper in the labyrinth—each testified to an inwardly sensible, gracious, and transforming encounter with the crucified Christ. And if we take their professions at face value, they sought through the medium of self-recollection to write more about the surprising graciousness of God than about themselves. This was what provided the unity in the diversity. For all their differences, Newton could still say to Cowper, 'Your case likewise has been pretty much like my own.'[71] We are able, therefore, in these autobiographies to hear distinctive changes rung on a still recognizable theme of evangelical conversion. The typological, intellectual, and psychological interpretations of the Olney autobiographers were, in the end, unique expressions of personal adherence to a common gospel.

conviction that he was 'damned below Judas'. There is some real pathos in Newton's comments to Cowper in 1780: 'How strange that your judgement should be so clouded in one point only, and that a point so obvious and strikingly clear to every body who knows you! . . . Though your comforts have been so long suspended, I know not that I ever saw you for a single day since your calamity came upon you, in which I could not perceive as clear and satisfactory evidence, that the grace of God was with you, as I could in your brighter and happier times' (Newton, *Works*, vi. 162); cf. the editorial comments of Madan (ed.), *Treatise on Christian Faith*, 39 n., drawing attention to the way accidental hindrances may obscure one's knowledge of one's faith, and yet not affect the safety of one's state.

[71] Newton, *Works*, vi. 152.

9

The Seventeenth Century Reprised: Conversion Narrative and the Gathered Church

As we observed in the first chapter of this book, it was in the mid-seventeenth century that autobiographical accounts of religious conversion became popular in England, and these narratives appeared first among the believers' churches in England and in New England. In this context it soon became a common practice to require prospective church members to make not only a public profession of orthodox belief, but also a declaration of the work of God upon their souls, giving evidence of their experience of saving grace as a prerequisite for admission to membership. This practice continued among many Dissenters after the Restoration and through the vicissitudes of political change in the late seventeenth century and into the eighteenth century, just as it continued among many later generations of New England Congregationalists. The resurgence of oral and written accounts of conversion during the Evangelical Revival took place for the most part outside this congregationalist polity, among evangelical Anglicans and Methodists. Yet the original occasion for conversion narrative continued in the eighteenth century among the direct lineal descendants of the Commonwealth sects. This chapter examines the narratives of some of these evangelical Dissenters, whose experience looked back to the seventeenth century while still resembling in other respects the experience of evangelical conversion among their contemporaries in other churches. In this context, however, conversion did not involve changing one's religious affiliation or entering into a new community; rather, it involved entering more deeply and personally into the community in which one was raised.

The Persistence of Conversion Narrative in the Gathered Church Tradition

In the late seventeenth century the Baptist minister Benjamin Keach described the ideal practice of a gathered church, laying it down that 'every Person before they are admitted Members . . . must declare to the Church (or to such with the Pastor, that they shall appoint) what God hath done for their Souls, or their Experiences of a Saving work of Grace upon their

Hearts'.[1] There is evidence in the church books of the Independents and the Baptists that this practice continued in the eighteenth century. For example, at the Baptist Church at Southill, near Bedford, the church book repeatedly recorded that candidates 'give in their experience' before being received into church fellowship.[2] The Blunham Baptist Church began in 1724 as a daughter church of Bunyan Meeting, Bedford, and right from the start they, too, recorded in their church book that this or that person 'was Joynd by Giving in theire Experaness'.[3] Such occasions were also recorded at Broadmead Baptist Church in Bristol and at Bury St Edmunds Independent Church in Suffolk.[4] In the church book at College Street Baptist Church in Northampton, where John Collett Ryland was pastor, a typical entry reads, 'At a Church Meeting Thursday Feb. 28 1760 Mr. William Cooper of the Drapery declared his Experience and his Consent to the Church Covenant, and was received into the Church with the Approbation of all the members.'[5] After a similar occasion a few months later, the church book recorded that 'several were deeply affected', or again, that there was a 'great melting of the church and auditory'. Some entries were a little fuller. On 13 April 1766, the entry declared, 'Mary Houghton Wife of Francis Houghton of Little Houghton—called and converted by Divine Grace about 2 years ago. The first occasion of her Conviction, was her seeing how Mary Whitney was filled with Horror on hearing some Farmers Servants curse and swear in a dreadful Manner in a Farmers Yard at their own Town.' Even John Cooke, who was deaf and dumb from birth, had to give a narrative of his spiritual experience, albeit through an interpreter, who began by explaining to the church in 1764, 'He came to me . . . and made me to understand he had a desire to be baptized . . .' The narrative continued for four pages in the church book at Northampton. Most entries were shorter than this, but they none the less recall the collections of similar experiences a century earlier by John Rogers, Henry Walker, and Thomas Shepard.

The church book of St Andrew's Street Baptist Church at Cambridge provides further evidence for this continued practice in the eighteenth century. Under the ministry of the ex-Methodist Robert Robinson, a man

---

[1] Benjamin Keach, *The Glory of a True Church and its Discipline Display'd. Wherein a True Gospel-Church is Described* (1697), 6.

[2] *Southill, Independent, later Baptist, Church: Church Book, 1693–1851*, transcribed for the Bedfordshire County Record Office (Bedford, 1981), 13–15 ff.

[3] *Blunham, The Old Meeting Baptist Church: Church Book, 1724–1891*, transcribed for the Bedfordshire County Record Office (Bedford, 1976), 2.

[4] Roger Hayden (ed.), *The Records of a Church of Christ in Bristol, 1640–1687* (Bristol, 1974); Michael R. Watts, *The Dissenters* (Oxford, 1978), i. 391.

[5] Church Book of Northampton College Street Baptist Church, 1733–81, bound MS, Northamptonshire Record Office, Northampton.

named Robert Silk was admitted as a member on 10 December 1761, and the whole procedure was described in detail:

R. Silk, having given notice of his design to the pastor, who had conversed with him in private, attended. The pastor stood at the head of the table; the deacons next him on each side, and the members in the table and adjoining pews: sitting. The pastor began by a short discourse . . . and closed by proposing R. Silk to them for a fellow citizen. Then he spent a few minutes in prayer. Silk, who stood at the bottom of the table-seat without, was asked to speak as in the presence of God the truth only.[6]

Thus warned of the seriousness of this occasion, Silk was told that faith and repentance were two prerequisites to church fellowship, and that he would be asked to speak and then would be questioned closely. 'The man then gave an account of his former profane life, and of his late change, declaring his faith in the gospel of Jesus Christ.' When finished, he was asked to step outside 'to give room for free debate'. The members discussed his life and character, and he was recalled and questioned further. It was decided that the pastor would enquire further into his character, and if there were no concerns, he would be baptized. So it transpired. At the next church meeting he was presented as a newly baptized candidate. 'The pastor asked whether the church was willing to receive him. They voted by holding up their hands.' Silk was approved and duly welcomed into full communion.[7]

The practice of requiring these sort of narratives certainly varied from church to church. The church book of the Blunham Baptist Church in Bedfordshire recorded a letter written in July 1741 to a sister church about twenty miles away at Ringstead, explaining why they could not transfer the membership of a woman named Mrs Wadkins, who had moved from the church at Ringstead to Blunham. Her husband Thomas had given an account of his experience and had been admitted as a member in January, but the letter complained that 'the Reason for Her not Joyning is because Her proud spirit would not submit to our order as a Church herein'. Her letter of dismission was in order, but that was not all that was required: 'We in the next place Intreat the person thus Joyning to give a plain faithful and impartiall account of the Dealing of God with their soul.' This was necessary for true spiritual fellowship and it was 'the Rule of the word which we Desire to walk by'.[8] No narrative, no admittance.

Only a few months before the Wadkins arrived at Blunham, Francis Okely's name appears in the church book. He was admitted as a member

---

[6] *Church Book: St Andrew's Street Baptist Church, Cambridge, 1720–1832*, transcribed by L. G. Champion for the Baptist Historical Society (n.p., 1991), 29.

[7] Ibid. 29–30.

[8] *Blunham Church Book*, 9–10.

and then commissioned for the work of the ministry. This was at the height of the early Evangelical Revival and Okely, who had been one of the so-called 'Cambridge Methodists', would join the Moravians within a few years.[9] His presence during these years at the Blunham Baptist Meeting is one indication that the culture of conversion preserved in Dissent was not entirely sealed off from the Evangelical Revival.

This practice of requiring narratives from candidates for admission to church membership helped to sustain traditions of narratable conversion among evangelical Dissenters, traditions that thus overlapped with the experience of contemporary Methodism, but that also looked back to seventeenth-century precedents. Just as conversion and revival were seen in Scotland and New England as in continuity with the past, so also these evangelical Dissenters in England experienced conversion within a long-standing tradition of faith and practice. Indeed, theological attention continued to fasten on the doctrine of conversion in this context, just as it had among the Puritans. For example, one of the most acute analyses of evangelical conversion in the century came from the pen of the Independent Philip Doddridge (1702–51), minister of the Castle Hill Church and tutor of a Dissenting academy in Northampton from 1730 until 1751. His eighth sermon in a series on regeneration was entitled, 'Of the various Methods of the Divine Operation in the Production of this saving change'.[10] His analysis of conversion in this sermon had its analogies both in the seventeenth century and in contemporary evangelical revival. Like Jonathan Edwards in his *Faithful Narrative*, Doddridge sought to delineate what was constant and what was variable in conversion, but in doing so he was guided, as was so often the case, by Richard Baxter's earlier reflections on conversion. His final peroration witnessed to a contemporary culture of conversion among Dissenters. He urged, 'Let Christians, in a prudent and humble manner, be ready to communicate their religious experiences to each other.' And he asked, 'Why may not intimate friends open their hearts to each other on such delightful topics? Why may not they who have met with any thing peculiar of this kind communicate it to their minister!'[11] The narrative culture thus extended beyond the practice of receiving oral relations from candidates for membership, or at least Doddridge expected that it would, as accounts of religious experience were exchanged in familiar conversation between intimate friends. But the practice of offering one's narrative to the church was still central. Doddridge did not lay down the

---

[9] John Walsh, 'The Cambridge Methodists', in Peter Brooks (ed.), *Christian Spirituality: Essays in Honour of Gordon Rupp* (1975), 251–83.

[10] Philip Doddridge, *Works*, ed. Edward Williams and Edward Parsons (Leeds, 1803), ii. 499–521.

[11] Ibid. 520.

practice as a law, as Keach did, but he argued prudentially for its importance and usefulness: 'And though I must in conscience declare against making it absolutely and universally a term of communion, yet I am well assured, that in some instances, a prudent and serious communication of those things to a christian society, when a person is to be admitted into fellowship with it, has often answered very valuable ends.'[12] The conversions related in this way by laypeople not only allowed pastors better to direct their people, but it also gave the pastors scope for further theological reflection, as it had for the ministers at Cambuslang. If truth be told, Doddridge confessed, 'It is by frequent conversations of this kind, that I have learnt many of the particulars on which I have grounded the preceding discourse.'[13]

In Doddridge's sermon and in most of the entries in the church books, it appears as though the lay practice of narrating religious experience was predominantly oral. There is evidence, however, that this passed over quickly into a manuscript culture of written narrative and, in due course, also into printed narrative. Written narratives were referred to in the church books as a concession to timid candidates, who trembled at the thought of having to speak before a large group—the fear of 'public speaking'. One expedient was for the candidate to speak privately to the pastor, and then allow the pastor to offer a précis of the account to the congregation. Frequently it was the women who were thus timid: 'Mrs [Hannah] Foster, having desired admission, and declaring that she had not courage to profess her faith and repentance in public before all the church, requested the pastor to repeat in public what she had said.'[14] This was in 1767 at St Andrew's Street Baptist Church at Cambridge. At Northampton the church book occasionally cross-referenced written documents. On 1 June 1770 Mary Pepper 'declared her experience' of the past eleven years: the death of her child, her many trials, and how she was finally set at liberty one year ago to the day. But it is uncertain whether she did this from her own mouth, since the church book recorded the postscript: 'See her written Experience.'[15]

John Ryland, jun., whose experience we will examine in detail below, succeeded his father in the ministry at Northampton and then moved to Bristol. There he found himself embroiled in a difficult dispute over 'written experiences' with the long-serving assistant pastor at the church, Henry Page. Ryland summarized their debate and made copies of their correspondence. The row began when a young man gave his experiences to

---

[12] Ibid.

[13] Ibid. 521.

[14] *Church Book: St Andrew's Street Baptist Church*, 40.

[15] Church Book of Northampton College Street Baptist Church. The church book also records the reception of Mary Churchill on 6 November 1760, when she declared her experience to the pastor and elders and deacons, and then 'by the Pastor's Mouth' to the congregation.

the church but found himself very embarrassed. Someone suggested it might have been better if he had written down the account of his conversion. Page disagreed strongly with this suggestion. A year and a half later, Ryland found a woman named Mary Ann Tozer in his study saying she really would not be able to speak before a vestry full of people. Ryland took up her cause and wrote to Page. Ryland acknowledged that some people had prejudices against written experiences just as they had prejudices against sermons preached from a prepared text rather than extempore. But Ryland pointed to the justice of the complaint often heard against their churches—namely, that they were too strict in this matter, 'requiring every timid female to speak out before a large company, and rejecting the fullest confession of faith in writing'.[16] Suppressing this prejudice, said Ryland, was one of the most important causes he had taken up at Bristol next to the suppression of false Calvinism. The issue evidently touched him in a tender place, since his own daughter was making herself ill by worrying about this exact ordeal.

As their epistolary dispute continued, Page and Ryland rehearsed the issues at stake in accepting written versus oral narratives. Indeed, Page enumerated a number of objections. Written narratives were more liable to imposture and bore more witness to the state of the mind than the heart; they made it impossible to assess sincerity; they privileged the rich over the poor; they contradicted the Bible's admonition that confession was to be made 'by the mouth'; they would make it likely that the individual would never speak openly to anyone about religion; they were an excuse for avoiding a difficulty that should be borne with self-denial; they were inevitably less touching; they were, like preaching from notes, second best; and, finally, they unduly privileged the minister–candidate relationship, when this trust should properly be shared by the whole congregation. Ryland responded to each of the criticisms in turn, but the main point of his reply was that some people are ready talkers and some not, and spoken words may deceive as readily as written ones. Conversely a written account might be just as touching as a spoken one—more so, if the speaker simply mumbled inaudibly. Ryland complained of the 'pride of some of the inconsiderate poor' who supposed that what a timid person writes cannot have the unction of the Spirit. In saying this, he claimed to plead not for the rich but for the timid. Moreover, he added two further advantages that attended written accounts in particular. First, they left 'a very precious memorial'; second, they left a standing witness against those who fell away.

---

[16] John Ryland, jun., 'Respecting Written Experiences', autograph copy of correspondence between Ryland and Henry Page about 'written experiences' in 1816, included in the second of two volumes of bound MSS containing miscellaneous papers of John Ryland, jun., Bristol Baptist College; photocopy at the Northamptonshire Record Office, Northampton.

This correspondence provides an important contemporary analysis of the narrative culture of at least one of the gathered churches. First of all, it bears witness to how longstanding and conventional the practice was of requiring these narratives before the church. It also demonstrates, contrary to what one might expect, that recourse to written narrative was sometimes a movement towards privacy rather than publicity. The debate reveals something of a possible social division in the narrative culture of Ryland's church, with the poor favouring oral narratives and the rich, written ones. The distinction here between poor and rich presumably also distinguished levels of literacy. But additionally, this correspondence bears witness to the appearance of writing as a stage along the path towards the fixing or reifying of identity, a stage midway between the oral and the printed narrative. Written accounts had the advantages, said Ryland, of serving as a memorial for those who continued pious, and a lasting embarrassment for those who fell away; that is, they had a permanence different from merely oral discourse. But, most important of all, this debate points to the central place held by spiritual autobiography in the culture of evangelical Dissent generally. The 'suppression of false Calvinism', referred to by Ryland, was one of the most celebrated theological causes among Baptists in the eighteenth century, but for Ryland the practical issue concerning how narratives were presented to the church came a close second.[17] The debate itself, leaving aside the different positions advanced, was predicated on the unequivocal importance of narratable evangelical conversion for these churches.

Many of the members of such churches had been taught the ways of conversion from childhood. In the context of the believers' church, children had many years to anticipate their own conversion (and the need there would be to translate this into personal narrative), since this was an expected stage of their own spiritual development. As one theorist of the genre of autobiography puts it, 'Lives that at some point issue in autobiography are typically lives lived in anticipation of that fact, lived in consciousness of their own narratability.'[18] This general point needs to be emphasized in the case of the gathered churches, where conversion narrative was highlighted as a requirement for coming of age spiritually. For young people hearing these oral relations as they grew up, conversion narrative was therefore in a sense proleptic. The stories they heard anticipated their own. As a candidate

---

[17] Robert Hall, jun. corresponded with Ryland about Henry Page, and this correspondence indicates something of the trial Page represented for Ryland. In August 1816 Hall wished Ryland to be relieved of Page: 'I am really afraid it will shorten your life.' And a year later Hall wrote again, saying he was happy that Ryland was at last free of Page. Geoffrey F. Nuttall, 'Letters from Robert Hall to John Ryland, 1791–1824', *Baptist Quarterly*, 34 (1991), 129, 130.

[18] Geoffrey Galt Harpham, 'Conversion and the Language of Autobiography', in James Olney (ed.), *Studies in Autobiography* (New York, 1988), 42.

announced her conversion to the listening members of her church, there were usually children present who awaited their own conversion and who knew that they too would someday be called upon to turn their experience into autobiography. Two cases illustrate this pattern of spiritual formation within a believers' church tradition, a pattern very different (or at least more protracted) than the experience of the typical Methodist convert. Anne Dutton and John Ryland, jun. were both associated with Northampton, a centre of evangelical Dissent in the eighteenth century, and each came to conversion not in the midst of revival, such as at Cambuslang, but in the normal course of spiritual formation within their church communities.

The Prolific 'A.D.': Anne Dutton's Spiritual Autobiography and Other Writings

Anne Dutton (1692–1765) is a precocious example of someone who, reared in this gathered church tradition, learned to speak in her own voice and who emerged into print in the eighteenth century as a widely respected writer and editor. According to her tombstone she published twenty-five volumes of letters and thirty-eight tracts on religious subjects. However, because her works were almost all published anonymously or under the initials 'A.D.', she remains to this day a little-known figure, and this despite the fact that she provides an early, well-spoken example of women's religious autobiography.

Although Dutton had published earlier works that were in large measure autobiographical, she began publishing a more extensive spiritual autobiography in the midst of the early years of the Evangelical Revival. The same year that Joseph Humphrey's hymn on 'The Progress of the Gospel in Various Parts of the World' was published, Dutton published her own *Brief Account of the Gracious Dealings of God, with a Poor, Sinful, Unworthy Creature* (1743).[19] By 1750 this would be expanded into a three-part work, with a large appendix to bring the narrative up to the present, and she included also a reprint of her *Letter... about the Lawfulness of Printing Any Thing Written by a Woman.* Her career as a writer began just as the Evangelical Revival was in its infancy, and by the end the 1740s she could list more than thirty publications to her credit, including personal narrative, poetry, spiritual letters, theological tracts, and controversial pieces. Whitefield was a favourite correspondent, and he urged her to continue especially with her letters. She also entered the Free Grace controversy with Wesley,

---

[19] Dutton recorded her spiritual autobiography in outline, particularly with respect to her establishment in full assurance of faith, in her earlier 'Brief Account How the Author was Brought into Gospel-Liberty', appended to her book, *A Discourse upon Walking with God* (1735), 158–69.

vindicating Calvinism in one open letter to him and opposing his doctrine of perfection in another. Thus, by the 1740s she was a leading figure among evangelical Dissenters whose public ministry extended beyond these bounds to include significant interaction with Methodism and other forms of evangelical faith and practice in the period. By 1743 her books were also being distributed in the American colonies.

Her autobiography helps to explain how she made the transition from private religious experience to public religious expression, and in this, conversion was central. In part one of her *Brief Account*, Dutton described Northampton as 'the Place of my *first*, and also of my *second* Birth'.[20] Although she does not tell us whether or not she gave an oral narrative of her conversion when at 15 years of age she joined the Independent Church at Castle Hill in Northampton, she was clearly raised within a religious culture that taught her the grammar of conversion prior to her own experience of it. She had 'the advantage of a religious education' from childhood, since her parents were earnest about this and faithfully brought her along to the Castle Hill meeting. 'From a Child' she read and memorized portions of the Bible and other devotional books—especially hymn books—and she prayed privately. 'From a Child' she also had a tender conscience and experienced both convictions and enlargement of soul. Above all, she knew well the way of salvation ('as it is alone by the Person, Blood, and Righteousness of Christ'). But the problem was that she had only 'Notions of these Things'.[21] She described herself as self-complacent and self-indulgent, at the same time a religious hypocrite and a vain young woman.

In the midst of this, she spoke of how God, having quickened her 'mystically', now quickened her 'influentially', or, again, that she was approaching the time of 'Love's Manifestation, not of Love's Beginning'.[22] This language is not only an introduction to her conversion narrative proper, but also an indication of the theological sophistication of her account and the high Calvinist perspective from which she was writing. As she told the story of her conversion she was simply recounting the temporal realization in her life of the eternal purposes of God in election. Her experience of conversion itself began at about 13 years of age, though she could not fix the exact time—and the reason she gave for this is a further indication of how encompassed she was by a culture that had already taught her what conversion was, for she claimed the time of her conversion was 'less discernible to me, by Reason of my being so frequently under Concern

---

[20] Anne Dutton, *A Brief Account of the Gracious Dealings of God, with a Poor, Sinful, Unworthy Creature* (1743), 1. 6. References to this work are by part and page number.

[21] Ibid. 1. 7.

[22] Ibid. 1. 8, 9.

of Soul before'.[23] As she gave the account of her conversion, there were
very few external references to her home life or her friends, and she offered
few anecdotes. Her story was a theological one, and the morphology of
conversion given four generations before by William Perkins provided a
close outline of her experience. She feared Hell but came to see the
spirituality of the law and to feel herself personally a damned sinner on
account of her own heart-sins. She understood the promises of salvation in
terms of general propositions but could not add the phrase 'for me'. She was
near despair and in this condition cast herself upon the mercy of God. In a
vivid picture she referred to herself as prostrate before the throne of God's
grace 'with a Rope about my Neck'.[24] Again, her language was both
theological and eloquent in its balanced periods: 'Out of the *Depths* of
Misery, I cry'd unto the *Depths* of Mercy.' Yet all of this work in her soul
thus far was preparatory, designed really to prise her away from self-
dependence. She learned to seek God in the means of grace, reading Scripture, hearing sermons, and so on, and by these means she was led to see
'such a ravishing Beauty, and transcendent Excellency in Christ', she says,
'that my Soul was ready to faint away with Desires after him'.[25] Notwithstanding this strikingly Edwardsian vision of the incandescent beauty of
Christ, still, she did not herself have an 'interest' in Christ. There are
indications in the midst of all this that she seemed to know what she was
experiencing—that she was now entering for herself into a long anticipated
and clearly outlined religious experience. For example, she offered this aside
about her convictions: 'I *dreaded* nothing more than that my Concern
should wear off, without saving Conversion to Christ.'[26] Or again, 'I
fear'd that what I felt should rise no higher than . . . *common Operations*.'[27]

A near-death illness proved the turning point. At one point her parents
were even led out of her room so that they would not need to see her in her
final demise. At this extremity, her desperation intensified her spiritual
quest: 'Like a Man Drowning, I catch'd at every Twig; I labour'd to take
hold of the Promises, to keep me from sinking.'[28] Finally, the breakthrough
came as she was able to take hold of a promise in John 6: 37 that often
recurred as a note of encouragement in Calvinist autobiography: 'Him that
cometh unto me, I will in no Wise cast out.' Something about this promise
on this occasion enabled her to believe, as she said, 'for myself', and as her
faith grew so also her body recovered. Religious duties became a delight to

---

[23] Dutton, *Brief Account*, 1. 9.
[24] Ibid. 1. 16.
[25] Ibid. 1. 19.
[26] Ibid. 1. 23.
[27] Ibid. 1. 24.
[28] Ibid. 1. 28.

her and she described her simultaneous vision of her own wretchedness and of Christ crucified in terms of exquisite compunction and joy mixed with mourning. This also introduced in her narrative a theme of bridal union, since she referred to this as 'the Time of my Espousals'.

As one would expect, given her high Calvinist milieu, her experience was tested by doubts and by the withdrawal of sensible communion with God. Picking up on the language in 1 Pet. 2: 1 of Christians as newborn babies who ought to crave pure spiritual milk, she referred to herself as being often laid to 'the Promise-Breast' where her faith revived.[29] After a year or more of this, her faith was more established and she learned the '*Strength of Faith* in the Dark'.[30]

Having thus narrated her childhood religious formation and her conversion, she continued by recounting the establishment of her faith. This commenced in about 1707 with her reception into church membership at Castle Hill at 15 years of age. Gradually, she was led to a more settled assurance by developing a more theocentric spirituality, looking less and less to her own past experiences or to self-examination or to religious feelings ('frames'), but rather making 'fresh acts of faith'. 'Being in some measure inured to a Life of Faith, I hasted away to Christ upon the first Assault. And have often found, that a *direct Act of Faith*, or a fresh Venture on Christ, has been attended with a *reflex Act*, or a full Persuasion of my eternal Safety in him.'[31] So with every new 'Soul-plunge' she sought to look directly to Christ. Her faith thus established, she experienced a return of ecstatic joy, 'a rich Overplus of spiritual *Sense*'.[32] She concluded this first part of her autobiography with applications to different sorts of readers in a variety of spiritual conditions, much as a preacher would wrap up a sermon with pointed application. Dutton had learned not only to read her life like a text, but to use it like a text to preach a gospel message. She entered the rhetoric of conversion as a child, owned it and experienced it for herself, and then she offered it up as an exemplary life for others. Conversion was the axis upon which her life turned not only from sin to grace, but also from private experience to public expression and indeed public advocacy.

Anne Dutton's autobiography thus began with an account of an adolescent conversion within a tightly knit community of faith. This was the way in which she came of age spiritually. The second and third instalments of her autobiography, with the appendix, continued her story. The theme of part

---

[29] Ibid. 1. 39, cf. 1. 42, where she says, 'I was often laid to the Breasts of Consolation, and being fed with the Milk of the Word . . . I grew thereby.' This is also her language in 2. 23, when, having returned to John Skepp's ministry in London, she was again 'laid to *Sion's Breasts*, and *milk'd out*'.

[30] Ibid. 1. 41.

[31] Ibid. 1. 46.

[32] Ibid. 1. 52.

two was providence, and particularly the way in which divine providence led her through a train of experiences that tested and deepened her faith and prepared her for public usefulness: 'how my Lord *prepar'd* me for his Service'. If this was a biography of a preacher, we would say that this was an account of her call to the ministry. Indeed, she described this period as that in which God 'call'd me to *feed his Lambs*' and '*extended* my Usefulness to *many* at a great Distance, by Writing, and Printing'.[33] As is the case in many women's autobiographies, her account was structured around the men in her life, as she recounted the various moves that she was called to make from one location to another due to her first and second marriages and her husband's work in each case, and how these moves helped or hindered her from enjoying the benefits of a good church. Her attachment to various ministers was intense and her narrative was organized in part around her passion for being under this or that gospel minister, and the enormous anxiety about parting from ministers whom she loved. There were four key figures in her life: John Hunt at Castle Hill in Northampton and the Baptists John Moore at The Watering Place (later College Lane) in Northampton, John Skepp in London, and William Grant at Wellingborough (West End).

When Dutton referred mildly to finding herself not edified after a time under Hunt and not agreeing with his judgement on various points, and when she explained that in contrast the doctrines of the gospel were 'clearly-stated' under John Moore, she was glossing a major controversy among the Congregationalist and Baptist churches of the period over high Calvinism ('Crispianism') and strictness of polity. The evangelistic rambles of the high Calvinist Richard Davis had led to rival churches in many places, and Dutton was one of several members of the Castle Hill meeting who were 'Rent Offe' to Mr Moore.[34] Thus the story of Anne Dutton's spiritual formation in the second part of her book was also an account of her theological transition into high Calvinism and more strict views of Baptist church order. She herself would contribute significantly to sustaining this high Calvinist tradition in many of the Baptist churches in the middle third of the eighteenth century.[35]

And yet the spiritual theme of this second part of her autobiography was in many ways the same as the first: her struggle to yield herself utterly to God's will in all things. Her alternating experience of consolation and desolation was expressed in intimate terms. When she enjoyed communion with God, she could say, 'But Oh, what Soul-ravishing Pleasures I then felt

---

[33] Dutton, *Brief Account*, 1. 162–3.

[34] Geoffrey F. Nuttall, 'Northamptonshire and *The Modern Question*: A Turning-Point in Eighteenth-Century Dissent', *Journal of Theological Studies*, NS 16 (1965), 105.

[35] Ibid. 119 n.

in Communion with *God* in *Love*! My Soul was as it were sensibly *clasp'd* in the sweet Embrace of Father, Son and Spirit!'[36] She was 'pained with Love-Desires' and languished in 'Love-sickness'. As with some of the Moravians, this strong language, and the spousal imagery that recurred in Dutton's use of the language of love in the Song of Solomon, made her often sound like Catherine of Siena, Mechthild of Magdeburg, or Julian of Norwich. Like Julian, she was also bold to think of God in maternal imagery. Remembering what a tender mother she had, and how her mother would pity her in times of illness, she recalled Isa. 49: 15 ('Can a Woman forget her sucking Child?') and 'was brought, in a Moment, into the *Bosom of* GOD'.[37] All along, she felt that God was making promises to her, and that God was speaking to her and applying passages of the Bible directly to her situation. In her use of Scripture, there was less rational application than there was loving intuition or *sensus allegoricus*. Her intimations and sense of special providences would no doubt have appeared naive or self-interested to some of her readers, and at points she seemed to regard herself as a favourite of heaven, but throughout there was a genuine vein of heightened spirituality that uniquely drew together her experience as a woman and her sophisticated appreciation of high Calvinism. If Catherine of Siena was a Third Order Dominican, then Anne Dutton must be reckoned something of a Third Order Baptist mystic.

And like many saints before (male or female), she was ambitious, notwithstanding her efforts to chasten this ambition and to spiritualize it. She wanted to exercise her gifts publicly. From all her trials and from her sense of God's leading, she was encouraged to think 'that the Lord had some Work for *me* to do; and that he would graciously *use* me for the Good of this People'.[38] By the end of this second and transitional part of her autobiography, she was settled at Great Gransden, and her writing was about to take off. The last part of the book (with the appendix) was a mixed genre of bibliographic essay and spiritual diary as she traced the spiritual history of each book she wrote and published. Again the theme was of resignation as in prayer she yielded to God her desires to publish or not publish in each case, and as to her delight her works found a larger and larger audience. This last part of her autobiography also made it clear that there was an element of apologia in her narrative, since she had received her share of censure on various occasions. Thus by providing the spiritual genealogy of her books, she was also defending her call to write.

---

[36] Dutton, *Brief Account*, 2. 25.

[37] Ibid. Dutton also used the image of a mother to describe her own sense of her spiritual joys when they came after travail. The frame of her soul was like 'a fond, affectionate Mother' who hugs her dear child all the more for having travailed to bring it to birth (2. 89).

[38] Ibid. 2. 148.

Just as the lives of the early Methodist preachers shared a common pattern of conversion, call to ministry, and public usefulness, so also Anne Dutton's life had this structure. Reared in a conservative religious culture, she nevertheless found in evangelical conversion an expansive dynamic that led her step by step into a sphere where her considerable gifts, theological acumen, and deep spirituality became known and valued by a large audience. The final item appended to her narrative was a twelve-page open letter on the lawfulness of a woman appearing in print, and though it appears almost an afterthought, it is in some ways the climax of her autobiography. In this letter she made several sophisticated arguments for the importance of women's gifts being recognized and used in the church, but her crucial argument was the counter-intuitive assertion that writing and communicating with readers through books was actually a private rather than a public exercise: 'For tho' what is printed is published to the *World*, and the Instruction thereby given, is in this regard *Publick*, in that it is presented to every ones View: Yet it is *Private* with respect to the *Church*.' Because the books were not read aloud in the gathered assembly of the church, but read individually in private homes, well then, they were just as private as any conversation between friends. 'Imagine then, my dear Friends', she says, 'when my *Books* come to your *Houses*, that I am come to give you a *Visit*.'[39] Her publishing list represented nothing more than a run of tête-à-têtes.

We need not take her arguments as cynical or disingenuous, just as we would be hasty to dismiss her spirituality as petty providentialism. Rather, it seems that she found a way to negotiate conflicting demands and desires in her life in a creative way. She grew up into her faith and sought to experience it as her own. Hers was not a conversion *away* from her family of origin or her community of faith, but *into* it more deeply. She wanted to yield herself wholly to the will of God and expressed the Calvinist aesthetic of *soli Deo Gloria* with some poignancy, expressing this through her experience as a woman in eighteenth-century England. But she also had a drive for evangelical usefulness and felt the call of the gospel to mission. The same dynamic of evangelical conversion that impelled laymen to preach impelled her to write and publish. How could she both submit to God and the teaching of Holy Scripture as she understood it, and proclaim the gospel to the multitudes? She did so precisely by reflecting on the boundaries between public and private spheres, boundaries that were shifting in significant ways in the wider society during her lifetime. According to the analysis of Jürgen Habermas, it was in the early eighteenth century that developments in continuous long-distance trade and continuous periodical publication largely created the public sphere and altered conceptions of privacy and

---

[39] Dutton, *Brief Account*, Appendix, 11.

publicity.[40] Given some of these same developments, Philippe Ariès could point to developments in England and call it the birthplace of privacy.[41] That Anne Dutton saw her own books as public from one point of view and private from another would no doubt have pleased both Habermas and Ariès.

FATHER AND SON: JOHN COLLETT RYLAND (1723–92) AND JOHN RYLAND, JUN. (1753–1825)

The two John Rylands, senior and junior, provide further insight into conversion narrative within the gathered church tradition in the eighteenth century. John Ryland, jun. was a fourth-generation Baptist on his father's side. His father, John Collett Ryland, was a well-known Baptist minister who moved to Northampton in 1759 to become the pastor of the College Lane Baptist Church, where he would serve for twenty-seven years. Like Doddridge earlier, the elder Ryland was a preacher and educator whose influence was felt throughout the region. He ran a well-known boarding school for boys, while one of his church members, Martha Smith (later Martha Trinder), kept a school for girls. It was in Northampton that John Ryland, jun. spent his childhood and adolescence. A timid boy, he grew up in his father's home, his father's church, and his father's school, and he was probably overawed by what one friend of the family called his father's 'excess of vehemence'.[42] His spiritual and theological formation was certainly dominated by his father's example and beliefs.

What kind of a man then was John Ryland, sen., and what kind of spiritual influence did he exert in Northampton and within his own family?[43] And how did conversion and spiritual autobiography figure in his own formation? The elder Ryland was by all accounts a colourful and forceful personality. At 18 years of age he was converted along with forty others in a local revival in 1741 at Bourton-on-the-Water under the ministry of the

---

[40] Jürgen Habermas, *The Structural Transformation of the Public Sphere*, trans. Thomas Burger (Cambridge, Mass., 1991), 14–26.

[41] Philippe Ariès, Introduction to Philippe Ariès and Georges Duby (eds.), *A History of Private Life* (Cambridge, Mass., 1989), iii. 5.

[42] Cf. the observation of Robert Hall, jun., who contrasted the younger Ryland's 'extreme gentleness' with the elder Ryland's 'excess of vehemence' and 'careless intrepidity of temper'. Grant Gordon, 'John Ryland, Jr. (1753–1825)', in Michael A. G. Haykin (ed.), *The British Particular Baptists, 1638–1910* (Springfield, Mo., 2000), ii. 82–3.

[43] On John Collett Ryland, see John Rippon, *The Gentle Dismission of Saints from Earth to Heaven: A Sermon Occasioned by the Decease of the Rev. John Ryland, Senior, A.M.* (1792); George Redford and John Angell (eds.), *Autobiography of William Jay* (1854; repr. Edinburgh, 1974), 286–96; William Newman, *Rylandiana* (1835); James Culross, *The Three Rylands* (1897); H. Wheeler Robinson, 'A Baptist Student—John Collett Ryland', *Baptist Quarterly* 3 (1926), 25–33; Peter Naylor, 'John Collett Ryland (1723–1792),' in *British Particular Baptists*, i. 185–201.

Baptist pastor Benjamin Beddome. This year was the high point of the early Evangelical Revival, and this local revival added yet another cluster of conversions to those appearing at the same time elsewhere in Britain and America. At Beddome's urging Ryland went to Bristol to train for the Baptist ministry, and while there he went through a period of profound spiritual darkness that lasted for eighteen months. Like many of his Nonconformist forebears Ryland kept a confessional diary at Bourton and Bristol, and this diary bears witness to an introspective piety that recalls Richard Kilby and the Puritan examen of conscience. Already in 1743 he was lamenting his sins ('My heart is exceeding full of sin and darkness,' etc.), and he wrote, for example, 'Rose and prayed . . . but could not absolutely apply any of the promises to myself, though I thought I could not live without them. I found great darkness, and my heart as hard as an adamant.'[44] Again, in 1745, '*Inward man*, for the most part, very dark, weak and wicked . . . My affections very carnal and corrupt.'[45] In a letter in 1751 he referred to his experience during this period, saying,

I have known what it is to be under the hidings of the Lord's face . . . I had no liberty in one prayer I put up in all that time, and no comfort in any one sermon I heard; no heart nor freedom for spiritual converse, and my life a load and burthen. I could not for a quarter of an hour . . . call God my God and Father. I could not say Christ was mine, nor feel any love to him, for my heart was estranged from him. I felt none of the sweet influences of the Holy Spirit, nor could I tell whether he dwelt in my soul or no. And part of the time I had dreadful atheism and rebellion working in my heart.[46]

Something of his grit and determination can also be seen in the entries in his diary while a student, as he sought to settle sinewy questions about the existence of God, the immortality of the soul, and other weighty theological matters. His questions were deeply personal. The key entry was noted with precision and decisiveness. On 25 June 1744, at ten o'clock in the evening, when he was '20 years, 8 months, 2 days' old, he recorded his resolve: 'If there is ever a God in heaven or earth, I vow and protest in his strength . . . I'll find him out; and I'll know whether he loves or hates me; or I'll die and perish, soul and body, in the pursuit and search. Witness, John Collet Ryland.'[47]

And yet at the same time that he was thus absorbed in self-examination and despondency, he knew what it was to unburden his soul to a colleague. Returning with a friend in February 1745 from hearing a sermon, he

---

[44] Newman, *Rylandiana*, 29.

[45] Robinson, 'Baptist Student', 27.

[46] Newman, *Rylandiana*, 8.

[47] Rippon, *Gentle Dismission*, 41. Rippon comments that 'few of God's people have experienced more spiritual conflict than he' (ibid. 47).

recalled, 'When we were coming home he told me the 1st beginnings of God with his soul and so on till he came to the Ministry and I told him of my first impressions . . .'[48] In this setting of ingenuous friendship, spiritual autobiography arose spontaneously and artlessly.

While he thus kept a diary and spoke of his spiritual experience, much like other evangelicals at the time, he had no use for the Arminianism of the Wesleys. He heard Charles Wesley preach in 1745 in Bristol and remarked in his diary that Wesley had 'positively asserted falling from Grace, in the strongest terms'.[49] As prophylactic against Wesley's ideas Ryland meditated during the preaching, while going home, and even during supper, on a discourse on the final perseverance of the saints by the Puritan Elisha Cole. This seemed to get him back on the straight path. The following month he gave proof of his Calvinism, since as he walked about town his thoughts were not on the 'universal redemption' of Charles Wesley but on the wonder of his own election by grace. He wrote, 'I had such a sense of Distinguishing Goodness of God to me—above the 100ds & 1000s yt Walk about ye Streets.'[50] Divine election rested on only one among hundreds or thousands in Bristol in 1745.

Ryland's spiritual darkness passed in time and he took up his first pastorate at Warwick in 1746 and it was there he began his boarding school and was married. It was also at Warwick that John Ryland, jun. was born in 1753, the first of five children. But the elder Ryland is remembered chiefly for his work at Northampton. His preaching was, by all reports, powerful for the awakening and conversion of sinners, and the numbers bear this out. When he arrived in 1759 he gave an account of his spiritual experience to some thirty members at the College Lane Church, and thereafter the church book recorded steady growth month by month as new members were received under his ministry. The brief accounts in the church book of the narratives of these new members makes it clear that many were awakened and converted under Ryland's preaching.[51] By the time of his death in 1792, 323 members had been added.[52]

---

[48] Quoted in Roger Hayden, 'Evangelical Calvinism among Eighteenth-Century British Baptists with Particular Reference to Bernard Foskett, Hugh and Caleb Evans and the Bristol Baptist Academy, 1690–1791', Ph.D. thesis (Keele, 1991), 134–5.

[49] Robinson, 'Baptist Student', 29.

[50] Ibid. 32.

[51] For example, Reuben Archer, sen. was a gardener for the Ryland family who came to church at first only because he thought it might please his employer, but soon he found 'there was a difference between his preaching and what he had before been accustomed to', and he recalled one sermon in particular by which he was led to repentance. Church Book of Northampton College Street Baptist Church, 9 May 1766.

[52] John Taylor, *Early History of College Lane Chapel* (Northampton, 1870), 15.

This energetic preaching and significant church growth is all the more interesting when one realizes that John Ryland, sen. was a gruff high Calvinist. Theologically, he was a follower of the Calvinist divines John Gill (1697–1771), John Brine (1703–65), and Joseph Hussey (1660–1726)—high predestinarians all of them. John Brine preached for Ryland at his ordination; Ryland returned the compliment by writing an elegy for Brine on the occasion of his death.[53] It is certainly not difficult to locate Ryland theologically, since he located himself when he said that he wanted to be buried at Bunhill Fields among the three great Johns: John Owen, John Gill, and John Brine.[54] Even more specifically, he asked to be placed between John Brine and John Skepp. That is about as precise a theological placement as we could ask for. John Ryland, sen. clearly identified strongly with the high Calvinism then dominant in London among leading Particular Baptists, rather than with the evangelical Calvinism that was more typical of the Western Association centred on Bristol.[55]

This is not the place to rehearse the fine details of the high Calvinism that Ryland imbibed from these writers, but for the younger generation of Baptist leaders who would move away from this theology, including Ryland's own son, the key issue was the free offer of the gospel.[56] If Christ died only for the elect, could one properly offer the gospel to all people indiscriminately? Could one claim that it was the duty of all sinners to believe the gospel? High Calvinists believed that you could not make this claim or extend this offer. As Joseph Hussey put it, that would be 'a piece of robbery against the Holy Spirit'.[57] What did John Ryland, sen. believe? We have a clue in an incomplete manuscript he drafted for a theological dictionary, under his entry for 'gospel':

[53] John Collett Ryland, *An Elegy on the Death of J. Brine* (1765), which includes the line, 'That Saints were freely choose 'ere Time began'—an indication perhaps of Brine's doctrine of eternal justification.

[54] The younger generation would generally distinguish Owen from these others as a 'strict' Calvinist, rather than a 'high' Calvinist. See further, John Ryland, jun., *Life and Death of the Reverend Andrew Fuller* (1816), 566–7.

[55] Roger Hayden argues that historians have wrongly focused on London Baptists such as Skepp, Gill, and Brine, who in this period were not typical of Particular Baptist life and thought. His focus is rather upon the Western Association and the Broadmead Baptist Church at Bristol, with its academy under the leadership of successive ministers Bernard Foskett, Hugh Evans, and Caleb Evans. These leaders remained faithful to the classic confession of 1689; they encouraged a covenant theology centred in Christian experience and passed on by catechesis; and they developed hymnody, supported missions, and trained students for the Baptist ministry. Hayden, 'Evangelical Calvinism'.

[56] On the terminology used by the younger generation to distinguish different varieties of Calvinism, see further, John Ryland, jun., *Life and Death of Fuller*, 566–7, and Bruce Hindmarsh, *John Newton and the English Evangelical Tradition* (Oxford, 1996), 120–5.

[57] Raymond Brown, *The English Baptists of the Eighteenth Century* (1986), 72.

Gospel... The word *offer* is not so proper as declaration, proposal, or gift. The gospel is a *declaration* of the free grace of God. It is a *proposal* of salvation by Jesus Christ, and it proclaims Christ as the free and absolute *gift* of God.—See *Hussey's* 'Operations of Grace and no Offers,' &c.; *Brine's* Answer to *Albery [sic] Jackson*: see, likewise, his 'Motives to Love and Unity Among Calvinists.'[58]

Under this scheme a preacher would be theologically correct to say that the grace of God was proclaimed, declared, or given in Jesus Christ, but not to say to a mixed congregation that Christ died for them. It is all the more remarkable then that under such theological constraints the ministry of John Ryland, sen. was so fruitful. Moreover, his high Calvinism did not lead to narrow sectarianism. On the contrary, he was an open-communion Baptist, and it was a matter of serious conviction for him that those baptized only as infants and those as adult believers be welcomed alike to the communion table, and that mode and age of baptism ought not to be a bar to full membership in the church. He went to press over this issue and there are extensive notes about it in the church book.[59] His personal friendships bear out his spiritual candour and openness, for he was a close friend of the Anglican evangelicals James Hervey and John Newton, and on intimate terms with George Whitefield and Rowland Hill; he was well acquainted likewise with Congregationalists such as Philip Doddridge in his early years and William Jay in his later years.

He was clearly of an older generation, however. He did not like the idea of the Baptist Missionary Society that was formed the year he died.[60] He was famously reported to have rebuffed William Carey when the young pastor proposed that the conversion of the heathen be taken seriously.[61] And he could not understand why Robert Hall, jun., Andrew Fuller, and his son were so preoccupied with this modern question of whether faith was the duty of all or just the elect. For the younger men, this was a theological crux upon which evangelism and world mission depended. William Carey said to Andrew Fuller, 'If it be the duty of all men when the Gospel comes to believe unto salvation, then it is the duty of those who are entrusted with the Gospel to endeavour to make it known among all nations for the obedience of faith.'[62] John Ryland, sen. responded with characteristic drollery about it all, remarking, 'The devil threw out an empty barrel for them to roll about, while they ought to have been drinking the wine of the

---

[58] Quoted in Newman, *Rylandiana*, 50.

[59] Naylor, 'John Collett Ryland', 195–7.

[60] 'At the end of his life he had the reputation of being a gruff hyper-Calvinist who sought to quash the idea for a Baptist Missionary Society, prior to its formation in 1792.' Hayden, 'Evangelical Calvinism', 125.

[61] The episode has been contested. See Naylor, 'John Collett Ryland', 193–4, 201; Culross, *Three Rylands*, 60–1.

[62] Culross, *Three Rylands*, 79.

kingdom. That old dog, lying in the dark, has drawn off many good men to whip syllabub, and to sift quiddities, under pretence of zeal for the truth.'[63] Ironically, then, the senior Ryland thought that the young evangelical Calvinists (not the high Calvinists) were the ones who were drawn off from vital spiritual life by useless theological debate about nice points of doctrine. The standard historiography of the rise of the missionary movement is, of course, exactly the opposite of this.

John Collett Ryland was thus a complex figure and a study in contrasts. He was a headstrong high Calvinist whose diary was characterized by melancholy introspection and whose theology constrained the free offer of the gospel to all sinners. And yet he was a zealous evangelist whose church grew through conversion. In one of his sermons he noted that 'some high Calvinists neglect the unconverted; but Paul left no case untouched'. Then he turned to address his congregation directly, 'O sinners, beware! . . . If you are condemned, I'll look you in the face at judgement, and say, "Lord I told that man—I told those boys and girls, on the 29th of August 1790—I warned them—they would not believe—and now they stand shivering before thy bar!"'[64] One can only suppose that preaching such as this would increase the seriousness of the young people. It was under this enigmatic John Collett Ryland, with all his high Calvinism and his zeal for conversion, that his son came to maturity at Northampton.

THE ADOLESCENT CONVERSION EXPERIENCE OF JOHN RYLAND, JUN.

It would not be until his late teen years that John Ryland, jun. would begin to question his father's theology. As a young person, his father's world was his world. He was a precocious child and the story was often told of his reading Psalm 23 in Hebrew to James Hervey when only 5 years old. At the age of 11 he had read the book of Genesis in Hebrew five times through; the Greek New Testament he had read through before he was 9. He preached his first sermon to the church when he was 17. He was a son of the manse in every sense and must have felt both the privileges and the constraints of his position. By any measure his spiritual and intellectual development was advanced for his age.[65]

At the Angus Library at Regent's Park College, Oxford, there is a bound volume with an eclectic arrangement of six printed pamphlets and three

---

[63] Newman, *Rylandiana*, 78.

[64] Ibid. 74.

[65] For John Ryland, jun., see Jonathan Edwards Ryland (ed.), *Pastoral Memorials* (1826); Culross, *Three Rylands*; Nuttall, 'Letters from Robert Hall'; Grant Gordon, 'The Call of Dr John Ryland Jr', *Baptist Quarterly* 34 (1992): 214–17; L. G. Champion, 'The Letters of John Newton to John Ryland', *Baptist Quarterly* 27 (1977), 157–63; Gordon, 'John Ryland, Jr.'.

manuscripts. On the flyleaf of the volume is the name 'William Button' and the date 1768. The same name appears on two of the printed pamphlets. From the documents themselves and from other records of the boarding school, it is evident that William Button (1754–1821) was a schoolfellow of John Ryland, jun. at Northampton.[66] The first manuscript is entitled, 'The Experience of Jo/n R.l.d. jun^r as wrote by himself in a Letter to Thos R..t dated Feb^y: 1770'.[67] The correspondent was Thomas Rutt, another boy from the boarding school. The second manuscript is entitled, 'An Account of the Rise and Progress of the Two Society's at Mr. Rylands and at Mrs Trinder's Boarding School in Northampton, drawn up by Iohn Ryland, junr', and this was dated 1768 and 1770. The last manuscript was written on the verso of John Ryland's 'Experience' and is a handwritten copy of a letter with the title, 'An Acct of the Lord's dealings with Miss Elizabeth Rutt written by herself in a Letter to her Parents on the Occasion of her joining the Church, Apr. 5. 1770'.[68] Together, these manuscripts provide an unparalleled portrait of adolescent spirituality within a leading Baptist community in the 1760s and 1770s. By comparing these accounts with the church book and the list of boarders kept by John Ryland, sen., and also with the later memoirs of John Ryland, jun., we can arrive at a detailed picture of the spiritual lives of these young people, children who had grown up anticipating both conversion and spiritual testimony as stages in their own future spiritual development.

The church book at Northampton recorded John Ryland, jun.'s reception into the church and his baptism on 13 September 1767. Three days before, at the Friday church meeting, he 'came before the church' and there made a profession of faith and gave an account of the work of grace in his soul.[69] He was then 14½ years old. He did not, however, write the manuscript account of his conversion on this occasion. The occasion for this arose two and a half years later, when Thomas Rutt asked him for an account of his spiritual experience. Rutt had joined the boarding school in 1767 and about a year later he was awakened to spiritual concern through a talk that John Ryland, sen. gave to the boys, as was his custom, on a Saturday evening. It appears that Rutt was still experiencing some anxiety about the state of his soul, and for this reason wanted a written account of what John Ryland, jun. had himself experienced. Ryland's letter, containing

---

[66] See C. A. Markham, 'The Rev. John Collet [sic] Ryland's Scholars', *Northamptonshire Notes and Queries*, NS 1 (1926), 18–31.

[67] This document is transcribed in H. Wheeler Robinson, 'The Experience of John Ryland', *Baptist Quarterly*, NS 4 (1928–9), 17–26.

[68] Given the records of the College Lane church book, Elizabeth Rutt's narrative was probably written in 1771, not 1770.

[69] John Ryland, jun., 'Autograph Reminiscences', bound MS, 24 October 1807, Bristol Baptist College, Bristol, p. 29.

this account, was dated 23 February 1770. The church book recorded Thomas Rutt's reception into the church more than a year later on 12 April 1771. Thus, the occasion of Ryland's written autobiographical account was not, as we might expect, his own reception into church membership, but rather the personal request of a schoolfellow in spiritual distress.

In his letter to Rutt, however, Ryland referred to a confessional diary that he began to keep in December 1766, and he quoted from it and referred to it at various points. This diary was the contemporary autobiographical document in which Ryland conducted his own self-examination once he sensed that the work of grace had begun in his soul, and this diary was no doubt the source underlying his oral narrative to the church in 1767, his autobiographical letter to Rutt in 1770, and his much later manuscript memoir in 1807.[70] This latter manuscript (which drew on both the earlier diary and the letter) was also the basis for a posthumous memoir published by his son.[71] Thus John Ryland, jun. laid down a series of layers of autobiographical reflection as the years went by, one on top of the other, and his autobiographical practice illustrates well the different occasions (personal and public) and motives (hortatory, doxological, and didactic) that prompt someone generally to speak or write about his or her spiritual experience.

In his letter, John Ryland, jun. explained that his own convictions began when in September 1766 he was brushed off by another boarder who spoke vaguely on one occasion about having something more important to talk about with someone else. When Ryland persisted he discovered that there was a group of three boys who regularly went for a turn in the garden to discuss the spiritual condition of their souls. Two of these, William Button and John Ray, had been shaken by the death of one of the boarders; the third boy, Thomas Brewer, had been spiritually awakened (like Thomas Rutt later) by one of John Ryland, sen.'s Saturday evening talks.[72] These three were the nucleus of a religious society formed among the boys, at their own initiative, two months later. But the immediate effect for 13-year-old John Ryland, jun. was to cause him to wonder if these three boys were going to heaven and he was not. In his words, 'The Lord showed me what a Wretch I was. I was convinced that I was undone. I felt it. I knew it in a manner before . . . but now I knew it indeed and I endeavoured to pray for Mercy.'[73]

---

[70] This last document was a 57-page memoir written late in life chiefly for his own children.

[71] Jonathan Edwards Ryland, 'Memoir', *Pastoral Memorials*, i. 1–61.

[72] Thomas Brewer was the son of the well-known pastor, Samuel Brewer, who had one of the largest Dissenting congregations in London at his Independent meeting in Stepney; both William Button and John Ray would go on to become ministers of Dissenting churches.

[73] Robinson, 'Experience of John Ryland', 18.

From this beginning, Ryland recounted in detail the fluctuating state of his soul over the following two years. In outline, he described three episodes of strong convictions in the autumn of 1766, which wore off but were renewed before the end of the year. Then, on 12 December he was at a church meeting where three women gave an account of their spiritual experience and were received into membership. As they walked past the pew where he was sitting, he felt 'a very great Love to all the Lord's people and had a little hope', and 'an earnest desire to have my lot among them'.[74] Just as he had not wanted to be excluded from his religiously minded peers, neither did he want to be left out of the inner circle of God's people at church. His time had come. He wanted entry into what one preacher called 'a garden inclosed, a spring shut up, a fountain sealed'.[75] In December he had his first experience of a promise from Scripture striking home personally and affording spiritual comfort. After this he described more than a dozen alternating occurrences of doubt and comfort right up to his baptism and reception into church membership in 1767. The same pattern continued after his baptism until August 1768 when he was at last substantially freed from serious doubts about his spiritual state. Before closing his letter, he offered some thoughts to Rutt on the nature of assurance and the kind of problems that still persisted to trouble his soul.

It is clear that the intellectually precocious Ryland had inherited a vast theological grammar before he entered the experience of travail for himself. Indeed, he remarked, 'Those who know how I was educated cannot suppose but I had head knowledge of these things,' and in his later memoir he recalled his childhood thoughts about conversion, and wrote, 'I used to purpose an alteration sometime, and thought at times, that I would begin such a period, when it might be noticed by others, how much I was altered from that particular season ... But tho' I often had slight convictions of sin, nothing of an abiding nature affected my mind till nearly the close of my thirteenth year.'[76] Consequently, there was almost a sense of relief when he came to experience the onset of spiritual labour for himself, since he knew well enough that he would have to go through this experience if he was to be soundly converted and received among the people of God.

Once conviction for sin had begun in earnest, Ryland knew immediately where to go for reading material: 'I read Allens Alarm, Baxters Call, Bunyans Grace Abounding, &c.' Joseph Alleine's *Alarm to the Unconverted*,

---

[74] Ibid. 19; John Ryland, jun., 'Autograph Reminiscences,' quoting earlier diary for 12 December 1766, p. 20.

[75] The words come from a sermon (based on Song of Songs 4: 12) bound up with Ryland's manuscript: John Lloyd, *The Well-Spring of Life Opened in Christ* (1768), 17.

[76] Robinson, 'Experience of John Ryland', 18; John Ryland, jun., 'Autograph Reminiscences', 14–15.

Richard Baxter's *Call to the Unconverted*, John Bunyan's *Grace Abounding*—these were the classical works on conversion by late seventeenth-century Puritans, and he had them at his fingertips. (One only wonders what all was contained in Ryland's '&c.') No more complete Puritan catechesis in all the ways of conversion could be found than in these influential works. Moreover, the pamphlets (thirty to forty-five pages each) bound up with John Ryland, jun.'s manuscript letter were drawn from a similar stock, and their provenance, the inscription of William Button on two of the title pages, and the presence of heavy underlining, point to these as constituting devotional reading for the young scholars in Northampton. In fact, the first two works were extracts from Joseph Alleine, prepared by John Ryland, sen. himself as part of his larger juvenile publication programme and an extension of his work as a tutor. This was his 'Christian Library'.[77]

The distinctive language John Ryland, jun. used tells us much about the theology that first stimulated and then explained his experience. He began his letter, 'Almost a year before the time of my first Convictions...', and proceeded to give an account of these other boys whom he would encounter and who would be the occasion of his spiritual awakening. But those first words were heavy-laden with preconceptions: the work of grace began with convictions, and these were perceptible and could be pinpointed. He described specific episodes in which 'convictions grew stronger', how these 'convictions wore off', and how he later feared all these might be nothing but 'common convictions'. This concern about 'common convictions' introduced the vocabulary of doubt and fear in his narrative, but once he faintly perceived the beginning of spiritual comfort he ceased speaking about convictions and began speaking of doubt or darkness. 'O how distress'd was I', he wrote, or 'the Lord withdrew & I fell a doubting', or, 'after this I was sometimes Cold, sometimes doubting'.[78] This doubting of his spiritual comforts was normal for one raised as an orthodox Calvinist. Not only was he seeking to discern whether he was truly elect, but he was wary of the possibility of merely 'temporary faith', as discussed by Calvin, the notion that it was possible for someone to experience all the signs of apparent conversion only to prove in the end a false Christian. Hence, he worried his were merely 'common convictions' or 'false comforts'. He probed his own experience, 'fearing...I was a deluded Hypocrite', or

---

[77] The six pamphlets bound up with the MSS were John Clarke, *The Good Tidings of Great Joy to All People* (1762); Joseph Alleine, *The Voice of God in His Promises*, ed. John Collett Ryland (1766); David Bradberry, *A Challenge Sent by the Lord of Hosts to the Chief of Sinners* (1766); Joseph Alleine, *The Believer's Triumph in God's Promises*, ed. John Collett Ryland (1767); R. Elliot, *For the Benefit of Six Orphans. A Funeral Discourse on the Death of Mr. John How* (1767); Lloyd, *Well-Spring of Life*.

[78] Robinson, 'Experience of John Ryland', 19.

'fearing all past Experience was a mere Delusion', or afraid that his faith was only 'Presumption'.[79]

Although the experience of doubt and the quest for assurance was altogether typical of the evangelical conversion narrative in its different forms, Ryland's experience of doubt was intensified by the high Calvinism of his father and his religious milieu generally. Included in the pamphlets bound up with Ryland's letter was a sermon by John Lloyd (1738–1801), *The Well-Spring of Life Opened in Christ: Or, an Invitation to Thirsty Souls, to Come and Take the Water of Life Freely*. The argument of this sermon was that the thirsty are invited to come because they have already been made thirsty by God, and this is a sign that they are saved. Prevenient grace was by no means solely the provenance of high Calvinism, but the logic of Lloyd's discourse could only have heightened the spiritual anxiety of Ryland, Button, and the other awakened boys in the school. Lloyd contended, 'This holy thirst after the water of life must be created in the soul, before the soul will desire to know any thing of Christ,' and he added, 'So must the creature be entirely passive as to any thing he can do towards giving himself this thirst after Christ, or the water of life.'[80] The Spirit of God 'does not propose eternal life to them in case they are disposed to accept of it, and leave it to their option'. One could only look within to discern whether one had been 'made willing' and was under the drawings of God. Then, but only then, said Lloyd, 'you have no cause to doubt of your acceptance by him'.[81] This sort of instruction goes far towards accounting for the sort of introspection Ryland conducted as an adolescent and the exchanges he and Thomas Rutt had on the subject of assurance. It was the old Puritan introspection writ large.

On the other side of the emotional scale from convictions or doubts was the vocabulary of 'comfort' and 'joy', but Ryland wrote about this in a way that was very precise. Spiritual comfort came from specific promises in Scripture being applied to his condition. This theologically precise language was evident again when he wrote of his experience in December 1766, saying, 'As yet I had not comfort,' and '[I] had a little hope—but never had a promise till December 15.' He was living, that is, in anticipation of an evangelical autobiography, looking forward to a narrative of his life that included his first experience of a biblical promise applied to his soul by the Spirit of God. Here also his reading would have prepared him for conversion. Alleine's *Voice of God in His Promises* was one of the pamphlets prepared by John Ryland, sen., and it was read closely and underlined, presumably by Button or Ryland. This work was essentially an anthology of scriptural

---

[79] Ibid. 21, 22, 24.
[80] Lloyd, *Well-Spring of Life*, 18–19.
[81] Ibid. 21, 23.

promises, paraphrased in the first person, so that the reader might hear the words as a personal address. For example, '*My son I give unto you in a marriage covenant for ever.* I make him over to you as wisdom, for your illumination; righteousness for your justification; sanctification, for the curing of your corruptions; redemption, for your deliverance from your enemies,' and so on.[82] After pages of such promises, a second part opened with 'The Voice of the Redeemed in reply to the Voice of God in his Promises', and here the first-person language was presented for the reader to borrow and use as his own in response to God. This was a very clear fill-in-the-blanks primer for both hearing God's voice and finding one's own voice in response. John Ryland's narrative followed precisely this pattern of promise and con- solation.

His first experience of relief from conviction came when he picked up a Bible and read at random a text from Hosea 13, 'I will ransom them from the power of the grave, I will redeem them from death.' According to the formula, this was the promise, and he commented on the effect: 'I hope they [the words] were applied. I had Comfort . . . & a good deal of joy.'[83] A little later the minister David Bradberry spoke at the meeting from Hos. 2: 14, and as in other contexts it was the allegorical language of love that spoke comfort to Ryland: 'I will allure her and bring her into the Wilderness & speak Comfortably to her.' Ryland said of the preacher, 'He mentioned many sweet promises which were precious Comforts to my soul.'[84] Ryland's narrative was woven out of the alternating strands of doubt and fear on the one hand, and comfort and hope on the other. In his diary he referred to a sermon preached on the day after his fourteenth birthday in January 1767 as the occasion upon which, he says, 'I was bro't into the kingdom of God.'[85] But doubts followed this conversion so quickly that in his letter to Thomas Rutt the event hardly stands out as any different than his other experiences of consolation and desolation.

This oscillating piety was characteristic of the Puritan introspective quest for assurance and for evidence of effectual calling. The so-called practical syllogism was a part of the Calvinist casuistry for discerning the reality of a work of grace in a person's life: All those who show certain infallible signs are among the elect (*All men are mortal*); I show those certain signs (*Socrates is a man*); therefore I am elect (*Socrates is mortal*). The difficulty was with the middle term. The signs might be good works, sincerity, faith, and repent- ance, or love for God, or, indeed, all of these, but could you be sure, given 'temporary faith', that the term could be fully distributed? Are *all* those who

---

[82] Alleine, *Voice of God*, 28.
[83] Robinson, 'Experience of John Ryland', 19.
[84] Ibid. 20.
[85] His diary is quoted in his late memoir, 'Autograph Reminiscences', p. 25.

do good works among the elect? Moreover, for the conclusion to be true to fact and not simply valid, the minor or particular premiss ('I show those certain signs') must correspond to reality. The only way to determine this was through the fallible process of self-examination. And given the 'spirituality of the law'—the belief that the law applied to inner motives and not just outward behaviour—this self-examination inevitably involved a deep probing of one's own sincerity and the workings of the heart. Many of the Calvinist converts at Cambuslang were able to short-circuit this process through an immediate, ecstatic self-evidencing experience, though even there this was tested by doubt after the fact. But what we see in John Ryland, jun. is a more drawn-out process, as a young boy of 13 or 14 with a precocious intellect, a tender conscience, and an enormous weight of orthodox Calvinist dogma sought to discern the state of his soul before God. This was, after all, what he had been taught and what he had witnessed. And so, he wrote:

I was afraid I was not a Child of God because I did not grow in Grace more. I write thus in my Diary, the 2d Sabbath in March [1767] in the Afternoon 'miserable, dull, doubting, fearing, sorrowfull, weeping, O what shall I do, have I begun or no? Mr. Austin, Mastr. Everard, my Mamma & dear Mastr. Ray tried to Comfort me but in vain for Jesus don't speak Comfort and I fear I shall never have any Joy any more.'[86]

Although he knew that many mature Christians experienced these same doubts, this did not help. In fact, one evening in May 1767 he heard his father talking with two other ministers: 'Mr. Edwards of Leeds, Mr. Hall of Arnsby & my papa talked together one Night & my papa said He had been 12 Yrs in the dark, Mr. Edwards 4. Mr. Hall 6. O thought I if there be such thinge as these in the way how shall I go on.'[87] Achieving assurance in this context was no simple matter of a few days or weeks or months, as it was in many other evangelical contexts. The idea that one could be without assurance for four to twelve years drove the young Ryland nearly to distraction.

In the summer and autumn of 1767 his crisis deepened and he really feared that he was self-deceived about the reality of his own convictions and comforts. He feared that it might all be nothing more than 'common Convictions' and 'false Comfort' and that he might be a 'deluded Hypocrite'.[88] He wanted to burn his diary, wished he was a pigeon or a stone, or anything but what he was.

In school time I was very sorrowful my papa ask'd me if I was sick I said no, Did my headach? no, so he thought I was sulky ... I burst out crying, he not knowing the

---

[86] Robinson, 'Experience of John Ryland', 20.
[87] Ibid. 21.
[88] Ibid. 22.

reason sent me out of school—my Mamma came to me and as[k]'d me the Reason so . . . I at last told her she and my papa then tried to comfort me & I got a little hope which insensibly increased to considerable Confidence.

He described his state now as 'middling', another indication of how precarious and subject to oscillation these feelings of assurance were. He was thus 'middling' until he was proposed to the church for baptism and membership. Perhaps the act of 'giving his experience' to the church increased his confidence. It certainly helped that he heard Whitefield preach on Isa. 61: 10 ('I will greatly rejoice in the Lord . . . ') between the Friday when he was proposed and the Sunday when he was received into membership. Hearing Whitefield on this joyful text, so full of bridal imagery, was 'a very good time to me'. Interestingly, his reception into the church was not straightforward. 'I joined the Church with Bror. B & Everard not without some opposition at first on account of our youth but the Lord at last made all willing to receive us & Sept. 13 we are baptized.'[89] It was thus with none other than William Button ('Bror. B') and another schoolboy, John Everard, that he entered into full church membership.[90] John Ryland, jun. was a little disappointed that his baptism and first communion were not more decisive experiences of inward spiritual consolation, but the mundane reality was that he was nervous about crying out at his baptism (presumably, on account of the coldness of the water). This, he said, 'hinder'd my Comfort'. However, he continued, 'I was much affected in ye water my papa lifting up his eyes to Heaven & crying out "Thanks be to God for this Boy" I shall never forget that sound while I live.'[91] The climactic experience of baptism was inseparable from the spiritual blessing of his own father. Perhaps there is even an intentional echo here of the words at Christ's baptism, 'This is my beloved son, in whom I am well pleased.'

This was by no means the end of Ryland's fluctuations of doubt and comfort, but these were resolved within the narrative over the course of the next year. Significantly, his father preached in May 1768 on the text in Isaiah, 'Comfort ye, Comfort ye my people,' and 'about this time', wrote the son, 'I was in general freed from Doubts. I have had some slight Attacks of that kind since but for these last 2 years I have hardly ever doubted of my state.'[92] Not unlike Wesley in his fourth *Journal*, he came to see that

---

[89] Robinson, 'Experience of John Ryland', 22.

[90] That there was some dispute about the boys' ages may explain why this sentence was underlined in William Button's copy of Joseph Alleine's memoirs: 'This our author appeared to have a very serious sense of religion at eleven years of age.' John Everard, the youngest of the three boys baptized, was also 11. This memoir of Alleine was by John Ryland, sen., forming a preface to the pamphlet bound up with the boys' manuscripts (Alleine, *Voice of God*, p. v).

[91] Robinson, 'Experience of John Ryland', 22.

[92] Ibid. 25.

assurance could be based either on the immediate apprehension of faith or on reason, but he placed more value upon the latter sort of assurance than Wesley. The inferences of reason left one with a settled assurance of one's eternal spiritual state ('I know I shall go to Heaven'), even under spiritual troubles of other kinds. Indeed, one of his greatest troubles now, claimed Ryland, was the concern he felt for the soul distress of others such as Thomas Rutt.

THE NARRATIVE CULTURE OF A GATHERED CHURCH: SECOND-GENERATION PIETY

Clearly, the need to discover a work of grace in the soul as a prerequisite for membership in the gathered church shaped a distinctive, Calvinistic, adolescent piety in Northampton, where the forceful John Ryland, sen. presided over the church and boarding school. John Ryland, jun. was not alone in his experience, and his manuscript account of the two religious societies among the boys and girls at the school, along with the church book with its record of those received into membership, bears witness to this. At least six of the other boys in the religious society were awakened by the lectures given by John Ryland, sen. on Saturday evenings. Likewise the girls' society began after three girls heard a lecture by the elder Ryland and gathered to pray together regularly. Other girls dated their first awakening or comfort to their experience of Ryland's ministry.

Although the narrative of the girls' society is less detailed than that of the boys', a manuscript copy of the conversion narrative of one these girls, Elizabeth Rutt, gives us some indication of the experience of the young girls.[93] She was the sister of Thomas Rutt, to whom John Ryland, jun. had addressed his letter in 1770 recounting his spiritual experience. Elizabeth Rutt declared her experience to the church at Northampton at 14 years of age on 12 May 1771, a month after her brother had been received into membership. Her narrative was preserved in a letter she wrote to her parents

---

[93] The narrative of the girls' society was less detailed and written at second hand by a frustrated John Ryland, jun., who complained that his narrative would be necessarily imperfect because of the girls 'not keeping a regular and exact Acct' of the origins of their group and, moreover, because of their 'not being very communicative' ('Some Account of the Society at Mrs. Trinders', forming the second part of John Ryland, jun., 'An Account of the Rise and Progress of the Two Society's at Mr. Rylands and at Mrs. Trinder's Boarding School in Northampton', 1768–70, Angus Library, Regent's Park College, Oxford). The account does list twenty-six girls who were at one time or another members of the society (including three names of backsliders written in Greek characters), and for several of the girls Ryland reconstructs at least the occasion of their awakening. The short entries are very much like what was recorded in the College Lane church book on the occasion of one being received into membership.

in London 'on the Occasion of her joining the Church', a copy of which was bound up with Ryland's narrative. She was the same age as John Ryland, jun. but her narrative was considerably shorter. Like Ryland, though, she began her account with the onset of her first convictions, and she rehearsed her 'Doubts & Fears' and fear of delusion, and then her comfort as various texts of Scripture were impressed on her mind. Just as Ryland had been moved by hearing the testimony of candidates in church, so also she found encouragement from the same source when most despondent: 'The only Thing that gave me Comfort In this dejected state was, when I Heard Christians talk of the Experience & found anything like Mine.'[94] Elizabeth Rutt's strong identification with this spoken testimony is another indication that these children were catechized in the way of conversion as they heard narratives in church. When John Ryland, sen. explained that a soul first enlightened is like a newborn lamb, a little, staggering creature that could barely walk, and that God did not break a bruised reed or quench the smoking flax, she was comforted.[95] She began to think, 'I had Reason to believe that my Sins were forgiven.'

The boys too made this transition to adult membership in the church through narrative, and through the preparatory discipline of their religious society. John Ryland, jun.'s friend, William Button, with whom he was baptized, was a founding member of the boys' society. Button was the son of a deacon at John Gill's church in London, and his experience was certainly shaped by a high Calvinist inheritance much like Ryland's.[96] The other boy baptized, John Everard, was a new boarder from London who immediately became a member of the religious society as well. Ryland noted in the society records that for Everard the work of grace had begun three years previously when he was reading a passage in the New Testament concerning the sufferings of Christ when he was only 8 years of age.

The religious society existed from 1766 to 1770, and after that we have no records of whether it continued or dissolved, but it was shortly after this that John Ryland, jun. made his first trial preaching publicly in church, and thereafter his pastoral responsibilities grew larger with every year. While the society existed, some twenty-two boys and three men (assistants in the school) were recorded among its members. Although it is difficult to determine the precise numbers in the school and in the society at any one time, the religious society was comprised of only a minority of the boys in

[94] 'The Lord's dealings with Elizabeth Rutt', MS copy of letter 1770 [1771?], Angus Library, Regent's Park College, Oxford.

[95] Ryland's sermons on these occasions were based on texts that had been well worked over in Puritan preaching: Isa. 40: 11 and 42: 3.

[96] Indeed, though the younger Ryland would later go on to champion evangelical Calvinism or 'Fullerism', Button emerged as one of its outspoken opponents. Brown, *English Baptists*, 94, 159.

the school. Several features of the society suggest that just as John Ryland, jun.'s piety was in some sense a mimetic, filial piety, so also the religious society was an attempt to imitate the gathered church discipline and polity of the adults within the community.

First, the society was gathered as a pure community from among the general population of the boarding school, and they were very concerned to keep their proceedings secret. The fifth rule laid down in February 1767 was that 'No member shall say anything about this Society to the other Boys.'[97] This was parallel to the 'Gospel Rules' spelled out in the College Lane church book about the same time, where rule number eight stated, 'We do promise to keep the Secrets of our Church jointly without divulging them to any that are not Members of this particular Body though they may be otherwise near and dear to us for we believe that the Church ought to be as a Garden enclosed and as a Fountain sealed.'[98]

Secondly, the church book recorded an Act of Excommunication of a member named William Faulkner in the same month as the boys in their society laid down their rules, and the boys imitated this form of discipline too. At least some of the boys had an opportunity to witness such proceedings. For example once the 'three little boys' were admitted members of the church, they participated fully in the congregational polity of the adult assembly, and indeed, John Ryland, jun. signed his name along with other church members to another act of excommunication in 1770 while the boys' religious society was still in operation. The boys too had a regulation for their society that was parallel to excommunication, and it read, 'Such as behave not according to these Rules & according to the Rules of Christ, or whose Conduct shall be disgraceful to their Profession shall be excluded after the 2d admonition.'[99] This could have been taken right out of Benjamin Keach's standard *Glory of a True Church and its Discipline Display'd* (1697). And it was not a dead letter on their books, for on 20 October 1766 two boys were excluded as backsliders—John Young and John Fauntleroy. In fact, John Young renewed his profession and then was described, in a wonderful construction, as having 'rebackslid'. These names, Young and Fauntleroy, appear in the register of the society and at several points in the narrative in Greek characters (phonetically, $Yovvγ$ and $Φαυντλεροι$) as a sign of their apostasy. It is as though the names themselves ceased to exist, having been written out of the book, as it were. It was something of an adolescent conceit on the part of John Ryland, and certainly the whole society partook

---

[97] John Ryland, jun., 'An Account of the Rise and Progress of the Two Society's at Mr. Rylands and at Mrs. Trinder's Boarding School in Northampton, drawn up by Iohn Ryland, Jun:", MS account, 1768–70, Angus Library, Oxford.

[98] Church Book of Northampton College Street Baptist Church, 91.

[99] John Ryland, jun., 'Account of the Two Society's'.

a little of the character of a secret boys' club, with an 'in group' and an 'out group'.

Thirdly, the boys' religious society functioned as a place to test spiritual gifts and to narrate spiritual experience. John Ryland, sen. recorded very brief accounts of many of those who spoke about their experiences to the church prior to being received into membership, and likewise, John Ryland, jun. recorded the religious experience of each member in an elaborate set of footnotes to his narrative of the society. They had meetings for telling their own experiences to one another, and twice a week they met for extemporaneous prayer. It would be an understatement to say that this was an apprenticeship for 'real church', since many of the members did indeed go on not only to membership but to ordained ministry. The person for whom the society offered the greatest scope for an apprenticeship was John Ryland, jun. himself. Recalling these years, his son and biographer later wrote, 'For some time he had united with several of his serious companions, in meetings for prayer and religious discourse. It was an easy step to address them in a more formal manner from a text of scripture. After frequent practice of these exercises, for upwards of two years, he commenced a more public trial of his abilities and received the approval of the church, March 10, 1771.'[100] We might think of that as his graduation ceremony from the make-believe gathered church to the real one.

Thus, as young people, John Ryland, jun. and his peers grew up within the piety and the theology of their elders and reproduced it in their private introspective narratives and their shared life as adolescent schoolchildren. At the stage of psycho-social development that Erik Erikson characterizes as one of 'identity diffusion', where the task before a young person is to establish a coherent identity, many of the young people in John Collett Ryland's boarding school strove to accomplish this by working through the interior soul struggle of conversion and following the example of the adults by establishing their own gathered church, which operated according to a discipline similar to a Congregationalist or Baptist chapel. This was the way a number of children made the passage to adulthood in Northampton in the 1760s and 1770s.

Since Philippe Ariès's *Centuries of Childhood*, debate among historians of the family has hinged upon the extent to which the idea of 'youth' existed at all as a stage in the life cycle, between childhood and adulthood, in the early modern period. With John Ryland, jun. and his schoolfellows we have an example of a group of young people with a corporate identity linked to their age and stage of life, but in all of this the religious impulse was central. The line between childhood and adulthood in the gathered church was marked by full admission as a member, and the rite of passage included oral

---

[100] Jonathan Edwards Ryland (ed.), *Pastoral Memorials*, i. 8.

testimony before the church and baptism, but preceding these rites was an adolescent period characterized by spiritual anxiety and the travail of conversion. And during this stage the young people instituted their own formal society as a social space in which they shared concerns common to themselves as religious youths. But the forms of this society and the piety of the young people did not set up a competition between the allegiances of the peer group and the allegiance owed to elders. At Northampton these values converged. The peer group ties had more to do with shared spiritual anxieties and what we might call, anachronistically, developmental tasks. Thus, in addition to courtship, apprenticeship, and other institutions that marked the transition from childhood to the responsibilities and privileges of adulthood in the early modern period, we must add this example of a formal religious youth society.[101]

William Button went on to become the pastor of a Baptist church in Dean Street, Southwark, the high Calvinist rump of John Gill's congregation. That John Ryland, jun. would later cast aside the high Calvinism of his father and join in the evangelical renewal of many structures of Baptist life points to a further stage in his own development, one that also drew him closer to other evangelicals outside the 'garden inclosed' of the gathered church and into the wider currents of revival. Indeed, when he looked back on his adolescent spiritual diary some forty years after his public profession of faith in the church at Northampton, he was a little embarrassed by some parts that seemed redundant, others that seemed trifling, and still others that seemed just too private. He realized that he had for many years been censuring others for the very sort of expressions he had recorded in his diary. He was chastened by this and planned to burn his diaries once he had summed up his memoirs in one last account for his family.[102]

The story of Ryland's later career is told elsewhere, from his friendship with John Newton and his discovery of Jonathan Edwards to his resolution of the 'modern question' and his championing of evangelical Calvinism ('Fullerism').[103] He co-pastored with his father at College Lane in Northampton beginning in 1781, took sole charge of the church in 1785, and founded several village churches in the area. He moved to Bristol in 1793 to pastor the important Broadmead Church and to take charge of the academy,

---

[101] On youth and adolescence in the early modern period, see further Philippe Ariès, *Centuries of Childhood*, trans. R. Baldick (New York, 1962); Michael Mitterauer, *A History of Youth* (Oxford, 1992); Ilana Krausman Ben-Amos, *Adolescence and Youth in Early Modern England* (New Haven, Conn., 1994).

[102] John Ryland, jun., 'Autograph Reminiscences', 21–2, 23, 28, 31.

[103] Gordon, 'John Ryland, Jr. (1753–1825)'; Bruce Hindmarsh, 'The Reception of Jonathan Edwards by Early Evangelicals in England', in *Jonathan Edwards at Home and Abroad* (Columbia, SC, 2003), 201–3, 207–11; Brian Stanley, *The History of the Baptist Missionary Society, 1792–1992* (1992), 1–35.

where he trained a new generation of Baptist leaders. He baptized and befriended the future missionary, William Carey, and took a leading part in the founding of the Particular Baptist Society for Propagating the Gospel among the Heathen (1792). This evangelistic work among non-Western peoples would open yet another chapter in the history of evangelical conversion narrative, since the very experience of evangelical conversion that propelled men and women into missionary service was itself often hard to reproduce overseas and led to new departures in autobiography.

Within the high Calvinist milieu of the Baptist churches in eighteenth-century England, however, the story had been one of spiritual formation within the community of faith. John Ryland, jun., like Anne Dutton, came to evangelical conversion as an adolescent in a church community that stood in continuity with the Commonwealth sects that had first required oral testimony of one's experience of grace as a test for admission to membership. Schooled in the ways of conversion from childhood, both Ryland and Dutton learned the grammar of conversion before ever they experienced it for themselves. Their conversion experiences therefore represented an act of affirmation, or a rite of passage, more than a protest against social custom or filial piety. Still, for all this, neither of them found their personalities diminished by this act of affirmation. On the contrary, it was through evangelical conversion that they became more secure in their identities and discovered the confidence to sustain a distinctive public voice as adults.

Questions about the conversion of the next generation would be raised not only among the Dissenters. These issues would exercise other leaders as the evangelical movement aged. Already in 1768 John Wesley worried out loud among his lay preachers, 'But what shall we do for the rising generation? Unless we take care of this, the present revival will be *res unius aetatis*; it will last only the age of a man.'[104] The evangelical movement did persist beyond one generation, however, and, as was the case among the Dissenters, conversion narrative itself proved to be one of the most potent means of passing the piety of one generation on to another.

---

[104] *Works of John Wesley*, ed. Thomas Jackson (3rd edn., 1872; repr. Grand Rapids, Mich., 1984), viii. 316; cf. Wesley, *Works* (BE), iii. 335.

10

After Christendom: Evangelical Conversion Narrative and its Alternatives

THE type of spiritual autobiography that flourished in England during the eighteenth century in the context of the Evangelical Revival was not unprecedented, since the evangelical narratives very much recalled the Puritan and Pietist conversion narratives of the last half of the seventeenth century. The context was, however, new, and the proliferation of the genre was spectacular. In the preceding chapters we have traced something of this proliferation not only across time but also across the principal communities that emerged from the original revival with a distinctive, if overlapping piety, and we observed this proliferation also in terms of literary form and the social location of the subjects.

The chronological development of the genre followed the progress of the Evangelical Revival itself from its origins in the 1730s, through its wider expansion, to the apparent permanence of evangelicalism as a part of English religious life by the end of the century. In this context the genre of conversion narrative that initially appeared as something novel became something more established within a generation. There was a charismatic phase of the early revival in the late 1730s and early 1740s, during which the subjects of the revival seemed to walk in a cloud of wonders. From this period we have not only the conversion narratives of key leaders such as George Whitefield and John and Charles Wesley, but we also have the testimony of those who responded to their first preaching. These artless narratives were characterized by an overwhelming sense of the spontaneity of divine grace, and the awareness of writing or speaking within a narrative tradition was negligible. Although the impression of a great transatlantic pentecost had passed by the late 1740s, evangelical conversions continued to multiply such that by the last third of the century, conversion narrative appeared if not more routine, certainly less novel than it was earlier. Yet to describe this process wholly in Weberian terms as a 'routinization of charisma' would be misleading, since this would too easily suggest a flattening out of conversion into the humdrum of everyday religious observance, and this was far from the case as the century progressed. Over time it became more possible to appeal to a tradition of conversion or to offer a rational account of conversion, but the sense that conversion involved a particular spiritual charism had not been eclipsed. There were still clusters of religious excitement and periods of fervour that led to the awakening of large numbers of women and men in numerous local revivals. Although there would be more young people like John Ryland and Anne Dutton, who would grow up within an evangelical culture of conversion, the experience itself was still more often described as an unexpected personal crisis than as an inherited ritual. Rather than 'routinization', then, it would be better to characterize the chronological development of the genre in the last two-thirds of the century as a process of proliferation and elaboration. In literary terms there was a greater richness and variety apparent by the end of the century. Indeed, the charisma of evangelical conversion was experienced again and again, and taken up into new keys, so that conversion came to characterize the whole of life and the most significant spiritual moments within it. The genre was more widespread and more public as increasing numbers of examples found their way into print, especially through the evangelical magazines, and this meant that the narrative conventions became more readily available and more firmly established. But still the genre was patient of elaboration in new ways, as Methodists discovered when they began in many instances to narrate sanctification as a further conversion experience. Conversion became not a moment in one's life, but the key to interpreting the meaning of one's life from beginning to end. The genre would also, of course, persist and flourish well into the nineteenth century and beyond as evangelicalism spread widely in the modern period.[1]

This chronological development in the eighteenth century corresponded in part to a literary elaboration of the genre. In Northrop Frye's essay on the theory of genres, he argues that generic distinctions in literature derive from what he calls 'the radical of presentation', or, in other words, from what we have referred to throughout this book as the 'occasion' of conversion narrative in various instances. Says Frye, 'The basis of generic criticism in any case is rhetorical, in the sense that the genre is determined by the conditions established between the poet and his public.' Conventions arise, that is, between speaker and audience, or between writer and reader. Again, Frye claims, 'The purpose of criticism by genres is not so much to classify as to clarify such traditions and affinities, thereby bringing out a large number of literary relationships that would not be noticed so long as there were no context established for them.'[2] Observing these contexts in the case of evangelical spiritual autobiography leads to a gradation of forms. Con-

---

[1] See e.g. David Bebbington, 'Evangelical Conversion, *c.* 1740–1850', Position Paper 21, North Atlantic Missiology Project (Cambridge, 1996), and Michael Watts, *The Dissenters* (1995), ii. 49–80.

[2] Northrop Frye, *Anatomy of Criticism* (Princeton, NJ, 1957), 246–8. Frye is concerned with a traditional canon of Western literature, with its roots in classical Greek forms, but he

version narrative persisted first as an oral genre, with a formal occasion in the context of a Methodist band meeting, a Moravian quarter hour, an interview in the Presbyterian manse, or a Baptist meeting for the admission of new members, and with an informal occasion in the ingenuous narratives that were so often spoken in passing in the context of familiar conversations. The journals and diaries kept by so many of the early evangelicals and by virtually all the leaders represented another form within which evangelical conversion might be narrated. Here the moments in one's life were captured in writing, but one was also able to continue day by day to reflect and to revise one's self-understanding, even in the journals made public at periodic intervals. This form was particularly characteristic of leaders such as Whitefield and Wesley who directed the movement. The ad hoc familiar letter was the most typical form assumed when laypeople had recourse to writing. In the case of those letters written soon after conversion, conversion appeared as an episode in the life of the writer, momentous and climactic, but not yet worked out in any detail as an authoritative interpretation of life from beginning to end. The letter remained, in the first instance, part of manuscript culture rather than print culture, for in a familiar letter one wrote not for a public but for an individual, usually for one's pastor. But the lines easily blurred, and the letter written to one's spiritual director, if that director was John Wesley, might easily find its way into print through his *Journal* and later through the *Arminian Magazine*. So it was that the lives of the Methodist lay preachers, specially commissioned by Wesley, pointed to a further literary elaboration of conversion narrative, since these accounts were only nominally letters. Like many of the Moravian *Lebensläufe*, these were in fact more like memoirs, written later in life, and providing a longer retrospective narrative in which conversion appeared as the leading theme. In many cases this led to highly individual accounts, but the shared vocation of the preachers, together with their shared experience of Methodist discipline under Wesley's direction, meant that this body of narratives had much in common in diction and incident. In the accounts of John Newton, William Cowper, and Thomas Scott, in contrast, it is possible to see evangelical conversion narrative not only as an authoritative act of retrospective self-interpretation, but also as a creative act of literary autobiography in which personality was not effaced by narrative conventions, but in fact explored creatively through those very conventions.

The preceding chapters have traced a chronological proliferation and literary elaboration of evangelical narratives of conversion, but our main principle of classification has still been religious and theological. The theo-

---

does analyse autobiography ('the confession form') as a specific case ('introverted, but intellectualized in content') of the continuous forms of prose fiction, in contrast to *epos* (the oral forms), drama, and lyric. Ibid. 307–8.

logical differences between Calvinists and Arminians, as between Methodists and Moravians, were significant enough to fracture the early undivided
revival movement in England and to create subtly different narrative cultures. In broad terms, the Arminian narratives influenced by Wesley were
agonistic, and the will was engaged throughout life in a painful contest first
in conversion and then ideally in its sequel, perfection. The Moravian
narratives influenced by Zinzendorf were, in contrast, self-abasing and
quietist, upholding an ideal of exquisite contemplation of the wounded
Saviour. The Calvinist narratives, influenced by various forms of seventeenth-century confessionalism, were introspective, providential, and more
rationalized in terms of the order of salvation, and the watchword of *soli Deo
gloria* was translated into a uniquely Calvinist sublime. Because of the close
pastoral supervision of lay converts and lay narratives in all these communities, nuances or distinctions that were significant at the level of theological
debate among leaders thus became significant at the level of personal
narrative and religious identity for large numbers of laypeople.

Although these theological schemes could at times overwhelm the personality of the subjects, the reverse was more often the case. The subjects
who gave an account of their conversion experiences during the Evangelical
Revival came from a wide range of social backgrounds, and these social
characteristics were accented and drawn out into narrative as the narrators
explored the conviction that this gospel message really was 'for me'. Few
other genres in the eighteenth century included authors from such a variety
of backgrounds in terms of gender, age, class, and (as we shall explore
below) race. Thus the genre included within its reach both women and
men, and allowed scope for many women in particular to speak about their
lives in ways few had done before. And although most of the subjects were
converted as young people, the narratives themselves were written by
people of all ages. Artisans, craftsmen, skilled and unskilled labourers,
apprentices, domestic servants—all these are amply represented in the extant
accounts, but so also are those with more education, social status, and
income. Against the barely literate Elizabeth Hinsome or Susannah Duree
must be placed the educated Martha Claggett and Martha Barham from
well-respected and propertied families. The evangelical conversion narrative was also a genre in which both pastors and laypeople participated.
Although the pastors significantly influenced the form and content of the
lay narratives, many were also called to revise their theology in the light of
the religious experience of the laity. And these laypeople frequently found
that the act of speaking or writing about their conversion implied a call to
more public usefulness. Becoming articulate about one's own conversion
was often the first step toward more public ministry for laypeople, women
and men alike.

Hence, a number of differences can be distinguished by analysing carefully the chronology, literary form, theology, and social conditions of the genre of evangelical conversion narrative. Still, notwithstanding these distinguishing characteristics, the similarities among the conversion narratives of this period remain the most striking feature of the genre as a whole. Indeed, it is the similarities or conventions that justify us describing these narratives as a genre at all, or allow us to use the definite article to refer to *the* evangelical conversion narrative. The Moravians and Methodists, the Anglicans and the Presbyterians, the women and the men, and the pastors and the people still recognized, for all their differences, that they shared a common experience of the gospel. As we observed in Ch. 2, they also understood the North Atlantic revivals in aggregate as part of one 'work' of God's Spirit. So, despite the subtle shades of difference from one community to another, these individuals had more in common with each other, in the end, than they did with those they regarded as 'unawakened' or nominal in their faith. David Bebbington's characterization of evangelicals as 'conversionist'—believing that 'conversion was the one gateway to vital Christianity'—has been confirmed repeatedly in the pages of this book.[3] Indeed, the heated debates that evangelicals had about conversion bore witness to the importance of the experience in their lives.

We began our account of the genre in the early chapters of this book with a description of some of the conditions that obtained in the early modern period to allow for the rise of conversion narrative, including the development among numbers of people of a heightened sense of introspective conscience and self-consciousness. In order to see the genre whole, however, and to appreciate the conditions in general under which people turned to this form of spiritual autobiography, it remains to look in this final chapter, first, at the ways in which the genre fared at the end of the eighteenth century in the context of evangelical mission enterprise beyond the borders of Christendom, and, second, at the ways in which it contrasted with the new forms of modern autobiography in England that appeared 'after Christendom'.

Such contrasting case studies provide insight into the close relationship between the conversion experience and the narratives themselves. Evidently it was not a matter of having a certain sort of experience and then 'writing it up'; it was more a matter of having an experience that was in principle narratable. Writing of Augustine's conversion, Geoffrey Galt Harpham likewise identifies 'the conversion that organizes the entire narrative around itself' as something that anticipates a second conversion, 'the conversion of life into textual self-representation'.[4] In her study of

---

[3] David W. Bebbington, *Evangelicalism in Modern Britain* (1989), 5–10.
[4] Geoffrey Galt Harpham, 'Conversion and the Language of Autobiography', in James Olney (ed.), *Studies in Autobiography* (New York, 1988), 42.

women's life writing, Carolyn Heilbrun points to this sort of close relationship between identity and narrative, even in the absence of written narrative, when she says, 'The woman may write her own life in advance of living it, unconsciously, and without recognizing or naming the process.'[5] It is this close relationship between conversion as experience and conversion as narrative identity among the early evangelicals that is exhibited most clearly by examining its alternatives in the non-Christendom contexts of the 'heathen' nations and the post-Christendom context of secular bourgeois autobiography. We turn then once more from general themes to specific case studies, since it is these case studies that will most help us to appreciate the close relationship of evangelical conversion narrative to the social and religious conditions in early modern England itself. By seeing the genre against its alternatives, we shall better be able to see it whole.

NON-WESTERN CONVERSION AND THE MISSIONARY EXPERIENCE: THREE CASE STUDIES

In the last chapter we observed how John Ryland, jun. became one of the leading figures in the transformation of the Particular Baptists at the end of the century into an expansive, missionary-oriented denomination. It was the experience of an evangelical conversion like that of Ryland that inspired the first English missionaries to spread the gospel to the non-Christian nations. The surprising discovery of many missionaries on the field, however, was that the narrative of evangelical conversion, which they held dear, was not always easy to reproduce and took different forms even when their converts embraced Christianity enthusiastically.

David Brainerd's Mission to the Delaware Indians in New Jersey, 1744–6

The first context in which we observe the conversion of aboriginal non-Western peoples was one that became famous through the writings of Jonathan Edwards, namely, the mission of David Brainerd (1718–47) to the Delaware Indians. While there had been earlier Protestant efforts to evangelize Native Americans, including, for example, the work of Thomas Mayhew, jun. (*c.*1620–57) on Martha's Vineyard in 1642, or the ministry of John Eliot (1604–90) among the Massachusetts Indians from 1646, it was the mission of Brainerd among a small band of Delawares in New Jersey during the Great Awakening that especially captured the imagination of evangelicals across the North Atlantic world when his diary was published by Jonathan Edwards in 1749. Brainerd's *Life* became a runaway best-seller and went through multiple editions.

---

[5] Carolyn Heilbrun, *Writing a Woman's Life* (New York, 1988), 11.

Brainerd's life was held up by Edwards as a specimen of the ideals expounded in his *Treatise on the Religious Affections*, much as Sarah Edwards had been earlier in *Some Thoughts Concerning the Revival*.[6] And Brainerd's piety was indeed inspirational for many evangelicals, not least for John Wesley, who abridged Brainerd's *Life* for his *Christian Library* and exhorted his preachers to read it as the most effective possible means of reviving the Methodist work where it had decayed.[7] If Brainerd's own conversion and example of self-dedication was inspirational, his work among the Delaware Indians was equally so, for Brainerd's *Life* recounts a religious awakening in 1744–6 that seemed to show all the Edwardsean signs of evangelical conversion and revival. During his first year among the Delaware band, he claimed to have baptized thirty-eight adults and thirty-nine children, including Moses Tinda Tautamy, his interpreter. The several cases of Indian conversion narrated by Brainerd very much followed the evangelical pattern of conversion, and, in fact, he appears to have judged these cases by the rules which he found in Edwards's *Distinguishing Marks*.[8]

Brainerd's interpretation of Indian conversion needs to be qualified, however. For instance, Brainerd described the conversion of one old Delaware who had been a murderer, drunkard, and conjurer, but in Brainerd's narrative, recounted in terms of awakening, soul-travail, relief, and so on, one can still hear a note of something foreign to the typical evangelical conversion in the European context. When Brainerd provided indirect quotation or paraphrase, the language of the Indian convert emphasized the kind of contest of the gods or power encounter we are familiar with from other mission settings, or indeed, from the conversion of Europe in the early Middle Ages. Brainerd reported at one point: 'And then, [the Indian convert] says, upon his feeling the Word of God in his heart (as he expresses it), his spirit of conjuration left him entirely, that he has had no more power of that nature since than any other man living; and declares that he don't now so much as know how he used to charm and conjure.'[9] And again later, when challenged by an old Indian at the Forks of Delaware who threatened to bewitch Brainerd and his people, this new convert 'challenged him to do his worst, telling him that himself [*sic*] had been as great a conjurer as he, and that notwithstanding as soon as he felt that Word in his heart which these people loved (meaning the Word of God), his power of conjuring immediately left him. "And So it would you," said he, "if you did

[6] Norman Pettit, Introduction to *WJE* vii. 5.

[7] Isabel Rivers, ' "Strangers and Pilgrims": Sources and Patterns of Methodist Narrative', in J. D. Hilson, M. M. B. Jones, and J. R. Watson (eds.), *Augustan Worlds* (Leicester, 1978), 195–6.

[8] Pettit, Introduction to *WJE* vii. 23.

[9] *WJE* vii. 392.

but once feel it in your heart; and you have no power to hurt them, nor so much as to touch one of them," etc.'[10] These elements bracket what is otherwise a carefully crafted account of conscience, travail, self-despair, and resignation, followed by divine illumination and moral transformation. But we can see that there is also something indigenous taking place, in terms of a confrontation of spiritual powers. Although it is hard to be sure, given the evidence we have, and in the absence of autograph narratives from the converts themselves, it seems that what Brainerd was seeing primarily in terms of 'the problems of conscience and their resolution' was seen by the Indian converts rather more in terms of Elijah on Mount Carmel. The language recalls the pagan conversion narratives of early medieval Europe, such as the account of Boniface and the Saxon Oak.

Moreover, if we look at the revival under Brainerd's ministry in terms of the stage of acculturation of the Indian band with whom he worked, we find that whites had occupied much of the surrounding territory for over a century, and that his displaced group of Indians were leading a marginal existence, decimated by disease, reduced to poverty by whiskey traders, and peddling home-made wares to their white neighbours.[11] Brainerd's ministry among them lasted only sixteen months. His younger brother, John, took over the work after his death and held it together over the next thirty years. But faced with the encroachment of the land-hungry white population, these Delawares were eventually forced onto reservations. By John's death in 1781 even this reservation had been seriously reduced by deaths and departures, and John was never replaced at the mission. In 1801 the last New Jersey Delawares sold their reservation and joined other refugee Indians at New Stockbridge, New York. So in the longer-term history of this particular group of Indians, their accession to evangelical Christian belief came at a point of advanced contact with a dominant white civilization. In this respect, it is significant that the band was located in the heartland of the Great Awakening in the Middle Colonies. Indeed, on one occasion, when Brainerd was absent on one of his many trips, the Delawares went a few miles up the road to attend the ministry of the famous revival preacher William Tennent ('whose house they frequented much while I was gone').[12] The Delawares were clearly not in a distant, pristine wilderness.[13]

This wider contextualizing of Brainerd's mission is not intended to discredit his interpretation of the Indian response to Christianity as an

---

[10] *WJE* vii. 395.

[11] Henry Warner Bowden, *American Indians and Christian Missions* (Chicago 1981), 153; cf. Pettit, Introduction to *WJE* vii. 26–8.

[12] *WJE* vii. 305.

[13] Robert Berkhofer has outlined several possible sequences of acculturation among Amerindians between 1760 and 1860 as they encountered Protestant missionaries. The situation of Brainerd's Delaware Indians seems most closely to approximate to his second

evangelical awakening. But it does suggest that from the perspective of the Native Americans themselves, hard as this perspective is to reconstruct from our sources, they were responding to Christianity against the background of a massive social change in which traditional religious patterns failed to satisfy or were powerless to cope with the new realities of their lives. In terms of conversion and conversion narrative, Brainerd's *Life* did much to spread the message that the pagan world could be expected to respond to the simple preaching of the law and gospel, much as men and women responded in the Evangelical Revival and the Great Awakening. However, conversion was not quite so straightforward among Brainerd's Indian hearers, and many missionaries in other contexts would be disheartened to find it even less so.

The Sierra Leone Colony, 1792–c.1830

The black African diaspora and Sierra Leone provide a second context for observing conversion in a non-Western context. Granville Sharp's founding Province of Freedom in Sierra Leone in West Africa was taken over by the Sierra Leone Company in 1791, and the few Old Settlers that remained were integrated into the new immigrant community of black Nova Scotians. Sierra Leone offers a unique case study in evangelical conversion, for if we cannot exactly say that the settler community of Nova Scotians, with the later recaptives, represented a purely non-Western society, neither can we say that they had a traditional European framework of Christian beliefs and practices.[14]

The black Baptist pastor David George (1743–1810) was one of those who migrated to Sierra Leone as part of the Clapham-inspired repatriation of former slaves after the American Revolutionary War. His spiritual autobiography was transcribed from spoken conversation and reported in John Rippon's *Baptist Annual Register* (1790–3). It provides the best specimen of the kind of background that the first Nova Scotian settlers brought to Sierra Leone.[15]

---

sequence, the 'Fragmented Community Sequence', in which the Indian social system, as well as its cultural system, is divided by response to Christianity. Instead of the original pagan society reintegrating in some manner, two new societies form, in each of which culture and society and political authority can be coterminous. So, for example, a new all-Christian village may be formed, as was done under Brainerd's ministry. Berkhofer observes that this process often occurs at about the time political autonomy is lost, just before reservation life commences, and, again, this seems to fit the chronological pattern of Brainerd's Delaware band. Robert F. Berkhofer, jun., 'Protestants, Pagans, and Sequences among the North American Indians, 1760–1860', *Ethnohistory* 10 (1963), 201–32.

[14] The standard history of Sierra Leone is Christopher Fyfe, *A History of Sierra Leone* (1962; repr. Aldershot, Hants, 1993).

[15] George's narrative is given in full in Grant Gordon, *From Slavery to Freedom: the Life of David George, Pioneer Black Baptist Minister* (Hansport, Nova Scotia, 1992), 168–83.

George's experience is also a case study of social dislocation if ever there was one. He was a second-generation African-American slave, born in Virginia, but he escaped his master to live for a time among the Creek Indians. Resold into slavery in South Carolina, he had only vague apprehensions of Christianity (he knew the Lord's prayer, for example), but after being confronted about his bad life by a passing slave, he came under conviction for sin, cast himself upon the mercy of God, and found relief from his distress. Soon afterward, George heard a sermon by the pioneer black Baptist pastor George Liele (1750–1828) and found himself confirmed in his conversion experience. He began to exhort and then to preach, but with the onset of the Revolutionary War he fled to Savannah, Georgia, and then to Charleston, South Carolina before being evacuated by the British to Nova Scotia, where he founded several black churches and became one of the key leaders in the black community. All this preceded his emigration, with many of his church members, to Sierra Leone in 1792.

It is because the Nova Scotia settlers brought this kind of background to Sierra Leone, and because the colony was itself inspired by the Clapham Sect, that Andrew Walls can describe Sierra Leone as the 'stepchild of the Evangelical Revival'.[16] Walls has also recounted the way in which these Nova Scotian settlers set the tone for the colony in religion as in other matters as Sierra Leone's population was enlarged by an increasing number of recaptives (slaves recaptured from ships intercepted along the West African coast).[17] These recaptives, having been uprooted from their own traditions, became in Sierra Leone 'the first mass movement to Christianity in modern Africa'.[18]

If America has been described as a melting pot of immigrant groups, then Sierra Leone was by the second decade of the nineteenth century a cauldron—with all its diverse African peoples, languages, and cultures. The only possibility for the recaptives in Sierra Leone was to take on a new identity, and what developed was a distinctively and self-consciously Christian and Europeanized Krio culture.[19] The Nova Scotian settlers' Christianity, along with the influence of governors and English missionaries, contributed to this identity.

What kind of evangelical piety did the recaptives encounter, then, when they integrated with the earlier settlers? David George and the Nova Scotian Baptists and Methodists brought to Sierra Leone a particularly radical

---

[16] Andrew F. Walls, 'A Christian Experiment: The Early Sierra Leone Colony', in G. J. Cuming (ed.), *The Mission of the Church and the Propagation of the Faith* (Cambridge, 1970), 107.

[17] Ibid. 116.

[18] Ibid. 128. See also Andrew F. Walls, 'A Colonial Concordat: Two Views of Christianity and Civilisation', in Derek Baker (ed.), *Church Society and Politics* (Oxford, 1975), 301.

[19] Ibid.

tradition of evangelicalism, which George Rawlyk has described as 'a peculiar antinomian blend of American Southern and Nova Scotian New Light popular evangelicalism'.[20] This can be seen with particular clarity when George's piety is viewed as a kind of foil to Zachary Macaulay's much more staid and stolid evangelicalism. Macaulay was governor of Sierra Leone (1793–9) and an intimate of the Wilberforce circle at Clapham. In Macaulay's journal, he recorded his observations after an interview with David George, saying:

Ask either one or the other [Methodists] how he knows himself to be a child of God, and the answer from both will be pretty much in the stile of David George, 'I know it,' not because of this or the other proof drawn from the word of God but because (perhaps) twenty years ago I saw a certain sight or heard certain words or passed thro a certain train of impressions varying from solicitude to deep concern & terror & despair & thence again thro fluctuations of fear & hope to peace & joy & assured confidence.[21]

Because the Nova Scotians had been so often disappointed by white American and European elites—through slavery in the South, through mistreatment and racism in Nova Scotia, and through mismanagement in Sierra Leone—their radical evangelicalism was, as often as not, also part of an expression of distinctive, and even dissenting, piety. The genre of conversion narrative was therefore appropriated to the Nova Scotians' own context in at least two significant ways.

First, there is a telling phrase in David George's conversion narrative. When George began to exhort and to preach after his conversion, he realized he needed to learn to read. His comment after learning a little was: 'I can now read the Bible, so that what I have in my heart, I can see again in the Scriptures'.[22] That is to say, the oral and the personal was anterior to the written and the discursive element in his experience. Indeed, George's phrase for many of his meetings with his people emphasized the oral context: they met 'to hear experiences'.[23] This spoken context of evangelical conversion narrative gave such testimonies a keen sense of immediacy. Whether in Bristol in 1741, in New Jersey among the Delawares in 1744, or in South Carolina in the 1770s, such 'live performances' represented, as we have observed, the most fundamental context for conversion narrative. In talking about what he had 'in his heart', David George was not talking about a strict Edwardsian piety in which the Calvinist

---

[20] G. A. Rawlyk, *The Canada Fire: Radical Evangelicalism in British North America, 1773–1812* (Kingston, 1994), 33.
[21] Ibid. 39; Gordon, *Slavery to Freedom*, 149.
[22] Ibid. 173.
[23] Ibid. 176, 179, 180.

ordo was carefully teased out from Scripture and rationalized in terms of intellectually grounded affective dispositions—he was talking about his *feelings*. And once he learned to read, there it was in the printed text, too, but only *ex post facto*. The heart strangely warmed by the spoken word came first.

Secondly, the spiritual autobiographies of ex-slaves such as George were often constructed not only around a theme of evangelical conversion, but also around the entirely sympathetic and biblical theme of emancipation and freedom from bondage. The key Scripture text in George's conversion—the one that resonated most deeply for him—was Matt. 11: 28: 'Come to me all ye that labour, and are heavy laden, and I will give you rest.' After he had heard Liele preach on this text, he went and told him that he was such a one, 'that I was weary and heavy laden, and that the grace of God had given me rest'.[24] In Sierra Leone itself, the Nova Scotian settlers were reported to have sung the song of Miriam as they marched ashore, celebrating their arrival and crossing of the Atlantic in terms of the Israelite exodus and crossing of the Red Sea. The exodus theme became a powerful organizing motif for slave narratives of spiritual conversion.[25] An unidentified European recorded a message preached by a black minister in Sierra Leone—very possibly David George himself—in which the Israelite exodus typology was made explicit: 'We all mind since it was so with us; we was in slavery not many years ago! Some maybe worse oppressed dan oders, but we was all under de yoke; and what den? God saw our afflictions, and heard our cry, and showed his salvation, in delivering us, and bringing us over de mighty waters to dis place.'[26]

One can easily appreciate that a piety revolving around evangelical conversion, so construed, would be sympathetic to the recaptive Africans whose identity-giving past had been so entirely obliterated. In forging a new identity, evangelical conversion came to play a key role, as the revivals of 1816 in Regent town under William Johnson, and afterwards, bore witness.

Did the recaptives have what we have described in the English context as a 'Christendom' inheritance? What of the 'introspective conscience of the West' that was developed through centuries of penitential discipline, and the assumptions writ large in early modern European culture about creation, providence, moral order, and eschatology? Although, no, they did not have

---

[24] Gordon, *Slavery to Freedom*, 172.

[25] Albert J. Raboteau, 'The Black Experience in American Evangelicalism: The Meaning of Slavery', in Leonard I. Sweet (ed.), *The Evangelical Tradition in America* (Macon, Ga., 1984), 194; Albert J. Raboteau, *Slave Religion* (New York, 1978), 3, 11–12.

[26] Gordon, *Slavery to Freedom*, 131–2, quoting an 'Extract of a letter from Sierra Leone, containing part of a sermon, by a Black Preacher in Freetown' in the *Missionary Magazine for 1796*.

this inheritance, what is particularly fascinating is how quickly they were given something like it through Governor Charles MacCarthy's programme of Europeanization, with virtual squire-parsons set up in an organized pattern of parish administration, including stone churches, parsonages, store-houses, schools, high-walled government buildings, and European-style dress, houses, furniture, and crockery. MacCarthy ordered bells, clocks, and weathercocks from England for the church towers, scales and weights for the local markets, forges for village blacksmiths, quill-pens, copy-books, prayer books, and arithmetic books for the schools, hats for the men, bonnets for the women, and so on.[27] This programme of Euro-peanization was so successful that these Sierra Leoneans have been rightly described as 'Black Europeans' and even contrasted ironically with the holiness-inspired missionaries of a slightly later period in Nigeria, whose ideals of indigenization—bringing the gospel into the day-to-day realities of African life—led them to dress as natives and hence to appear as 'White Africans'.[28] These European missionaries would be quick to lament the prevalence of nominal faith among West Africans, much as evangelical preachers scorned the Christianity of nominal churchgoers in Britain.

Evangelical Missions to the South Pacific, 1797–c.1830

The closest situation we have to cultural contact with a pure and undiluted non-Western society, where missionaries were in the vanguard of cross-cultural encounter, is in the evangelical mission enterprises in the South Pacific from roughly the end of the eighteenth century to the third decade of the nineteenth century. The story of Western contact with the peoples of Australasia has been told elsewhere, along with the missionary history from the sailing of the London Missionary Society (LMS) ship, the *Duff*, and the landing of ill-prepared missionaries on Tahiti and other islands in the Marquesas and Tonga, and the revivals throughout Polynesia from 1830 to 1850.[29] What we may note here in particular is the early missionary reflection on the islanders' experience of conversion.

Missionaries to the South Seas, many of whom had been inspired by Brainerd's diary, were often perplexed that islanders experienced so little abject misery in the first stages of conversion when made aware of their past wrongdoing—even when this wrongdoing included infanticide, cannibal-ism, or human sacrifice. There was often a complete lack of emotion in

---

[27] Fyfe, *Sierra Leone*, 129–31.

[28] Andrew F. Walls, *The Missionary Movement in Christian History* (Edinburgh, 1996), 102–10.

[29] See Niel Gunson, *Messengers of Grace: Evangelical Missionaries in the South Seas, 1797–1860* (Melbourne, 1978); K. R. Howe, *Where the Waves Fall: A New South Sea Islands History from First Settlement to Colonial Rule* (Sydney, 1984).

conversion. One missionary to the Society Islands, William Ellis (1794–1872), wrote: 'Under declarations of the nature and dreadful consequences of sin...the denunciation of the penalties of the law of God, and even under the awakenings of their own consciences to a conviction of sin, we seldom perceive that deep and acute distress of mind, which in circumstances of a similar kind we should have expected.'[30] Likewise, upon being made to understand the doctrine of the cross, the islanders did not frequently express 'that sudden relief, and that exstatic [*sic*] joy, which is often manifested in other parts of the world, by individuals in corresponding circumstances'. Again, Ellis reflected, 'the varied representations of the punishment and sufferings of the wicked, and the corresponding views of heaven, as the state of the greatest blessedness, being to them partial and new, the impressions were probably vague and indistinct; while with us, from long familiarity, they are at once vivid and powerful'.[31] Ellis, then, would appear to confirm the hypothesis of the need for a certain level of Christianization of conscience as a condition of evangelical conversion narrative. In any case, the missionaries worked hard to change this attitude of indifference into real contrition through both civil and ecclesiastical discipline, and through the preaching of sin and hell, since as Neil Gunson comments, 'they wished their converts really to feel their guilt'.[32]

Ellis's consternation at the absence of typical patterns of response to the evangelical message is also apparent in the comments of other missionaries. Sometimes this came out in correspondence between the field and mission authorities back in England. There was a tendency for home authorities to regard the success of mission work according to standards derived from their own experience. 'I often wish', wrote one LMS missionary to the directors, 'that our joy on the shores of Tahiti were in some measure proportionate to yours on the platform in Exeter Hall.' It was difficult for those at home to realize that change in the islands was a very gradual process, and that mass conversion to Christianity was more often the beginning than the climax of mission work.[33]

The usual pattern after the arrival of the first missionaries was initial resistance, next perhaps a few conversions of marginal members of an island society, then the conversion of the chief, followed by a mass conversion of the island, and the beginnings of long-term process of instruction to make the nominal faith of the group more personally meaningful for its members.[34] One historian of the South Seas describes this phenomenon of mass

---

[30] Gunson, *Messengers of Grace*, 223.

[31] Ibid.

[32] Ibid.

[33] Ibid. 131.

[34] Cf. Berkhofer's first sequence of community reintegration in 'Protestants, Pagans, and Sequences among Indians', 206–8, and Kenneth Scott Latourette, *A History of Christianity*

conversion under the influence of the chief by analogy with the conversion of the Germanic peoples of early medieval Europe. The way in which Tahitians acceded to Christianity after Pomare II went to war in the name of Jehovah, and united the island under his rule in 1815, is thus the Polynesian equivalent of the Christianization of Spain by Charlemagne. K. R. Howe's concluding observation on Tahiti is that 'the doctrine of *cuius regio, eius religio* (as the King, so the religion) has universal, not just European application'.[35]

The result of this pattern of conversion was that many of the South Sea islands came to embody more of a 'parish' than a 'gathered' model of church and to embrace a 'mixed body' (Augustine's *corpus permixtum*) of Christians in which there was a profound distinction between nominal and earnest Christian allegiance. Consequently, the lament of missionaries in this situation was often the same as that of evangelicals in Europe. When George Pritchard complained in 1826 'that nine-tenths, of those who were in Church fellowship [were] strangers to the power of vital Godliness', he could as easily have been John Berridge opening his evangelical ministry at Everton, as an LMS missionary to Tahiti.[36] Because Christianity in the islands was eventually adjusted to the existing tribal structure of society, the most difficult problem for the missionaries was often the role of the chiefs in the religious life of the community. Here too there is an analogy to the long history of church–state tension in Europe from the German Investiture Controversy in the high Middle Ages to the Scottish Disruption of 1843 over the voluntary principle.

In the South Pacific, Gunson concludes that there were two types of conversion experienced by the islanders:

There was the experience of heart-acceptance or faith, and there was the outward profession necessitated by a national change of religion. Even this nominal

(San Francisco, 1975), ii. 1298–9. Note, however, that in the large-scale conversion of the Maoris in New Zealand, where the native population was more decentralized into small groups, often at war with each other, conversion followed more of a bottom-up pattern, and came to be associated with reconciliation and peace-making, rather than with the victory of a warrior patron such as Pomare II. Extensive debate about the reasons and conditions of Maori conversion may be followed in Harrison M. Wright, *New Zealand, 1769–1840* (Cambridge, Mass., 1959); Judith Binney, *The Legacy of Guilt: A Life of Thomas Kendall* (Christchurch, NZ, 1968); J. M. R. Owens, 'Christianity and the Maoris to 1840', *New Zealand Journal of History* 2 (1968), 18–40; Judith Binney, 'Christianity and the Maoris to 1840: A Comment', ibid. 3 (1969), 143–65; K. R. Howe, 'The Maori Response to Christianity in the Thames-Waikato Area, 1833–1840', ibid. 7 (1973), 28–46; Robin Fisher, 'Henry Williams' Leadership of the CMS Mission to New Zealand', ibid. 9 (1975), 142–53; Howe, *Where the Waves Fall*, 224–6.

[35] Howe, *Where the Waves Fall*, 145. On the Christianization of Europe, see Anton Wessels, *Europe: Was it Ever Really Christian?*, trans. J. Bowden (1994).

[36] Gunson, *Messengers of Grace*, 303.

profession, or renunciation of the old gods, was a major break with the past . . . However, this was only part of the pattern. Old superstitions persisted, and it was only the
heartfelt conversion in which the missionaries found satisfaction.[37]

And, indeed, revivals of the latter sort often came later, as was the case in
1845 on Fiji.

The uniqueness of mission history in the South Pacific, fragmented as the
region was into thousands of isolated island communities that preserved
their indigenous autonomy as social decision-making units, has attracted the
attention of cultural anthropologists. Alan Tippett is one missionary anthropologist who has developed a sequential model to illustrate the dominant
pattern of conversion among the peoples of Oceania, in particular, over the
last century. In the transition of such societies from the old pagan to the new
Christian context, Tippett sees first a period of awareness, which climaxes in
a point of realization when the new faith is not just an idea but a meaningful
possibility, and which introduces a further period of decision-making. This
period in turn climaxes in a point of commitment, when, if Christianity is
embraced, then this commitment is symbolized by an ocular demonstration
of their rejection of paganism (such as fetish-burning) and acceptance of
Christianity (usually through baptism). After this follows a period of incorporation and catechesis into the new faith. Having developed his model
thus far, Tippett later adds a further point of consummation or confirmation, followed by a further period of maturity. Tippett acknowledges that
he grounds this further stage in his own Wesleyan-holiness theology, but he
also comments,

The early mission records in the Wesleyan fields of the south Pacific speak of 'two
conversions,' one from heathenism to Christianity as a system, a faith experience or
power encounter . . . and the second, a little later, a faith experience leading to a
positive *assurance of new birth*. In many cases still further 'manifestations of grace'
have been recorded, experiences of *sanctification*, associated with revivals rather than
awakenings.[38]

THE CONDITIONS FOR NARRATABLE EVANGELICAL CONVERSION

In the first two mission contexts we observed a significant history of
European contact, although the process of Christianization was perhaps
less advanced among the Delaware Indians of New Jersey than among the
Nova Scotian settlers and recaptives of Sierra Leone. We also saw distinctive

---

[37] Gunson, *Messengers of Grace*, 220.

[38] Alan R. Tippett, 'Conversion as a Dynamic Process in Christian Mission', *Missiology*
2 (1977), 219. A sequential model similar to Tippett's, but elaborated through extensive
cross-disciplinary research, is given in Lewis R. Rambo, *Understanding Religious Conversion*
(New Haven, 1993).

forms of recognizable evangelical conversion narrative, such as the account of the unnamed old Indian convert under Brainerd's ministry, who weaved into his testimony a concern with the loss of spiritual power, or the narrative of David George, who looked back on a remarkable spiritual and geographical migration and integrated an exodus theme into his narrative. Among the Pacific Islanders whose national conversions, such as under Pomare II in Tahiti, brought about a change of religion to Christianity without initially disrupting their social system in a significant way, missionary testimony bears witness to the absence of recognizable evangelical conversion until the later revivals of the mid-century. What may we conclude from this, and how can these case studies shed light on the conditions for narratable evangelical conversion in early modern England?

Again, it seems that there are two key interrelated conditions: first, the development of a keen sense of introspective conscience, and secondly, the rise of a sense of distinctive self-consciousness. As argued in the first chapters of this book, these conditions were essential to the rise of the genre itself in the early modern period. Protestant catechesis, penitential discipline, the contritional emphasis of the liturgy, and the inheritance of law did much to supply the first condition among European peoples, and arguably these influences had been brought to bear to some extent in the Christian formation of the Delaware Indians and the Black African diaspora (in the American South, Nova Scotia, and Sierra Leone), where there was a long history of cultural encounter dominated by white Europeans and Protestant missionaries. But what of the second condition—a distinctive sense of the self?

Charles Taylor writes, 'Along with [modern] forms of narrativity go new understandings of society and forms of living together. Corresponding to the free, disengaged subject is a view of society as made up of and by the consent of free individuals.' Taylor argues that we do not have selves the way we have hearts and livers, 'as an interpretation-free given', but that our sense of personal identity is shaped by our moral topography and our conception of society, or what it is to be a human agent among other agents—in other words, by both what makes up our consciences and our self-consciousness.[39] The modern identity or sense of the self goes hand in hand then with societies in which self-determination is given significant scope, for it is in these situations that the individual may construe his or her life not in terms of a traditional role handed down, but rather of a goal-directed narrative, where past and present choices of certain courses of action, among many possibilities, are projected into an open-ended future. The kinds of society in which such a sense of the self may be expected to appear are those that comprehend relatively more pluralism, that is, those in

---

[39] Charles Taylor, *Sources of the Self* (Cambridge, 1992), 105–6.

which responsibility devolves upon the individual to make significant choices among viable alternatives that affect his or her destiny. To the extent that these choices move me towards or away from what I conceive to be good or ideal, to that extent I am also understanding myself in narrative terms.[40]

Now my narrative, if it is articulated, may come in many forms. It may be curriculum vitae, apologia, memoir, travelogue, or a rags-to-riches tale. But one of the forms it took in early modern England, given the importance of conscience and the dissemination of Protestant teaching concerning the order of salvation, was a narrative of spiritual conversion. Many recent comparative studies of evangelicalism have highlighted the way in which this evangelical impulse has thrived in situations of social disruption, the cross-pollination of peoples, and even political revolution.[41] The North Atlantic evangelical revivals of the eighteenth century arose themselves in the midst of unprecedented movements of people and a heightened awareness of other nations through forced and voluntary migrations and through increasingly efficient means of transportation and communication. That kind of stirring of the international pot is also certainly what we witness in Sierra Leone, spectacularly, but also among the Native American Indians in New Jersey. So these are situations, it may be argued, in which a narrative form of self-understanding and expression may be expected to flourish. In the South Pacific, where traditional patterns of society were not disrupted, even in national conversions to Christianity, we get a different situation, in which the kind of questions that might prompt a personal narrative as an answer do not arise.

To return then to the question posed in the early chapters of this book concerning why the seventeenth century offered 'the autobiographical moment' in the Western Christian tradition, it should be clear now that in addition to a sense of introspective conscience—which was acute already among the sixteenth-century reformers—evangelical conversion narrative required the conditions of modern society, in which the individual has

---

[40] Cf. Alasdair MacIntyre, *After Virtue: A Study in Moral Theory* (2nd edn., 1985), 218–19.

[41] 'In almost all North Atlantic regions, evangelicalism was already present as a religious impulse before the onset of political revolution. Perhaps with only one or two exceptions, however, evangelicalism did not exert a broad, culture-shaping influence in these societies until after the experience of revolution.... [Such a survey indicates] how extraordinarily adaptable the evangelical impulse was in North Atlantic societies during an age of revolution.... More than anything else, it was evangelicalism's singular combination of Protestant biblicism and experiential faith that enabled it to flourish in revolutionary settings, precisely because it was able to offer, when other props gave way, meaning for persons, order for society, and hope for the future.' Mark A. Noll, 'Revolution and the Rise of Evangelical Social Influence in North Atlantic Societies', in M. A. Noll, D. W. Bebbington, and G. A. Rawlyk (eds.), *Evangelicalism* (New York, 1994), 114–15.

greater scope for self-determination. Clearly, there was something distinctive about the conditions of the early modern period that helped to foster the
evangelical narrative and to compel countless women and men to resort to
confessional diaries, oral testimony, and written autobiographies to interpret
their own religious experience as a story of conversion.

It is a commonplace of intellectual history that Western Europe did see an
increasing involution or individuation of consciousness in the early modern
period. From the complex psychology of a character like Lear in Elizabethan drama to the preoccupation with self-portraiture on the part of
Rembrandt, from Descartes's *cogito* to Locke's *tabula rasa*, there seems to
be a new anthropocentrism and self-reflectiveness in Western society that
sets the period apart. Georges Gusdorf highlights the novelty of this self-
consciousness by contrasting it with what came before:

> The conscious awareness of the singularity of each individual life is the late product
> of a specific civilization. Throughout most of human history, the individual does
> not oppose himself to all others; he does not feel himself to exist outside of others,
> and still less against others, but very much *with* others in an interdependent
> existence that asserts its rhythms everywhere in the community. No one is rightful
> possessor of his life or his death; lives are so thoroughly entangled that each of them
> has its center everywhere and its circumference nowhere. The important unit is
> thus never the isolated being—or, rather, isolation is impossible in such a scheme of
> total cohesiveness as this. Community life unfolds like a great drama, with its
> climactic moments originally fixed by the gods being repeated from age to age.
> Each man thus appears as the possessor of a role, already performed by the ancestors
> and to be performed again by descendants.[42]

Gusdorf's picture here of pre-modern consciousness, however idealized,
compares well with evangelical missionary experience on Tahiti and elsewhere in the South Pacific and helps to explain one of the missing conditions of evangelical conversion narrative in that context.

In contrast, Gusdorf describes the new consciousness in Western society
that autobiography reflects, arguing that autobiographical practice 'obliges
me to situate what I am in the perspective of what I have been . . . It adds to
experience itself consciousness of it.'[43] Or, again, '[autobiography] asserts a
kind of tradition between myself and me that establishes an ancient and new
fidelity, for the past drawn up into the present is also a pledge and prophecy
of the future.'[44] This was precisely what happened in evangelical narratives

---

[42] Georges Gusdorf, 'Conditions and Limits of Autobiography', in James Olney (ed.),
Autobiography: Essays Theoretical and Critical (Princeton, NJ, 1980), 29–30. Gusdorf's account
is developed in a more detailed and nuanced way in Michael Mascuch, *Origins of the
Individualist Self: Autobiography & Self-Identity in England, 1591–1791* (Cambridge, 1997),
6–9, 13–24.

[43] Gusdorf, 'Conditions and Limits', 38.

[44] Ibid. 44.

of conversion, in which the autobiographer placed herself personally along the curve of salvation history. In W. R. Ward's words, these narratives expressed a 'wish to realize the history of salvation not only as an objective and outward fact but as an event of the soul'.[45] The self is projected into a future that follows the order of salvation—growth in holiness, Christian service, and a pious death, with the expectation of eternal felicity hereafter. But this abstract pattern was read in personal terms from the details of one's own past and present life.

From the vantage point of evangelical mission experience in Tahiti, where there were conversions but a total absence of conversion narratives, we can see more clearly the appearance of evangelical conversion narrative as an episode in Western history. The evangelical conversion narrative flourished, then, when Christendom, or Christian civil society, had eroded far enough to allow for toleration, dissent, experimentation, and the manifestation of nominal and sincere forms of adherence to faith, but not so far as to elide a traditional sense of Christian moral norms and basic theological and cosmological assumptions. It was precisely in the seventeenth and eighteenth centuries that the emerging modern identity could cross paths with the fading Christian moral hegemony. Evangelical conversion narrative appeared on the trailing edge of Christendom and the leading edge of modernity. These were the conditions under which large numbers of men and women found that the pattern and experience of evangelical conversion expressed their deepest religious aspirations.[46]

JAMES LACKINGTON: AN UNCONVERSION NARRATIVE

In contrast then to these non-Western case studies, conversion narrative among the early English evangelicals owed something to an individuation of conscience and consciousness that appears characteristic of early modern Europe. However, if one accepts a certain steady secularization of consciousness as a key development of late eighteenth-century English society, then conversion narrative appears as an increasingly anachronistic form of sectarian literature. Indeed, cultural historians have pointed to the emergence of a modernist, bourgeois narrative identity in precisely the same period in which we have traced the flourishing of the evangelical conversion narrative. The autobiography of the ex-Methodist James Lackington (1746–1815) is an *un*conversion narrative of this sort, and it provides a final literary foil to the evangelical genre, particularly since Michael Mascuch regards Lackington's *Memoirs* as an early and seminal example of the modern

---

[45] W. R. Ward, Introduction to Wesley, *Works* (BE), xviii. 9.
[46] Cf. Andrew Walls, 'The Evangelical Revival, The Missionary Movement, and Africa', in Noll, Bebbington, and Rawlyk (eds.), *Evangelicalism*, 313–14.

identity.[47] We have said that evangelical conversion narrative appears not only as Christendom recedes but also as modernity advances. Lackington's narrative allows us to test the modernity of the genre.

James Lackington was a 16-year-old in London who went along to a Methodist meeting in 1762. His conscience was awakened under the preaching and a month later he found peace with God. He tried to make a living as a journeyman shoemaker, but by the time he was 28, he was penniless. He was able to get a small business loan of five pounds from John Wesley, and with that money he started retailing books. Beginning with a bag of books he bought for a guinea and sold in an obscure passageway, he built an enormously successful bookselling business in London, so that some seventeen years later, he boasted an income of £5,000 a year. His secret was the invention of the practice we know today as remaindering—buying and selling unsold books at below the cover price. In 1793 he bought a block of houses in Finsbury Square for a new shop that he christened 'The Temple of the Muses'. The main floor was large enough to drive a coach and six horses around, and the shop quickly became one of the sights to see in London.

Two years after Lackington started this business, with the loan from Wesley, he left the Methodists and abandoned his evangelical faith altogether. Consequently, when he wrote his *Memoirs* in 1791, he wrote not a conversion narrative but an *un*conversion narrative. Mascuch emphasizes that Lackington's story was deliberately structured to develop and direct his own identity without reference to divine providence or piety of any kind. These were not simply the disconnected anecdotes of an old man either. His story had a point. The frontispiece of Lackington's autobiography was an engraved portrait of the author with the caption, 'I. Lackington. Who a few years since, began Business with five Pounds; now sells one Hundred Thousand Volumes Annually.' The complete title of the American edition of the book communicates the same message of Lackington as a self-made man: *Memoirs of James Lackington, Who from the Humble Station of a Journeyman Shoemaker, by Great Industry, Amassed a Large Fortune and now Lives in a Splendid Style in London Containing among other Curious and Facetious Anecdotes, a Succinct Account of . . . the Methodists. Written by himself.*

A part of what made his book so successful was his witty (indeed scurrilous) exposé of the Methodists as one who had been an insider. The cover hinted of kiss-and-tell revelations in his book. For example, he tells a story of George Whitefield out field-preaching. A young woman in the front of the crowd fell backwards, just below the great evangelist, and lay there kicking up her heels. Seeing her in a kind of convulsion, some of the crowd moved to help her and the women drew her petticoats and apron

---

[47] Mascuch, *Origins of the Individualist Self*, 2; James Lackington, *Memoirs of the First Forty-Five Years of the Life of James Lackington*, corrected and enlarged edn. (1792).

down over her feet, but Whitefield cried out, 'Let her alone! Let her alone! A glorious sight! A glorious sight!' meaning of course that it was wonderful to see a soul overwhelmed in spiritual emotion. But the young men construed his meaning somewhat differently, and when the audience could not stop laughing, Whitefield had to dismiss them. It became a saying among the young men ever after, when reeling home from the pub, 'A glorious sight, A glorious sight!'[48]

Again, Lackington recounts his previous amours and how he was infatuated with one Methodist sister after another, moving easily from spiritual advice to kisses: 'I assure you, my friend, that we were sometimes like the Galatians of old; we began in the *spirit*, and ended in the *flesh*.'[49] None of this did much for the reputation of Methodism, but it certainly established Lackington's own ethos as a witty, urbane man-about-town. And that, of course, was precisely what he was trying to do.

Entertaining stories such as these were embedded in an overall story of Lackington's progress from rags to riches by dint of his own enterprise and stoic self-discipline. Lackington took control of his own identity in secular terms. He constructed his own story, owned his own copyright, and acted as his own distributor. He took advantage of the new legal mechanisms of intellectual property rights, and he made his life into a successful commodity: he literally traded on his own identity. And he was good at it. There were thirteen editions of his *Memoirs* in his lifetime. He successfully persuaded a vast, anonymous public to sanction his self-identity as a uniquely successful bookseller.

So, Lackington is a good specimen, and an early one, of the modern self-understanding that has been so much discussed by moral philosophers, literary theorists, cultural historians, and social scientists. Lackington understood himself as clearly bounded, unique, and neatly integrated. He was the product of his own choices, and he could narrate his life in a way that organized the aimless drift of experience into a coherent story, one that pointed authoritatively to a single retrospective meaning. And he was the one to declare this meaning and persuade others of it. This form of narrative identity is sometimes called modern or modernist, bourgeois, or individualist. It arises alongside historicism and it similarly champions the sort of narrative in which the meaning or significance of the story rehearsed is wholly immanent and springs, as it were, genetically, out of resources of the subject itself, without reference to external authority. In the modern context, then, authoring an autobiography has become quite literally self-authorization. The 'we-narrative' of converts in early medieval Europe and early nineteenth-century Polynesia has become the secular 'I-narrative' of modernity.

---

[48] Lackington, *Memoirs*, 186.
[49] Ibid. 243.

Reshaping Individualism: The Evangelical
Narrative Community

Literary studies of 'the rise of the novel' have sought to account for the changes in narrative prose fiction during the mid-eighteenth century at least partly in terms of the changes in the relationship of the individual to society during this period. Ian Watt famously argued, for example, that Daniel Defoe's *Robinson Crusoe* was the quintessential embodiment of economic and spiritual individualism.[50] Michael Mascuch has extended the argument, claiming that if *Robinson Crusoe* was thus the first expression of early modern individualism in narrative fiction, then James Lackington's *Memoirs* offers the first expression of that same individualism in non-fiction narrative.[51]

Large numbers of evangelicals found their voice through a different kind of narrative than this, however. Societal changes could lead to competing versions of what it meant to be a moral agent among other moral agents. What then was distinctive about the evangelical self-identity? What was the difference between James Lackington and, say, Martha Claggett, the lay evangelical whom we discussed in Ch. 5? Clearly enough, Lackington was deep in what Michel Foucault decried as the 'anthropological sleep' of the modern self, quietly and blissfully eliding the contribution that others had made to his identity and the extent to which his autobiography was his own fiction.[52] But what about these evangelicals? Were they a little drowsy too?

It has been argued by a number of historians that evangelicals were uniquely adapted to the emerging consumer culture in the eighteenth century, and that they effectively hawked the gospel as a commodity in the marketplace and addressed people as religious consumers—all of this in contrast to the traditional monopoly over religion presumed to exist in the Church as established by law and by custom.[53] On this reading, evangelicals were profoundly individualist, and when seen against the sense of community identity in Polynesia or in pre-modern Europe this seems indisputably

---

[50] Ian Watt, *The Rise of the Novel* (Berkeley, Calif., 1957), 60–92. Watt's so-called 'triple-rise thesis' was that the rise of the novel was parallel with the rise of individualism in early industrial capitalism, the rise of a literate middle class, and the spread of Protestantism, especially in its Calvinist and Puritan forms. Watt's thesis has been fully explored, challenged, and revised in the last half century, but the concern to see the origins of the novel in terms of wider, complex changes in social and intellectual life has, if anything, intensified. See e.g. Michael McKeon, *The Origins of the English Novel, 1600–1740* (Baltimore, Md., 1987); John Richetti (ed.), *The Cambridge Companion to the Eighteenth-Century Novel* (Cambridge, 1996); and David Blewett (ed.), *Reconsidering the Rise of the Novel*, a special issue of *Eighteenth-Century Fiction* 12 (Jan.–Apr., 2000), in honour of Ian Watt who died in 1999.

[51] Mascuch, *Origins of the Individualist Self*, 26.

[52] Michel Foucault, *The Order of Things* (1970), 340–3.

[53] See e.g. Harry S. Stout, *The Divine Dramatist: George Whitefield and the Rise of Modern Evangelicalism* (Grand Rapids, Mich., 1991), and Frank Lambert, *'Pedlar in Divinity': George Whitefield and the Transatlantic Revivals, 1737–1770* (Princeton, NJ, 1994).

true. And yet, if we look closely at the stories told by the evangelicals, we find a surprisingly strong countervailing emphasis upon the community of faith as well, a community that was as much discovered as it was constructed by human agency. As noted in Ch. 4, if the evangelicals who wrote autobiographies were individualists of a sort, they were also communitarians of a sort. The evangelical self-identity owed much to the rise of the individual, but this identity differed markedly from the solipsism of the secular, modern version of the self with its naive claim to derive the meaning of one's life immanently, wholly from the resources of the autonomous ego. The evangelical conversion narrative bore witness, therefore, to an important alternative version of Enlightenment individuality.

Many voices today would describe Western individualism as pathological. Noni Jabavu speaks of the contrast in this respect between African and Western autobiography. Speaking of his own Xhosa and Zulu peoples, he recollects,

I was thankful that we were each brought up to feel ourselves a symbol, 'a representative of a group' not of a family only, and not as a private person. '*Umntu ngumntu ngabantu.* A person is a person (is what he is) because of and through other people.' Otherwise success too often leads to conceit and failure to humiliation that would be an intolerably lonely burden. As it was, sharing gave a sense of proportion.[54]

What of the early evangelicals? While evangelicals bore witness to a keen sense of individuation and uniqueness, called out into narrative by the gospel message, we also hear again and again in their narratives about friendships and intimate group meetings, where the fellowship was close and people spoke more freely to each other than ever they had before. When Thomas Oliver or Margaret Austin expressed such strong yearnings to join the Methodist band meetings, they acknowledged not only that they needed new hearts, but also that they needed a new community. When such people were converted, they felt that they were born again not in isolation, but into a new family of brothers and sisters. John Newton wrote a hymn to dedicate a new meeting place for his religious society, and it includes the stanza,

> Within these walls let holy peace,
> And love, and concord dwell;
> Here give the troubled conscience ease,
> The wounded spirit heal.[55]

---

[54] Quoted in James Olney, *Tell Me Africa: An Approach to African Literature* (Princeton, NJ, 1973), 69.

[55] *The Olney Hymns* (1779), 234.

It was within precisely this kind of *koinonia* that ordinary women and men discovered a new way to understand their religious identity.

These groups, and the preachers who led them, fostered a culture in which one discovered the possibilities of a narrative identity shaped by a gospel message. It was within these meetings that you would hear the testimonies and sing the hymns. Here you would begin to learn the story and ask yourself, Could my life be like that in any way? How might I 'enact' or experience that sort of autobiography? The evangelical conversion narrative is a genre, which means that it has certain conventions, and one recognizes the form by these features, just as one recognizes a familiar letter by the presence of a conventional salutation, closing, and so on. Such conventions do not come out of thin air; they arise within a community, or a tradition (a community expressed through time). They arise, that is, according to Frye's 'radical of presentation'. These conventions bound one narrative to another. This does not mean that everyone's story was the same. All Elizabethan sonnets are not the same, even though they might be written in fourteen lines of iambic pentameter with a limited range of rhyme schemes. We noted how the Puritan Richard Baxter went through some travail over whether he was only socialized as a Christian, rather than truly regenerated. At the end of his anxious soul-searching, he wrote, 'At last I came to realize that God breaketh not all men's hearts alike.'[56] There was scope for the personal and unique, even within the larger story, but these evangelical subjects witnessed at the same time to a painful shattering of their false selves, the ego that Luther described as *in se incurvatus*, or 'curved in upon itself'.

What was the pattern that structured these narratives? Unlike Lackington's story, an escalator of progress, Martha Claggett's story, like that of many other evangelicals, was a narrative of suffering, humiliation, and redemption. Northrop Frye argues that the pattern of original prosperity, descent into humiliation, and return is the overall structure of the biblical story and of the small narratives within it, such as the parable of the prodigal son. He also argues that this pattern has distinctively shaped much of Western literature.[57] This was true for a figure such as John Newton, and it has also been true for the narrative identity of many Christians throughout history. Their personal story replicated the biblical story in miniature and often took the form of an episode in the larger story of God so that their narratives have the same shape as the larger drama of salvation history. The most famous example is Augustine. His story of stealing fruit from an orchard nicely echoes the epic fall from paradise in Genesis, and his later conversion in a garden at Milan corresponds to paradise restored, and so on.

[56] Richard Baxter, *Reliquiae Baxterianae* (1696), 7.
[57] Northrop Frye, *The Great Code* (1982), 198.

Martha Claggett read this pattern in her life, too, as she remembered the relative innocence of a Bible-reading childhood and the hardening of her heart in adolescence at boarding school. Then, just as the promise of redemption follows the biblical fall, so also the word of God entered her experience with Whitefield's preaching and began the process of return. Again, even as the climax of salvation history comes with the advent of the Messiah and the pentecostal experience of the Holy Spirit, so also Martha Claggett and other converts bore witness to a joyous sense of sins forgiven and a sense of new life. Finally, the biblical prophecy of a future new heaven and earth has its counterpart in the hopeful curve of these conversion narratives, projecting the hope of growth in grace, pious death, and joy hereafter. Margaret Austin concluded her narrative, saying, 'I see there is a great work to be wrought still in my soul: but he that has begun the work will surely finish; he that is the author will be the finisher.'[58] It is a telling metaphor, God as the author who will finish his work, who will complete the 'life' in the double sense of the written narrative and the living experience of the author. In this sense at least, these evangelical autobiographers did not essentialize the self, since they recognized in the last analysis that they were seeking not to author their own stories but to discern, even if sometimes through a glass darkly, the story that God was authoring and for which their lives were the text.

This is the way the gospel actually went to work as 'theory' to shape early evangelical narrative identity. But again, this larger story (of creation, fall, redemption, new creation) was explored within a deeply personal narrative of *my* life, since the autobiographer had the vivid sense that this story had to do with *me*. The pattern offered an opportunity for men and women to locate themselves personally in a kind of spiritual and moral space and to explore how their story uniquely reflected common themes. So was this identity *constructed*, like a modern identity, or *bestowed*, like a pre-modern identity? Again, located on the cusp of modernity but also sharing all the assumptions of a fading Christian hegemony, the evangelical sense of self involved *both* creativity and discovery, *both* individuation and community.

Like evangelical conversion narrative, medieval hagiography had similarly strongly etched patterns, but without the same sense of strong individuation. Saints' lives were woven together out of topoi, literary commonplaces or patterns, that overwhelmed the personality of the subjects. Richard Fletcher gives an example in his study of early medieval conversion.[59] Bede's *Life of Cuthbert*, written in the eighth century, tells how the saint was brought pig's lard by a pair of ravens, and Bede says

---

[58] Margaret Austin (19 May 1740), EMV.

[59] Richard Fletcher, *The Barbarian Conversion: From Paganism to Christianity* (New York, 1997), 11–12.

outright that this was 'after the example' of the *Life of Benedict*, written a couple of centuries earlier by Gregory the Great. Behind Benedict's story was yet another story of the hermits, Paul and Anthony, who were sustained by bread brought to them by ravens in the desert. And, of course, all this sounds a lot like the account in 1 Kings 17 of the prophet Elijah, who was fed by ravens by the brook Cherith. What this one example illustrates is the way that the medieval biographer could draw on a pool of stock tales, themes, and phrases and apply these to his subject without restraint or acknowledgement. Behind this lay a theological conception of the communion of saints and the essential unity of sanctity across the ages: there was really only one life of a saint.[60] But the effect of all this was, in many cases, to efface the personality of the saint, not to mention leaving modern historians scratching their heads and wondering how exactly to use this information.

Some cultural historians, such as Roy Porter, think that evangelical conversion narrative is really a hangover of this kind of hagiographical writing, a sectarian or fundamentalist backwater in the modern era, a literary remnant of a spirit-drenched universe that does not properly fit in the age of Enlightenment and rational religion.[61] But this really is not true. The evangelical genre is not primarily biographical, but autobiographical, and moreover, it is truly popular, written by women and men from a wide range of backgrounds. That in itself should be enough to place evangelical narrative self-identity squarely in the modern period. And as we have observed, the genre first emerged uniquely in the mid-seventeenth century at the outset of the modern period, and it was not Luther and Calvin who wrote conversion narratives—we have to piece the details of their spiritual biographies together from fragments in their theological writings—but their later descendants. The evangelical genre thus reflects a high level of individuation. This is what you would expect under the conditions of the early modern world as the individual began to count for more in all sorts of ways.

And yet Arminians and Calvinists alike echoed the language of the prayer of general thanksgiving in the Prayer Book when they routinely spoke of a certain number of ordained 'means of grace', such as preaching, holy communion, the reading of Scripture, prayer, and Christian conversation and friendship. These were given things, received and not constructed. But it was in the midst of these shared practices that one experienced the travail of new birth and discovered a uniquely personal faith. This led to the ironic situation in which a whole *group* of people sang, 'His blood can make the foulest clean, | His blood avail'd for *me*.' The evangelical conversion

---

[60] Thomas J. Heffernan, *Sacred Biography: Saints and their Biographers in the Middle Ages* (New York, 1988), 130–2, 157, 165.

[61] Roy Porter, *Mind-Forg'd Manacles: A History of Madness in England from the Restoration to the Regency* (London, 1990), 66–7, 72–3, 80, 265, 279.

narrative owed much to the rise of a new individualism in modern society, but at the same time the self-identity of evangelicals contrasted sharply with the pathological autonomy of the secular individualist self that has often been taken as the normative development of the Enlightenment.

In 1804, nearly 60 years old, James Lackington wrote another autobiographical book which is less well known. It was called *The Confessions of James Lackington*, and it was a full retraction of his earlier *Memoirs*.[62] He wrote, 'When I look into my memoirs, I shudder to see what I have done. I have wantonly treated of, and sported with the most solemn and precious truths of the gospel. O God, lay not this sin to my charge.'[63] He had turned back again to the Methodists and renewed his faith. Indeed, he became a local preacher, and between 1805 and his death in 1815 he built and endowed three Methodist chapels. The *Confessions* is comprised of a series of thirty edited letters that trace the gradual progress of Lackington, like Thomas Scott earlier, from agnosticism to orthodoxy ('revealed religion') to evangelical piety. His narrative recounts the intellectual arguments and literary influences that led him to change his mind. He had also become anxious about the moral disorder he witnessed around him, and he had lived long enough to see some of his 'infidel' and 'libertine' acquaintances come to a poor end at the close of their lives. In his twenty-fifth letter, Lackington recounts how he began reading John Whitehead's two-volume *Life of the Rev. John Wesley* (1793) in order 'to see in what state of mind Mr. Wesley died'. While reading he came to a conviction of his error in having rejected the faith of the Methodists many years earlier:

To describe the conflict, and the different commotions which passed in my mind, while we were reading this excellent work is impossible . . . That divine power which has been felt by thousands and tens of thousands under the preaching of Mr. Wesley, his brother Charles, and others of his preachers, again humbled me in the dust. I sunk down at the feet of Christ and washed them with my tears. Sorrow, joy, and love, were sweetly mingled together in my soul . . . I was now convinced that the pardoning love of God, which forty years since was first manifested to my soul, was a divine reality, and not the effect of a heated imagination.[64]

The *Confessions* was thus a *re*-conversion narrative. Michael Mascuch sees all of this as just one more act of self-revisioning, one more indication that Lackington was master of his own identity, able to remake himself once more at the end of his life, and he therefore dismisses the *Confessions* as more or less unimportant.[65] I think this is too hasty. Lackington himself pointed

---

[62] James Lackington, *The Confessions of J. Lackington, Late Bookseller . . . in a Series of Letters to a Friend* (1804; repr. New York, 1978).

[63] Ibid. 185.

[64] Ibid. 167.

[65] Mascuch, *Origins of the Individualist Self*, 208–9.

to the significance of the early modern genre examined in the pages of this book, impressed that there were 'thousands, and tens of thousands' during his lifetime who had 'borne testimony to the truth of this doctrine'.[66] Between the *Memoirs* and the *Confessions* he discovered, through painful experience, that his ideals of moral and spiritual self-sufficiency could not finally be sustained. Within his own lifetime James Lackington came to realize that the modern self was insupportable. Given the many voices today calling for the decentring, deconstruction, or death of the modern self, and the rejection of any essentialist notion of the self, it is surely significant that Lackington, as a pioneer of the modernist identity, shudders back from the brink and reposes in the end in the community of faith and the self-transcending word of the gospel.

[66] Lackington, *Confessions*, 167.

Bibliography

1. MANUSCRIPTS

Angus Library, Regent's Park College, Oxford
Elizabeth Rutt, 'The Lord's dealings with Elizabeth Rutt', autograph copy of letter, 1770 [1771?].
John Ryland, jun., 'An Account of the Rise and Progress of the Two Society's at Mr. Rylands and at Mrs. Trinder's Boarding School in Northampton', 1768–70.
—— 'The Experience of Jo/n R.l.d. jun' as wrote by himself in a Letter to Tho' R..t dated Feb': 1770.'

Bodleian Library, Oxford
John Newton to Wilberforce, 1 Nov. 1787, Add. Wilberforce Papers, c. 49.

Bristol Baptist College, Bristol
John Ryland, jun., 'Autograph Reminiscences', 24 October 1807.

Cowper and Newton Museum, Olney, Buckinghamshire
John Newton, 'Vol. 5. Lectures on Rom. ch. viii', MS sermon notebook, no. 14.

Firestone Library, Princeton University
John Newton, autograph diaries, 1751–6 and 1773–1805.

John Rylands Library, Manchester
Early Methodist Volume, chiefly letters to Charles Wesley, c.1738–88.
Notebook containing account of religious experiences sent to Charles Wesley by Susanna Design, Sarah Colston, and Betty Brown, 1742.

Moravian Church House, London
Memorials, c.1772–1847 (2 packets).
Memoirs [Fetter Lane], c.1760–1850.
Memoirs [Fulneck], c.1775–1850.
Letters of Application to the London Congregation, 1740s [Fetter Lane].
Fetter Lane Congregation Diary, 1742–1928, 41 vols.
Minutes of the General Synod at Marienborn, 1 July – 17 Sept. 1769.
Resolutions of the General Synod at Marienborn, 2 July – 22 Aug. 1764.
Harmony of the Synods of 1764, 1769, 1775, and 1782.
Extracts from the London Archives of the United Brethren [1850].
E. Seymour Cooper, 'Analytical Index to the first and second volumes of the London Congregation Diary,' bound typescript (1904–7).

Mills Memorial Library, McMaster University, Hamilton, Ontario
John Newton, shorthand autograph copy of William Cowper's memoir.

New College, Edinburgh
William McCulloch, 'Examinations of persons under spiritual concern at Cambuslang, during the Revival in 1741–42', 2 vols.

Northamptonshire Record Office, Northampton
John Ryland, jun., 'Respecting Written Experiences,' autograph copy of correspondence between Ryland and Henry Page in 1816, Bristol Baptist College; photocopy at the Northamptonshire Record Office.
Church Book of Northampton College Street Baptist Church, 1733–81.

Ockbrook Moravian Church and Settlement, Ockbrook, Derbyshire
Memoir of Henrietta Mary Louisa v. Hayn, d. 1782.
Memoir of John Rogers, d. 1765.
Memoir of Anna Kriegabstein, d. *c.*1778.

2. PRINTED PRIMARY SOURCES

'Brief Memoir of the Late Revd Wm Richardson', prefixed to *Sermons by the Late Rev. William Richardson*, 2 vols. (York, 1822), 1–71.
ADAM, THOMAS, *Private Thoughts* (York, 1795).
ALLEINE, JOSEPH, *The Believer's Triumph in God's Promises*, ed. John Collett Ryland (1767).
—— *The Voice of God in His Promises*, ed. John Collett Ryland (1766).
AMBROSE, ISAAC, *Media: the Middle Things in Reference to the First and Last Things: or, The Means, Duties, Ordinances, both Secret, Private and Publike, for Continuance and Increase of a Godly Life, Once Begun, till We Come to Heaven* (1649).
An Apology for the Presbyterians of Scotland who are the Hearers of The Reverend Mr. George Whitefield, Shewing that their Keeping Communion with Him, in the Ordinances of the Gospel, Stands Justified by the Principles and Practice of the Church of Scotland from the Reformation to this Day, Especially by the Westminster Confession of Faith and Solemn League and Covenant (Edinburgh, 1742).
The Arminian Magazine (1778–97).
An Authentick Relation of the Many Hardships and Sufferings of a Dutch Sailor, Who was put on shore on the Uninhabited Isle of Ascension . . . Taken from the Original Journal, found . . . by some Sailors . . . in January 1725/6 (1728).
BACON, FRANCIS, 'Of Travel', *The Essays* (1701).
BALBANI, NICOLO, *The Italian Convert: Newes from Italy of a Second Moses; or, The Life of Galeacivs Caracciolvs, the Noble Marquesse of Vico. Containing the Story of his Admirable Conversion from Popery* (1635).
BARBOUR, HUGH, and ROBERTS, ARTHUR O. (eds.), *Early Quaker Writings, 1650–1700* (Grand Rapids, Mich., 1973).
BARRY, JONATHAN, and MORGAN, KENNETH (eds.), *Reformation and Revival in Eighteenth-Century Bristol* (Bristol, 1994).
BAXTER, RICHARD, *The Mischiefs of Self-Ignorance and the Benefits of Self-Acquaintance* (1662).

—— *Reliquiae Baxterianae* (1696).

BEADLE, JOHN, *The Journal or Diary of a Thankful Christian* (1656).

BENHAM, DANIEL, *Memoirs of James Hutton* (1856).

BENNET, JOHN, *Mirror of the Soul: The Diary of an Early Methodist Preacher, John Bennet (1714–1754)*, ed. Simon Valentine (Werrington, Peterborough, 2002).

BERRIDGE, JOHN, *The Works of the Rev. John Berridge . . . with an Enlarged Memoir of his Life*, ed. Richard Whittingham (1838).

Blunham, The Old Meeting Baptist Church: Church Book, 1724–1891, transcribed for the Bedfordshire County Record Office (Bedford, 1976).

BRADBERRY, DAVID, *A Challenge Sent by the Lord of Hosts to the Chief of Sinners* (1766).

[BREWER, SAMUEL], 'Life of the Rev. Samuel Brewer', *Evangelical Magazine* 5 (1797), 5–18.

The Brotherly Agreement and Declaration Touching the Rules and Orders of the Brethren's Congregation at London (1776).

BULL, JOSIAH, *John Newton of Olney and St Mary Woolnoth* (1868).

BUNYAN, JOHN, *Grace Abounding to the Chief of Sinners*, ed. Roger Sharrock (Oxford, 1962).

BURNHAM, RICHARD, *Pious Memorials; or, the Power of Religion . . . in the Experience of many Divines and other Eminent Persons* (1753).

CECIL, RICHARD, *Memoirs of the Rev. John Newton* (1808).

CENNICK, JOHN, *The Bloody Issue Healed* (1744).

—— *Extracts from the Journals of John Cennick*, ed. J. H. Cooper (Glengormley, Co. Antrim, 1996).

—— *The Life and Hymns of John Cennick*, ed. J. R. Broome (Harpenden, Herts, 1988).

—— *The Life of Mr. J. Cennick* (Bristol, 1745).

—— *The New Birth, Being the Substance of a Discourse Delivered at Malmsbury in Wiltshire in the Year 1741* (1788).

—— *Sacred Hymns For the Use of Religious Societies* (1764).

—— *Sacred Hymns For the Use of Religious Societies. Generally composed in Dialogues*, part 2 (Bristol, 1743).

—— *A Short Account of the Experience of Mrs. Anne Beaker* (1744).

The Christian History, Containing Accounts of the Revival and Propagation of Religion in Great-Britain & America (Boston, 1743–5).

The Christian Monthly History: or, an Account of the Revival and Progress of Religion Abroad and at Home (1743–6).

The Christian's Amusement: Containing Letters Concerning the Progress of the Gospel both at Home and Abroad, etc. (1740–1).

Church Book: St Andrew's Street Baptist Church, Cambridge, 1720–1832, transcribed by L. G. Champion for the Baptist Historical Society (n.p., 1991).

CLARKE, JOHN, *The Good Tidings of Great Joy to All People* (1762).

A Collection of Hymns . . . Designed Chiefly for the Use of the Congregations in Union with the Brethren's Church (1754).

A Collection of Hymns for the Use of the People Called Methodists . . . With a New Supplement (1877).

COOKE, EDWARD, *A Voyage to the South Sea, and Round the World, Perform'd in the Years 1708, 1709, 1710, and 1711. Containing a Journal of all Memorable Transactions* (1712).

COWPER, WILLIAM, *Letters and Prose Writings of William Cowper*, ed. James King and Charles Ryskamp, 5 vols. (Oxford, 1979).

—— *Memoir of the Early Life of William Cowper* (1816).

—— *Memoirs of the Most Remarkable and Interesting Parts of the Life of William Cowper, Esq., of the Inner Temple, Detailing Particularly the Exercises of His Mind in Regard to Religion* (1816).

CULROSS, JAMES, *The Three Rylands* (1897).

DARWIN, ERASMUS, *Zoonomia*, 2 vols. (1794, 1796).

DEFOE, DANIEL, *A Journal of the Plague Year, Being Observations or Memories of the most Remarkable Occurrences, as well Publick as Private, which Happened in London During the Last Great Visitation in 1665*, ed. Louis Lanada (1969).

DODDRIDGE, PHILIP, 'Free Thoughts on the Most Probable Means of Reviving the Dissenting Interest', in *The Works of Philip Doddridge*, 5 vols. (1804), v. 383–412.

—— *The Works of . . . P. Doddridge*, ed. Edward Williams and Edward Parsons, 5 vols. (Leeds, 1803).

DOE, CHARLES (ed.), *A Collection of Experience of the Work of Grace (never before Printed): or the Spirit of God Working upon the Souls of several Persons; whereby is Demonstrated their Conversion to Christ* (1700).

DUTTON, ANNE, *A Brief Account of the Gracious Dealings of God, with a Poor, Sinful, Unworthy Creature* (1743).

—— *A Discourse upon Walking with God* (1735).

EDWARDS, JONATHAN, *The Works of Jonathan Edwards*, ed. Perry Miller, John E. Smith, and Harry Stout (New Haven, Conn., 1957–).

ELLIOT, R., *For the Benefit of Six Orphans. A Funeral Discourse on the Death of Mr. John How* (1767).

ERB, PETER C. (ed.), *Pietists: Selected Writings* (1983).

ERSKINE, JOHN, *Signs of the Times Considered, or the High Probability that the Present Appearances in New England, and the West of Scotland, are a Prelude of the Glorious Things Promised to the Church in the Latter Ages* (Edinburgh, 1742).

The Evangelical Magazine (1793–1812).

An Exact Account of the Wonderful Preservation of a Gentlewoman from Shipwrack (1739).

A Faithful Narrative of the Life and Character of the Reverend Mr. Whitefield, B. D., From his Birth to the Present Time. Containing an Account of His Doctrine and Morals; His Motives for Going to Georgia, and His Travels through Several Parts of England (1739).

A Familiar Letter of Reproof and Humiliation to the Rev. Thomas Towle (1785).

FAULL, KATHERINE M. (ed.), *Moravian Women's Memoirs: Their Related Lives, 1750–1820* (Syracuse, NY, 1997).

FAWCETT, BENJAMIN, *Extracts from the Diary, Meditations and Letters of Mr. Joseph Williams of Kidderminster, Who Died December 21, 1755, Aged 63* (Shrewsbury, 1779).

FIRMIN, GILES, *The Real Christian, or, A Treatise of Effectual Calling* (1670).

FRANCKE, AUGUST HERMANN, *Nicodemus: or, a Treatise on the Fear of Man. Written in German by August Herman Franck. Abridged by John Wesley* (3rd. edn., Newcastle upon Tyne, 1744).

—— *Pietas Hallensis: or a Publick Demonstration of the Foot-steps of a Divine Being yet in the World: in an Historical Narration of the Orphan-House, and Other Charitable Institutions, at Glaucha near Hall in Saxony* (1705).

FRASER, JAMES, *Memoirs of the Life of the Very Reverend Mr. James Fraser of Brea* (Edinburgh, 1738).

GIB, T., *Remarks on the Reverend Mr. Whitefield's Journal. Wherein His many Inconsistencies are Pointed out, and His Tenets Consider'd* [signed T.G.] (1738).

GILBERT, MARY, *An Extract of Miss Mary Gilbert's Journal* (4th edn., 1787).

GILLIES, JOHN (ed.), *Historical Collections Relating to Remarkable Periods of the Success of the Gospel* (Glasgow, 1754).

—— (ed.), *Historical Collections Relating to Remarkable Periods of the Success of the Gospel* (rev. edn. 1845; repr. Edinburgh, 1981).

—— *Memoirs of the Life of the Reverend George Whitefield* (1772).

The Glasgow Weekly-History Relating to the Late Progress of the Gospel at Home and Abroad (Glasgow, 1742).

GODWIN, EDWARD, *A Brief Account of God's Dealings with Edward Godwin. Written by Himself* (2nd edn., Bristol, 1744).

The Gospel Magazine (1766–83).

GOUGH, STRICKLAND, *An Enquiry into the Causes of Decay of the Dissenting Interest* (2nd edn., 1730).

GREY, ZACHARY, *The Quaker and Methodist Compared. In an Abstract of George Fox's Journal . . . And of the Reverend Mr. George Whitefield's Journals* (1740).

GRIMSHAW, WILLIAM, *An Answer to a Sermon Lately Published against the Methodists by the Rev. Mr George White* (Preston, 1749).

HAIME, JOHN, *A Short Account of God's Dealings with Mr. John Haime* (1785).

HAMILTON, KENNETH G. (ed.), *The Bethlehem Diary: Volume 1, 1742–1744* (Bethlehem, Penn., 1971).

HARRIS, HOWELL, *A Brief Account of the Life of Howell Harris, Esq; Extracted from Papers Written by Himself* (Trevecka, 1791).

HART, JOSEPH, *Hymns . . . With a Preface, Containing a Brief and Summary Account of the Author's Experience* (1759).

HAWKINS, JOHN, *Clavis Commercii; or, the Key of Commerce: Shewing, the True Method of Keeping Merchants Books, . . . With a Practical Waste-Book, Journal and Ledger* (1718).

HAYDEN, ROGER (ed.), *The Records of a Church of Christ in Bristol, 1640–1687* (Bristol, 1974).

HERVEY, JAMES, *Theron and Aspasio: or, a Series of Dialogues and Letters upon the Most Important and Interesting Subjects* (1755).

HOLLAND, HENRY, 'Preface to the Reader' in *The Workes of Richard Greenham* (1605).

HOOKER, THOMAS, *The Application of Redemption . . . Printed from the Author's Papers . . . by Thomas Goodwin, and Philip Nye* (1657).

HUMPHREYS, JOSEPH, *An Answer to Everyman That asketh a Reason Of the Hope that is in Us* (2nd edn., Bristol, 1744).

—— *A Discourse on the Parable or Story of Dives and Lazarus. . . . Design'd for Those who are Convinc'd of the Way of Truth, to Lend or Give to Such of their Unconvinc'd Friends or Relations who will not Come to Hear the Word of Life* (Bristol, 1744).

—— *Joseph Humphreys's Experience of the Work of Grace upon his Heart* (Bristol, 1742)

—— *Our Lord's Grace to the Thief upon the Cross . . . now Publish'd for a Pattern of Mercy to the Chief of Sinners, and Especially Condemn'd Malefactors, who shall hereafter Believe on Jesus Christ to Life Everlasting* (Bristol, 1744).

INGHAM, BENJAMIN, *Diary of an Oxford Methodist, Benjamin Ingham, 1733–1734*, ed. Richard P. Heitzenrater (Durham, NC, 1985).

JACKSON, THOMAS (ed.), *Lives of Early Methodist Preachers*, 6 vols. (4th edn., 1871; repr. in 3 vols., Stoke-on-Trent, 1998).

JANEWAY, JAMES, *A Token for Children* (1671).

The Journal of the Honourable House of Representatives, of His Majesty's Province of the Massachusetts-Bay in New England Begun and Held at Boston, in the County of Suffolk, on Wednesday the Thirtieth Day of May, Annoque Domini, 1739 (Boston, 1739).

KEACH, BENJAMIN, *The Glory of a True Church and its Discipline Display'd. Wherein a True Gospel-Church is Described* (1697).

KILBY, RICHARD, *The Burthen of a Loaden Conscience: or, The Miserie of Sinne: Set Forth by the Confession of a Miserable Sinner* (Cambridge, 1616).

—— *Hallelu-iah. Praise yee the Lord. For the Unburthening of a Loaden Conscience. By his Grace in Iesus Christ, Vouchsafed unto the Worst Sinner of All the World* (1632).

KNAPPEN, M. M. (ed.), *Two Elizabethan Puritan Diaries* (Chicago, 1933).

LA MOTTE, PHILÉMON DE, *Several Voyages to Barbary. Containing an Historical and Geographical Account of the Country . . . With a Journal of the Late Siege and Surrender of Oran . . . by Captain Henry Boyde* (1736).

LACKINGTON, JAMES, *The Confessions of J. Lackington, Late Bookseller . . . in a Series of Letters to a Friend* (1804; repr. New York, 1978).

—— *Memoirs of the First Forty-Five Years of the Life of James Lackington* (corrected and enlarged edn., 1792).

LAVINGTON, GEORGE, *The Enthusiasm of Methodists and Papists Compared*, 3 vols. (1754).

LINDSEY, THEOPHILUS, *The Apology of Theophilus Lindsey, M.A., on Resigning the Vicarage of Catterick, Yorkshire* (1774).

—— *A Sequel to the Apology on Resigning the Vicarage of Catterick, Yorkshire* (1776).

LLOYD, JOHN, *The Well-Spring of Life Opened in Christ* (1768).

LUMLE, GEORGE, *A Journal of the Squadron, under the Command of Nicholas Haddock, Esq; Rear Admiral of the Red, &c. from Spithead to Mahon: Introduced with Impartial Thoughts, upon the Past and Present State of our Affairs* (1739).

MADAN, MARTIN (ed.), *A Treatise on Christian Faith, Extracted and Translated from the Latin of Hermannus Witsius* (1761).

—— *A Scriptural Comment upon the Thirty-Nine Articles of the Church of England* (1772).

MANNERS, NICHOLAS, *Some Particulars of the Life and Experience of Nicholas Manners* (York, 1785).

MANTON, THOMAS, *The Complete Works of Thomas Manton*, 22 vols. (1870).

MAWSON, CAPTAIN, *The Just Vengeance of Heaven Exemplify'd. In a Journal Lately Found by Captain Mawson . . . All Wrote with his Own Hand, and Found Lying near the Skeleton* (1730).

The Methodist Magazine (1798–).

A Miscellaneous Collection of Satirical Pieces . . . Respecting the Extraordinary, Unprecedented and Scandalous Conduct of Master Tommy Dishclout . . . (1785).

MITCHELL, THOMAS, *A Short Account of the Life of Mr. Thomas Mitchell* (1781).

MOORE, HENRY (ed.), *The Life of Mrs. Mary Fletcher* (6th edn., 1824).

—— (ed.), *The Life of Mrs. Mary Fletcher* (New York, 1848).

MONTAIGNE, MICHEL DE, *The Essayes*, trans. John Florio (1904).

MORGAN, JAMES, *The Life and Death of Mr. Thomas Walsh, Composed in Great Part from the Accounts Left by Himself* (1762 [1763]).

MUGGLETON, LODOWICKE, *The Acts of the Witnesses of the Spirit . . . By Lodowick Muggleton: One of the Two Witnesses, and True Prophets of the Only High, Immortal, Glorious God, Christ Jesus. Left by Him to be Publish'd After's Death* (1699).

NELSON, JOHN, *The Case of John Nelson, Written by Himself* (1745).

—— *An Extract of J. Nelson's Journal* (Bristol, 1767).

The New Spiritual Magazine (1783–5).

NEWMAN, WILLIAM, *Rylandiana* (1835).

NEWTON, JOHN, *An Authentic Narrative of Some Remarkable and Interesting Particulars in the Life of* ******* (1764).

—— *The Works of the Rev. John Newton*, 6 vols. (1808–9).

—— and COWPER, WILLIAM, *The Olney Hymns* (1779).

PAYNE, THOMAS, *Redeeming Grace Displayed to the Chief of Sinners* (York, 1780).

PERKINS, WILLIAM, *A Case of Conscience, the Greatest that Ever Was; How a Man May Know Whether He Be the Childe of God or No* (1592).

—— *The Workes of that Famous and Worthy Minister of Christ in the Universitie of Cambridge, Mr. William Perkins*, 3 vols. (1613).

—— *The Workes of that Famous and Worthy Minister of Christ in the Universitie of Cambridge, Mr. William Perkins*, 3 vols. (1626).

PETTO, SAMUEL, 'Epistle to the Reader', prefixed to *Roses from Sharon* (1654), n.p.

POWELL, VAVASOR, 'Epistle to the Sober and Spirituall Readers of this Booke', prefixed to *Spirituall Experiences, of Sundry Beleevers* (1653), n.p.

Praise out of the Mouth of Babes: or, a Particular Account of some Extraordinary Pious Motions and Devout Exercises, Observ'd of Late in Many Children in Silesia (1708).

REDFORD, GEORGE, and ANGELL, JOHN (eds.), *Autobiography of William Jay* (1854; repr. Edinburgh, 1974).

RIPPON, JOHN, *The Gentle Dismission of Saints from Earth to Heaven: A Sermon Occasioned by the Decease of the Rev. John Ryland, Senior, A.M.* (1792).

ROBE, JAMES, *A Faithful Narrative of the Extraordinary Work of the Spirit of God, at Kilsyth* (Glasgow, 1742).

—— *Narratives of the Extraordinary Work of the Spirit of God, at Cambuslang, Kilsyth, &c* (Glasgow, 1790).

—— *A Short Narrative of the Extraordinary Work at Cambuslang* (Glasgow, 1742).

ROBINSON, H. WHEELER, 'The Experience of John Ryland', *Baptist Quarterly*, NS 4 (1928–9), 17–26.

ROGERS, JOHN, *Ohel or Beth-shemesh. A Tabernacle for the Sun: or Irenicum Evangelicum. An Idea of Church Discipline, In the Theorick and Practick Parts . . . Published for the Benefit of All Gathered Churches, More Especially in England, Ireland, and Scotland* (1653).

ROGERS, RICHARD, *Seven Treatises, Containing such Direction as is Gathered out of the Holie Scriptures, Leading and Guiding to True Happines* (1603).

ROGERS, WOODES, *Cruising Voyage Round the World: First to the South-Sea, thence to the East-Indies, and Homewards by the Cape of Good Hope. Begun in 1708, and Finish'd in 1711* (1718).

RYLAND, JOHN COLLETT, *An Elegy on the Death of J. Brine* (1765).

RYLAND, JOHN, JUN., *Life and Death of the Reverend Andrew Fuller* (1816).

RYLAND, JONATHAN EDWARDS (ed.), *Pastoral Memorials: Selected from the Manuscripts of the Late Revd. John Ryland, D. D. of Bristol, with a Memoir of the Author*, 2 vols. (1826).

A Saint Indeed: or, the Great Work of a Christian . . . to which is added, a Faithful and Succinct Narrative of some Late and Wonderful Sea-Deliverances (Glasgow, 1754).

SCOTT, JOHN, *Life of the Rev. Thomas Scott* (6th edn., London, 1824).

SCOTT, THOMAS, *Commentary on the Holy Bible*, 3 vols. (6th edn., 1823).

—— *The Force of Truth: An Authentic Narrative* (1779).

—— *Theological Works*, 5 vols. (Buckingham 1805–8).

The Secret Patient's Diary: also the Gout and Weakness Diaries. Being each a Practical Journal or Scheme (1725).

SEWARD, WILLIAM, *Journal of a Voyage from Savannah to Philadelphia, and from Philadelphia to England* (1740).

SHEPARD, THOMAS, *Thomas Shepard's 'Confessions'*, ed. George Selement and Bruce C. Wooley (Boston, 1981).

—— *God's Plot: The Paradoxes of Puritan Piety, being the Autobiography and Journal of Thomas Shepard*, ed. Michael McGiffert (Amherst, Mass., 1972).

A Short Account of the Remarkable Conversions at Cambuslang in a Letter from a Gentleman in the West-Country to his Friend at Edinburgh (Glasgow, 1742), 5.

SIMONS, MENNO, *The Complete Writings of Menno Simons, c. 1496–1561*, ed. J. C. Wenger, trans. L. Verduin (Kitchener, Ont., 1984).

Southill, Independent, later Baptist, Church: Church Book, 1693–1851, transcribed for the Bedfordshire County Record Office (Bedford, 1981).

SPENER, PHILIPP JAKOB, *Pia Desideria: or Heartfelt Desires for a God-Pleasing Improvement of the True Protestant Church*, trans. Theodore G. Tappert (Philadelphia, 1964).

TAYLOR, THOMAS, *Redeeming Grace Displayed to the Chief of Sinners* (York, 1780).

TELFORD, JOHN (ed.), *Wesley's Veterans*, 7 vols. (1912–14).

The Theological Miscellany (1784–9).

TOLD, SILAS, *An Account of the Life, and Dealings of God with Silas Told* (1786).

TRAHERNE, THOMAS, *Selected Poems and Prose*, ed. Alan Bradford (1991).

TRAPNEL, ANNA, *A Legacy for Saints; being several Experiences of the Dealings of God with Anna Trapnel, in, and after her Conversion* (1654).

TURNER, JANE, *Choice Experiences of the Kind Dealings of God before, in, and after Conversion* (1653).

TYNDALE, WILLIAM, 'A Pathway into the Holy Scripture', *Doctrinal Treatises*, ed. Henry Walter (Cambridge, 1848).

VAN BROECK, ADRIAN, *The Life and Adventures of Capt. John Avery, the Famous English Pirate, (Rais'd from a Cabbin-Boy, to a King) Now in Possession of Madagascar . . . Written by a Person who made his Escape from thence, and Faithfully Extracted from his Journal* (1709).

VENN, JOHN, *Life and . . . Letters of the Late Rev. Henry Venn* (2nd edn., 1835).

WALKER, HENRY (ed.) [attrib.], *Spirituall Experiences of Sundry Beleevers* (1653).

The Weekly History: or, An Account of the Most Remarkable Particulars Relating to the Present Progress of the Gospel (1741–2).

The Weekly Miscellany . . . by Richard Hooker, of the Temple, Esq. (1732–41).

WELCH, EDWIN (ed.), *The Bedford Moravian Church in the Eighteenth Century* (Bedford, 1989).

WESLEY, CHARLES, *A Short Account of the Death of Mrs. Hannah Richardson* (1741).

—— *Journal of the Rev. Charles Wesley*, ed. Thomas Jackson, 2 vols. (1849).

—— *The Journal of the Rev. Charles Wesley, M.A., Sometime Student of Christ Church, Oxford*, ed. Thomas Jackson, 2 vols. (1849).

—— *The Sermons of Charles Wesley: A Critical Edition with Introduction and Notes*, ed. Kenneth G. C. Newport (Oxford, 2001).

WESLEY, JOHN, *The Bicentennial Edition of the Works of John Wesley*, ed. Frank Baker and Richard P. Heitzenrater (Nashville, 1976–).

—— *Journal of John Wesley*, ed. Nehemiah Curnock, 8 vols. (1909–16).

—— *Letters of John Wesley*, ed. John Telford, 8 vols. (1931).

—— *The Works of John Wesley*, ed. Thomas Jackson, 14 vols. (3rd edn., 1872; repr. Grand Rapids, Mich., 1984).

—— and WESLEY, CHARLES, *A Short View of the Difference between the Moravian Brethren, Lately in England, and the Reverend Mr. John and Charles Wesley* (2nd edn., Bristol, 1748).

WHITEFIELD, GEORGE, *A Collection of Papers, Lately Printed in the Daily Advertiser* (1740).

—— *George Whitefield's Journals* (5th edn., Edinburgh, 1960).

—— *Letters of George Whitefield for the Period 1734–1742* (Edinburgh, 1976).

—— *The Marks of the New Birth: A Sermon Preached at the Parish Church of St. Mary, White-Chapel, London* (1739).

—— *Saul's Conversion: A Lecture, Preached on . . . September 12th, 1741, in the High-Church-Yard of Glasgow* (Glasgow, 1741).

—— *The Works of the Reverend George Whitefield, M.A.*, ed. John Gillies, 6 vols. (1771).

WILCOX, THOMAS, *Choice Drop of Honey from the Rock Christ* (1690).

WILLIAMS, JOSEPH, *Enlarged Series of Extracts from the Diary, Meditations and Letters*, ed. Benjamin Hanbury (1815).

WINTHROP, JOHN, *Winthrop's Journal, 'History of New England', 1630–1649*, ed. J. K. Hosmer, 2 vols. (New York, 1908).

ZINZENDORF, NICOLAUS LUDWIG, *Extract of Count Zinzendorf's Discourses on the Redemption of Man by the Death of Christ. By John Wesley* (Newcastle-upon-Tyne, 1744).

—— *Nine Public Lectures on Important Subjects in Religion, Preached in Fetter Lane Chapel in London in the Year 1746* (Iowa City, Ia., 1973).

—— *Sixteen Discourses on the Redemption of Man by the Death of Christ, Preached at Berlin* (1740).

3. SECONDARY SOURCES

ABBEY, CHARLES J., and OVERTON, JOHN H., *The English Church in the Eighteenth Century*, 2 vols. (1878).

AGNOS, PETER, *The Queer Dutchman Castaway on Ascension* (New York, 1978).

ALTHOLZ, JOSEPH L., *The Religious Press in Britain, 1760–1900* (New York, 1989).

ANDERSON, HOWARD, and EHRENPREIS, IRVIN, 'The Familiar Letter in the Eighteenth Century: Some Generalizations', in H. Anderson, P. B. Daghlian, and I. Ehrenpreis (eds.), *The Familiar Letter in the Eighteenth Century* (Lawrence, Kan., 1966), 269–82.

ARIÈS, PHILIPPE, *Centuries of Childhood*, trans. Robert Baldick (New York, 1962).

—— and DUBY, GEORGES (eds.), *A History of Private Life* (Cambridge, Mass., 1989), iii. 1–11.

ARISTOTLE, *Poetics*, Loeb Classical Library (1995).

ARMINIUS, JAMES, *Works of James Arminius*, trans. James Nichols and William Nichols, 3 vols. (1825; repr. Grand Rapids, Mich., 1991).

ARNOLD, MATTHEW, *St. Paul and Protestantism* (1892).

ATWOOD, CRAIG D. 'Blood, Sex, and Death: Life and Liturgy in Zinzendorf's Bethlehem', Ph.D. thesis (Princeton Theological Seminary, 1995).

—— 'The Mother of God's People: The Adoration of the Holy Spirit in the Eighteenth-Century Brüdergemeine', *Church History* 68 (1999), 886–909.

—— 'Sleeping in the Arms of Christ: Sanctifying Sexuality in the Eighteenth-Century Moravian Church', *Journal of the History of Sexuality* 8 (1997), 25–51.

—— 'Zinzendorf's "Litany of the Wounds" ', *Lutheran Quarterly* 11 (1997), 189–214.

—— 'Zinzendorf's 1749 Reprimand to the *Brüdergemeine*', *Transactions of the Moravian Historical Society* 29 (1996), 59–84.

—— and VOGT, PETER (eds.), *The Distinctiveness of Moravian Culture: Essays and Documents in Moravian History in Honor of Vernon H. Nelson* (Nazareth, Penn., 2003).

AUGUSTINE, *Confessions*, trans. R. S. Pine-Coffin (1961).

BALIE, W. D., *The Six Mile Water Revival of 1625* (Belfast, 1976).

BANGS, CARL, *Arminius* (Nashville, 1971).

BEBBINGTON, DAVID W., 'Evangelical Conversion, *c.* 1740–1850', Position Paper 21, North Atlantic Missiology Project (Cambridge, 1996).

—— *Evangelicalism in Modern Britain* (1989).

BEN-AMOS, ILANA KRAUSMAN, *Adolescence and Youth in Early Modern England* (New Haven, Conn., 1994).

BENSON, ROBERT, and CONSTABLE, GILES (eds.), *Renaissance and Renewal in the Twelfth Century* (Cambridge, Mass., 1982; repr. Toronto, Ont., 1991).

BERGER, PETER, *The Sacred Canopy* (New York, 1967).

BERKHOFER, ROBERT F., JUN., 'Protestants, Pagans, and Sequences among the North American Indians, 1760–1860', *Ethnohistory* 10 (1963), 201–32.

BERNARD OF CLAIRVAUX, *Sermons on Conversion*, trans. Marie-Bernard Saïd (Kalamazoo, Mich., 1981).

BINNEY, JUDITH, 'Christianity and the Maoris to 1840: A Comment', *New Zealand Journal of History* 3 (1969), 143–65.

—— *The Legacy of Guilt: A Life of Thomas Kendall* (Christchurch, NZ, 1968).

BLAUVELT, MARTHA TOMHAVE, and KELLER, ROSEMARY SKINNER, 'Women and Revivalism: The Puritan and Wesleyan Traditions', in Rosemary Radford

Ruether and Rosemary Skinner Keller (eds.), *Women and Religion in America*, 2 vols. (San Francisco, 1983), ii. 316–67.

BLEWETT, DAVID (ed.), *Reconsidering the Rise of the Novel*, a special issue of *Eighteenth-Century Fiction* 12 (Jan.–Apr. 2000).

BOWDEN, HENRY WARNER, *American Indians and Christian Missions* (Chicago 1981).

BRAUER, JERALD C., 'Conversion: From Puritanism to Revivalism', *Journal of Religion* 58 (1978), 227–43.

BREKUS, CATHERINE A., *Strangers and Pilgrims: Female Preaching in America, 1740–1845* (Chapel Hill, NC, 1998).

BRERETON, VIRGINIA LIESON, *From Sin to Salvation: Stories of Women's Conversions, 1800 to the Present* (Bloomington, 1991).

BRETHERTON, F. F., ' "Early Methodist Preachers" and "Wesley's Veterans" ', *Proceedings of the Wesley Historical Society* 22 (1940), 102–5.

BRINTON, HOWARD H., *Quaker Journals* (Wallingford, Penn., 1972).

BROWN, PETER, *Augustine of Hippo: A Biography* (Berkeley, 1969).

BROWN, RAYMOND, *The English Baptists of the Eighteenth Century* (1986).

BULLOCK, F. W. B., *Evangelical Conversion in Great Britain, 1696–1845* (St Leonards on Sea, 1959).

—— *Evangelical Conversion in Great Britain, 1516–1695* (St Leonards on Sea, 1966).

BURCKHARDT, JACOB, *The Civilization of the Renaissance in Italy*, 2 vols. (New York, 1958).

BURKE, PETER, 'Representations of the Self from Petrarch to Descartes', in Roy Porter (ed.), *Rewriting the Self: Histories from the Renaissance to the Present* (1997), 17–28.

BURTON-CHRISTIE, DOUGLAS, *The Word in the Desert* (New York, 1993).

BUTLER, JON, 'Enthusiasm Described and Decried: The Great Awakening as Interpretive Fiction', *Journal of American History* 69 (1982), 325

CALDWELL, PATRICIA, *The Puritan Conversion Narrative* (Cambridge, 1983).

CALVIN, JOHN, *Institutes of the Christian Religion*, ed. John T. McNeill, trans. Ford Lewis Battles, 2 vols. (Philadelphia, 1960).

—— *Calvin: Commentaries*, trans. and ed. J. Haroutunian and L. P. Smith (Philadelphia, 1958).

CAMPBELL, TED A., *The Religion of the Heart: A Study of European Religious Life in the Seventeenth and Eighteenth Centuries* (Columbia, SC, 1991).

CHADWICK, HENRY, *Augustine* (Oxford, 1986).

—— Introduction to Augustine, *Confessions* (Oxford, 1991), pp. ix–xxviii.

CHAMPION, L. G., 'The Letters of John Newton to John Ryland', *Baptist Quarterly* 27 (1977), 157–63.

CHARTIER, ROGER, 'The Practical Impact of Writing', in Philippe Ariès and Georges Duby (eds.), *A History of Private Life* (Cambridge, Mass., 1989), iii. 111–59.

CHILCOTE, PAUL WESLEY, *John Wesley and the Women Preachers of Early Methodism* (Metuchen, NJ, 1991).

CHURCH, LESLIE F., *The Early Methodist People* (1948).

—— *More about the Early Methodist People* (1949).

CLARK, J. C. D., *English Society, 1688–1832* (Cambridge, 1985).

COHEN, CHARLES LLOYD, *God's Caress: The Psychology of the Puritan Religious Experience* (Oxford, 1986).

COLLEY, LINDA, *Captives: Britain, Empire and the World, 1600–1850* (2002).

COLLINS, JAMES, *Pilgrim in Love: An Introduction to Dante and His Spirituality* (Chicago, 1984).

COLLINS, KENNETH J., 'Other Thoughts on Aldersgate: Has the Conversionist Paradigm Collapsed?' *Methodist History* 30 (1991), 10–25.

—— 'Twentieth-Century Interpretations of John Wesley's Aldersgate Experience: Coherence or Confusion?' *Wesleyan Theological Journal* 24 (1989), 18–31.

COLLINSON, PATRICK, *The Elizabethan Puritan Movement* (Oxford, 1990).

CONWAY, JILL KER, *When Memory Speaks: Reflections on Autobiography* (New York, 1998).

CRAIN, WILLIAM C., *Theories of Development* (Englewood Cliffs, NJ, 1980).

CRAWFORD, MICHAEL J., 'Origins of the Eighteenth Century Evangelical Revival: England and New England Compared', *Journal of British Studies* 26 (1987), 361–97.

—— *Seasons of Grace: Colonial New England's Revival Tradition in its British Context* (New York, 1991).

CRESSY, DAVID, *Literacy and the Social Order: Reading and Writing in Tudor and Stuart England* (Cambridge, 1980).

CUBIE, DAVID L., 'Placing Aldersgate in John Wesley's Order of Salvation', *Wesleyan Theological Journal* 24 (1989), 32–53.

CURRIE, ROBERT, HORSLEY, LEE S., and GILBERT, ALAN D., *Churches and Churchgoers: Patterns of Church Growth in the British Isles Since 1700* (Oxford, 1977).

DALLIMORE, ARNOLD, *George Whitefield*, 2 vols. (Edinburgh, 1990).

DANTE ALIGHIERI, *The New Life*, trans. C. E. Norton (Boston, 1909).

DAVIES, G. C. B., *The Early Cornish Evangelicals, 1735–1760* (1951).

DAVIS, JOHN F., 'The Trials of Thomas Bylney and the English Reformation', *Historical Journal* 24 (1981), 775–90.

DELUMEAU, JEAN, *Sin and Fear: The Emergence of a Western Guilt Culture, 13th–18th Centuries*, trans. Eric Nicholson (New York, 1990).

DRESSER, MADGE, 'Sisters and Brethren: Power, Propriety and Gender among the Bristol Moravians, 1746–1833', *Social History* 21 (1996), 304–29.

DREYER, FREDERICK, 'Faith and Experience in the Thought of John Wesley', *American Historical Review* 87 (1983), 12–30.

—— *The Genesis of Methodism* (1999).

DURDEN, SUSAN, 'A Study of the First Evangelical Magazines, 1740–1748', *Journal of Ecclesiastical History* 27 (1976), 255–75.

ELLA, GEORGE, *William Cowper* (Darlington, 1993).

ELLIOTT-BINNS, L. E., *The Early Evangelicals: A Religious and Social Study* (1953).

EVANS, RICHARD, 'The Relations of George Whitefield and Howell Harris, Fathers of Calvinistic Methodism', *Church History* 30 (1961), 179–90.

FAULL, KATHERINE M., 'The American *Lebenslauf*: Women's Autobiography in Eighteenth-Century Moravian Bethlehem', *Yearbook of German-American Studies* 27 (1992), 23–48.

FAWCETT, ARTHUR, *The Cambuslang Revival* (Edinburgh, 1971).

FERGUSON, WALLACE, *The Renaissance in Historical Thought: Five Centuries of Inter-pretation* (Boston, 1948).

FISHER, ROBIN, 'Henry Williams' Leadership of the CMS Mission to New Zealand', *New Zealand Journal of History* 9 (1975), 142–53.

FITZPATRICK, MARTIN, 'Latitudinarianism at the Parting of the Ways: a Suggestion', in John Walsh, Colin Haydon, and Stephen Taylor (eds.), *The Church of England, c.1689–c.1833* (Cambridge, 1993), 209–27.

FLETCHER, RICHARD, *The Barbarian Conversion: From Paganism to Christianity* (New York, 1997).

FOUCAULT, MICHEL, *The Order of Things: An Archaelogy of the Human Sciences* (1970).

FOWLER, JAMES W., 'The Enlightenment and Faith Development', in Jeff Astley and Leslie J. Francis (eds.), *Christian Perspectives on Faith Development* (Leominster, 1992), 15–28.

FOXE, JOHN, *The Acts and Monuments of John Foxe*, 8 vols. (New York, 1965).

FRYE, NORTHROP, *Anatomy of Criticism* (Princeton, NJ, 1957).

—— *The Great Code: The Bible and Literature* (1982).

FYFE, CHRISTOPHER, *A History of Sierra Leone* (1962; repr. edn., Aldershot, Hants, 1993).

GASCOIGNE, JOHN, 'Anglican Latitudinarianism and Political Radicalism in the Late Eighteenth Century', *History* 71 (1986), 22–38.

—— *Cambridge in the Age of Enlightenment* (Cambridge, 1989).

GIBBEN, CRAWFORD, *The Puritan Millennium* (Dublin, 2000).

GILBERT, ALAN D., *Religion and Society in Industrial England* (1976).

GOLDEN, MORRIS, *In Search of Stability: The Poetry of William Cowper* (New York, 1960).

GORDON, GRANT, 'The Call of Dr John Ryland Jr', *Baptist Quarterly* 34 (1992), 214–17.

—— *From Slavery to Freedom: The Life of David George, Pioneer Black Baptist Minister* (Hansport, Nova Scotia, 1992).

—— 'John Ryland, Jr. (1753–1825)', in Michael A. G. Haykin (ed.), *The British Particular Baptists, 1638–1910*, 2 vols. (Springfield, Mo., 1998, 2000), ii. 77–95.

GRIMES, MARY COCHRAN, 'Saving Grace Among Puritans and Quakers: A Study of 17th and 18th Century Conversion Experiences', *Quaker History* 72 (1983), 3–26.

GUIBERT OF NOGENT, *A Monk's Confession: The Memoirs of Guibert of Nogent*, trans. P. J. Archambault (University Park, Penn., 1996).

GUNSON, NIEL, *Messengers of Grace: Evangelical Missionaries in the South Seas, 1797–1860* (Melbourne, 1978).

GUSDORF, GEORGES, 'Conditions and Limits of Autobiography', in James Olney (ed.), *Autobiography: Essays Theoretical and Critical* (Princeton, 1980), 28–48.

HABERMAS, JÜRGEN, *The Structural Transformation of the Public Sphere*, trans. T. Burger with F. Lawrence (Cambridge, Mass., 1991).

HALLER, WILLIAM, *The Rise of Puritanism* (1938; repr. New York, 1957).

HAMBRICK-STOWE, CHARLES E., *The Practice of Piety: Puritan Devotional Disciplines in Seventeenth-Century New England* (Chapel Hill, NC, 1982).

HARPHAM, GEOFFREY GALT, 'Conversion and the Language of Autobiography', in James Olney (ed.), *Studies in Autobiography* (New York, 1988), 42–50.

HARRAN, MARILYN J., *Luther on Conversion* (Ithaca, NY, 1983).

HARTLEY, LODWICK, 'Cowper and the Evangelicals: Notes on Early Biographical Interpretations', *Proceedings of the Modern Languages Association* 65 (1950), 719–31.

—— *William Cowper: The Continuing Revaluation* (Chapel Hill, NC, 1960).

HASKINS, CHARLES HOMER, *The Renaissance of the Twelfth Century* (Cambridge, Mass., 1927).

HATCH, NATHAN O., and STOUT, HARRY S. (eds.), *Jonathan Edwards and the American Experience* (New York, 1988).

HAYDEN, ROGER, 'Evangelical Calvinism among Eighteenth-Century British Baptists with Particular Reference to Bernard Foskett, Hugh and Caleb Evans and the Bristol Baptist Academy, 1690–1791', Ph.D. thesis (Keele, 1991).

HAYKIN, MICHAEL (ed.), *The Revived Puritan: The Spirituality of George Whitefield* (Dundas, Ont., 2000).

HEFFERNAN, THOMAS J., *Sacred Biography: Saints and their Biographers in the Middle Ages* (New York, 1988).

HEIDEGGER, MARTIN, *Being and Time*, trans. J. Macquarrie and E. Robinson (New York, 1962).

HEILBRUN, CAROLYN, *Writing a Woman's Life* (New York, 1988).

HEITZENRATER, RICHARD P., *The Elusive Mr. Wesley*, 2 vols. (Nashville, 1984).

—— 'Great Expectations: Aldersgate and the Evidences of Genuine Christianity', in Randy L. Maddox (ed.), *Aldersgate Reconsidered* (Nashville, 1990), 49–91.

—— *Mirror and Memory: Reflections on Early Methodism* (Nashville, Tenn., 1989).

—— 'Wesley and His Diary', in John Stacey (ed.), *John Wesley: Contemporary Perspectives* (1988), 11–22.

HILLHOUSE, JAMES T., *The Grub-Street Journal* (Durham, NC, 1928).

HINDMARSH, BRUCE, *John Newton and the English Evangelical Tradition: Between the Conversions of Wesley and Wilberforce* (Oxford, 1996).

—— 'The Reception of Jonathan Edwards by Early Evangelicals in England', in D. W. Kling and D. A. Sweeney (eds.), *Jonathan Edwards at Home and Abroad* (Columbia, SC, 2003), 201–21.

HOWE, K. R. 'The Maori Response to Christianity in the Thames-Waikato Area, 1833–1840', *New Zealand Journal of History* 7 (1973), 28–46.

—— *Where the Waves Fall: A New South Sea Islands History from First Settlement to Colonial Rule* (Sydney, 1984).

HURTADO, LARRY W., 'Convert, Apostate or Apostle to the Nations: The "Conversion" of Paul in Recent Scholarship', *Studies in Religion* 22 (1993), 283–4.

JACOB, W. M., *Lay People and Religion in the Early Eighteenth Century* (Cambridge, 1996).

JAMES, WILLIAM, *The Varieties of Religious Experience* (2nd edn., 1902).

—— *Writings, 1902–1910*, ed. Bruce Kuklick (New York, 1987).

JONES, MARGARET, 'From "The State of My Soul" to "Exalted Piety": Women's Voices in the Arminian Magazine/Methodist Magazine, 1778–1821', in R. N. Swanson (ed.), *Gender and Christian Religion* (Woodbridge, Suffolk, 1998), 273–86.

KENT, JOHN, *Wesley and the Wesleyans: Religion in Eighteenth-Century Britain* (Cambridge, 2002).

KING, JAMES, 'Cowper's *Adelphi* Restored: the Excisions to Cowper's Narrative', *Review of English Studies* 30 (1979), 291–305.

—— *William Cowper* (Durham, NC, 1986).

KNAPPEN, MARSHALL MASON, *Tudor Puritanism* (Chicago, 1939).

LAKE, PETER, *Moderate Puritans and the Elizabethan Church* (Cambridge, 1982).

LAMBERT, FRANK, *Inventing the 'Great Awakening'* (Princeton, 1999).

—— 'Pedlar in Divinity: George Whitefield and the Great Awakening, 1737–1745', *Journal of American History* 77 (1990), 812–37.

—— *'Pedlar in Divinity': George Whitefield and the Transatlantic Revivals, 1737–1770* (Princeton, 1994).

LANDSMAN, NED, 'Evangelists and Their Hearers: Popular Interpretation of Revivalist Preaching in Eighteenth-Century Scotland', *Journal of British Studies* 28 (1989), 120–49.

LANGFORD, PAUL, *A Polite and Commercial People: England, 1727–1783* (Oxford, 1990).

LATOURETTE, KENNETH SCOTT, *A History of Christianity*, 2 vols. (San Francisco, 1975).

LONGNECKER, RICHARD (ed.), *The Road from Damascus* (Grand Rapids, Mich., 1997).

LOVEGROVE, DERYCK W. (ed.), *The Rise of the Laity in Evangelical Protestantism* (2002).

LUTHER, MARTIN, 'Preface to the Complete Edition of Luther's Latin Writings, 1545', trans. Lewis W. Spitz, Sen., *Luther's Works* (Philadelphia, 1960), xxxiv. 323–38.

LYLES, ALBERT M., *Methodism Mocked: The Satiric Reaction to Methodism in the Eighteenth Century* (1960).

MACDONALD, MICHAEL, *Mystical Bedlam: Madness, Anxiety, and Healing in Seventeenth-Century England* (Cambridge, 1981).

—— and MURPHY, TERENCE R., *Sleepless Souls: Suicide in Early Modern England* (Oxford, 1990).

MACFARLAN, DUNCAN, *The Revivals of the Eighteenth Century, Particularly at Cambuslang* (1845; repr. Glasgow, 1988).

MACFARLANE, ALAN, *The Origins of English Individualism: The Family, Property and Social Transition* (New York, 1979).

MACINTYRE, ALASDAIR, *After Virtue: A Study in Moral Theory* (2nd edn., 1985).

MCKENDRICK, NEIL, BREWER, JOHN, and PLUMB, J. H. (eds.), *The Birth of a Consumer Society: The Commercialization of Eighteenth-Century England* (Bloomington, Ind., 1982).

MCKEON, MICHAEL, *The Origins of the English Novel, 1600–1740* (Baltimore, Md., 1987).

MADDOX, RANDY L., 'Aldersgate: A Tradition History', in Randy L. Maddox (ed.), *Aldersgate Reconsidered* (Nashville, 1990), 133–46.

—— (ed.), *Aldersgate Reconsidered* (Nashville, 1990).

—— 'Celebrating Wesley—When?' *Methodist History* 29 (1991), 63–75.

—— 'Continuing the Conversation', *Methodist History* 30 (1991), 235–41.

Margaret Ebner: Major Works, trans. L. P. Hindsley (New York, 1993).

MARGERY KEMPE, *The Book of Margery Kempe*, trans. B. Windeatt (1994).

MARKHAM, C. A., 'The Rev. John Collet [*sic*] Ryland's Scholars', *Northamptonshire Notes and Queries*, NS I (1926), 18–31.

MARSDEN, GEORGE M., *Jonathan Edwards* (New Haven, Conn., 2003).

Martin Luther's Basic Theological Writings, ed. T. F. Lull (Minneapolis, Minn., 1989).

MARTIN, BERNARD, *John Newton* (1950).

MASCUCH, MICHAEL, 'Continuity and Change in Patronage Society: The Social Mobility of British Autobiographers, 1600–1750', *Journal of Historical Sociology* 7 (1994), 177–97.

—— *Origins of the Individualist Self: Autobiography and Self-Identity in England, 1591–1791* (Cambridge, 1997).

—— 'Social Mobility and Middling Self-Identity: The Ethos of British Autobiographers, 1600–1750', *Social History* 20 (1995), 45–61.

MASON, J. C. S., *The Moravian Church and the Missionary Awakening in England, 1760–1800* (Woodbridge, Suffolk, 2001).

MASON, MARY G., 'The Other Voice: Autobiographies of Women Writers', in James Olney (ed.), *Autobiography: Essays Theoretical and Critical* (Princeton, 1980), 207–35.

MATTHEWS, WILLIAM, *British Autobiography: An Annotated Bibliography of British Autobiographies Published or Written Before 1951* (Berkeley, 1955).

MEALING, S. R., *The Jesuit Relations and Allied Documents: A Selection* (Toronto, Ont., 1963).

MILLS, KENNETH, and GRAFTON, ANTHONY (eds.), *Conversion: Old Worlds and New* (Rochester, NY, 2003).

—— (eds.), *Conversion in Late Antiquity and the Early Middle Ages: Seeing and Believing* (Rochester, NY, 2003).

MISCH, GEORG, *A History of Autobiography in Antiquity*, trans. E.W. Dickes, 2 vols. (1950), 678–81.

MITCHELL, CHRISTOPHER, 'Jonathan Edwards's Scottish Connection', in David W. Kling and Douglas A. Sweeney (eds.), *Jonathan Edwards at Home and Abroad* (Columbia, SC, 2003), 222–47.

MITTERAUER, MICHAEL, *A History of Youth* (Oxford, 1992).

MORGAN, EDMUND S., *Visible Saints* (New York, 1963).

MULDOON, JAMES, (ed.), *Varieties of Religious Conversion in the Middle Ages* (Gainesville, Fla., 1997).

NAYLOR, PETER, 'John Collett Ryland (1723–1792)', in Michael A. G. Haykin (ed.), *The British Particular Baptists, 1638–1910,* 2 vols. (Springfield, Mo., 1998, 2000), i. 185–201.

—— *Picking up a Pin for the Lord: English Particular Baptists from 1688 to the Early Nineteenth Century* (1992).

NIETZSCHE, FRIEDRICH, *The Will to Power*, trans. A. M. Ludovici, 2 vols. (New York, 1964).

NOLL, MARK A., 'Revolution and the Rise of Evangelical Social Influence in North Atlantic Societies', in Mark A. Noll, David W. Bebbington, and George A. Rawlyk (eds.), *Evangelicalism: Comparative Studies of Popular Protestantism in North America, the British Isles, and Beyond, 1700–1990* (New York, 1994), 113–36.

NOLL, MARK A., *The Rise of Evangelicalism: The Age of Edwards, Whitefield and the Wesleys* (Leicester, 2004).

—— BEBBINGTON, DAVID W., and RAWLYK, GEORGE A. (eds.), *Evangelicalism: Comparative Studies of Popular Protestantism in North America, the British Isles, and Beyond, 1700–1990* (New York, 1994).

NUSSBAUM, FELICITY A., *The Autobiographical Subject: Gender and Ideology in Eighteenth-Century England* (Baltimore, 1989).

—— 'Private subjects in William Cowper's "Memoir" ', in Paul Korshin (ed.), *The Age of Johnson* (New York, 1987), i. 307–26.

NUTTALL, GEOFFREY F., 'Continental Pietism and the Evangelical Movement in Britain', in J. van den Berg and J. P. van Dooren (eds.), *Pietismus und Reveil* (Leiden, 1978), 207–36.

—— 'George Whitefield's 'Curate': Gloucestershire Dissent and the Revival', *Journal of Ecclesiastical History* 27 (1976), 369–86.

—— 'Letters from Robert Hall to John Ryland, 1791–1824', *Baptist Quarterly* 34 (1991), 127–31.

—— 'Methodism and the Older Dissent: Some Perspectives', *United Reformed Church Historical Society Journal* 2 (1981), 259–74.

—— 'Northamptonshire and the Modern Question: A Turning-Point in Eighteenth-Century Dissent', *Journal of Theological Studies*, NS 16 (1965), 101–23.

—— *Visible Saints: The Congregational Way, 1640–1660* (Oxford, 1957).

OBERMAN, HEIKO A., *Luther: Man between God and the Devil*, trans. E. Walliser-Schwarzbart (New Haven, Conn., 1989).

O'BRIEN, SUSAN, 'Eighteenth-Century Publishing Networks in the First Years of Transatlantic Evangelicalism', in Mark A. Noll, David W. Bebbington, and George A. Rawlyk (eds.), *Evangelicalism: Comparative Studies of Popular Protestantism in North America, the British Isles, and Beyond, 1700–1990* (New York, 1994), 38–57.

—— 'A Transatlantic Community of Saints: The Great Awakening and the First Evangelical Network, 1735–1755', *American Historical Review* 91 (1986), 811–32.

OLNEY, JAMES, 'Autobiography and the Cultural Moment: A Thematic, Historical, and Bibliographical Introduction,' in James Olney (ed.), *Autobiography: Essays Theoretical and Critical* (Princeton, 1980), 3–27.

—— (ed.), *Autobiography: Essays Theoretical and Critical* (Princeton, 1980).

—— *Tell Me Africa: An Approach to African Literature* (Princeton, NJ, 1973).

OWENS, J. M. R., 'Christianity and the Maoris to 1840', *New Zealand Journal of History* 2 (1968), 18–40.

PACKER, JAMES I., 'The Puritan View of Preaching the Gospel', in *Among God's Giants: The Puritan Vision of the Christian Life* (Eastbourne, 1991).

PATRICK, ST, *The Works of St. Patrick,* trans. Ludwig Bieler (New York, 1953).

PETERSON, LINDA, 'Gender and Autobiographical Form: The Case of Spiritual Autobiography', in James Olney (ed.), *Studies in Autobiography* (New York, 1988), 211–22.

—— 'Newman's *Apologia* and English Spiritual Autobiography', *Proceedings of the Modern Languages Association* 100 (1985), 300–14.

PETRARCH, FRANCESCO, *Letters from Petrarch*, trans. M. Bishop (Bloomington, Ind., 1966).

—— *Petrarch's Secret*, trans. W. H. Draper (1911; repr. Norwood, Penn., 1975).

PETTIT, NORMAN, *The Heart Prepared: Grace and Conversion in Puritan Spiritual Life* (1966; 2nd edn., Middletown, Conn., 1989).

PICKERING, HENRY, *Twice-Born Men* (1934).

PODMORE, COLIN, *The Moravian Church in England, 1728–1760* (Oxford, 1998).

POLLMANN, JUDITH, 'A Different Road to God: The Protestant Experience of Conversion in the Sixteenth Century', in Peter van der Veer (ed.), *Conversion to Modernities* (New York, 1996), 47–64.

PORTER, ROY, *English Society in the Eighteenth Century* (1990).

—— *Mind-Forg'd Manacles: A History of Madness in England from the Restoration to the Regency* (1990).

—— *A Social History of Madness: Stories of the Insane* (1987).

PRESTWICH, MENNA, *International Calvinism, 1541–1715* (Oxford, 1985).

QUESTIER, MICHAEL C., *Conversion, Politics and Religion in England, 1580–1625* (Cambridge, 1996).

RABOTEAU, ALBERT J., 'The Black Experience in American Evangelicalism: The Meaning of Slavery', in Leonard I. Sweet (ed.), *The Evangelical Tradition in America* (Macon, Ga., 1984).

—— *Slave Religion* (New York, 1978).

RACK, HENRY D., 'Evangelical Endings: Death-Beds in Evangelical Biography', *Bulletin of the John Rylands University Library of Manchester* 74 (1992), 39–56.

—— 'John Wesley and Early Methodist Conversion', Position Paper 28, North Atlantic Missiology Project (Cambridge, 1997).

—— *Reasonable Enthusiast: John Wesley and the Rise of Methodism* (1989).

RAMBO, LEWIS, *Understanding Religious Conversion* (New Haven, Conn., 1993).

RAWLYK, G. A., *The Canada Fire: Radical Evangelicalism in British North America* (Kingston, Ont., 1994).

RICHETTI, JOHN (ed.), *The Cambridge Companion to the Eighteenth-Century Novel* (Cambridge, 1996).

RICŒUR, PAUL, *The Rule of Metaphor* (Toronto, Ont., 1977).

RIVERS, ISABEL, 'Shaftesburian Enthusiasm and the Evangelical Revival', in Jane Garnett and Colin Matthew (eds.), *Revival and Religion since 1700* (1993), 21–39.

—— ' "Strangers and Pilgrims": Sources and Patterns of Methodist Narrative', in J. D. Hilson, M. M. B. Jones, and J. R. Watson (eds.), *Augustan Worlds* (Leicester, 1978), 189–203.

ROBINSON, H. WHEELER, 'A Baptist Student—John Collett Ryland', *Baptist Quarterly* 3 (1926), 25–33.

ROBISON, OLIN C., 'The Particular Baptists in England, 1760–1820', D.Phil. thesis (Oxford, 1963).

ROUTLEY, ERIK, *Conversion* (Philadelphia, 1960).

RUPP, GORDON. *Religion in England: 1688–1791* (Oxford, 1986).

RUSSELL, NORMA, *A Bibliography of William Cowper to 1837* (Oxford, 1963).

SCHAEFER, PAUL R., 'The Spiritual Brotherhood on the Habits of the Heart: Cambridge Protestants and the Doctrine of Sanctification from William Perkins to Thomas Shepard', D.Phil. thesis (Oxford, 1994).

SCHMIDT, JEAN MILLER, ' "Strangely Warmed": The Place of Aldersgate in the Methodist Canon', in Randy Maddox (ed.), *Aldersgate Reconsidered* (Nashville, 1990), 109–19.

SCHMIDT, LEIGH ERIC, *Holy Fairs: Scottish Communions and American Revivals in the Early Modern Period* (Princeton, 1989).

SHANTZ, DOUGLAS, 'Women, Men, and their Experience of God: Comparing Spiritual Autobiographies', *Canadian Evangelical Review* 22 (2001), 2–18.

SHEA, DANIEL B., JUN., *Spiritual Autobiography in Early America* (Princeton, 1968).

SHUMAKER, WAYNE, *English Autobiography: Its Emergence, Materials, and Form* (Berkeley, 1954).

SMABY, BEVERLY PRIOR, 'Female Piety Among Eighteenth Century Moravians', *Pennsylvania History* 64 (1997), 151–67.

—— *The Transformation of Moravian Bethlehem* (Philadelphia, Penn., 1988).

SMOUT, T. C., 'Born Again at Cambuslang: New Evidence on Popular Religion and Literacy in Eighteenth-Century Scotland', *Past and Present* 97 (1982), 114–27.

SNADER, JOE, *Caught between Worlds: British Captivity Narratives in Fact and Fiction* (Lexington, Ky., 2000).

SPACKS, PATRICA MEYER, 'Female Rhetorics', in Shari Benstock (ed.), *The Private Self: Theory and Practice of Women's Autobiographical Writings* (Chapel Hill, 1988).

STANLEY, BRIAN, *The History of the Baptist Missionary Society, 1792–1992* (1992).

STARR, G. A., *Defoe and Spiritual Autobiography* (New York, 1971).

STAUFFER, DONALD, *The Art of Biography in Eighteenth-Century England* (Princeton, 1941).

—— *English Biography Before 1700* (Cambridge, Mass., 1930).

STEIN, STEPHEN J., 'A Note on Anne Dutton, Eighteenth-Century Evangelical', *Church History* 44 (1975), 485–91.

STEINMETZ, DAVID C., 'Reformation and Conversion,' *Theology Today* 35 (1978), 25–32.

STENDAHL, KRISTER, 'The Apostle Paul and the Introspective Conscience of the West', in Krister Stendahl (ed.), *Paul Among the Jews and Gentiles and Other Essays* (1976), 78–96.

STEPHEN, LESLIE, *History of English Thought in the Eighteenth Century*, 2 vols. (1876).

STOEFFLER, F. ERNEST, *German Pietism During the Eighteenth Century* (Leiden 1973).

—— *The Rise of Evangelical Pietism* (Leiden, 1971).

STOEVER, WILLIAM K. B., *'A Faire and Easie Way to Heaven': Covenant Theology and Antinomianism in Early Massachusetts* (Middletown, Conn., 1978).

STONE, LAWRENCE, 'The Educational Revolution in England, 1560–1640', *Past and Present* 28 (1964), 41–80.

STOUT, HARRY S., *The Divine Dramatist: George Whitefield and the Rise of Modern Evangelicalism* (Grand Rapids, Mich., 1991).

—— 'George Whitefield in Three Countries', in Mark A. Noll, David W. Bebbington, and George A. Rawlyk (eds.), *Evangelicalism: Comparative Studies of Popular Protestantism in North America, the British Isles, and Beyond, 1700–1990* (New York, 1994), 58–72.

SUTHERLAND, JAMES, *Defoe* (1937).

TAFT, ZECHARIAH, *Biographical Sketches of the Lives and Public Ministry of Various Holy Women*, 2 vols. (1825; repr. Peterborough, 1992).

TAVES, ANN, *Fits, Trances, & Visions: Experiencing Religion and Explaining Experience from Wesley to James* (Princeton, 1999).

TAYLOR, CHARLES, *Sources of the Self: The Making of the Modern Identity* (Cambridge, 1992).

TAYLOR, JOHN, *Early History of College Lane Chapel* (Northampton, 1870).

TELFORD, JOHN, *The Life of John Wesley* (New York, 1898).

TIPPETT, ALAN R., 'Conversion as a Dynamic Process in Christian Mission', *Missiology* 2 (1977), 203–21.

TIPSON, LYNN BAIRD, JUN., 'The Development of a Puritan Understanding of Conversion', Ph.D. thesis (Yale, 1972).

TOMALIN, CLAIRE, *Samuel Pepys: The Unequalled Self* (2002).

TORRANCE, THOMAS F., *The School of Faith: The Catechisms of the Reformed Church* (1959).

TUDUR, GERAINT, *Howell Harris: From Conversion to Separation, 1735–1750* (Cardiff, 2000).

TYERMAN, LUKE, *The Life and Times of the Rev. John Wesley, M. A., Founder of the Methodists*, 3 vols. (3rd edn., 1876).

—— *The Life of the Rev. George Whitefield, B.A., of Pembroke College, Oxford*, 2 vols. (1876–7).

—— *The Oxford Methodists* (New York, 1873).

VALENTINE, SIMON, *John Bennet and the Origins of Methodism and the Evangelical Revival in England* (1997).

VAN BRAGHT, THIELEMAN J. (ed.), *The Bloody Theater, or, Martyrs' Mirror*, trans. Joseph F. Sohm (Scottdale, Penn., 1987).

VAN DER VEER, PETER (ed.), *Conversion to Modernities: The Globalization of Christianity* (New York, 1996).

VOGT, PETER, 'A Voice for Themselves: Women as Participants in Congregational Discourse in the Eighteenth-Century Moravian Movement', in Beverly Mayne Kienzle and Pamela J. Walker (eds.), *Women Preachers and Prophets Through Two Millennia of Christianity* (Berkeley, Calif., 1998), 227–47.

VON ROHR, JOHN, *The Covenant of Grace in Puritan Thought* (Atlanta, 1986).

WALLACE, DEWEY D., JUN., *Puritans and Predestination: Grace in English Protestant Theology, 1525–1695* (Chapel Hill, NC, 1982).

WALLS, ANDREW F., 'A Christian Experiment: The Early Sierra Leone Colony', in G. J. Cuming (ed.), *The Mission of the Church and the Propagation of the Faith* (Cambridge, 1970), 107–30.

—— 'A Colonial Concordat: Two Views of Christianity and Civilisation', in Derek Baker (ed.), *Church Society and Politics* (Oxford, 1975), 293–302.

—— 'The Evangelical Revival, The Missionary Movement, and Africa', in Mark A. Noll, David W. Bebbington, and George A. Rawlyk (eds.), *Evangelicalism: Comparative Studies of Popular Protestantism in North America, the British Isles, and Beyond, 1700–1990* (New York, 1994), 310–30.

—— *The Missionary Movement in Christian History* (Edinburgh, 1996).

WALSH, JOHN, 'The Anglican Evangelicals in the Eighteenth Century', in Marcel Simon (ed.), *Aspects de L'Anglicanisme* (Paris, 1974), 87–102.

—— 'The Cambridge Methodists', in Peter Brooks (ed.), *Christian Spirituality: Essays in Honour of Gordon Rupp* (1975), 251–83.

—— 'Methodism and the Mob in the Eighteenth Century', in G. J. Cumming and Derek Baker (eds.), *Popular Belief and Practice* (Cambridge, 1972), 213–27.

—— ' "Methodism" and the Origins of English-Speaking Evangelicalism', in Mark A. Noll, David W. Bebbington, and George A. Rawlyk (eds.), *Evangelicalism: Comparative Studies of Popular Protestantism in North America, the British Isles, and Beyond, 1700–1990* (New York, 1994), 19–37.

—— 'Origins of the Evangelical Revival', in Gareth V. Bennett and John D. Walsh (eds.), *Essays in Modern English Church History in Memory of Norman Sykes* (Oxford, 1966), 132–62.

—— 'The Yorkshire Evangelicals in the Eighteenth Century: With Special Reference to Methodism', Ph.D. thesis (Cambridge, 1956).

—— and TAYLOR, STEPHEN, 'Introduction: The Church and Anglicanism in the "Long" Eighteenth Century', in John Walsh, Colin Haydon, and Stephen Taylor (eds.), *The Church of England, c.1689–c.1833* (Cambridge, 1993), 1–64.

WARD, W. R., *Christianity under the Ancien Régime* (Cambridge, 1999).

—— *Faith and Faction* (1993).

—— 'John Wesley, Traveller', in *Faith and Faction* (1993), 249–63.

—— 'Power and Piety: The Origins of Religious Revival in the Early Eighteenth Century', in *Faith and Faction*, 75–93.

—— *The Protestant Evangelical Awakening* (Cambridge, 1992).

WATKINS, OWEN, *The Puritan Experience* (1972).

WATSON, J. R., *The English Hymn: A Critical and Historical Study* (Oxford, 1999).

WATT, IAN, *The Rise of the Novel: Studies in Defoe, Richardson and Fielding* (Berkeley, Calif., 1957).

WATTS, MICHAEL R., *The Dissenters*, 2 vols. (Oxford, 1978, 1995).

WEBSTER, TOM, 'Writing to Redundancy: Approaches to Spiritual Journals and Early Modern Spirituality', *The Historical Journal* 39 (1996), 33–56.

WEINTRAUB, KARL J., 'Autobiography and Historical Consciousness', *Critical Inquiry* 1 (1975), 821–48.

WESSELS, ANTON, *Europe: Was it Ever Really Christian?* trans. John Bowden (1994).

WESTERKAMP, MARILYN J., *Triumph of the Laity: Scots-Irish Piety and the Great Awakening, 1625–1760* (New York, 1988).

WHITEBROOK, J. C., 'The Life and Works of Mrs. Ann Dutton', *Transactions of the Baptist Historical Society* 7 (1920–1), 129–46.

WILCOX, PETER, 'Conversion in the Thought and Experience of John Calvin', *Anvil* 14 (1997), 113–128.

—— 'Restoration, Reformation and the Progress of the Kingdom of Christ: Evangelisation in the Thought and Practice of John Calvin, 1555–1564', D.Phil. thesis (Oxford, 1993).

WILLIAMS, CHARLES, *The Descent of the Dove* (New York, 1956).

WILLMER, HADDON, 'Evangelicalism, 1785–1835', unpublished Hulsean Prize Essay (Cambridge, 1962).

WILSON, LINDA, 'Conversion Amongst Female Methodists, 1825–75', *Proceedings of the Wesley Historical Society* 51 (1998), 217–25.

WRIGHT, HARRISON M., *New Zealand, 1769–1840* (Cambridge, Mass., 1959).

Index